HANDBOOKS

COLORADO

STEVE KNOPPER

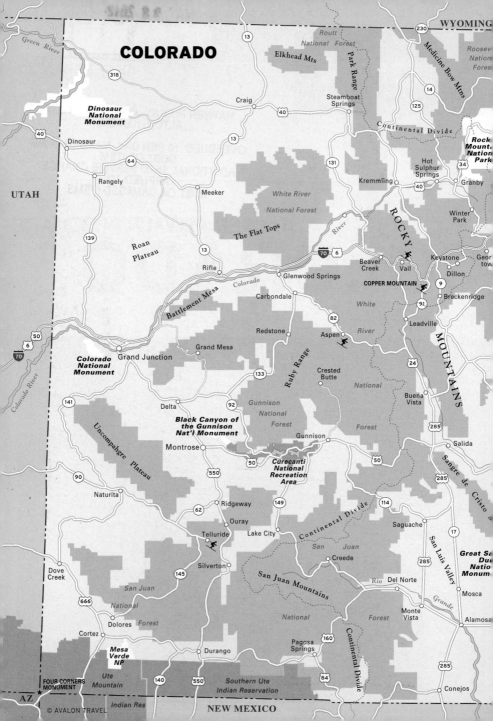

Contents

Discover Colorado

The mountains are everything in Colorado. Looming over cities and towns, parks and forests, fields and stadiums, at elevations of 11,000–14,000 feet, they make themselves known even when hidden from view. From the Rockies in the north to the San Juans in the southwest, the mountains have spawned multibillion-dollar tourism industries, including internationally renowned ski and snowboard resorts such as Aspen and Vail. They've also messed with visiting baseball pitchers at Coors Field, who've given up hundreds of home runs in the mile-high altitude and thin air. And they've attracted endless visitors to the state, many of whom have glanced at the backdrop and then moved here immediately. They're the main reason I like living in Colorado: Every now and then I'll be lost in thought, contemplating Denver rush-hour traffic, and look west to see the Rockies peeking through the skyline. During these moments I know why I always return to Colorado, no matter where else I've been.

The High Rockies are just as fun to explore on foot (or snowboard or snowshoe or 4WD vehicle) as they are on skis. Boulder is practically a country unto itself – an aggressively liberal, environmentalist one – with smoke-free restaurants grouped around the downtown redbrick Pearl

Street Mall. Denver continues its downtown renaissance, offering Major League Baseball and the Elitch Gardens amusement park at the heart of the city, plus zoos, parks, and trails on the outskirts. Skiers (and bluegrass fans who attend its gigantic festival every June) know Telluride for its scenic waterfalls and friendly hippie bars. And in the northwest, Colorado and Utah share the sprawling Dinosaur National Monument, complete with giant skeletons, while the south-central region is home to a huge alligator farm. Even the flat eastern third of the state contains historical charms, such as the Summit Springs Battlefield, which marks an 1869 epic battle between Cheyennes, Arapahos, and pioneers.

Almost anywhere you live or visit in Colorado is within weekend-getaway distance of something really amazing to look at — a mesa, a valley, a river, an ancient cliff dwelling, or, most obvious and satisfying of all, a mountain peak.

Planning Your Trip

▶ WHERE TO GO

Denver

Although many travelers still consider Denver a mere gateway to ski resorts or the Rocky Mountains, the city has jumped several notches on the sophistication scale in recent years. The 1990s brought a successful new airport—and Major League Baseball—to a resurgent part of downtown known as LoDo (Lower Downtown). Since then, gourmet restaurants and hip clubs have joined the renaissance, invigorating shopping districts like Larimer Square. Prices aren't bad, sightseeing is plentiful, and hotels are available at all levels of luxury.

The College Towns: Boulder and Fort Collins

Travelers perceive Boulder, home of the University of Colorado, as some kind of utopia—it's in a scenic bowl directly beneath the Rocky Mountain foothills. And while "The People's Republic of Boulder" has grown more expensive and yuppie-centric over the years, the restaurants are diverse, and the pedestrian Pearl Street Mall is charmingly filled with guitarists and acrobats. Fort Collins, just an hour's drive to the northeast, has Colorado State University and the historic shopping district Old Town Square.

Aspen and the Ski Towns

Colorado's top ski resorts—Aspen, Vail, Breckenridge, Winter Park, Arapahoe Basin, Copper Mountain, and others—are bunched up along I-70 in the spectacular High Rockies, about 2–3 hours west of Denver. Every ski area has its own personality, in terms of moguls, prices, and general

IF YOU HAVE...

- **THREE DAYS:** Visit Denver, Boulder, and Estes Park or Rocky Mountain National Park.

- **ONE WEEK:** Add Breckenridge, Keystone, and Vail.

- **TWO WEEKS:** Add Aspen, Redstone, Leadville, Glenwood Springs, and Crested Butte.

- **THREE WEEKS:** Add Telluride, Silverton, Ouray, Durango, Mesa Verde National Park, and the Four Corners.

- **FOUR WEEKS:** Add Grand Junction, Dinosaur National Monument, Steamboat Springs, Pueblo, Colorado Springs, and Great Sand Dunes National Park.

the town of Telluride, tucked within aspen trees

the Big Blue Bear, by local artist Lawrence Argent, at the Colorado Convention Center in downtown Denver

feel of the surrounding town, so regulars tend to pick their favorites and stick with them. Aspen and Vail, for example, emphasize shopping and general ritziness, while Winter Park and Breckenridge are less pretentious and snag more townies than travelers.

Grand Junction and Northwest Colorado

Grand Junction is the only major town (pop. 30,000) between Salt Lake City and Denver.

It's at the confluence of the Colorado and Gunnison Rivers, and nearby are such sights as the Little Book Cliffs (flat, steep mountains that extend for miles across the landscape), the Grand Mesa National Forest, and the Colorado National Monument. Northwest Colorado's cycling, cross-country skiing, and horseback-riding opportunities are surprisingly fertile. Dinosaur National Monument straddles the Colorado-Utah border.

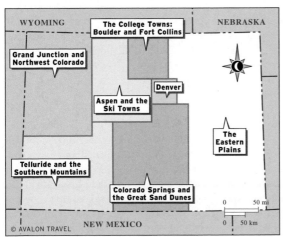

Telluride and the Southern Mountains

Underneath the towering San Juans, Telluride is filled with tall waterfalls, breathtaking mountain views, trails, summer festivals, hot springs, and a ski area. Given the five-hour drive from Denver, the region is hard to reach, but isolation only adds to its appeal. Other sights in southwestern Colorado: dramatically steep Black Canyon of the Gunnison National Park; historic mining towns

hiking near Durango

Ouray and Silverton; the Durango & Silverton Narrow Gauge Railroad; and Four Corners, where you can touch four states simultaneously.

Colorado Springs and the Great Sand Dunes

Colorado Springs is famous these days for two basic reasons: It's home to majestic Pikes Peak and to a conservative, religious, and politically influential group called Focus on the Family. The city's lodging centerpiece is The Broadmoor, with hiking trails, a small lake, and frilly pillows on four-corner beds. To the south, Pueblo is a big city with interesting historic sites and museums, while Great Sand Dunes National Monument, outside Alamosa, has 900-foot hills for climbing and "sand skiing."

The Eastern Plains

The drive from endless Nebraska or Kansas through eastern Colorado is flat and uneventful, especially compared to the vibrant Rocky Mountain regions that await in the rest of the state, but the farm- and ranch-filled plains are not without regional charms. You'll feel the car begin to climb around Sterling, home of the Native American Overland Trail Museum, and might consider a stop in Crook, including the 7,000-acre Tamarack Ranch State Wildlife Area, or Fort Morgan, which includes the big-rock-among-the-plains Pawnee National Grassland.

▶ WHEN TO GO

The majority of Colorado visitors arrive during ski season, roughly October–April, although certain resorts such as Arapahoe Basin are open into early summer. In ski towns such as Vail and Steamboat Springs, crowds are plentiful this time of year, and hotels and restaurants are significantly pricier. The weeks of Christmas, Thanksgiving, and New Year's Eve are even more crowded and expensive. Many experienced skiers know to look for off-season deals. Colorado blizzards are in full swing this time of year, which can wreak havoc on travelers but are like manna from heaven for skiers already staying at the resorts.

During summer, ski towns such as Steamboat Springs, Telluride, Aspen, and Vail as well as tourist towns like Pagosa Springs, Estes Park, and Silverton transform into quaint little districts packed with shops and bakeries. Plus, Colorado is a huge summer-festival state, from Telluride Bluegrass to a variety of farming, cycling, hiking, running, and historical events. Temperatures frequently hit 100°F, although humidity is low.

In spring and fall, Colorado weather is especially unpredictable, with 80°F days and blizzards arriving out of nowhere. Deals at ski-town hotels, restaurants, and bars are especially fruitful at these times of year, and crowds are small. Still, call first before traveling in the off-season: In the ongoing economic downturn, many hotels and restaurants in ski towns have cut costs by drastically reducing their hours or even closing during the slow seasons (meaning roughly spring and fall). For example, in 2011 Aspen's three top hotels, the Little Nell, the St. Regis, and the Hotel Jerome, closed for maintenance during much of April–May. Also in Aspen, roughly 30 popular restaurants closed for two weeks in May, including Cache Cache and Syzygy.

Before traveling to national parks in Colorado during the winter, check the websites for seasonal hours. At Black Canyon of the Gunnison National Park, the easygoing South Rim Road is open to cars only to a point; after that it's snowshoes and cross-country skis only, and the North Rim Road is closed entirely. Garden of the Gods, in Colorado Springs, has reduced hours, and certain ranger stations, visitors centers, and campgrounds are closed in well-known parks such as Rocky Mountain National Park and Mesa Verde National Park.

The weather in Colorado changes quickly, so pack accordingly. In January, even in the mountains, the sun can come out in the middle of a blizzard and you'll need shorts. In July, the wind can whip up and you'll need a coat. Bring sunscreen no matter what. For the most part, Coloradoans pride themselves on a sort of cowboy-skier informality, so even the fanciest restaurants in Aspen or Telluride tend not to require suits or dresses.

columbine and other wildflowers on a grassy slope near Ophir in southwestern Colorado

Explore Colorado

▶ THE BEST OF COLORADO

Colorado's top attractions—the ski resorts—bunch up along the High Rockies in the north-central part of the state, so most travelers get a skewed vision of what this square, land-locked state is all about. For ambitious visitors, here's a (literally!) up-and-down itinerary that begins in the big city and spirals through not only the Summit County ski areas but also the southwestern San Juan Mountains and the Black Canyon of the Gunnison National Park. Unless you're inclined to make the endless drive through Kansas, Nebraska, Utah, Wyoming, or Texas, plan to book a flight into Denver International Airport (DIA) and rent a car. This strategy focuses on winter travel, so pack the skis and boots—and be flexible about extending your stay in a given hotel in case you're snowed in.

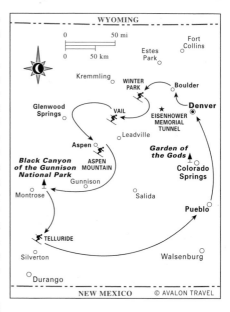

Sports Authority Field at Mile High in Denver, with "The Broncos" by sculptor Sergio Benvenuti

Day 1

Fly into DIA, rent a car (consider a 4WD vehicle for mountain highways in blizzard season), and take I-70 and I-25 to downtown Denver. Check in for a two-night stay at the Brown Palace, the Hotel Monaco, the Adam's Mark, or any of the city's centrally located hotels.

Day 2

Explore Denver, beginning with the Denver Museum of Nature & Science in City Park, about a 10-minute trip by car on Colorado Boulevard south of I-70. The third floor has the city's best view of the Rocky Mountains.

Return to downtown and hop on one of the free 16th Street Mall buses for an afternoon of

BEST OF COLORADO – IN THE SUMMER

For summer trips, follow the Best of Colorado itinerary with the following substitutions:

- **Day 2:** Catch a Rockies game at **Coors Field** in LoDo rather than braving the cold at Sports Authority Field at Mile High or catching the Avs or Nuggets.

- **Day 4: Winter Park**'s ski trails are generally open to hiking and cycling, and the restaurants and hotels are noticeably cheaper this time of year.

- **Day 5: Vail** is a hub of outdoor summer sports, with white-water rafting available in nearby towns as well as abundant rock climbing and cycling in town and on the slopes. Contact **Lakota Guides** about rafting or **Paragon Sports** for climbing and cycling information.

- **Day 6: Aspen,** surrounded by the Roaring Fork Valley, is an outdoor-sports haven. With a pretty, well-kept town square, it's also a

mountain biking through an aspen grove in Vail

Garden of the Gods

great place to kill a lazy afternoon. Consider stopping for a day at the giant **Hot Springs Pool** in Glenwood Springs.

- **Day 7: Black Canyon of the Gunnison National Park** provides easy hikes for visitors at the top and intense white-water rafting at the bottom for adventurers.

- **Days 8-9:** In the San Juan Valley, **Telluride, Silverton,** and **Ouray** are popular summer playgrounds. The gondola runs full-time in Telluride, delivering guests in the mountain village to the laid-back downtown wine bars, shops, restaurants, and music clubs. And it doesn't take long to find superb hiking trails, Jeep rentals, and hot springs.

- **Days 11-12:** Consider spending extra time at **Pikes Peak** and **Garden of the Gods,** which are more accommodating to picnickers during the warm months.

shopping. Later, catch a Denver Broncos game at Sports Authority Field at Mile High (you might have to buy scalped tickets on eBay or StubHub, or, yes, the streets around the stadium) or the Denver Nuggets or Colorado Avalanche at the Pepsi Center. For dinner, try one of the city's gourmet restaurants, such as Mizuna, Rioja, or Fruition. Budget-conscious travelers should consider a Fat Tire beer and a buffalo burger at My Brother's Bar. Late-nighters might venture into El Chapultepec for live jazz and atmosphere.

Day 3

Drive half an hour down U.S. 36 to Boulder and stay in the Hotel Boulderado, just in the shadow of the foothills. Tour the University of Colorado campus (off Broadway, south of downtown) and shop at the Pearl Street Mall.

Day 4

Take I-70 west directly through the Rocky Mountains to begin a tour of select ski-resort towns. Go through the Eisenhower Memorial Tunnel and watch for the scenic Continental Divide. (Note: When traveling I-70 in the winter, avoid heavy-traffic days, notably Saturday and Sunday afternoons, unless you enjoy sitting in the car for hours at a time.) First stop: Winter Park, home of affordable ski trails, notably the legendary Mary Jane, as well as a laid-back spirit of ski bums, college students, and locals.

Day 5

Next stop (farther west along I-70, about an hour west of the Eisenhower Tunnel): Vail, home of beautifully coiffed ski rats, three huge ski villages, pricey shopping, some of the best mountain scenery in the High Rockies, and, of course, legendary ski trails, particularly the seven Back Bowls and, beyond that, the Blue Sky Basin.

town of Vail at twilight

Day 6

Drive another hour down I-70, then head south at Glenwood Springs on Highway 82 to Aspen. Spend the night at the Little Nell, luxurious mountain home to the stars. Ski one of the four mountains, all of which have distinct personalities: Buttermilk offers predominantly beginner trails, while Aspen Mountain favors insane, fast-plunging expert runs.

Day 7

Return east to U.S. 24, drive to U.S. 285, turn west on U.S. 50, and make the five-hour drive southwest to the San Juan Mountains. Spend a luxurious few hours driving and venture quickly into the Black Canyon of the Gunnison National Park, using South Rim Road, which is open up to a point. If you happen to have cross-country skis or snowshoes, you can venture farther.

Black Canyon of the Gunnison National Park

Days 8-9

Take U.S. 50 west to U.S. 550, then turn south toward breathtaking Telluride and Silverton. These picturesque mountain hamlets have amazing ski trails—Telluride rivals Vail and Aspen for luxury, variety, and extremity, while Silverton's expert runs are ridiculously steep and high in elevation. For a change of pace, the hiking trails outside Ouray lead to world-class ice climbing in the winter. Check into one of the many beautiful hotels,

and explore the restaurants and gift shops in these charming Old West-style towns.

Day 10

Head back toward Denver via U.S. 160 and I-25, spending the night in Pueblo for a break.

Days 11-12

Explore Colorado Springs (an hour north of Pueblo on I-25), specifically Garden of the Gods, and be sure to stay at the tony Broadmoor Hotel, which seems extra-peaceful under a fresh blanket of snow. Ambitious hikers may want to tackle Pikes Peak, which offers numerous trails, open in the winter although often more difficult and dangerous. Also consider driving the Pikes Peak Highway, three hours up and back, a twisty road straight uphill to the Summit House restaurant and gift shop.

Day 13

Drive back to Denver (about 1.5 hours north of Colorado Springs on I-25) and spend the last night checking out the hip bars and live-music nightclubs of LoDo. Pick another downtown hotel for the last night.

Day 14

Return home via DIA.

▶ EXTREME ADVENTURE: SKIING AND BEYOND

Colorado is built for adventure, whether you're skiing or snowboarding in Vail or Snowmass, training for a cycling race in Boulder, or hiking Pikes Peak in Colorado Springs. Pretty much every outdoor sport—with the possible exception of waterskiing—is huge here. And there are outlets all over the state for hiking, mountain biking, rock climbing, kayaking, ice climbing, cycling, snowboarding, snowshoeing, and, of course, skiing. Below are

just a few ways of experiencing the sport in Colorado, but there's plenty of variety. Just be sure to reserve bicycles, cars, and hotels on your itinerary before showing up; even in laid-back Colorado, it's possible to lose your place.

Skiing and Snowboarding

All the major ski resorts offer extreme runs for downhill experts and terrain parks for jumpers and tricksters. Begin with the home of the

PLANNING A SKI TRIP

Colorado's ski resorts are legendarily crowded, so it pays to plan in advance. Here are some tips.

Choose what kind of ski trip you'd like to have. For the full-on luxury experience, you'll want a highfalutin hotel in Aspen or Telluride, which means more money and (usually) more crowds. But it also means a larger variety of trails, better restaurants, more open ski-school slots, and just plain higher-quality skiing. If you're just hauling the family for a quickie day trip or weekend getaway, consider a more affordable resort, ranging from tiny, no-frills Monarch and Ski Cooper to Copper Mountain and Arapahoe Basin to Winter Park. Also influencing your choice: the vertical-drop information listed on the resort websites, which gives you an idea of how long each run or trail will last.

High season is roughly mid-February–end of March, when the powder is best, as well as Christmas week and New Year's Eve, although the skiing isn't quite as consistently excellent during December. For those months, especially at the big resorts, book hotels, lift tickets, and restaurant reservations as early as possible, preferably as much as a year ahead. Of course, there are always last-minute deals, especially since the onset of the economic downturn – on a recent February weekend, LivingSocial offered a quality room for two at Vail Cascade Resort for $75 (!). During less-popular months, last-minute deals are far more plentiful, so pay attention to newspaper coupons, Groupon alerts, value sites such as www.vailonsale.com, and the resort websites themselves. (Sign up for email alerts on each of these sites.) Generally, it's easier to be spontaneous if you're looking at Arapahoe Basin and Copper Mountain as opposed to Aspen, Vail, Steamboat Springs, or Telluride.

Ideas for keeping expenses down in general:

skiing Blue Sky Basin, Vail

- **Buy gas on the road,** particularly if you're coming up U.S. 24 from Colorado Springs, rather than indulging in one of the super-expensive stations in Aspen or Vail.

- **Stay in "satellite" ski towns** such as Minturn or Edwards (for Vail) or Carbondale or Basalt (for Aspen).

- **Season ski passes,** especially for Colorado residents, can be super-cheap, such as a recent Aspen deal for $450; ski shops in Boulder, Denver, Colorado Springs, and elsewhere often offer lift-ticket discounts. Check www.epicpass.com or www.coloradopass.com for deals.

- **Look for last year's models** for gear, rent in your hometown in advance, or just go to REI or another store for a free or cheap deal on waxing and tune-ups.

- **Buy lunch along the way,** at one of the many sandwich or fast-food shops, rather than waiting to eat at an overpriced ski-village bistro.

- **Consider staying at a hostel,** offering bunks for roughly $20–45, depending on the city, such as the Fireside Inn Bed and Breakfast (Breckenridge) or the Crested Butte International Lodge and Hostel.

cycling the Colorado National Monument

annual Winter X-Games—Aspen. The resort contains several different parks, including Snowmass's new one, full of boxes and steep jumps that shoot skiers and boarders straight into the air.

Hiking

In Telluride, two trails, Sneffels High Line Trail and the more famous Bridal Veil Falls, are about 10 miles each way through steep, rough terrain. Plan to stay in Telluride, as both trails are a short drive (or long bike ride) from town.

Biking

Just outside Grand Junction, the 23-mile path up 2,000-foot Rim Rock Drive, in Colorado National Monument, takes you through a menagerie of giant red rocks and an endless pageant of mesas, valleys, and canyons. The cement bike path is filled with hairpin curves and at one point seems to take you straight into the rock before breaking into the artificial "Half Tunnel."

Independence Pass, from Aspen to Leadville, is a difficult, 32-mile, 12,000-foot-high route, but worth it for the mountain views. Consider spending a night or two in Leadville, checking out some historic buildings and nice restaurants, to decompress after the intense ride.

White-Water Rafting

Along the Arkansas River, near the "twin cities" of Salida and Buena Vista, is a mountainous waterway known as Brown's Canyon. Here you'll find the steep, rocky drop-offs that local outfitters such as River Runners (www.whitewater.net) have named Zoomflume, Devil's Punchbowl, and Seidel's Suckhole.

Ballooning

Hot-air balloons are plentiful in mountain towns, and while they involve dragging yourself out of bed at daybreak, they're a great way to experience mountain scenery. Book a trip with San Juan Balloon Adventures, based in rural Ridgway, outside of Telluride.

Kayaking

There are many insane kayak routes in Colorado's rock-filled mountain rivers, but consider a change of pace: Rent a steed at the REI Store in northwest Denver, then take it along the South Platte River, just behind the store. It's a great urban ride with the skyline in the background.

Rock Climbing

Outside of Del Norte, near Alamosa in south-central Colorado, Penitente Canyon contains giant slabs of red boulders with long, flat, frequently craggy sides—perfect for climbers. They have names like Bullet the Blue Sky, A Virgin No More, and Air Jordan.

Ice Climbing

The primary outlet for this more-extreme-than-plain-old-rock-climbing sport is the Ouray Ice Park, in a small historic town outside Telluride. Run by the city, the park includes 40 paths that are a sort of pretty, crystallized blue color and only somewhat treacherous.

▶ THE OLD WEST IN TWO WEEKS

Colorado was largely founded in the late 1800s, when fortune seekers around the United States cried, "Pikes Peak or bust!" and uprooted their lives and families to move here. Some got lucky, most didn't, but almost all wound up stuck in Colorado trying to figure out how to make money. Most cities, big and small, have some kind of museum or historical marker recalling these days—and many go even farther back, to the Utes and Arapahos who wandered the mountains and valleys before white people showed up.

Day 1

Fly into the Durango-La Plata County Airport in southwest Colorado, take the 25-minute shuttle to the 1887 Strater Hotel, and spend the late afternoon exploring the historic miners' buildings of downtown Durango. Drivers can easily get to Durango by heading north on U.S. 550 from New Mexico.

Days 2-3

The hotel will tell you how to get to the Durango & Silverton Narrow Gauge Railroad, a 45-mile line through the

mountains that transported miners and their families as early as 1882. Once in Silverton, wander the early-1900s jail, hotel, and other buildings in the National Historic District downtown. Stay a night at Silverton's 1882 Grand Imperial Hotel. The next day, arrange for a shuttle at Mountain Limo to drive

the Beaumont Hotel, Ouray

SIX GREAT SPOTS FOR NATIVE AMERICAN HERITAGE

The **Four Corners Monument,** run by the Navajo Nation, is the only place in the United States where you can touch four states simultaneously; it's in Colorado's southwestern corner. Not far away is the **Southern Ute Indian Reservation,** along the Colorado–New Mexico border, which often plays host to public music, art, and dance events. Check the official Southern Ute Indian Tribe site (www.southern-ute.nsn.us).

Earmark an entire day for **Mesa Verde National Park,** just southwest of Durango. In addition to being a scenic outdoor attraction – 80 square miles of canyons and cliffs – it's the largest collection of Anasazi cliff dwellings in the state. On the premises are an archaeological museum, a visitors center, and several trails.

Near Cortez, in the southwest part of the state, **Hovenweep National Monument** is a breathtaking 20-mile stretch of canyons and vistas containing more remnants of Anasazi cliff dwellings.

In Montrose, the **Ute Indian Museum** is on the original 8.65-acre homestead owned by Chief Ouray and his wife, Chipeta. Ouray, the great diplomatic leader of the southern Utes in the 1800s, died in 1881. At the museum, you'll find one of the biggest collections of Native American artifacts in the state as well as Chipeta's crypt and a variety of educational programs and exhibits.

On a less upbeat note, tiny **Meeker,** in the northwest near Grand Junction, was the site of a horrible 1870s clash between white reformers and disgruntled Utes that left 10 white men dead. The "Meeker Massacre" became a political issue and resulted in the Utes giving up key pieces of land they'd possessed for decades. Today, Meeker is an uneventful town of about 2,200 people, well-situated for trips to the White River National Forest and Grand Junction, but hardly the dramatic hub it was in the Old West.

dwellings in Mesa Verde National Park

Durango & Silverton Narrow Gauge Railroad

the 14 or so miles over steep mountain curves to Telluride. Arrange to rent a car there.

Days 4-5

In Telluride, stay at the New Sheridan Hotel, built in 1895, and spend a day looking at the downtown historic district. Miners settled here in the late 1800s, and according to legend, the name Telluride comes from skeptics who told their prospector friends, "To hell you ride."

Days 6-7

Drive north (take Highway 145 to Highway 62, then turn north on U.S. 550, about 45 minutes) to Ouray, another old mining town that maintains its Old West feel, and spend the night at the 1887 Beaumont Hotel, where Teddy Roosevelt and other luminaries stayed. The next morning, drive north on U.S. 550 to Montrose (about 30 minutes) and visit the Ute Indian Museum (just off the highway). Spend the night at a functional hotel in Montrose.

Days 8-9

Drive an hour east on U.S. 50 to Gunnison, then another hour north on Highway 135 to Crested Butte, where miners discovered gold in nearby Washington Gulch in the 1860s. Crested Butte is beautiful and funky, with several skier-oriented hotels. Try the Grand Lodge Resort & Suites, in the mountain village area a couple of miles from town.

Day 10

Drive north on the bumpy dirt County Road 12 west from Crested Butte, then catch Highway 133 north to Redstone, about 45 minutes from Crested Butte. (Note that Kebler Pass is closed during the winter, so you might need to take an alternate route.) Redstone is a history buff's dream, with the old Redstone Castle, the historic Redstone Inn, and remnants of the Coke Ovens, all recalling the life of John C. Osgood, the railroad magnate who developed this area.

town of Crested Butte

Days 11-12

Continue north another 30 minutes on Highway 133 to I-70, and stay at Glenwood Springs's Hotel Colorado. Built in 1893, it was once known as Colorado's "grande dame" and has drawn guests from Al Capone to Teddy Roosevelt (their pictures hang on the lobby walls).

Day 13

Drive east on I-70 and, depending on how much time you have, stop in ski towns like Vail or Breckenridge, both of which were once mining towns that in the mid-20th century shifted to tourism. Just before Denver, make the small history museums off the highway in Georgetown and Idaho Springs a priority—these small, quiet, scenic regions were mining boomtowns in the late 1800s, and many of the buildings have been carefully preserved. It takes about three hours to get from Glenwood Springs to Denver in optimum traffic conditions.

If you have an extra day or two, just before Vail, take U.S. 24 south from I-70, about an hour each way, and stop in Leadville, former home of the tragic mining-era couple Horace and Baby Doe Tabor; numerous historic sites mark their time here, including the well-preserved Augusta Tabor Home.

the historic Molly Brown House Museum, Denver

FROM RED ROCKS TO BLUEGRASS: LIVE MUSIC IN COLORADO

concertgoers enjoying an evening of entertainment at Red Rocks Amphitheatre

One of Colorado's great secrets is the diversity of its live music scene. From the Astronauts in the 1960s to Firefall in the 1970s to Big Head Todd and the Monsters in the 1980s and 1990s to The Fray, the Flobots, and DeVotchKa in recent years, Colorado has produced a diversity of stars almost as rich as the state's music festivals. Note that times, dates, and artist lineups of the festivals change yearly, so check out the Colorado Music Association's website (www. coloradomusic.org) for updates.

Anchor your trip on one of the many summer festivals. Late June's **Telluride Bluegrass Festival** attracts country and bluegrass acts, but it branches out so far that you may find yourself wondering about the title. Late July's **Music in the Mountains,** in Durango, is far from Denver but worth it for a variety of classical and chamber-music orchestras. The **Rocky Mountain Folks Festival,** in Lyons during late August, draws the rock-and-rollier side of folk music, including Todd Snider and the Subdudes.

Other great Colorado music experiences:

Red Rocks Amphitheatre in Morrison, about a half-hour west of Denver along I-70, is one of the best and most beautiful outdoor concert venues in the United States, and big-time acts that include Coldplay, the White Stripes, and Peter Gabriel continue to play there regularly. Back in Denver, check out the **Fillmore Auditorium,** a medium-sized club with superb acoustics and a nice ambience underneath a large chandelier.

Catch a concert at the **Lion's Lair** for rugged rock and roll, the **Soiled Dove** for slightly more muted rock and roll, **Dazzle** for jazz, or the **Ogden Theatre** for larger shows. For old-fashioned country music, not to mention line-dancing lessons and boot shopping, drive to the **Grizzly Rose,** along I-25.

In Boulder, the **Fox Theatre** always has something going on, whether it's a top national act like the Reverend Horton Heat or a rising local band such as Rose Hill Drive. Other top live-music spots include the **Boulder Theater** and numerous venues on the University of Colorado campus, including **Macky Auditorium.** Boulder is also the home of superb record stores, including **Albums on the Hill.**

Drive west to Golden to hit the **Buffalo Rose,** a homey mountain club that plays host to national blues, country, and rock acts such as Hot Tuna and jamming locals. The mountain-town scene has several notable clubs, many specializing in Grateful Dead–style rock and blues: the **Mishawaka Amphitheatre** near Rocky Mountain National Park and Fort Collins, **The Llama** in Telluride, **The Eldo** in Crested Butte, and many others.

Telluride is home to numerous major music festivals, beginning with the aforementioned bluegrass extravaganza in late June. Also noteworthy is the **Telluride Blues and Brews Festival** in mid-October. Check various town websites for information on other summer festivals, such as the **Breckenridge Music Festival,** which is mostly classical; **Rockygrass** in Lyons; and the **Bravo! Vail Valley Music Festival,** also classical.

Day 14

On your last day, check out some of Denver's history museums, including the Molly Brown House Museum and, on the 16th Street Mall, the Daniels and Fisher Tower. For decades in the late 1800s, Colorado represented affluence and opportunity, and miners traveled to Denver from the western Rockies while presidents and kings came here from all over the world. Fly out from DIA, or take an extra day or two for the return driving trip—the fastest route is I-70 west to U.S. 550 south into New Mexico.

▶ THE ROCKY MOUNTAINS SANS SKIING

Some of us Coloradoans are forever doomed to answer no to the question "Do you ski?" It's expensive, and cold, and full of traffic and crowds. And maybe we're just not that coordinated. We make up for it by venturing into the mountains during the summer—camping, hiking, biking, and generally enjoying the scenery. Ideas for building a vacation around this philosophy (you can generally flip them for the winter by adding snowshoes or cross-country skis):

Camping

Outside Estes Park and Boulder, Rocky Mountain National Park has incredible mountain scenery and, outside of Telluride, is the best place to check out the fall color. It also has five drive-in campgrounds, 200 backcountry campsites, and 350-plus miles of hiking trails, including the moderate, nearly three-mile Mills Lake, overlooking a terrific view of Long's Peak.

Hiking

Boulder is filled with excellent trails, most obviously the 5.5-mile Creek Path at the center of town. Try the mildly strenuous 3.2-mile Royal Arch, which goes straight into

elk in Moraine Park Campground, Rocky Mountain National Park

sailing on the Dillon Reservoir

the foothills from pretty Chautauqua Park; you'll know you're at the top upon spotting the red rocky arch itself and a full-range overhead view of the city from the mountains.

Boating

It's not a natural pond, but Dillon Reservoir, owned by the public utility Denver Water, is a 3,233-acre water-sports playground with an island in the middle and the Rockies in the background. Its marinas, operated by the nearby towns of Dillon and Frisco, allow canoes, kayaks, sailboats, and motorboats in addition to fishing and windsurfing.

Fishing

It's hard to hit the wrong spot along the Colorado River, which begins its 1,450 miles at 12,000 feet of elevation in the northern Rockies and flows to the flat Glenwood Springs area. Look for the spot where the river merges with the Roaring Fork River and widens into an angler's haven, with all kinds of trout scurrying in every direction.

Lodging

Need a break from sleeping on the ground? Venture to the Westcliffe Inn, in tiny Westcliffe, in the brief flat area between the Sangre de Cristo Range and the Wet Mountains. It's a little out of the way, 52 miles west of Pueblo, and closed in the winter, but it's worth the extra drive.

Eating

The quintessential mountain restaurant is BeauJo's, a venerable thick-crust pizza joint in downtown Idaho Springs (and other locations near Denver, but this one has the best atmosphere). It's off I-70, just west of Denver en route to Winter Park, Breckenridge, Vail, and the rest.

DENVER

The blizzards in Denver are memorable, exhilarating, legendary—and all the better because within a week or two, the snow disappears, the temperatures rise, and suddenly it's spring again for the rest of the month. In a little more than a century, this onetime Old West outpost has boomed into a metropolis of 500,000 with a young, vibrant downtown core. Why? First, the weather—the snow is dramatic, you won't miss the rain, and even the high-90s days in July and August are bearable due to the lack of humidity. Second, the altitude—5,280 feet, which explains the "Mile High City" nickname and attitude. And finally, the air—the city has cleaned up its "Brown Cloud" and major pollution problems of the 1970s and 1980s, and locals can breathe clearly again.

After the recession of the early 1990s, visionary leaders such as then-mayor Federico Peña revitalized several key parts of the city: Denver International Airport became one of the world's top transportation hubs; the Colorado Rockies brought Major League Baseball and built the old-school, purple-and-brown Coors Field as the heart of Lower Downtown (LoDo); and the classic amusement park Elitch Gardens moved from the outskirts to the center of town.

Over the next decade, the NFL's Denver Broncos built a new stadium, and the NBA's Denver Nuggets built a new arena. With a new young mayor (Michael Hancock, the former city council president who attended high school in the city) and an economy doing better than the rest of the country, Denver has transformed even troubled neighborhoods

© RON RUHOFF / VISIT DENVER

HIGHLIGHTS

◖ Denver Botanic Gardens: Along with 32,000 plants from all over the world, arranged along calm walking paths, the Botanic Gardens has one of the best outdoor concert stages in the city (page 35).

◖ Elitch Gardens: If rides like the Mind Eraser don't tear apart your stomach *and* your mind, enjoy the prime central-Denver location of this classic amusement park (page 38).

◖ State Capitol: Built in 1886, the gold leaf-domed State Capitol is one of the city's most distinctive and stately buildings (page 38).

◖ City Park: A 314-acre park in the northeast part of town, City Park is home to the Denver Zoo and the Denver Museum of Nature & Science— and it's a great place to walk a dog, kick a soccer ball, roll around on the grass, or fly a kite (page 38).

◖ Coors Field: The Colorado Rockies haven't been much to see in recent years, but their modern-and-retro purple-and-black Major League Baseball park was an instant classic as soon as it went up in 1995 (page 41).

◖ Larimer Square: The shops, restaurants, and bars at the heart of LoDo are almost always jammed, and thankfully, former mayor John Hickenlooper made the parking-meter charges far more reasonable as soon as he took office (page 56).

◖ Tattered Cover: The Cherry Creek outlet of this two-bookstore chain is the best – every book you could want, attentive clerks, a huge magazine collection, a strong children's section, and a comfortable atmosphere with cushy chairs and coffee (page 57).

◖ Denver Flagship REI: With a mountain-bike track, a climbing wall, a kayaking haven out back, and tents and hiking equipment everywhere, the REI store is a place for outdoors types to get lost for hours at a time – and there's even a playground for kids (page 59).

◖ Red Rocks Amphitheatre: Whether Van Morrison, Peter Gabriel, Norah Jones, or Alan Jackson, to name a few recent performers, is your thing, Red Rocks is perhaps the most spectacular venue to see a concert in the entire United States (page 77).

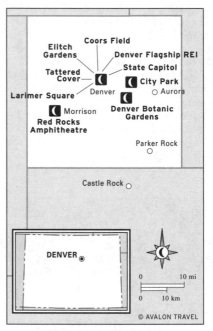

© AVALON TRAVEL

LOOK FOR ◖ TO FIND RECOMMENDED SIGHTS, ACTIVITIES, DINING, AND LODGING.

DENVER

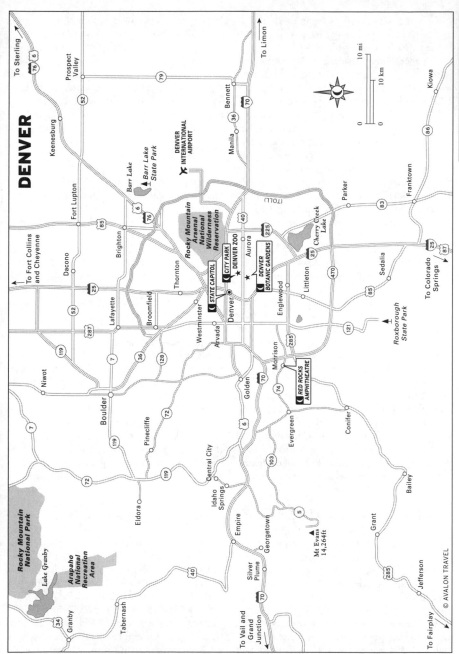

DENVER

To Sterling

Prospect Valley

Keensburg

Fort Lupton

Barr Lake
▲ Barr Lake
State Park

Dacono

Brighton

Thornton

Broomfield

Westminster

Arvada

Denver

Rocky Mountain
Arsenal
National
Wildlife
Reservation

■ STATE CAPITOL
★ CITY PARK
★ DENVER ZOO

★ DENVER
BOTANIC GARDENS

Aurora

Englewood

Littleton

Cherry Creek
Lake

Parker

Sedalia

To Colorado
Springs

Franktown

Kiowa

Roxborough
State Park

To Fort Collins
and Cheyenne

Niwot

Lafayette

Boulder

Pinecliffe

Central City

Idaho
Springs

Eldora

Empire

Georgetown

Silver
Plume

Morrison

Golden

■ RED ROCKS
AMPHITHEATRE

Evergreen

Conifer

Bailey

Grant

Mt Evans
14,264ft

Rocky Mountain
National Park

Arapaho
National
Recreation
Area

Lake Granby

Granby

Tabernash

To Vail and
Grand
Junction

Jefferson

To Fairplay

Prospect
Valley

Bennett

Manila

DENVER
INTERNATIONAL
AIRPORT ✈

To Limon

10 mi

10 km

© AVALON TRAVEL

such as the northwest's venerable Highlands and Sunnyside into trendy havens filled with hip restaurants and townie bars.

The recession of the early 2000s hit Denver hard, especially among the many high-tech workers who'd relocated here through the 1990s, and now in the Great Recession era, politicians have had to make tough choices on cutting the city budget and eliminating services. But Denver continues to expand and grow: The city's five-line light-rail system, which cost billions of dollars during better times, is efficient and popular, linking key LoDo spots such as Union Station and the theater district to Sports Authority Field, the University of Denver, and the suburbs of Littleton, Englewood, and Greenwood Village. The city's Hispanic population, already at 31.8 percent, is growing at a rapid rate, its cultural influence spreading everywhere, from the numerous salsa nights throughout the city to the arena shows by visiting Latin American superstars such as Mexican singer-songwriters Marco Antonio Solís and Ana Gabriel to the many ramshackle chili pepper stands that line Federal Boulevard on the north side of town.

Denver's biggest national moment came in late August 2008, when Barack Obama accepted his nomination for the presidency at a packed Invesco Field (which has since changed its name to Sports Authority Field at Mile High). Although the crowds made driving and walking downtown nearly impossible for four days, the city managed the influx of delegates, media, protesters, and celebrities such as Kanye West and Oprah Winfrey.

PLANNING YOUR TIME

As with many big U.S. cities, it's possible to get a good feel for Denver in just a weekend—hit the LoDo bars and restaurants, stay in a nice hotel like the Brown Palace or the Four Seasons, maybe take in a Rockies game or a trip to the mountains. But to truly capture the local flavor, spend a week. Fly into Denver International Airport, book a few nights at a few different hotels, and check out the less-publicized riches of the Denver Museum of

Nature & Science or people-watch for hours on the 16th Street Mall. Day trips are nice—Central City and Black Hawk may well be the most charming gambling towns in the United States, and Golden has the MillerCoors Brewery tours in addition to a nice old historic gold-mining district—but leave at least a few nights to get to the bottom of LoDo and the many diverse theaters and jazz and rock clubs.

HISTORY

When gold prospectors pushed to Colorado in the 1850s, they shouted, "Pikes Peak or bust!"—but they first discovered gold at the intersection of Cherry Creek and the South Platte River, about 100 miles to the north. The discovery, on November 22, 1858, kicked off the gold rush, beginning a migration of 100,000 people to Colorado; the U.S. government established the state in 1861, and founders named the town for James W. Denver, governor of the Kansas Territory (which, at the time, included eastern Colorado).

Civilization spread quickly after that—to the detriment of fur trappers, traders, and particularly the Cheyennes and Arapahos, whose reservations had been on this land for decades. At first, Native Americans helped Western settlers traverse Kansas and Colorado—they had traded with Anglo settlers for decades—but they were starting to get frustrated over unfavorable U.S. government treaties that forced them to surrender land and deplete their resources. As the Colorado gold rush turned into a boom, bands attacked the new settlers, infamously massacring the Hungate family on its ranch 30 miles from Denver in 1864 and marauding against wagon trains and miner camps.

The settlers fought back, and according to *Colorado: A History of the Centennial State* (1994), John Chivington, a Methodist preacher and colonel of the Third Regiment of the Colorado Volunteer Cavalry, said: "I am fully satisfied that to kill them is the only way to have peace and quiet." Massacres ensued, including a November 29, 1864, ambush of a Cheyenne camp in southeastern Colorado in which U.S. soldiers killed more than 100 Cheyennes and, according to history books, raped and mutilated their women and shot their children. This led to a flurry of treaty negotiations, but skirmishes continued throughout the state until the natives were thoroughly displaced.

Having rid themselves of what they cynically called the "native problem," Americans in Denver built railroads, banks, breweries (including Coors), and meatpacking plants, turning the city into a major agricultural hub. From 1870 to 1890, Denver grew from 4,800 to 107,000 people, making it the second-biggest city in the West, after San Francisco. Although the 1893 depression and the U.S. government's decision to demonetize silver ended this massive growth, Denver businessmen turned to farming wheat, sugar beets, and cows—thus the "Cowtown" label.

In the early 1900s, ambitious but sickly businessman Robert W. Speer came from Pennsylvania to Denver, declared the city "the Paris of America," and in 1904 became mayor until he died in office of influenza 14 years later. During that time, Speer landscaped Civic Center, added zoological gardens to City Park, encouraged local philanthropists to build the Colorado Museum of Natural History (now the Denver Museum of Nature & Science) and other attractions, planted 110,000 trees, built parks, and generally turned Denver into what he called a "city beautiful." These innovations have defined Denver's character ever since.

Denver has since endured several busts (notably the Great Depression) and booms (the city took particular advantage of Franklin D. Roosevelt's New Deal, allowing his Civilian Conservation Corps to build Red Rocks Amphitheatre, in nearby Morrison, in the 1930s). Beginning in the 1960s, given nearby skiing tourism, the oil and gas industry, and an influx of federal employees at the U.S. Mint and other offices, Denver has grown into a stable Western metropolis, able to withstand trauma such as the 1980s oil bust, the bursting of the Internet bubble, and, one hopes, the post-2008-crash budget-cutting.

In 1995, thanks to the efforts of mayors Federico Peña and Wellington Webb, the city opened the $5 billion Denver International Airport, leading to a new boom and a resurgence of the downtown area. The old Mile High Stadium, home of the Denver Broncos, gave way to the flashy Sports Authority Field at Mile High, Major League Baseball planted the Colorado Rockies in a beautiful retro stadium downtown, the LoDo bar and shopping district flourished with fancy restaurants and a free downtown bus, and the metro area population hit more than 2.5 million in 2010 (including fast-growing suburbs like Broomfield and Aurora).

For a more elaborate version of Denver's history, go to www.denvergov.org/AboutDenver/history.asp, an excellent resource.

ORIENTATION

Downtown Denver is about an hour's drive from Denver International Airport off I-70. The main highways are the east–west I-70 and the north–south I-25, both of which provide access to the city's many suburbs—Westminster, Thornton, and Arvada to the north; Littleton, Englewood, and Lakewood to the south; and Aurora to the east. The mountains are due west on I-70, while Boulder is northwest on Highway 36.

This chapter divides the Denver area into seven general regions: **LoDo/Central Denver** refers to Lower Downtown, the heart of the city, including Coors Field and various warehouses turned brewpubs, as well as nearby neighborhoods such as Civic Center and Capitol Hill; **Highlands/Northwest** is a growing, heavily Hispanic part of town with tons of restaurants at the intersection of 32nd Avenue and Lowell Boulevard, Sloan's Lake park, and numerous old Victorian houses (just southeast of this area, **Lower Highland** has transformed recently into a walking and cycling paradise, from the REI flagship store and Confluence Park to the new 18th Street Pedestrian Bridge leading into a cluster of condos and restaurants); **City Park** is a relatively small area east of downtown, but it's notable

DENVER

for attractions such as the Denver Zoo and the Denver Museum of Nature & Science as well as the sprawling park itself; **Cherry Creek** is perhaps Denver's fanciest area, with beautiful old houses and a giant high-end mall; **South Denver** refers to the entire southern part of the city, including the university and neighborhoods such as Hampden and Wellshire, as well as the heavily Hispanic **La Alma/Lincoln Park,** near the Auraria Campus; and **Greater Denver** includes the suburbs, from Aurora to Broomfield to Greenwood Village. Also mentioned, but not as regularly, is **East Denver,** which includes the corridor surrounding East Colfax Avenue, and **South Federal Boulevard,** in the southwestern part of the city, an area heavy with Asian immigrants as well as some of the best Asian restaurants in town.

SAFETY

Denver has its share of gang, drug, and crime problems, but police are fairly aggressive, and most neighborhoods are safe. As always, use caution at night, lock your car doors, and don't walk alone. The emergency number, of course, is 911, or call 720/913-2000 for less pressing police or fire issues.

Sights

LODO/CENTRAL DENVER
Downtown Aquarium

Landry's Restaurants has owned the Downtown Aquarium (700 Water St., 303/561-4450, www.aquariumrestaurants.com/downtown-aquariumdenver, 10 A.M.–9 P.M. Sun.–Thurs., 10 A.M.–9:30 P.M. Fri.–Sat., $16) since 2003, including, with no acknowledgment of the irony, a seafood restaurant on the first floor. The aquarium is packed with fish of all shapes, sizes, and colors, several octopuses, manta rays, sharks, and tigers who occasionally scratch a massive log to tatters. It's a fine city aquarium, although Landry's emphasizes tight, streamlined paths to the exhibits, with cheap stuff to buy along the way.

Denver Public Library

A trip to the Denver Public Library's 540,000-square-foot **Central Library** (10 W. 14th Ave., 720/865-1111, www.denverlibrary. org, 10 A.M.–8 P.M. Mon.–Tues., 10 A.M.–6 P.M. Wed.–Fri., 9 A.M.–5 P.M. Sat., 1–5 P.M. Sun.) is a lot less boring than you'd think. Built in the 1950s and renovated a decade ago, the complex includes a three-story atrium, a bunch of interesting sculptures (including a giant horse on a chair outside), and weirdly shaped windows that give it a fort-like ambience. Inside, look for expansive collections of American West art,

© STAN OBERT / VISIT DENVER

viewing fish at Denver's Downtown Aquarium

books, maps, memorabilia, and, among other works, Edward Ruscha's 130-yard Western-landscape mural on the main floor. The children's room is stocked with all the Dr. Seuss you could ever want, and the periodicals room carries almost every major magazine.

RELIVING *ON THE ROAD*

Much of the late Beat poet Jack Kerouac's classic wanderlust novel *On the Road* takes place in Denver. That's mostly thanks to real-life Denver native Neal Cassady, a charming, fast-moving, near-manic 1940s graduate of the state reformatory who met Kerouac and fellow Beat Allen Ginsberg on a trip to Manhattan. Cassady boasted of stealing 500 cars before he was 21, but he also knew his important philosophers and made a huge impression on the burgeoning Beat scene at the time. Kerouac immortalized Cassady as Dean Moriarty, the main character of *On the Road*.

Before he raised a family in San Francisco and died of hypothermia near a Mexican railroad track in 1968, Cassady brought Kerouac to Denver. Some visitors still stroke their goatees and listen to bebop jazz while checking out the following Kerouacian sights – as well as places where Cassady, Ginsberg, and others lived, worked, and committed drug-induced mayhem. Note that the City of Denver maintains a Beat Poetry Driving Tour at www.denvergov.org (some of which is the source of this information).

Begin at the **City and County Building** (1437 Bannock St., 720/865-9000, www.denvergov.org), immortalized in Ginsberg's poem "The Green Automobile," and get your bearings by looking at the large clock face on the side. To the right is the former May Company store building, where Ginsberg worked as a vacuum salesman and Cassady guided customers in 1947. About seven blocks southeast, at 980 Grant Street, is the site of the former Colburn Hotel (although the building isn't there anymore), where Kerouac and Moriarty stay in a fictionalized, anonymous version simply known as "the hotel." In real life, the Colburn was the site of cosmic discussions and Benzedrine inhaling by Kerouac, Ginsberg, and Cassady.

At 23rd and Welton Streets, **Sonny Lawson Field** remains a functional softball field in the Five Points area. Here, in the book, a reflective, downcast Kerouac watched a game and observed: "The strange young heroes of all kinds, white, colored, Mexican, pure Indian, were on the field, performing with heartbreaking seriousness. Just sandlot kids in uniform." The Five Points area was also in Kerouac's novel, mostly as the site of the great jazz nightclub shows that Moriarty loved so much. Sadly, today, not much jazz or blues goes on in Five Points. You have to venture to LoDo for the best stuff.

In *On the Road*, Kerouac describes the fictional Moriarty as "the son of a wino," a kid who grew up on the mean streets around Larimer Street in downtown Denver. This was more or less true in Cassady's case; he saw Larimer as a vibrant skid row where all the action took place. Today, most of Cassady's beloved old buildings are gone, although some at 15th and Larimer Streets have been restored and converted into shops.

My Brother's Bar (2376 15th St., 303/455-9991) is not mentioned in *On the Road*, but it was one of Cassady's favorite hangouts for years. Pictures of Kerouac and articles about the Beats still hang on the wall, and Beat enthusiasts should ask the owner to see a copy of Cassady's original letter authorizing a friend to pay his bar tab. Around back (behind the huge REI building) is Confluence Park, another Cassady favorite.

Finally, Kerouac's first house, a nondescript one-story, still stands at 6100 West Center Avenue in Lakewood. The writer spent his $1,000 advance from *The Town and the City* on it, and moved his mother and other members of his family here. They showed up, didn't like it, and moved back east after a month. But Kerouac found the house quiet and inspirational, and wrote some of *On the Road* here.

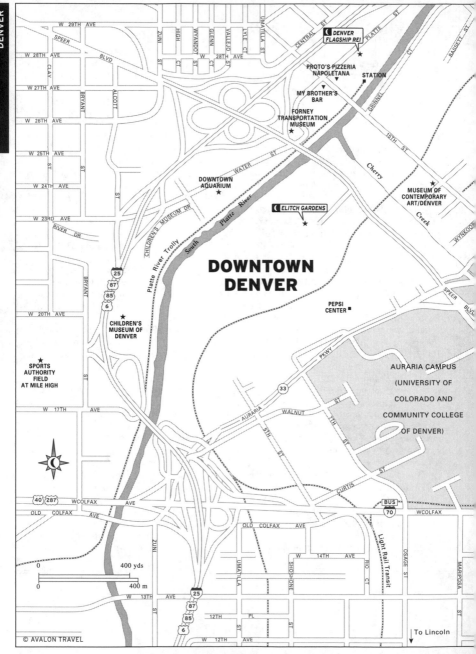

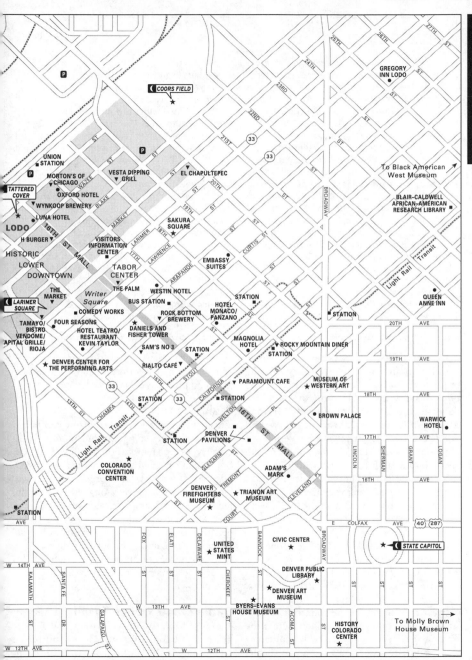

COORS FIELD

GREGORY INN LODO

To Black American West Museum

BLAIR-CALDWELL AFRICAN-AMERICAN RESEARCH LIBRARY

UNION STATION

MORTON'S OF CHICAGO

VESTA DIPPING GRILL

EL CHAPULTEPEC

TATTERED COVER

OXFORD HOTEL

WYNKOOP BREWERY

LUNA HOTEL

LODO

H BURGER

SAKURA SQUARE

VISITORS INFORMATION CENTER

HISTORIC LOWER DOWNTOWN

EMBASSY SUITES

TABOR CENTER

THE MARKET

THE PALM

WESTIN HOTEL

STATION

QUEEN ANNE INN

LARIMER SQUARE

Writer Square

BUS STATION

COMEDY WORKS

ROCK BOTTOM BREWERY

HOTEL MONACO/ PANZANO

STATION

20TH AVE

TAMAYO/ BISTRO VENDOME/ APITAL GRILLE/ RIOJA

FOUR SEASONS

HOTEL TEATRO/ RESTAURANT KEVIN TAYLOR

DANIELS AND FISHER TOWER

SAM'S NO 3

MAGNOLIA HOTEL

ROCKY MOUNTAIN DINER

STATION

19TH AVE

DENVER CENTER FOR THE PERFORMING ARTS

STATION

RIALTO CAFÉ

STATION

PARAMOUNT CAFE

MUSEUM OF WESTERN ART

18TH AVE

STATION

STATION

BROWN PALACE

WARWICK HOTEL

17TH AVE

DENVER PAVILIONS

16TH ST MALL

COLORADO CONVENTION CENTER

STATION

ADAM'S MARK

16TH AVE

DENVER FIREFIGHTERS MUSEUM

TRIANON ART MUSEUM

STATION

E COLFAX AVE

40 287

STATION

UNITED STATES MINT

CIVIC CENTER

STATE CAPITOL

W 14TH AVE

DENVER PUBLIC LIBRARY

DENVER ART MUSEUM

BYERS-EVANS HOUSE MUSEUM

W 13TH AVE

HISTORY COLORADO CENTER

To Molly Brown House Museum

W 12TH AVE

FIVE POINTS

Jazz giants Charlie Parker, Duke Ellington, and Lionel Hampton were regular attractions at Five Points clubs in the 1940s, and the neighborhood along Welton Street, northeast of downtown, remains the city's African American cultural center today. The neighborhood, bounded by Park Avenue, Downing Street, Stout Street, and Tremont Place, has suffered from diminished cultural influence. There's no major club anymore, unless you count **Cervantes Masterpiece Ballroom** (2637 Welton St., 303/297-1772, www.cervantesmasterpiece.com), located in the old Casino Cabaret, where James Brown, Ray Charles, Duke Ellington, Count Basie, Muddy Waters, B.B. King, and a host of other legends once commanded the stage. Today the club focuses mainly on funk, rock, and hip-hop acts, from the Radiators to Dizzee Rascal to members of the Roots.

The historic Rossonian Hotel is no longer open for business, and most of the old clubs and attractions have shut down. However, Five Points is growing in a different direction, adding restaurants, barber shops, boutiques, and a bank.

Attractions include the **Black American West Museum** (3091 California St., 303/242-7428, www.blackamericanwestmuseum.com), the **Cleo Robinson Dance Ensemble** (119 Park Ave. W., 303/295-1759, www.cleoparkerdance. org), and the informal **Juneteenth Festival** (www.juneteenth-denver.org), an annual party that draws 150,000–200,000 people to the neighborhood, in commemoration of the day Texas released all slaves two years after the Emancipation Proclamation.

The annual **Five Points Jazz Festival,** usually in April or May, includes local and small national acts such as the Hugh Ragin Ensemble and the Queen City Jazz Band. For information, contact the **Denver Office of Cultural Affairs** (1245 Champa St., 720/865-4320, www.denvergov.org/doca).

Denver's public library system is also superb, with tiny branches all over the city offering broad selections of magazines and children's books and videos. Of note, in the Five Points area, is the **Blair-Caldwell African-American Research Library** (2401 Welton St., 720/865-2401, http://aarl.denverlibrary. org, noon–8 P.M. Mon., 10 A.M.–6 P.M. Wed. and Fri., 9 A.M.–5 P.M. Sat.), which has rare collections of Black Panther leader Eldridge Cleaver's writings along with interesting documents about black settlers in the Old West.

U.S. Mint

The U.S. Mint (320 W. Colfax Ave., 303/405-4761, www.usmint.gov, guided tours 8 A.M.–2 P.M. Mon.–Fri., free) is literally where the money is. One of four official U.S. mints, Denver's branch produces 14 billion coins per year and maintains the country's second-largest gold supply. The gift shop, across the street at the Tremont Center, sells commemorative coins, and walk-up tours are available, although you have to submit your name in a complex street-side lottery system and may not get in on busy days. Try weekday mornings.

Civic Center

The centerpiece of Mayor Robert Speer's "City Beautiful" campaign in the early 20th century, Civic Center (bounded by Bannock St., Broadway, Colfax Ave., and 14th Ave., 303/331-4060, www.denvergov.org) is three blocks of grass and trees along with a recently renovated Greek amphitheater and 1920s-era Old West statues such as *Bronco Buster.* It's a beautiful part of the city, and festivals such as Cinco de Mayo and Taste of Colorado run here every spring and summer, but be careful walking around at night. Crime can be heavy in this part of town.

Daniels and Fisher Tower

The 375-foot, 20-story Daniels and Fisher Tower (1601 Arapahoe St.) was the third-tallest building in the United States in 1910, when developer William Cooke Daniels built it next to his five-story department store. Although the city razed the store in the 1970s, preservationists kept the tower intact, and it's now a historic site that doubles as an office building. Its clock is 16 feet tall.

Sakura Square

"Tiny Tokyo" centers on Sakura Square (bounded by Larimer St., Lawrence St., 19th St., and 20th St. in LoDo), a one-block development built in 1972 and heavily populated by post–World War II internment-camp refugees and their descendants. In addition to a market, restaurants, a barbershop, and an apartment building, the centerpiece is the **Tri-State/ Denver Buddhist Temple** (1947 Lawrence St., 303/295-1844, www.tsdbt.org), which serves a heavily Japanese immigrant population (many belong to the Jodo Shinshu Buddhist sect). The temple offers services, classes, and a bookstore, and organizes the **Cherry Blossom Festival** in the same downtown area in late June.

◖ Denver Botanic Gardens

The Denver Botanic Gardens (1005 York St., 720/865-3500, www.botanicgardens.org, 9 A.M.–5 P.M. daily Oct.–Apr., 9 A.M.–9 P.M. daily May–Sept., $12.50) make up a serene 23-acre spot filled with 33,000 kinds of plants from all over the world. Check out the "cloud forest tree," inside the Tropical Conservatory, which looks like a huge green giant about to give somebody a bear hug. The Gardens provide dozens of classes, from birdhouse-building workshops for kids to a seminar called "Why Did My Good Plant Go Bad?" The Gardens are also the best place in town to see an outdoor concert; artists from singer-songwriter Rosanne Cash to country chanteuse k. d. lang have played here.

Denver Art Museum

The Denver Art Museum (100 W. 14th Ave., 720/865-5000, www.denverartmuseum.org, 10 A.M.–5 P.M. Tues.–Thurs., 10 A.M.–8 P.M. Fri., 10 A.M.–5 P.M. Sat.–Sun., Colorado residents $10, nonresidents $13) is just a notch or

two below the world-class level of New York's Guggenheim or the Art Institute of Chicago, with works by Claude Monet, Pablo Picasso, and numerous other masters. The Institute of Western American Art is one of the most comprehensive of its kind, including Frederic Remington's bronze *The Cheyenne* and Charles Deas's *Long Jakes,* and its North American Indian collection contains 19,000 pieces illustrating all cultures and ethnic groups. The museum is also a relaxing place to spend some time, both inside and out—a concrete outdoor plaza leads to the public library next door. The museum's huge, metallic, and geometric Frederic C. Hamilton Building was designed by architect Daniel Libeskind, who's heading up the World Trade Center reconstruction in New York City.

Byers-Evans House Museum

Built in 1883 by William Byers, publisher of the *Rocky Mountain News* and an important founder of Denver as we know it, the Byers-Evans House Museum (1310 Bannock St., 303/620-4933, www.historycolorado.

a pond at the Denver Botanic Gardens

a view of the Denver Art Museum's Hamilton Building and its public art display

org/museums/byers-evans-house-museum, 10 A.M.–4 P.M. Tues.–Sun., $6) maintains the furnishings of its original residents. Byers sold it in 1889 to William G. Evans of the Denver Tramway Company, and his family kept it elegant for 80 years. Guided tours run every 30 minutes 10:30 A.M.–2:30 P.M.

History Colorado Center

Scheduled to open downtown in spring 2012, the History Colorado Center (1060 Broadway, 303/447-8679, www.historycolorado.org/museums/history-colorado-center) is in a $111 million building, under construction since 2009, where the Judicial Department used to be. As with the former, much smaller, 130-year-old Colorado History Museum, the center will dig into every aspect of Colorado's past—from Paleo-Indians to gold miners in covered wagons to the Sand Creek Massacre to the ski-pioneering 10th Mountain Division. The most iconic display is Colorado TimeScape, a 10- by 8-foot map and timeline that plays out the region's 10,000-year history in scale models, lasers, and artifacts.

Denver Firefighters Museum

The Denver Firefighters Museum (1326 Tremont Ave., 303/892-1436, www.denverfirefightersmuseum.org, 10 A.M.–4 P.M. Mon.–Sat., $6) was the city's first firehouse, built in 1909, and today houses artifacts such as hoses, alarm bells, and trucks—plus photos tracing the history of firefighting, from rickety old wagons to modern red trucks. Of course, visitors can slide down the pole.

Molly Brown House Museum

Denver philanthropist and society maven Molly Brown is best remembered for her role on the *Titanic*—or, perhaps, Kathy Bates's role in the movie *Titanic*. The Molly Brown House Museum (1340 Pennsylvania St., 303/832-4092, www.mollybrown.org, tours 10 A.M.–3:30 P.M. Tues.–Sat., noon–3:30 P.M. Sun. Sept.–May, 10 A.M.–3:30 P.M. Tues.–Sat., noon–3:30 P.M. Sun. June–Aug., $8) documents her life with her wealthy husband, J. J., in this opulent stone-and-sandstone home. Eventually, after the couple separated, Brown rented the building to families and stayed at the Brown Palace whenever she returned to Denver. She died in 1932, and the still-furnished house is open for tours.

The Children's Museum of Denver

The Children's Museum of Denver (2121 Children's Museum Dr., 303/433-7444, www.mychildsmuseum.org, 9 A.M.–4 P.M. Mon.–Tues. and Thurs.–Fri., 10 A.M.–5 P.M. Sat.–Sun., $8) is a high-class, hands-on city kids' museum with a tree-decorated, pillowy playground in the basement for infants and a fire truck, basketball court, and grocery store for bigger kids upstairs. The exhibits aren't super-high-tech, but they keep the target market busy.

Museum of Contemporary Art/Denver

You'll know the MCA Denver (1485 Delgany St., 303/298-7554, www.mcadenver.org, 10 A.M.–6 P.M. Tues.–Thurs. and Sat.–Sun., 10 A.M.–10 P.M. Fri., $10) upon spotting the large, bright-red, flashing-neon heart with a sparkly sword cutting through it in front of the sleek, 25,000-square-foot, mostly glass building between LoDo and the Highlands. (The sad heart is called *Toxic Schizophrenia,* by British artists Tim Noble and Sue Webster.) The exhibits here, meaningful whoopee cushions, light-and-shadow mazes, wineglass chandeliers, and other works by mostly Colorado artists, are thought-provoking, colorful, and even fun for kids. Check out the MCA Café, which occasionally devises cupcakes that match the exhibits.

Black American West Museum

Among the revelations at the Black American West Museum (3091 California St., 720/242-7428, www.blackamericanwestmuseum.com, 10 A.M.–2 P.M. Thurs.–Sat., 1–4 P.M. Sun., $8): One of the first Colorado miners to discover gold, Henry Parker of Idaho Springs, was African American; the all-black 10th Cavalry was instrumental in helping Teddy Roosevelt capture San Juan Hill in 1898; and

© BOB ASH / VISIT DENVER

the Colorado State Capitol building

DENVER

black families headed west like everybody else in the late 1800s, establishing all-black cities throughout Colorado.

Elitch Gardens

This popular amusement park (2000 Elitch Circle, 303/595-4386, www.elitchgardens. com, hours vary, $43), which opened in 1890 as a zoological park in northwest Denver, relocated to the middle of downtown in 1995 and is now famous for rides such as the Mind Eraser (it climbs higher than 10 stories, drops abruptly, goes upside-down, and hits speeds of 50 mph). Kids love the place, especially given tie-in rides with Bugs Bunny and Batman and an elaborate new adventure water park. Grown-ups—well, those whose minds don't need erasing—can hold hands on the 100-foot-tall Ferris wheel overlooking Denver and the Rockies. The park also plays host to summer concerts by the likes of *iCarly* star and singer Miranda Cosgrove and *cumbia* stars Los Tucanes de Tijuana.

State Capitol

One of the most distinctive sights in the city, the gold leaf–domed State Capitol (200 E. Colfax Ave., 303/866-2604, www.colorado. gov/capitoltour, historical tours 10 A.M.–3 P.M. Mon.–Fri., dome tours 9 A.M.–2:30 P.M. Mon.–Fri.) was built in 1886 out of granite, white marble, onyx, sandstone, and other materials at the time unique to Colorado. The legislature usually convenes January–May, and people can watch from third-floor viewing areas. Also check out the rotunda—which is sporadically open to the public these days—for great views of the city. Tours run on the hour; a self-guided tour includes a 99-step hike into the dome and a museum called "Mr. Brown's Attic."

CITY PARK

Many experience this 314-acre park (17th Ave. and Colorado Blvd., 720/913-0696) by visiting the zoo or the Museum of Nature & Science, then jumping back in the car to return home. But the park itself is a beautiful, quiet kite-flying spot with a public golf course, tennis

courts, a large lake (and several smaller ones), flower gardens, and various fountains. The city first acquired the property in 1881.

Denver Zoo

The Denver Zoo (2300 Steele St., 303/376-4800, www.denverzoo.org, 9 A.M.–5 P.M. daily Mar.–Oct., 10 A.M.–4 P.M. daily Nov.–Feb., $13 Mar.–Oct., $10 Nov.–Feb.) is a great city zoo, with a pair of elephants at the center; monkeys of every conceivable shape, age, and size; and an elaborate aquatic section full of polar bears and fish. It's spread out, so bring comfortable shoes and a stroller for the kids—who will probably insist on rides on the animal-themed carousel and mini-train.

Denver Museum of Nature & Science

Cramming many levels of science and history under one roof, the recently renovated and expanded Denver Museum of Nature & Science (2001 Colorado Blvd., 303/322-7009, www.

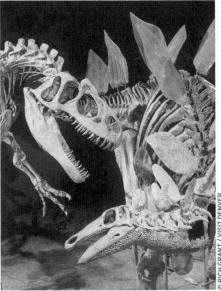

© RICH GRANT / VISIT DENVER

dinosaur fossils on display at the Denver Museum of Nature & Science

dmns.org, 9 A.M.–5 P.M. daily, $12) has two superb anchoring exhibits—Space Odyssey, which lets visitors ride in actual moon-visiting spacecraft, and the dinosaur-filled Prehistoric Journey. The IMAX theater is worth the additional price. Before leaving, save time to check out the rear of the museum, where the third floor overlooks perhaps the best view in the city of the Rockies—just behind the Denver skyline.

HIGHLANDS/NORTHWEST

A little less congested than the celebrated Elitch Gardens, **Lakeside Amusement Park** (4601 Sheridan Blvd., 303/477-1621, www. lakesideamusementpark.com, hours vary by season, $2.50) stars the 90-second wooden-car Cyclone along with throwback rides such as Tilt-A-Whirl, Wild Chipmunk, and Rock-O-Plane. The park was built in the mid-1800s, and toddlers particularly love its nonscary kids' park.

All that's left of the old **Elitch Gardens** site, supported by the Historic Elitch Gardens Theatre Foundation (1228 15th St., 303/623-0216, www.historicelitchtheatre.org), is a modest theater and a small pavilion built in 1925. Although Edward G. Robinson, Grace Kelly, Jessica Tandy, and numerous others have performed here, the location is better known these days for its weekly summer farmers markets and other community events.

LA ALMA/LINCOLN PARK

One of Denver's oldest neighborhoods, La Alma/Lincoln Park (just south of the Auraria Higher Education Center campus, bounded by W. Colfax Ave., W. 6th Ave., Speer Blvd., and the South Platte River) is rich with Hispanic culture and growing fast, thanks in part to the light-rail station at 10th Avenue and Osage Street. In the 1870s the area was part of Auraria City and attracted affluent residents who built homes here, some of which survived the Cherry Creek floods of the early 1900s. Denver officials bought a 15-acre chunk of the region in 1885 and turned it into a park; in later years Hispanics immigrated to the city

and settled in this neighborhood, nicknaming it "La Alma," meaning "spirit" or "soul." The Spanish name stuck, and the area today is officially double-named.

Museo de las Americas

Since it opened in the early 1990s, the cultural centerpiece of La Alma/Lincoln Park has been the Museo de las Americas (861 Santa Fe Dr., 303/571-4401, www.museo.org, 10 A.M.–5 P.M. Tues.–Fri., noon–5 P.M. Sat.–Sun., $5). Long-standing exhibitions include statues and pottery from Mexico and South America before the Europeans showed up as well as a display of 20th-century painter David Alfaro Siqueiros's brightly colored works. The museum offers programs, films, slide shows, and workshops. The museum is also a social center, with a Spanish happy hour every third Friday of the month; plan to drink beer (Coors is a sponsor!), speak Spanish, and take the occasional dance lesson.

SOUTH FEDERAL BOULEVARD

The **Far East Center** (Federal Blvd. between W. Alameda Ave. and W. Mississippi Ave.) refers to both a two-story strip mall in this south Denver area and the surrounding food-dominated cultural center for Thai, Vietnamese, and other southeast-Asian refugees who settled in this area after the Vietnam War. One of the key attractions here is *pho,* a traditional and very delicious Vietnamese rice-noodle soup dish usually filled with beef or chicken. The **Little Saigon Supermarket** (375 S. Federal Blvd., 303/937-8860), as you might expect, has a gigantic section of Asian noodles as well as live lobsters, crabs, chicken feet, and pork tail. The house specialty at **Bakery Vinh-Xuong** (375 S. Federal Blvd., 303/922-4968) is a sloppy French-meets-Vietnamese sandwich filled with ham, pork, chicken, and vegetables; the bakery also sells puddings and pastries, some with sugar, others with, uh, meat.

The mall itself, with a distinctive arch in the parking lot at 333 South Federal Boulevard, is filled with Asian supermarkets (look for the live eel tanks!), bakeries, restaurants, and various shops and businesses.

GREATER DENVER

For a city obsessed with souped-up cars and "cruising" streets such as Federal Boulevard, the small **Forney Transportation Museum** (4303 Brighton Blvd., 303/297-1113, www.forneymuseum.org, 10 A.M.–4 P.M. Mon.–Sat., $8) provides sleek historical perspective. The six-cylinder, six-wheel, bright-yellow Model H6A is a Barcelona-built luxury car, supposedly for a king of Greece in the early 1920s. There's also a Rolls Royce, a locomotive, and a train car known as "Big Boy."

The main attraction of the peaceful **Butterfly Pavilion** (6252 W. 104th Ave., Westminster, 303/469-5441, www.butterflies.org, 9 A.M.–5 P.M. daily, $8.50) is a greenhouse filled with plants and butterflies of all colors and sizes (not to mention caterpillars and cocoons). It also has an iguana, fish in a pond, various large insects, huge plastic grasshopper statues, starfish available for petting, and other hands-on stuff for kids.

Denver's Asian population is just under 4 percent, but it's growing. In addition to the Far East Center, suburban Aurora has a Korean American–dominated district (bounded by S. Havana St., S. Peoria St., E. Mississippi Ave., and S. Parker Rd.), known colloquially as "Koreatown." There are tons of excellent restaurants here, including **Han Kang** (1910 S. Havana St., Aurora, 303/873-6800, www.hankangkoreancuisine.com, 8 A.M.–10 P.M. Mon.–Sat., 8 A.M.–9 P.M. Sun., $9), which *Westword* recently cited for "Best Barbecued Bacon." Also in the area are Korean-focused grocery stores, churches, and shops.

Sports and Recreation

SPECTATOR SPORTS

No matter how many Stanley Cups the Colorado Avalanche ice hockey team wins, Denver will always be a football town—quarterback John Elway's two Super Bowl victories in the late 1990s merely confirmed it. **Sports Authority Field at Mile High** (1701 Bryant St., 720/258-3000, www.sportsauthorityfieldatmilehigh.com), where the **Denver Broncos** play, is a steel-and-glass monolith that replaced the classic old Mile High Stadium. The stadium is a comfortable, well-maintained place to watch a game (or the occasional rock concert), and the concession snacks tend to be more diverse than just hot dogs and beer. In summer 2011, Sports Authority paid $32 million to take over the naming rights to the stadium for the next 10 years, replacing Invesco, a mutual-fund company.

The **Colorado Avalanche,** 1996 and 2001 Stanley Cup champions, play at the **Pepsi Center** (1000 Chopper Circle, 303/405-1100, www.pepsicenter.com), downtown across the parking lot from Elitch Gardens. The Pepsi Center also houses the **Denver Nuggets** professional basketball team, who were forced to trade their dynamic superstar, Carmelo Anthony, to the New York Knicks for a bunch of promising young players. Nuggets games are oddly designed to entertain nonfans, with prominent cheerleaders, a daredevil mascot named Rocky, games, and contests during every conceivable break in the action. The Pepsi Center also plays host to the Colorado Mammoth (lacrosse), big-name concerts such as Taylor Swift, Eminem, 50 Cent, Bruce Springsteen, and Paul McCartney, and events that include World Wrestling Entertainment, Cirque du Soleil, and monster-truck rallies. Note that the Pepsi Center has an in-house ticketing service, not Ticketmaster, called TicketHorse (866/461-6556, www.tickethorse.com).

Dick's Sporting Goods Park (6000 Victory Way, Commerce City, 303/727-3500, www.dickssportinggoodspark.com) is a sprawling complex with 24 fields and good sight lines pretty much everywhere. (The downside is that you have to go to Commerce City, an industry-heavy suburb of Denver that is not known for its pleasant outdoor smells.) The home team is the **Colorado Rapids** professional soccer club, who have been improving in recent years thanks to exciting players such as high-scoring forward Conor Casey. As one of the biggest concert venues in the Denver area, Dick's often plays host to popular music events such as jam band Phish and country singer Kenny Chesney.

The University of Denver's Pioneers ice hockey team is almost always good—in 2005 they became the seventh team in NCAA history to win two straight titles. They play at the college's **Magness Arena** (2240 Buchtel Blvd., 303/871-2336, www.denverpioneers.com), a rowdy bowl of a sports arena that doubles as a concert venue—Christina Aguilera, Jane's Addiction, the Pixies, Sting, and Luis Miguel have performed here in recent years. DU also has teams in men's and women's basketball and soccer, gymnastics, volleyball, and lacrosse.

Denver has not one but two female Roller Derby teams. I can't vouch for the **Rocky Mountain Rollergirls** (www.rockymountainrollergirls.com), who have regular bouts throughout Denver, Colorado Springs, and Durango, but I am a fan of such sharp-elbowed heroines as Inga Lorious and Angela Death of the **Denver Roller Dolls** (www.denverrollerdolls.org). Their bouts run every few months at theaters and arenas in the Denver area, and they're both campy (dig the burlesque outfits) and exciting (taking the time to study the rules is strongly recommended).

◖ Coors Field

The **Colorado Rockies** pro baseball team made it to the World Series in 2007, losing to the Boston Red Sox, but that was their peak; since then, the team has been spiraling downward, eventually shedding their best pitcher, Ubaldo Jiménez, in a trade four years later. But the team that brought baseball to LoDo and Coors Field (2001 Blake St., 303/292-0200, www.rockies.mlb.com) is fun to watch no matter how well they play. This Major League

Coors Field

Baseball park, built in 1995, is all purple, black, and brown, with a classic ambience and excellent snacks.

GOLF

The golf courses in Denver aren't as world-renowned as their counterparts in, say, Vail or Aspen, but some have won awards, and they're convenient for weekend travelers. The 6,318-yard, par-72 **City Park** (2500 York St., 303/295-2096, www.cityofdenvergolf.com/citypark, $26 weekdays, $35 weekends) has a 1.5-acre lake. **Foothills** (3901 S. Carr St., 303/409-2400, www.foothillsgolf.org, $30–40), opened in 1933, is one of the city's highest-traffic courses. **Overland** (1801 S. Huron St., 303/777-7331, www.overlandgolfcourse.com, $26 weekdays, $35 weekends) was built in 1895 and was the Denver Country Club for years; today, it's known for high trees and narrow fairways. **Willis Case** (4999 Vrain St., 720/865-0700, www.cityofdenvergolf.com/williscase.htm, $26 weekdays, $35 weekends) is an OK course, but the views of Denver and the Rockies are incredible. The 27-hole, putting-oriented **Kennedy** (10500 E. Hampden Ave., 720/865-0720, www.cityofdenvergolf.com/kennedy, $23 weekdays, $31 weekends), along Cherry Creek, has serious water hazards. One of the most challenging courses in town, **Wellshire** (3333 S. Colorado Blvd., 303/692-5636, www.cityofdenvergolf.com/wellshire, $26 weekdays, $35 weekends) has two holes known as "Amen Corner."

Just outside Denver, the **Omni Interlocken Resort** (500 Interlocken Blvd., Broomfield, 303/438-6600, www.omnihotels.com/golf/denver, $105–130) has one 18-hole course and three nine-hole courses designed by 1981 U.S. Open champion David Graham and his partner, Gary Panks. The John Elway Celebrity Classic Golf Tournament, a big deal in these parts, is held here every year. In Littleton, a suburb just south of the city, the **Arrowhead Golf Course** (10850 W. Sundown Trail, Littleton, 303/973-9614, www.arrowheadcolorado.com, $79–119) overlooks Roxborough State Park and has some of the most beautiful

golf-course scenery in the state, if not the country. Its VIP packages also offer luxurious (if unnecessary) touches like GPS systems on the carts.

HIKING AND BIKING

The **Denver Parks Department** (201 W. Colfax Ave., Dept. 601, 720/913-1311, www.denvergov.org/Parks) operates more than 200 parks, including massive crown jewels such as the flowery, 165-acre **Washington Park** (701 S. Franklin St., 303/698-4962) and the urban 314-acre **City Park** (17th Ave. and York St.). The parks are generally well kept, often with elaborate flower arrangements, tennis courts, baseball diamonds, and jogging paths. Spend some time in the city and you'll notice people riding around on beautiful new red bicycles; these come from a city-approved program called **Denver Bike Sharing** (2737A Larimer St., 303/825-3325, www.denverbikesharing.org), also known as Denver B-cycle, which allows people to check out bikes for ridiculously cheap rates—free for up to 30 minutes,

Bicyclists ride along Cherry Creek on the Cherry Creek Trail.

© STEVE CRECELIUS / VISIT DENVER

$1 for the first hour, or $6 per day. They're conveniently located throughout downtown, and some in the city plan their weekend nights around getting tipsy at LoDo bars then B-cycling back home.

The **Cherry Creek Trail** is a paved path that connects Cherry Creek Reservoir along the creek to the network of concrete paths in downtown Denver. The **Highline Canal** is a quiet, tree-lined, paved path that runs 66 miles through Douglas, Arapahoe, and Denver Counties—it starts south of Highway 470 and Wadsworth and ends at the Rocky Mountain Arsenal in northeast Denver.

Once a horribly polluted area shunned by city officials and residents, the **Platte River Greenway** underwent a massive cleanup effort in the mid-1970s that continues today. The best spot to "jump in" is at **Confluence Park,** just behind REI across I-25 from Sports Authority Field, a pretty little spot where the river turns into rapids and forms a small pool (with a wooden bridge). Kayakers and dogs love it here, and the Platte River extends in three directions—east to the suburbs, west to the football stadium, and south to LoDo. The surrounding cement paths are great for biking and walking.

On various plots west of Denver, **Jefferson County Open Space** (700 Jefferson County Pkwy., Golden, 303/271-5925, http://openspace.jeffco.us) operates more than 51,000 acres of fully staffed public land. This includes more than 23 parks, most of which are equipped with well-maintained trails (210 miles overall) through some of the most beautiful land in Colorado. **Elk Meadows Park,** for example, has 13.1 miles of trails. I've hiked the 3.7-mile **Bergen Peak,** which rises about 1,500 vertical feet and contains frequent rocky switchbacks en route to an amazing summit overlooking several "fourteeners" (14,000-foot peaks), including Mount Evans, Grays Peak, and Torreys Peak. To get to the trailhead, take I-70 west from Denver, exit onto Highway 74, drive 2.25 miles, turn right on Lewis Ridge Road, and turn right into the parking lot. **Matthews-Winters Park** is a forest- and wildlife-heavy park ideal for hikers and mountain bikers, extending to Red Rocks Park and the town of Golden. To get there, take I-70 to Highway 26, turn south, and drive about 500 feet to the park entrance. Also in Jefferson County is **Deer Creek Canyon,** a 1,881-acre park that was once a campground for wandering Utes and Jesse James. To get there, take I-70, turn south on C-470 to Kipling, exit south to South Deer Creek Canyon Road, turn west to Grizzly Drive, and go about 0.25 miles to the parking lot. Almost all of these trails are open to cyclists, but most are not for novices; I passed half a dozen beefy mountain-bikers on the Bergen Peak Trail and most were huffing, puffing, and pushing their bikes over the steepest and rockiest parts.

South of the city in Littleton, **Chatfield State Park** (11500 N. Roxborough Park Rd., 303/791-7275, http://parks.state.co.us/parks/chatfield) has a reservoir, a marina, and a variety of wildlife and birds, including 80 pairs of blue herons. The park's three trails include the **Chatfield Internal Bikeway,** a 10-mile paved ride that links to other trails in the south suburbs. One of these is the **Mary Carter Greenway,** an eight-mile concrete path that runs along the South Platte River from Chatfield Park to the border of Englewood and Denver. (It's also a great stretch of water for paddlers.) The park has four campgrounds with a total of 197 sites; they're $22 per night. Chatfield Park is also a hotbed for hot air: Although the Rocky Mountain Balloon Festival closed in 2009, **Rocky Mountain Hot Air** (5075 W. Alaska Place, Denver, 303/936-0292, www.rockymountainhotair.com) uses Chatfield Park as its home base, giving private balloon trips on dirigibles of all shapes, sizes, and colors.

In Brighton, northeast of Denver, **Barr Lake State Park** (13401 Picadilly Rd., 303/659-6005, http://parks.state.co.us/parks/barrlake) includes a flat, easy walk and a chance to see some of the 350 different species of birds, snakes, and other creatures that live in this wildlife sanctuary. Barr Lake is also headquarters for the **Rocky Mountain Bird Observatory** (14500 Lark Bunting Lane, 303/659-4348, www.rmbo.org), so it attracts serious birders.

The loop around the lake is 8.8 miles, but you can take the shorter **Neidrach Nature Loop** (0.6 miles) or the three-mile Gazebo Boardwalk Trail, which swings by a bald eagle nest.

Denver is stuffed with bike shops, including **Salvagetti Bicycle Workshop** (1611 Platte St., 303/691-5595, www.salvagetti.com), in the Highlands neighborhood not far from downtown; it's a bit of a hipster spot, but the staff is helpful and knowledgeable, and during the summer the shop opens a side window for cyclists to grab a quick coffee and pastry during their commutes. Suburban **Wheat Ridge Cyclery** (7085 W. 38th Ave., 303/424-3221, http://ridewrc.com) is larger and more traditional than Salvagetti's, but its employees are just as cheerful, particularly in the service department.

WATER SPORTS

Paddlers who aren't in the mood for a long Rocky Mountain day trip tend to congregate along the **South Platte River,** which flows from Park County, southwest of Denver, through Chatfield State Park in Littleton, then through the entire city of Denver before traveling northeast into the Eastern Plains and Nebraska. In Denver itself, there are several access points for paddlers, including **Globeville Landing** (38th St. and Arkins Court), near the Denver Coliseum, and **Overland Park** (Florida Ave. and South Platte River Dr.). The river pools into an artificial concrete recreation area just behind the REI store at **Confluence Park,** near 15th and Platte Streets. This park is a haven for kayakers and dogs.

For kayak rentals and resources, **Confluence Kayaks** (2373 15th St., Unit B, 303/433-3676, www.confluencekayaks.com) is centrally located, not far from Confluence Park.

Fishing opportunities at city and state parks in the Denver area aren't on par with, say, those at Horsetooth Reservoir or on the Fryingpan River elsewhere in Colorado. But at **Cherry Creek State Park** (4201 S. Parker Rd., Aurora, 303/690-1166), the Colorado Division of Wildlife fills the reservoir with rainbow trout, and two dozen species can be found here, including walleye, tiger muskie, and northern pike. **Chatfield**

Confluence Park on the South Platte River bustles with river enthusiasts.

© STAN OBERT / VISIT DENVER

State Park (11500 N. Roxborough Park Rd., Littleton, http://parks.state.co.us/parks/chatfield, 303/791-7275) also has a reservoir stocked with channel catfish, yellow perch, crappie, carp, and rainbow trout. In Brighton, northeast of the city, **Barr Lake State Park** (13401 Picadilly Rd., 303/659-6005, www.parks.state.co.us/parks/barrlake/Pages/BarrLakeHome.aspx) is stocked with rainbow trout in the spring and other species year-round. For more information on urban or suburban fishing, contact **Colorado State Parks** (1313 Sherman St., Suite 618, Denver, 303/866-3437, www.parks.state.co.us/Pages/HomePage.aspx) or **Denver Parks and Recreation** (720/865-9000, www.denvergov.org/Parks_Recreation). For equipment, guided tours, and other resources, try **The Flyfisher Guide Service** (1303 E. 6th Ave., Suite 200, 303/733-2672, www.theflyfisher.com) or **Bass Pro Shops Outdoor World** (7970 Northfield Blvd., 720/385-3600, www.basspro.com), which was designated "Best Place to Hook a He-Man" in *Westword* not long ago, just for your information.

FITNESS

Denver has tons of health clubs all over the city, but start with the 29 **Denver Recreation Centers** (720/913-0693, www.denvergov.org/recreation), which charge $10 per day for an adult nonresident for access to swimming pools, basketball courts, weight-lifting equipment, classes, and child-care programs. The most impressive center is the **Colorado Athletic Club** (1630 Welton St., 303/623-2100, www.coloradoac.com), a 40,000-square-foot facility that truly pampers its clients with a pool, tanning beds, massage chairs, and saunas along with cutting-edge weight-training equipment and a basketball court. Similarly high quality, but even more convenient to downtown, is the **Forza Fitness and Performance Club** (1849 Curtis St., 303/294-9494, www.forzadenver.com), two blocks from the 16th Street Mall. One of the club's owners is Steve Hess, strength and conditioning coach for the Denver Nuggets.

About 10 minutes from central Denver, the **Lakeshore Athletic Club–Flatiron** (300 Summit Blvd., Broomfield, 303/729-4300, www.lsac-flatiron.com) is, at 100,000 square feet, more than twice the size of the downtown Colorado Athletic Club, with an NBA-sized basketball court, 50-foot rock-climbing wall, Junior Olympic–sized pool, and tons of classes for kids and adults, from yoga to healthy cooking.

Entertainment and Nightlife

The centerpiece of Denver entertainment and culture is the **Denver Performing Arts Complex** (14th St. and Curtis St., 303/893-4100, www.denvercenter.org, box office 10 A.M.–6 P.M. Mon.–Sat.), a collection of 11 large and small theaters (11,260 seats in all) spread over four city blocks. With a huge curved glass "ceiling" covering much of the gray-brick complex, the center dominates downtown Denver even on nights without a popular show. Built in 1974 and run by the Denver Center for the Performing Arts, the complex's anchors are the in-the-round Boettcher Concert Hall, the ornate Temple Hoyne Buell Theatre, and the newest venue, the Ellie Caulkins Opera House. Among the attractions over the years: Disney's *Lion King* and *The Little Mermaid; Les Misérables; I Love You, You're Perfect, Now Change;* Lyle Lovett; Jerry Seinfeld; *Hello Dolly* with Carol Channing; Penn and Teller; the ballet and opera seasons; and, of course, the Colorado Symphony Orchestra. The main promoter for theatrical productions here is **Denver Center Attractions,** which imports many of the big touring shows to Denver.

THEATER

While it's tough to make it as an actor or director in Denver, the theater scene is supportive, talent quickly rises to the top, and there are enough stages (in all genres, from

DENVER'S MUSIC SCENE

Rock, jazz, and blues fans accustomed to the bursting weekends of New York, Chicago, Los Angeles, and Austin endure a temporary letdown upon relocating to Denver. They have a right to be disappointed: A month's worth of musical entertainment here is equivalent to a weekend in those places. But have some patience, and pick your spots. Every single major touring act, with rare exceptions, winds up in Denver or Boulder before long, owing to the city's location halfway between Chicago and LA (where else are bands going to play? Salt Lake City? Cheyenne?) And on the club level, the city maintains a "scene" for almost every genre – blues, jazz, punk, folk, and hippie jamming music have venues of their own, and while Denver is unlikely to become the next Seattle and spawn its own style, its diversity is a plus.

RED ROCKS AND BIG TENTS

Summer is the best time of year for music lovers, as the inimitable Red Rocks Amphitheatre and the suburban Comfort Dental Amphitheatre fill up with superstar acts, while the midsize downtown Fillmore Auditorium and the nearby Ogden Theatre draw the smaller, Elvis Costello–grade names. If you're a true live-music lover, though, don't lose sight of clubs like the Bluebird, El Chapultepec, and Herman's Hideaway – they thrive in spring and fall, and their shows can be both intimate and star-powered. *The Denver Post* does a good job of chronicling these scenes, especially in its Friday sections, but pick up *Westword* (www.westword.com) for more thorough listings, critics' picks, and reviews of local music. Here's a rundown of music venues:

The single best place to see a show is **Red Rocks Amphitheatre** (2901 Ship Rock Rd., Morrison, 303/640-2637, www.redrocksonline.com), where the acoustics are almost as breathtaking as the scenery. Bands from the Beatles to U2 have performed legendary

shows here, and every summer the crowded, general-admission, 9,000-capacity amphitheater snags a solid half dozen amazing acts – depending on your age, if you're from Denver, you're probably still talking about R.E.M., local heroes Big Head Todd and the Monsters, B.B. King, the Pretenders, Paul Simon, Bonnie Raitt, or Sonic Youth.

Far less charming, in the south suburbs, is **Comfort Dental Amphitheatre** (6350 Greenwood Plaza Blvd., Greenwood Village, 303/220-7000, www.livenation.com), which handles more customers at a time and has hosted everything from all six Lollapaloozas to Jay-Z and 50 Cent to Ringo Starr's All-Starr Band. Hosting concerts year-round is the downtown **Pepsi Center** (1000 Chopper Circle, 303/405-1100, www.pepsicenter.com), which gets the likes of Bruce Springsteen, Shakira, and Taylor Swift, and the **Denver Coliseum** (4600 Humboldt St., 303/295-4444, www.denvercoliseum.com), a less-slick sports arena that has played host to Nirvana, George Jones, and Slipknot over the years and remains a central hub for Spanish-language pop, folk, and rock music, including Los Tigres del Norte (not to mention the circus).

HISTORIC VENUES, ROCKIN' BANDS

Denver is blessed with three terrific midsize theaters where major musicians play regularly: the **Paramount Theatre** (1621 Glenarm Place, 303/623-0106, www.denverparamount.com), which opened in 1930 and has a beautiful old Wurlitzer organ to go with a classic interior and a comfortable, carpeted lobby; the **Fillmore Auditorium** (1510 Clarkson St., 303/837-0360, www.livenation.com), a lovingly refinished, chandelier-topped, former ice-skating rink (in the 1910s), hockey arena (in the 1940s), and heavy-metal club (in the 1990s), which draws some of the biggest bands in the city; and the **Ogden Theatre** (935 E. Colfax Ave., 303/832-1874, www.ogdentheatre.net), down the street from the Fillmore, which is grungier but has an excellent sound system and also regularly draws top acts. The remodeled **Gothic Theatre** (3263 S. Broadway, Englewood, 303/788-0984, www.gothictheatre.com) is famous for hosting punk, metal, and grunge shows throughout the 1990s – memorably Nirvana, the Red Hot Chili Peppers, the Butthole Surfers, and the Pixies played here; the venue isn't quite as influential as it used to be, but it still draws alternative-rock and punk bands. The circa-1917 **Bluebird Theater** (3317 E. Colfax Ave., 303/377-1666, www.bluebirdtheater.net) is sort of a mini-Ogden, a nicely refinished, intimate place to see The Wedding Present or Slim Cessna's Auto Club.

Club-wise, the city has at least one venue for almost any kind of music you can name. The legendary jazz venue is **El Chapultepec** (1962 Market St., 303/295-9126), which has hosted Ella Fitzgerald, Sarah Vaughan, Frank Sinatra, Tony Bennett, Chet Baker, Wynton Marsalis, and hundreds of others since it switched from mariachi to jazz music after it opened in the 1950s. Owner Jerry Krantz, who serves only beer and disallows dancing, told the *Rocky Mountain News* that members of U2 stopped by in 1992 with underage girls in tow – and Krantz told them to get lost. A more recent addition to Denver's jazz circuit is **Dazzle** (930 Lincoln St., 303/839-5100, www.dazzlejazz.com), which has mirror-lined walls, modern performers (including many locals) such as Kenny Garrett, and excellent Sunday brunches.

APPROVED BY RAMONES FANS

Punkers love the **Lion's Lair** (2022 E. Colfax Ave., 303/320-9200, www.myspace.com/lionslairdenver), where bands play on a raised stage behind a bar literally at the center of the room – I saw an incredible show there once by British pub-rocker Graham Parker. Also punk-leaning is the venerable **Aztlan Theatre** (974 Santa Fe Dr., 303/573-0188). Revered in the 1980s and 1990s as a punk club called Seven South, the **Hi-Dive** (7 S. Broadway, 720/570-4500, www.hi-dive.com) reinvented itself in 2003 as a hipster hangout (there are almost always lines out the door on weekends) with a backdrop of DJs, local stars like Dressy Bessy, and up-and-coming national acts like Slim Cessna's Auto Club. The **Soiled Dove** (7401 E. 1st Ave., 303/830-9214, www.tavernhg.com/soiled_dove) also draws national acts that are softer and more folkie and countryish than the other clubs, such as Over the Rhine and Ian Tyson.

The center of the folk-and-bluegrass (which is to say, "acoustic music") scene is the **Swallow Hill Music Hall** (71 E. Yale Ave., 303/777-1003 or 877/214-7013, www.swallowhill.com), a 2,000-member organization that has put on live shows and classes since the 1960s.

Country line-dancers, or just people who like to take in the occasional Willie Nelson or Tanya Tucker show, flock to the **Grizzly Rose** (5450 N. Valley Hwy., 303/295-1330, www.grizzlyrose.com), an old-school country club where everything's made of wood. Faith Hill, Tim McGraw, Brooks and Dunn, and Garth Brooks, to name just a few, stopped here on their way to the top.

Finally, for plain old rock and roll – by which I think of a Dave Alvin show in the early 1990s, with the Skeletons as his backup band, which kicked my behind all over the floor – **Herman's Hideaway** (1578 S. Broadway, 303/777-5840, www.hermanshideaway.com) has a warm, beer-drinking vibe. Local heroes Big Head Todd and the Monsters and the Subdudes, among others, have made it their home base.

But even big-city snobs know Denver isn't the only place to see live music. Boulder is filled with excellent clubs and theaters, and world-class clubs and festivals are in Telluride, Fort Collins, Lyons, Nederland, and many other places. If you're planning to stay awhile, check out as many as you can.

© STEVE KNOPPER

Most of Denver's top theaters are located in the Denver Performing Arts Complex, a colorful, covered area downtown.

comedy to drama) to maintain a diversity of mainstream and truly weird productions. The **Denver Center Theatre Company** (Denver Performing Arts Complex, 1245 Champa St., 303/893-4100, www.denvercenter.org) has booked acclaimed Broadway-style shows such as *Hair* and *It Ain't Nothin' but the Blues* to the biggest theaters in town, particularly the four-stage Helen Bonfils Theatre Complex.

Opened in 1971, when Chicano theater was a relatively new phenomenon in the United States, **Su Teatro** (721 Santa Fe Dr., 303/296-0219, www.martinezled.com) began as a student-run theater group, and it bought and moved into the former Denver Civic Theatre in 2010. It focuses on Latino art and culture, including plays that explore issues of mortality and religion, such as *Little Hands Hold the Wind* and *The Miracle at Tepeyac*. Located in the La Alma/Lincoln Park neighborhood southeast of downtown, Su Teatro also plays host to an annual Chicano Music Festival and Auction, which recently starred Los Cenzontles, Mariachi Vasquez, and Jazz del Barrio.

On a smaller scale, the **Bug Theatre Company** (3654 Navajo St., 303/477-9984, www.bugtheatre.org, shows begin 7–8 P.M.), in a 1912 nickelodeon movie house, is at the center of this scene, sponsoring regular improv-oriented events such as *Freak Train,* in which actors of all levels stand up to give hilarious impromptu performances.

Opened with a $500 production of *Innocent Thoughts* in 1997, the **Shadow Theatre Company** (721 Santa Fe Dr., 720/857-8000, www.shadowtheatre.com, box office 9 A.M.–6 P.M. Mon.–Thurs., 1–5 P.M. Fri.) focuses on African American dramas, such as, recently, Arnold King's three-part *The Final Mile to Providence.* Productions take place at the Su Teatro and other small local theater venues.

Even smaller—so small that it bills itself as "the runt stepchild of small nonprofit theaters"—is **Germinal Stage Denver** (2450 W. 44th Ave., 303/455-7108, www2.priva-tei.com/~gsden, shows begin 8 P.M. Fri. and Sat., 7 P.M. Sun.), which formed in 1974 and tackles Tennessee Williams, Eugene O'Neill,

Albert Camus, and other masters in a tiny theater on the northwest side. The **Buntport Theatre** (717 Lipan St., 720/946-1388, www.buntport.com, shows begin 8 P.M., days vary) puts on small comedic productions such as *Kafka on Ice* and the warped magic show *Jugged Rabbit Stew*. The **Mizel Center for Arts and Culture** (350 S. Dahlia St., 303/316-6360, www.maccjcc.org, box office 9 A.M.–5 P.M. Mon.–Fri.) is a large Jewish cultural facility that often produces plays in its 300-seat theater—including *Romeo and Juliet* and the Israeli drama *Apples from the Desert*.

The **Aurora Fox Arts Center** (9900 E. Colfax Ave., Aurora, 303/739-1970, www.aurorafoxartscenter.org, shows begin 7:30 P.M. Fri.–Sat., 2 P.M. Sun.) puts on small but

---

LATINO MUSIC CLUBS IN DENVER

The Denver area's Hispanic population reached 200,000 a few years ago, and it's growing fast – which means Latinos of Mexican, Cuban, Puerto Rican, Central American, and Caribbean descent need radio stations and dance clubs to remind them of home. Some of the city's most popular radio stations are in Spanish-language format, including KXPK (96.5 FM), which specializes in regional Mexican pop songs. Top Latino pop stars, from Juanes to Luis Miguel to Ricky Martin, regularly fill large concert venues such as the University of Denver's Magness Arena and the Pepsi Center. And dozens of nightclubs, from D-Note to Tequila Le Club, hire DJs and live bands to create a dance-music mix of *cumbia*, salsa, merengue, *reggaeton*, *norteño*, and Latin-jazz songs and rhythm tracks.

Here are some of the top clubs and venues in most of the major genres:

Reggaeton: Thumping-dance-floor clubs for young Latinos come and go in Denver, but **Club Vinyl** (1082 Broadway, 303/832-8628) sponsors a reliable Latin night, focusing on merengue, *reggaeton*, *cumbia*, and other youth-oriented pop songs, usually drawn from Mexican and Latino Top 40 playlists; it's mostly DJs. The club's other theme nights are generally gringo-themed.

Salsa: La Rumba (99 W. 9th Ave., 303/572-8006, www.larumba-denver.com) is open only three nights a week – Thursday-Saturday – and one of those nights, the popular "Lipgloss," focuses on indie rock. The other two nights are devoted to this snappy Caribbean dance-music genre. Don't know

the steps? No problem – the club has free lessons and workshops in rooms beyond the big dance floor.

Latin jazz: Inspired by Latin stars from Tito Puente to Paquito D'Rivera, Latin-jazz artists in Denver have developed an audience big enough to play regular nights at local jazz clubs like **Dazzle** (930 Lincoln St., 303/839-5100, www.dazzlejazz.com) and restaurants like **Vita** (1575 Boulder St., Suite A, 303/477-4600, www.vitadenver.com). One popular club fixture is the heavily improvisational Manuel Lopez Latin Jazz Project, starring the bandleader on percussion and local trumpeter extraordinaire Hugh Ragin on trumpet.

Tejano/Tex-Mex/New Mexico: Open on the weekends, **Rick's Tavern** (6762 Lowell Blvd., 303/427-3427, www.rickgarciaband.com) hires singers and bands that play the strumming guitar-heavy folk-and-pop music that comes from Tejanos in central Texas and New Mexico. In addition to live acts that perform in the tradition of the late Selena, La Mafia, Kumbia Kings, and Los Lobos, Rick's has a karaoke night, line-dancing lessons, and DJ nights.

Mariachi: A number of Denver-area clubs and restaurants play host to live traditional-Mexican guitar-violin-trumpet music. These include **Ajuua! Family Mexican Restaurant** (4490 Peoria St., 720/374-9001, www.ajuua.com) and **Que Bueno!** (10633 Westminster Blvd., Suite 600, Westminster, 303/464-1171, www.quebuenomexicangrill.com), where the entertainment is provided by popular local band Mariachi Vasquez.

well-reviewed plays in the suburb's small East End Arts District—recent shows have included *Rashomon* and *The Elephant Man*. The **Arvada Center for the Arts and Humanities** (6901 Wadsworth Blvd., Arvada, 720/898-7200, www.arvadacenter.org, box office 9 A.M.–6 P.M. Mon.–Fri., 9 A.M.–5 P.M. Sat., 1–5 P.M. Sun.) has kids' classes and art exhibits, but lately it has been better known for mainstream plays like *Ragtime* and a variety of Shakespeare productions. Its outdoor amphitheater puts on live music shows by acts such as rocker George Thorogood and the Destroyers and bluesman Jonny Lang.

CLASSICAL MUSIC AND DANCE

The Denver Performing Arts Complex is pretty much one-stop shopping for the high-class musical arts—including the Jeffrey Kahane–conducted **Colorado Symphony Orchestra** (Boettcher Concert Hall, 1000 14th St., 303/623-7876, www.coloradosymphony. org, box office 10 A.M.–6 P.M. Mon.–Sat., noon–6 P.M. Sun.), which plays at Boettcher Concert Hall and various locations throughout the state; **Opera Colorado** (695 S. Colorado Blvd., Suite 20, 303/778-1500, www.opera-colorado.org), which goes for the big names like *The Marriage of Figaro* but occasionally experiments with the likes of *Nixon in China;* and the **Colorado Ballet** (1278 Lincoln St., 303/837-8888, www.coloradoballet.org, box office 10 A.M.–4 P.M. Mon.–Fri.), founded as a ballet school in 1951.

DANCE CLUBS

Throbbing, electronic, updated disco clubs are alive and well in Denver, especially downtown. Many of the city's top dance clubs are owned by longtime impresario Regas Christou, who lately has been taking advantage of the "bottle service" trend—expensive bottles of vodka or rum that cost an average of $200 per table. Christou's upscale clubs include **The Church** (1160 Lincoln St., 303/832-2383, www.co-clubs.com/venue/detail/the-church), which books well-known live DJs (like the Utah

Saints) and locals alike to build a low-key electronic vibe for laid-back beautiful people; the **Funky Buddha Lounge** (776 Lincoln St., 303/832-5075, www.coclubs.com/venue/detail/funky-buddha), built on The Ginger Bar, a heated outdoor patio, and multiple DJ-and-dance nights, with a clientele of hypersexy hipsters in skimpy clothes and tall shoes; and **Vinyl** (1082 Broadway, 303/860-8469, www.coclubs.com/venue/detail/club-vinyl-), whose DJs play more upbeat techno than those at The Church, with rooftop views of Denver's skyline.

Blue Ice Martini Lounge (22 Broadway, 303/777-3433, 4 P.M.–2 A.M. Mon.–Fri., 6 P.M.–2 A.M. Sat.–Sun.) has one of the best hip-hop nights in town as well as a serious selection of champagne and other high-end drinks, plus Cuban dishes to supplement the liquids. The lounge also has reggae and salsa nights.

24K (1414 Market St., 303/888-0655, http://24k.lotusclubs.com, 9 P.M.–2 A.M. daily) was a popular hangout for MTV's *The Real World: Denver* cast before the show aired in 2006. It's not quite as much fun as naked hot-tub high jinks with reality-show stars, but the club is exclusive and high-end, with a strict dress code, occasional free-drink specials for women, and ritzy events like Milan-style fashion shows. The liquor is expensive, and the DJs emphasize pop and Top 40.

Beta (1909 Blake St., 303/383-1909, www.betanightclub.com) puts on fashion shows and hot DJs from around the country, playing a range of electronic dance music. The crowd is slightly more casual and granola than that of, say, The Church or Monarck. Removed from the main dance floor, Beta's Beatport Lounge is more of a performance space where the DJs can show off.

Befitting its name, **Sutra** (1109 Lincoln St., 303/861-4272, www.sutradenver.com) contains several "bed rooms," a stripper pole, a swing, and a large mirror next to the two small dance floors. But even with all the emphasis on sex, the club is less snooty and more relaxed than most high-end Denver dance halls.

DENVER

BARS

Although Denver doesn't have quite the same amazing bar-per-capita ratio of Chicago or New York City, several of its watering holes are world-class. Below is a sampling, or pick your own spot by scouring *Westword*'s Best-of-Denver listings (www.westword.com/bestof).

LoDo/Central Denver

Although it's not quite as self-contained as Boulder's Pearl Street "Mall Crawl," LoDo has a critical mass of bars and brewpubs to sustain anybody for one solid night of debauchery. Begin with the **Wynkoop Brewing Co.** (1634 18th St., 303/297-2700, www.wynkoop. com, 11 A.M.–2 A.M. daily), where owner John Hickenlooper began his political career before becoming mayor in 2002, then Colorado governor in 2010. It serves dozens of distinctive brews, notably the signature Rail Yard Ale and something called Cow Town Milk Stout.

Wazee Supper Club (1600 15th St., 303/623-9518, www.wazeesupperclub.com, 11 A.M.–2 A.M. Mon.–Sat., noon–midnight Sun.) is one of those centrally located joints where, after 20 minutes of wandering the streets for the perfect spot, somebody in your party finally says, "Let's just go to the Wazee Supper Club." The beer is cheap, the food is solid, local sports are always on TV, and the black-and-white checked floor creates a down-to-earth ambience.

Several sports bars line the streets surrounding Coors Field, and they're all equally nondescript—with the exception of the **Falling Rock Tap House** (1919 Blake St., 303/293-8338,

10 NOTEWORTHY COLORADO BEERS

Jay Dedrick, former beer columnist for the *Rocky Mountain News*, compiled this list of notable Colorado-brewed beers— and supplied the commentary.

- **Avalanche Ale, Breckenridge Brewery, Denver:** A malty amber ale that got its start in the mountain town of Breckenridge. Now brewed at the biggest microbrewery in Denver.

- **Coors, MillerCoors Brewing Co., Golden:** Easily the lightest beer on the list, and easily found across the country. But, hey, you're in Colorado— how can you ignore it?

- **Dale's Pale Ale, Oskar Blues, Lyons:** It spawned a legion of imitators by becoming the first craft beer to be sold in cans. And it's darn tasty.

- **Denver Pale Ale, Great Divide Brewing Co., Denver:** They're brewing great stuff just a few blocks from Coors Field. This flagship beer is crisp and balanced.

- **Easy Street Wheat, Odell Brewing Co., Fort Collins:** A taste of the state's amber waves of grain in liquid form. Smooth and citrusy, it's a warm-weather refresher.

- **Ellie's Brown Ale, Avery Brewing Co., Boulder:** Ellie was a chocolate lab, and her namesake beverage is indeed chocolaty. Plus, the pooch looks cute on the label.

- **Fat Tire Amber Ale, New Belgium Brewing Co., Fort Collins:** The slightly nutty, malty brew that roared, helping to make New Belgium the third-biggest craft brewery in the United States.

- **Hazed and Infused, Boulder Beer Co., Boulder:** Kind of sweet, kind of hoppy, kind of hard to explain. Forget definitions and just enjoy its forest-like aroma and taste.

- **Milk Stout, Left Hand Brewing Co., Longmont:** A coffee-dark brew with roasty flavor that could make a certain Seattle java company feel inferior.

- **Steam Engine Lager, Steamworks Brewing Co., Durango:** Outstanding craft brew isn't exclusive to the Front Range; from the southwest comes this easy-drinking amber.

www.fallingrocktaphouse.com, 11 A.M.–2 A.M. daily), which supplements its brick walls and wood floors with an amazing selection of beers (more than 75 on tap and another 130 in bottles). Also worthwhile in this area is a decidedly non-Rockies-fanatic kind of place: **9th Door** (1808 Blake St., 303/292-2229, www.theninthdoor.com, 4:30–9:30 P.M. Sun.–Mon., 4:30–10 P.M. Tues.–Wed., 4:30–10:30 P.M. Thurs., 4:30 P.M.–1:30 A.M. Fri., 5 P.M.–1:30 A.M. Sat.), which serves high-class cocktails (mojitos *and* mijitas) along with live-but-quiet Spanish music and reasonably priced tapas.

Old Chicago (1415 Market St., 303/893-1806, www.oldchicago.com, 11 A.M.–1:15 A.M. daily) is part of a Colorado chain, and the Boulder outlet is a smidgen better, food-wise, but the pool tables, televised sports, central location, and signature homemade deep-dish pizza make it one of LoDo's most popular bar-restaurants. Part of the same chain is the **Rock Bottom Brewery** (1001 16th St., 303/534-7616, www.rockbottom.com/denver-downtown, 11 A.M.–2 A.M. daily), with several locations in the Denver area, but none as convenient as this one, on the 16th Street Mall.

Attached to the Courtyard by Marriott hotel on the 16th Street Mall, the **Rialto Café** (934 16th St., 303/893-2233, www.rialtocafe.com, 6:30 A.M.–10 P.M. Mon.–Thurs., 6:30 A.M.–11 P.M. Fri., 8 A.M.–11 P.M. Sat., 8 A.M.–10 P.M. Sun.) is an easygoing pub-restaurant with steaks and appetizers.

Remember the lounge-music revival of the late 1990s? The **Cruise Room Bar** (1600 17th St., 303/825-1107, www.theoxfordhotel.com/the-cruise-room.html, 4:30–11:45 P.M. Sun.–Thurs., 4:30 P.M.–12:45 A.M. Fri.–Sat.) continues to traffic in this kind of Mel Tormé-on-the-jukebox vibe, with a wide range of affordable martinis and decor that recalls 1933, when the bar first opened. It's located in the Oxford Hotel.

For red-and-white drinkers, the **Paris on the Platte Café and Bar** (1553 Platte St., 303/455-2451, www.parisontheplattecafeandbar.com, 7 A.M.–1 A.M. Mon.–Thurs., 7 A.M.–2 A.M. Fri., 8 A.M.–2 A.M. Sat., 8 A.M.–1 A.M. Sun.)

supplements its selections with beer, martinis, sandwiches, soup, and brunch.

Consider branching to the Colfax Avenue drinking district, including **Irish Snug** (1201 E. Colfax Ave., 303/839-1394, www.irishsnug.com, 11 A.M.–2 A.M. Mon.–Fri., 10 A.M.–2 A.M. Sat.–Sun.), which, as per Irish tradition, refers to the one-person drinking booth on the premises. It also serves brunch on weekends.

Around the corner from the art museum and the library, **Pints Pub** (221 W. 13th Ave., 303/534-7543, www.pintspub.com, 11 A.M.–10 P.M. Sun.–Wed., 11 A.M.–midnight Thurs.–Sat.) wraps itself in the British flag, playing pretty much all Beatles and David Bowie all the time on the speakers. The beers are tall and varied, the waitstaff barely notice you when you come in, and the thick wood tables make you want to hang around forever. Tip: Chocolate Lovers Torte.

Northwest/Highlands

Once a biker bar, **Mead Street Station** (3625 W. 32nd Ave., 303/433-2138, www.meadststation.com, 11 A.M.–midnight Mon.–Thurs., 11 A.M.–1 A.M. Fri.–Sat.) is a dark, loud, smoky neighborhood joint that just happens to have great food—try the portobello mushroom wraps ($9) and the vegetarian chili ($5). Live bands play occasionally.

El Camino (3628 W. 32nd Ave., 720/889-7946, http://elcaminotavern.t83.net, 11 A.M.–midnight Mon.–Thurs., 11 A.M.–1 A.M. Fri., 10 A.M.–1 A.M. Sat., 10 A.M.–midnight Sun.) is a lively, high-end burrito joint that serves $1 tacos on Tuesdays as well as alcohol at night in a dark, narrow room with a bright pink facade. Another cozy spot in this area, down the street, is the **Coral Room** (3489 W. 32nd Ave., 303/433-2535, www.coralroom.com, 9 A.M.–2 P.M. and 4–10 P.M. Mon.–Thurs., 9 A.M.–2 P.M. and 4–10:30 P.M. Fri.–Sat., 9 A.M.–2 P.M. and 4–9:30 P.M. Sun.), where the pan-Asian menu is pretty good but is no match for the inviting throwback martini lounge–style bar.

In the East Highlands area, **Lechugas** (3609 Tejon St., 303/455-1502, http://

lechugasitalianrestaurantandlounge.lbu.com, 10 A.M.–9 P.M. Mon.–Thurs., 10 A.M.–10 P.M. Fri.–Sat.) is a homey Italian restaurant and lounge with no-frills decor and a no-nonsense staff.

South Denver

For all its highfalutin shopping and ritzy reputation, Cherry Creek has a number of easygoing bars—maybe it's so the spouses of the upscale shoppers have a place to sit. Among them: **Bull and Bush Brewery** (4700 Cherry Creek S. Dr., 303/759-0333, www.bullandbush.com, 11 A.M.–2 A.M. Mon.–Fri., 10 A.M.–2 A.M. Sat.–Sun.), where very little light gets in to supplement the huge bourbon and scotch selection and fish-and-chips; **Brandon's Pub** (3027 E. 2nd Ave., 303/399-0092, 11 A.M.–10 P.M. daily), a laid-back beer-drinking paradise replete with flat-screen TVs and Mexican snacks; and, known for its burgers, **The Cherry Cricket** (2641 E. 2nd Ave., 303/322-7666, www.cherrycricket.com, 11 A.M.–2 A.M. daily), which attracts a young sports-loving crowd and is almost always jammed on weekend nights.

A little farther south, **The Village Cork** (1300 S. Pearl St., 303/282-8399, www.villagecork.com, 4–10:30 P.M. Mon.–Thurs., 4 P.M.–midnight Fri., 5 P.M.–midnight Sat.) serves a $16 cheese plate, which gives you an indication of the clientele, but it's small, cozy, and seems to be designed for amorous wine-drinking. On the other end of the ambience spectrum, the **Pearl Street Grill** (1477 S. Pearl St., 303/778-6475, www.pearlstreetgrilldenver.com, 11 A.M.–midnight Mon.–Thurs., 11 A.M.–1 A.M. Fri.–Sat., 10 A.M.–midnight Sun.) is bright and boisterous, serving many kinds of beer to go with barbecued ribs, nachos, and chicken wings.

East Denver

Colfax Avenue, long populated by adult-movie theaters and other shady goings-on, is less notorious than it used to be, but it's still a great area for sitting at a barstool and watching the action. Across the street from the Bluebird

Theatre, **Goosetown Tavern** (3242 E. Colfax Ave., 303/399-9703, www.goosetowntavern.com, 11 A.M.–2 A.M. daily) is homebrew heaven, serving pizza and sandwiches too. The **PS Lounge** (3416 E. Colfax Ave., 303/320-1200, 3 P.M.–2 A.M. daily) is what many locals consider a "real bar," with football on TV, Johnny Cash on the jukebox, flowers for the women, beer in bottles only, and a house shot called the Alabama Slammer. Along those lines, **Gabor's** (1223 E. 13th Ave., 303/832-3108, 5 P.M.–2 A.M. Mon.–Fri., 1 P.M.–2 A.M. Sat.–Sun.) is the kind of place where black-and-white movie-star photos (Frank Sinatra and Clint Eastwood, naturally) line the walls, and the crowd is mostly young locals.

Greater Denver

In Greenwood Village, along I-25 south of Denver, **Water 2 Wine** (9608 E. Arapahoe Rd., 303/799-9463, http://water2wine.us, noon–8 P.M. Tues.–Sat.) serves 100 different types of wine from 13 countries, by the bottle (28–30 types) or glass. It also provides equipment and instruction for budding winemakers, although there's a 45-day wait between choosing your flavor and style and returning for the bottling process. **C.B. & Potts** (1257 W. 120th Ave., Westminster, 303/451-5767, www.cbpotts.com, 11 A.M.–midnight Mon.–Thurs., 11 A.M.–2 A.M. Fri., 10 A.M.–2 A.M. Sat., 10 A.M.–midnight Sun.), a spin-off of a popular Fort Collins joint, has large burgers and friendly servers.

LoDo's Bar and Grill (8545 S. Quebec St., Highlands Ranch, 303/346-2930, www.lodosbarandgrill.com, 11 A.M.–2 A.M. daily) attempts to bring the downtown Denver feel to the suburbs—and has grown in stature to the point that the well-known rock band Goo Goo Dolls recently played its rooftop patio.

Olde Town Arvada, just northwest of the city, is a growing shopping district centered on a large (well, much larger than it looks from the outside) bar called **The D Note** (7519 Grandview Ave., Arvada, 303/463-6683, www.dnote.us, 3 P.M.–midnight Mon.–Thurs., 11 A.M.–2 A.M. Fri.–Sun.). Live entertainment of all kinds dominates the club, with salsa nights, kids playing music on stage on Sundays, and jamming Latin bands.

Country-music fans taking a break from the Grizzly Rose flock to **Stampede** (2430 S. Havana St., Aurora, 303/696-7686, www. stampedeclub.net, 5 P.M.–2 A.M. Wed.–Fri., 6 P.M.–2 A.M. Sat.). It has all the cowboy trimmings: a mechanical bull for *Urban Cowboy* nostalgics, live bands, line-dancing (and Western-swing dancing, for Bob Wills fans), and even a hat doctor on hand for emergency service.

Englewood, the neighborhood just south of Denver that runs along South Broadway, is sort of a Music Row for lesser-known punk, alt-rock, and country bands. Down the street from the Gothic Theatre, **Herman's Hideaway** (1578 S. Broadway, 303/777-5840, www.hermanshideaway.com) is a classic watering hole that puts on live music just about every night. Many years ago, rockers Dave Alvin and the Skeletons played one of the best bar-band shows I've ever seen, in no small measure due to the intimate room and consistently great acoustics.

COMEDY

Denver's comedy scene is surprisingly rich, with local stars from onetime *Last Comic Standing* winner Josh Blue to the international trio A.C.E.—not to mention a regular influx of traveling funnypeople, from Jerry Seinfeld to Louis C.K. The **Impulse Theater** (1634 18th St., 303/297-2111, www.impulsetheater.com) is the local version of Chicago's Second City. **Bovine Metropolis Theatre** (1527 Champa St., 303/758-4722, www.bovinemetropolis. com) is young and hungry, and the comedians who star in the ACME sketch and improv shows are some of the best talent in town. **Comedy Works** (1226 15th St., 720/274-6800, www.comedyworks.com) snags traveling A-minus-list comedians such as Bob Saget and Jon Lovitz.

EVENTS

Denver's mild weather, views of the Rockies, and clean, laid-back downtown make it a natural fit for festivals, and the roster of annual events has been growing since the LoDo renaissance in the early 1990s.

An annual two-week extravaganza of hootin', hollerin', and celebratin' the beef industry, the January **National Western Stock Show** (Denver Coliseum, 4655 Humboldt St., 303/297-1166, www.nationalwestern.com) is one of the most fascinating Western rodeo events you'll ever attend. The rodeo itself is exciting, with nationally known riders roping steers and attempting to stay on bucking broncos. There's also Mutton Bustin', in which helmeted little kids hang onto sprinting sheep for dear life. The booths are also faintly surreal, selling everything from cowboy hats to bull-semen contracts (did I mention that attendees are primarily from the beef industry?). As of this writing, National Western officials were negotiating with Denver officials to release the Stock Show from its long-term contract in order to move to Aurora and hook up with a new $824 million hotel and conference center. At the time of writing, Denver officials expressed optimism that they could make a deal with the Stock Show to keep it at its Denver location for years to come.

Every year in May, celebrants from all over the city flock to Civic Center Park for a huge **Cinco de Mayo** party. True Cinco celebrants, however, flock to North Federal Boulevard, in the northwestern part of Denver, to show off their flag-equipped, souped-up hot rods for an all-day-and-night cruising extravaganza. (Noncelebrants should plan alternate routes around the always heavily trafficked Federal Boulevard in early May.)

For July 4 weekend, the **Cherry Creek Arts Festival** (3rd Ave. and Steele St., 303/355-2787, www.cherryarts.org) draws hundreds of thousands of people to see the works of 200 artists. If you get bored of the various high-end paintings, ceramics, glass, and sculpture, you can always hit the mall across the street.

Denver's most spectacular event is the late September–early October **Great American Beer Festival** (Colorado Convention Center, Welton St., 303/447-0816, www.

longhorn steer leaving Union Station at the beginning of the National Western Stock Show Parade in downtown Denver

greatamericanbeerfestival.com), which serves more than 2,200 different beers from 450 U.S. breweries in one-ounce sample cups.

The early-December **Parade of Lights** (www.denverparadeoflights.com), with its huge floats and holiday festivity, gets everybody all excited—except the grumpy drivers who have to pass through congested downtown on their way to almost anywhere else.

Smaller extravaganzas of all types play out at Denver-area parks: The early-June **Capitol Hill People's Fair** (303/830-1651, www.peoplesfair.com), which recently celebrated its 40th anniversary, includes arts, crafts, food, wine

tastings, and auctions; the late-July **Colorado Dragon Boat Festival** (303/953-7277, www.cdbf.org) celebrates Asian culture at Sloan's Lake Park (W. 17th Ave. and Sheridan Blvd.) with decorative boat races, tons of food, and colorful dancing and music; and the **Colorado Black Arts Festival** (720/339-1693, www.colbaf.org), at City Park West (bounded by Downing St., 23rd Ave., York St., and Colfax Ave.), celebrates local African American culture with music, dance, and theater events. Check the **Denver Parks and Recreation** website (www.denvergov.org/parks_recreation) for schedules—particularly in the summer.

Shopping

LODO/CENTRAL DENVER

Those of us who still prefer flipping through record-store racks to clicking through iTunes or Spotify tend to camp out at **Wax Trax** (638 E. 13th Ave., 303/831-7246, www.waxtraxrecords.com, 10 A.M.–7 P.M. Mon.–Thurs., 10 A.M.–8 P.M. Fri.–Sat., 11 A.M.–6 P.M. Sun.), a hipster joint that focuses on cutting-edge punk and techno titles; **Independent Records & Video** (937 E. Colfax Ave., 303/863-8668, www.beindependent.com, 10 A.M.–11 P.M. Mon.–Sat., 10 A.M.–10 P.M. Sun.), a spin-off of a venerable Colorado Springs chain that sells a mix of CDs, vinyl, DVDs, and Blu-Ray; and **3 Kings Tavern** (60 S. Broadway, 303/777-7352, 2 P.M.–2 A.M. Mon.–Fri., noon–2 A.M. Sat.–Sun.), a live-music bar that plays host to Suburban Home Records' **Punk Rock Flea Market** (noon–5 P.M. every second Sat. of the month).

Even if you're not a celebrity, **Rockmount Ranchwear** (1626 Wazee St., 303/629-7777, www.rockmount.com, 8 A.M.–6 P.M. Mon.–Fri., 10 A.M.–6 P.M. Sat., 11 A.M.–4 P.M. Sun.) is worth a visit for the superhip Western jackets, hats, belts, boots, and many other leather-and-fringe items. As the aggressively self-marketing Denver fixture likes to point out, rock stars Elvis Presley and Bruce Springsteen as well as movie stars Dennis Quaid and Tom Hanks have modeled the distinctive brand on stage and in films.

◖ Larimer Square

When miners first settled in Denver, Larimer Square (bounded by Market St., Lawrence St., 14th Ave., and 15th Ave., 303/534-2367, www.larimersquare.com) was the central part of town with the first bank, a bookstore, a dry-goods store, and racy Gahan's Saloon, allegedly the site of backroom poker games and a

Rockmount Ranchwear manufactures Western shirts, hats, and accessories and sells them worldwide.

© STEVE CRECELIUS / VISIT DENVER

basement speakeasy in the 1920s. Today, the area is a clean and easily accessible bar-and-restaurant district with some of the best shopping in Denver—chains like **Ann Taylor** have mostly given way to distinctive local outlets such as the cowkid-fashion **Cry Baby Ranch** (1421 Larimer St., 303/623-3979 or 888/279-2229, www.crybabyranch.com, 10 A.M.–7 P.M. Mon.–Fri., 10 A.M.–6 P.M. Sat., noon–5 P.M. Sun.) and the high-end women's clothing boutique **Eve** (1413 Larimer St., 720/932-9382, www.eveinc.net, 10 A.M.–7 P.M. daily).

16th Street Mall

Around the corner from Larimer Square is the 16th Street Mall (16th St. from Broadway to Wynkoop St., 303/534-6161), a gray-brick, 16-block, pedestrian-only strip of hotels, restaurants, and shops. A free city bus operates regularly, which is a huge bonus, and even if some of the local high school students get a little boisterous at times, the mall is a great place to shop and hang out.

Many of the stores are chains, but the **Writer Square** (1512 Larimer St.) portion of the mall has originals such as the **Knox Gallery** (1512 Larimer St., Suite R15, 303/820-2324, www.knoxgalleries.com, 11:30 A.M.–6 P.M. Mon.–Tues. and Thurs.–Sat.) and practical stuff such as the **UPS Store** (1550 Larimer St., 303/825-8060, www.theupsstore.com, 7:30 A.M.–6 P.M. Mon.–Fri., 10 A.M.–3:30 P.M. Sat.) and **Rocky Mountain Chocolate Factory** (1512 Larimer St., 303/629-5500, http://rmcf.com/CO/Denver50771, 9:30 A.M.–10:30 P.M. Mon.–Thurs., 9:30 A.M.–11:30 P.M. Fri.–Sat., 10:30 A.M.–9:30 P.M. Sun.), depending on your definition of "practical." Also on the mall is **Denver Pavilions** (500 16th St., 303/260-6000, www.denverpavilions.com, 10 A.M.–8 P.M. Mon.–Sat., noon–6 P.M. Sun.), a four-level plaza anchored with a multiplex movie theater and megachains such as H&M, Barnes & Noble, Gap, Virgin Megastore, and the restaurant Maggiano's Little Italy. The **Tabor Center** (1201 16th St., 303/628-1000, www.taborcenter.com, 10 A.M.–7 P.M. Mon.–Sat.), between Arapahoe and Larimer Streets,

is a tall glass-enclosed mall-within-a-mall that includes a Corner Bakery and a Cheesecake Factory.

(Tattered Cover

In the Amazon.com age, which finally dealt Borders Books a death blow in 2011, Tattered Cover (2526 E. Colfax Ave., 303/322-7727, www.tatteredcover.com, 9 A.M.–9 P.M. Mon.–Sat., 10 A.M.–6 P.M. Sun.) remains one of those classic bookstores, with sink-into-the-couch ambience, regular local-author signings, coffee and pastries, and kids' activities. Its 150,000-title book collection is almost intimidating, with an entire large room devoted to maps and travel (with an emphasis on Colorado, of course), and the best magazine racks in the city. Immediately next door, **Twist & Shout** (2508 E. Colfax Ave., 303/722-1943, www.twistandshout.com, 10 A.M.–10 P.M. Mon.–Sat., 10 A.M.–8 P.M. Sun.) is similarly a survivor in the era after physical record buying, with friendly, knowledgeable, and passionate employees who are happy to help navigate the endless genres and subgenres of music, from a wall full of DVDs to rooms devoted to hip-hop, jazz, and country music.

Tattered Cover's second location (1628 16th St., 303/436-1070, 6:30 A.M.–9 P.M. Mon.–Fri., 9 A.M.–9 P.M. Sat., 10 A.M.–6 P.M. Sun.), with similar ambience and almost as big a book collection, is on the west end of the 16th Street Mall downtown. In 2004 the store opened a third outlet, in suburban Highlands Ranch (9315 Dorchester St., 303/470-7050, 9 A.M.–9 P.M. Mon.–Sat., 10 A.M.–6 P.M. Sun.).

CHERRY CREEK

The ritziest shopping area in Denver is just northeast of the intersection of University and Speer Boulevards. Standing at this corner, facing east, you'll see the indoor **Cherry Creek Mall** to your right and the outdoor, impeccably maintained **Cherry Creek North** to your left. Cherry Creek Mall (3000 E. 1st Ave., 303/388-3900, www.shopcherrycreek.com, 10 A.M.–9 P.M. Mon.–Sat., 11 A.M.–6 P.M. Sun.) is Denver's biggest mall, a high-class joint

the exterior of Cherry Creek Mall

with mostly top-of-the-line stores—Burberry, Louis Vuitton, Ralph Lauren, Neiman Marcus, Tiffany & Co., and (my personal favorite) the only Apple Computer Store within the city limits. Cherry Creek North (299 Milwaukee St., Suite 201, 303/394-2904, www.cherry-creeknorth.com, hours vary by store) has much more personality, even if it's pricey and the see-and-be-seen nature of the shopping rivals that of Aspen.

The best of the Cherry Creek North shops include: **Kazoo & Company** (2930 E. 2nd Ave., 303/322-0973, www.kazootoys.com, 10 A.M.–8 P.M. Mon.–Fri., 10 A.M.–5:30 P.M. Sat., noon–5 P.M. Sun.), a kids' store that supplements name brands like Groovy Girls and Ryan's Room with lesser-known gems like the Edushape Toddler Orchestra; **Outdoor DIVAS** (2717 E. 3rd Ave., 303/320-3482, www.out-doordivas.com, 10 A.M.–6 P.M. Mon.–Sat., noon–5 P.M. Sun.), a store for active hikers, cyclists, skiers, and snowboarders with large budgets; **MAX** (264 Detroit St., 303/321-4949, www.maxfashion.com, 10 A.M.–6 P.M.

Mon.–Sat., noon–5 P.M. Sun.), a chic boutique that carries all the big names, including Stella McCartney shoes, Yves Saint Laurent bags, and Prada everything; **HW Home** (199 Clayton Lane, 303/394-9222, www.hwhome.com, 10 A.M.–6 P.M. Mon.–Thurs., 10 A.M.–7 P.M. Fri.–Sat., 11 A.M.–5 P.M. Sun.), a small Denver-area chain that carries cushy beds, dressers, and throw cushions; and **Andrisen Morton** (270 St. Paul St., 303/321-0404, www.andrisenmorton.com, 9:30 A.M.–6 P.M. Mon.–Sat.), which, in addition to selling clothes for men and women, specializes in high-end bridal fashion.

HIGHLANDS/NORTHWEST
The Highlands neighborhood is known for its restaurants, but shopping is an unexpected bonus. A few blocks from the intersection of 32nd Avenue and Lowell Boulevard is **Starlet** (3450 W. 32nd Ave., 303/433-7827, www.shopstarlet.com, 11 A.M.–6 P.M. Mon.–Fri., 10 A.M.–6 P.M. Sat., 11 A.M.–5 P.M. Sun.), a clothing boutique with colorful, flowery hats, jewelry, belts, and purses, and

Babareeba! (3629 W. 32nd Ave., 303/458-5712, 10:30 A.M.–5 P.M. Tues.–Wed. and Sun., 10:30 A.M.–6:30 P.M. Thurs.–Sat.), which sells vintage dresses, purses, and jewelry, with everything from animal prints to sequins.

Beyond West Highlands, as the 32nd-and-Lowell area is known, the **Tennyson** neighborhood (http://tennysonst.com) centers on the intersection of West 44th Avenue and Tennyson Street and restaurant fixtures such as Parisi and Swing Thai. There's a lot of turnover in this area, but **Tenn Street Coffee & Books** (4418 Tennyson St., 303/455-0279, www.tennstreetcoffee.com, 6:30 A.M.–9 P.M. Mon.–Fri., 7 A.M.–9 P.M. Sat., 7 A.M.–6 P.M. Sun.), a quiet, cozy place to study or work and grab a coffee or smoothie afterward, has survived for some time. The anchor of this rising district is **Tennyson Hardware** (4034 Tennyson St., 303/455-9282, 8 A.M.–7 P.M. Mon.–Fri., 8 A.M.–6 P.M. Sat., 9 A.M.–5 P.M. Sun.), one of those old-fashioned nail-and-caulk stores that has just about anything a home-repair enthusiast needs and patient clerks on hand for advice and directions.

◖ Denver Flagship REI

The REI store (1416 Platte St., 303/756-3100, www.rei.com/stores/denverflagship, 9 A.M.–9 P.M. Mon.–Fri., 9 A.M.–9 P.M. Sat., 10 A.M.–6 P.M. Sun.) is not only a huge warehouse building visible when driving along I-25, it's the Colorado flagship for the outdoor-supply chain, with more tents, fishing rods, bicycles, camping stoves, and freeze-dried peas and corn than you could ever possibly want. The store includes a nice climbing wall, a Starbucks, and a third-floor, stream-themed jungle gym for entertaining the kids. Behind the store is the Platte River Greenway, a pretty little spot where dogs swim, kayakers practice, and kids run around.

SOUTH DENVER

Denver's big-name furniture scene changed dramatically in the last few years, as downtown fixture Kacey Fine Furniture's owner died and the store shut down in 2010, while **Ikea** (9800 E. Ikea Way, Centennial, 303/768-9164, www.ikea.com, 10 A.M.–9 P.M. Mon.–Sat., 10 A.M.–8 P.M. Sun.) opened in the nearby suburbs in spring 2011. For bargain hunters who prefer to avoid giant corporate stores, the city's charming antiques district is South Broadway between 1st Avenue and Evans Street, and **Village Antique Mall** (827 Corona St., 303/813-1113, 10 A.M.–5 P.M. Mon.–Sat., noon–5 P.M. Sun.) is as good a place to start as any.

Denver's Art District on Santa Fe (Santa Fe Dr. between 4th Ave. and 12th Ave., www.artdistrictonsantafe.com, hours vary by store), which has more than 40 art galleries as well as shops and restaurants, overlaps a large part of the La Alma/Lincoln Park neighborhood south of downtown. **The Sandra Phillips Gallery** (744 Santa Fe Dr., 303/573-5969, www.thesandraphillipsgallery.com, 12:30–5 P.M. Wed.–Fri., 12:30–4 P.M. Sat., by appointment Sun.–Mon.) is in a former beauty parlor, selling a diverse mix of paintings, sculptures, and ceramics, with an emphasis on the oddly colorful and brightly oblong. **John Fielder's Colorado** (833 Santa Fe Dr., 303/744-7979, www.johnfielder.com, 10 A.M.–6 P.M. Tues.–Sat.) displays the owner's photography, particularly rich scenes of waterfalls and flowers in the San Juans and Rocky Mountains. The **Van Stratten Gallery** (760 Santa Fe Dr., 303/573-8585, www.vanstrattengallery.com) is in a huge space, exhibiting a wide range of artists who specialize in colorful etchings, steel prints, cartoon cityscapes, and acrylic paintings. **Nepali Bazaar** (38 Broadway, 720/570-0649, 11 A.M.–7 P.M. Mon.–Fri., 11 A.M.–7:30 P.M. Sat.–Sun.) is the perfect shop for Denverites searching for the most potent incense (as well as tie-dyed T-shirts, homemade wall-hangings, and other nice-smelling goods) for their meditations.

Old South Gaylord Street (S. Gaylord St. between Mississippi St. and Tennessee St., www.southgaylordstreet.com) is one of the oldest business districts in Denver, having begun near a cable-car turnaround in 1924. Numerous shops and galleries are here, including **Pome** (1071 S. Gaylord St., 303/722-2900, www.pomedenver.com, 10 A.M.–6 P.M. Mon.–Sat., 11 A.M.–5 P.M. Sun.), a haven of hanging beads, old typewriters, flower-festooned hats, and other old-meets-new fashions; the **Pine Creek Clothing Company** (1099 S. Gaylord St., 303/733-4848, www.pinecreek-clothing.com, 10 A.M.–6 P.M. Mon.–Sat., 11:30 A.M.–5 P.M. Sun.), a women's clothing boutique that sells colorful hats, leopard-print handbags, dresses of all brands and styles, and bracelets and other accessories; and the self-explanatory **Lil' Angel Pet Boutique and Gallery** (1014 S. Gaylord St., 303/777-0224, www.megapetportraits.com, 10 A.M.–6 P.M. Mon.–Sat., 10 A.M.–4 P.M. Sun.).

The **Old South Pearl Street** district (www.oldsouthpearlstreet.com) is a nine-block stretch of South Pearl Street from I-25 to Evans Avenue. Hanging around this area during summer, it's hard to miss an event or festival, such as the mid-July **BrewGrass** (yes, beer and live bluegrass), the early-August **Blues & Brews** (beer and live blues), the every-Sunday **Farmers Market** (S. Pearl St. between Florida Ave. and Iowa Ave.), and the **First Fridays ArtWalk.** Some of the best shops in this district include **5 Green Boxes** (1596 S. Pearl St., 303/777-2331, and 1705 S. Pearl St., 303/282-5481, www.5greenboxes.com, 10 A.M.–6 P.M. Mon.–Sat., noon–5 P.M. Sun.), which, counter to its name, is not a container store but a quaint all-purpose furniture, beads, and baubles outlet; and the **Old South Frame & Gallery** (1588 S. Pearl St., 303/715-3828, www.oldartgallery. com, 10 A.M.–6 P.M. Mon.–Sat.), which sells custom frames to go with its prints of vintage advertisements and contemporary paintings.

The "SoBo District," short for South Broadway, runs along a huge, crowded, traffic-filled road. (Art-movie buffs are directed to the **Landmark Mayan Theatre** (110 Broadway, 303/744-6883, www.landmarktheatres.com), just north of the shopping district; although it's part of a large chain, the theater was built in 1930, has a certain art deco–mobster ambience, and serves alcoholic beverages on the second floor.) SoBo is an urban shopping experience,

for sure, and many of the stores here are of the dusty-book and sexy-game variety. The street is still fun to explore: **True Love Shoes** (42 Broadway, 303/860-8783, www.trueloveshoes. com, 11 A.M.–7 P.M. daily) sells pumps, sandals, and just about everything else at very affordable prices—and leather-free; **Fancy Tiger** (1 S. Broadway, 303/282-6590, www.fan-cytiger.com, 10 A.M.–7 P.M. Mon. and Wed.–Sat., 10 A.M.–9 P.M. Tues., 11 A.M.–6 P.M. Sun.) is a do-it-yourself utopia, providing supplies and know-how for customers to design everything from soap to jewelry to musical recordings and, especially, clothes; **Lee Alex Décor** (24 Broadway, Suite 104, 303/777-0862, www. leealexdecor.com, 10 A.M.–6 P.M. Mon.–Thurs. and Sat., 10 A.M.–7 P.M. Fri., noon–5 P.M. Sun.) sells space-age lamps, tinted martini glasses, vinyl sofas, rings, earrings, and other stuff with *Mad Men* ambience; **Decade** (56 S. Broadway, 303/733-2288, www.decade-gifts. com, 10 A.M.–6 P.M. Mon.–Sat., 11 A.M.–5 P.M. Sun.) has expanded beyond its roots as a furniture store into a 3,000-square-foot menagerie of flowery dresses, colorful scarves, and baby and pet knickknacks, with an old cat called Stella the Fella watching over the merchandise; and **T-Trove Asian Décor** (189 S. Broadway, 303/722-0949, www.t-trove.com, 10 A.M.–5:30 P.M. Mon.–Fri., 10 A.M.–5 P.M. Sat.), which looks like an urn warehouse from the outside but is a beautifully cluttered showroom of smiling Buddhas, wooden lamps, designer fountains, and hand-painted leather cabinets.

GREATER DENVER

The next-best mall in the Denver area, after Cherry Creek and 16th Street, is **Colorado Mills** (14500 W. Colfax Ave., Lakewood, 303/384-3000, www.simon.com, 10 A.M.–9 P.M. Mon.–Sat., 11 A.M.–6 P.M. Sun.), with all the big chains, including Build-A-Bear Workshop, Starbucks, and a Banana Republic factory store. Other fine places to carry a credit card: **Outlets at Castle Rock** (5050 Factory Shops Blvd., Castle Rock, 303/688-2800, www.outletsatcastlerock.com, 10 A.M.–8 P.M. Mon.–Sat., 11 A.M.–6 P.M.

Sun.), about halfway between Denver and Colorado Springs on I-25; **FlatIron Crossing Mall** (1 W. FlatIron Circle, Broomfield, 720/887-7467, www.flatironcrossing.com, 10 A.M.–9 P.M. Mon.–Sat., 11 A.M.–6 P.M. Sun.), with a high-class food court, a dinosaur playground for kids, and an excellent selection of gumball machines, in addition to a Dick's Sporting Goods, Macy's, and Nordstrom; and **Park Meadows Mall** (8401 Park Meadows Center Dr., Lone Tree, 303/792-2999, www. parkmeadows.com, 10 A.M.–9 P.M. Mon.–Sat., 11 A.M.–6 P.M. Sun.), near Littleton, which has Nordstrom, Dillard's, and JCPenney.

Some of the suburbs have excellent shopping districts. Littleton's Main Street is a historic district with churches and courthouses dating to the late 1800s. Chains haven't overrun the area—yet—so it's a quaint place to find deals in mom-and-pop stores. **Willow– An Artisan's Market** (2400 W. Main St., Littleton, 303/730-8521, www.willowartisansmarket.com, 10 A.M.–6 P.M. Mon.–Sat., noon–4 P.M. Sun.) is a hub for artists specializing in offbeat art and fashion, including bracelets, pins, T-shirts, and plenty of stuff covered in beads. **Savory Spice Shop** (2650 W. Main St., Littleton, 720/283-2232 or 888/677-3322, www.savoryspiceshop.com, 10 A.M.–6 P.M. Mon.–Fri., 10 A.M.–5 P.M. Sat., 11 A.M.–4 P.M. Sun.) has more kinds of cinnamon, spices, chilies, and blends than most people ever thought existed, from achiote paste to wasabi powder.

For years, Olde Town Arvada was the forgotten older sibling of New Arvada, a suburb with a Home Depot and a Radio Shack.

But this 1860s gold-mining area, west of Denver surrounding the corner of Wadsworth Boulevard and Ralston Road, has grown beyond what was once just a water tower and a closed flour mill. Today, it's a shopping area with a large concert venue (the D Note) and several restaurants. Don't miss the **Rheinlander Bakery** (5721 Olde Wadsworth Blvd., 303/467-1810, www.rheinlanderbakery.com, 8:30 A.M.–6:30 P.M. Mon.–Sat., 9 A.M.–5 P.M. Sun.), which in addition to the usual cakes and buns has traditional German sweets like two-pound apple- or cherry-filled strudel and *pfeffernüsse* cookies.

Southwest of Denver, **Belmar** (408 S. Teller St., 303/742-1520, www.belmarcolorado.com, 10 A.M.–8 P.M. Mon.–Thurs., 10 A.M.–9 P.M. Fri.–Sat., 11 A.M.–6 P.M. Sun.) is an outdoor mall with dominant chains such as Banana Republic and Whole Foods as well as a popular ice rink in the center. Despite the big chains, it's hard to find a more original store than **Gimme Gimme Pillow Toast** (445 S. Saulsbury St., Lakewood, 303/872-7706, www.gimmegimmepillowtoast.com, noon–7 P.M. Wed.–Sun.), which carries a wide range of Japanese pop-culture artifacts, such as Gloomy Bear key chains and Bruce Lee candles.

In suburban Glendale, along a functional stretch of suburban shopping sprawl not far from the Cherry Creek Mall, one of the best deals in town for buying and selling used CDs is **Second Spin** (1485 S. Colorado Blvd., 303/753-8822, www.secondspin.com, 10 A.M.–9 P.M. Mon.–Thurs., 10 A.M.–10 P.M. Fri.–Sat., 11 A.M.–9 P.M. Sun.), despite its nondescript location in a suburban strip mall.

DENVER

Accommodations

LODO/CENTRAL DENVER
Under $100

"As comfortable as you remember Grandma's house to be" is the motto of the **Holiday Chalet B&B** (1820 E. Colfax Ave., 303/437-8245 or 800/626-4497, www.denver-bed-breakfast. com, $94–145), and family heirlooms and lacy curtains back it up. In an 1896 Victorian building, the inn has 10 guest rooms decorated with elaborate flower-print patterns, antiques, and wicker chairs in the lobby. Sightseeing buses stop out front, a hint that the chalet's clientele tends to be on the older side.

$100-150

Concentrating on the business customer, **The Warwick Hotel** (1776 Grant St., 303/861-2000, www.warwickdenver.com, $139–189) has extra-large guest rooms, Internet data ports, and wireless access throughout the hotel as well as a decent restaurant (Randolph's) and marble-and-antique elegance.

The guest rooms at the **Capitol Hill Mansion Bed & Breakfast Inn** (1207 Pennsylvania St., 800/839-9329, www.capitolhillmansion.com, $119–219) are almost as charming as their names: the Elk Thistle Suite, the Shooting Star Balcony Room, the Paintbrush Room, and the Pasque Flower Room, all with vivid touches, like a 28-foot alpine-tree mural and a four-poster canopy bed. If you have $455 to spend, or two other couples to share with, consider reserving the entire third floor—a seriously luxurious experience that includes a balcony and a whirlpool tub.

With six rooms named after famous composers—that's Handel, Vivaldi, and Debussy, by the way, not Lennon and McCartney or Jones and Strummer—the **Adagio Bed & Breakfast Hotel** (1430 Race St., www.adagiobb.com, 303/370-6911 or 800/533-4640, $115–225) is in a large 1880s mansion a little removed from downtown. Visitors to City Park attractions like the Denver Zoo will find this the most convenient hotel in town; everybody else will need a car.

The Burnsley (1000 Grant St., 303/830-1000 or 800/231-3915, www.burnsley.com, $129–329) was a hotel and jazz club in the 1960s, and loyal touring jazz musicians continue to stay here after gigs—the Roy Haynes Quintet, trumpeter Nicholas Payton, and singer-pianist Freddy "Nat's Brother" Cole are among the guests proudly listed on the hotel's website. The guest rooms are all suites, which means they're large and pricey, although the "studio suites" are just 520 square feet and somewhat more affordable.

In a horizontal brick-and-wood building, the **Gregory Inn LoDo** (2500 Arapahoe St., 303/295-6570 or 800/925-6570, www.gregoryinn.com, $139–219) was the last home in Denver to switch to electricity from gas lighting; today its website boasts of "the leading edge of fiber-optic communications, high-speed computer linkups, and liquid-crystal television projection systems." The eight guest rooms (plus a more expensive carriage house) are festooned with antiques. None are so old and mysterious as the grave marker underneath a locust tree outside: Kate A. Priole, 19, born in 1886, two years before the home was built. Inn employees can't say why Kate, and not her parents, is buried here.

Usually, naming rooms after famous painters or musicians is a gimmick, but the **Queen Anne Bed & Breakfast** (2147–51 Tremont Place, 303/296-6666, www.queenannebnb. com, $135–215) decorates the Alexander Calder Suite with red, yellow, and blue paintings from the artist himself, along with herky-jerky bedspread colors and diagonally arranged antique furniture. The Norman Rockwell Suite, of course, is more traditional. All 14 guest rooms have writing desks and piped-in classical music, a few have fireplaces, and the overall effect is quirky and artsy.

$150-200

The Oxford Hotel (1600 17th St., 303/628-5400 or 800/228-5838, www.theoxfordhotel.

com, $170–400) is a five-story redbrick building that truly looks like it came from 1891, when it was built by the same architect who designed the Brown Palace. The guest rooms are a mixture of art deco and Victorian, with reds and blues all over the place, and in addition to the usual amenities such as in-room high-speed Internet access and CD players, the hotel's driver will take you out in a hotel Cadillac.

Although it's part of a (small) chain, the (**Magnolia Hotel** (818 17th St., 303/607-9000 or 888/915-1110, www.magnoliahoteldenver.com, $161–181) is one of Denver's most distinctive hotels. Built in a 1906 downtown structure, its guest rooms are rich in red and brown, large, and thoughtful, with fireplaces and perfect spots for baby cribs. Harry's Bar is a swanky neon spot for drinking martinis.

Luxury hotels in downtown Denver are usually large and filled with amenities, but **The Jet Hotel** (1612 Wazee St., 303/572-3300, www.thejethotel.com, $169–219) has 20 modern and cozy guest rooms in its redbrick-facade building at the center of LoDo. No children allowed.

With light-colored, almost glowing guest rooms, the modern but stately (**Hotel Teatro** (1100 14th St., 303/228-1100 or 888/727-1200, www.hotelteatro.com, $179–309) borrows ambience from the Denver Center Theatre Company, part of the Denver Performing Arts Complex, across the street. The lobby is filled with black-and-white photos of old theater productions along with props and costumes. One of Denver's top chefs runs two high-end eateries here—Restaurant Kevin Taylor and the healthy Italian Prima, which replaces Taylor's Bistro Jou Jou.

The **Hyatt Regency Denver** (650 15th St., 303/436-1234, http://denverregency.hyatt.com/hyatt/hotels, $165–409) is a tall rectangular building with 1,100 guest rooms that have excellent views of the city to go with a classy restaurant (Altitude) and the usual Hyatt amenities.

The (**Brown Palace** (321 17th St., 303/297-3111 or 800/321-2599, www.

the atrium at the Brown Palace in downtown Denver

© RICH GRANT / VISIT DENVER

brownpalace.com, $169–1,400) opened in 1892 in a triangular (and brown) high-rise at the center of the city. It has since served Teddy Roosevelt (who wanted a "tub of ice water"), Dwight D. Eisenhower, and countless rock stars, actors, and prime ministers. I once watched as an entire Los Angeles Lakers team, including Shaquille O'Neal and Kobe Bryant, got off a bus and walked to their rooms. Don't let "old" scare you off—the lobby is filled with cozy couches and waitstaff serving drinks, there's wireless Internet access, and the guest rooms declare not "frilly bed-and-breakfast" but "modern comfort for the business traveler."

$200-300

Directly next to the historic Daniels and Fisher clock tower, at the center of the 16th Street Mall, the recently renovated **Westin Tabor Center** (1672 Lawrence St., 303/572-9100, www.starwoodhotels.com, $199–369) has an indoor-outdoor pool overlooking the Rockies, large guest rooms with wide beds, concierges who will provide complimentary tickets to

Hyatt Regency Denver

weekend Denver Performing Arts Complex shows, and an old-school-fancy, star-pampering, steak-and-seafood restaurant called The Palm.

The Curtis (1405 Curtis St., 303/571-0300 or 800/525-6651, www.thecurtis.com, $219–389) has basic guest rooms with generic bedspreads and floor patterns and almost nothing on the walls. Its resources go instead to an on-site fitness center, including one of the largest pools in downtown Denver, an outdoor tennis court, and two indoor racquetball courts.

The **Hilton Garden Inn** (1400 Welton St., 303/603-8000, www.hgidenverdowntown.com, $209–400) is one of Denver's newest luxury hotels, a tall brick building on a street corner with clean, modular design and comfortable guest rooms. With large desks, ergonomic chairs, and high-speed Internet access, the hotel caters to business travelers.

Where the Brown Palace has the pedigree and the Hotel Teatro has the style, the **Sheraton Denver** (1550 Court Place, 303/893-3333 or 800/325-3535, www.

sheratondenverdowntown.com, $229–264), formerly the Adam's Mark, has the size. One of the 25 biggest hotels in the country, it's tall and wide, with 1,231 guest rooms and 133,000 square feet of meeting space.

After opening in late 2010, the **Four Seasons** (1111 14th St., 303/389-3000, www.fourseasons.com/Denver, $245–305) quickly became one of Denver's top hotels, taking up the first 17 floors of a 45-story building in the center of LoDo (the higher floors are expensive private residences). The building has a glowing spire at the top, but its beige and boxy architecture is otherwise unremarkable. The guest rooms, however, are terrific, with large windows showing off the city and the mountains, stone fireplaces in some suites, and marble baths. There's a rooftop pool on the third-floor terrace.

$300-400
The ◖ **Hotel Monaco** (1717 Champa St., 303/296-1717 or 800/990-1303, www.monaco-denver.com, $299–309) at first seems like a throwback, located in the 1917 Railway Exchange Building. But it proves super-modern, with pink-and-red-striped lobby walls, an explosion of bright colors in the guest rooms, and suites named after rocker John Lennon and jazzman Miles Davis. Lonely? Request a goldfish from the front desk.

SOUTH DENVER
$100-150
Loews Denver Hotel (4150 E. Mississippi Ave., 303/782-9300, www.loewshotels.com/hotels/denver, $129–149) one-ups the name-dropping Brown Palace by recalling past guests such as President George W. Bush, Sting, and the New York Giants. The 11-story hotel is old-fashioned Italian, with large classic murals, marble columns, and a facade made of glass and black metal. Despite conveniences like a health club and the Tuscany restaurant, it's a little out of the way, so guests will almost certainly want to rent a car if they're planning to explore downtown Denver.

GREATER DENVER
$200-300

The **《 Omni Interlocken Resort** (500 Interlocken Blvd., Broomfield, 303/438-6600, www.omnihotels.com, $199–219) is a massive complex off Highway 36 between Denver and Boulder, with 390 guest rooms, 34,000 square feet of meeting space, and all the trimmings— a highly rated golf course, high-speed Internet in every room, a spa and health club, and an outdoor pool and whirlpool. It is a little generic, but the views are great.

Food

LODO/CENTRAL DENVER
Snacks, Cafés, and Breakfast

Olivea (719 E. 17th Ave., 303/861-5050, http://olivearestaurant.com, 5–10 P.M. Mon.–Fri., 10 A.M.–2 P.M. and 5–10 P.M. Sat., 10 A.M.–2 P.M. and 5–9 P.M. Sun., $10) serves dinner nightly, but it's most renowned downtown for its weekend brunch, beginning with the fresh-baked pastries ($9), then moving on to the ricotta French toast ($9) or the breakfast flat bread, with crème fraîche, bacon, onions, and eggs sunny-side up ($9).

《 The Market (1445 Larimer Square, 303/534-5140, http://themarketatlarimer. com, 6 A.M.–11 P.M. Mon.–Thurs., 6 A.M.– midnight Fri.–Sat., 6 A.M.–10 P.M. Sun., $9) is the unofficial food anchor of Larimer Square, serving just about everything you could want, deli-style—pastries of all types, sandwiches, potato salad, beef and poultry dishes, and natural sodas. Avoid the lunch rush, when it's so packed you can barely move; at other times it's a great spot to sit on a rickety wire chair and read a book all afternoon.

Pete's Kitchen (1962 E. Colfax Ave., 303/321-3139, www.petesrestaurantstoo. com/petesKitchen.html, 24 hours daily, $8) is a classic diner—Colorado Governor John Hickenlooper's favorite, in fact—with a neon sign depicting a jovial, white-hatted chef flipping pancakes. Even if you sit at the counter for the renowned breakfast burritos (or omelets or pancakes), expect a long wait.

Casual

If you see a huge line on the 16th Street Mall, get on it. The source is **Biker Jim's Dogs** (16th St. and Arapahoe St., www.bikerjimsdogs.com, $5), where former repo man Jim Pittenger and his minions pleasantly serve fresh dogs made of Alaska reindeer sausage, elk, German veal, Hebrew National beef, and my favorite, buffalo (with green chili, chipotle peppers, and cumin adding a kick). Grab a bag of chips and a soda from the cooler and pull up an outdoor table or a section of curb. Biker Jim recently expanded to a bona fide restaurant (2148 Larimer St., 720/746-9355, 11 A.M.–10 P.M. Mon.–Thurs., 11 A.M.–3 A.M. Fri.–Sat.).

Gloriously basic and cozy, **《 My Brother's Bar** (2376 15th St., 303/455-9991, 11 A.M.–2 A.M. Mon.–Sat., $8) is down the street from REI and serves nongreasy fries and burgers (both beef and buffalo), sandwiches, and, naturally, beer. It's open until 2 A.M., and the tree-covered back porch, blaring with classical music, is the perfect summer drinking spot.

Sam's No. 3 (1500 Curtis St., 303/534-1927, www.samsno3.com, 6 A.M.–8 P.M. Mon., 6 A.M.–9 P.M. Tues.–Wed., 6 A.M.–10 P.M. Thurs., 6 A.M.–midnight Fri., 7 A.M.–midnight Sat., 7 A.M.–8 P.M. Sun., $10) has a menu almost as thick as the phone book, with an emphasis on green chili–covered burritos and potato-filled breakfast skillets. (The "No. 3" refers to original owner Sam Armatas's third of five Coney Islands; his son and grandsons reopened the restaurant in 1998.)

The **《 Spicy Pickle Sub Shop** (988 Lincoln St., 303/860-0730, www.spicy-pickle.com, 10:30 A.M.–7 P.M. Mon.–Thurs., 10:30 A.M.–6 P.M. Fri., 11 A.M.–6 P.M. Sat.–Sun., $7) is a Colorado franchise that walks all over Subway and Schlotzsky's—try the Sausalito turkey on whole wheat. Also, order an extra-tall beverage because the pickles really are spicy.

A number of local food critics have pinpointed Denver's best burger at **CityGrille** (3575 S. Yosemite St., 303/694-0454, www.citygrille.com, 11 A.M.–11 P.M. Sun.–Thurs., 11 A.M.–midnight Fri.–Sat., $9), which offers a giant steak burger ($8) along with a variety of salads and deli sandwiches.

A grocery store, not a restaurant, **Spinelli's Market** (4621 E. 23rd Ave., 303/329-8143, www.spinellismarket.com, 9 A.M.–7 P.M. Mon.–Fri., 8 A.M.–6 P.M. Sat., 9 A.M.–3 P.M. Sun., $6.50) has nonetheless been serving some of the city's best sandwiches since it opened in a questionable area in 1994. Both the neighborhood and market are booming today, and Spinelli's is a sort of community center, the kind of place where you'd advertise for a bassist for your band on the wall out front. Even on Spinelli's worst day, the meats and cheeses are fresher than Safeway or King Sooper.

Modeled after the Place Vendôme square in Paris, **Bistro Vendôme** (1420 Larimer St., 303/825-3232, www.bistrovendome. com, 5–10 P.M. Mon.–Thurs., 5–11 P.M. Fri., 10 A.M.–2 P.M. and 5–11 P.M. Sat., 10 A.M.–2 P.M. and 5–9 P.M. Sun., $20) is as French as anything you'll find in Denver and a lot more easygoing than France itself. The restaurant's goal is "French soul food," and the chef achieves this with dishes such as rabbit blanquette with truffles and fava beans. You expected maybe grits and collard greens?

Racines Restaurant (650 Sherman St., 303/595-0418, www.racinesrestaurant.com, 7 A.M.–11 P.M. Mon.–Wed., 7 A.M.–midnight Thurs.–Fri., 8 A.M.–midnight Sat., 8 A.M.–11 P.M. Sun., $10) has a massive menu of salads, steaks, fajitas, and seafood, but its greatest strength is dessert—15 items, including peach cobbler, banana cream pie, and a famous brownie parfait with almost as many strawberries as pieces of brownie.

Steuben's (523 E. 17th Ave., 303/830-1001, www.steubens.com, 11 A.M.–11 P.M. Mon.–Thurs., 11 A.M.–midnight Fri., 10 A.M.–midnight Sat., 10 A.M.–11 P.M. Sun., $13) takes the

diner concept to a whole new level of creativity, putting a gourmet spin onto comfort-food classics such as baked meatballs ($8), mac and cheese ($8), fried chicken ($16), ribs ($14–21), and meatloaf ($14). It seems at first like one of those throwback Johnny Rockets concepts, but it's far more than that. Watch for the blue, brown, and orange **Steuben's Truck** (www.steubens.com/truck, 303/475-9636), which helped usher in the popular food-truck concept throughout the city, puttering around town.

Because it's in the exact center of LoDo, the clientele so metropolitan and the ambience so sleek, metallic, and modern, my wife and I like to fool ourselves that what we eat at **H Burger** (1555 Blake St., Suite 102, 720/524-4345, noon–8 P.M. Sun., 11 A.M.–9 P.M. Mon.–Thurs., 11 A.M.–10 P.M. Fri., noon–10 P.M. Sat., $18) is good for us. That's sadly not the case, but we still consider the burgers and fries here among the best in town; try the buffalo burger, full of spices, topped with a fried onion ring. Top it off with a liquid-nitrogen shake: The Nutella Marshmallow ($8) contains vodka, hazelnut liquor, vanilla ice cream, and roasted marshmallows in addition to the Nutella.

Steakhouses

It's hard to walk a step in central Denver without running into a decent steakhouse. Among the best are: **The Palm Restaurant** (1672 Lawrence St., 303/825-7256, www.thepalm.com, 11 A.M.–11 P.M. Mon.–Fri., 5–11 P.M. Sat., 5–10 P.M. Sun., $80), an elegant chain outlet in the Westin Hotel; the **Buckhorn Exchange** (1000 Osage St., 303/534-9505, www.buckhorn.com, 11 A.M.–2 P.M. and 5:30–9 P.M. Mon.–Thurs., 11 A.M.–2 P.M. and 5–10 P.M. Fri., 5–10 P.M. Sat., 5–9 P.M. Sun., $35); and **Denver ChopHouse & Brewery** (1735 19th St., Suite 100, 303/296-0800, www.denverchophouse.com, 11 A.M.–11 P.M. Mon.–Thurs., 11 A.M.–midnight Fri.–Sat., 11 A.M.–10 P.M. Sun., $25). But I recommend **The Capital Grille** (1450 Larimer St., 303/539-2500, www.thecapitalgrille.com, 11:30 A.M.–2:30 P.M. and 5–10 P.M. Mon.–Thurs., 11:30 A.M.–2:30 P.M. and 5–11 P.M. Fri., 5–11 P.M. Sat., 4–9 P.M.

Sun., $72) for its dry-aged steaks plus creative high-class appetizers like caviar and pan-fried calamari with cherry tomatoes. *5280* magazine recommends **EDGE Restaurant and Bar** (1111 14th St., 303/389-3343, 6:30–10:30 A.M., 11 A.M.–2:30 P.M., and 5–10 P.M. Mon.–Fri., 9 A.M.–2 P.M. and 5–10 P.M. Sat.–Sun., $45) for its "perfectly seasoned and buttery-tender filet, no sauce needed." And while **Morton's of Chicago** (1710 Wynkoop St., 303/825-3353, www.mortons.com/Denver, 5:30–10 P.M. Mon.–Thurs., 5:30–11 P.M. Fri.–Sat., 5–10 P.M. Sun., $65) is one of the larger chain steakhouses, that just means its employees are really, really good at bringing slabs of raw porterhouse and filet mignon to your table before cooking it with béarnaise sauce or au poivre.

Asian

With its neon sign and plain-brick location on South Broadway, **Imperial Chinese** (431 S. Broadway, 303/698-2800, www.imperial-chinese.com, 11 A.M.–9:30 P.M. Mon.–Thurs., 11 A.M.–10 P.M. Fri., noon–10 P.M. Sat., 4–9:30 P.M. Sun., $22) looks from a distance like a fast-food joint. It's actually one of the nicest Chinese restaurants in Denver, with goldfish and fountains gleaming in a large red room and some of the best spring rolls and dumplings in town. They're not kidding when they say the sesame chicken ($10) is spicy.

The namesake of local-celebrity chef Lon Symensma, **ChoLon Modern Asian Bistro** (1555 Blake St., Suite 101, 303/353-5223, www.cholon.com, 11 A.M.–10 P.M. Mon.–Thurs., 11 A.M.–11 P.M. Fri., 2–11 P.M. Sat., $22) goes several steps beyond Asian standbys, with cutting-edge dishes such as yellow curry mussels with pork belly ($12) and "porkerhouse" with watermelon, tomatoes, and corn puree ($25).

Thai Wrap @ Tuk Tuk (605 Grant St., 720/917-1111, www.tuktukrocks.com, 11 A.M.–9 P.M. Mon.–Sat., $7), named for the three-wheeled taxis of Thailand, is your basic Thai restaurant—pad thai ($6), panang chicken ($5), and the like—only everything is wrapped in a flour tortilla. Top it off with an iced Thai coffee.

Two of the best sushi restaurants in town are **Sushi Den** (1487 S. Pearl St., 303/777-0826, www.sushiden.net, 11:30 A.M.–2:30 P.M. and 4:45–10:30 P.M. Mon.–Thurs., 11:30 A.M.–2:30 P.M. and 4:45–11:30 P.M. Fri., 4:30–11:30 P.M. Sat., 5–10:30 P.M. Sun., $8 per order), which has employees to regularly handpick fresh fish in Japan and ship it to Denver, and **Sushi Tazu** (300 Fillmore St., 303/320-1672, www.sushitazu.com, 11:30 A.M.–10 P.M. Mon.–Thurs., 11:30 A.M.–11 P.M. Fri.–Sat., noon–10 P.M. Sun., $15.50), which serves rice balls, halibut, and the standard sushi stuff with just the right feel and proportions.

Dim sum aficionados swear by **Super Star Asian Bistro** (2200 W. Alameda Ave., 303/727-9889, 10 A.M.–midnight daily, $18), a dumpling paradise that also does dishes like Peking duck and sea cucumber with goose web.

Mexican/Southwestern

"Modern Mexican" is the catchphrase at 🄲 **Tamayo** (1400 Larimer St., 720/946-1433, www.richardsandoval.com/tamayo, 11 A.M.–2 P.M. and 5–10 P.M. Sun.–Thurs., 11 A.M.–2 P.M. and 5–11 P.M. Fri., 5–11 P.M. Sat., 5–10 P.M. Sun., $25), owing to owner-chef Richard Sandoval's style, both here and at New York City's Pampano and San Francisco's Maya. Some find this white-tablecloth restaurant a little pretentious in a heavily Hispanic city filled with all kinds of Mexican restaurants. But the guacamole ($8) and margaritas are truly among the best in town, and I can't get enough of the fruit-filled empanadas for dessert.

Italian

The Hotel Monaco's **Panzano** (909 17th St., 303/296-3525, www.panzano-denver.com, 6:30–10 A.M. and 11 A.M.–10 P.M. Mon.–Thurs., 6:30–10 A.M. and 11 A.M.–11 P.M. Fri., 8 A.M.–2:30 P.M. and 5–11 P.M. Sat., 8 A.M.–2:30 P.M. and 4–9:30 P.M. Sun., $22) has an elaborate menu that includes a risotto and *fagioli borlotti,* plus multiple interpretations of mussels, chicken, mushrooms, and everything else that goes with pasta. The pastry-dominated Sunday brunch is also excellent.

Jennifer Jasinski may be Denver's best-known chef, and her (**Rioja** (1431 Larimer St., 303/820-2282, www.riojadenver.com, 5–10 P.M. Mon.–Tues., 11:30 A.M.–2:30 P.M. and 5–11 P.M. Fri., 10 A.M.–2:30 P.M. and 5–11 P.M. Sat., 10 A.M.–2:30 P.M. and 5–10 P.M. Sun., $25) is her attempt to reproduce Panzano according to her own personal style—everything is homemade, notably the mozzarella in prosciutto and oven-baked chicken.

Denver's top three pizza joints are (in this order, and if you don't believe me, go find your own): **Basil Doc's** (various locations, including 2170 E. Virginia Ave., 303/778-7747, www.basildocspizzeria.com, hours vary but roughly 4:30–10 P.M. daily, $23), which has thin, gushy crusts, small chunks of fruity tomatoes in the sauce, unusually fresh ingredients, and off-beat, mildly spicy flavorings befitting the restaurant's name; **BeauJo's** (various locations, including 2710 S. Colorado Blvd., 303/758-1519, www.beaujos.com, 11 A.M.–9:30 P.M. Sun.–Thurs., 11 A.M.–10 P.M. Fri.–Sat., $13), whose thick crusts (perfect with honey) might have topped this list if the quaint wooden-wall ambience of the Idaho Springs outlet were somehow harnessed in the South Denver or Westminster location; and **Proto's Pizzeria Napoletana** (various locations, including 2401 15th St., 720/855-9400, www.protospizza.com, 11 A.M.–9:30 P.M. daily, $15), which lets you watch as the cooks shove the super-thin crusts and salad-fresh ingredients into the huge ovens.

Seafood
Owned by Landry's Restaurants, which runs the Downtown Aquarium and the seafood restaurant inside, the **Oceanaire Seafood Room** (1400 Arapahoe St., 303/991-2277, www.theoceanaire.com, 5–10 P.M. Mon.–Sat., 5–9 P.M. Sun., $40) plays to the high end—the *plateau de fruits de mer* costs $79, and entrées like the Alaskan halibut and Copper River salmon start at $19 and just go up from there. But it's comfortable, diverse (try the oyster bar!), and everything is fresh.

Jax Fish House (1539 17th St., 303/292-5767, www.jaxfishhousedenver.com, 4–10 P.M. Mon.–Thurs., 4–11 P.M. Fri.–Sat., 4–9 P.M. Sun., $25) can be loud and boisterous, but fish-lovers appreciate its salmon, oysters, and especially its lighter-than-average fried dishes.

Upscale
Run by another Denver celebrity chef, Frank Bonanno, (**Mizuna** (225 E. 7th Ave., 303/832-4778, www.mizunadenver.com, 5–10 P.M. Tues.–Sat., $35) is a mixture of French, Italian, Asian, and American styles, with a particular emphasis on butter and cream (but not in a fatty kind of way). The secret ingredient in the macaroni and cheese appetizer ($15) is lobster. Bonanno also runs **Luca D'Italia** (711 Grant St., 303/832-6600, www.lucadenver.com, 5–10 P.M. Tues.–Sat., $40), which twists traditional Italian dishes with unexpected ingredients—chicken-liver ravioli ($8), for example, or rabbit three ways ($19). A *third* Bonanno restaurant is **Osteria Marco** (1453 Larimer St., 303/534-5855, www.osteriamarco.com, 11 A.M.–10 P.M. Sun.–Thurs., 11 A.M.–11 P.M. Fri.–Sat., $15), named Best Italian Restaurant in *5280* magazine in 2008, which has the usual gourmet pizzas, shaved-lamb salad, organically grown chicken, and, oh, yes, slow-roasted suckling pig.

Venerable **Restaurant Kevin Taylor** (1100 14th St., 303/820-2600, www.restaurantkevintaylor.com, 5:30–10:30 P.M. Mon.–Sat., $50), in the Hotel Teatro downtown, rests on the 15-year reputation of its namesake chef. The titles tell the story: roasted Broken Arrow Ranch axis venison with black truffle brioche pudding and caramelized apples ($36).

Some say the concept overwhelms the actual food at (**Vesta Dipping Grill** (1822 Blake St., 303/296-1970, www.vestagrill.com, 5–10 P.M. Sun.–Thurs., 5–11 P.M. Fri.–Sat., $25), where almost everything on the menu comes in small bites with a variety of fruity, spicy, and creamy salsas and sauces. I love the place. It recalls Spanish tapas and Chinese dim

© STEVE CRECELIUS / VISIT DENVER

Vesta Dipping Grill

sum, only with more flavors (try the pineapple basil salsa and the Blake Street barbecue sauce together and listen to your tongue explode) and different things (chips and pita) for dipping.

CHERRY CREEK/ SOUTH DENVER
American

The heart of **Cherry Cricket** (2641 E. 2nd Ave., 303/322-7666, www.cherrycricket.com, 11 A.M.–2 A.M. daily, $13) is steak and burgers—beware the "very well done," in which "moderation is thrown to the wind." But the lengthy menu also includes a hot meatloaf sandwich ($7), beef burritos ($8), and many-sized bowls of pork-filled green chili.

Although the former Denver Broncos quarterback and current team executive does *not* sling steaks around in the kitchen, his namesake restaurant, **Elway's** (2500 E. 1st Ave., 303/399-5353, www.elways.com, 11 A.M.–10 P.M. Mon.–Thurs., 11 A.M.–11 P.M. Fri.–Sat., 11 A.M.–9 P.M. Sun., $75), has an all-star chef, Tyler Wiard. His frequently Asian-inflected

dishes, from Japanese sea bass to Australian lobster tail, complement American standards like burgers and twice-baked potatoes.

As the name implies, the **Bull & Bush Pub and Brewery** (4700 Cherry Creek S. Dr., 303/759-0333, www.bullandbush.com, 11 A.M.–2 A.M. Mon.–Fri., 10 A.M.–2 A.M. Sat.–Sun., $15) is best known as a drinking establishment, but the burgers and steaks are huge, and the pub food includes creative ideas like street tacos, mashed potatoes with green chili, and almond chicken tenders in addition to the usual quesadillas and nachos.

South of Cherry Creek, **Fruition** (1313 E. 6th Ave., 303/831-1962, www.fruitionrestaurant.com, 5–10 P.M. Mon.–Sat., 5–8 P.M. Sun., $26) is the brainchild of *Food & Wine* star Alex Seidel, who raises his own ingredients on his 10-acre Larkspur farm. "He's making his own cheese and growing various crops, and it's literally his farm to his table," says John Lehndorff, a longtime Denver-area food writer. The menu usually has just seven main courses or so, but see if you can resist pan-roasted New Zealand bass, with stuffed cannellini-bean *agnolotti,* tomato-braised baby artichokes, and chanterelle mushroom vinaigrette ($27).

Asian

Little Ollie's Asian Café (2364 E. 3rd Ave., 303/316-8888, http://littleolliescherrycreek.com, 11 A.M.–10 P.M. Mon.–Fri., 11:30 A.M.–10 P.M. Sat.–Sun., $9) is a solid Chinese restaurant with all the basics—crispy duck, sesame chicken—and curveballs like barbecue baby back ribs. It's also comfortable and large, with a surprisingly long wine list.

Italian

Abrusci's Italian Restaurant (300 Fillmore St., 303/462-0513, www.abruscis.com, 5–9 P.M. Sun.–Thurs., 5–10 P.M. Fri.–Sat., $18) is a straight-down-the-middle Italian place, with excellent veal marsala ($19), chicken saltimbocca ($16), penne gorgonzola ($17), and long wine and dessert lists.

Spanish

In a city that skews Mexican and Southwestern far more than Spanish, **Ondo's Spanish Tapas** (250 Steele St., Suite 100, 303/975-6514, www.ondostapas.com, 4–10 P.M. Mon.–Thurs., 4–11 P.M. Fri., 5–11 P.M. Sat., $10) is a rare tapas specialist—begin with the *chorizo y datiles* ($6), work up to the *patatas bravas con salsa romesco* ($4), then peak with the *solomillo con salsa queso valdeón* ($15).

HIGHLANDS/NORTHWEST

I admit to a certain bias when writing about Highlands, the northwest Denver neighborhood about 1.5 miles from LoDo. My family bought a house here in 2001, near the intersection of Lowell Boulevard and West 32nd Avenue, where no less than 15 restaurants, from a corporate Chipotle to the distinctively local Julia Blackbird's, sit within a few hundred yards. Although weighed down with gangs and crack in the early 1990s, the neighborhood made a comeback with the Internet boom, and its solid 19th-century Victorian homes, proximity to downtown, and foundation of

immigrant families make it unlikely to fall again anytime soon (or so housing prices would indicate, even during the recession). The cuddly coffee shop Common Grounds and down-to-earth deli Heidi's took root more than a decade ago, and stroller-pushing hipsters have long since followed.

Snacks, Cafés, and Breakfast

Governor John Hickenlooper is one of the many local businesspeople who have held meetings at the homey, home-brewed coffee shop **⟨ Common Grounds** (3484 W. 32nd Ave., 303/458-5248, www.commongroundscoffeehouse.com, 6:30 A.M.–11 P.M. daily, sandwiches $7). Supplement your caffeine drinks with sandwiches, soups, and salad, and commandeer a spot near the piano. Kids love the board games in the back room. Trivia: The other Common Grounds location (1601 17th St.) in LoDo, employs onetime *Survivor* contestant Ami Cusack as a barista.

Denver Bread Company (3200 Irving St., 303/455-7194, www.thedenverbreadcompany.com, 10 A.M.–6 P.M. Sun.–Fri., 9 A.M.–5 P.M. Sat., $7 per loaf) is a brick-walled Highlands fixture that contains no comfy couches for customers to enjoy their fragrant homemade loaves, so grab the sourdough, rye, focaccia, and Swedish peasant breads to go.

Casual

Heidi's Brooklyn Deli (3130 Lowell Blvd., 303/477-2605, www.heidisbrooklyndeli.com, 6:30 A.M.–9 P.M. Sun.–Thurs., 6:30 A.M.–10 P.M. Fri.–Sat., $8) has six Denver locations, but none more prominent than this one, the quirky red-and-white centerpiece of the bustling 32nd-and-Lowell restaurant district. The bread and bagels are baked fresh daily—try the *ciabatta.* The plastic-wrapped brownies and muffins are surprisingly fresh, and the ice cream is a nice bonus. The service is mixed; Highlands residents have learned to drop by during off-hours.

Closer to downtown, near the Highland Bridge, the **Masterpiece Delicatessen** (1575 Central St., 303/561-3354, www.

masterpiecedeli.com, 8 A.M.–4 P.M. Mon.–Fri., 9 A.M.–4 P.M. Sat.–Sun., $10) is pricey for sandwiches, but the ingredients are super-fresh, and the variety is top-notch for a deli—try the Cubano ($9.75), the braised-beef brisket ($9.75), the wild ahi tuna ($10.75), or the white-truffle egg salad ($8.50).

Mexican/Southwestern

Down the street from North High School, in the rising Potter Highlands neighborhood, **(Taqueria Patzcuaro** (2616 W. 32nd Ave., 303/455-4389, www.patzcuaros.com, 11 A.M.–9 P.M. daily, $7) is cheap, greasy, totally no-nonsense, and delicious. The basic burritos, enchiladas, and mouth-burning green salsa, along with thick guacamole and a variety of fish, pork, beef, and chicken, are a match for the wooden tables and chili-stained menus.

Jack-N-Grill (2524 Federal Blvd., 303/964-9544, www.jackngrill.com, 7 A.M.–9 P.M. Sun.–Thurs., 7 A.M.–10 P.M. Fri.–Sat., $9) lost a smidgen of charm when it recently expanded its building and modernized its facade on the east side of bustling Federal Boulevard. But it didn't lose any burrito heft—these things are gigantic, and sloppy with cheese and the house-specialty green chili—and the freshly cooked chiles rellenos and enchiladas are among the best in town.

Never mind the strawberry lemonade arriving in fluorescent pink cups. **Julia Blackbird's New Mexican Café** (3434 W. 32nd Ave., 303/433-2688, 11 A.M.–2 P.M. and 5–9 P.M. Mon.–Thurs., 11 A.M.–2 P.M. and 5–10 P.M. Fri., 11 A.M.–10 P.M. Sat., 10 A.M.–8 P.M. Sun., $10) is worthy of discerning, Latino-populated northwest Denver. The enchiladas covered with feta cheese and pinto beans are spicy, but not as spicy as the incredible salsa, which comes with fresh blue-and-yellow corn chips and which my family takes home by the carton.

Brazilian

(Café Brazil (4408 Lowell Blvd., 303/480-1877, www.cafebrazildenver.com, 5–10 P.M. Tues.–Sat., $17) is a colorful little restaurant with fruity, spicy salsas and appetizers (the black bean soup is especially great) that match the owners' enthusiasm and the boisterous conversational buzz you notice as soon as you step inside. The entrées can be a little expensive, but the jumbo shrimp and fried bananas are certainly worth the splurge. Make reservations in advance or you won't get in, especially on the weekend.

Italian

(Parisi (4401 Tennyson St., 303/561-0234, www.parisidenver.com, 11 A.M.–9 P.M. Mon.–Thurs., 11 A.M.–10 P.M. Fri.–Sat., $11) is both a restaurant with eggplant-and-portobello panini sandwiches, smooth risotto Milanese, and gourmet pizzas and an Italian market selling premade frozen pizzas, gourmet meats, olives, and gelato. Two tips: They'll give serious dirty looks if you try to make pizza substitutions, and you should show up before 6 P.M. to avoid long lines.

American

Don't make the tourist mistake of walking through the front door at **Bang!** (3472 W. 32nd Ave., 303/455-1117, www.bangdenver.com, 11 A.M.–9 P.M. Tues.–Fri., 10 A.M.–9 P.M. Sat., 10 A.M.–2 P.M. Sun., $15); the way in is a narrow alley just west of the pastel-colored facade. Weird layouts aside, Bang is one of the best restaurants in town for high-end comfort food, such as meatloaf and gingerbread.

Root Down (1600 W. 33rd Ave., 303/993-4200, www.rootdowndenver.com, 5–10 P.M. Mon.–Thurs., 5–11 P.M. Fri., 10 A.M.–2:30 P.M. and 5–11 P.M. Sat., 10 A.M.–2:30 P.M. and 5–9 P.M. Sun., $15) takes normal-sounding food and puts an oddly delicious spin on it, like organic carrot and Thai red curry soup ($5–7), sweet-potato falafel ($8), and duck confit sliders ($7–13).

Denver isn't known for its barbecue, but the bright-red **Brickyard BBQ** (4243 W. 38th Ave., 303/561-4875, www.brickyardbbq.com, 11 A.M.–9 P.M. Mon.–Sat., noon–6 P.M. Sun., $11) has a nice sauce, plus the usual trimmings of ribs, chicken, baked beans, white bread, and corn. Plus, the musical and photographic themes of Billie Holiday and Louis Armstrong create a nice atmosphere—even if it isn't enough to make you feel like you're eating in Texas or Louisiana.

Upscale

The fanciest restaurant on the 32nd Avenue corridor, **Highland's Garden Café** (3927 W. 32nd Ave., 303/458-5920, www.highlandsgardencafe.com, 11 A.M.–2 P.M. and 5–9 P.M. Tues.–Sat., $30) serves pan-seared halibut, vegetarian five-cheese lasagna, and grilled quail inside a beautiful roomy old house and adjoining tree-lined patio.

Duo (2413 W. 32nd Ave., 303/477-4141, http://duodenver.com, 5–10 P.M. Mon.–Fri., 10 A.M.–2 P.M. and 5–10 P.M. Sat., 10 A.M.–2 P.M. and 5–9 P.M. Sun., $22) is in a restored-brick building just outside the Highlands area; chef-owner John Broening, formerly of downtown Brasserie Rouge, has a way of turning open-faced ravioli ($18) or rib eye with potatoes ($26) into what *5280* magazine recently called "often unexpected but always keen flavors."

SOUTH DENVER
Asian

South Federal Boulevard, which includes the **Far East Center,** is a hidden vault of Asian restaurants in Denver, and while many are located in nondescript strip malls, the food is generally superb. The Vietnamese restaurants here are known for their *pho,* a noodle soup in a beef or chicken broth that includes rice noodles and vegetables such as bean sprouts and cilantro. Drawing the late-night *pho* crowd on weekends, **Pho 555** (1098 S. Federal Blvd., 303/936-1000, 10 A.M.–9 P.M. Sun.–Thurs., 10 A.M.–3 A.M. Fri.–Sat., $6) puts consistently fresh ingredients into its *pho* and supplements it with excellent egg rolls. (**Pho 79** (781 S. Federal Blvd., 303/922-2930, 9 A.M.–9 P.M. daily, $5) and **Pho Duy** (945 S. Federal Blvd., Suite G, 303/937-1609, 9 A.M.–9 P.M. daily, $6) are also superb. **J's Noodles Star Thai** (945 S. Federal Blvd., 303/922-5495, www.

jsnoodlesstarthai.blogspot.com, 11 A.M.–9 P.M. Mon.–Thurs., 11 A.M.–10 P.M. Fri.–Sat., noon–9 P.M. Sun., $8–15) is inside yet another South Federal strip mall, but the service and Thai food are superb.

Formerly on South Federal, in a new location a few miles east, **JJ Chinese Dim Sum Restaurant** (2500 W. Alameda Ave., 303/934-8888, 11 A.M.–midnight Mon.–Fri., 10:30 A.M.–midnight Sat.–Sun.) will scare the bejesus out of you by responding to a crab order by fishing a live one out of a tank—but it's worth it. And so is the calamari.

Farther south along I-25, **Star Kitchen** (2917 W. Mississippi Ave., 303/936-0089, www.starkitchendenver.com, 10:30 A.M.–10 P.M. Sun.–Thurs., 10:30 A.M.–1 A.M. Fri.–Sat., $15) depicts two pretty, pastel-colored fish on its website, a symbol of this restaurant's specialty—lobster, oysters, clams, shrimp, smelt, and squid. The massive menu contains plenty of alternatives too, as well as some of the city's best dim sum.

American

Dedria and Joe Catalano of **Nonna's Chicago Bistro** (6603 Leetsdale Dr., 303/399-2000, www.coloradoeats.com/nonnas, 11 A.M.–2:30 P.M. and 5–9 P.M. Mon.–Fri., 5–10:30 P.M. Sat., 5–9 P.M. Sun., $18) owned restaurants in Littleton and Greenwood Village before opening this Italian comfort-food place that specializes in hot, homemade bread and thick red sauces.

On the University of Denver campus around the corner from a Ben & Jerry's, **Mustard's Last Stand** (2081 S. University Blvd., 303/722-7936, 10:30 A.M.–9 P.M. Mon.–Fri., 11 A.M.–9 P.M. Sat.–Sun., $4), befitting the name, has pretty much the best restaurant hot dogs in town. Also tasty are the hamburgers and buffalo burgers, the very salty and spiced-up fries, and a chunky vegetable chili that goes perfectly with big crackers.

Indian

(**India's Restaurant** (7400 E. Hamden Ave., 303/755-4284, www.indiasrestaurant.

com, 11:30 A.M.–2:15 P.M. and 5:30–9:15 P.M. Mon.–Thurs., 11:30 A.M.–2:15 P.M. and 5:30–9:45 P.M. Fri., noon–2:15 P.M. and 5:30–9:45 P.M. Sat., 5:30–8:45 P.M. Sun., $15), in a strip mall, has beautifully spiced and frustratingly filling dishes—from tandoori chicken to coconut shrimp curry, with green and red sauces perfectly capturing sweet and spicy. Show up for the lunch buffet, if only for the garlic naan bread.

Mexican

One of Denver's handful of local-celebrity chefs, Sean Yontz, opened **El Diablo Cocina Y Tequileria** (101 Broadway, 303/954-0324, 7 A.M.–2 A.M. daily, $15) in a huge open room in the SoBo neighborhood in 2010. The margaritas are some of the best in the city, the bar serves 200 different kinds of tequila, and the food isn't bad—several different salsa flavors arrive with the chips, and the chefs do an excellent job of mixing them up as well as other sauces and chili on the various pork, lamb, chicken, duck, beef, and veggie dishes.

El Noa Noa Restaurant (722 Santa Fe Dr., 303/623-9968, http://denvermexicanrestaurants.net, 9 A.M.–10 P.M. Mon.–Sat., 10 A.M.–9 P.M. Sun., $5) is a standard Mexican restaurant—burritos, guacamole—with two major distinctions: first, the margaritas; second, the large patio garden, which has mariachi bands and other live music in the summer.

Ethiopian

Denver has several superb Ethiopian restaurants, all of which teach American diners a new way of eating: Rather than using spoons, they scoop up the main dishes with their fingers and a squishy kind of bread known as *injera*. The two best are **Abyssinia Market Café Ethiopian Restaurant** (4116 E. Colfax Ave., 303/316-8830, 11:30 A.M.–11 P.M. Wed.–Mon.), which seems run-down until you sit down and receive a lot of attention from the waitstaff and taste the rich garlic and ginger spices; and **Arada** (750 Santa Fe Dr., 303/329-3344, www.aradarestaurant.com, noon–3 P.M. and 5–10 P.M. Mon.–Sat., 5–10 P.M. Sun.,

$10), which is tasty, but its real edge is quantity: huge piles of lamb *wat,* ground beef, and liver *dulet.*

Middle Eastern

The University of Denver campus, just south of downtown, is rich with diverse ethnic restaurants. **Jerusalem Restaurant** (1890 E. Evans Ave., 303/777-8828, www.jerusalemrestaurant.com, 9 A.M.–4 A.M. Sun.–Thurs., 9 A.M.–5 A.M. Fri.–Sat., $8) is packed just about every hour of the day thanks to its affordable and very delicious baba ghanoush, hummus, and shish kebab. A little farther south, **Damascus** (2276 S. Colorado Blvd., 303/757-3515, 11 A.M.–10 P.M. Sun.–Thurs., 11 A.M.–11 P.M. Fri.–Sat., $10) is similar to Jerusalem Restaurant, only with a Syrian bent. And the Lebanese **House of Kabob** (2246 S. Colorado Blvd., 303/756-0744, www.houseofkabobrestaurant.com, 11 A.M.–11 P.M. Mon.–Thurs., 11 A.M.–3 A.M. Fri.–Sat., 11:30 A.M.–10 P.M. Sun., $15) offers nighttime belly dancers to go with its traditional lamb, beef, and chicken kebab meals.

Dessert

The beloved **Bonnie Brae Ice Cream** (799 S. University Blvd., 303/777-0808, www.bonniebraeicecream.com, 11 A.M.–10 P.M. Sun.–Thurs., 11 A.M.–11 P.M. Fri.–Sat.) has been drawing long lines since 1986 for its heavy, sugary ice cream, with flavors that include apple pie, triple-death chocolate, and yes, vanilla.

GREATER DENVER

Denver's suburbs aren't as far away as you'd think—Wheat Ridge is just a 10-minute drive from LoDo, and Englewood is practically indistinguishable from much of south Denver. And while none of the surrounding towns have the restaurant volume of the big city, each has several places worth a meal.

Tiny Parker is the last place you'd expect to find an upscale Japanese-and-French (yes, Japanese *and* French) restaurant, but **Junz** (1121 S. Dransfeldt Rd., Suite 100, Parker, www.junzrestaurant.com, 720/851-1005, 11:30 A.M.–2:30 P.M. and 5–9 P.M.

Sun.–Thurs., 11:30 A.M.–2:30 P.M. and 5–9:30 P.M. Fri.–Sat., $19) pulls off the unique combination. It serves sushi and filet mignon ($24), chicken teriyaki ($15), and lamb chops with rosemary potatoes ($22).

Although **Bloom** (1 W. FlatIron Circle, Broomfield, 720/887-2800, www.foxrc.com/ bloom.html, 11 A.M.–9 P.M. Mon.–Thurs., 11 A.M.–10 P.M. Fri.–Sat., 11 A.M.–8 P.M. Sun., $22) is a chain restaurant in a suburban shopping mall, it's the best chain restaurant in a suburban shopping mall. The green-apple martinis are an excellent way to psych yourself up for the meal, and my favorite dish is bow-tie pasta with chicken, spinach, and sun-dried tomatoes.

Café Paprika (13160 E. Mississippi Ave., Aurora, 303/755-4150, www.cafepaprika.com, 11 A.M.–3 P.M. and 5–9:30 P.M. Mon.–Thurs. and Sat., 4–9:30 P.M. Fri., $10) is one of the best Middle Eastern restaurants in the Denver area, and its hummus, baba ghanoush, and chicken, lamb, and fish *tajines* are available for take-out.

Aurora is also known as a settling place for a small number of African immigrants, and a couple of excellent restaurants cater to this community. The **Hessini Roots Café** (2044 Clinton St., Aurora, 303/317-6531, www.hessiniroots.com, 10 A.M.–8 P.M. Mon.–Sat., $7–12) is absurdly culturally diverse, with a menu of soul, African, and Mexican food, which means on the same menu you get burritos, catfish nuggets, and Nigerian *edikaikong* soup. **Nile Ethiopian Restaurant** (1951 S. Havana St., 720/748-0239, www.nileethiorestaurant.com, 11 A.M.–2 A.M. daily, $12) is a great place for collard greens, lentils, and *doro wat*.

Seared tuna peanut butter and jelly. That's right, seared tuna peanut butter and jelly. For this dish, at **Opus Restaurant** (2575 W. Main St., Littleton, 303/703-6787, www.opusdine.com, 11 A.M.–3 P.M. and 5–10 P.M. Sun.–Thurs., 11 A.M.–3 P.M. and 5–11 P.M. Fri.–Sat., $35), former *Westword* food critic Jason Sheehan praised head chef Michael Long's "necessary revolutionary spirit of New American cuisine." The menu is incredibly long, careening through eggs Carolina with pecan biscuits, ham, and gravy ($11), mushroom escargot tart with blue cheese, garlic, and spinach ($11), and French-fried Florida lobster ($35). Opus is the best of a handful of restaurant gems populating Littleton's quaint historic downtown shopping district.

240 Union (240 Union Blvd., Lakewood, 303/989-3562, www.240union.com, 11 A.M.–10 P.M. Mon.–Fri., 5–10 P.M. Sat., 5–9 P.M. Sun., $24) has a huge dining room and an almost-as-large open kitchen along with a knack for spicy chipotle sauces. The entrées are mostly fish and beef, but curveballs like Israeli couscous ($14), baba ghanoush ($8), and Szechuan duck pizza with shiitake mushrooms ($11) add to the broadly international feel.

Twin Dragon Restaurant (3021 S. Broadway, Englewood, 303/781-8068, www.twindragonrestaurant.com, 11 A.M.–3:30 P.M. and 4–9:30 P.M. Mon.–Thurs., 11 A.M.–3:30 P.M. and 4–10 P.M. Fri., noon–3:30 P.M. and 4–10 P.M. Sat., 4–9:30 P.M. Sun., $13) is in many ways like every other Chinese restaurant—noodle bowls, egg rolls, egg foo yong—but it's also a rare gem whose takeout food is just as hot and flavorful as its sit-down meals.

Greenwood Village is basically a bunch of office buildings and the outdoor Comfort Dental Amphitheatre, but, of course, office workers and rock-and-roll roadies have to eat. The **Cool River Café** (8000 E. Belleview Ave., Suite C10, Greenwood Village, 303/771-4117, www.coolrivercafe.com, 11 A.M.–10 P.M. Mon.–Fri., 4–10 P.M. Sat., 9:30 A.M.–2 P.M. and 5–9 P.M. Sun., $30) has pool tables and a cigar-and-cognac lounge, plus steak, seafood, poultry, and what *5280* magazine considers the best smoked-pork sandwich in the city.

How can any Denverite forget **Casa Bonita** (6715 W. Colfax Ave., Lakewood, 303/232-5115, www.casabonitadenver.com, 11 A.M.–9 P.M. Sun.–Thurs., 11 A.M.–10 P.M. Fri.–Sat., $13)? A requisite for kids, it's more of a show than a restaurant, with divers jumping off cliffs, explorable caves, a gorilla (or at least a dude dressed like one), and all the shopping and video games you could ever want.

The food? Let's just say Casa has been serving the same recipe of chicken-and-beef enchiladas and tacos roughly since it opened in 1974. "Go for the cliff-divers and the fish!" says John Lehndorff, a longtime Denver restaurant critic. "Other than that, the biggest thing, of course, is the beer."

Wheat Ridge is one of the smallest suburbs, almost indistinguishable from Denver and Westminster, but its handful of excellent eateries includes **Red Tango** (5807 W. 38th Ave., Wheat Ridge, 303/420-2203, 11 A.M.–9 P.M. Mon.–Fri., noon–9 P.M. Sat., $18). The flavors here are the selling point—onions, cocoa mole, chili, avocado *pico de gallo,* and, above all, fried plantains.

Information and Services

TOURIST INFORMATION

The main number for Denver's **city government** is 720/913-1311, and www.denvergov.org has numerous resources, from parks to police. Also helpful is the **Denver Chamber of Commerce** (1445 Market St., 303/534-8500, www.denverchamber.org) and **Visit Denver** (www.denver.org).

NEWSPAPERS, RADIO, AND TELEVISION

After the *Rocky Mountain News* folded in 2009 after running continuously since 1859, the *Denver Post* (www.denverpost.com) is the main newspaper in town, and it seems to be hanging in there despite the Internet, iPads, and iPhones. Also still kicking are the alternative weekly *Westword* (www.westword.com) plus neighborhood publications such as the *North Denver Tribune.* Denver's best-known news-radio stations include **KOA** (850 AM), **KHOW** (630 AM, more talk-oriented), **KNUS** (710 AM), and the Spanish-language **KNRV** (1150 AM). The major local-news television stations are **9 News** (NBC, www.9news.com), CBS4 (http://cbs4denver.com), **KWGN** (The CW, http://cw2.trb.com), **7News** (ABC, www.thedenverchannel.com), and **Fox** (Channel 31, www.myfoxcolorado.com).

HOSPITALS

The top area hospitals include **Rose Medical Center** (4567 E. 9th Ave., 303/320-2121, www.rosemed.com), **Presbyterian/St. Luke's Medical Center** (1719 E. 19th Ave., 303/839-6000, www.pslmc.com), **St. Anthony Central Hospital** (11600 W. 2nd Place, Lakewood, 720/321-0000, www.stanthonyhosp.org), the University of Colorado-Denver's **Anschutz Medical Center** (13001 E. 17th Place, Aurora, 303/372-0000, www.ucdenver.edu), and the **National Jewish Medical and Research Center** (1400 Jackson St., 800/423-8891, www.nationaljewish.org).

POST OFFICES

U.S. Postal Service outlets are scattered throughout the city. The main office (450 W. 14th Ave., 800/275-8777) is located downtown.

LAUNDRY AND DRY CLEANING

Laundries are available throughout Denver and the surrounding area, including **Dependable Cleaners** (several locations including 1701 S. Broadway, 303/777-2673, www.thedependablecleaners.com) and the **32nd Avenue Laundromat and Cleaners** (3481 W. 32nd Ave., 303/480-9647). **Highland Mobile Dry Cleaning** (303/948-0300, www.highlandmdc.com) is based in Aurora but picks up dirty clothes and delivers them clean.

Getting There and Around

Denver International Airport (DIA, 8500 Pena Blvd., 303/342-2000, www.flydenver.com) opened in 1995 as a state-of-the-art hub for almost every major airline. Its early controversies, like a shaky baggage system and traffic-slowing toll roads, are almost completely resolved, and DIA, built on 53 square miles with fancy-looking tepee structures on top, is one of the most comfortable and easiest major airports in the United States. Little touches like windmill art in the train tunnels and decent restaurants in the food courts make all the difference to weary and occasionally frightened travelers. As you're driving in or out of the airport along Pena Boulevard, look for the striking, 32-foot-tall, fiberglass *Mustang* sculpture not far from the road. The rearing horse with blood-red eyes made its debut in February 2008, almost two years after its master sculptor, 65-year-old Luis Jiménez, died in an industrial accident in Hondo, New Mexico. You can't possibly miss it.

Within Denver, the **Regional Transportation District** (RTD, 1600 Blake St., 303/299-6000, www.rtd-denver.com) is an effective bus service—RTD is not as reliable, or relied-on, as bus networks in Chicago or New York City, but at $1.10–5 per ride, depending on the duration, you can't beat the price.

As for traffic and congestion, Denver's highways aren't nearly as bad as those in Los Angeles, Chicago, or Washington, D.C., but they have their moments, especially during rush hour. The **Transportation Expansion Project,** or T-REX, a highway-improvement project costing $1.67 billion, spent the earlier part of the last decade renovating 17 miles of key highways, including stretches of I-25, so they have more lanes, smoother ramps, improved bridges, and other improvements. But the primary T-REX benefit is a city- and suburb-wide RTD-run **light-rail system** (303/299-6000, www.rtd-denver.com/light-rail, $1.75–4), which hits Union Station, the University of Denver, and other key city destinations as well as Littleton, Greenwood Village, and other spots. It's fast, efficient, usually on time, and certainly beats paying more than $4 (at the time of this writing) per gallon of gas.

All the major car-rental companies, including Hertz, Budget, Enterprise, Avis, and Alamo, have outlets in Denver. Contact them at DIA. The rental-car website, containing all the phone numbers, is http://flydenver.com/rentalcars, and the airport's ground transportation staff can be reached at 303/342-4059 or 800/247-2336.

West of Denver

When driving out of Denver west along I-70 toward the ski towns in the High Rockies, consider leaving time for a day trip to Golden, Morrison, Black Hawk, and Central City. Although Morrison is tiny (just 426 residents), it's home to the renowned Red Rocks Amphitheatre and surrounding park; Black Hawk and Central City have transformed over the past century and a half from Old West mining towns to tourist traps and low-stakes gambling meccas; and Golden is home to MillerCoors Brewery, Buffalo Bill's gravesite,

and the Colorado School of Mines. All are quiet and pretty, with mountain scenery and fun stuff to do.

MORRISON

With a population of 427, Morrison is hardly a teeming mountain metropolis. But it does have Red Rocks Amphitheatre, which many traveling musicians consider the most spectacular outdoor arena in the United States— the Beatles and U2, to name just a few, have played legendary shows here. Founded in

1874 as a railroad town—it was supposed to be an important hub but wound up as a last stop—Morrison is tiny and beautiful, and its "downtown" area is filled with restaurants and shops catering to concertgoers. Thanks to Red Rocks, it's also a haven for hikers and cyclists.

◖ Red Rocks Amphitheatre

Red Rocks (2605 Red Rocks Park Rd., 720/865-2477, www.redrocksonline.com) is the site of numerous rock-and-roll happenings—perhaps most famously, U2's June 5, 1983, concert in which singer Bono declared, "This song is not a rebel song; this song is 'Sunday, Bloody Sunday.'" The show became legendary after U2 turned it into an album and concert video called *Under a Blood Red Sky*. The Beatles, Bruce Springsteen, the Pretenders, R.E.M., Sonic Youth, Wilco, Norah Jones, the Dave Matthews Band, Peter Gabriel, Death Cab for Cutie, and many others have performed here in their prime, and almost every one comes away marveling at the giant sandstone boulders surrounding the stage and the natural quality of the acoustics.

Sports and Recreation

Red Rocks Park (18300 W. Alameda Pkwy., 720/865-2494, www.redrocksonline.com, 5 A.M.–11 P.M. daily, free), surrounding the concert amphitheater, is great for hikers and cyclists. The official park trail is the 1.4-mile **Trading Post Trail,** which goes straight up through a meadow, some valleys, and, of course, those rocks. Visitors to the park can't miss the Trading Post, where the trail begins; just go into the park entrance from the highway, then head straight up, just before the concert venue.

Knee-shredding enthusiasts all over the world swamp the amphitheater to hike the 193 steps from the bottom (in front of the stage) to the top. "And they get so upset when you have to stop them for a concert," says Ron Garrison, Red Rocks' guest services manager. Garrison notes that a horizontal run across each row of the venue, essentially crisscrossing the stands, totals 2.472 miles. It seems much longer.

Note that rock climbing is prohibited in the park, no matter how tempting it may be.

Nearby is **Dinosaur Ridge** (16831 W.

© BOB ASH / VISIT DENVER

an aerial view of Red Rocks Amphitheatre in Morrison

Alameda Pkwy., 303/697-3466, www.di-noridge.org, 10 A.M.–3 P.M. daily, free), a visitors center where, in 1877, scientists discovered 145-million-year-old brontosaurus, diplodocus, stegosaurus, and other fossils. The ridge has guided tours, classes, and a gift shop.

Just west of Morrison is **Mount Falcon Park** (northwest of the intersection of U.S. 285 and Hwy. 8, 303/271-5925, www.jeffco.us/openspace/openspace_T56_R16.htm), with a slew of easy-to-find trails—begin with **Eagle Eye Shelter,** which provides wide, pretty views of Evergreen, Mount Evans, and Indian Hills. One of the two trailheads is at 21004 Mount Falcon Road in Indian Hills; to get there, take U.S. 285 to the Indian Hills turn-off, continue on Parmalee Gulch Road for five miles, then look for the west parking area once you reach Picutis Road.

Just north of Red Rocks and Morrison, **Matthews/Winters Park** (303/271-5925, www.jeffco.us/openspace/openspace_T56_R1.htm) is an area that was, in the 1800s, a mountain route to Central City gold fields. It's a beautiful spot, with nice views of the foothills in one direction and the plains in the other. The three hiking-biking trails here go straight up to Red Rocks, some overlooking the park itself. The 2.2-mile **Dakota Ridge** is steep and rocky, so be sure to carry plenty of water and make sure you're in shape; it begins at Highway 26, just past the I-70 underpass, and ends at the highway leading up to Red Rocks Amphitheatre, so it's especially convenient for cyclists. **Red Rocks Trail** is 2.8 miles long, with nice views of the amphitheater, and it leads to the curvy, 1.2-mile **Morrison Slide Trail,** which offers an amazing view of the city from the top. To get to the park, take I-70 to Highway 26, turn south, and look for the entrance. There's a short (less than one mile) trail leading to the other three.

Lair O' the Bear Park (4 miles west of Morrison on Hwy. 74, parking area and trailhead on the south side of Hwy. 74, 303/271-5925, www.jeffco.us/openspace/openspace_T56_R11.htm) is an all-time favorite of families with little kids. The Jefferson County park has a flat 1.5-mile trail that runs along Bear Creek, with lots of coolness and shade for summertime outings. There's also a picnic area and an accessible fishing pier. If you're up for a longer hike, the Lair O' the Bear Trail connects to two of the Denver Mountain Parks at either end: Pence Park and Little Park.

In addition to Red Rocks, the other giant attraction in tiny Morrison is **Bandimere Speedway** (3051 S. Rooney Rd., 303/697-6001, www.bandimere.com), an official course for National Hot Rod Association championship drag racing during the summer, and host to events from motorcycling to extreme snowmobiling throughout the year.

Entertainment

The **Morrison Holiday Bar** (403 Bear Creek Ave., 303/697-5658, www.morrisonholidaybar.com, 10 P.M.–2 A.M. daily), otherwise known as "The Local Cure," is a recently renovated joint in which 1890s-era ceiling fans whir above the din of plasma television sets, coin-operated video games, foosball, and darts. For those with the munchies, next door is the **Mill Street Deli** (401 Bear Creek Ave., 303/697-1700, www.morrisonholidaybar.com, 11 A.M.–10 P.M. Sun.–Thurs., 11 A.M.–midnight Fri.–Sat., $4–9), which serves sandwiches, of course, as well as pizza, calzones, and salads.

Food

Inspired by Bent's Fort, the 1830s trading post on the Santa Fe Trail, Samuel P. Arnold built a fort-like home here in 1962 and installed a restaurant on the lower floor. **The Fort** (19192 Hwy. 8, 303/697-4771, www.thefort.com, 5:30–10 P.M. Mon.–Fri., 5–10 P.M. Sat., 5–9 P.M. Sun., $35–50) serves hefty slabs of beef, poultry, and game along with an irresistible dish called peanut butter–stuffed jalapeños *escabeche*.

Information and Services

The **Town of Morrison** (321 Hwy. 8, 303/697-8749, http://town.morrison.co.us) will answer most of your questions, including those about Red Rocks.

GOLDEN

Once a rival to Denver for territorial capital status in Colorado—this was in the 1860s—Golden has since slipped into a comfortable zone as a sleepy mountain town with plenty of heavy industry and jobs. The most interesting of these are at the MillerCoors Brewery, built in 1873, and the engineering-oriented Colorado School of Mines, emblazoned with a giant "M" on the side of a mountain. It's easily accessible from both Boulder (about 20 miles via Hwy. 93) and Denver (20 miles via Hwy. 58), and its historical sites are among the richest in the greater Denver metropolitan area.

Sights

Everything in Colorado seems to be named after Coors—baseball's Coors Field, the University of Colorado's Coors Event Center, onetime U.S. Senate candidate Pete Coors, and, especially, the **MillerCoors Brewery** (13th St. and Ford St., 303/277-2337 or 800/642-6116, www.millercoors.com/who-we-are/locations.aspx#Golden,

10 A.M.–4 P.M. Mon.–Sat., noon–4 P.M. Sun. June–Labor Day, 10 A.M.–4 P.M. Thurs.–Mon., noon–4 P.M. Sun. Labor Day–May), which Prussian-born Adolph Coors founded here in 1873. In 2008, Coors merged with competitor Miller and officially changed its name to MillerCoors. The brewery offers free 30-minute tours throughout weekdays, and, yes, those over 21 are given free samples at the end. Some 250,000 take these tours every year, which seems like a lot until you consider the company sells 32.7 million *barrels* (that's 31 gallons each) of beer per year.

The mountainside **Colorado School of Mines** (1500 Illinois St., 303/273-3000 or 800/446-9488, www.mines.edu) has a world-class mineral-engineering program, which isn't exactly what makes it a fun campus to visit (and the Princeton Review once named it the campus with the unhappiest students). In addition to the high jinks of hard-partying engineers, CSM has a **Geology Museum** (1310 Maple St., 303/273-3823, www.mines.edu/Geology_Museum, 9 A.M.–4 P.M. Mon.–Sat.,

© STEVE KNOPPER

"Howdy Folks!": inviting downtown Golden

1–4 P.M. Sun., free) containing 50,000 minerals and fossils of every shape, size, and color from all over the globe. Also on campus is the **USGS Earthquake Information Center** (1711 Illinois St., 303/273-8420, http://earthquake. usgs.gov/regional/neic/tours.php, tours by appointment), which quickly analyses data about the world's earthquakes and sends out information to relevant agencies everywhere.

Buffalo Bill Museum and Grave (987½ Lookout Mountain Rd., 303/526-0744, www. buffalobill.org, 9 A.M.–5 P.M. daily May–Oct., 9 A.M.–4 P.M. Tues.–Sun. Nov.–Apr., $3) is the final resting spot of Col. William F. "Buffalo Bill" Cody, the Old West trapper, frontiersman, and Civil War scout who starred in plays about his own exploits. The museum, on top of Lookout Mountain, has incredible views, and some people visit this area just for the hiking. Numerous trails are at the top of Lookout Mountain along with the **Lookout Mountain Nature Center and Preserve** (910 Colorow Rd., 720/497-7600), a 110-acre park with trails, picnic areas, and exhibits on migrating birds and the ponderosa pine forest. Also here is the Boettcher Mansion, onetime summer home of famous Denver entrepreneur Charles Boettcher, open today for weddings and business meetings.

Any kid who ever picked up a Thomas train will enjoy the **Colorado Railroad Museum** (17155 W. 44th Ave., 303/279-4591 or 800/365-6263, www.crrm.org, 9 A.M.–5 P.M. daily, $8), in an 1880s-style depot stocked with a 317-ton Burlington locomotive, a 1937 stainless-steel observation car from the Santa Fe *Super Chief,* various pieces of vintage equipment, an art gallery, and a gift shop.

Golden has many other historic areas. **Heritage Square** (18301 W. Colfax Ave., on U.S. 40 between I-70 and W. 6th Ave., 303/277-0040, www.heritagesquare.info, 10 A.M.–8 P.M. Sun.–Fri., 11 A.M.–8 P.M. Sat.) recreates a late-1800s village in Victorian style (in addition to its alpine slide). The **American Alpine Club** (710 10th St., 303/384-0110,

© STEVE KNOPPER

The creek path from downtown Golden into the mountains is a pretty place to hang out during the summer.

www.americanalpineclub.org) has a 17,000-volume library devoted to all things mountain. **Clear Creek History Park** and **Astor House Museum** (11th St. and Arapahoe St., 303/278-3557, www.clearcreekhistorypark.org, $5 donation) make up a complex with an 1860s-era replica prospectors' park and a Victorian-style 1890s-era hotel. And **12th Street** is a National Historic District of late-19th-century brick buildings, including the **National Guard Armory** at 13th and Arapahoe Streets.

Sports and Recreation

Running through Golden the way the Boulder Creek Path runs through Boulder, the **Clear Creek Trail** (303/384-8000, http://ci.golden.co.us) leads directly from downtown to the bottom of the foothills. On sunny summer days, the concrete path is great for walking, cycling, and, in the creek, kayaking. Access points include Vanover Park (Water St. and Ford St.) and the Jefferson County Library (10th St. and Illinois St.). Just head west, toward the big "M" in the mountains.

Golden Gate Canyon State Park (north of Golden near Hwy. 93 and Golden Gate Canyon Rd., 303/582-3707, http://parks.state.co.us/Parks/goldengatecanyon) has 35 miles of hiking trails, 19 miles of trails for bikers and horseback riders, and many ponds full of rainbow trout for fishing. In the winter it's also a hot spot for snowshoeing, cross-country skiing, ice fishing, and ice-skating. Look for really good sledding hills near the visitors center and above Kriley Pond.

The biggest campground here is **Reverend's Ridge** (Gap Rd., 303/642-3856, $18–22), which has 97 sites, flush toilets, hot showers, and a laundry room. The smaller, quieter **Aspen Meadows Campground** (Golden Gate Canyon State Park, 92 Crawford Gulch Rd., 303/470-1144, $18) has 35 tent sites, nonflush toilets, tables, fire rings, and one water pump. Two of the sites are horse-friendly. Golden Gate also has four open-air huts ($12 per night) for up to six people each; permits are available at the visitors center. The park also has 20 more remote backcountry tent campsites surrounded by 10,000-foot peaks and flowery meadows. No fires are allowed, and you have to hike in for about a mile. Also, yurts are available for up to six people per structure, as well as cabins and guesthouses (303/470-1144, http://parks.state.co.us/reservations, $70).

Entertainment

Golden's **Buffalo Rose** (1119 Washington Ave., 303/278-6800, www.buffalorose.net, 11 A.M.–1:30 A.M. daily) is a classic mountain bar, with wooden walls and furniture and die-hard Broncos fans who loyally show up every Sunday in the fall. It's also a surprisingly great concert venue, drawing up-and-coming local bands (mostly of the jam-rock or acoustic-folk variety) and excellent has-beens such as The Fixx and Molly Hatchet.

Billing itself as "Golden's second-largest brewery," **Golden City** (920 12th St., 303/279-8092, http://gcbrewery.com, 11:30 A.M.–6:30 P.M. daily) is a small bar in a house-like building that caters to a grizzled crowd of students and townies. Ask for the Legendary Red Ale on tap.

Shopping

Golden's shopping district has grown in recent years with its downtown creek walk area. **Baby Doe's Clothing** (1116 Washington Ave., 303/279-8100 or 888/385-8420, www.babydoesclothing.com, 10 A.M.–5 P.M. Mon. and Sat., 10 A.M.–6 P.M. Tues.–Fri., noon–4 P.M. Sun.) carries hipster women's clothing with brands such as True Grit, Royal Robbins, and Horny Toad. It's in a building known to old Goldenites as the former home of the Fair Variety Store, a sort of mountain Woolworth's.

Accommodations

Whereas the downtown Table Mountain Inn and other chain hotels are no-frills, **The Golden Hotel** (800 11th St., 303/279-0100 or 800/233-7214, www.thegoldenhotel.com, $149–189) is known for its luxurious touches, like fireplaces in some guest rooms, wide and pillowy beds, and the huge Creekside Suite.

Food

The **Table Mountain Inn** (1310 Washington Ave., 303/277-9898, www.tablemountaininn.com, 6:30–10:30 A.M., 11 A.M.–3 P.M., and 4:30–10 P.M. Mon.–Fri., 7 A.M.–2 P.M. and 4:30–10 P.M. Sat.–Sun., $15) is a hotel restaurant that serves bar food—but it's really good bar food, with a Southwestern flavor that gives a zip to the enchiladas and a bit of soul to the burgers. Think Rock Bottom Brewery in an adobe building.

Information and Services

The **City of Golden** (1445 10th St., 303/384-8151, http://ci.golden.co.us) website focuses on waterlines and planning-board meetings, but it's somewhat useful for visitors.

CENTRAL CITY/BLACK HAWK

Until 1991, these twin mountain towns were quaint, historic, Old West mining areas—they celebrated and replicated the 1880s, when somebody discovered gold in western Kansas territory and prospectors in raggedy tents spilled into the area known as Gregory's Gulch. But by the mid-20th century, long after the miners disappeared, both towns were in decline, with little money to maintain buildings and roads.

Low-stakes gambling—meaning you can't bet more than $5 on one hand—rescued Central City and Black Hawk from permanent ghostville. Suddenly, given the growing number of corporate casinos, huge hotels, and buffet-style restaurants, the towns were tourism destinations, with the added bonus that visitors could go to historic sites such as the Central City Opera House and the Thomas House Museum.

Although some antigambling crusaders continue to criticize Central City and Black Hawk for selling out to vice and establishing a "poor tax" on Colorado residents, it's obvious the towns are revitalized. Their main drags have old-fashioned candy and souvenir shops and capture the spirit of debauched miner settlements. Plus, the casinos are well kept, the gambling is fun, and country-and-imitator bands

provide the cornball entertainment. Central City was initially the dominant gambling area, but its sibling town has since taken over much of the business. In recent years, after much political wrangling, both cities have banned smoking in casinos and eliminated the long-running $5 limits on tables.

Sights

Despite the large casinos and busloads of slot-machine players, both Black Hawk and Central City are acutely aware of their history as Colorado mining towns—historic buildings and districts are everywhere, notably the **Mountain City Historic Park** (Gregory St., Black Hawk, 303/582-5221, free), a collection of 12 historic Victorian and Gothic homes that were moved to accommodate the casinos.

Built in 1878 for (temporarily) rich miners, the **Central City Opera House** (124 Eureka St., Central City, 303/292-6500, www.centralcityopera.org) hit hard times in the early 1900s when the gold rush ended. In 1932, local volunteers refurbished and reopened the house—its first opera was *Camille,* starring Lillian Gish, and it has been open ever since for productions such as *The Ballad of Baby Doe* and *Gabriel's Daughter.* The large stone building, with its curved front doors and second-floor balcony, and famous performers' names carved into the red seats, is worth visiting even if you're not an opera fan. There's no dress code, by the way—business attire is more than acceptable.

The **Gilpin County Historical Society Museum** (228 E. 1st High St., Central City, 303/582-5283, www.gilpinhistory.org, 10 A.M.–4 P.M. Tues.–Fri., 9 A.M.–4 P.M. Sat.–Sun. Memorial Day–Labor Day, $5) is a two-story stone building that functioned as a school for miners' kids beginning in 1870—and continued through the 1960s. Its exhibits recreate a doctor's office and barbershop from the old days, displaying kerosene lamps and scale models of local mills. Also part of the complex is the **Thomas House Museum** (228 E. 1st High St., Central City, 303/582-5283, www.gilpinhistory.org, 11 A.M.–4 P.M. Tues.–Sun.

Memorial Day–Labor Day, $5), an 1874 frame building where Ben and Marsha Thomas lived in the 1920s and beyond.

Teller House (120 Eureka St., Central City, 303/582-5283, www.gilpinhistory.org, 10:30 A.M.–4:30 P.M. daily Memorial Day–Labor Day, call for hours in other seasons), in an 1872 building, is perhaps the most impressive in the Central City/Black Hawk region. Built by former U.S. senator and U.S. Secretary of the Interior Henry M. Teller, it was once a lavish hotel—Teller's friend Ulysses S. Grant stayed here and was reputed to have been irritated by the solid-silver path mine owners laid en route to the entrance (Grant supposedly took a different path).

Accommodations

Many of the larger casinos offer lodging, including the **Fortune Valley Hotel & Casino** (321 Gregory St., Central City, 303/582-0800, www.fortunevalleycasino.com, $71–169), which has 118 guest rooms and is the largest hotel in the region. While they're adequate for a night or two on a gambling vacation, visitors may choose to stay at some of the nicer properties, including several bed-and-breakfasts, in both Central City and Black Hawk.

The **Hooper Homestead** (210 Hooper St., Central City, 303/582-5828 or 866/582-5828, www.hooperhomestead.com, $125–149) is in an 1878 house built by Thomas Hooper, inventor of the "Hooper Brick," used to reconstruct Central City after a major fire in 1874. It's on top of a hill, with great views of the city and mountains, and its two suites and one guest room are a combination of wooden Old West colors and modern elegance.

Food

Inside The Lodge casino, the **White Buffalo Grille** (240 Main St., Black Hawk, 303/582-1771, www.thelodgecasino.com, 5–9 P.M. Sun.–Thurs., 5–10:30 P.M. Fri.–Sat., $25) is one of the few nice restaurants in the area (which is to say, other than the casino cattle-call buffets). Its menu is pretty basic, with steak and salmon dishes in the $19–23 range and

appetizers ranging from Buffalo wings to crab cakes.

Information and Services

Try the **Central City Visitors Center** (103 Eureka St., 303/582-3345, www.centralcitycolorado.us/tourism/cc-bh-vistors-center) for information. For more on Central City and Black Hawk—heavy on casino advertisements—check their websites at www.centralcitycolorado.com and www.blackhawkcolorado.com. The official Black Hawk government website (www.cityofblackhawk.org) is more sparse.

For medical services, the **Mountain Family Health Centers** (562 Gregory St., Black Hawk, 303/582-5276, www.mountainfamily.org) is a community health center funded by the U.S. government. It has on-call doctors, nurses, and nurse practitioners and handles emergencies since big-city hospitals are far away.

Getting There and Around

Twisty, steep, narrow mountain highways take drivers to Black Hawk and Central City. From Denver, drive west on I-70 toward the Eisenhower Memorial Tunnel, then head north on Highway 279 from Idaho Springs. Central City is on the left, and Black Hawk is a mile up the road. From Boulder, head west to Nederland—a good area to stop for lunch or dinner—then follow the many hairpin curves along Highway 119 to Black Hawk. Denver and Boulder cabs and limousines are available to shuttle gamblers, but beware of snowstorms.

EVERGREEN

Before my family moved from Livonia, Michigan, to Colorado in 1982, my parents bought an empty tract of land here so we could visit it every summer on family vacations. Back then, Evergreen was (mostly) empty and undeveloped, and the aspen, pine, and blue spruce forests at 7,000 feet resembled real-life backdrops for the *Grizzly Adams* TV show. The mountains seemed steep and endless, the air impossibly clean, and the world impossibly quiet.

Although Evergreen has filled in quite a bit, particularly around the main drag, Bear Creek Road, it retains those silent, empty, crisp, endless qualities. The town's 130 square miles stretch from 14,260-foot-tall Mount Evans to Lookout Mountain, with tiny mountain towns Conifer and Aspen Park on the southern border. Once a resort town, Evergreen is today a prime day-trip destination for Denver residents some 40 miles to the northeast as well as home base for sprawl escapees and commuters who prefer the scenic drive along Highway 74, I-70, and U.S. 6 rather than a more conventional suburban drive.

Like many other towns in these parts, Evergreen was once home to the Ute Indians, until gold-rushers showed up in the late 1800s. The local homesteader was Thomas Bergen, who drifted here from the mines and built a ranch and hotel. The forests were jammed with trees back then, and many ranchers and harvesters followed, building sawmills and producing lumber for the booming home business in nearby Denver. Evergreen ranchers raised cattle, hay, potatoes, and peas for the new arrivals. The town boomed from 200 people back then to roughly 600 in the 1920s and 1930s, and when automobiles arrived in Colorado, Evergreen shifted from a logging-and-ranching community to a Denver commuter town. Willie Nelson, Trey Parker of *South Park,* former U.S. senator Gary Hart, and Olympic skater Scott Hamilton are among the notables who've lived in this area. Today, some 9,200 residents live in this growing part of Jefferson County, enjoying the best-of-both-worlds spirit of living in the mountains and working in a major metropolitan city.

Sports and Recreation

About 20 miles west of Evergreen and south of Idaho Springs, **Echo Mountain Park** (19285 Hwy. 103, Idaho Springs, 303/325-7347, www.echomtnpark.com) opened in 2005 as a skiing and snowboarding haven that emphasizes extreme sports. The terrain park contains trails with names like Mousetrap, Grimace, and the Junkyard, and the tricks include the Monster Launch Box and the Neff Roller. The park is especially kid-friendly, catering to beginners with an elaborate Ski and Ride School and a magic-carpet lift known as Thumper. Lift tickets as of the 2011–2012 season were $159.

Another popular Evergreen winter sport is ice-skating on **Evergreen Lake** (29614 Upper Bear Creek Rd., 720/880-1300, www.evergreenrecreation.com, $5, plus $6 for rentals), which also allows reservations for broomball. In the summer, the 40-acre lake converts to a nice tree-lined area for sailboats, paddle boats, canoes, and fishing boats ($4 per day, $35 season pass). The lake is also stocked with rainbow trout for fishers, and hikers and joggers can run the 1.3-mile **Evergreen Lake Trail** around the water.

Evergreen shares numerous hiking trails and scenic parks with Morrison, its neighbor to the east, including Lair O' the Bear Park and Mount Falcon Park. More specific to Evergreen is **Alderfer/Three Sisters Park,** just west of town, with 10 miles of trails leading to huge boulders and open meadows. The trail winds past a massive chunk of quartz known as the Three Sisters and up another one called the Brothers, where hikers can view the entire town of Evergreen and a bunch of pretty valleys. To get to the park, take Highway 73 south of Evergreen, turn right on Buffalo Park Road, and watch for the east parking lot after about a mile. Northwest of town, **Elk Meadow Park** is wider and more expansive, leading through a valley up to Bergen Peak, where on a clear day you can see all the way out to the foothills and the Eastern Plains, as well as the Continental Divide in the other direction. The park is accessible by taking Highway 74 north from Evergreen, turning left on Stagecoach Boulevard, then driving 1.25 miles to the south parking lot. Other parks in the broader Evergreen area include **Flying J Ranch Park** and **Meyer Ranch Park,** both closer to Aspen Park, a few miles south of Evergreen along Highway 74. For more information on parks and trails in this area, including detailed maps, contact **Jefferson County Open Space** (700 Jefferson County Pkwy.,

Golden, 303/271-5925, www.co.jefferson. co.us/openspace).

Evergreen is a nice escape for golfers bored of urban courses. Opened in 1962, **Hiwan Golf Club** (30671 Clubhouse Lane, 303/674-3366, www.hiwan.com) has hosted big events such as the Colorado Open (from 1964 to 1991) and the Junior America's Cup (ongoing). It is members-only, but banquet and catering facilities are available to everybody, and nonmembers can play the courses if they get a member to sponsor them. **Evergreen** (29614 Upper Bear Creek Rd., Evergreen, 303/674-6351, www. cityofdenvergolf.com/evergreen.htm, $22 weekdays, $30 weekends) is the only city-run golf course outside of Denver.

Entertainment

The **Little Bear** (27895 Hwy. 74, 303/674-9991, www.littlebearsaloon.com, 11 A.M.–9:30 P.M. Mon., 11 A.M.–11 P.M. Tues.–Thurs., 11 A.M.–1 A.M. Fri.–Sat., 11 A.M.–9 P.M. Sun.) is a brown wooden bar on the corner of two mountain roads, formerly a church and a drugstore. It has been open for decades, legendary for its inebriated crowds of townies and visiting skiers, emphasizing live musical acts of the blues and rock persuasions, from bluesman Tab Benoit to the Young Dubliners.

Shopping

Although Evergreen doesn't have a tourist strip quite as established as those of Estes Park or even Grand Lake, Bear Creek Road, or Highway 74, has a number of excellent shops that make it worth visiting. Sniffing the candles at **Evergreen Candleworks** (9124 Armadillo Trail, 303/506-9692, www.evergreencandleworks.com) is like sniffing the actual pine trees surrounding Evergreen, and the merchandise is made of environmentally friendly soy, with wicks of pure cotton. In the Bergen Village Shopping Center, the **DARE Boutique** (1260 Bergen Pkwy., Suite C130, 303/670-9900, www.dareboutique.net, 10 A.M.–6 P.M. Mon.–Fri., 10 A.M.–5 P.M. Sat.) carries the hippest women's clothing brands, like Michael Stars sportswear tops and Dolce Cabo sweaters.

Accommodations

With 11 guest rooms, three levels of outdoor porches, and a hot tub, the **Bears Inn** (27425 Spruce Lane, 303/670-1205 or 800/863-1205, www.bearsinn.com, $145–225) is the best of a handful of woodsy cabins in the Evergreen area.

Food

At the Evergreen golf course, **Keys on the Green** (29614 Upper Bear Creek, 303/674-4095, www.evergreengolf-dine.com, 11 A.M.–9 P.M. Mon.–Sat., 9 A.M.–2 P.M. and 4–9 P.M. Sun.) is in a wooden cabin with a stone fireplace. Its menu is steak, steak, steak, and a few concessions to non–meat eaters such as chicken, salad, and seared ahi tuna. Due south of Evergreen and Conifer, near tiny Pine, the **Bucksnort Saloon and Family Restaurant** (15921 Elk Creek Rd., Pine, www.thebucksnortsaloon.com, noon–9 P.M. Mon.–Thurs., noon–11:30 P.M. Fri., 11 A.M.–11:30 P.M. Sat., 11 A.M.–9 P.M. Sun.) is a legendary biker bar in a small log shack, complete with barstools made out of logs and graffiti-covered walls. It's famous for its burgers—the menu calls them "the biggest, juiciest, most sizzling, messiest, sloppiest, hardest-to-eat, hand-pattied half pound of fresh ground beef on a kaiser roll"—but has a bunch of other stuff as well, like ice cream pie and beer.

Information

Located in the historic Evergreen Hotel building, the **Evergreen Area Chamber of Commerce** (28065 Hwy. 74, Suite 201, 303/674-3412, www.evergreenchamber.org) has a bit of helpful visitor information and town history. While we lived in Michigan and pined for our mountainside property in Evergreen, my family subscribed to the *Canyon Courier* (www.canyoncourier.com), a classic small-town newspaper. Back then, it printed plenty of random police-blotter items about lost dogs and cats in trees, and while it's more sophisticated today, the cranky letters to the editor remain.

THE COLLEGE TOWNS: BOULDER AND FORT COLLINS

The time to nap in the car is not when you're on I-36, heading west from Denver to Boulder. After twisting through the suburban sprawl of Westminster, Broomfield, Louisville, Lafayette, and Superior, the highway leads up one final steep hill, then…*bam*. What looks like a color postcard of the Rocky Mountain foothills suddenly appears in a full panorama, just below the hill in front of you. Flagstaff Mountain, rising out of the red-roofed University of Colorado campus, is to your left. The flat-headed Longs Peak is in the distance to your right. This view is just the beginning of why so many people—more than 90,000, in the last census—settle in tranquil, soothing Boulder.

The outdoor activities are obvious just from one glance at the city, but once you start driving around the foothills, the Front Range, and spectacular wilderness areas like Rocky Mountain National Park and Grand County, it's hard to overcome an addiction to clean air and mountain scenery. Plus, when locals feel they've had enough of the University of Colorado, Fort Collins and Colorado State University are just 40 minutes north. Boulder's Achilles' heel is its lack of diversity—the African American population hovers in the low single digits, and Latinos tend to populate Denver and its surrounding suburbs instead. And even though smaller satellite towns such as Louisville, Superior, Niwot, and Erie have filled in over the past few years, housing prices remain so exorbitant that only people at a certain socioeconomic level, generally speaking, can afford to live here.

HIGHLIGHTS

◀ **Pearl Street Mall:** With street performers climbing tightropes, kids playing on frog and snail statues, some of the best shops, bars, and restaurants in Colorado, and a red-brick ambience that attracts travelers, locals, and beggars alike, Boulder's downtown mall is just as vibrant as it was when it opened in 1977 (page 94).

◀ **Chautauqua Park:** The grassy park is a great place to play Frisbee or just laze around underneath the foothills for an afternoon, and the hiking trails, restaurant, and concert hall are an elegantly down-home combination – plus, you can rent cabins (page 95).

◀ **Flagstaff Mountain:** Drive up a steep road of hairpin curves for the city's most renowned restaurant (Flagstaff House) and panoramic views of Boulder (page 96).

◀ **Boulder Theater:** The distinctive marquee just off the Pearl Street Mall hints at the grandeur inside this 1906 former opera house, which continues to grab big-name concerts and excellent second-run movies (page 103).

◀ **Bolder Boulder:** This Memorial Day footrace has three parts – one for world-class competitive runners; one for regular citizens (some of whom are pretty fast); and one for wheelchair racers. The streets close and most of Boulder comes out to watch if they aren't running (page 103).

◀ **Hiking in Rocky Mountain National Park:** It's hard to adequately describe this 265,000-acre nature preserve of gigantic mountains, green meadows, intimidating snow-filled tundra, and endless hiking trails, campgrounds, and picnic areas, but let's just say it's one of the most beautiful spots in Colorado (page 117).

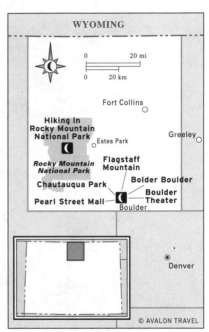

LOOK FOR ◀ TO FIND RECOMMENDED SIGHTS, ACTIVITIES, DINING, AND LODGING.

PLANNING YOUR TIME

It only takes a few days to get a feel for Boulder, with its combination of college hangouts, yuppie shops on the Pearl Street Mall, mountain scenery, and perfectly paved biking trails. Any of the hotels will do for a weekend, and while some feel pressured to get into the mountains as soon as possible, Boulder is a relaxed city that more than rewards lazy days on outdoor restaurant patios.

If you have more time, consider splitting the trip between mountain excursions, hikes in Chautauqua Park, and a sampling of the surprisingly world-class restaurants clustered around the Pearl Street Mall. Just be careful not to fall in love with the city, or you'll wind up giving up your high-powered career in New York or Los Angeles, buying Birkenstocks, and living here (while complaining about crowds) forever.

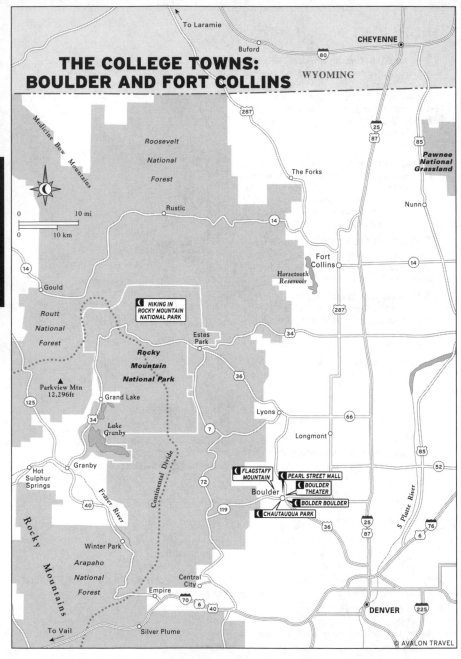

Boulder's downtown hotels make a perfect base to explore the many sights in northern Colorado. **Estes Park** and the nearby **Rocky Mountain National Park** are about half an hour's drive from the city; hikers and mountain climbers should plan to spend at least a weekend in that area (the local hotels and restaurants in Estes Park are well above functional, if not luxurious). The tiny hippie town **Nederland** is half an hour into the mountains and well worth visiting, although many locals consider it a pit stop en route to mountain sightseeing towns such as **Georgetown** and **Idaho Springs** or the ski resorts farther west along I-70. **Fort Collins,** home of Colorado State University and an easygoing college town, is about 40 minutes' drive north of Boulder. Other pretty mountain day trips include **Grand Lake, Hot Sulphur Springs,** and **Granby,** all within about 45 minutes of Boulder.

Boulder and Vicinity

Since the 1960s, Boulder has become known throughout the state as "The People's Republic of Boulder," as hippies put down roots, transformed into yuppies, and started driving Saabs with "Visualize Whirled Peas" stickers between the Wild Oats and Celestial Seasonings Tea outlets. Although the college campus is more famous for partying skiers than political activism, Boulder is by far the state's most liberal, and certainly most environmentalist, city—although ex-CU football coach Bill McCartney formed the stadium-sized conservative-Christian men's group Promise Keepers here in 1990. Equally notorious are its weird quirks, from the annual Kinetic Sculpture Challenge, in which thousands head to Boulder Reservoir to race their homemade contraptions while wearing elaborate costumes, to the buskers, balloon twisters, tightrope walkers, artists, beggars,

COURTESY OF BOULDER CONVENTION AND VISITORS BUREAU

an aerial view of Boulder

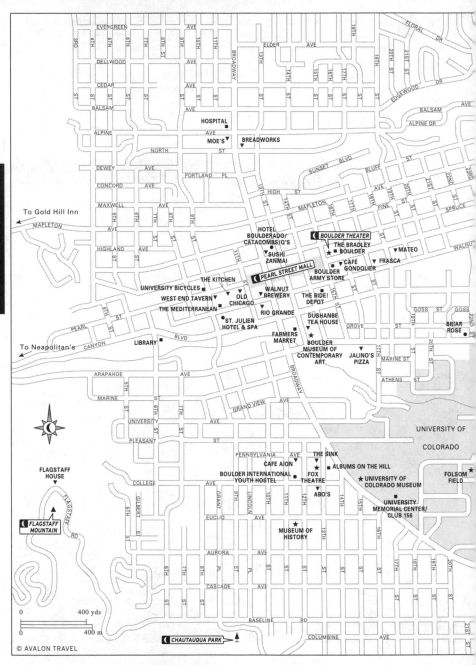

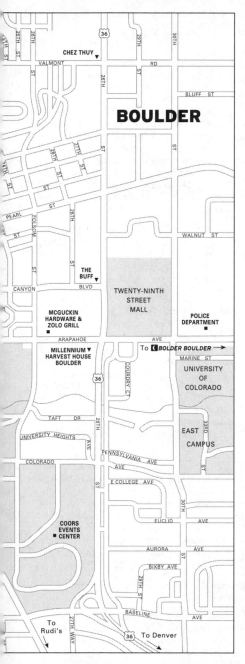

and bar-crawling college students who populate the visitor-friendly Pearl Street Mall.

HISTORY

Boulder's incredible mountain scenery has been a magnet for civilizations, businesses, students, and travelers for centuries, from the Arapahos in the early 1800s to European settlers and gold-seekers who arrived during the "Pikes Peak or bust!" movement in 1858 to the University of Colorado in 1877.

"Boulder City" became a town, officially, in 1859, and it immediately became the county's fastest-growing region. Thanks to CU's role as a picturesque economic, intellectual, and social center, and the city's smart purchases of Chautauqua Park at the base of the Flatirons and open space west of Boulder, entities such as the National Center for Atmospheric Research and IBM set up headquarters here in the early 1960s. Although Boulder has attempted to limit growth since 1959, growth happened anyhow.

Beaded, pot-smoking hippies flooded the area in the 1960s, and bars (The Sink), concert halls (Tulagi), and rock-and-roll bands (the Astronauts) sprang up to accommodate them. They were the first group to give CU its reputation as a ski-bum party school, despite occasional protests of the Vietnam War and a countercultural attitude that reflected the activism in Berkeley and Ann Arbor at the time. Local businesses established the colorful "Hill" area to cater to the 6,000 students who attended by the late 1800s.

The Pearl Street Mall opened downtown in 1977, the same year the city adopted the Danish Plan, the most powerful of many long-standing laws intended to protect views of the mountains and prevent the kind of sprawl that would later afflict Denver and its suburbs. But the antigrowth laws backfired, to an extent, as Boulder expanded by 19,000 people and 27,000 jobs from 1980 to 1995. Residents spilled into nearby Louisville, Lafayette, and Niwot, and housing prices jumped almost to San Francisco levels. But despite all these problems, Boulder remains as

ONLY IN BOULDER

The phrase "only in Boulder" may have originated in the 1950s, when city officials dug up dirt near 63rd Street to create a dam and build Boulder Reservoir. The resulting hole turned into Coot Lake, where locals swam and sunbathed nude for more than 30 years. *Newsweek* made a big deal of this charmingly weird and countercultural vision of Boulder in a 1980 story called "Where the Hip Meet to Trip." Drug use, undoubtedly, had something to do with it as well. But however the phrase came about, it pops up every time some Boulder citizen – usually of the liberal persuasion – does something that freaks out the rest of the state. Here are a few examples:

- Shortly after September 11, 2001, a Boulder Public Library director rejected an employee's request to hang a large American flag just inside the entrance. This created an uproar. Two weeks later, the library authorized an art exhibit that included a set of colorful glazed ceramic penises. This created an even louder uproar. To put an exclamation point on this strange chain of events, someone calling himself "El Dildo Bandito" made off with the offending penises – and was arrested at gunpoint.

- In 2007, local high school students were required to attend a Conference on World Affairs panel titled "STDs: Sex, Teens and Drugs" at the University of Colorado. One panelist told the audience: "I'm going to encourage you to have sex, and I'm going to encourage you to use drugs appropriately." This created huge statewide outrage that resulted in parental protests and Republican senators calling for principals' firings.

- In 2005, a police officer uprooted several healthy marijuana plants from a tulip bed prominently displayed on the Pearl Street Mall as passersby giggled.

- Patrick Murphy, a Boulder botanist, videotaped a woman and confronted a man in separate incidents after both neglected to clean up after their dogs. Murphy even tailed the woman to her office in an attempt to discern her identity. He was charged with harassment in 2001. It gets worse: According to *The Denver Post,* Murphy employed GPS technology to chronicle 663 piles of dog poop throughout Boulder. Later, he was interviewed on Comedy Central's *Daily Show;* his website is www.myxyz.org/phmurphy/patsdogimp1.htm.

- In 1995, Boulder became one of the first cities in the United States to ban smoking in restaurants. This seemed very strange at the time, but dozens of cities, including Denver, have since followed.

- In the late 1980s, when a cat named Gatsby became stuck in a drainpipe, the local *Daily Camera* printed updates on the front page for several days. A group of mischievous college students responded by building a tribute to Gatsby – a diorama made from small plastic dinosaurs and bugs they'd won at a local arcade. They wrote a deadpan letter to the editor, including their phone number, and numerous locals called, in all seriousness, pledging support and asking to bring children over for private viewings.

- In the 1980s, the Pearl Street Mall was the site of a massive Halloween "Crawl," drawing 20,000-35,000 elbow-to-elbow revelers dressed in elaborately funny costumes – like Shriners, complete with fake cars, and a woman dressed as a lumberjack with a man dressed as a fir tree. But the Crawl went bad in 1988, drawing pot smokers and fistfighters, so the city shut the whole thing down by 1992.

beatific as ever, and it's a great place to grow up, work, or visit.

ORIENTATION

Boulder is in a bowl, surrounded by the Flatiron Mountains on the Front Range. It's an easy half hour drive from Denver, west on U.S. 36, and it's the central city in a rich open-space area including Estes Park, Grand Lake, and Rocky Mountain National Park to the north; Louisville, Lafayette, and Superior to the south; and Fort Collins, Longmont, Loveland, and Niwot to the east and northeast.

SAFETY

Although Boulder has in recent years dealt with violence, gangs, and racial harassment, like any other city, it remains one of the safest metropolitan areas in Colorado. It's the kind of place where people leave their car doors unlocked while they run into stores, although the local police probably wouldn't recommend it. Solo walkers and bikers should be careful to stay in well-lit areas after dark. The **Boulder Police Department** (1805 33rd St., 303/441-3300, www.ci.boulder.co.us/police) has more or less recovered its reputation after its bumbling investigation of the JonBenét Ramsey murder in 1996. Its officers are friendly and receptive and are generally happy to answer visitors' questions.

SIGHTS
University of Colorado

The 30,000-student **University of Colorado at Boulder** (303/492-1411, www.colorado.edu) is infamous as one of the nation's top party schools, with high-profile scandals in recent years involving football players, alleged sexual assaults, and various other activities and government investigations (although CU dropped off the Princeton Review's nonscientific party-school rankings in 2005). I indulged in CU parties myself in my younger days—none involving football players or illicit behavior, but several with rousing games of Quarters and Viking Master—and can attest that it's one of the most fun and relaxed institutions on earth.

It's also strong, education-wise, with a Nobel Prize–winner (Eric Cornell) on the physics faculty and excellent departments in science, journalism, and music (the huge Norlin Library isn't shabby either).

CU, founded in 1877, is also a great place to hang around. Centered on the **Norlin Quadrangle,** a wide, grassy area where students chill out on sunny afternoons, it's filled with impeccable cement walkways and buildings with red-tiled Italian-style tops that are strikingly visible from the hills and mountains around Boulder. The **University Memorial Center** and its fountain-dominated plaza is just south of the Quad, and its movies, cafeteria, and bowling alley, complete with the live-music Club 156 and numerous video and pinball games, are open to the public as well as students.

If you're in the mood to take a break from bowling and beer to study local history, the **University of Colorado Heritage Center** (Old Main Building, Pleasant St., 303/492-6329, http://cuheritage.org, 10 A.M.–5 P.M. Mon.–Fri., free) sponsors exhibits on Shakespeare, bison, bats, and other important stuff. The **University of Colorado Museum of Natural History** (Henderson Building, 15th St. and Broadway, 303/492-6892, http://cumuseum.colorado.edu, 9 A.M.–5 P.M. Mon.–Fri., 9 A.M.–4 P.M. Sat., 10 A.M.–4 P.M. Sun., $3) has more than 4 million artifacts, mostly of the dinosaur-and-fossil variety.

Fiske Planetarium (southwest of the CU Events Center, 303/492-5002, http://fiske.colorado.edu, 9 A.M.–4 P.M. Mon.–Fri., free) has been putting on laser shows (check out Pink Floyd, dude, it's cosmic) and astronomy workshops and lectures for decades in a domed building that's surprisingly roomy on the inside. Nearby is **Sommers-Bausch Observatory,** an amazing stargazing spot that includes a 24-inch reflector and other gigantic university-owned telescopes. It often puts on lectures and observation sessions after the shows at Fiske.

CU's social center is **University Hill** (13th St. between Pennsylvania St. and College

Ave.), also known as "The Hill," a cement playground for students, concertgoers, album buyers, pizza and ice cream eaters, souvenir shoppers, and people who like wandering into The Sink to see the cartoon depictions of former student Robert Redford and other luminaries. University Hill actually refers to the fraternity-heavy neighborhood that surrounds The Hill, and it gets loud and raucous on weekend nights—which can be a plus or a minus depending on your age and attitude.

Downtown

The **Boulder History Museum** (1206 Euclid Ave., 303/449-3464, www.boulderhistorymuseum.org, 10 A.M.–5 P.M. Tues.–Fri., noon–4 P.M. Sat.–Sun., $6), founded by *Daily Camera* publisher A. A. "Gov" Paddock in the 1940s, displays more than 30,000 objects dating from the 1800s to the present. Some of the best stuff involves costumes, like women's boots and round pillbox hats of previous Boulder eras.

Surrounding the Mall are rows of downtown Victorians that command huge real-estate prices. One of them, at 1619 Pine Street, is where *Mork and Mindy* was filmed, and some 1980s TV aficionados still make pilgrimages there. The **Downtown Boulder Historic District** (Spruce St. between 10th St. and 16th St., Walnut St. between Broadway and 9th St., Pearl St. between 9th St. and 16th St.) encompasses a bunch of late-19th-century rock-and-brick buildings with Roman and Italian architecture, and the **Mapleton Historic District** (Broadway, Pearl St., 4th St., and Dewey St.) includes the 1899 Inn at Mapleton Hill and the 1903 Lewis-Cobb House.

◖ Pearl Street Mall

The Mall (Downtown Boulder, 1942 Broadway, Suite 301, 303/449-3774, www.boulderdowntown.com), which extends down Pearl Street from 10th Street to 15th Street, opened in 1977 as a pedestrian-only response to the then-flourishing Crossroads Mall a few

The redbrick Pearl Street Mall is filled with tourists, musicians, shoppers, balloon-benders, and acrobats.

© STEVE KNOPPER

miles to the east. Over the years, the five-block redbrick area has exceeded even the most ambitious city planners' expectations, drawing visitors by the thousands and street performers who walk tightropes, strum Neil Young songs on their guitars, paint portraits, and tie balloons into animal shapes for kids. The mall's former businesses remain as famous as their extant counterparts—the Blue Note nightclub drew legends from punk trio Hüsker Dü to comedian Robin Williams in the 1980s; Pearl's and Potter's were notorious college bars; and the New York Deli was a great sandwich shop whose facade was prominently featured on *Mork and Mindy*. Remaining are fixtures such as Old Chicago, the Boulder Theater, and the Walnut Brewery, as well as world-class shops Boulder Bookstore, Peppercorn, and others, not to mention chains like Abercrombie & Fitch.

Contact **Historic Boulder** (1123 Spruce St., 303/444-5192, www.historicboulder.org, 9 A.M.–4 P.M. Mon.–Fri.) for guided tours and other historical information.

Boulder Museum of Contemporary Art

The solid Boulder Museum of Contemporary Art (1750 13th St., 303/443-2122, www.bmoca.org, 11 A.M.–5 P.M. Tues.–Fri., 9 A.M.–4 P.M. Sat., 11 A.M.–4 P.M. Sun., $5) is in a comfortable orange-brick building near the farmers market a few blocks from the Mall. It puts on striking exhibitions of international artists such as Brooklyn, New York–based comic book–style painter Casey McGlynn as well as dance concerts and other events.

Twenty-ninth Street

For years, the Pearl Street Mall was locked in a competition with Crossroads, which finally closed in the early 1990s but recently transformed into Twenty-ninth Street (1710 29th St., 303/444-0722, www.twentyninthstreet.com, 10 A.M.–9 P.M. Mon.–Sat., 11 A.M.–6 P.M. Sun.), a modern outdoor mall that isn't as quaint as Pearl Street but certainly has a more convenient parking situation. Shops include Anthropologie, Coldwater Creek, Eddie Bauer, Gymboree, and Home Depot; the restaurants cover most styles of upscale fast food, including California Pizza Kitchen, Daphne's Greek Café, Panera Bread, and Rumbi Island Grill.

◖ Chautauqua Park

This area for walking, Frisbee-throwing, picnicking, and afternoon napping is literally in the shadow of Flagstaff Mountain; the large grassy park is at the bottom, along Baseline Road, and it gets more rocky and forested as it rises into the foothills. Locals love the hiking and biking trails, there's a great old restaurant on the park grounds, and the wooden Chautauqua Auditorium is, as many performers have observed, like spending some time inside a giant acoustic guitar. For information on events, and to some extent the park, contact the **Colorado Chautauqua Association** (900 Baseline Rd., 303/442-3282, www.chautauqua.com).

Celestial Seasonings

Mo Siegel discovered a certain kind of wild herb in Boulder around 1969, and the first teas from his Celestial Seasonings (4600 Sleepytime Dr., 303/581-1202 or 800/434-4246, www.celestialseasonings.com, tours 10 A.M.–4 P.M. Mon.–Sat., 11 A.M.–3 P.M. Sun., free) came out shortly thereafter—notably the Red Zinger brand in 1971. Today, Siegel's tea empire is corporate-owned and serves some 1.2 billion cups of tea per year, although it remains a landmark on Sleepytime Drive. The company offers tours, including the factory, where 8 million tea bags come out every day, an herb garden, the intensely scented Mint Room, a gift shop—and free samples.

National Center for Atmospheric Research

The website refers to "the west end of Table Mesa Drive," but that hardly does justice to the location of the National Center for Atmospheric Research (NCAR, 1850 Table Mesa Dr., 303/497-1000, http://ncar.ucar.edu, 8 A.M.–5 P.M. Mon.–Fri., 9 A.M.–4 P.M.

Sat.–Sun., free)—the Mesa Laboratory and Fleischmann Building are literally on the edge of a cliff, part of a complex of boxy, orange, I. M. Pei–designed buildings with the foothills as a magnificent backdrop. NCAR itself is a federal research center that studies the sun, the earth's atmosphere, and above all, the weather; tours and exhibits include a telescopic camera as well as tornado and lightning demonstrations. The outdoor "weather trail" has various hands-on science exhibits—kids eat this stuff up—in addition to excellent views.

◖ Flagstaff Mountain

Continue driving past Chautauqua Park, west on Baseline Road, straight into this steep mountain, where the switchbacks and U-turns go straight uphill. Flagstaff is mostly famous for its crystal-clear views of the entire city—get your bearings by picking out the red-topped University of Colorado buildings on your right—but is also home to Boulder's fanciest restaurant, Flagstaff House. During the holidays, the city lights up a giant star on the side of the mountain, and mischievous types occasionally like to mess with it, cutting wires or changing its shape into various slogans. (I am not condoning this illegal activity—at least, I haven't condoned it since 1986.)

The Leanin' Tree Museum of Western Art

The Leanin' Tree Museum (6055 Longbow Dr., 303/530-1442 or 800/777-8716, www.leanintreemuseum.com, 8 A.M.–5 P.M. Mon.–Fri., 10 A.M.–5 P.M. Sat.–Sun., free) is a fun destination that started with four 1949 Christmas cards depicting cowboys and their horses. It has since expanded into a massive greeting-card business that ships more than 30 million cards per year, all out of this boxlike building south of Boulder, with a bronze statue out front and a museum of Old West paintings and sculpture inside, along with a sculpture garden.

SPORTS AND RECREATION

Before venturing into Boulder's many parks and miles of open space, contact the **City of**

Boulder Open Space & Mountain Parks (1777 Broadway, 303/441-3440, www.osmp.org), which has trail maps, weather and safety information, and helpful experts on hand to answer questions.

Hiking and Biking

Everything you've heard about Boulder's reputation as an outdoor-sports city is true: Where hikers and cyclists in, say, Chicago have to drive miles out of town to find a scenic trail, around here they're everywhere. Tour de France cyclists and Olympic runners have trained in Boulder for decades, and even the paved city streets have clearly marked bike lanes, along with (mostly) respectful drivers who look in all directions before turning.

When all else fails, walk or ride west into the mountains. Just about any road will do. West of Broadway, Mapleton Avenue leads to **Sunshine Canyon,** a pretty, tree-lined ride among pricey, secluded homes, and the site of a popular 3.3-mile-loop trail, full of steep rock stairways, called **Mount Sanitas.** To access the trailhead, go to the intersection of Broadway and Mapleton Avenue, turn west on Mapleton, go another five blocks, pass Mapleton Medical Center, and then look for the parking spots near the trailhead on your right. It's usually hard to find parking here on a nice day. This is one of the most popular spots for a day hike in Boulder (horses are allowed, but not bikes).

Also in this general area are smaller, more casually scenic trails such as **Red Rocks** and **Boulder Falls.** Red Rocks is at the very far (west) end of Pearl Street, where it intersects with Canyon Boulevard near the bottom of the mountains. **Canyon Boulevard** goes straight into Boulder Canyon. This beginner-to-intermediate trail, 5.5 miles round-trip, is steep in places. To get to the trail, which is mostly dirt road, go to the west end of Pearl Street where it intersects with Canyon Boulevard, then look for the parking area and trailhead in Settler's Park. The park earned its name when the first nonnative settlers hunkered behind the dramatic red-rock fins sticking out of the ground. The half-mile trail, which is wheelchair

FOR SKATEBOARDERS ONLY

When skateboarding took off in the late 1970s, it was a renegade street sport, beloved by punks in Vans sneakers, celebrated in movies like *Back to the Future,* and detested by city officials who didn't much like black marks on their sidewalks, concrete steps, and flat handrails. Today, it's under consideration as an Olympic sport for 2016 – and Colorado's budding Tony Hawkses have more half-pipes than ever to practice their Ollies and kick-turns. Helmets and pads are usually required. The parks are generally free and open 5 A.M.–11 P.M. daily year-round.

Designed by Arizona boarder-turned-architect Michael McIntyre, **Boulder Skatepark** (1505 30th St., Boulder, 303/441-3429) has a gigantic bowl filled with steep drops and unexpected bumps. It's the center of a longtime skateboard scene in which kids still find more natural terrain on the Pearl Street Mall and the Hill.

The 18,200-square-foot **Aurora Wheel Park** (2500 S. Wheel Park Circle, Aurora, 303/739-7160), near a BMX track, has two bowls and a sizable flow course, which means an open area where boarders have room to freestyle.

Opened in 2005 after numerous delays, **City Park** (W. 104th Ave. and Sheridan Rd., Westminster, 303/658-2400) is known for

perhaps the tallest and steepest bowl in the state, recommended for advanced skaters.

Like Boulder, Denver is known for its street skating, but **Skatepark** (2205 19th St., Denver, 720/913-1311), built on 60,000 square feet for $2.9 million in 2001, is a haven of concrete curves and long rails. It's also in a prime location in the South Platte River District.

Colorado Springs's best-known skate park is a small concrete jungle at the **Gossage Youth Sports Complex** (3225-3950 Mark Dabling Blvd., Colorado Springs, 719/385-5940), named for native son and Baseball Hall of Famer Goose Gossage. Also in Colorado Springs is Memorial Park, opened in 2008, a $1 million facility next to Sertich Ice Center, near the corner of Pikes Peak Avenue and Union Boulevard. It emphasizes barriers and obstacles, but there are bowls too.

Other Colorado skate parks include **Action Park** (200 E. 16th St., Rifle, 970/625-2151), **Rio Grande** (Rio Grande Place, Aspen, 970/920-5120), **Breckenridge Skate Park** (880 Airport Rd., Breckenridge, 970/453-1734), **Montrose Skate Park** (540 Rio Grand Ave., Montrose, 970/249-7705), and **Tolla Brown Skate Park** (N. Division Ave. and Washington St., Sterling, 970/522-7882).

BOULDER AND FORT COLLINS

accessible, ends at Centennial Park, close to the Mount Sanitas trailhead and the opening of Sunshine Canyon.

Boulder Falls sits 11 miles outside town, between Boulder and Nederland on the north side of Boulder Canyon Drive (Hwy. 119). Visitors like to stop here for picnics on their way to the high country. Look for the dramatic 70-foot waterfall. It's fun to poke your head through the hole in the boulder next to the falls, aptly named "picture rock."

Farther from downtown, take Broadway due north to the edge of Boulder, then turn left at **Lee Hill Road;** it goes into Boulder Heights, a steep route (not for squeamish cyclists) filled with hairpin turns and perfect city views.

South of downtown, Baseline Road becomes

Flagstaff Mountain, one of the most breathtaking routes in the city, a wiggly road full of scenic Boulder views. This road offers access points to numerous popular trailheads. At the very top of the mountain, about 3.2 miles from the base, is the Inspiration Point parking area on the right side. Follow the signs here to the trailhead for the 0.5-mile, sort-of loop **Sensory Trail,** an easy forest walk with views of Boulder and the Continental Divide. This trailhead also leads to the 1.5-mile **May's Point.** When overlooking Boulder, watch for the red tops of the University of Colorado buildings to get your bearings.

Flagstaff Road also accesses **Walker Ranch,** about eight miles west of town; it's a difficult, 7.5-mile bike ride with great mountain views. Walker Ranch totals 3,778 acres, with 12 miles of marked trails open to hikers and horseback riders. Look for the trailhead to the best-known trail, **Meyer's Homestead,** on the west side of Flagstaff Road about 7.5 miles west of Baseline Road. This is a surprisingly rich area for fishing too, as South Boulder Creek flows through the ranch en route from Gross Reservoir. To get to a stream stocked with rainbow trout, take Flagstaff Road to the top of the mountain, then turn left on Bison Road; look for the Ethel Harrold trailhead, and use that to access the **South Boulder Creek Trail.** For more information on Flagstaff Mountain trails and maps, contact **Boulder County Parks & Open Space** (5201 St. Vrain Rd., Longmont, 303/678-6200, www.bouldercounty.org/openspace).

Eldorado Canyon State Park (9 Kneale Rd., Eldorado Springs, 303/494-3943, http://parks.state.co.us/parks/eldoradocanyon, dawn–dusk daily, $8 per vehicle) is most famous for its rock climbing—it has more than 500 routes, and the granite mountain edges are packed with dangling adventurers when the weather is mild. It's also known for incredible views of mountains, rocks, canyons, and vistas; trout fishing and kayaking in South Boulder Creek; bird and wildlife watching just about everywhere; and more than 40 picnic sites, although camping isn't allowed. It's especially great for hiking, with five locally renowned trails, including **Rattlesnake Gulch,** a three-mile walk that shows the Continental Divide, and **Fowler,** which goes past the abandoned tracks of the 19th-century Colorado–Southern Utah Railroad and the burned-down (in 1912) Crags Hotel. The park is about five miles southwest of Boulder. To get to the Rattlesnake Gulch trail from the intersection of Broadway and Baseline Road, go south on Broadway three miles, then turn right on Eldorado Springs Drive. The trailhead is three miles ahead on the left. A bookstore and visitors center are about one mile beyond the entrance. To reach Fowler Trail, start at the Rattlesnake Gulch trailhead, then take the left fork after 0.2 miles.

The park's trails are also open to cyclists and snowshoers; the canyon is eight miles south of Boulder, near the intersection of Highway 93 and Highway 170. The park entrance is west of Eldorado Springs.

A network of trails spreads from **Chautauqua Park** to Flagstaff Mountain, Saddle Rock, and Green Mountain, and they range from easy jaunts to steep and somewhat technical paths through sharp rocks and bumpy dirt paths. All have spectacular views: My favorite is **Royal Arch,** just under one mile each way, which passes pretty Tangen Spring before shooting straight up to the naturally occurring arch and great views of the city. Also popular is the seven-mile **Mesa Trail,** a long up-and-down path leading through forests and meadows, all under the mountains. A good starting point is at the intersection of Grant Street and Baseline Road, where you can find a map and many of the trailheads. A parking area, picnic tables, and a Ranger Cottage (with helpful staff available during the day) are in this area.

The paved and well-maintained **Boulder Creek Path** is one of the city's best attributes, a nine-mile artery connecting Fourmile Canyon (to the west) with the flat intersection of Arapahoe Avenue and Cherryvale Road (to the east). Along the way, it passes downtown Boulder. (I used to bike it every day from my apartment near CU to my job at the *Daily Camera* downtown.) Be careful during rush hour, including sunny Saturdays and Sundays, because the flood of bikers, in-line skaters, joggers, walkers, stroller-pushers, and CU football fans can make for grumpy congestion. Access points to the path are fairly obvious once you walk around Boulder—just for a starting point, walk south on Broadway from Canyon Boulevard toward Arapahoe Avenue, and you'll run right into it (or over it).

Brainard Lake Recreation Area (off Hwy. 102, about 60 miles west of Boulder, near the Peak-to-Peak Hwy.) takes hikers into the Indian Peaks Wilderness via several trails, notably the eight-mile (round-trip) **Mount Audubon,** overlooking the entire range of snowcapped peaks, and the five-mile **Blue Lake,** a difficult path directly underneath the 13,000-foot-tall Mount Toll. The area is west of Ward, off Highway 72. For more information on hikes and trails in this area, as well as fishing spots, contact the **USDA Forest Service** (2150 Centre Ave., Bldg. E, Fort Collins, 970/295-6600, www.fs.fed.us/r2/arnf/recreation/brainard). Access requires an $8 fee per vehicle for five days.

Left Hand Canyon, northwest of Boulder, is a paved road that snakes between the foothills and displays plenty of views. It leads to tiny towns like Rowena and Ward and numerous hidden hiking trails. To get to Left Hand, take Broadway north from Boulder, then turn left on Lee Hill Road; go about five miles straight up the mountain, past several hairpin curves, then down the other side; turn left at the first stop sign, which is Left Hand Canyon Road. Watch traffic carefully, though, because cars and bikes don't always get along on this serpentine mountain road.

For cyclists with more time, a nice longer ride goes from U.S. 36 via Ward to the **Peak-to-Peak Highway.** For an easier ride, stop at the Foothills trailhead, which intersects with Lee Hill Road, about 0.2 miles west of Broadway. Look for the open space sign and parking area. This trail loops around at the base of the mountains. It passes through rolling meadows with few hills.

My parents, who've hiked at least once a week in Boulder since 1982, have a favorite walk: Nugget Hill, about one mile west of the intersection of Lee Hill Drive and Left Hand Canyon Drive, about one mile outside Rowena. You'll see a rusty gold storage box, which marks the trailhead; the dirt path goes up about 1,500 feet, past several mines and an abandoned family cemetery.

Other good hiking-and-biking routes in Boulder include the forest-heavy **Switzerland Trail** (5 miles west of Broadway on Canyon Blvd., then turn right onto Sugarloaf Rd., and right again on Sugarloaf Mountain Rd.), a gentle up-and-down path that was once a narrow-gauge railroad track; the **Marshall Mesa/Community Ditch Trail,** which begins in South Boulder, just east of the intersection of Broadway and Marshall Drive, and goes about 2.5 miles each way past coal-mining ruins, forest and mountains, and occasional wildlife (horned owls are fairly common); and the 14-mile **East Boulder & Teller Farm Trails** (off Arapahoe Ave., about 7 miles east of downtown), which, in lieu of mountains and canyons, contains flat swampy marshes, perfect for bird-watching in the Gunbarrel Farm area.

Cyclists can rent and repair bikes at several stores in Boulder. **University Bicycles** (839 Pearl St., 303/444-4196 or 800/451-3950, www.ubikes.com) opened in 1985 and frequently hires competitive (but not snobby) riders who know their way around goosenecks and sprockets. **Full Cycle** (1795 Pearl St., 303/404-1002; 1211 13th St., 303/440-7771, www.fullcyclebikes.com) has been in Boulder for 30 years. Part of a large national chain, the **Performance Bike** (2450 Arapahoe Ave., 303/444-5044, www.performancebike.com) outlet in Boulder is a small-enough shop where salespeople spend plenty of time ensuring the right fit.

Fishing

Despite its outdoor-recreation reputation, Boulder isn't a major fishing hot spot, although **Walden and Sawhill Ponds** (N. 75th St., north of Valmont Dr.) are collections of 20 small bodies of water, some of which are stocked with bluegill, pumpkinseed, and yellow perch. The bird-watching here is excellent—check out the songbirds and raptors. For fishing equipment, tours, and advice, try **Rocky Mountain Anglers** (1904 Arapahoe Ave., 303/447-2400, www.rockymtanglers.com), known for its experienced guides.

Golf

Boulder County has two major courses: **Flatirons** (5706 Arapahoe Ave., 303/442-7851, www.flatironsgolf.com, $27–34), open since 1933, and the Hale Irwin–designed **Indian Peaks** (2300 Indian Peaks Trail, Lafayette, 303/666-4706, www.indianpeaksgolf.com,

$32–47), 10 miles east of Boulder but worth the trip to play in view of several 14,000-foot peaks. Both have 18 holes.

Skiing and Snowshoeing

Pretty much wherever you can walk, you can take a pair of cross-country skis or snowshoes, so feel free to explore Chautauqua Park, Flagstaff Mountain, Brainard Lake, and Left Hand Canyon this way. The **Boulder Outdoor Center** (2525 Arapahoe Ave., Suite E4-228, 303/444-8420, www.boc123.com) rents equipment and provides expertise on trails, directions, and laws and permits.

Water Sports

"The Res," or **Boulder Reservoir** (5565 N. 51st St., 303/441-3461, www.boulderrez.org), is Boulder's lone major body of water—it may not satisfy visitors from the coasts, but it's a pretty fun place to hang out. Sailboating, canoeing, swimming, fishing, and barbecuing are kosher here, but the predominant sport (especially among local high school students) is sitting on the loose gravel beach observing members of the opposite sex. The dirt path around the reservoir is a nice walk on sunny days.

Kayaking is popular in numerous local streams, including the Boulder Creek Path (which has surprisingly choppy currents), Left Hand Canyon, and the South Platte River. The **Boulder Outdoor Center** (2525 Arapahoe Ave., Suite E4-228, 303/444-8420, www.boc123.com) is an excellent resource for kayakers.

Boulder Creek is also open to a nutty do-it-yourself local sport—tubing—in which swimmers sit in giant, puffed-up tire inner tubes and navigate currents, rocks, and cement walls. The **Conoco** gas station (1201 Arapahoe Ave., 303/442-6293) sells tubes for $12; the creek is just a block away.

Spectator Sports

The University of Colorado is a Division I college, and it fields competitive teams in soccer, golf, tennis, volleyball, and, naturally, skiing.

COURTESY OF BOULDER CONVENTION AND VISITORS BUREAU

paddling down Boulder Creek

But the sport that owns Boulder residents' hearts is football—fans are still sore about the national championships that got away in the early 1990s, although they pack **Folsom Field** (2400 Colorado Ave.) regularly to root against arch-enemies such as Nebraska and Oklahoma. The basketball Buffs (traditionally mediocre) and Lady Buffs (traditionally pretty good) play at the **Coors Events Center** (950 Regent Dr.). For tickets to all the sports—and directions to the arenas and stadiums—call 303/492-8337 or visit www.cubuffs.com.

ENTERTAINMENT AND EVENTS
Nightlife

Boulder's live music scene has been thriving since the 1960s, when a local surf band, the Astronauts, briefly attempted to challenge the Beach Boys for national dominance. Since then, artists such as the Eagles, Firefall, former Buffalo Springfield member Richie Furay, and Big Head Todd and the Monsters have lived here (some temporarily), and clubs from the

JAM BANDS

The Grateful Dead was one of the most influential rock bands of all time, and through endless concerts until guitarist Jerry Garcia died in 1995, it spread the seeds of improvisational music all over the world. These took root in the early 1990s, when similarly improvisational bands such as Phish, Blues Traveler, the Dave Matthews Band, and the Samples became hugely popular among a crowd of neo-hippies who attended concerts and danced for hours in a nonstop twirling motion.

Boulder, with its college crowd and laid-back mountain atmosphere, became ground zero for this "jam band" scene. From the Samples and Big Head Todd and the Monsters to early-1990s local club acts like Acoustic Junction and the Reejers, the scene shifted from small clubs to large venues – by the early 2000s, homegrown bands Leftover Salmon and String

Cheese Incident graduated to national recognition, selling out venues all over the United States and even racking up CD sales. Meanwhile, established national acts like Matthews, who once opened for the Samples, continue to sell out regularly at Red Rocks Amphitheatre and elsewhere.

Although many such bands don't like being lumped into the hippie-Grateful Dead-jamming category, and their styles are diverse and occasionally revolutionary, they share an improvisational quality. It's not uncommon for a song to stretch to more than 15 or 20 minutes onstage, driving Ramones fans a little crazy, but these bands pack festivals like Bonnaroo in Manchester, Tennessee, drawing 90,000 people a year. Plus, in recent summers, Phish has drawn tens of thousands of people to Telluride for several concerts at a time.

late lamented Tulagi to the still-thriving Fox Theatre continue to draw big touring names away from Denver. The predominant musical style is hippie jamming music, including local stars like String Cheese Incident and national vagabonds like the Grateful Dead and Dave Matthews Band, but Boulder has pockets of folk, blues, bluegrass, country, and punk fans as well. Nirvana performed at a small club here in 1989.

CU's student-run **Program Council** (303/492-7704, www.programcouncil.com) sponsors many live shows, some of which are just as great as the ones you'd see at the Boulder Theater or Denver's Fillmore Auditorium. **Club 156,** inside the University Memorial Center (UMC), is a tiny, brick-walled lounge that famously played host to the Red Hot Chili Peppers and Toad the Wet Sprocket in their early days. Also in the UMC, the **Glenn Miller Ballroom** is a large room that snags bigger names; rapper Ice-T and his heavy-metal band, Body Count, once nearly tore the paint off the walls in front of Miller's benign, grinning portrait. **Macky Auditorium,** a few blocks away

on campus, is also an excellent place to see a show.

Several blocks from CU, **Chautauqua Music Hall** (900 Baseline Rd., 303/442-3282, www.chautauqua.com) has a summer music series that's the best in town. Many of the concerts are of the soft and classical variety, but Los Lobos, Randy Newman, John Prine, Michelle Shocked, Richard Thompson, Dr. John, and other folk and rock acts show up on a regular basis.

About 10 miles northeast of Boulder, the **Left Hand Grange Hall** (195 2nd Ave., Niwot, 303/444-4640) is a tiny facility that runs occasional folk and bluegrass concerts on nights the Boy Scouts, Girl Scouts, Niwot Rotary, bridge club, and beekeepers haven't reserved the room.

With one of the country's biggest party colleges as the clientele, Boulder is a city of late-night brewpubs and taverns, with raucous see-and-be-seen happy hours and frequent live-music backdrops. Just off Pearl Street, the **Walnut Brewery** (1123 Walnut St., 303/447-1345, www.walnutbrewery.com, 11 A.M.–11:30 P.M. daily) is an upscale brewpub with numerous different kinds of beer, some of which come from the huge silver vats stored in the back. It's often crowded, especially on nights when small bands play.

Other bars that are part of the "mall crawl": **The Walrus** (1173 Walnut St., 303/443-9902, http://boulderwalrus.com, 4 P.M.–2 A.M. Mon.–Sat., 7 P.M.–2 A.M. Sun.), a downstairs joint with underwhelming food, cheap beers in tall glasses, and a decent jukebox; the **Rio Grande Mexican Restaurant** (1101 Walnut St., www.riograndemexican.com, 303/444-3690, 11 A.M.–10 P.M. Sun.–Wed., 11 A.M.–midnight Thurs.–Sat.), which has superb margarita specials, better-than-average food and snacks, and the most beautiful of the beautiful people; **Absinthe House** (1109 Walnut St., 303/443-8600, www.boulderabsinthehouse.com, 4–10 P.M. Mon., 4 P.M.–midnight Tues.–Wed., 4 P.M.–2 A.M. Thurs.–Fri., noon–2 A.M. Sat., noon–10 P.M. Sun.) is in a space that has been many things over the years, from the concert hall Marquee Club to the pool-heavy Foundry, and this particular second it happens to be an adult dance club with hot local DJs and a nice outdoor terrace; the **Corner Bar** (2115 13th St., 303/442-4880, www.qsboulder.com/thecornerbar, 11:30 A.M.–midnight Mon.–Fri., 11 A.M.–midnight Sat.–Sun.), a relaxing indoor-outdoor bar in the Hotel Boulderado; **Catacombs Bar** (2115 13th St., 303/443-0486, www.boulderado.com/catacombs.html, 4 P.M.–1:30 A.M. Mon.–Fri., 6:30 P.M.–1:30 A.M. Sat.–Sun.), a basement bar that lives up to its name, with live entertainment including an open-mike night and live weekend DJs; and the **West End Tavern** (926 Pearl St., 303/444-3535, www.thewestendtavern.com, 11:30 A.M.–10:30 P.M. Sun.–Mon., 11:30 A.M.–midnight Tues.–Wed., 11:30 A.M.–12:45 A.M. Thurs.–Sat.), with a rooftop bar overlooking the mountains.

Removed from the mall crawl is **The Kitchen Upstairs** (1039 Pearl St., 303/544-5973, www.thekitchencafe.com/winelounge.shtml, 5:30–11 P.M. Sun.–Mon., 11 A.M.–midnight Tues.–Sat.), which draws from the upscale restaurant downstairs for its 750 wines and 50 beers. Just keep in mind, this is high-class, Boulder-style luxury, with a quiet, low-lit ambience and beer that can cost as much as $28 per pint. On the eastern side of the mall, **Mountain Sun Pub & Brewery** (1700 Vine St., 303/388-2337, 4 P.M.–1 A.M. Mon., 11 A.M.–1 A.M. Tues.–Sat.) explicitly caters to the hippie crowd (even the murals on the wall are of psychedelic earth mothers), but its homebrews (try the Illusion Dweller IPA) are among the best in Boulder.

Up on the Hill, **The Sink** (1165 13th St., 303/444-7465, www.thesink.com, 11 A.M.–2 A.M. daily) is as wild as it was when Robert Redford partied here in the 1960s. If you must scrawl graffiti on something, make it the ceiling rather than the hallowed artwork.

Catering to an older clientele, **Rodeway Inn & Suites Boulder Broker** (555 30th St., 303/444-3330, www.rodewayinn.com/hotel-boulder-colorado-CO223, 3 P.M.–2 A.M. daily) has a dark bar—Bentley's Lounge—where countless karaoke singers have warbled over the years. It will always be known locally as "The Broker."

Consider venturing off the Mall for a night trip to the small towns surrounding Boulder. Halfway between Boulder and Longmont, beyond a minuscule downtown area off the Diagonal Highway, the **Niwot Tavern** (7960 Niwot Rd., Niwot, 303/652-0200, www.niwottavern.com, 11 A.M.–11 P.M. daily) has a talkative townie crowd.

In the other direction, off U.S. 36 en route to Denver, the **Old Louisville Inn** (740 Front St., Louisville, 303/666-9982, www.olirish.com, 11 A.M.–9 P.M. Sun.–Tues., 11 A.M.–10 P.M. Wed.–Thurs. and Sat., 11 A.M.–midnight Fri.) has a cherry, birch, and mahogany bar built in the 1880s. During the gold-mining days, it was a brothel in a red-light district. All of this means it will withstand almost any kind of mischief you can come up with after a night of beer, wine, burgers, corned beef and cabbage, and tapas.

Named somewhat tongue-in-cheek for the nearby nuclear-weapons facility that attracted protests galore until it closed in the late 1980s, the **Rocky Flats Lounge** (11229 Hwy. 93, 303/499-4242, 11 A.M.–close daily) retains its townie, removed-from-the-college atmosphere. On the outside, along the highway south of Boulder, it looks like the seediest joint in the Rockies. On the inside, especially on fish-fry Friday nights, it feels like the warmest. (Note: I called to find out exactly what time the bar closes, and was told, "It depends on what time the road closes outside at night—sometimes 7 o'clock, but if you're in here, you're in here." Beyond that, "It depends how crazy it gets.")

◖ Boulder Theater

Although it surrenders many big shows to the Fox Theatre, the Boulder Theater (2032 14th St., 303/786-7030, www.bouldertheater.com), a 1906 former opera house, has a neon marquee, a renovated ceiling, and comfortable old chairs on the main floor and balcony. Its "house act" since the early 1990s has been *E-Town,* a

© STEVE KNOPPER

The Boulder Theater has played host to numerous concerts over the decades.

music-and-environment variety show hosted by former Hot Rize bassist Nick Forster and his wife, Helen, that brings big names like James Taylor, Los Lobos, Lyle Lovett, and others onstage for a few songs with Forster's crack band. The theater itself has regular movie nights as well as national touring acts—recently, singer-songwriter Brandi Carlile, the bluegrass Yonder Mountain String Band, and *Saturday Night Live* comedian Seth Meyers.

Fox Theatre

The Fox Theatre (1135 13th St., 303/447-0095, www.foxtheatre.com, shows usually at 7 P.M.) was a movie house on the Hill for decades until some adventurous local promoters turned it into the city's premier live-music club. In the early 1990s I saw Sheryl Crow, the Gin Blossoms, Uncle Tupelo, and many others here on their way up, and while the club's moneymaking acts are jam bands, its owners aim for diversity, including heavy metal, punk, folk, and hip-hop—recent headliners have been Band of Horses, Yelawolf, Odd Future, and Ziggy Marley.

Performing Arts

The **Boulder Philharmonic Orchestra** (Dairy Center for the Arts, 2590 Walnut St., 303/449-1343, ext. 2, www.boulderphil.org) performs pieces by Brahms, Tchaikovsky, Stravinsky, and others, mostly at CU's Macky Auditorium. **Boulder's Dinner Theatre** (5501 Arapahoe Ave., 303/449-6000 or 800/448-5501, www.theatreinboulder.com) is a nice meal with a bunch of singing people in the background, performing classic Broadway plays like *Phantom of the Opera* and *Cats.*

CU has a superb **College of Music** (Imig Music Building, 18th St. and Euclid Ave., 303/492-6352, www.colorado.edu/music); check the schedule for year-round concerts by faculty, students, and guests in many genres. Concerts take place at the Music School as well as Macky Auditorium and other CU halls.

◖ Bolder Boulder

You can't swing a shoelace without hitting a

THE BIG WHEEL RALLY

Early one summer morning in 1993, my friend Jim and I walked out of a bar on the Pearl Street Mall when we spotted about a dozen full-sized adults slamming into each other while riding Big Wheels. We immediately remembered these plastic tricycle contraptions from our youths in the 1970s, and as *Daily Camera* reporters, we set to interviewing the participants and writing a feature story.

Today, thanks to the efforts of leader Matt "Captain Obvious" Armbruster, who wears an impressive gold cape and silver helmet, the **Almost-Annual Matt Armbruster Memorial Big Wheel Rally** has become a semiregular tradition at downtown Boulder institutions (the kind that serve beer, that is). Armbruster's fleet gathers at, say, the Walrus, then spends the night driving up and down various bar staircases.

Armbruster soups up some of these Big Wheels himself and sells them for charity. The rally is open to anybody with an above-average sense of humor and a threshold for pain. For information, check out www.bigwheelrally.com. In recent years, Armbruster's rallies have been benefits for the Saint Joseph Hospital's neonatal intensive-care unit.

stand on sidewalks throughout the city to cheer, and dozens of live bands play on strategic street corners to serenade the runners. Many people walk, although I have a yearly tradition of sleeping through it. Note that during Bolder Boulder hours, roughly 7 A.M.–noon on Memorial Day, it's very difficult to drive or even walk through the city, as main roads are closed off. Check the race website for maps and updates.

Kinetic Sculpture Challenge

Since 1980, this alcohol-fueled event (Boulder Reservoir, 5565 N. 51st St.) in early May has attracted goofy engineers and masochistic athletes for a competitive morning of zooming over dry land, paddling through Boulder Reservoir, and attempting not to sink in stinky, quicksand-like mud. The idea is to build the best nonmotorized craft by hand, and teams make up names like "Whizzers of Oz," "Inbredibles," and "Radioactive Sushi." A panel of local celebrity judges picks the best-costumed teams.

Boulder Creek Festival

This Memorial Day Weekend event (bounded by Canyon Blvd., Arapahoe Ave., 9th St., and 13th St., 303/449-3137, www.bouldercreekfestival.com) is a typical city art fair, with crafts, games, and small rides for kids, but it's in a great location, in the park near City Hall along Boulder Creek.

Colorado Shakespeare Festival

A recent website design for this world-class festival (Mary Rippon Theatre, University of Colorado, 303/492-0554, www.coloradoshakes.org) depicts the bard sailing through the sky on a skateboard, which gives you a clue of how classics like *Twelfth Night* and *Othello* come across on stage. The Mary Rippon Theatre is a cozy "in the round" area in the middle of campus, and Shakespeare's words are perfect when the July and August nighttime breeze hits you just the right way—although sirens and other traffic noise from nearby Broadway and Arapahoe Avenue can be distracting.

jogger in Boulder, and that's in part thanks to the all-ages Bolder Boulder (www.bolderboulder.com), a Memorial Day 10-kilometer footrace in three stages: the early one for elite runners from around the world; a more lackadaisical later one for citizens, some of whom dress up in goofy costumes, including Father Time and Elvis Presley; and a third one for wheelchair users. Meandering through the city, from a bank near Iris Avenue and 30th Street through the Pearl Street Mall area up a hill to the University of Colorado, the race began in 1979 with 2,700 people and today attracts more than 50,000. Hundreds of thousands of people

FROZEN DEAD GUY DAYS

The annual Frozen Dead Guy Days festival, every March in Nederland, begins with an *actual* dead guy. His name was Bredo Morstøl, and he was a retired parks and recreation director in Baerum County, Norway, when he suffered a fatal heart attack in 1989. And that's when he really became famous. Morstøl's grandson, Boulder resident and Norwegian transplant Trygve Bauge, has a weird obsession with frozen cryonic storage of dead bodies. But Norway doesn't allow such a thing. So Bauge had Grandpa Bredo moved from Norway to a California cryonics facility and then to a Nederland freezer-cum-sarcophagus and shack behind a local house in 1993.

A whole lot of bizarre things happened after that. First, Nederland town officials decided they didn't need any frozen dead guys lying around, so they passed an emergency law banning dead humans and animals on local property. But the law came after the fact, so Morstøl was "grandfathered in." Second, Bauge became surreally famous. The U.S. Immigration and Naturalization Service took notice and deported him to Norway, where he lives to this day.

Finally, Teresa Warren, an events director for Nederland's Chamber of Commerce,

decided her little mountain town needed a weird festival on par with Fruita's Mike the Headless Chicken Days. So in 2002 she came up with the **Frozen Dead Guy Days Festival** (303/258-3936, www.nederlandchamber.org/events_fdgd-home.html), which runs every March, starring coffin races, a plunge into an icy lake, a pancake breakfast, and plenty of Frozen Dead Guy-flavored ice cream (it's an official Glacier brand– blue, of course– mixed with sour Gummi worms and crushed Oreos). "I guess when you live out in Nederland and Rollinsville you need something like this to entertain yourself," local Joann Upcott told the *Rocky Mountain News.* Some 5,000 celebrants showed up in this 1,400-person town during the 2007 festival. Trygve Bauge himself once endorsed the festival in the Boulder *Daily Camera,* calling it the "Mardi Gras of cryonics." He has since had an apparent falling-out with festival organizers and Nederland officials and doesn't say much about it at all.

As for Grandpa Bredo, he's still not kicking. Local "planetary ecologist" Bo "Ice Man" Shaffer (who went on *The Tonight Show with Jay Leno* in 2005) fills Bredo's sarcophagus with 1,500 pounds of dry ice, at -90°F, every month.

Colorado Music Festival

This classical and chamber-music extravaganza (900 Baseline Rd., 303/449-1397, www.coloradomusicfest.org), late June–early August, combines traditional pieces with selections from *West Side Story,* fiddle performances from bluegrass musician Mark O'Connor, and other off-the-beaten-path styles.

SHOPPING

For years, Boulder had two malls: the **Pearl Street Mall** (Pearl St. from 9th St. to 15th St., 303/449-3774, www.boulderdowntown.com) and Crossroads Mall, but after a brief period of dominance in the early 1990s, Crossroads succumbed to the nearby FlatIron Crossing in Broomfield. The situation may soon reverse,

however, because major national chains such as The Gap have moved out, perhaps signaling rough times ahead for Pearl Street. **Twenty-ninth Street** (1710 29th St., 303/449-1189, www.twentyninthstreet.com, 10 A.M.–9 P.M. Mon.–Sat., 11 A.M.–6 P.M. Sun.) is the latest incarnation of the mall formerly known as Crossroads. The anchor stores here are well-known chains, such as Home Depot, Ann Taylor, Lady Foot Locker, Victoria's Secret, and The North Face.

Pearl Street

As for Pearl Street—meaning the mall and its several surrounding blocks—the shopping is still magnificent, if you like tourist-oriented knickknacks and high-priced clothing. Chains haven't completely taken over here, as the Mall emphasizes colorful stores such as **Color Me Mine** (1938 Pearl St., 303/443-3469, www. boulder.colormemine.com, 10 A.M.–6 P.M. Sun.–Mon., 10 A.M.–8 P.M. Tues.–Sat.), a do-it-yourself ceramics studio; **Alpaca Connection** (1326 Pearl St., 303/447-2047 or 888/447-2047, www.thealpacaconnection. com, 11 A.M.–6 P.M. daily), which sells distinctive Peruvian rugs and sweaters; and the funky T-shirt store **Where the Buffalo Roam** (1320 Pearl St., 303/938-1424, 10 A.M.–10 P.M. Mon.–Sat., 10 A.M.–9 P.M. Sun.).

On the Mall's west side, **Boulder Bookstore** (1107 Pearl St., 303/447-2074 or 800/244-4651, http://boulderbookstore.indiebound.com, 10 A.M.–10 P.M. Mon.–Thurs., 10 A.M.–11 P.M. Fri.–Sat., 10 A.M.–8 P.M. Sun.) is a friendly, wood-floored, two-story, somewhat cramped literary fixture that has withstood challenges from Barnes & Noble, the recently defunct Borders, and many others over the years; Toward the east side, **Peppercorn** (1235 Pearl St., 303/449-5847 or 303/449-8105, www.peppercorn.com, 10 A.M.–6 P.M. Mon.–Thurs., 10 A.M.–8 P.M. Fri.–Sat., 11 A.M.–6 P.M. Sun.) is a fruity candle–smelling kitchen-and-bathroom store where I and every single person I knew in high school bought Mother's Day presents for four straight years. Bongo the Balloon Man generally ties his monstrous pink-and-green creations for adoring kids outside Peppercorn. Run by longtime Boulder fashion merchant Debra Mazur, **Common Era** (1500D Pearl St., 303/444-1799, www.mycommonera.com, 11 A.M.–6 P.M. Sun.–Wed., 11 A.M.–7 P.M. Thurs.–Sat.) is an affordable women's clothing shop selling hip brands like Adrianna and Lush and onetime finds like homemade Yarn Series necklaces, multicolor jeans, and those ubiquitous very tall boots you see all over the Denver-Boulder area.

Specialty bookstores in the Pearl Street area include: **Trident Booksellers** (940 Pearl St., 303/443-3133, http://tridentcafe.com, 6:30 A.M.–11 P.M. Mon.–Sat., 7 A.M.–11 P.M. Sun.), a used store that has sold coffee and

dog-eared New Age books to bohemian customers for decades; and, in a tiny nook east of the Mall, the **Beat Book Shop** (1717 Pearl St., www.abebooks.com/home/beatbookshop, 303/444-7111, 3–8 P.M. Sun.–Tues., 1–10 P.M. Wed.–Sat.), which will never compete with Barnes & Noble but has an irresistible collection of Allen Ginsberg's writings and a box of used vinyl records that range from punk to jazz to psychedelic rock. It's sometimes closed at weird times.

I've bought gas masks, camping equipment, hiking boots, and random artifacts over the years at the **Boulder Army Store** (1545 Pearl St., 303/442-7616, http://boulderarmystore. com, 9 A.M.–8 P.M. Mon.–Fri., 9 A.M.–6 P.M. Sat., 11 A.M.–5 P.M. Sun.), just east of the mall, once a desolate area but now a high-end shopping district.

A little farther east, **Grandrabbit's Toy Shoppe** (2525 Arapahoe Ave., 303/443-0780 or 866/522-1207, www.grtoys.com, 9:30 A.M.–6 P.M. Mon.–Sat., 10 A.M.–5 P.M. Sun.) has just about every kind of stuffed animal you can imagine, as well as sticker and coloring books, DVDs, models, trains, balls, and assorted stocking-stuffers.

Art Galleries and Shops

Boulder has numerous art galleries and arty stores, including: **Art Mart** (1326 Pearl St., 303/443-8248 or 888/556-4438, www.artmartgifts.com, 9:30 A.M.–10 P.M. Mon.–Thurs., 9:30 A.M.–11 P.M. Fri., 9 A.M.–11 P.M. Sat., 10 A.M.–9 P.M. Sun.), which caters to a hippieish clientele, selling hammocks, tie-dyed T-shirts, and Chinese earrings; **Art Source International** (1237 Pearl St., 303/444-4079 or 800/304-5029, www.rare-maps.com, 10 A.M.–6 P.M. Mon.–Sat., 11 A.M.–6 P.M. Sun.), a map store that doesn't tell you where to go but stocks old globes and rare parchments; the **Boulder Arts & Crafts Cooperative** (1421 Pearl St., 303/443-3683 or 866/656-2667, www.boulderartsandcrafts.com, 10 A.M.–6 P.M. Mon.–Wed., 10 A.M.–9 P.M. Thurs.–Sat., 11 A.M.–6 P.M. Sun.), which since 1971 has sold (mostly) locally made pottery, ceramics, paintings, leather, and jewelry; and the **Smith Klein Gallery** (1116 Pearl St., 303/444-7200, www.smithklein.com, 10 A.M.–5 P.M. Mon., 10 A.M.–6 P.M. Tues.–Thurs., 10 A.M.–7 P.M. Fri.–Sat., noon–5 P.M. Sun.), selling a variety of different styles, from large pewter statues to handblown glass designs.

Farmers Market and Natural Foods

The **Boulder County Farmers Market** (13th St. between Canyon Blvd. and Arapahoe Ave., 303/910-2236, www.boulderfarmers. org, 8 A.M.–2 P.M. Sat. early Apr.–early Nov., 4–8 P.M. Wed. early May–early Oct.) is not only a great place to buy locally grown fruits, vegetables, and flowers, it's an excuse to drag yourself out of bed and get outside on sunny Saturday mornings. It's in a perfect location near the Mall and various parks; kids love it.

Other Interesting Shops

Absolutely everything is at **McGuckin**

Hardware (2525 Arapahoe Ave., 303/443-1822 or 866/624-8254, www.mcguckin.com, 7:30 A.M.–8 P.M. Mon.–Fri., 8 A.M.–6 P.M. Sat., 9 A.M.–6 P.M. Sun.), which continues to more than hold its own even after a Home Depot moved in down the street. McGuckin carries nails, spray paint, and plants of all types, to name just a few items in the long aisles, and clerks in green aprons are happy to help you navigate the occasionally intimidating maze of high shelves.

University Hill has several interesting shops, although most are geared to students; step into one of the several tattoo-and-piercing boutiques for fashion or terror, depending on your age. My favorite record store in Colorado is **Albums on the Hill** (1128 13th St., 303/447-0159, www.albumson-thehill.com, 10 A.M.–9 P.M. Mon.–Sat., noon–6 P.M. Sun.), in a basement dungeon filled with new and used CDs, a roomful of LPs, and staff knowledgeable in every genre. The **Colorado Bookstore** (1111 Broadway, 303/442-5051, http://colorado.bncollege.com,

Boulder County Farmers Market

8:30 A.M.–7 P.M. Mon.–Wed., 8:30 A.M.–6 P.M. Thurs., 8:30 A.M.–5 P.M. Fri., 10 A.M.–5 P.M. Sat., 11 A.M.–5 P.M. Sun.) is geared toward students, of course, but it's surprisingly practical for civilians looking for art and writing supplies as well as CU paraphernalia.

ACCOMMODATIONS
Under $100
Pawnee Campground (Brainard Lake Rd., 5 miles west of Hwy. 72, Ward, 303/541-2500, $17) is part of Brainard Lake Recreation Area, about 17 miles west of Boulder, which means it captures the high-mountain splendor of Indian Peaks Wilderness. Hiking trails are everywhere.

The family-run **Foot of the Mountain** (200 W. Arapahoe Ave., 303/442-5688 or 866/773-5489, www.footofthemountainmotel.com, $90), near the Arapahoe Avenue path up Boulder Canyon, is a fairly basic motel made of wood, with striking red highlights near the cabin doors.

$100-150
The **Millennium Harvest House Boulder** (1345 28th St., 303/443-3850 or 866/866-8086, www.millenniumhotels.com/millenniumboulder, $109–175) has for years been the city's largest hotel, and while it's part of a national chain and isn't particularly distinctive inside, it's a comfortable stop for business travelers. Its outdoor restaurant and patio, just a few hundred feet from Boulder Creek, make it prime real estate for weddings, conferences, and class reunions.

The **Briar Rose B&B** (2151 Arapahoe Ave., 303/442-3007 or 888/786-8440, www.briarrosebb.com, $139–179) has 10 nicely furnished guest rooms named after Colorado mountain peaks. Lest you forget this is Boulder, it has a meditation room and offers an organic breakfast.

$150-200
The **Bradley Boulder** (2040 16th St., 303/545-5200 or 800/858-5811, www.thebradleyboulder.com, $175–245) is a 12-room

bed-and-breakfast with a stone fireplace and fireplaces in the guest rooms—as well as a business-oriented hotel with 1,500 square feet of meeting space and wireless Internet service everywhere. Just down the street from the Pearl Street Mall, it's also conveniently located, with a bread-and-fruit breakfast and free health-club services at the nearby Pulse fitness center.

The **Colorado Chautauqua Association** (900 Baseline Rd., 303/442-3282, www.chautauqua.com, $150–200) owns 99

A PLACE THAT MAKES YOU SAY "OM"

Because meditation is far more than sitting in the Lotus position and chanting mantras slowly to yourself, consider a soothing trip to the **Shambhala Mountain Center** (4921 County Rd. 68C, Red Feather Lakes, 970/881-2184, www.shambhala-mountain.org). Located on 600 acres northwest of Fort Collins, the center's Buddhist principles are the foundation for classes such as "Learn to Meditate" and "Turning the Mind into an Ally." Yoga enthusiasts will find this place ideal, and even skeptics of Boulder-style meditation culture will have trouble resisting the generally mild weather, serene forests, and grassy hiking paths. The Dalai Lama spoke here in 2006 and Sting – yes, that Sting – once dropped by when he wasn't performing "Roxanne."

Don't leave without checking out the 108-foot Great Stupa of Dharmakaya, a red, white, and gold "expression of the aspiration for peace, harmony, and equanimity for all beings." A *Colorado Springs Gazette-Telegraph* reporter described it as a "cross between a shrine and a spaceship" and noted that, in keeping with Buddhist tradition, it contains the skull of 20th-century Tibetan teacher Vidyadhara Chogyam Trungpa, who helped create a worldwide network of about 140 Shambhala centers.

apartment-style cottages with long porches at the edge of Chautauqua Park, off Baseline Road near the bottom of Flagstaff Mountain. The association rents 60 of them year-round, although some are slightly run-down—but hey, in 1898 they were canvas tents, so don't complain. Larger, more expensive lodges are available as well.

In tiny Niwot, the town named for the Arapaho chief Niwot, about 10 miles northeast of Boulder on the Diagonal Highway, the **Niwot Inn** (342 2nd Ave., Niwot, 303/652-8452, www.niwotinn.com, $159–189) has spare, quiet guest rooms named for various 14,000-foot Colorado peaks. (There's no Longs Peak room, although that fourteener is the nearest to this location.) It has conveniences like high-speed Internet access in the guest rooms, but really, if you're planning to spend significant time in Boulder, the inn is a little inconvenient—and don't even think about it if you're not planning to rent a car.

$200-300

The **Hotel Boulderado** (2115 13th St., 303/442-4344 or 800/433-4344, www.boulderado.com, $229–399) is a local classic that takes up half a city block and makes you feel like you've stepped into the Old West upon entering the lobby. The redbrick structure looks modern from the outside, but the lobby has a huge cherrywood staircase, stained-glass ceiling, and flowery carpets and wallpaper, and even the baths recall the hotel's 1909 origins. The Catacombs bar, which has live blues bands on several nights, is downstairs, and Q's Restaurant is next to the lobby.

$300-400

The **St. Julien Hotel and Spa** (900 Walnut St., 720/406-9696 or 877/303-0900, www.stjulien.com, $299–309) has a fancy restaurant (Jill's), a bar (T-Zero), and a spa, and for the last several years it has challenged the Boulderado's almost 100 years of local lodging dominance.

FOOD
Snacks, Cafés, and Breakfast
Formerly the popular posthangover

The historic Hotel Boulderado in downtown Boulder is a city landmark.

college joint Burnt Toast, **Café Aion** (1235 Pennsylvania Ave., 303/993-8131, www. cafeaion.com, 9 A.M.–3 P.M. and 5–11 P.M. Tues.–Sat., 9 A.M.–3 P.M. Sun.–Mon., $15) transformed recently into a tapas bar run by a chef from Boulder's Kitchen. Scrambled eggs are still on the menu, but they include things like sautéed chard and feta; tapas include tempura squash blossoms with aioli and smoked paprika tapas or paella with saffron rice, linguica sausage, and clams.

The bottom line of **Breadworks** (2644 N. Broadway, 303/444-5667, www.breadworks. net, 7 A.M.–7 P.M. Mon.–Fri., 7 A.M.–6 P.M. Sat.–Sun., $7) is bread, of course, from baguettes and *batards* to challah, but its sandwiches, homemade soups (including several organic kinds), and desserts make the hippieish restaurant a great place to hang out. For breakfast and lunch, **Moe's Broadway Bagel** (2650 Broadway, 303/444-3252, www.moesbroadwaybagel.com, 5:30 A.M.–5 P.M. daily, $8) eclipsed the Bagel Bakery sometime in the early 1990s and has been serving its thick, homemade, and very tasty breakfasts to most of Boulder ever since.

The Buff (1725 28th St., 303/442-9150, www.buffrestaurant.com, 6:30 A.M.–2 P.M. Mon.–Fri., 7 A.M.–2 P.M. Sat.–Sun., $11) is a one-story breakfast classic that's part of the Best Western Golden Buff Lodge near the corner of Canyon Boulevard and 28th Street. It's your basic eggs, toast, and bacon—with, befitting its host city, an emphasis on vegetarian dishes and organically grown ingredients.

Casual

Millions—no, it has to be *zillions*—of college students with the munchies have stopped by **Abo's on the Hill** (1124 13th St., 303/443-3199, www.abosonthehill.com, 11 A.M.–1 A.M. daily, $3 slice, $15 large pizza) for a huge slice of New York–style crunchy pizza slapped onto a white paper plate with plenty of grated cheese and spices available. Abo's has slowly grown into a Colorado chain, with several locations in the Boulder-Denver area.

Opened in 1923, **The Sink** (1165 13th St.,

303/444-7465, www.thesink.com, 11 A.M.–10 P.M. daily, $9) is a mythical CU bar and restaurant and Hill anchor that is still best known for providing beer and pizza to Robert Redford when he was a student in the late 1960s. Although it changed names briefly in the 1980s—my pal Jonathan and I ate the last-ever pizza of the Herbie's Deli era—it's The Sink for good, with above-average burgers, sandwiches, and pizza, a bar that stays packed until 2 A.M., an often-raucous outdoor patio, and large, weirdly friendly bouncers.

C Jalino's Pizza (1647 Arapahoe Ave., http://jalinospizza.com, 303/443-6300, 10:30 A.M.–midnight Sun.–Thurs., 10:30 A.M.–2 A.M. Fri.–Sat., $10), across the street from Boulder High School, is a hidden gem in a city renowned for its restaurants— the pizza has thin crust and a spicy sauce, with thick cheese and a huge topping selection, and it's the most reliable pizza delivery in Boulder. Avoid lunch on weekdays or you'll have to wait in line behind dozens of high school students.

Focusing on a Salvadoran dish that's sort of a thicker, corn-tortilla taco, **Pupusas Sabor Hispano** (4500 Broadway, 303/444-1729, 10 A.M.–9 P.M. Mon.–Sat., 10 A.M.–8 P.M. Sun., $4) is out of the way in a strip mall on the north edge of town but worth visiting for its variety of salsas and fresh, unexpected ingredients such as fiddlehead ferns.

The Mediterranean (1002 Walnut St., 303/444-5335, www.themedboulder.com, 11 A.M.–10 P.M. Mon.–Thurs., 11 A.M.–11 P.M. Fri.–Sat., 11 A.M.–9 P.M. Sun., $18), just west of the Pearl Street Mall on Walnut Street, is a hipster hot spot with a crowded bar and frontroom dining area, but the food makes it well worth the occasionally long wait for a table. The menu is tapas-heavy, with changing fish and pizza specials as well as superb chicken and beef mainstays.

Yes, **Old Chicago** (1102 Pearl St., 303/443-5031, www.oldchicago.com, 11 A.M.–2 A.M. daily, $12) is part of a Denver-based national chain, and there's nothing spectacular about the menu for this western Pearl Street Mall fixture. But the clientele is a comfortable combination of drinkers sampling hundreds of brands of beer in the bar and families eating thick-crust pizza and big cookies with ice cream in the restaurant.

The **West End Tavern** (926 Pearl St., 303/444-3535, www.thewestendtavern.com, 11:30 A.M.–10 P.M. daily, $15) has been famous for years for its rooftop deck overlooking the mall and the mountains (although new construction has somewhat obstructed the view in recent years). Chef Dave Query has transformed the menu from bar food to comfort food, with his high-end take on macaroni and cheese and mahimahi sandwiches.

Now that Tom's Tavern, a meat-eating institution in a sea of vegans on the western edge of the Pearl Street Mall, has closed, the **Dark Horse** (2922 Baseline Rd., 303/442-8162, http://darkhorsebar.com, 11 A.M.–2 A.M. daily, $8) is the best place in town to get a greasy-spoon burger. It's a popular college hangout, which means noise, sports, and videogames, but the Horse has a certain grungy charm. Alumni relive their boisterous youth here before CU games.

Asian

Run by longtime Colorado chef Thuy Le, a native of Vietnam, **Chez Thuy** (2655 28th St., 303/442-1700, www.chezthuy.com, 11 A.M.–10 P.M. Mon.–Sat., 4–10 P.M. Sun., $17) looks at first like a kitschy Asian restaurant (check out the plastic flowers, statues, and bead curtains near the entrance), but its long menu is diverse and elegant. The yam-heavy Vietnamese curry stew ($9) is the house specialty, but Buddha Delight ($7), with vegetables and tofu, is one of many varied choices.

The Japanese seafood dishes at **Sushi Zanmai** (1221 Spruce St., 303/440-0733, www.sushizanmai.com, 11:30 A.M.–2 P.M. and 5–10 P.M. Mon.–Fri., 5 P.M.–midnight Sat., 5–10 P.M. Sun., $18) are pretty excellent, but few show up solely for the food. Karaoke is every Saturday from 10 P.M.–midnight, and Boulder residents excel at making idiots of themselves. Far more humorous and quasi-professional than the customers are the sushi-bar

chefs, who sing while they chop up the raw fish. Also check out the sake bar next door, **Izakaya Amu** (1221 Spruce St., 303/440-0807, www.izakayaamu.com, 5–10 P.M. Mon.–Thurs., 5–10:30 P.M. Fri.–Sat., 5–9:30 P.M. Sun., $12), also serving Japanese entrées.

Just down the hill from the Hill, **Khow Thai Café** (1600 Broadway, 303/447-0273, www.khow-thai.com, 11 A.M.–10 P.M. Mon.–Fri., noon–10 P.M. Sat.–Sun., $10) is purely no-frills—it resembles a smaller version of a high school cafeteria. The exception is the food, from curry-heavy vegetables to spicy seafood and pad thai to coconut ice cream and banana desserts.

Mexican/Latin American

Centro Latin Kitchen & Refreshment Palace (950 Pearl St., 303/442-7771, www.centrolatinkitchen.com, 11:30 A.M.–10 P.M. Mon.–Fri., 9:30 A.M.–10 P.M. Sat., 9:30 A.M.–9 P.M. Sun., $20) features exotic Latin American soul food, whereas chef Dave Query's other restaurant, the West End Tavern, is all about American comfort food. The pork bellies get all the attention, but the huge meals hit every taste, from grilled blue marlin to *barbacoa*-lacquered short ribs. Everybody in town is familiar with Centro's festive outdoor patio and desirable location less than a block west of the Pearl Street Mall, so arrive early for a good seat, and order the chips with three kinds of rich salsa.

In a large yellow house in Lafayette, one of the suburb-like small towns east of Boulder along U.S. 36, ◖ **Efrain's** (101 E. Cleveland St., Lafayette, 303/666-7544, 11 A.M.–9 P.M. Wed.–Mon., $8) is perhaps the best Mexican restaurant in Boulder County. It's a friendly, family-style kind of place, with excellent blue-corn enchiladas and chips and salsa. There's another location in east Boulder (63rd St. and Arapahoe Ave., 303/440-4045).

Italian

On the fancy-restaurant scale, **Radda Trattoria** (1265 Alpine Ave., 303/442-6100, www.raddatrattoria.com, 11 A.M.–10 P.M. Mon.–Fri., 9 A.M.–10 P.M. Sat.–Sun., $13) is almost the exact midpoint between the very casual Café Gondolier and the very high-end Frasca. It's small but with plenty of parking in overcongested Boulder, and *Westword* said its basic chicken-and-pasta dishes have a "beautiful simplicity and a passionate understanding of ingredient over artifice."

I've been eating at **Café Gondolier** (1600 Pearl St., Suite 1, 303/443-5015, www.gondolieronpearl.com, 11:30 A.M.–9 P.M. Mon.–Thurs., 11:30 A.M.–10 P.M. Fri.–Sat., noon–9:30 P.M. Sun., $15) since roughly 1982, and the restaurant's long, squishy noodles, red sauce, and sausage-based minestrone soup haven't changed a bit since then. The silver-metal beast of an espresso machine dates to 1903 and was the first of its kind in Boulder. Sadly, the restaurant recently abandoned its all-you-can-eat spaghetti special, which drew roughly 1,478,869 college and high school students over the years.

DaGabi Cucina (3970 N. Broadway, 303/786-9004, www.dagabicucina.com, 5–10 P.M. daily, $16) is a little hard to find—it's behind the Lucky's Market on Broadway, north of Iris Avenue—but with the exception of downtown's more casual Café Gondolier, it's pretty much Boulder's only traditional Italian restaurant. The linguini with fresh clams ($14) and the risotto with rock shrimp ($15) are among the best dishes.

Indian

Boulder's best Indian restaurant is the venerable **Royal Peacock** (5290 Arapahoe Ave., 303/447-1409, www.royalpeacocklounge.com/index2.htm, 11:30 A.M.–2:30 P.M. and 5:30–9:30 P.M. Mon.–Fri., 5:30–9:30 P.M. Sat.–Sun., $18), which eschews belly dancers and other ethnic bells and whistles in favor of the basics—such as perfectly spiced versions of tandoori chicken and boti kebab.

Upscale

It may seem a little random to have a fancy Tajik restaurant at the center of Boulder, but the **Boulder Dushanbe Teahouse** (1770 13th St., 303/442-4993, www.boulderteahouse.com, 8 A.M.–9 P.M. daily, $15) grew out of the Dushanbe, Tajikistan, mayor's 1987 announcement of sister-city ties. The teahouse took a while to build—40 artisans from all over the once-Persian country spent three years hand-carving its complex ceramic decorations and hand-painting its ceiling, tables, and columns. Today, it's a full-service restaurant with an international menu of Spanish seafood *pimienta* ($12), Chinese plum pork ($11), and German flank steak ($14).

The Pinyon (1710 Pearl St., 720/306-8248, www.thepinyon.com, 5 P.M.–close Tues.–Fri., 10 A.M.–2 P.M. and 5 P.M.–close Sat.–Sun., $17) makes fried chicken ($18) "so juicy it slobbers," according to *Westword,* and supplements this menu centerpiece with ribs, steak, ham, soft-shell crab, fennel sausage, chicken-liver pâté, and other stuff for fancy people who like to eat a lot.

C Flagstaff House (1138 Flagstaff Rd., 303/442-4640, www.flagstaffhouse.com, 6–10 P.M. Sun.–Fri., 5–10 P.M. Sat., $60) has always been the gold standard of Boulder fine dining, and even though chef Mark Monette replaced his father, founder Don Monette, in 1985, very little has changed. Dishes include Maine lobster ($59) and Hawaiian big-eye tuna ($36). Supplementing the elegance is one of the best mountain views of Boulder.

Zolo Grill (2525 Arapahoe Ave., 303/449-0444, www.zologrill.com, 11 A.M.–9 P.M. Mon., 11 A.M.–10 P.M. Tues.–Sat., 11 A.M.–2:30 P.M. and 4–9 P.M. Sun., $21) is Southwestern and fancy—but neither too Southwestern nor too fancy. Casual dishes like smoked cheese enchiladas offset the white-tablecloth decor, and elegant dishes like tortilla-crusted and seared ahi tuna offset the funky Boulder-style modern art on the walls and the occasionally raucous 100-tequila bar.

If **C The Kitchen** (1039 Pearl St., 303/544-5973, www.thekitchencafe.com, 11 A.M.–9 P.M. Mon., 11 A.M.–10 P.M. Tues.–Fri., 9 A.M.–2 P.M. and 5:30–10 P.M. Sat., 9 A.M.–2 P.M. Sun., $29) co-owner and former celebrity chef Hugo Matheson's dishes are good enough for Mick Jagger, Sting, and

Pink Floyd, they're certainly good enough for Boulder. Regularly listed as one of Boulder's finest restaurants in local and national magazines, The Kitchen is a cozy little Pearl Street bistro that serves a mean eggplant-and-olive antipasti as well as pork, lamb, steak, and salmon entrées.

Even more critically acclaimed than The Kitchen, **Frasca** (1738 Pearl St., 303/442-6966, www.frascafoodandwine.com, 5:30–10 P.M. Mon.–Sat., $62 for 4 courses) serves scintillatingly named meals (hand-cut tagliatelle with Colorado sweet corn, oregano and piave cream and Long Family Farm shaved pork leg with red plums, pancetta, and *sugo naturale*) that go perfectly with the sommelier's selections. Make reservations early, because Frasca is every Boulderite's ultimate date night venue, and the wait list is usually long.

It's not in the greatest location—in the strip mall at 28th Street and Iris Avenue—but **Arugula** (2785 Iris Ave., 303/443-5100, 11 A.M.–2:30 P.M. and 4:30–9:30 P.M. Mon.–Thurs., 11 A.M.–2:30 P.M. and 4:30–10 P.M. Fri., 4:30–10 P.M. Sat., $20) is one of Boulder's sleeper Italian restaurants, serving the usual pastas, fish, and steaks with comforting, colorful twists. The sausage and goat-cheese penne ($17) contains caramelized onions, and the chicken and zucchini penne ($18) has lemon and snap peas.

The small Provence-style bistro **Mateo** (1837 Pearl St., 303/443-7766, www.mateorestaurant.com, 11:30 A.M.–3 P.M. and 5–10 P.M. Mon.–Fri., 5–10 P.M. Sat., $22) can be noisy and crowded if too many people are eating or drinking in the bar at once, but it's worth trying if only for the amazing french fries, which actually taste like potatoes.

Inside the Hotel Boulderado, **Q's Restaurant** (2115 13th St., 303/442-4880, www.qsboulder.com, 6:30 A.M.–2 P.M. and 5–10 P.M. Mon.–Fri., 7 A.M.–10 P.M. Sat.–Sun., $21) is both funky and stately, with a green-and-white ceiling, pillars, and stained-glass windows, and a menu that stretches from foie gras to chicken tortilla soup. With an outdoor patio and huge windows in the dining room, it's also the perfect spot for Pearl Street people-watching.

To get to **Gold Hill Inn** (401 Main St., 303/443-6461, www.goldhillinn.com, 6–9 P.M. Wed.–Sat., 5–8 P.M. Sun. May and Oct., 6–9 P.M. Mon. and Wed.–Sat., 5–8 P.M. Sun. June–Sept., 6–8:30 P.M. Fri.–Sat., 5–7:30 P.M. Sun. Nov.–Dec., $31 for 6 courses), take Mapleton Avenue through Sunshine Canyon, straight up until you come to a rickety dirt-road town at the intersection of the excellently named Lickskillet Drive. It's in an old log cabin—which perfectly fits its surroundings—but the food inside is Flagstaff House–worthy. The six-course meal ($31) includes your choice of lamb venison, roast pork loin, salmon, roast duck, or broiled smoked trout.

INFORMATION

The **City of Boulder** (1777 Broadway, 303/441-3388, www.bouldercolorado.gov) is packed with parks and recreation resources as well as city services and general details. The **Boulder Convention & Visitors Bureau** (2440 Pearl St., 303/442-2911 or 800/444-0447, www.bouldercoloradousa.com) is more geared toward visitors and business travelers. The **University of Colorado** can be reached at 303/492-1411 and www.colorado.edu.

Boulder has a surprisingly large number of newspapers for a midsize city: the *Daily Camera* (www.dailycamera.com) is the morning daily; now owned by the same newspaper chain as the *Camera,* the once fiercely independent *Colorado Daily* (www.coloradodaily.com) focuses on CU but also covers local news; the *Boulder Weekly* (www.boulderweekly.com) is sort of a mini-*Westword* focusing on Boulder; and CU's student-run *Independent* (www.cuindependent.com) is often informative. Most of these publications, as well as *Westword* and various trade weeklies, pile up in the vestibules of local record stores, restaurants, grocery stores, and theaters.

Boulder's best-known radio station, **KBCO** (97.3 FM), has grown from country rock and new wave in the early 1980s to a pioneering format called "adult alternative" in the 1990s, but today it's a corporate rock station owned by Clear Channel and programmed from Denver. (Even its studio, long visible from the street in Boulder, has moved to Denver.) The community radio station, which emphasizes local musicians and news, is the eclectic **KGNU** (88.5 FM, 4700 Walnut St., 303/449-4885, www.kgnu.org).

Boulder's main **post office** (1905 15th St., 800/275-8777) is just off the Pearl Street Mall.

The top hospitals are the **Boulder Medical Center** (2750 Broadway, 303/440-3000, www.bouldermedicalcenter.com), **Boulder Community Hospital** (1100 Balsam, 303/440-2273, www.bch.org), and the **University Family Medicine–Boulder** (350 Broadway, Suite 130, 720/848-2604, www.uch.edu/locations/get-care/ufm-boulder). About 20 minutes northeast of Boulder, **Longmont United Hospital** (1950 Mountain View Ave., Longmont, 303/651-1111, www.luhcares.org) provides care on the same level as the Boulder hospitals.

Centrally located laundries include **Boulder Cleaners** (5280 Spine Rd., 303/581-0630, www.bouldercleaners.com) and **John's Cleaners** (3325 28th St., 303/444-2877, www.johnsdrycleaners.com).

GETTING THERE AND AROUND

In addition to the standard RTD buses (1400 Walnut St., 303/442-7332, www.rtd-denver.com), which serve the entire city as well as Denver and points between, Boulder has a superb mini transportation system. Colorful shuttles known as Hop, Skip, Jump, and others are quick and easy rides. For more information, contact the **City of Boulder Transportation Division** (1739 Broadway, 303/441-3200, www.bouldercolorado.gov).

Denver International Airport (DIA) is still the best way to get to Boulder from out of town, but you'll need to take a car or a bus. A few small airports, such as the **Rocky Mountain Metropolitan Airport** (11755 Airport Way, Broomfield, 303/271-4850, www.airnav.com/airport/BJC) accommodate smaller planes and private pilots.

NEDERLAND

Some say Boulder is the quintessential hippie town, having discovered marijuana and the Grateful Dead in the 1960s, and never let go. But Boulder has transformed into a city with more to life—for the most part—than where the next round of snacks will come from. So where have all the hippies gone? To "Ned," a tiny former mining town at the intersection of Highways 72 and 119, surrounded by placid hills and valleys. The people who live here are taking a break from civilization, in a good way.

Sights

The 55-mile **Peak-to-Peak Highway** begins in Estes Park as Highway 7 and twists through several tiny mountain towns—notably sleeping-dog-in-the-road Ward and gambling meccas Central City and Blackhawk—before intersecting with I-70, just west of Idaho Springs. Built in 1918, the highway winds through some of the most scenic terrain in Colorado, including Rocky Mountain National Park, Arapahoe and Roosevelt National Forests, and the Indian Peaks Wilderness Area. Views of the scenic Continental Divide pop up unexpectedly along the way. It's a narrow, mostly two-lane paved road, and the easiest way to access it is in Nederland, where Highway 119 comes in from Longmont and Niwot.

Skiing

Here is where I confess that I cannot ski. I've tried twice at **Eldora Mountain Resort** (2861 Eldora Ski Rd. 140, on Hwy. 119, five miles west of Nederland, 303/440-8700, www.eldora.com, $69), and each time involved stumbling off the lift at the top, with irritated grumbles and catcalls from the experienced skiers below. My vast network of skiing sources assures me that Eldora, despite its reputation as a beginner's stop en route to Winter Park, Vail, or Aspen, is fun and relaxed, with plenty of powder. The resort reports Eldora gets 300 inches of snow per year, the summit is 10,800 feet above sea level, the sharpest vertical drop is 1,400 feet, the longest run is three miles, and there are 50 miles of skiable terrain totaling 680 acres.

Hiking and Biking

Just south of Rocky Mountain National Park and blending with Roosevelt National Forest to the east, **Indian Peaks Wilderness** is almost 77,000 acres with a range of triangular 13,000-foot granite peaks for a backdrop. The park is filled with hiking trails, although the parking areas are small and it's a little hard to get to some of them. The **Arapaho Glacier Trail** goes six miles and gains about 1,500 vertical feet to a beautiful overlook of 13,000-foot South Arapaho and North Arapahoe peaks as well as the namesake glacier. After that, it continues downhill another 1.6 miles to the Fourth of July Mine. To access the trailhead, head north on Highway 72 out of Nederland, turn west onto Forest Road 298 (marked with a "CU Mountain Research" sign), and go five miles until you see a parking area. Shorter and a little easier is the **Mount Audubon Trail,** which climbs 3.7 miles and almost 3,000 vertical feet to the top of Mount Audubon, above the tree line. To get to the trailhead, go 13 miles north from Nederland on Highway 72, turn west onto County Road 102 (at the "Brainerd Lake Recreation Area" sign), then follow the signs to the Mitchell Lake trailhead parking area.

For more detail on the 30-some trails in this wilderness area, contact the **USDA Forest Service's Boulder Ranger District** (2140 Yarmouth Ave., Boulder, 303/541-2500, www.fs.fed.us/r2/arnf/recreation/wilderness/indianpeaks). You can also find information here about backcountry camping permits.

Entertainment

The **Pioneer Inn** (15 E. 1st St., 303/258-7733, www.pioneerinnnederland.net, 11 A.M.–2 A.M. daily) is a live-music club on the mountain circuit, which includes Golden's Buffalo Rose

and the Mishawaka Inn near Fort Collins. It has a legendary pedigree—in the early 1970s, when rock stars such as Billy Joel, Rod Stewart, Carole King, and Dan Fogelberg showed up to record at the Caribou Ranch studio nearby, they wound up jamming at the Pioneer Inn. Today, most of the bands that play here are of the hippie-jamming variety, but it snags strong local talent as well.

Accommodations

Nederland is more popular as a pit stop en route to Central City, Blackhawk, Rocky Mountain National Park, and Boulder than as a destination in itself, so few nonchain hotels have sprung up over the years. There is one excellent campground in the vicinity: **Kelly Dahl** (Hwy. 119, four miles south of Nederland, 877/444-6777, $17), near gambling casinos *and* excellent hiking trails.

Food

Black Forest Restaurant (24 Big Springs Dr., 303/279-2333 or 303/582-9971, www.blackforestrest.com, 11 A.M.–9 P.M. Mon.–Sat., 11 A.M.–8 P.M. Sun., $25) is a German eatery that looks the part—big triangular roof, building trim out of *Pippi Longstocking,* and menu items like Hungarian goulash and wiener schnitzel. It's maybe not the best place to stop on a quick drive, but you might crave the protein after a day at Eldora.

Information

The **Nederland Chamber of Commerce** (303/258-3936, www.nederlandchamber.org) provides information about pretty much every business in town and is the primary source of news for such required local events as Frozen Dead Guy Days. The local weekly is the *Mountain Ear* (www.themountainear.com).

Although based in Black Hawk, **Mountain Family Health Centers** (562 Gregory St., Black Hawk, 303/582-5276, www.mountainfamily.org) serve Nederland as well.

Rocky Mountain National Park

With flat, 14,000-foot Longs Peak standing watch over a landscape of massive mountains as well as meadows, lakes, and wilderness, the 265,000-acre Rocky Mountain National Park is one of Colorado's most exhilarating attractions and a user-friendly nature preserve with 359 miles of meticulously crafted trails. Its valleys are "only" about 8,000 feet high, but the elevations shift abruptly; Longs Peak is the sole fourteener, and more than 75 mountain peaks rise above 12,000 feet.

The park has endless nooks and crannies for the 3 million hikers, rock climbers, campers, and picnickers who visit every year, and they're all consistently rewarded with clean mountain air; sightings of elk, deer, coyotes, eagles, and many other kinds of wildlife; and fields full of summer wildflowers.

Artists and poets should visit the park regularly for inspiration. You can get lost staring into a single mountain range, with its layers of green, red, and yellow earth and trees. In the background, some of the tallest peaks maintain their snow caps as late as June. From high vantage points throughout the park, it's possible to wedge green meadows, blue lakes, relaxing cow elk, and twisty brown streams into one broad camera view. The scenery is so endless it's almost frustrating; travelers need at least a few days to properly experience it.

Although it didn't become a national park until 1915, the area formed tens of thousands of years ago when active volcanoes and moving glaciers left mountains, valleys, and tundra behind. (Even in the dead of summer, it can be extremely cold as you walk or drive higher up the mountains, so be sure to pack accordingly.) A variety of Native American groups lived and hunted here for centuries, until gold miners took over in the late 1800s; remnants of both can still be found in the park.

© STEVE KNOPPER

Even in late June, snowcaps are still visible in the Rockies above Rocky Mountain National Park.

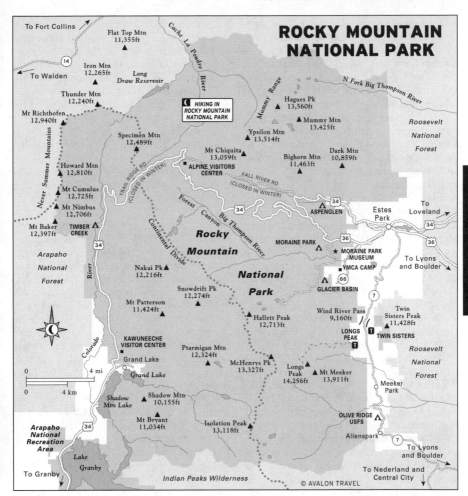

SPORTS AND RECREATION
Hiking

Biking isn't allowed in the park—just on 23 miles of the paved Trail Ridge Road—but **hiking** trails are everywhere. The park can get amazingly crowded, especially in the summer, so if you're looking for seclusion, or at least a walk without running into people, contact park officials beforehand (970/586-1206) for maps and advice.

The park's most famous trail is **Longs Peak** (Hwy. 7, near the park's southeast corner, about 6 miles north of Allenspark), which is Colorado's version of Mount Everest (well, minus the Sherpas and life-threatening elevations). The eight-mile trip begins at 9,400 feet of elevation and climbs to more than 14,200 feet at the summit, and it's one of the most technically difficult climbs in the state; some hikers have died while climbing, so be sure to equip yourself with windbreakers and water, and make pre-hike calls to local rangers for conditions. There are shorter and (in some cases) less strenuous routes up the mountain, including the four-mile (one-way) trails to **Chasm Lake** and **Twin Sisters Peaks,** both moderately difficult and totally worth it for the breathtaking views. But there's nothing like looking down from the Longs summit.

Of the miles and miles of hiking trails within the park, among the best and most popular are **Bear Lake** (Bear Lake Rd., 11 miles from Beaver Meadows Visitors Center), a 0.6-mile loop that meanders around the base of two large mountains and overlooks the lake and waterfalls; **Coyote Valley** (5 miles north of Kawuneeche Visitors Center), an easy one-mile trail with elk and moose as frequent guest stars; the **Colorado River Trail** (on the park's west side), a 3.7-mile (one-way) walk that goes along a onetime stagecoach road into an abandoned gold-mining town, Lulu City; and the five-mile (one-way) **Ouzel Lake** (off Hwy. 7, at the Wild Basin Ranger Station parking lot, 2 miles northwest of Allenspark), along the frantic waterfall-like North St. Vrain Creek, leading toward several lakes near the end.

Alberta Falls is an easy one-mile trek to scenic waterfalls. Head south from the Beaver Meadows park entrance, about nine miles along Bear Lake Road. Park and look for the shuttle bus to the Glacier Gorge trail junction.

The musical name of the four-mile (round-trip) **Calypso Cascades** matches the sounds of the flowing creeks and waterfalls along the way. The trail was named for an orchid that grows in the area. Find the trailhead near the Wild Basin Ranger Station parking area. For more of a workout, tack on a visit to Ouzel Lake.

Wildlife-Watching

On a recent summer drive into the park, along the Fall River entrance just west of Estes Park, my daughter and I encountered so many animals we could barely pay attention to the road. Just a few hundred yards past the ranger station we saw dozens of cow elk resting in a green meadow. Strolling slowly past them were a half-dozen white mountain goats. Eventually

rangers were forced to halt car traffic on U.S. 34 so they could cross the road; drivers stopped to take photos as one of the smallest goats stopped for 15 minutes in the middle of the highway to look around. He soon rejoined his colleagues as they marched up a hill on the other side. Later, chipmunks begged us for food at an observation area.

Rocky Mountain National Park is one of the best and most diverse settings for wildlife-watching in the state. At any moment, visitors can spot bighorn sheep, foxes, mule deer, coyotes, elk, moose, and (be careful) mountain lions and black bears. Bird-watchers have reported 280 species since the area became a park in 1915; these include white-tailed ptarmigans, three-toed woodpeckers, Townsend's solitaires, Virginia's warblers, and northern pygmy owls.

Generally, you have an excellent chance of spotting just about any kind of wildlife (except for certain endangered ones, such as the bald eagle or the Canada lynx) anywhere in the park. Elk, deer, and bighorn sheep are especially prevalent along Old Fall River Road and throughout Horseshoe Park, just beyond the northern entrance to the park along U.S. 34. To the south, elk and bighorn sheep often roam throughout Upper Beaver Meadows and Moraine Park, closer to the U.S. 36 entrance. On the western edge of the park, near Grand Lake, moose and elk are prevalent along the stretch of U.S. 34 from the Grand Lake Entrance to the Alpine Visitors Center.

Rock Climbing

Rock climbers have flocked to the park for decades, particularly the east side of Longs Peak, where difficult alpine-wall climbs like **The Diamond** (accessible from the mountain trailhead) have become so crowded that enthusiasts have stopped telling their friends about it. Another popular climbing destination within the park is **Lumpy Ridge** (off MacGregor Ave., Estes Park), a huge chunk of granite that makes veterans rapturous. For gear, maps, and advice, go to the **Colorado Mountain School** (341 Moraine Ave., Estes Park, 970/586-4677 or 800/836-4008, www.totalclimbing.com).

Skiing and Snowshoeing

Most of the hiking trails open in the summer are accessible in the winter for backcountry skiers and snowshoers. Call the park for weather conditions—avalanches happen now and then in this terrain—before heading out, and be sure to bring at least one partner. **Outdoor World** (156 E. Elkhorn Ave., Estes Park, 970/586-2114 or 800/679-3600, www.rmconnection.com) rents equipment and gives tips.

Fishing

With lakes everywhere, fishing is also common in the park; **Kirk's Fly Shop** (230 E. Elkhorn Ave., Estes Park, 970/577-0790 or 877/669-1859, www.kirksflyshop.com) rents rods, tackle boxes, and other equipment and provides guided tours, including some with llamas (yes, llamas) carrying your packs.

ACCOMMODATIONS AND CAMPING

There are no hotels in Rocky Mountain National Park—you'll have to stay in nearby Estes Park for luxury, or at least indoor plumbing—but several campgrounds are among the best in the state.

Car Camping

The park provides six official camping areas, accessible by car. All sites in the campgrounds cost $20 per night or $3 pp for the group sites, although some are cheaper in the fall, when the running water is turned off. Some campsites are open year-round, others just in the summer. For maps and to confirm the details, contact the National Park Service (888/448-1474 or 877/444-6777, www.nps.gov/romo/planyourvisit/camping.htm). Only Glacier Basin and Moraine Park take reservations, up to six months in advance.

Aspenglen is along U.S. 34, west of the Fall River Entrance Station, and has 54 sites; **Glacier Basin,** on Bear Lake Road, about six miles south of the Beaver Meadows Entrance Station, has 150 individual sites as well as group sites for up to 40 people; **Longs Peak,** on Highway 7, nine miles south of Estes Park,

has 26 sites; **Moraine Park,** on Bear Lake Road, 2.5 miles south of the Beaver Meadows station, is the largest camping area, with 245 sites as well as group sites for up to 40 people; and **Timber Creek,** on U.S. 34 eight miles east of the Grand Lake Entrance Station, has 98 sites.

Consider the "unofficial" car-camping areas as well. **Olive Ridge Campground** (Hwy. 7, 25 miles northwest of Boulder, 303/541-2500, $14) is near the trail that peak-baggers use to climb Longs Peak, the most recognizable fourteener in the Boulder area. For that reason, it fills up early during warm summer weekends, even though it has 56 campsites, so try to visit during the week or very early on Friday. Bonus for parents: There's a playground, in addition to the usual toilets, tables, and fire rings. **Meeker Park** (Hwy. 7, 13 miles south of Estes Park, www.fs.fed.us/r2/arnf/recreation/camping-picnicking/developed/brd/meekerpark.shtml, 303/541-2500, $9) is a smaller campground (29 sites) with great access to all kinds of trails and activities. Again, it pays to get here early on summer weekends, because you can't reserve these spots in advance. Also, the roads can be rough, so this campground is especially suited for tent camping.

Backcountry Camping

Many park enthusiasts swear by the backcountry camping, most of which is incredibly scenic and involves hiking to the sites, but backpackers cannot just plop down anywhere in the park, as is allowed on most U.S. Forest Service land; you have to camp at designated sites and reserve them ahead of time. You also need a special permit: The National Park Service issues them at the Beaver Meadows and Kawuneechee visitors centers. For more information, call 970/586-1242. Here's a sampling of the most popular and notable backcountry campsites:

You can see three gorgeous alpine lakes plus two waterfalls at **The Loch, Glass Lake,** and **Sky Pond**—accessible via a nine-mile (round-trip) hike. Enter the park from the Beaver Meadows Entrance Station, turn left on Bear Lake Road, and drive 8.4 miles to the Glacier Gorge Trailhead. You can hike for 0.5 miles, take in beautiful but crowded Alberta Falls, then keep going all the way to Sky Pond. Double back to spend the night at the Andrews Creek backcountry campsite, the only designated spot to lay your head between the Glacier Gorge trailhead and Sky Pond. Look for the campsites beside Andrews Creek, along the Andrews Glacier Trail (one mile past The Loch).

Longs Peak is the flat-head fourteener visible from many high-country spots in Boulder and Longmont. It's probably the most popular mountain to climb in the park. A trail leads eight miles to the 14,255-foot summit. It's challenging, with a 4,855-foot elevation gain, but many hikers try to do it in one day. Since rangers strongly advise getting off the summit by noon to avoid storms, most groups start their trek at 2 or 3 A.M. A better plan might be to stay in one of the backcountry campsites near Longs Peak the night before. That way you can split the hike in two. Set up camp the first day, rest and get used to the altitude, then enjoy the views from the summit the next morning. One Longs Peak camping option is **Moore Park,** with two sites next to a meadow with views of Twin Sisters and Estes Cone. To get here, drive nine miles south of Estes Park on Highway 7, turn into the Longs Peak Ranger Station, and park. Look for the Longs Peak trailhead near the ranger station, then hike 1.7 miles to Moore Park. Another is the **Boulder Field,** two miles from the summit, for hardy souls who like to sleep in windy, rocky beds above the tree line. These eight campsites, at 12,000 feet, have fine views of the peak's East Face and the Keyhole. Boulder Field sites are available by reservation only, and they fill up fast, so call way before your trip.

Sprague Lake is a wheelchair-accessible camping site 0.5 miles from the Sprague Lake Picnic Area parking lot (seven miles from the Beaver Meadows park entrance). The hike to the campsite hugs a lake (well-stocked for fishing) with a nice nature trail. This backcountry site is ideal for families with small kids, wheelchair

users, and those who can't stand car-camping. It has beautiful views of the Continental Divide, especially when the sun rises.

Lake Nokoni and **Lake Nanita** involve a difficult hike, but at the end you'll enjoy two of the most scenic lakes in the park. Start at the North Inlet Trailhead (off Hwy. 278, north of Grand Lake and Trail Ridge Rd.), then hike 9–11 miles to get to the lakes. Backcountry campsites are scattered all along this route, which starts out flat and gentle. Save your energy for steep switchbacks near the end. Moose, elk, deer, and thundering waterfalls are among the sights you'll encounter. The campsites along this trail fill up fast in summer, so reserve one well in advance.

The **Lone Pine Lake** campground is next to a stunning alpine lake in relative solitude. The hike on the less-busy west side of Rocky Mountain National Park attracts relatively few visitors. Start at the East Inlet Trailhead (off Hwy. 278, 2.7 miles from Trail Ridge Rd., on the east shore of Grand Lake across from the boat launch). The moderate hike is 11 miles round-trip, with many waterfalls, streams, and the chance to see a moose munching his breakfast.

Finally, an underutilized part of the park is the northeast section, including the **Boundary Creek** backcountry campsite near the Comanche Peak Wilderness. If you visit in early September, you might find a sun-ripened patch of wild raspberries. It's about a five-mile hike on the North Fork Trail. Take Devil's Gulch Road till you see a "Forest Service Access" sign, then follow the Forest Service dirt road to a parking area and trailhead.

FOOD

There are no food services in the park itself. Most visitors stock up at the cafés and restaurants of Estes Park (to the east) or Grand Lake (to the southwest) before making a prolonged day trip.

INFORMATION AND SERVICES
Visitors Centers

The park's visitors centers are **Alpine** (Fall

River Pass, Trail Ridge Rd. and Old Fall River Rd., 970/586-1222); **Beaver Meadows** (U.S. 36, at the park entrance, 3 miles from Estes Park); **Fall River** (U.S. 34, at the park's Fall River entrance, 5 miles west of Estes Park); **Hozwarth** (U.S. 34, at the park entrance, 7 miles north of Grand Lake); **Kawuneeche** (U.S. 34, at the park entrance, 1 mile north of Grand Lake, 970/586-1513); and **Moraine Park** (off Bear Lake Rd., 1.5 miles from the Beaver Meadows entrance). Check the park website (www.nps.gov/romo) for hours, as they vary from season to season; unless noted above, call 970/586-1206 for information.

Entrance Stations

It costs $20 per car for a week at the park, or $10 for bicyclists and motorcyclists. For maps and other information, try the **Rocky Mountain Nature Association** (970/586-0108, www.rmna.org).

GETTING THERE

The town of Estes Park, at the intersection of U.S. 34, U.S. 36, and Highway 7, is the eastern gateway to Rocky Mountain National Park. To get here from Denver, drive west on U.S. 36, which turns into 28th Street in Boulder, and continue through Lyons to Estes Park. From Estes Park, U.S. 34 forks north to the park's Fall River entrance, and U.S. 36 forks north to the Beaver Meadows entrance. Visitors centers are just inside each entrance.

The western edge of the park is accessible via the tiny mountain town of Grand Lake. Take I-70 west to U.S. 40, and turn onto U.S. 34 in Granby. Just past the Kawuneeche Visitors Center on the right, continue north along U.S. 36 into the park.

GETTING AROUND

U.S. 34 is also known as **Trail Ridge Road,** a 48-mile paved highway that peaks at 12,183 feet and rises dramatically above the trees, straight into 11 miles of alpine tundra that often includes unexpected patches of snow. (This is where you might have to switch from the air conditioner to the heater in your car.)

Bring a camera for the incredible roadside views. Most of the road is open all year, but the central stretch is usually closed mid-October–late May.

Almost as scenic is nine-mile **Bear Lake Road,** which begins at the **Moraine Park Museum** (off U.S. 36, Estes Park, 970/586-8842, 9 A.M.–4:30 P.M. daily May–early Oct., free), and which overlooks Longs Peak and numerous waterfalls en route to the pretty lake and its surrounding trails. The road and parking lot are often cluttered with cars, so consider stopping three miles past the museum to take a U.S. Park Service shuttle.

The 11-mile **Old Fall River Road** (from Fall River to Alpine Visitors Centers) is sort of a shortcut, but a tough one—one-way, unpaved, 15 mph maximum, and no RVs allowed. The views from the nearly 12,000-foot Fall River Pass and potential detours into relaxing Horseshoe and Willow Parks are worth it if you can stand the driving conditions. Four-wheel drive is helpful.

Two **shuttles** transport visitors throughout the park. The Bear Lake and Moraine Park buses service several trailheads, the Moraine Park Visitors Center, and the Moraine Park and Glacier Basin Campgrounds. They operate every 10–15 minutes (Bear Lake) or every 30 minutes (Moraine Park) on weekends May 28–June 5, beginning from the Park & Ride stop across from the Glacier Basin Campground. An express all-day Hiker Shuttle goes between the Town of Estes Park Visitors Center (500 Big Thompson Ave., Estes Park, 800/443-7837, www.estesparkcvb.com), the park's Beaver Meadows Visitors Center, and the Park & Ride stop across from the Glacier Basin Campground; it runs daily June 25–September 5, then weekends September 5–October 2. Check www.nps.gov/romo/planyourvisit/shuttle_bus_route.htm for maps and other details, including information about the summer Visitor Shuttle in Estes Park.

ESTES PARK

Estes Park is the entry point to Rocky Mountain National Park, some of the most magnificent mountain-and-valley country in

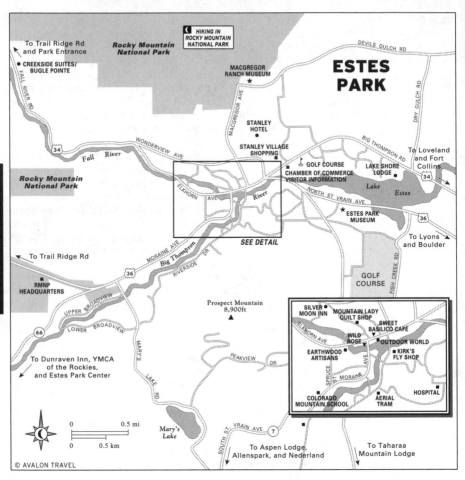

To Trail Ridge Rd and Park Entrance

Rocky Mountain National Park

HIKING IN ROCKY MOUNTAIN NATIONAL PARK

DEVILS GULCH RD

ESTES PARK

CREEKSIDE SUITES/ BUGLE POINTE

MACGREGOR RANCH MUSEUM

DRY GULCH RD

FALL RIVER RD

WONDERVIEW AVE

MACGREGOR AVE

STANLEY HOTEL

STANLEY VILLAGE SHOPPING

BIG THOMPSON RD

To Loveland and Fort Collins

Fall River

GOLF COURSE
CHAMBER OF COMMERCE
VISITOR INFORMATION

LAKE SHORE LODGE

Rocky Mountain National Park

ELKHORN AVE

River

NORTH ST VRAIN AVE

Lake Estes

ESTES PARK MUSEUM

To Lyons and Boulder

SEE DETAIL

To Trail Ridge Rd

MORAINE AVE

Big Thompson

RIVERSIDE DR

FISH CREEK RD

RMNP HEADQUARTERS

GOLF COURSE

UPPER BROADVIEW

LOWER BROADVIEW

Prospect Mountain 8,900ft

SILVER MOON INN

MOUNTAIN LADY QUILT SHOP

SWEET BASILICO CAFE

ELKHORN AVE

WILD ROSE

OUTDOOR WORLD

EARTHWOOD ARTISANS

KIRK'S FLY SHOP

To Dunraven Inn, YMCA of the Rockies, and Estes Park Center

MARY'S LAKE RD

PEAKVIEW DR

SPRUCE ST

MORAINE

COLORADO MOUNTAIN SCHOOL

AERIAL TRAM

HOSPITAL

0   0.5 mi
0   0.5 km

Mary's Lake

SOUTH ST VRAIN AVE

To Aspen Lodge, Allenspark, and Nederland

To Taharaa Mountain Lodge

© AVALON TRAVEL

Colorado, but the town itself is surprisingly unmagnificent. Except for the huge Stanley Hotel (itself a bit run-down these days), the old hotels are nothing special, most of the nonfastfood restaurants are of the burger-and-billiards variety, and the tourist-trap stores sell a combination of polished gemstones and kids' toys.

The town is a fine detour en route to the national park, but its lack of elegant food and lodging discourages long stays, especially in the winter, when most travelers have moved on to the ski resorts.

Native Americans were the first to live here,

but Estes Park's first nonnative settler was hunter Joel Estes, who stumbled on the mountain valley in 1859 and relocated his family to two log cabins in order to build a cattle ranch. Word spread among Estes's friends, and by 1877 the Irish Earl of Dunraven had built a hotel for European visitors. Stanley Steamer inventor F. O. Stanley took over as the primary developer at the turn of the 20th century; sick with tuberculosis, he built his massive white Stanley Hotel in 1909.

The Stanley became famous in the 1980s after Stephen King stayed here and was inspired to write a portion of *The Shining*,

a view of Estes Park, the tourist town just outside Rocky Mountain National Park

although the famously creepy Jack Nicholson film wasn't filmed in Estes Park. After two major floods, Estes Park became known as "The Gutsiest Little Town in Colorado."

Sights

Among the exhibits in the small **Estes Park Museum** (200 4th St., 970/586-6256, www.estesnet.com/museum, 10 A.M.–5 P.M. Mon.–Sat., 1–5 P.M. Sun., free) is an actual Stanley Steamer automobile, in honor of F. O. Stanley and his hotel, as well as a log cabin and various photos and postcards from the old days.

Founded in 1883, the **MacGregor Ranch Museum** (180 MacGregor Lane, 970/586-3749, www.macgregorranch.org, 10 A.M.–4 P.M. Tues.–Sat. June–Aug., school-group tours year-round by appointment, free) displays the original family's personal paintings, clothing, and rock collections in a historic house on a huge ranch underneath Longs Peak.

Sports and Recreation

Nearby Rocky Mountain National Park is the place to go for hiking, biking, snowshoeing, and the like, but Estes Park has the **Big Thompson River** (on U.S. 34 east of town) and **Peter's Pond** (510 Moraine Ave., 970/586-5171, www.etonnant.com/catch_wild_trout), which is regularly stocked with wild trout. For equipment, maps, and tour information, contact **Rocky Mountain Adventures** (1117 N. Hwy. 287, 970/493-4005 or 800/858-6808, www.shoprma.com), which also focuses on the Cache La Poudre River.

For white-water rafting, the Cache La Poudre River begins in Estes Park and flows fairly ruggedly into the Fort Collins area, and **Rapid Transit Rafting** (161 Virginia Dr., 800/367-8523, www.rapidtransitrafting.com) tags along, providing the proper guides, rental rafts, equipment, and lessons.

The **Estes Park Golf Club** (1080 S. St. Vrain Ave., 970/586-8146 or 866/586-8146, http://golfestes.com/golf/golf-course-info, $46) has a park district–run 18-hole course that's scenic and no-nonsense—unless you count the occasional deer, elk, or coyote wandering onto the greens.

Entertainment and Nightlife

Although Wall of Dogs and Ricky and the Red Hot Voodoo Devils are unlikely to challenge the Rolling Stones for national live-concert dominance, shows featuring local bands at **Lonigans** (110 W. Elkhorn Ave., 970/586-4346, www.lonigans.com, 11 A.M.–2 A.M. daily) are usually raucous, bluesy, and fun. It has decent bar food too. Townie bars like the **Wheel Bar** (132 E. Elkhorn Ave., 970/586-9381, www.thewheelbar.com, 10 A.M.–2 A.M. daily) are scattered along Elkhorn Avenue, inviting travelers to step in for some pool, darts, or a glimpse of sports on television.

Shopping

The Estes Park shopping district centers on Elkhorn Avenue, the town's main drag, with all the Christmas knickknacks, kids' toys, wooden wildlife sculptures, and shiny rocks you could ever want. Some of the more unique shops include the **Mountain Lady Quilt Shop** (930 Big Thompson Ave., 970/586-5330, www.mtnladyquilt.com, 10 A.M.–4 P.M. Mon.–Fri., 10 A.M.–5 P.M. Sat., 12:30–4:30 P.M. Sun.), which has colorful fabric art panels of mountain scenes and holiday themes; **Earthwood Artisans** (141 E. Elkhorn Ave., 970/586-2151, www.earthwoodartisans.com, hours vary), a large gallery of pottery, photographs, paintings, and many other styles, mostly by local artists; and **Estes Ark** (521 Lone Pine Dr., 970/586-6483, 10 A.M.–5 P.M. Thurs.–Sat. and Mon.–Tues., 1–5 P.M. Sun.), which specializes in both talking teddy bears and slot cars, and is a requisite stop for embattled parents tired of saying no to their kids as they wander through Estes Park in search of food.

Accommodations

$100-150

On an 860-acre ranch with tall hills for sledding and backcountry skiing, the **Estes Park Center/YMCA of the Rockies** (2515 Tunnel Rd., 970/586-3341 or 800/777-9622, www.ymcarockies.org, $109–169) has four lodges and several log cabins. It's the most affordable lodging in town for large groups, and the conference dining rooms have all-you-can-eat buffets.

The **Aspen Lodge at Estes Park Ranch Resort and Conference Center** (6120 Hwy. 7, 970/586-8133 or 800/332-6867, www.aspenlodge.net, $139–159) is on an 82-acre ranch of meadows and evergreens that are almost always open for guest hikers, snowshoers, and, of course, horseback riders. The ranch has an on-site livery, with horses available for all different riding levels. As for the 52-room lodge itself, it's a giant log cabin with a fireplace in the cowboy-style lobby. Be careful when exiting your room onto the wooden balcony, however; my wife and I once locked ourselves out and had to ask a bride, who was preparing for her wedding on the ranch in 15 minutes, to let us back in through her room.

The green-roofed **Lake Shore Lodge** (1700 Big Thompson Ave., 970/577-6400, www.lakeshorelodge.com, $139–229) is great for hiking and mountain viewing—the steps down from the hotel's deck lead directly to the 3.7-mile Lake Estes Trail, which is a pretty walk, and the outdoor patio at the Silverado Restaurant overlooks both the lake and the mountains.

$150-200

Happy hour, in front of a stone fireplace beyond the lobby, is the best part about the **Taharaa Mountain Lodge** (3110 S. St. Vrain Ave., 970/577-0098 or 800/597-0098, www.taharaa.com, $159–199). The lodge is a larger-than-usual bed-and-breakfast with helpful owners, Ken and Diane Harlen, who patiently answer questions. Large windows let in plenty of blue sky and mountain views.

Creekside Suites (1400 David Dr., 970/577-0068 or 800/349-1003, www.estescondos.com/creekside, $185–255) is a collection of wooden suites with decks overlooking the Fall River. Some of the guest rooms are small, but most have fireplaces and whirlpools. Many other local hotels and condos are along Fall River, including **Bugle Pointe** (1400 David Dr., 970/577-0068 or 800/349-1003, www.estescondos.com/buglepointe,

$185–255) and **Silver Moon Inn** (175 Spruce Dr., 970/586-6006 or 800/818-6006, http://silvermooninn.com, $152–250), a two-story, ski resort–style hotel.

Upon viewing the **Stanley Hotel** (333 Wonderview Ave., 970/577-4000 or 800/976-1377, www.stanleyhotel.com, $179–600), underneath a huge mountain peak overlooking the town of Estes Park, you might be tempted to stare through a door and declare, *"Honey, I'm home."* But Jack Nicholson, who delivered that line in *The Shining,* never filmed in this massive white building; author Stephen King stayed briefly at the hotel and was inspired to write the book that inspired the movie. Filming did not take place at the hotel, which F. O. Stanley, of Stanley Steamer automobile fame, built it while dying of tuberculosis in the early 1900s. The hotel remains an ornate fixture with red carpets on the floor, wide staircases, large windows that show off the best mountain views, and a restaurant that's the perfect wedding location. The only downfall is that the hotel is, well, old, and it feels like it.

Food

There's nothing wrong with a good tourist-trap burger joint with beer and pool, and **Ed's Cantina** (390 E. Elkhorn Ave., 970/586-2919, www.edscantina.com, 11 A.M.–11 P.M. Mon.–Thurs., 7 A.M.–11 P.M. Fri.–Sun. summer, 11 A.M.–11 P.M. Mon.–Fri., 7 A.M.–11 P.M. Sat.–Sun. winter, $11) is one of many such restaurants clustered around Estes Park's main drag, Elkhorn Avenue. But the one-room Italian restaurant **Sweet Basilico Café** (430 Prospect Village Dr., 970/586-3899, www.sweetbasilico.com, 11 A.M.–10 P.M. Mon.–Fri., 11:30 A.M.–10 P.M. Sat.–Sun. summer, 11 A.M.–9 P.M. Tues.–Fri., 11:30 A.M.–10 P.M. Sat.–Sun. winter, $16) is an exception, geared to fine-diners en route to Rocky Mountain National Park. The homemade dishes include lasagna and excellent minestrone soup. Grab a table in the window and watch all the travelers.

Other upscale Estes Park eateries include the **Wild Rose** (157 W. Elkhorn Ave., 970/586-2806, www.wildroserestaurant.

com, 11 A.M.–10 P.M. daily, $18), which has a long wine list to go with a European menu of seafood, pasta, and steak; **Nicky's Famous Steakhouse** (1350 Fall River Rd., 970/586-5376, www.nickysestespark.com, 7 A.M.–10 P.M. daily Apr.–Sept., 11 A.M.–9:30 P.M. Mon.–Thurs., 8 A.M.–9:30 P.M. Fri.–Sun. Oct.–May, $24), a Greek-style steak restaurant with a wooden interior to match the mountain ambience outside; and the **Dunraven Inn** (2470 Hwy. 66, 970/586-6409, www.dunraveninn.com, 5–9 P.M. daily, $25), an Italian place a few miles from town specializing in seafood and steaks.

Information and Services

For general information on Estes Park, the **Municipal Building** (170 MacGregor Ave., 970/586-5331, www.estesnet.com) has a variety of boilerplate details for locals and visitors. You can also contact the local chamber of commerce (500 Big Thompson Ave., 800/443-7837) or visit www.estesparkcvb.com.

The **Estes Park Medical Center** (555 Prospect Ave., 970/586-2317, www.epmedcenter.com) is a full-service hospital in the area.

LYONS

An arty, hippieish community of 2,000 people, Lyons is 13 miles northwest of Boulder at the intersection of two pretty rivers, the North St. Vrain and South St. Vrain, and two canyons of the same name. It's in the perfect location for mountain travelers, as Highway 7 (S. St. Vrain Dr., toward the Peak-to-Peak Hwy.) and U.S. 36 (N. St. Vrain Dr., toward Estes Park and Rocky Mountain National Park) fork in opposite directions into the foothills. Which, by the way, look spectacular from Main Street in Lyons: green, brown, and red, hovering right over the town without looking too tall or intimidating. Lyons's Main Street is hardly metropolitan, but it has been growing more popular among travelers and beer drinkers in recent years, thanks mostly to a funky brewpub and concert hall called Oskar Blues. Also, perhaps due to the proximity to the foothills, the weather in Lyons is unusually mild year-round: "As the locals say, it's about five degrees cooler than surrounding areas in the summer and about five degrees warmer in the winter," reports one town press release.

History

Sandstone built this town after the Civil War. The red rocks visible in the surrounding mountains were created from sand-dune deposits ages ago, and disappointed men who had traveled to Colorado in the 1880s to find gold in the hills had drifted to pretty areas on the edge of the foothills. One of these was Edward S. Lyon of Connecticut; he and his partners were among the first to open the sandstone-building companies that would ultimately erect numerous buildings in town—liveries, banks, a storage shed for dynamite, and a schoolhouse. By 1890 the red-sandstone building business was booming in Lyons as structures made of this unique and sturdy material, transported by newly built local railroads, popped up in prestigious places, such as the 1893 Chicago World's Fair. Soon, seven quarry companies were employing hundreds of workers in the valley.

The boom lasted 30 years, until the spread of cement gutted the demand for Lyons sandstone. Today, the sandstone industry is considerably smaller, with the venerable Loukonen Brothers Stone, founded by Finnish tanner John Gust Loukonen in 1890, still operated by his six grandchildren.

Fifteen historic buildings made of the original sandstone remain in Lyons, including the **Lyons Redstone Museum** (340 High St., 303/823-5271, www.lyonsredstonemuseum. com, 9:30 A.M.–4 P.M. Mon.–Sat., 12:30–4:30 P.M. Sun. June–Sept., by appointment in other seasons, free), site of the original 1880s schoolhouse. The museum's artifacts include Old West saddles, arrowheads, high-school yearbook photos, and, my particular favorite, a "fainting couch" owned by one W. A. Colt, who helped build several important local roads.

Sports and Recreation

Lyons is centrally located between Rocky Mountain National Park, Boulder County Open Space, and Roosevelt National Park. One of the best Open Space areas is **Rabbit Mountain,** about two miles east of town on the north side of Highway 66; its five miles of trails are especially popular in the spring for the plentiful wildflowers and views of snow-covered peaks. In the portion of the vast Roosevelt National Park that's near Lyons, check out the tree-covered picnic area surrounded by tall canyon walls. It's about eight miles west of Lyons, along Highway 7 next to the south fork of St. Vrain Creek. **Button Rock Preserve** and **Ralph Price Reservoir** are popular local getaways, with Longs Peak and equally pretty Mount Meeker hovering over the water. The best hiking here is the five-mile Sleepy Lion Trail, which climbs from about 6,000 feet elevation to about 6,600 feet. To get to the trailhead, take U.S. 36 four miles from Lyons to County Road 80, turn left, then drive another 2.8 miles to the parking lot at the end of the road. Fishing is allowed at the reservoir, but you'll need a special permit. Permits are $10 and are available from the Longmont City Clerk's Office (350 Kimbark St., Longmont, 303/651-8649, www.ci.longmont.co.us/city_clerk/licenses/fishing.htm).

The best wildlife sightings in the area are at **Heil Valley Ranch** and **Hall Ranch,** both on the southwest edge of Lyons, about one mile from downtown. Take Highway 7 south, turn left onto Highway 84/Old St. Vrain Road, then turn left again onto Red Gulch Road. Here you'll find hawks, elk, bighorn sheep, deer, coyotes, eagles, and (be careful!) mountain lions and rattlesnakes. Most of the trailheads in this broad North Foothills Open Space area are closer to Boulder, but the 5.5-mile **Picture Rock Trail** begins at Red Gulch Road and is beloved by cyclists trying to improve their balance skills on narrow, hilly pathways underneath the foothills. Also try the 3.7-mile **Bitterbush Trail** or the 2.2-mile **Nelson Loop.** The entrance is off Highway 7, about one mile west of Lyons.

The several parks in Lyons itself include **Meadow Park,** west of the intersection of

Highway 7 and Railroad Avenue, home of the beginning of the North St. Vrain River. Tubers and kayakers swear by the Old Swimming Hole, and there are also playgrounds, picnic areas, and RV camping.

For those of us who believe old-school arcade games are a sport, **Lyons Classic Pinball** (339-A Main St., 303/823-6100, www.lyonspinball.com/intro.htm, 5–10 P.M. Thurs., 3–11 P.M. Fri.–Sat., 3–9 P.M. Sun.) is a retro oasis in a PlayStation, Xbox, and iPad world. The games include a giant 1979 Atari-made Hercules pinball machine as well as more familiar stuff like Galaga, Ms. Pacman, and Addams Family pinball.

Entertainment and Nightlife

Planet Bluegrass (500 W. Main St., 800/624-2422, www.bluegrass.com), which runs the Telluride Bluegrass Festival, relocated here years ago. The company's biggest Lyons festivals are the **Rocky Mountain Folks Festival,** the third week in August, featuring stars such as Arlo Guthrie, Steve Earle, Joan Armatrading, and Wilco's Jeff Tweedy; and **RockyGrass,** which draws new bands and legends such as Doc Watson in late July. On a smaller scale, **Lyons Good Old Days** (www.lyons-colorado.com/goodolddays) sponsors various local jazz, rock, and bluegrass artists in Sandstone Park (4th Ave. and Railroad Ave.) all summer.

Club-wise, **Oskar Blues Grill & Brew** (303 Main St., 303/823-6685, www.oskarblues.com, 11 A.M.–10 P.M. Sun.–Thurs., 11 A.M.–2 A.M. Fri.–Sat.) manages to transfer its weird hippie-with-an-edge home-brewing philosophy to its nightly live shows, mostly local acts who specialize in alternative country, reggae, soul, and, of course, blues. The grill opened in 2002 using a home-brewing machine that sealed its cans of Dale's Pale Ale one at a time, and has since expanded to numerous other flavors, including G'Night Imperial Red and Ten Fidy. Next door is **The Old Chubway Expeditious Chow Dispensary** (303 Main St., 303/823-9292, www.oskarblues.com/restaurant/the-old-chubway-expeditious-chow-dispensary), a diner-style lunch spot that puts home brew in the sauces, oils, and even ice cream (although teetotalers have options too).

Shopping

Main Street is jammed with tiny shops devoted to quilting, art, and furniture, and while the shopping scene isn't quite as refined as those in tourist-oriented mountain towns like Steamboat Springs and Estes Park, it's a great strip for bargain-hunters. The **Lyons Outdoor Market** (www.lyonsoutdoormarket.com, 10 A.M.–3 P.M. Sat. mid-May–mid-Oct.) is a combination farmers market and art fair, with 20-some do-it-yourself jewelry artists, farmers, and live musicians competing for strollers' attention. **Red Canyon Art Co.** (400 Main St., 303/823-5900, www.redcanyonart.com, 11 A.M.–5 P.M. daily) has colorful Western paintings of horses and landscapes as well as stained-glass works of all sizes, jewelry, gifts, and the odd wooden bird carving.

Accommodations

Longmont, nine miles away, is the place to go for chain hotels. Lyons's specialty is woodsy cabins such as **Apple Valley Farmstead** (416 Apple Valley Rd., 303/823-6875 or 877/823-6875, www.applevalleyfarmstead.com, $100–150), which has a few different down-home buildings. The Carriage House, for example, has a wooden spiral staircase and a wide balcony; the grounds are full of surprises, from a koi pond to an old tree house to a variety of apple trees.

Food

Formerly Cilantro Mary, **Lyons Fork** (450 Main St., 303/823-5014, www.lyonsfork.com, 11 A.M.–2 P.M. and 4–9 P.M. Mon.–Fri., 8 A.M.–2 P.M. and 4–9 P.M. Sat.–Sun., $14–22) is a family restaurant that has shifted focus from salsa-dominated Mexican food to a diverse menu of chicken pot pie, haystack goat-cheese gnocchi, veal bolognese, and churros. The beers are imported from private brewpubs in Durango, Boulder, San Diego, and elsewhere.

Information

The **Lyons Area Chamber of Commerce** (303/823-5215 or 877/596-6726, www.lyons-colorado.com) has no physical location (an administrator runs it out of her home office) but the website is filled with colorful information about the town. The **Town of Lyons** (432 5th Ave., 303/823-6622, www.townoflyons.com) provides information about spring cleanup days and jogging events, but generally it's more relevant to locals than visitors.

North of Winter Park

Grand County is a spectacular area in the northern Rockies that includes portions of the Routt National Forest, Arapaho National Forest, numerous reservoirs and wilderness areas, Rocky Mountain National Park, and along the northern border, the Continental Divide. This region is perhaps best known for its popular ski town, Winter Park, but it also includes quaint small towns such as Granby, Grand Lake, and Hot Sulphur Springs. The most popular of these for visitors is Grand Lake, with its proximity to three large lakes and all the fishing and sailing that go with them. All three towns are north of Winter Park. To get from the ski resort to Granby, take U.S. 40 northwest about 36 miles; Hot Sulphur Springs is another 11 miles west along U.S. 40. To get to Grand Lake, take U.S. 40 northwest from Winter Park, then turn onto to U.S. 34 and head northeast. All three towns are also accessible from Fort Collins and Estes Park.

GRAND LAKE

On the west edge of Rocky Mountain National Park, Grand Lake has been a high-class tourism area since miners discovered gold in nearby mountain towns in the late 1800s. It has three huge lakes, including Grand Lake itself, the largest natural body of water in Colorado. For centuries, though, the Utes avoided what they called "Spirit Lake." They believed rival tribes, after massacring the men and pushing rafts of women and children into the lake to capsize and die, created evil spirits from the lake mists.

These days, Grand Lake has plenty of fishing, sailing, and golf—and tourism. The shops here have an Old West feel, like those in nearby Estes Park, but the shopping district is fairly substantive for a tourist town.

Sights

At 69 miles one-way, the **Colorado River Headwaters & Scenic Byway** is a little inconvenient for drivers who just want to get from Rocky Mountain National Park to Steamboat Springs. But travelers with a couple of hours to kill should experience it for the scenery—mountains, canyons, springs, lakes, a weirdly out-of-place desert, and, of course, the Colorado River, which runs parallel. The byway begins as U.S. 34 in Grand Lake, heads south to Granby, then curves west through Hot Sulphur Springs, Kremmling, and Radium before ending at State Bridge. From there, look for Highway 131 north, which runs into U.S. 40 and, ultimately, Steamboat Springs. There's a good map at www.coloradodirectory.com/maps/coriver.html.

Sports and Recreation

According to the Grand County Tourism Board, the Grand Lake area has 1,000 miles of streams, 1,000 acres of lakes, and 11,000 acres of reservoirs—most of which contain many different kinds of trout and salmon. The three main lakes are Grand Lake and the bigger reservoirs Lake Granby and Shadow Mountain Lake, and they're all open for ice fishing, sailing, canoeing, and other water sports. On Lake Granby, the **Beacon Landing Marina** (1026 County Rd. 64, 1 mile from U.S. 34, 970/627-3671, www.beaconlanding.us), in business since 1952, offers guided **fishing** trips and rents rods, reels, and boats as well as a place to launch them.

In addition to ice fishing, Grand Lake is

© MATT INDEN/WEAVER MULTIMEDIA GROUP/COLORADO TOURISM OFFICE

Grand Lake

famous for its **snowmobiling**—and has a decent reputation for cross-country skiing and snowshoeing as well. The area has 150 miles of groomed snowmobiling trails—as well as another 150 for bushwhackers—and several companies that rent the vehicles. One of the best is **On the Trail Rentals** (1447 County Rd. 491, 970/627-0171, www.onthetrailrentals.com).

Cross-country skiers and **snowshoers**—not to mention hikers and bikers—find numerous trails, groomed and otherwise, in nearby Arapahoe National Recreation Area, Rocky Mountain National Park, and Indian Peaks Wilderness Area. For access to 18 miles of groomed trails, check out the **Grand Lake Metropolitan Recreation District** (1415 County Rd. 48, 970/627-8872, http://grandlakerecreation.com). For equipment rental, the **Grand Lake Touring Center** (U.S. 34 at County Rd. 48, 0.25 miles west of Grand Lake, 970/627-8008, www.grandlakecolorado.com/touringcenter) has a low-key ski shop.

The city-run **Grand Lake Golf Course** (1415 County Rd. 48, 970/627-8008, http://grandlakerecreation.com/golfmain.html, $64 late June–mid-Sept., $44 mid-May–late June and mid-Sept.–late Oct.) has 18 holes as well as tennis courts and a restaurant.

Nightlife

The **Rocky Mountain Repertory Theatre** (Town Park, 970/627-5087, www.rockymountainrep.com) has been producing local plays, including a regular lineup of youth productions, for decades. Recent shows include *Guys and Dolls* and *Beauty and the Beast.*

Shopping

Grand Avenue is the main drag for visitors and shoppers. Among the best galleries and stores are **Jackstraw Mountain Gallery** (1030 Grand Ave., 970/627-8111, http://jackstrawgallery.com, 10 A.M.–6 P.M. daily summer, 11 A.M.–5 P.M. Mon.–Fri., 10 A.M.–6 P.M. Sat. winter), specializing in watercolor and oil paintings and selling digital prints, and **Humphrey's Cabin Fever** (1100 Grand Ave., 970/627-8939, 10 A.M.–6 P.M. Mon.–Fri., 10 A.M.–7 P.M. Sat.–Sun. summer, reduced hours in winter), selling a range of home products such as furnishings and clothes.

Accommodations

The **Rapids Lodge** (209 Rapids Lane, 970/627-3707, www.rapidslodge.com, $85–185) is in a secluded house on the Tonahutu River, with classic B&B-style guest rooms, many with old-fashioned patterned wallpaper, four-poster beds, and snow-shoes hanging on the walls. The large dark-wood lodge has seven guest rooms, and several smaller log cabins are available as well.

The **Western Riviera** (419 Garfield St., 970/627-3580, www.westernriv.com, $115–300) is the only Grand Lake motel on the lake itself. It's not the fanciest joint in the world—the guest rooms are basic, and the second-floor balconies have plastic deck furniture—but you can't beat the location.

Mountain Lakes Lodge (10480 U.S. 34, 970/627-8448 or 877/627-3220, www. mountainlakeslodge.com, $99–159) has 10 log cabins, built in 1950, as well as the three-bedroom Little Log House, in the middle of the woods about four miles from town. The guest rooms are funky and a little strange, with huge log beds and various sports pictures on the walls. A "good caster" can actually fish from the outdoor deck, according to the lodge website.

Directly next to Rocky Mountain National Park, the pine-built **Grand Lake Lodge** (15500 U.S. 34, 970/627-9495 or 855/585-0004, www.grandlakelodge.com, $125–145) has been renting small cabins since the 1920s—Henry Ford once stayed here, and one of the cabins is named after him. Although it's not super-luxurious, the lodge is worth it for its proximity to Grand and Shadow Mountain Lakes.

Food
Inside the Inn at Grand Lake, the **Sagebrush BBQ & Grille** (1101 Grand Ave., 970/627-1404 or 866/900-1404, www.sagebrushbbq.com, 7 A.M.–10 P.M. daily, $12) displays 1883 iron jail doors on the walls and has some of the best burgers (including vegetarian ones) in town. It also serves seafood, pork, burritos, and, of course, barbecue.

Information
The **Grand Lake Area Chamber of Commerce** (West Portal Rd. and U.S. 34, 970/627-3402 or 800/531-1019, www.grandlakechamber.com) is geared to travelers, posting restaurant, hotel, and recreation listings. The **Town of Grand Lake** (1026 Park Ave., 970/627-3435, www. townofgrandlake.com) is more geared to locals, with information about zoning and permits.

GRANBY
Never mind that Granby is a ranching town in the mountains near Winter Park and Rocky Mountain National Park, or that several rodeos are staged here every year. What most Coloradoans associate wwith Granby these days is a bulldozer. In June 2004 a 51-year-old muffler-shop owner, Marvin Heemeyer, was reportedly upset about a local zoning-board decision and all but destroyed the town with a 75-ton armor-plated bulldozer he rigged himself. After demolishing several Agate Avenue businesses, including a general store and the local newspaper office, Heemeyer ended the carnage by shooting himself to death.

It's a freaky story, even more so because Granby, founded in 1905, is a mountain town at an elevation of 7,935 feet with an otherwise uneventful history, famous for its cowboy culture and history as a major lettuce-production hub. There's not much here, other than ranches and mountain views, but Granby is conveniently located within a few miles of the Winter Park, Arapahoe Basin, Copper Mountain, Keystone, and Loveland ski areas as well as Rocky Mountain National Park and Hot Sulphur Springs.

Sports and Recreation
Colorado State Forest State Park (56750 Hwy. 14, near Walden, 53 miles north of Granby, 970/723-8366, http://parks.state.co.us/parks/stateforest) is almost 71,000 acres of wilderness with 50 miles of clearly marked **hiking** trails and spots to watch elk, antelope, moose, and buffalo. The mountain views here are terrific, thanks especially to the Medicine Bow range, which hits 12,000 feet at some plateaus.

Bird-watching is the primary sport in Granby—other than rodeo—and the **Windy Gap Reservoir** (U.S. 40 and Hwy. 125, about 2 miles west of Granby, 970/725-6200, free) has a wildlife area where it's possible to spot pelicans, eagles, swans, and many other birds.

Anglers are generally better served with the three massive lakes of nearby Grand Lake, but some of the connecting waterways, such as the **Colorado River,** are great for **fishing.** Other places to fetch a giant trout or two are the **Fraser River** and **Willow Creek.** For fishing information—on Lake Granby, Grand Lake, and Shadow Mountain Reservoir, in addition to the Granby spots—contact the **Beacon Landing Marina** (1026 County Rd. 64, 970/627-3671 or 800/864-4372, http://beaconlanding.us).

Granby Ranch (999 Village Rd., 2 miles south of Granby, 970/887-2709 for golf, 800/757-7669 for skiing, www.granbyranch.com, golf $55–75, skiing $61, lower rates off-season) is the only resort in Colorado to give equal billing to both skiing and golfing. The SolVista Basin ski resort is a little invisible, given that Winter Park and Mary Jane are just 15 minutes north, but its 220 inches of snow per year, summit elevation of 9,202 feet, 406 acres of skiable terrain, and a balanced mix of trails for beginners and experts make it an unexpected pleasure. Golf-wise, the club has 18 holes alongside the pretty Fraser River. Also on the premises is a bike park and hiking trails.

The other Granby golf facility is the **Grand Elk Ranch & Club** (1300 Ten Mile Dr., 970/887-9122, www.grandelk.com, $39–95 depending on the season), an 18-hole, par-71 course designed by Craig Stadler and Tripp Davis in 2002.

Accommodations

The **C Lazy U Guest Ranch** (3640 Hwy. 125, 970/887-3344, www.clazyu.com, $2,800–2,900 pp per week, 6 nights minimum) emphasizes horseback riding—there's a 12,000-square-foot indoor riding area—but also offers a pool, tennis and basketball courts, trap-shooting, and hayrides. The lodge is a large wooden building on a 1919 ranch, and it's so luxurious that even celebrities show up with their kids.

Food

The **Longbranch Restaurant** (185 E. Agate Ave., 970/887-2209, 5–9:30 P.M. Mon.–Sat., $15) has an Old West theme—dig the wagon wheels!—despite an unusual predisposition for German food amid the American and Mexican dishes. More family-oriented is **Remington's** (52 4th St., 970/887-3632, www.remingtonsrestaurant.us, 11 A.M.–9 P.M. Mon., 6:30 A.M.–9 P.M. Tues.–Sat., $18), with a wide variety of entrées, including enchiladas, trout, and bacon double cheeseburgers.

Information

The **Grand Lake Area Chamber of Commerce** (970/627-3402 or 800/531-1019) is at www.grandlakechamber.com. And while its focus is real estate, www.grandlakecolorado.com has helpful tourism information as well.

The **Greater Granby Chamber of Commerce** is at 970/887-2311 or 800/325-1661 and www.granbychamber.com. The Granby newspaper, the *Sky-Hi News* (www.skyhidailynews.com), recovered from its brush with the bulldozer and continues to publish once a week.

St. Anthony Granby Medical Center (480 E. Agate Ave., 970/887-7400, www.granbymedicalcenter.org) is a 24-hour hospital that serves the 12,000 regular residents of this area and the additional 48,000 visitors who show up during the summer.

HOT SULPHUR SPRINGS

With a population of 521, Hot Sulphur Springs is a cattle-ranching town with some of the best scenery in tiny Grand County—the Continental Divide, Colorado River, and various tree-lined meadows and hills are within striking distance. But the town's best quality is something the Utes and Arapahos discovered some 9,000 years ago: the springs themselves, which the Utes named "big medicine" and "healing waters." The pools, ranging 104–126°F in temperature, are best experienced at the local spa and resort.

Sights

The **Grand County Historical Association** (110 E. Byers Ave., 970/725-3939, www.grandcountymuseum.com) operates three museums:

the **Pioneer Village Complex** (U.S. 40, east end of Hot Sulphur Springs, 10 A.M.–5 P.M. Tues.–Sat. summer, 10 A.M.–4 P.M. Wed.–Sat. winter, $5), which is in a brick 1924 school building and displays Old West tools and artifacts; the **Cozens Ranch Museum** (U.S. 40 between Winter Park and Fraser, 970/726-5488, 11 A.M.–5 P.M. Wed.–Sat. summer, 10 A.M.–4 P.M. Wed.–Sat. winter, $5), named for the Canadian-born sheriff of Central City and showing various original ranch-house wallpaper and carpet pieces; and the **Heritage Park Museum** (Kremmling, 17 miles west of Hot Sulphur Springs, 970/724-9390, 10 A.M.–5 P.M. Fri.–Sat. summer, $4), in an 1885 two-story log building recently relocated from nearby Wolford Mountain Reservoir.

Accommodations

The **❰ Hot Sulphur Springs Resort & Spa** (5609 County Rd. 20, 20 miles west of Grand Lake, 970/725-3306 or 800/510-6235, www.hotsulphursprings.com, $108–225) has 21 natural mineral springs, some in standard outdoor pools and some at the bottom of rocky holes. The 17 motel rooms and one large 1840s log cabin are wooden and minimalist, with just beds and showers, no telephones or TVs.

Latigo Ranch (Kremmling, about 17 miles west of Hot Sulphur Springs, 970/724-9008 or 800/227-9655, www.latigotrails.com, $2,350–2,750 pp per week) is one of the few secluded mountain lodging properties in Colorado that encourages parents to bring their kids. The horseback-riding and hiking trails wind around lakes and meadows and overlook mountains and forests, and the log-cabin rooms have old-fashioned metal fireplaces and comfortable chairs and couches.

Information

The **Grand County Visitors Center** (www.rkymtnhi.com/visitors/grandtour.html) site has excellent information on Hot Sulphur Springs, a town so small it doesn't have its own website. For details on the springs themselves, contact the resort at 970/725-3306 or www.hotsulphursprings.com.

Fort Collins

Home of both Colorado State University and a wide-open swath of farms and ranches, Fort Collins is a 126,000-resident college town that lacks the loopy yuppies of Boulder and the conservative red-staters of fellow northern Colorado towns like Greeley and Fort Morgan. It's on the Cache La Poudre, a tree-lined river that flows from Rocky Mountain National Park and the Front Range, so it attracts outdoors enthusiasts of all types, and at 60 miles north of Denver it's the perfect combination of isolated and populated.

Fort Collins came into being in 1862, when U.S. soldiers arrived to watch over the Cherokee Trail and the Overland Stage Line, but the "old fort" lasted only four years. Its future arrived in 1860, when settlers created an irrigation ditch for the Cache La Poudre; farmers, ranchers, and a major railroad followed shortly thereafter. CSU opened in 1870 with 25,000 students, and although the student body has shrunk somewhat since then, the college provides the city's largest number of jobs.

Today, Fort Collins is a medium-sized city with a downtown area (historic Old Town Square) that resembles Boulder's University Hill, with all the pierced-nosed kids, sweatshirt-wearing alumni, and microbreweries, microbreweries, and more microbreweries that implies.

SIGHTS
Old Town Square

Old Town Square (Mountain Ave. and College Ave.) was a business district in the late 1800s; some of the few remaining original buildings include a drugstore called Old Grout on the corner of Mountain and College Avenues. A National Historic District, the square is known

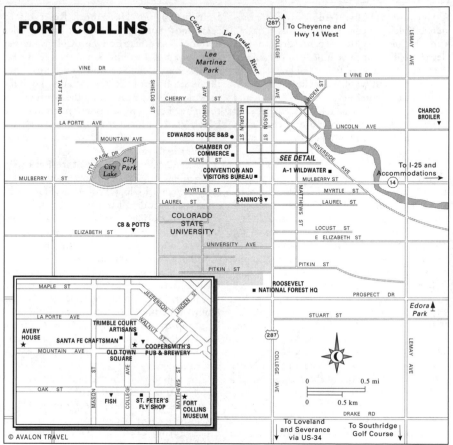

© AVALON TRAVEL

today as the center of college life, with a lively mix of bars and restaurants, shops, and galleries. One of the best-known buildings is the sandstone **Avery House** (328 W. Mountain Ave., 970/221-0533, www.poudrelandmarks.com, 1–4 P.M. Sat.–Sun., free), named for original Fort Collins street builder, bank founder, and agricultural pioneer Franklin Avery, who built this family home in 1879.

Fort Collins Museum and Discovery Science Center

The Fort Collins Museum (200 Mathews St., 970/221-6738, www.ci.fort-collins. co.us/museum, 10 A.M.–5 P.M. Tues.–Sat., noon–5 P.M. Sun., $4) has three late-1800s buildings in its courtyard and a main gallery of sugar beet–farming artifacts and a mud wagon. Andrew Carnegie coughed up $12,500 to fund the museum's sandstone building, originally the city's public library, in 1904. Recently the museum partnered with the Discovery Science Center, expanding the museum's focus to electricity experiments, planetarium shows, and kids' science classes.

Environmental Learning Center

The Environmental Learning Center (2400 S.

County Rd. 9, 970/491-1661, http://elc.war-nercnr.colostate.edu, sunrise–sunset daily), run by Colorado State's Natural Resources department about three miles east of campus, preserves 212 acres of forest and grassland for local hikers and wildlife watchers. There's an information center and a 1.2-mile trail, and staff members are on hand for guided tours and questions. Also on the premises is the Rocky Mountain Raptor Program, a haven for a variety of birds.

Brewery Tours
It's a little random that the St. Louis company **Anheuser-Busch** (2351 Busch Dr., 970/490-4691, www.budweisertours.com/toursFTC.htm, 10 A.M.–4 P.M. Thurs.–Mon. Oct.–May, 10 A.M.–4 P.M. daily June–Sept., free) runs brewery tours in Fort Collins, but this is one of five tour locations in the United States.

Fort Collins is also a huge microbrewery town, and several of those give tours as well—the **Odell Brewing Co.** (800 E. Lincoln Ave., 970/498-9070 or 888/887-2797, www.odell-brewing.com, 11 A.M.–6 P.M. Mon.–Thurs., 11 A.M.–7 P.M. Fri.–Sat., tours at 1, 2, and 3 P.M. Mon.–Sat., free), which in the late 1980s sold its homebrews out of the back of a truck, is the most interesting.

Swetsville Zoo
Noted in the bible of goofy American traveling attractions *Roadside America,* Swetsville Zoo (4801 E. Harmony Rd., 970/484-9509, dawn–dusk daily, free) is ex-farmer Bill Swets's menagerie of dinosaurs, ducks, and robots constructed from scraps of old cars and farm machines. Do not miss the Autosaurus II, a fully operable monstrosity with huge eyes, a tongue, and a Ford 351 engine.

SPORTS AND RECREATION
Hiking and Biking
Fort Collins isn't far from Rocky Mountain National Park and the foothills of Boulder, of course, but its own 2,700-acre, waterfall-strewn **Horsetooth Mountain Open Space** is a local hiker-and-biker paradise, climbing

from 5,430-foot Horsetooth Reservoir to 7,255-foot Horsetooth Rock. It has 29 miles of trails. To get there from Fort Collins, start at Harmony and Taft Hill Road, then turn west onto County Road 38E until you get to either the South Bay or Inlet Bay entrance. Look for parking and the trailhead on the north side of the road. For more information, contact the **Bison Visitors Center** (1800 S. County Rd. 31, Loveland, 970/679-4570, www.larimer.org/parks/htmp.htm).

Also at 2,500 acres, **Lory State Park** (708 Lodgepole Dr., 970/493-1623, www.parks.state.co.us/parks/lory/Pages/LoryStatePark.aspx) has 25 miles of trails for hikers, bikers, and horseback riders—it's a great spot for looking at wildlife, birds, and wildflowers too. It's on the northwest side of Horsetooth Reservoir. Try the 1.7-mile **Arthur's Rock Trail;** the views of the reservoir and the mountains at the top are worth the difficult uphill stretch. Just inside the park entrance is **Corral Center Mountain Bike Park,** one of the only public pump tracks in the state. (A pump track has a series of dirt berms and jumps to help beginning mountain bikers learn in a safe environment.)

Other good trails in the Fort Collins area: **Poudre River** (N. Taft Hill Rd., near the Environmental Learning Center on E. Drake Rd.), which goes along the river for about eight miles; **Spring Creek** (W. Drake Rd., at the intersection of the Poudre Trail), a 6.6-mile path that goes through many parks, including Southwest Community Park; and **Foothills** (along Horsetooth Reservoir, beginning at Dixon Reservoir), a 5.8-mile trip through rough terrain. For more information on these trails, as well as on parks and a bike map, contact the city's **Parks Department** (413 S. Bryan Ave., 970/221-6660, www.fcgov.com/parks).

Fishing
The 6.5-mile-long **Horsetooth Reservoir** (County Rd. 38E, west of Harmony Rd. and Taft Hill Rd., 970/498-7000, www.co.larimer.co.us/parks/horsetooth.htm, $7), north of Fort Collins, includes the massive Horsetooth

Rock, which, according to Native American legend, was once a giant slain by heroic Chief Maunamoku. It's the best fishing spot in the area and also has facilities for boating, waterskiing, and picnicking. Part of Larimer County Natural Resources, the reservoir has two main camping areas (970/679-4570, www.larimercamping.com, $15–20), the South Bay Campground and the Inlet Bay Campground.

Other excellent fishing holes: the **Cache La Poudre River,** which passes through Fort Collins between the Rockies and the South Platte River, and **Red Feather Lakes,** about 30 miles northwest of the city, north of the intersection of Rist Canyon Road and Manhattan Road. Red Feather Lakes has several campgrounds and a small grocery nearby; **West Lake Campground** (877/444-6777, $15), with 35 sites, has the most privacy. Some sites have views of the lake or Rocky Mountain National Park.

Fort Collins is also home of the superb **St. Peter's Fly Shop** (202 Remington St., 970/498-8968, www.stpetes.com), whose guided tours, not to mention tips and information, span northern Colorado and part of Wyoming.

White-Water Rafting

The Cache La Poudre River can get pretty choppy as it descends from Rocky Mountain National Park to the Fort Collins area, and **A-1 Wildwater** (2801 N. Shields St., 970/224-3379 or 800/369-4165, www.a1wildwater.com) gives tours for all the degrees of rafting difficulty, from placid to wild.

Golf

The **Collindale Golf Course** (1441 East Horsetooth Rd., 970/221-6651, www.fcgov.com/golf/collindale.php, $30–33) is a city-run 18-hole course that occasionally sponsors local qualifying matches for the U.S. Open. The clubhouse is new, the course is spread out, and the lessons are first-rate.

Spectator Sports

Colorado State University operates in the

kayaking the Cache La Poudre River near Fort Collins

shadow of the University of Colorado at Boulder, but its Rams sports teams occasionally bludgeon the Buffaloes. Although the college competes in volleyball, basketball, baseball, and swimming, its most popular sport is football—**Hughes Stadium** (800/491-7267, www.csurams.com/facilities/hughes-stadium.html) is the home of the Rams. CSU and CU face off in football just about every fall at Denver's Sports Authority Field at Mile High Stadium.

NIGHTLIFE

Although it's part of a Colorado-and-Wyoming chain, Fort Collins's **C.B. & Potts** (1415 W. Elizabeth St., 970/221-1139, www.cbpotts.com/colorado/fortcollins.shtml, 11 A.M.–2 A.M. Mon.–Fri., 10 A.M.–2 A.M. Sat.–Sun.) has far more character—and better buffalo wings—than its counterparts. **Coopersmith's Pub & Brewery** (5 Old Town Square, 970/498-0483, http://coopersmithspub.com, 11 A.M.–11 P.M. Sun.–Thurs., 11 A.M.–1 A.M. Fri.–Sat.) is the college-leaning pub alter ego of the pool hall and pizza joint across the nearby walkway. If you can get in, the teeny-tiny **Town Pump** (124 N. College Ave., 970/493-4404, www.fortcollinstownpump.com, 3 P.M.–midnight Mon.–Fri., noon–midnight Sat., 11 A.M.–midnight Sun.) has some of the city's best atmosphere.

For live music, the **Mishawaka Amphitheatre** (13714 Poudre Canyon Hwy., Bellvue, 970/482-4420, www.themishawaka.com) is one of those cozy little mountain clubs, like the Buffalo Rose in Golden, and it attracts mostly local performers, although national acts such as David Grisman and Marc Cohn have headlined in recent years. In Fort Collins itself, **Avogadro's Number** (605 S. Mason St., 970/493-5555, www.avogadros.com, 7 A.M.–1:15 A.M. daily) has been booking bands since 1971; acts in recent years have included folk singers Greg Brown and Tish Hinojosa.

SHOPPING

Fort Collins's two main shopping districts are Old Town Square and Foothills Mall. **Old Town Square** (Mountain Ave. and College Ave.) has funky little boutiques and shops such as the gem- and fossil-selling **Nature's Own** (201 Linden Ave., 970/484-9701, www.naturesown.com, 10 A.M.–6 P.M. Mon.–Sat., 11 A.M.–5 P.M. Sun.) and the Southwestern jewelry and pottery gift store **Santa Fe Craftsman Inc.** (118 N. College Ave., 970/224-1415, www.santafecraftsman.com, 10 A.M.–7 P.M. Mon.–Fri., 10 A.M.–6 P.M. Sat., noon–5 P.M. Sun.). **Foothills Mall** (215 E. Foothills Pkwy., 970/226-5555, www.shopfoothills.com, 10 A.M.–9 P.M. Mon.–Sat., 11 A.M.–6 P.M. Sun.) is anchored by Sears and Macy's.

The city's best-known art gallery is **Trimble Court Artisans** (118 Trimble Court, 970/221-0051, www.trimblecourt.com, 10 A.M.–6 P.M. Mon.–Sat., noon–5 P.M. Sun.), which has operated here since 1971 and has grown to a co-op of 50 mostly local artists who contribute pottery, paintings, jewelry, stained glass, and other media.

ACCOMMODATIONS

Fort Collins has one hotel from roughly every major chain, and unlike Boulder or Denver, just a few are unique locally owned hotels or bed-and-breakfasts.

A beautiful Victorian home built in 1904, **◖ Edwards House B&B** (402 W. Mountain Ave., 970/493-9191 or 800/281-9190, www.edwardshouse.com, $99–175) has high ceilings, wooden floors, stained-glass windows, a large wooden staircase, excellent breakfast, whirlpools and claw-foot tubs in the guest rooms, and all the other amenities you'd expect from a bed-and-breakfast—only a little more solid, as if the inn were of a piece with the large surrounding trees.

The guest rooms at the business-oriented **Plaza Hotel Fort Collins** (3836 E. Mulberry St., 970/484-4660, http://plazahotelftcollins.com, $60–90) are pretty basic, like what you'd find at a Marriott or Holiday Inn, but the inn's real advantage is a large indoor-outdoor heated pool, along with a sauna and a hot tub. An alternative at the same price is the **Guesthouse Inns and Suites** (4333 E. Mulberry St., 970/493-9000 or 800/234-5548, www.mulberry-inn.com, $65–75), formerly the

Mulberry Inn, with hot tubs in every room and an outdoor pool.

The 800,000-acre **Roosevelt National Forest** (2150 Centre Ave., 970/295-6600, www.fs.fed.us/r2/arnf/recreation) has 53 campgrounds with more than 1,000 sites in various locations, most with running water, toilets, picnic tables, and grates for making fires.

FOOD

The **Back Porch Café** (1101 E. Lincoln Ave., 970/224-2338, http://thebackporchcafe.com, 7 A.M.–2 P.M. daily, $16) is perhaps best known for its breakfasts (the green chili–covered breakfast burritos with chorizo are especially popular), but it also serves solid American dinner fare like ribs, chicken-fried steak, and fried fish.

Fish (150 W. Oak St., 970/224-1188, www.fishmkt.com, 11 A.M.–9 P.M. Mon.–Sat., 4–8 P.M. Sun., $20) is an upscale but affordable seafood (duh) restaurant.

Canino's (613 S. College Ave., 970/493-7205, www.caninositalianrestaurant.com, 11 A.M.–9 P.M. daily, $18) is Fort Collins's predominant Italian restaurant, in a classic old house, with homemade desserts to go with the usual pasta and eggplant parmigiana dishes.

The **Charco Broiler** (1716 E. Mulberry St., 970/482-1472, www.charcobroiler.com, 6 A.M.–10 P.M. Sun.–Thurs., 11 A.M.–10:30 P.M. Fri.–Sat., $15) is one of those old-school steakhouses with a dark 1970s ambience. For years it has been one of Fort Collins's best restaurants, although it's not exactly hip and modern these days.

Yum Yum Restaurant (1300 W. Elizabeth St., 970/493-7937, www.yumyumsfortcollins.com, 11 A.M.–9 P.M. Mon.–Sat., $10) is a Lebanese fixture, operating since 1991, with Middle Eastern standbys such as hummus, baba ghanoush, falafel, stuffed grape leaves, and chicken *shawarma*.

The Nepalese **Mt. Everest Café** (1113 W. Drake Rd., 970/223-8212, http://mteverestcafe.com, 11 A.M.–2:30 P.M. and 5–9:30 P.M. daily, $13) draws the campus crowd with its $12.95 all-you-can-eat dinner buffet ($8.95 at lunchtime), and dishes from the requisite

chicken tikka masala to the more elaborate Sherpa stew bring in the slightly older crowd.

In Severance, about 16 miles southeast of Fort Collins, the only famous attraction is the Rocky Mountain oyster, known more technically as—and there's really no elegant way of saying this—bull testicles. The delicacy has achieved quite the reputation statewide in recent decades, but one of the first to serve it was **Bruce's Bar** (123 1st St., Severance, 970/686-2320, 10 A.M.–9:30 P.M. Sun.–Thurs., 10 A.M.–2 A.M. Fri.–Sat., $10). The restaurant closed in 2006 when founder Bruce Ruth died, and her son failed to secure a liquor-license transfer. In a strange and wonderful twist, Jairo Landeros and Bruce Carron purchased the bar and reopened it in 2008. The new owners' sons had been wrestlers for nearby Berthoud High School who endured a car accident, lost their legs, and became well-known in local media for their courage.

INFORMATION AND SERVICES

The **City of Fort Collins** (300 LaPorte Ave., 970/221-6505, www.fcgov.com) is particularly helpful with parks-and-recreation listings, but its website is also a key stop for local residents. Travelers may find the **Fort Collins Convention & Visitors Bureau** (19 Old Town Square, Suite 137, 970/232-3840 or 800/274-3678, http://visit.ftcollins.com) more useful. The local newspaper is the *Coloradoan* (www.coloradoan.com), and it posts dining listings and restaurant reviews online. For CSU information, contact the college (College Ave., 970/491-1101, www.colostate.edu).

Fort Collins has a community radio station: **KRFC** (88.9 FM), which focuses on folk and blues music as well as local news and public affairs.

The Fort Collins area's main hospital is the **Poudre Valley Hospital** (1024 S. Lemay Ave., 970/495-7000, http://pvhs.org/pvh).

The central post office is at 301 East Boardwalk Drive.

Laundries include **Country Clean Coin-Op Laundry** (3765 S. College Ave., 970/223-4860) and the **Laundry Basket** (925 S. Taft Hill Rd., 970/484-4980).

ASPEN AND THE SKI TOWNS

Since the first ski resort, Howelsen Ski Hill, opened in Steamboat Springs almost a century ago, those long slats attached to people's feet have defined Colorado's identity and propped up its massive tourism industry. What's the appeal for the 11 million visitors who come to the state's 25 ski resorts every year? Just the opportunity to stand on the edge of a giant snow-covered bowl, with evergreen-covered skylines in the distance, impossibly fresh air in their faces, and a bumpy plunge from a 12,000-foot mountain.

Most of Colorado's best-known ski areas bunch up around I-70, near the Continental Divide, the backbone of the Rocky Mountains. Aspen, Vail, Keystone, Winter Park, Breckenridge, Steamboat Springs, and Arapahoe Basin, just to name the best-known resorts, have for decades created a local culture. The nearby University of Colorado is a haven for hard-partying ski bums, and hippie rock bands such as String Cheese Incident and Leftover Salmon have perfectly captured the laid-back mentality of the knit-cap-and-hiking-boot set. (For a while, punk-rocking snowboarders threatened to puncture this culture, but in recent years boarders and skiers have come to a sort of détente—and all major Colorado ski areas offer snowboarding lessons.)

Each resort has a well-defined personality—Vail and Aspen attract the ritziest clientele and have the high-priced shopping districts to prove it, while A-Basin has far fewer frills to go with its amazing mountain views, and the City of Denver–owned Winter Park is full of unpretentious townie bars and restaurants.

HIGHLIGHTS

◖ Wheeler Opera House: The cultural heart of Aspen since 1889, the Wheeler continues to bring great entertainment to town, from bluegrass to blues and independent films (page 144).

◖ Snowmass Mountain: Each of Aspen's four mountains has its advantages, but none is as diverse as Snowmass, with its trails for beginners and experts alike (page 157).

◖ Vail Mountain: Skiers argue endlessly about the virtues of Aspen over Steamboat Springs or A-Basin over Copper Mountain. But everybody agrees that Vail's 3,000-acre Back Bowls are incomparable (page 167).

◖ Arapahoe Basin: A local favorite, A-Basin is the highest ski area in the United States, staying open through June or July; "Beachin' at the Basin" is Colorado's largest tailgate party (page 198).

◖ Mount Evans Scenic and Historic Byway: Other than Pikes Peak, this is the only 14,000-foot-high mountain in the United States open for automobile traffic; the views are worth it (page 213).

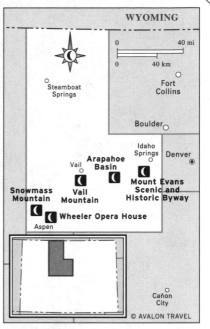

LOOK FOR ◖ TO FIND RECOMMENDED SIGHTS, ACTIVITIES, DINING, AND LODGING.

Expect crowds during the high season, roughly November through February, especially when the sun is out after a large snowfall. But Coloradoans know to avoid the crush and look for off-season deals.

The best of these happen away from ski season, in April and October, when hotels and restaurants are amazingly cheap and the weather remains nice enough for hiking and cycling excursions. In addition to the slopes and moguls, the High Rockies are filled with breathtaking forests and parks, such as the White River National Forest in Aspen and the Devil's Thumb Ranch north of Winter Park. Whitewater rafting, sailing, hot-air ballooning, and hang gliding are just some of the other popular summer sports in these parts.

PLANNING YOUR TIME

Spending time in all the major Summit County ski areas—that is, the ones along I-70, not counting Telluride, several hours to the southwest—will require at least a few weeks and a willingness to drive vast distances. Most out-of-state skiers pick their favorite resort and stick with it for a long weekend; they often take shuttle buses from Denver International Airport or nearby towns such as Boulder and Colorado Springs. Once you're there, the resorts are pretty much self-contained, and you'll have food, entertainment, and, of course, skiing within walking or shuttle-bus distance.

More ambitious trips, hitting several areas, require greater planning. The most manageable strategy is to drive from the Denver

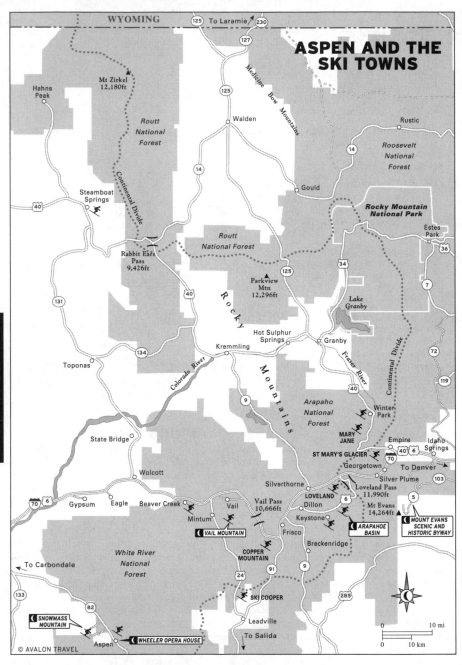

ASPEN AND THE SKI TOWNS

WYOMING

To Laramie

Mt Zirkel
12,180ft

Hahns Peak

Routt National Forest

Walden

Medicine Bow Mountains

Rustic

Roosevelt National Forest

Steamboat Springs

Continental Divide

Gould

Rocky Mountain National Park

Estes Park

Rabbit Ears Pass
9,426ft

Routt National Forest

Parkview Mtn
12,296ft

Lake Granby

Toponas

Hot Sulphur Springs

Kremmling

Granby

Fraser River

Colorado River

Rocky Mountains

Continental Divide

State Bridge

Arapaho National Forest

Winter Park

MARY JANE

Empire

Idaho Springs

Wolcott

ST MARY'S GLACIER

Georgetown

Silver Plume

Silverthorne

Loveland Pass
11,990ft

To Denver

Gypsum

Eagle

Beaver Creek

Vail

Vail Pass
10,666ft

LOVELAND
Dillon

Loveland Pass
11,990ft

Mt Evans
14,264ft

MOUNT EVANS SCENIC AND HISTORIC BYWAY

To Carbondale

Mintum

VAIL MOUNTAIN

White River National Forest

COPPER MOUNTAIN

Frisco

Keystone

ARAPAHOE BASIN

Breckenridge

SNOWMASS MOUNTAIN

SKI COOPER

WHEELER OPERA HOUSE

Aspen

Leadville

To Salida

© AVALON TRAVEL

0   10 mi

0   10 km

© STEVE KNOPPER

Consider planning your ski trip to return home along I-70 outside of rush hour – Sunday afternoons and evenings are the worst.

airport—and you'll definitely need a car, some maps, and weather reports—and begin the trip on the eastern edge of the Rockies. Check out Idaho Springs, with its surprisingly great restaurants, and Georgetown, which has superb views and the nearby Mount Evans, then make your first stop in Keystone and hit Arapahoe Basin just a few miles away. Skiers will want to plan full days at each resort; explorers and hikers may find it easier to wander around a bit before moving to the next area.

Winter Park is about an hour off I-70, so it's almost certain to be a separate trip. Then get back on I-70, head west, and cover the Dillon/ Silverthorne, Frisco, and Copper Mountain areas before settling in Vail. Beaver Creek is half an hour to the west, and you should save time for an evening trip to perfect little Minturn.

Note that the climate in the Rockies is far more extreme and unpredictable than in Denver or Boulder, so pack a mixture of outfits even in the heart of summer or winter. And check driving conditions in advance; it's not uncommon for a snowstorm to slow I-70 to a crawl around the Eisenhower Tunnel. There are other routes back to the Denver airport, but they all involve tinier and more vulnerable mountain roads.

Aspen and Vicinity

While wandering the streets of downtown Aspen, glance at the housing prices in the realtors' windows. They're incredible—mountain hamlet homes in the tens of millions of dollars. They demonstrate why Aspen is among the most in-demand and expensive cities in Colorado's Rocky Mountains. The city has a charming downtown area filled with superb hotels and gourmet restaurants, and it's located directly beneath four towering mountains: Snowmass, Aspen Highlands, Aspen Mountain, and Buttermilk. But with home prices averaging $4 million, it's one of the most expensive cities in the United States, so celebrities such as Jack Nicholson, Kevin Costner, Kurt Russell, Goldie Hawn, and Chris Evert are among the elite few who can live here.

But Aspen is an irresistible place to visit because it gets the best of everything in Colorado. No single hotel in the state, and almost none in the country, is as luxurious as the Little Nell. The country's best chefs and sommeliers have migrated to restaurants of incredible diversity and quality, from the sushi temple Matsuhisa to the Asian-and-Southwestern Syzygy. The bars are inviting, the town square centers on the serene Aspen Fountain, and there's no better place to wander, whether it's through the town square or in the surrounding mountain wilderness.

Town & Country magazine once called Aspen Mountain—the one that looms directly over the city, with the Silver Queen Gondola—"the great equalizer." It doesn't matter how much money you have or how well you're dressed as long as you're a skier who can navigate the slippery drops and complex masses of trees and steep moguls. That's true, and Aspen Mountain's 11,000-foot views of the city are stunning enough to impress skiers, hikers, and shoppers of any socioeconomic level. But the city has, over the past 140 years, taken on the identity of a rich person's town, and some out-of-town skiers and Coloradoans deliberately avoid its overwhelming fashion consciousness and high prices in favor of A-Basin or Winter Park.

People who've never been to Aspen may envision streets lined with gold and fur coats in every window. They should visit. It's also oddly laid-back, and even the snootiest restaurants and hotels aim to make guests relax, rather than be uptight in their tuxedos and cocktail dresses. Plus, the late, great gonzo journalist Hunter S. Thompson lived in nearby Woody Creek for decades. So how pretentious can it be?

Despite sticker-shock prices on gas and food, it's still possible to find good deals, like the ultramodern Sky Hotel (especially in the off-season).

HISTORY

Although the Utes first discovered the Aspen region, calling it "Shining Mountain," silver miners arrived in the 1870s, attempting to strike it rich during the Colorado gold rush. Twenty years later, though, the U.S. government demonetized silver, and the poor sap who subsequently discovered a 2,350-pound nugget was out of luck. Aspen descended into relative poverty for the next five decades—even Jerome B. Wheeler, the Macy's department store magnate who built the Wheeler Opera House and the Hotel Jerome, declared bankruptcy in 1901—but it discovered a far richer substance to replace silver in the 1930s.

Snow became Aspen's primary business around 1936, and while World War II delayed investors' plans for a major ski area, out-of-town industrialists founded Aspen Skiing Corp. within a decade. Condominiums boomed throughout the region in the 1960s, and Snowmass grew into a resort of its own; by the 1970s, Aspen had developed a worldwide reputation for high-class skiing. Developers and celebrities have moved to town ever since, and as a result Aspen's outdoor charms have become out of reach for almost everybody else.

SIGHTS
Wheeler-Stallard House Museum

One of several houses built by founding father Jerome B. Wheeler, the Wheeler-Stallard House Museum (620 W. Bleecker St., 970/925-3721 or 800/925-3721, www.heritageaspen.org/wsh.html, 1–5 P.M. Tues.–Sat., $6) is an 1888 Victorian building that frequently undergoes renovations and updates. The high-class Spirit of Aspen exhibit, which includes a full-floor tribute to late local singer-songwriter John Denver, is open most of the year.

Aspen Art Museum

The Aspen Art Museum (590 N. Mill St., 970/925-8050, www.aspenartmuseum.org, 10 A.M.–6 P.M. Tues.–Wed. and Fri.–Sat.,

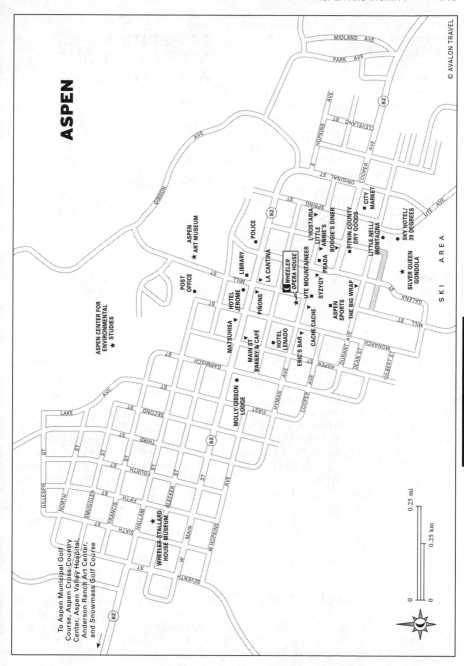

ASPEN

© AVALON TRAVEL

To Aspen Municipal Golf
Course, Aspen Cross-Country
Center, Aspen Valley Hospital,
Anderson Ranch Art Center,
and Snowmass Golf Course

★ ASPEN CENTER FOR ENVIRONMENTAL STUDIES

★ ASPEN ART MUSEUM

★ WHEELER-STALLARD HOUSE MUSEUM

POST OFFICE

HOTEL JEROME

LIBRARY

POLICE

PIÑONS

LA CANTINA

MATSUHISA

MAIN ST BAKERY & CAFÉ

HOTEL LENADO

ERIC'S BAR

MOLLY GIBSON LODGE

WHEELER OPERA HOUSE

UTE MOUNTAINEER

SYZYGY

CACHE CACHE

L'HOSTARIA

LITTLE ANNIE'S

PRADA

BOOGIE'S DINER

ASPEN SPORTS

THE BIG WRAP

PITKIN COUNTY DRY GOODS

LITTLE NELL

MONTAGNA

CITY MARKET

SKY HOTEL/ 39 DEGREES

SILVER QUEEN GONDOLA

SKI AREA

ASPEN AND THE SKI TOWNS

0   0.25 mi

0   0.25 km

10 A.M.–7 P.M. Thurs., noon–6 P.M. Sun., free) emphasizes modern art, such as (in recent exhibits) Donald Judd's minimalist *Green Desk with Two Chairs* and Haegue Yang's three-dimensional sci-fi constructions made out of wires, light bulbs, and pine cones. Eventually the museum will relocate to a building designed by architect Shigeru Ban, at South Spring Street and East Hyman Avenue, which will ultimately contain 12,500 square feet of space for exhibitions, a sculpture garden on the roof, and various new bookstores and classrooms. The new building, which will cost an estimated $30 million in donations, had a groundbreaking ceremony in August 2011; construction was to begin in early 2012, and the project was supposed to be completed by late 2013.

◖ Wheeler Opera House

It's appropriate that Aspen's best-known historical sight, the Wheeler Opera House (320 E. Hyman St., 970/920-5770, www.wheeleroperahouse.com, box office 11 A.M.–7 P.M. daily), is named for a wealthy New Yorker. Wheeler arrived in 1883 to get a piece of the silver-mining boom, and he wound up building a good portion of the town, including his own home, the Hotel Jerome, the Wheeler Bank, and this still-ornate building. When built, it had crimson velvet drapes, gold plush seats, and a silver star–studded azure ceiling. Today, after a $4.5 million renovation completed in 1984, it's open for about 300 events a year, including movies, touring bands, and a new comedy event called the Laff Festival. (Sadly, the HBO-sponsored U.S. Comedy Arts Festival, which drew big names such as Conan O'Brien and reunited Cheech & Chong, recently changed its name and relocated to Las Vegas.) The house is open for individual concerts and events as well as tours.

SPORTS AND RECREATION
Downhill Skiing and Snowboarding

Since 1950, when Olympic skier Dick Durrance took a job at the Aspen Skiing Co.

CELEBRITIES OF ASPEN (PART-TIME, AT LEAST)

- Jack Nicholson

- Kurt Russell, Goldie Hawn, and daughter Kate Hudson

- Antonio Banderas and Melanie Griffith

- Robert Wagner and Jill St. John

- Glenn Frey of the Eagles

- Kevin Costner

- John Oates of Hall & Oates

- Don Johnson

- Catherine Zeta-Jones and Michael Douglas

- Nick Nolte

- Martina Navratilova

Sources: *The Denver Post, Rocky Mountain News*

---

and brought the FIS World Championships to town, Aspen has been prime territory in a state that knows its chutes and moguls. Aspen's resort is actually four mountains—Snowmass, Buttermilk, Aspen Highlands, and Aspen Mountain (or Ajax, the big one that overshadows the town). They're all within 14 miles of each other, and together they encompass 4,993 acres of ski trails.

With a summit elevation of 11,200 feet, **Aspen Mountain** is known for its massive bumps and expert runs (it has no trails for beginners). The longest run is three miles, and some of the groomed paths take skiers almost directly into town. The mountain has eight lifts, and the Silver Queen Gondola goes from bottom to top in 14 minutes; many skiers, after spending the morning on high-up Ruthie's

Road or Buckhorn, break for lunch at the mountainside restaurant Bonnie's. Shrines to Jimi Hendrix, Elvis Presley, John Denver, and Jerry Garcia are among the wacky snow-covered sights. Extreme-sports enthusiasts are directed instead to the terrain parks at Snowmass and Buttermilk mountains; Aspen Mountain didn't even allow boarders until 2001.

Many consider **Aspen Highlands** the best skiing mountain not only in Aspen but in the entire state. Locals worship it for the frighteningly steep and bumpy Highland Bowl, Olympic Bowl, and Steeplechase runs. Its disadvantage used to be old, poky lifts, but today it has four, including three high-speed quads. The Highlands has far more beginner runs than Aspen Mountain, including the short and popular Red Onion and Exhibition, and there are seven restaurants on the mountain, notably Cloud Nine Alpine Bistro. The majestic views of the Maroon Bells and Pyramid Peak defy description.

Buttermilk, site of ESPN's Winter X Games for six straight years, is sort of the reverse image of Aspen Mountain. The runs are predominantly for beginners, and there are no expert trails whatsoever. The Ski & Snowboard School is also here, areas are available for kids, and the mood is considerably less intense and show-offy than the other Aspen mountains. Buttermilk is especially inviting for boarders, given its five terrain parks, from the expert-only X Park to the entry-level S3 Park (which includes a ski and snowboard school). The mountain contains 100 features overall, including barrel bonks, propane tanks, flat boxes, side hits, and a 22-foot Zaugg-cut superpipe.

The **Ski & Snowboard School** has 1,200 pros from all over the world, and it offers lessons to skiers of all ages and skill levels. The typical group lesson is $140, but private lessons are more expensive, as are beginners lessons and courses tailored to women and other special groups. Call 970/925-1227 (Aspen Mountain), 970/544-3020 (Highlands), or 970/920-0788 (Buttermilk) to set something up.

The **Aspen Skiing Company** (970/925-1220 or 800/308-6935, www.aspensnowmass.com, lift tickets $104) operates the ski area at all four mountains; information on the website comes directly from the company. For equipment rental, the resort recommends **Aspen/Snowmass Four-Mountain Sports** (8 locations at Aspen and Snowmass, 970/923-1227 or 877/282-7736, www.aspensnowmass.com/onmountain/rentals/dandesports.cfm) and **D&E Ski & Snowboard Shop** (520 E. Durant Ave., 970/920-2337, www.aspensnowmass.com/onmountain/rentals/danderetail.cfm), but experienced locals look for better deals at the many sporting-goods stores in the area. **Aspen Sports** (408 E. Cooper Ave., 970/925-6331, www.aspensports.com) and **Pomeroy Sports** (614 E. Durant Ave., 970/925-7875, www.pomeroysports.com) have wide selections and helpful staff.

Cross-Country Skiing and Other Winter Sports

For skiers who find Aspen's official resort runs a bit too limiting, the Roaring Fork Valley is filled with out-of-the-way paths. Inexperienced backcountry skiers should start with guided tours: **Aspen Mountain Powder Tours** (Aspen Mountain, Silver Queen Gondola Bldg., 970/920-0720 or 800/525-6200, ext. 3720, www.aspensnowmass.com/onmountain/moremountainfun/powdertours.cfm) brings groups of snowcat skiers at 8:15 A.M. daily to trails on 1,000 acres of the backside of the mountain. Also giving guided tours, only via standard chairlifts rather than snowcats, are **Aspen Alpine Guides** (970/925-6618, www.aspenalpine.com) and **Aspen Expeditions** (115 Boomerang Rd., Suite 5201A, Aspen Highlands, 970/925-7625, www.aspenexpeditions.com).

For solo exploring, backcountry skiers should look for the best warm-weather hiking trails. One is **Conundrum Creek,** which begins 0.5 miles west of Aspen on Highway 82, then five miles up Castle Creek Road, then right on Conundrum Road for 1.1 miles to a parking lot. It's moderately difficult, about

THE BASICS OF SKIING

© DREAMSTIME.COM

skiing in an aspen glade with fresh snow

1. **Lift tickets:** Lift tickets will run about $71 for a one-day pass, depending on the resort; as with everything else, Aspen is more expensive than, say, Arapahoe Basin. But truly, only suckers pay that amount. Scan local newspapers as well as websites for *Westword*, *The Denver Post*, and others for deals and coupons. Also, contact resort hotels in advance for lift-and-lodging packages. Also consider skiing during off-season periods – Christmas week tends to be packed and expensive, while it's a serious buyer's market (Keystone lift tickets are $39) in April.

2. **Lessons:** Every resort has a ski and snowboard school, with group and private lessons for kids (usually over age three) and adults of all skill levels. Some resort lessons are basic – train 'em and herd 'em to the lifts – while the instructors at Steamboat and Vail know hundreds of languages and may have competed on a super-high level. Again, rates depend on the season and the resort, but $100 for a one-day group lesson (including lift ticket and lunch) is about average.

3. **Renting equipment:** Every resort has its own rental shop, which is usually a bit more expensive than the "unsanctioned" shops lining the surrounding area. I'd recommend stopping at an outside town – for example, the outlet malls at Dillon or Silverthorne, if you're heading to Breckenridge or Keystone – for better deals. Some of the big sporting-goods names are Christy Sports (877/754-7627, www.christysports.com) and Gart Sports (www.gartsports.com), and you won't be able to miss shops like this in a ski town. Forty bucks per day for skis, poles, and boots, or $30 for a snowboard, is about average.

8.5 miles each way, and passes three rivers, a few creeks, and several meadows before getting to a hot springs toward the end. There's also **Montezuma Basin Road,** which begins at the Ashcroft Ski-Touring parking area, 0.5 miles west of Aspen; take Highway 82 to the roundabout, then turn right onto Castle Creek Road. This is an eight-mile (one-way) path that starts off level and easy before elevating sharply after about 2.5 miles. Note: These trails work for snowshoers too, but beware of avalanches! The **Colorado Avalanche Information Center** (325 Broadway, Boulder, 303/499-9650, http://avalanche.state.co.us) provides forecasts. An excellent trail resource for this area is the **U.S. Forest Service's White River National Forest Division** (900 Grand Ave., Glenwood Springs, 970/945-2521, www.fs.fed.us/r2/whiteriver).

There's also hut-to-hut skiing, in which backcountry aficionados follow up-and-down trails for several days in a row and sleep at small cottages in the woods. The best outlet is the **10th Mountain Hut & Trail System** (1280 Ute Ave., Suite 21, 970/925-5775, www.huts.org), which presides over hundreds of miles of trails in the wide area between Vail Valley and Aspen. These include the **Alfred A. Braun Hut System,** which goes from the Ashcroft Ski Touring Center to the Maroon Bells–Snowmass Wilderness. The 10th Mountain website also provides a wealth of information about trailheads such as Hunter Creek and Lenado, which go up steep mountain paths. Snowshoes are allowed on these trails, but snowmobiles are discouraged.

For guided tours and other information, try the **Aspen/Snowmass Nordic Council** (970/429-2039, http://aspennordic.com), which maintains the Roaring Fork Valley's 48 miles of groomed trails. The **Aspen Cross-Country Center** (39551 W. Hwy. 82, 970/925-2145, www.aspennordic.com) gives lessons and sponsors annual events such as the all-ages, all-skill-levels **Town Cross-Country Series** late December–late February, with results announced on the website in early March. The **Ute Mountaineer** (210 S. Galena St.,

970/925-2849, www.utemountaineer.com) rents equipment.

Snowmobiling trails are also common in Aspen. The 4.5-mile **Little Annie Road Trail** begins 0.5 miles west of Aspen along Highway 82. At the traffic circle, turn right onto Castle Creek Road, then go seven miles to Little Annie Road. It starts out on the main road, but gets steeper as it climbs up Midnight Mine Road to the top of Aspen Mountain—be sure to check out the views. To get to **Smuggler Mountain Road,** take Highway 82 into Aspen, turn north onto Mill Street, turn right onto Gibson Street, bear left onto South Avenue, turn right onto Park Circle, and watch for the road on the left. It's six miles each way, getting steeper as it heads toward Warren Lakes. For more information, try the **Aspen Ranger District** (806 W. Hallam St., 970/925-3445, www.fs.fed.us/r2/whiteriver/contact).

Hiking and Mountain Biking

Surrounding Aspen, the forest includes alpine valleys such as Maroon Creek, Castle Creek, and Hunter Creek, all of which are open to hikers and cyclists (mostly in spring and summer). Hundreds of miles of trails, both official and unofficial, are in this area; excellent resources include the **Aspen Ranger District** (806 W. Hallam St., 970/925-3445, www.fs.fed.us/r2/whiteriver/contact), the **U.S. Forest Service's White River National Forest Division** (900 Grand Ave., Glenwood Springs, 970/945-2521, www.fs.fed.us/r2/whiteriver), and the **Aspen Chamber of Commerce** (970/925-1940 or 800/670-0792, www.aspenchamber.org).

The most user-friendly trails involve Silver Queen Gondola trips up Aspen Mountain. They range in difficulty from the easygoing 0.9-mile **Nature Trail** to the 2.5-mile **Ute Trail,** which is steep but unfolds into an amazing view of the city at the rock-covered high point. Note that the gondola runs every day June–August but just on weekends in May and September—and while it's kosher to hike down Aspen Mountain, it's 3,000 steep vertical feet. These trails (and the gondola) are also open to mountain bikers; rentals are available

FIVE EXTREME-SPORTS EVENTS YOU SHOULD SEE

© MATT INDEN/WEAVER MULTIMEDIA GROUP/COLORADO TOURISM OFFICE

A skier gains big air during the superpipe competition at Aspen's Winter X Games.

Flame-haired snowboard superstar Shaun White regularly dominates the **Winter X Games** (Aspen-Snowmass, late Jan., www.aspensnowmass.com/travelinfo/events), held at the base of Buttermilk Mountain and broadcast comprehensively on ESPN. Generally speaking, the competitions are in skiing, snowboarding, and snowmobiling. Specifically speaking, White once pulled off a "front-side double-cork 1080, Cab double-cork 1080, front-side stale-fish 540, double McTwist 1260 and alley-oop rodeo" in the same event, according to one report.

If you're a 24-year-old skier or snowboarder in the **Winter Park Freeskiing Open** (Mar., www.rlyrd.com/freeski_open.html), you're considered a grizzled elder statesman. The wide variety of competitions are slope-style, which means they emphasize mid-air spins, aerobic back-flips, and board-grabbing tricks. And they're not for the squeamish— in 2011, Indiana's Chris Laker, 17, had the best overall run, winning $2,000 after shattering his two front teeth, then breaking a corrective dental plate. "Knees to jaw," he told *The Denver Post* afterward.

Past winners of **Rock the Mach** (Breckenridge, late Jan., www.breckenridge.com), a two-run event in which skiers navigate steep moguls and 33-degree drop-aways, have included Olympic medalists Donna Weinbrecht, Jonny Moseley, and Toby Dawson. The event is named for Derk Slottow, a 21-year-old Dillon mogul-jumper, hard-rock fan, and outdoor adventurist who died in 2009 after his kayak flipped.

The two-day **Extreme Telemark Freeskiing Championships** (Crested Butte, mid-Mar., www.skicb.com/cbmr/things-to-do/telemark-extremes.aspx) involve lunatic super-skiers jumping off sharp rocks and navigating through clumps of trees. The woodsy courses have titles like Bodybag and Deadend Chutes.

Cody's Challenge (Steamboat Springs, early Apr., http://codyschallenge.tcsjf.org) is an endurance race for cross-country skiers that begins at the top of the gondola on Mount Werner in Steamboat. It's a specialized type of skiing called *randonnée,* which refers to a specific way of locking the boots and bindings to the skis. The race is named for Cody St. John, a 29-year-old local ski patroller who died in an auto accident in 2007; proceeds go to medical-education scholarships for fellow patrollers.

at nearby **Four-Mountain Sports/D&E Ski & Snowboard Shop** (520 E. Durant Ave., 970/920-2337), which also has an outlet in Snowmass.

Bikers who want to venture far from the tourist areas might try 12,000-foot **Independence Pass,** a super-strenuous, 10-mile, straight-up-a-mountain path that points at the end (with more downhills) into Leadville. It's not hard to find this route: Just take Highway 82 east from Aspen and keep going.

Beyond that, the dozens of trails in the Aspen region range from treacherous multiple-day trips up 14,000-foot mountains to easy meadow strolls. It's impossible to list all of these hikes in this space, but here are a few examples, beginning with the toughest:

Maroon Bells is a 10-mile round-trip hike-cum-climb that starts at 10,000 feet and ends at a 14,156-foot summit. It's as incredible, scenery-wise, as you would think, but beware—Aspen rangers call these unstable, often-crumbling mountains of sedimentary rock "unbelievably deceptive." A guide is recommended, or at least climbing experience, as well as a rope and a hard hat. To get to this area, take Highway 82 west of Aspen, then turn left on Maroon Creek Road and drive 11 miles to the parking area.

A less arduous way to experience the beautiful Maroon Bells is via the **Maroon/Snowmass Trail,** a popular 4.8-mile (one-way) trail that begins at Maroon Lake and rises almost 3,000 vertical feet to a beautiful rocky summit before descending into Crater Lake. Streams and meadows are all over the place. Maroon Creek Road is mostly closed throughout the summer, although early risers (before 8 A.M.) can take Highway 82 west of Aspen to the traffic circle, then turn right on Maroon Creek Road, driving 9.5 miles to the parking lot. Otherwise, a shuttle leaves regularly from the Aspen Highlands ski area. There are campsites along the route if you want to break it up a bit.

Lost Man Lake is a moderate walk through the Hunter-Fryingpan Wilderness Area, about nine miles each way. The route follows Lost Man Creek and passes Lost Man Lake, one of those gorgeous alpine lakes surrounded by a glacial cirque. To reach the trailhead, take Highway 82 about 18.5 miles east of Aspen, and watch for the Lost Man trailhead at the point where the highway crosses the Roaring Fork River.

Buckskin Pass is 9.5 miles (round-trip), climbing from 9,600 to 12,462 feet in the Maroon-Snowmass Wilderness area. It's steep and rocky, but includes views of the Maroon Bells, Pyramid Peak, and Crater Lake. To get there, take Highway 82 west of Aspen to the traffic circle, then turn right on Maroon Creek Road, driving 9.5 miles to the parking lot.

Although it's longer, the 16-mile **Rio Grande Trail** is less difficult than the previous ones. It follows the Roaring Fork River through thick forest to Woody Creek; look for the trailhead near the Aspen Post Office.

An extremely easy, pleasant walk past trickling creeks, bridges, aspen groves, and views of the Elk Mountain Range is the **Hunter Creek Trail.** Going north on Mill Street in Aspen, turn left onto Red Mountain Road, then go 1.3 miles to Hunter Creek Road; turn right, then left up a hill into the parking lot.

Smuggler Mountain, an 8.5-mile loop outside Aspen, is one of the most popular routes in the area for moderate and intermediate mountain bikers, and it has a lot of variety and scenery. To reach the trailhead from Aspen, cross over the Roaring Fork River on Highway 82, turn left on Park Avenue, turn right on Park Circle, then turn right into the parking area on Smuggler Mountain Road.

For maps and other information, check in with the **Forest Service** (806 W. Hallam St., 970/925-3445) or the **Aspen Parks Department** (585 Cemetery Lane, 970/920-5120, www.aspenrecreation.com). Also, **Ajax Bike & Sports** (400 E. Cooper Ave., 970/925-7662, www.ajaxbikeandsport.com) is one of several local sporting-goods stores that rents bicycles, and **Blazing Adventures** (Snowmass Village, 970/923-4544 or 800/282-7238, www.blazingadventures.com) leads guided tours for all skill levels.

ASPEN AND THE SKI TOWNS

Fishing

Outside of Basalt, a tiny mountain town northwest of Aspen on Highway 82, **Fryingpan River** leads to **Ruedi Reservoir,** and anglers get that drooly look on their faces when they start thinking about it. The fish here are huge, there are plenty of bugs for them to eat, and the dry-fly fishing is legendary among local and visiting anglers. Built by the U.S. Bureau of Reclamation in 1968, the 13.5-mile-long reservoir flows from a dam, then west to the Fryingpan River all the way to the Roaring Fork River around Basalt. To get to this "Gold Waters" fishing site, take Highway 82 to Basalt and head east on Fryingpan Road. You'll find yourself following the river to the reservoir.

The stretch from Basalt to Ruedi Dam includes a number of historic areas, such as a sandstone quarry used from 1888 to 1908 that provided stone material in local landmarks such as Aspen's Wheeler Opera House. Also, in addition to fish, keep your eyes open for bald eagles, bighorn sheep, mountain lions, and peregrine falcons.

There's a campground in this area too: **Chapman** (970/963-2266 or 970/927-9406, $18), just southwest of the reservoir along the river, 29 miles east of Basalt along Fryingpan Road. It has 84 campsites, plus restrooms and pressurized water.

For directions and other information, contact the **Roaring Fork Conservancy** (970/927-1290, www.roaringfork.org), the **Basalt Chamber of Commerce** (970/927-4031, www.basaltchamber.com), or the **Colorado Division of Wildlife** (970/947-2920, www.wildlife.state.co.us).

Golf

Befitting a town with amazing scenery, great weather, and wealthy residents, Aspen has several acclaimed private courses, including **Maroon Creek** (10 Club Circle, 970/920-1533, www.mccaspen.com, $195 guests), designed by Tom Fazio and filled with creeks and ponds at the base of Buttermilk Mountain, and **Roaring Fork** (100 Arbaney Ranch Rd., Basalt, 970/927-2727, www.roaringforkclub.com, $85 guests), designed by Jack Nicklaus and built along the Roaring Fork River.

Aspen also has a public course: **Aspen Golf and Tennis Club** (39551 Hwy. 82, 970/429-1949, www.aspengolf.com, $39–135), with 18 holes and a nice restaurant.

White-Water Rafting

White-water rafting is available through **Blazing Adventures** (Snowmass Village, 970/923-4544 or 800/282-7238, www.blazingadventures.com).

ENTERTAINMENT AND NIGHTLIFE

Aspen's primary musical entertainment is of the classical and chamber variety: **Aspen Music Festival and School** (2 Music School Rd., 970/925-3254, www.aspenmusicfestival.com) draws hordes of college-student prodigies to woodsy residence halls every June and August. The concerts they put on are affordable and often revelatory. **Wheeler Opera House** (320 E. Hyman Ave., 970/920-5770, www.wheeleroperahouse.com) has a diverse summer schedule of jazz, pop, and opera concerts. The early September **Jazz Aspen Snowmass** (970/920-4996, www.jazzaspensnowmass.org) isn't as stuffy as its name, having booked rock, country, and pop artists such as James Brown, Macy Gray, and Lyle Lovett to go with the standard jazz combos. The mid-June **Aspen Food & Wine Classic** (www.foodandwine.com/promo/classic-in-aspen) draws renowned chefs from all over the world for wine tastings, cooking classes, and other events. Around the same time of year, in Snowmass Village, the **Annual Chili Pepper and Brewfest** (970/925-1663, www.snowmasschiliandbrew.com) shows off 40 microbreweries to go with an International Chili Society competition and national music acts such as (in recent years) Spearhead and the Tedeschi Trucks Band.

Bars and Clubs

Aspen's bars are world-class, even when they're not as celebrity-packed and luxurious as the nearby restaurants and hotels. The **J-Bar** (330 E. Main St., 970/920-1000, http://hoteljerome. rockresorts.com/info/din.jbar.asp, 11:30 A.M.–midnight daily), inside the Hotel Jerome, is a laid-back place to hang out, attracting tons of locals, with beer and burgers that rival any eatery in town. Another excellent hotel bar, this one of the hipster variety, is the Sky Hotel's **39 Degrees** (709 E. Durant Ave., 970/925-6760, www.theskyhotel.com/sky-dining, 11:30 A.M.–midnight Sun.–Thurs., 11:30 A.M.–2 A.M. Fri.–Sat., reduced hours off-season), which has comfortable couches and a huge flat-panel TV for sports enthusiasts. **Eric's Bar** (315 E. Hyman Ave., 970/920-1488, 7 A.M.–2 A.M. daily, reduced hours off-season) is far homier, with an emphasis on malt scotch. And most famous of all is the **Woody Creek Tavern** (002 Woody Creek Plaza, 2858 Upper River Rd., Woody Creek, 970/923-4585, www.woodycreektavern.com, 11 A.M.–10 P.M. daily), which offers a few pool tables, beer, comfort, and an opportunity to raise a glass to late regular Hunter S. Thompson.

A number of high-class Aspen eateries double as wine-drenched party destinations; the ages of the clientele drop noticeably during event weekends like the X Games. Tip for experiencing Aspen on the cheap: Sit at the bar and order from the bar menu. Tip for undercutting the previous tip: Order a lot of wine from the wine list. Bars in this genre include **L'Hostaria** (620 E. Hyman Ave., 970/925-9022, www.hostaria.com, 5:30–9:30 P.M. daily, reduced hours off-season), which has a wine list of hundreds of brands as well as an affordable bar menu of pastas and salads; **Campo de Fiori** (205 S. Mill St., 970/920-7717, www.campodefiori.net, 5:30–10:30 P.M. daily, reduced hours off-season), an inviting little trattoria with colorful murals and a long wine list; **Jimmy's** (205 S. Mill St., 970/925-6020, www.jimmysaspen.com, 5:30 P.M.–1:45 A.M. daily), which specializes in harder stuff like tequila and mescal to go with Saturday-night salsa, merengue, and tango dancing; and **Brunelleschi's Dome Pizza** (205 S. Mill St., 970/544-4644, http://zgpizza.com,

11 A.M.–10 P.M. daily), a family-friendly pizza joint doubling as a fully stocked bar for skiers with the munchies.

Inside the St. Regis hotel, the **Shadow Mountain Lounge** (315 E. Dean St., 970/920-3300, www.stregisaspen.com/dining/lounge, 11 A.M.–midnight daily) supplements its mountain luxury—big chairs, granite fireplace, Aspen Mountain views—with live jazz and piano music.

Belly Up Aspen (450 S. Galena St., 970/544-9800, www.bellyupaspen.com, open daily, hours vary by show) is Aspen's primary live-music club, supplementing movie nights and local hippie-rock bands with high-quality national headliners such as DeVotchKa, Snoop Dogg, Chromeo, and, in recent years, B. B. King. **Syzygy** (308 E. Hopkins Ave., 970/925-3700, www.syzygyrestaurant.com, music 10 P.M. daily) is better known as a bar and restaurant, but it has jazz and dancing on weekends and DJs for special events such as New Year's Eve.

SHOPPING

Shopping in Aspen, as the *New York Times* once called it, is a "mix of the insanely expensive (movie stars) and the insanely inexpensive (ski bums)." I've yet to see anything that can be reasonably described as "insanely inexpensive" in Aspen, but the article's example—**Susie's Limited** (623 E. Hopkins Ave., 970/920-2376, 9:30 A.M.–5:30 P.M. Mon.–Sat., noon–5 P.M. Sun.)—is as good a place as any to find such deals as a $30–60 ski jacket or sweater.

Clothing

The insanely expensive is much easier to find: The **Prada Store** (312 S. Galena St., 970/925-7001, www.prada.com, 10 A.M.–6 P.M. Mon.–Sat., noon–5 P.M. Sun.) has drawn celebrities such as Ivana Trump, Nicky and Paris Hilton, and Monica Lewinsky over the past decade. At one point, according to the *Denver Post,* it sold a $14,160 mink sleeping bag. Family owned for years, **Pitkin County Dry Goods** (520 E. Cooper Ave., 970/925-1681, http://pitkincountydrygoods.com, 11 A.M.–6 P.M.

daily) isn't nearly as ostentatious, but it has sleek menswear and stylish women's clothing, jewelry, and purses. For shoe enthusiasts, **Bloomingbirds** (304 S. Galena Ave., 970/925-2241, 10 A.M.–6 P.M. Mon.–Sat., 11 A.M.–6 P.M. Sun.) has a high-end mix of tennis, formal, and ski. **Brigi** (1232 Vine St., 970/379-7749, www.brigipj.com) sells the most elaborately luxurious women's pajamas you've ever seen. And we're not talking Victoria's Secret, either—these are mostly two-piece ensembles, made of silk and such, festooned with cartoons of topless cowboys, kittens, and butterflies.

Galleries

Aspen's galleries are also among the best in the region, and there are dozens of them in a small area (and that's not even counting satellite towns such as Carbondale and Basalt): The **David Floria Gallery** (525 E. Cooper Ave., 970/544-5705, www.floriagallery.com, 10 A.M.–6 P.M. Mon.–Sat., noon–6 P.M. Sun.) has a huge roster of top new artists, from Joseph Scheer and his large butterflies to James Surls and his jittery bug sculptures. The **212 Gallery** (525 E. Cooper, Suite 201, 970/925-7117, www.212gallery.com, 10 A.M.–7 P.M. Mon.–Fri., 10 A.M.–6 P.M. Sat.–Sun.) traffics primarily in modern images, such as Karl Hollinger's *Hello Larry,* a collage of peace signs, dogs, and beatnik expressions like "howl."

Antiques

Another high-end vein to tap is antiques, notably **Daniels Antiques** (431 E. Hyman Ave., 970/544-9282, www.blackforestantiques.com, 10 A.M.–6 P.M. Mon.–Sat.), which sells intricate wood-carved chairs, animal carvings, and clocks, as well as vintage slot machines and pistols, and **Paris Underground** (205 S. Mill St., Suite 231, 970/544-0137, http://parisunderground.com/store, 10 A.M.–5 P.M. Mon.–Wed., 10 A.M.–6 P.M. Thurs.–Fri.), which carries furniture, pottery, and chandeliers by 1930s and 1940s French designers.

Ski Equipment

Super-fashionable skiers go to **Performance**

Ski (408 S. Hunter St., 970/925-8657, 10 A.M.–5 P.M. daily), where Cindy Crawford and other big names are said to have shopped, and **Pomeroy Sports** (614 E. Durant Ave., 970/925-7875, www.pomeroysports.com, 10 A.M.–5 P.M. daily), a family-run store that caters both to top athletes and to beginners craving personal attention.

ACCOMMODATIONS

Hotels in Aspen are the most amazing and luxurious in Colorado, if not the entire country, but they're *expensive,* especially during ski season and major weekend holidays. Fractional ownership, in which somewhat rich guests can pay for permanent lodging shares, is the new thing—the St. Regis Resort has tried it, and the Little Nell and Hyatt Grand Aspen reportedly have plans in the works. And, of course, there are condos.

Some travelers opt to stay just outside of Aspen, in more affordable mountain towns such as Leadville and Carbondale. This is somewhat inconvenient geographically, especially for a prolonged ski trip, but it's a way to experience Aspen without spending every cent you have.

Under $100

In Carbondale, 30 miles from Aspen, the woodsy **Ambiance Inn** (66 N. 2nd St., Carbondale, 970/963-3597 or 800/350-1515, www.ambianceinn.com, $90–100) is a cozy B&B with four guest rooms in patchwork colors and furnishings. Be sure to ask for a private bath. In even tinier Basalt, the straightforward **Aspenalt Lodge** (157 Basalt Center Cir., Basalt, 970/927-3191 or 877/379-6476, www.aspenalt.com, $99–109) overlooks the Fryingpan River and has a hot tub on an outdoor deck. Not far from there is the **Green Drake** (200 Midland Ave., Basalt, 970/927-4747 or 800/905-6797, www.green-drake.com, $89–209), also in an excellent location near the rivers and underneath the mountains.

$150-200

The **Aspen Meadows Resort** (845 Meadows

Rd., 970/925-4240 or 800/452-4240, www.
dolce-aspen-hotel.com, $150–250) has large
guest rooms with balconies that overlook the
mountains and the Roaring Fork River. It's
also the headquarters of the Aspen Institute
(www.theaspeninstitute.org), a longtime nonprofit group that organizes influential public-
policy seminars (former CNN executive Walter
Isaacson, author of the best-selling *Steve Jobs,* is
the president and CEO these days).

Aria's Loft (370 Euclid Ave., Carbondale,
970/963-3832, www.ariasloft.com, $145)
looks like a regular family home in the center
of Carbondale, with a garden, a second-floor
balcony, and couches in the living room; it's
actually a comfortable hotel.

It's probably best to get a fireplace room at
the **Molly Gibson Lodge** (101 W. Main St.,
970/925-3434 or 888/271-2304, www.mol-
lygibson.com, $175–345), as the basic guest
rooms are nondescript. But it's a nice place in
a mountain location three blocks from downtown, with a heated outdoor pool, whirlpool
tubs, and complimentary wireless Internet access throughout the hotel.

Hotel Lenado (200 S. Aspen St., 970/925-
6246 or 800/321-3457, www.hotellenado.com,
$175–495) has two kinds of guest rooms: the
very basic Larkspur, with shared balconies, and
the deluxe Smuggler, with four-corner wooden
beds. The Smuggler is far preferable, with in-
room hot tubs and (in some cases) private balconies and wood-burning stoves. Either way,
it's in a central location next to the town's
Whitaker Park and worth trying out.

$200-300

The **Hearthstone House** (134 E. Hyman
Ave., 970/925-7632 or 888/925-7632, www.
hearthstonehouse.com, $269–309) is in a two-
story building with flat, angular architecture
reminiscent of Frank Lloyd Wright. The guest
rooms are almost as nice-looking, and they
take on a certain glow when you factor in the
mountain views. Also on the premises is the
Aspen Club & Spa.

The **◖ Sky Hotel** (709 E. Durant Ave.,
970/925-6760 or 800/882-2582, www.

theskyhotel.com, $199–249) is new and mod-
ern, in stark contrast to the rustic Little Nell
and the mainstream St. Regis. Hipsters hang
out at the curvy outdoor pool and party in the
hot-tub area late at night; the guest rooms have
touches of bright red and green to go with the
cream-colored walls and beds, and tall, car-
toonish white chairs are in the lobby along
with board games for kids.

$300-400

Built in 1889, the **◖ Hotel Jerome** (330 E.
Main St., 970/920-1000 or 877/412-7625,
www.hoteljerome.com, $299–459) takes the
down-home Colorado approach to luxury
Aspen hotels, with a genuine Wild West ambience throughout the building, with moose
heads on the walls and numerous crystal chandeliers. Locals in cowboy boots love the place
for its hard-drinking ambience, especially in
the J-Bar, an inexpensive and homey little place
with excellent burgers.

Luxury isn't a big priority at the **Limelight
Lodge** (355 S. Monarch St., 970/925-3025 or
800/433-0832, www.limelightlodge.com, $325–
800), but location is—the tree-lined wooden
building is a short walk from the gondola. It also
has two pools and two whirlpool tubs.

Over $400

Many say the **◖ Little Nell** (675 E. Durant
Ave., 970/920-4600 or 888/843-6355, www.
thelittlenell.com, $420–880) is the best hotel
between the coasts, and its pampering is beloved among guests. In a city where the pool of
talented, experienced hotel workers isn't nearly
as big as, say, New York or Los Angeles, the
Nell grabs all of them. "What do you need?" is
a common refrain among the staff. In addition
to that, it's beautiful: Even the standard guest
rooms have gas fireplaces and down sofas (and
some have balconies), and the mountain views
are unlike any in the Rockies.

Just a notch down from the Nell, but still
very nice, is **The St. Regis Resort** (315 E.
Dean St., 970/920-3300, www.stregisaspen.
com, $499–839), which is at the base of Aspen
Mountain. A few years ago it underwent a

major renovation, adding the 15,000-square-foot Remede Spa, plus the St. Regis Residence Club Aspen, which sells fractions of a residence for $300,000–1.5 million apiece.

Little Red Ski Haus (118 E. Cooper Ave., 970/925-3333 or 866/630-6119, www.thelittleredskihaus.com, $2,500–3,500) is one of the town's first bed-and-breakfasts, in a late-1880s Victorian. It rents the entire building—all nine bedrooms—rather than individual units.

FOOD

While every visitor ought to have a solid $200 meal (with wine) at the Century Room, Matsuhisa, or Range, it's surprisingly affordable to get by for a few days on J-Bar burgers, The Big Wrap sandwiches, and Main Street Bakery & Café pastries. An excellent resource is the website of *Aspen Times Weekly* (www.aspentimes.com, click on "Dining"), in which food critics never take too seriously the luxuries so prominent in this glittery town. Note: Hours, prices, and menus often change seasonally, or even from week to week.

Snacks, Cafés, and Breakfast

The **Main Street Bakery & Café** (201 E. Main St., 970/925-6446, 7 A.M.–4 P.M. daily, $10) is on every travel writer's "Aspen on the cheap" list. It serves pastries, cakes, and croissants, plus homemade soups and granola—for as little as $5 per entrée. While it's locally famous for breakfast, it also serves lunch and dinner, and it has mountain views too.

Casual

La Cantina (411 E. Main St., 970/925-3663, www.cantina-aspen.com, 11 A.M.–9:30 P.M. Mon.–Thurs., 11 A.M.–10 P.M. Fri.–Sat., 10:30 A.M.–9:30 P.M. Sun., $15) is a festive Mexican restaurant that serves the usual stuff—fajitas, enchiladas, tacos, burritos, and, of course, delicious guacamole and margaritas. To save a little dough, drop by for lunch.

The aggressive 1950s rock-and-roll theme makes **Boogie's Diner** (534 E. Cooper St., 970/925-6111 or 888/245-8121, www.boogiesaspen.com, 11 A.M.–8 P.M. Sun.–Thurs.,

11 A.M.–9 P.M. Fri.–Sat., $7) as much of a gimmick as a restaurant—ever been to Ed Debevic's in Chicago?—but it's a fun place to eat dinner, and the half-pound burgers anchor a diverse menu (with vegetarian options).

Little Annie's Eating House (517 E. Hyman Ave., 970/925-1098, www.littleannies.com, 11:30 A.M.–10 P.M. daily, $20) competes with the Hotel Jerome's J-Bar for the "best burger" prize, and **The Big Wrap** (520 E. Durant Ave., 970/544-1700, 10 A.M.–6 P.M. Mon.–Sat., $7) has tortilla-covered healthy sandwiches that inspire this scene at the *Times Weekly* offices: "Every time the intercom crackles with 'Big Wrap in the front office,' the sound of a half dozen pairs of feet resounds through the rickety building." Try the wrap with hummus and Greek veggie salad ($6).

Upscale

Now that the beloved Century Room has closed, the best eating option in the Hotel Jerome is the **Garden Terrace** (330 E. Main St., 970/920-1000, http://hoteljerome.rockresorts.com/info/din.terrace.asp, generally 7 A.M.–9:30 P.M. daily, hours vary by season, $38), a classy steak-and-fish joint where the lamb sirloin comes with grilled soft white polenta and the duck breast comes with duck confit orecchiette casserole.

Run by sommelier Rob Ittner, **Rustique** (216 S. Monarch St., 970/920-2555, www.rustiquebistro.com, 5:30–10:30 P.M. daily, reduced hours off-season, $33) has a few familiar entrées, like roasted chicken with mushroom sauce, but its menu also includes venison loin with roasted beets and self-described "weird dishes" like calf's liver with bacon and onion.

◖ **Montagna** (675 E. Durant Ave., 970/920-4600, www.thelittlenell.com/restaurants/montagna-restaurant.aspx, 7–10:30 A.M., 11:30 A.M.–2:30 P.M., and 6–10 P.M. Mon.–Sat., 6–10:30 A.M., 11 A.M.–2:30 P.M., and 6–10 P.M. Sun., $33), in the Little Nell, is a one-of-a-kind destination restaurant around which out-of-town visitors plan entire vacations. Master sommelier Richard Betts, presiding over a 15,000-bottle wine cellar, is one of the best in the country. The menu's charms range from seared yellowfin tuna ($36) for dinner, eggplant bruschetta ($6) for lunch, and a two-person doughnut tasting ($15) for brunch.

Piñons (105 S. Mill St., 970/920-2021, www.pinons.net, 5:30–9:30 P.M. daily, $35), named after New Mexico's state tree, is an American-style restaurant with Southwestern decor, serving elk, pork, and beef tenderloins. Lobster strudel is a specialty of chef Rob Mobillian, and the appetizers range from potato-crusted scallops to beluga caviar.

Cache Cache (205 S. Mill St., 970/925-3835, www.cachecache.com, 5:30–10:30 P.M. daily, $45) is so well known for its use of garlic, rosemary, and vinaigrettes that it's almost impossible to get a table, even midweek. Every menu item has some kind of oddly perfect flavoring: The calf's liver is in caramelized onion sauce, the pork tenderloin is in apple-brandy sauce, and even the filet mignon comes with Dijon-peppercorn sauce.

Gisella (415 E. Main St., 970/925-8222, www.gisellaaspen.com, 6 P.M.–close Tues.–Sat., $30) is a beautiful Italian restaurant with an elegant look that says both "white tablecloths" and "people eat a *lot* here." The menu is basic Italian, so expect plenty of pasta, with straightforward shadings—tortelloni with pesto, goat cheese, and pine nuts, beef tenderloin with mashed potatoes, spinach with garlic, and the like.

Aspen imported **Matsuhisa** (303 E. Main St., 970/544-6628, www.nobumatsuhisa.com, 6–10 P.M. daily, $34), the namesake of chef Nobu Matsuhisa, after his restaurants earned acclaim in Beverly Hills, Malibu, and New York City. It's famous for sushi, but entrées such as the halibut cheeks with pepper sauce ($29)—supplemented, of course, with miso soup—are superb alternatives. The restaurant strongly recommends making a reservation a month in advance.

Social Restaurant (304 E. Hopkins Ave., 970/925-9700, www.social-aspen.com, 5:50–10 P.M. daily, $30) opened in late 2007 in the former R Cuisine space. The menu is predominantly tapas, and the lively Social serves the same food and drinks in both the restaurant and lounge.

Regularly named one of the best restaurants in Aspen, **Syzygy** (308 E. Hopkins Ave., 970/925-3700, www.syzygyrestaurant.com, 6–10:30 P.M. daily, $50) captures all the little things that take an eatery to the next level—perfectly arranged flowers on the table, live jazz that's just the right volume, miniature waterfalls, and, oh, yes, the food. Chef Martin Oswald, an expert in cooking game, combines Asian and Southwestern influences into dishes like hazelnut-crusted lamb loin.

INFORMATION AND SERVICES

The ski resort's website (www.aspensnowmass.com) has information about everything from live music to hotels, or call 970/925-1220 or 800/525-6200. The **Aspen Chamber Resort Association** (970/925-1940 or 800/670-0792, www.aspenchamber.org) has an elaborate website geared toward travelers. Aspen's weekly newspaper, the **Aspen Times** (www.aspentimes.com), is sophisticated for a small town and includes well-written restaurant reviews. The ski resort also maintains a separate Snowmass website (www.snowmass.com), or call 800/923-8920.

Aspen Valley Hospital (0401 Castle Creek Rd., 970/925-1120, www.aspenvalleyhospital.org) is the primary resource for medical care in the Aspen-Snowmass area, although the ski area provides emergency services.

GETTING THERE

Aspen is almost a 2.5-hour drive west from Denver International Airport, and once you're here, the Roaring Fork Valley region is so self-contained it's hard to wander around and explore the rest of the Rockies. In part, that's why Aspen has become such a destination town. To get here, take I-70 west to Glenwood Springs, then turn left (southeast) and backtrack along Highway 82 to get to Aspen. Especially in winter, the high, curvy highway can be treacherous. Also, be sure to gas up along I-70, as

ASPEN AND THE SKI TOWNS

TIPS FOR DRIVING IN THE MOUNTAINS

Snowy mountain roads, even big ones like I-70, are dangerous. Highway crews can be slow to react with plows after blizzards, so icy conditions are common – and even if stretches of blacktop look dry, "black ice" can fool even the savviest of mountain drivers. Obviously, it's safer in warmer weather, but beware of unexpected hairpin curves and icy patches in the high country. Some tips:

- Slow down in the winter. Plan in advance, and allow extra travel time. And if the sports car behind you is following too close, ignore it – and find a safe shoulder to pull over and let faster traffic pass.

- Avoid sudden moves.

- In the mountains, deer and other animals can leap in front of cars at any time, so pay attention to the deer-crossing signs and drive slowly enough to stop.

- Pass only when you're absolutely certain it's safe. Pay attention to the "Do Not Pass" signs and the solid and broken lines on the highway. Make sure you have a clear vision of the entire road before doing so. When in doubt, don't do it. Entering the opposing lane at the wrong time can be catastrophic.

- Avoid using cruise control, especially when it's slippery.

- When it's icy, pump the brakes to stop rather than slamming on them.

- When driving downhill in slippery conditions, try to avoid braking on snowy or icy patches. It's best to find what looks like a dry spot and slow yourself down there. However, you should be going slowly enough so this doesn't become a factor – and never be afraid to brake if you feel you're in an unsafe situation.

- Downhill, if you're driving 30-40 miles per hour, slow yourself down by shifting into a lower gear (this works with both automatic and manual transmissions).

- Don't tailgate.

- Make sure your car has good tires. Experts recommend buying tires with the worst possible driving conditions in mind; also, tread depth in snowy conditions should be three-sixteenths of an inch.

- Use your brights at night, but if it's foggy or snowy, turn them off to avoid confusing reflections.

- If you need further information, check with local governments in mountain towns. The Summit County Chamber of Commerce (970/668-2051) gives tips on local tire dealers. For **road conditions,** call 303/639-1111, or watch for the blue radio-station signs on the highway.

Aspen's prices are among the most expensive in the state—sometimes as much as $0.50 per gallon more than Denver. Snowmass is about 14 miles northeast of Aspen along Highway 82.

A popular alternate route to Aspen is I-70 to U.S. 24, just east of Copper Mountain, then passing through Leadville before turning right onto Highway 82 into Aspen. It makes for a slightly longer trip, but many Denver-to-Aspen regulars swear by the Old West ambience and friendly restaurants of Leadville. It's also a nice change of pace from the crowded interstate highway.

Most affluent visitors and residents—which is to say, a lot of people—indulge in the **Aspen/ Pitkin County Airport** (0233 E. Airport Rd., 970/920-5384, www.aspenairport.com), three miles from the city of Aspen and six from Snowmass Village. It has service by United, Frontier, and Delta. Punters can fly into Denver, Colorado Springs, or Grand Junction airports, rent a car, and take I-70 to Highway 82.

GETTING AROUND

Free shuttle buses serve all four Aspen mountains during the day, and the **Roaring Fork**

Transit Authority (Rubey Park, Durant St., 970/925-8484, www.rfta.com) provides free and convenient city buses within the city during the day and between Aspen and Snowmass Village from evening until night.

SNOWMASS

Since it opened in 1967, Snowmass Village and its one-mountain ski area have been a sleepier alternative to ritzy Aspen. Residents have come to like it that way, although developers have pumped in more than $1 billion in improvements since 2003. These include the Treehouse Kids' Adventure Center on the mountain, and, in the base village, 600 new condos, bars, restaurants, and shops.

Although Snowmass has managed to retain its homey identity, for the most part these changes complete the town's transformation from a townie-oriented, best-kept-secret type of resort that has more in common with Copper Mountain than Aspen or Vail. To prove the point: Russian billionaire Roman Abromavich bought a Wildcat Ridge mansion for $36.375 million in May 2008—the third-most-expensive property in Pitkin County history. Then again, Snowmass has been building up to this transformation for years, with additions to its resort area in the mid-1990s and the opening of super-expert ski runs that attract more death-defying snowboarders and extreme skiers than laidback beginners.

◀ Snowmass Mountain

Snowmass is the largest of the four mountains in the Aspen-Snowmass range; its specialty is expert-only terrain, but 6 percent of its runs are geared to beginners. With the Winter X Games coming to the Aspen area on a regular basis in recent years, a new group of extreme snowboarders and skiers have come to dominate the mountain, and the resort responded by opening acres of terrain on the high-up Cirque's Burn Side Cliffs. The new runs, including Leap 'n' Land, Gluteus, and Triple Jump, have huge cliff drops and complement expert standbys such as the Hanging Valley Wall.

But with 3,100 acres of ski trails on the mountain, Snowmass has a variety of runs for just about every type of skier and skill level. The most popular of six distinct areas is Big Burn, for intermediates, which seems endless and open. Toward the bottom of the mountain are numerous short and smooth runs for beginners and kids. In recent years, the mountain has unveiled several multimillion-dollar renovations, including new lifts such as the Sky Cab and Elk Camp gondolas, the latter of which leads to a six-acre beginners' ski area.

For boarders, Snowmass has three terrain parks—**Lowdown,** with 5–15-foot tabletop jumps and other boxes and rails, mostly designed for beginners; **Little Makaha,** with 25 features, geared to advanced riders learning new tricks; and **Snowmass,** with mostly advanced and experts features, including flat boxes, rails, wall rides, and a superpipe. In late March, the resort offers a Snowboard Boot Camp aimed at kids.

Snowmass also is an excellent setting for cyclists and hikers—in some ways better than Aspen. During summer, the ski-resort mountains open to various bike trails, including Village Bound (for beginners) and Sam's Knob (for experts), both of which require trips up the ski lift. "Discovery Zones," for mountain bikers and BMX riders alike, are located inside the Snowmass Village Mall.

Lift tickets cost roughly $104 per day, the same as at Aspen.

The **Treehouse Kids' Adventure Center** (at the intersection of the three new ski lifts on Fanny Hill, www.aspensnowmass.com/snowmass/treehouse.cfm) is a $17 million glorified recreation center that opened for the 2007–2008 season. Inside are a climbing gym, retail shops, and age-appropriate activities for kids beginning at eight weeks old.

Biking

Fit and ambitious cyclists can circle Snowmass on one continuous loop of single track that surrounds the town. **Snowmass Loop** includes a total elevation gain of 3,000 feet and, at 24 miles, takes up at least half a day. One popular approach is to start at the Ridge/Blake Trail near the Snowmass Village Mall, cross Owl Creek Road, then take the Highline Trail to the Rim Trail and ride back to the mall.

Outside of ski season, cyclists can ride the 12-mile **Government Trail** all the way to Aspen. Take the Burlingame chairlift up Snowmass Mountain and begin the ride at the top.

Entertainment and Nightlife

Popular Snowmass Village bar spots include **Cirque Café** (125 Daly Lane, 970/923-8686), with frequent live music and a nice outdoor deck; the **Big Hoss Grill** (45 Village Square, Store 10, 970/923-2597, www.bighossgrill. com, 7:30 A.M.–2 A.M. daily, reduced hours off-season), which advertises nice-and-simple "burgers, beer and BBQ," and **Zane's Tavern** (10 Village Square, 970/923-3515, www.zanes-tavern.com, 11 A.M.–2 A.M. daily, reduced hours off-season), which has your basic burritos, onion rings, and Philly cheesesteaks to go with pool tables and drinks. In the Silvertree Hotel, the **Fireside Lounge** (100 Elbert Lane, 5th Fl., 970/923-8285, www.brothers-grille.com, 7–11 A.M., 11:30 A.M.–2:30 P.M., 3–5 P.M., and 5:30–10 P.M. daily) serves drinks beside a, um, fireplace—and has great mountain views as a bonus.

Accommodations

Snowmass hotels and condos spent $33.7 million on renovations in 2007, just before the recession kicked in, which has meant more options and more luxury. Condos are scattered all over town—some of the most centrally located rental companies include **Laurelwood Condominiums** (Snowmass Village, 970/923-3110 or 866/356-7669, www.laurelwoodcondo-miniums.com, $125–295) and **Shadowbrook Condominiums** (Snowmass Village, 970/923-8500 or 800/201-2391, www.shadowbrook-condos.com, $355–850 for 2 bedrooms). For a fairly comprehensive roundup of lodging properties, go to www.snowmassvillage.com/stay/accomodation.html.

A stumpy box of a building, the **Stonebridge Inn** (300 Carriage Way, 970/923-2420 or 866/939-2471, www.stonebridgeinn.com, $95–115) exemplifies the difference between Aspen and Snowmass—Aspen's best hotels are elaborately luxurious, while Snowmass's best is functional and convenient. It's two blocks from the Village Mall, the guest rooms are comfortable but nothing fancy, and it has all the amenities you need, like a heated outdoor pool and a cozy bar and restaurant. Side by side, the **Pokolodi Lodge** (25 Daly Lane, 970/923-4310 or 800/666-4556, www.pokolodi.com, $79–219) and the **Snowmass Inn** (67 Daly Lane, 970/923-3900 or 800/843-1579, www.mountainchalet.com, $95) are within 100 yards of the slopes and immediately next to the village. They're basic and affordable, and ensconced in the mountains, making for excellent views. The Naked Lady Pub, a local favorite, is in the Snowmass Inn. (To make things especially confusing, the Snowmass Mountain Chalet manages the Snowmass Inn.)

Also in keeping with Snowmass's personality—comfort over luxury—is the higher-end **Silvertree Hotel** (100 Elbert Lane,

Snowmass ski resort

970/923-3520 or 800/837-4255, www.silver-treehotel.com, $139–349), which has the feel of a Marriott, only with better scenery and several bars and restaurants in the lobby.

The town's most charming hotel is the **Snowmass Mountain Chalet** (115 Daly Lane, 970/923-3900 or 800/843-1579, www.mountainchalet.com, $150–160), a 64-room B&B-style lodge with log furniture, a lobby fireplace, and complimentary breakfast.

Food

Krabloonik (4250 Divide Rd., 970/923-3953, www.krabloonik.com, 11 A.M.–2 P.M. and 5:30–9 P.M. daily mid-Dec.–mid-Apr., reduced hours off-season, $50) is unique in the Aspen-Snowmass area, mainly because its full title is "Krabloonik Restaurant and Kennel." Yes, while guests in this serene log-cabin restaurant dine on the house-specialty wild mushroom soup ($5), 200 sled-pulling huskies eat dog food in the kennel next door. (They're available for sled tours throughout the area.)

Good Italian restaurants are hard to find in the mountains, but **Il Poggio** (73 Elbert Lane, 970/923-4292, 5:30–9:30 P.M. daily, $30) is the kind of casual pasta specialist that wouldn't seem out of place in the heart of New York or Chicago. It does great things with garlic, and the sweet-potato ravioli ($16), in a hazelnut cream sauce with goat cheese, is a highlight.

LEADVILLE

Many travelers know Leadville as the quaint little mountain town with friendly old cafés and restaurants that they pass through en route to Aspen. It also gave Colorado some of its most famous characters, from the mining-era couple Horace and Baby Doe Tabor to the Old West outlaw Doc Holliday.

As the story goes, Kansas farmer Horace Tabor moved his wife and son to what would become Leadville to take advantage of the mining boom. He opened a grocery store, and in 1878, two German immigrants showed up and asked Tabor to grubstake them for their future silver discoveries. He gave them $17, and within months they'd each made $10,000.

Tabor used this money to make his fortune and become the symbolic master of the mining boom. He bought the Matchless Mine, developed a fortune worth a reported $3 million, and fell in love with a new Leadville resident, divorcée Elizabeth Bonduel McCourt Doe. Before long, Tabor was asking his wife, Augusta, for a divorce. Against her wishes, he married "Baby Doe" in 1882.

The story of one of the most famous people in Colorado history ends in tragedy. Congress repealed the Sherman Silver Act in 1893, dissipating Tabor's fortune and those of countless others. Tabor became destitute and begged Baby Doe on his deathbed (according to the history section of Leadville's website) to "hold on to the Matchless as it will pay millions again"—although some dispute those were actually his words. The mine never paid millions again, and Baby Doe died of a heart attack in her icy cold Matchless Mine cabin.

The ostentatious Baby Doe and Tabor, who became a U.S. senator, have since been immortalized in the opera *The Ballad of Baby Doe*, among many other fictional works. Leadville is now a quaint tourist town, a sort of gateway from Denver to Aspen, but the original Matchless Mine (and Baby Doe's shack) still exist in historical-museum form.

Sights

The **Matchless Mine** (E. 7th St., 719/486-1229, www.matchlessmine.com, 10 A.M.–5 P.M. daily June–Oct., $7) preserves the original cabin where Baby Doe died in 1935—some say she froze to death, but historical records show it was actually a heart attack. The mine is more or less as it was, and an on-site museum exists primarily to sell books and videotapes about the Tabor story. Also obsessed with Tabor family history is the **Tabor Opera House** (308 Harrison Ave., 719/486-8409, www.taboroperahouse.net, tours 10 A.M.–5 P.M. Mon.–Sat. summer, $5), once so regal it drew performers such as Harry Houdini, John Philip Sousa, and Oscar Wilde. The **Augusta Tabor Home** (116 E. 5th St., 719/486-2092, www.cityofleadville.com, call

Downtown Leadville's streets are lined with the historic features of an old mining town.

for appointment information) was a happy place for a few years when Horace and loyal Augusta first lived here, but Horace took off for mistress Baby Doe in 1881. Branching beyond the Tabor family, the **National Mining Hall of Fame & Museum** (120 W. 9th St., 719/486-1229, www.mininghalloffame. org, 11 A.M.–4 P.M. daily, $7) has a walkthrough replica of an 1880s mine, a miniature model Colorado railroad, and a Hall of Fame honoring dozens of miners past. The **Heritage Museum** (9th St. and Harrison Ave., 719/486-1878, 9 A.M.–5 P.M. daily May–Oct., 11 A.M.–4 P.M. daily Nov.–Apr., $7) displays Victorian furniture of the time and a model replica of the town's 1896-era "palace of ice."

The scenic **Leadville, Colorado, and Southern Railroad** (326 E. 7th St., 719/486-3936 or 866/386-3936, www.leadville-train.com) follows the Arkansas River between the tiny towns of Leadville and Climax along the Continental Divide. The depot is an 1893 building filled with historical artifacts and a gift shop.

Sports and Recreation

It's a little nuts to travel all the way to Colorado and ski at the dinky **Ski Cooper** (U.S. 24, about 9 miles west of Leadville, 719/486-3684 or 800/707-6114, www.skicooper.com, all-day lift tickets $44), but the slopes are rarely crowded, and the four lifts serve 400 skiable acres (a snowcat delivers backcountry skiers to 2,400 more available acres). Backcountry skiers should consider the Mineral Belt Trail, opened in 2000, a 12.5-mile loop around Leadville with views of two large mountain ranges and stops at various historic mining areas. Also, the **Tennessee Pass Nordic Center** (U.S. 24, 719/486-1750, www.tennesseepass.com/skiing. htm, trail pass $14) offers backcountry skiing lessons and access to trails halfway between Leadville and Minturn off U.S. 24. Billing itself as the highest golf course (elevation-wise) in North America, the nine-hole **Mt. Massive Golf Course** (259 County Rd. 5, 719/486-2176, www.mtmassivegolf.com, $36) is miles from the nearest condo.

Leadville is terrific for hikers due to its

proximity to several gigantic mountain peaks. **Mount Sherman,** part of the Mosquito Range, is renowned as the easiest-to-climb fourteener in Colorado. In fact, mountaineers can be kind of snobby about it. But don't let them stop you if you're eager to try a fourteener and you don't have tons of experience on the big mountains. With a 2,000-foot elevation gain, Mount Sherman is a gentle climb, with a shorter round-trip route to the summit (5.25 miles) than other big peaks. From Fairplay, take U.S. 285 to County Road 18 (Four Mile Creek Rd.) and drive 10 miles to the parking area. Walk past a gate and some mine shacks; a cairn marks the summit trail on a 13,140-foot saddle. From here it's just a quick one-mile scramble to the summit.

A greater fourteener challenge is **Mount Harvard,** which demands some technical rock climbing just before the summit. From Denver, take U.S. 285 southwest to Highway 24 north into Buena Vista; go west on County Road 350, then right on County Road 361; take a sharp left on County Road 365, enter the San Isabel National Forest, and find the trailhead and parking area where the pavement ends.

Boating enthusiasts will appreciate a weekend getaway at **Turquoise Lake,** which has two launches, as well as hiking trails and ample room for campers. **May Queen** (719/486-0749, $16) is one of the prettiest of the eight campgrounds in this area, with 27 campsites at an elevation of 9,900 feet, and it has excellent mountain views. To get here, take Harrison Street to West 6th Street, then turn right on Turquoise Lake Road (Forest Rd. 104); May Queen is 10 miles past the dam.

Events

The weirdest event in Leadville is the International Pack Burro Race, which began in 1949, when people presumably still asked burros to carry all their heavy stuff. The race, a surreal part of Leadville's early-August **Boom Days** (www.leadville.com/boomdays) celebration, demands that participants lead burros over a 21-mile course, some of which goes over the 13,183-foot Mosquito Pass summit. Oh, and the burros carry 35-pound packs.

Accommodations

Leadville is a great one-night stopover on the way to Aspen or Snowmass, with several excellent bed-and-breakfasts in the town's historic district. **McGinnis Cottage** (809 Spruce St., 719/486-3110 or 800/288-1775, www.mcginniscottage.com, $130–160) has three guest rooms in a restored Victorian, all with down mattresses and views of nearby fourteeners. **Peri & Ed's Mountain Hideaway** (201 W. 8th St., 719/486-0716 or 800/933-3715, www.mountainhideaway.com/bb, $49–159) is surrounded by pine trees with mountains in the distance.

Food

For upscale diners willing to travel to a yurt via cross-country skis, snowshoes, or snowmobile, the **Tennessee Pass Cookhouse** (U.S. 24, 719/486-8114, www.tennesseepass.com/cookhouse.htm, 5:30–9 P.M. daily late Nov.–mid-Apr., 5:30–9 P.M. Thurs.–Sun. early July–early Oct., $75 for 4 courses) has meals of elk tenderloin, rack of lamb, salmon, chicken, and vegetables. In downtown Leadville, The **Grill Bar and Café** (715 Elm St., 719/486-9930, www.grillbarcafe.com, 4–9 P.M. Wed.–Mon., noon–9 P.M. Sun. summer, 4–9 P.M. Wed.–Mon. winter, $12) has a usually packed patio overlooking Mount Massive. The margaritas, green chili, and hand-roasted peppers from Hatch, New Mexico, are well worth a stopover meal.

Information and Services

The **Leadville Lake County Chamber** (809 Harrison Ave., 719/486-3900, www.leadvilleusa.com) provides information about town history and businesses.

Medical services are available at **St. Vincent's Hospital** (822 W. 4th St., 719/486-0230, www.svghd.org).

CARBONDALE

The most exhilarating and meditative thing to do in Carbondale, about 30 miles northwest of Aspen, is gaze southward at the 12,965-foot-high, usually snowcapped, double-peaked

Mount Sopris. It gives Carbondale a kind of grandeur, even though the tiny town at the center of the Maroon Bells–Snowmass Wilderness is otherwise known as a less crowded, slightly less expensive alternative to Aspen. The restaurants, hiking trails, and shopping here are amazing, though, and Carbondale is definitely worth a separate trip.

Carbondale's history mirrors several towns in the Colorado Rockies. The Ute Indians settled here first and flourished until gold prospectors pushed them out in the 1880s. Local settlers opened cattle and sheep ranches and made so much money from potatoes that they were able to open a prestigious railroad depot. Depressions in 1893 and the 1930s stalled the rapid growth, however, and Carbondale's population dropped until Aspen began to boom as a ski town and tourism made the entire Roaring Fork Valley region affluent and upscale. For a long time, Carbondale was an inexpensive way to experience Aspen, but since the early 1990s, the town has boomed right alongside its chichi neighbor.

Sports and Recreation

Mount Sopris is totally climbable, but it's long (13 miles) and tough, elevating past several pretty lakes (including Dinkle and Thomas), yards of rocky terrain, and a couple of frustrating false summits. It's worth it, though, because the view from the real summit includes Glenwood Springs, Carbondale, a huge swath of the Roaring Fork Valley, Chair Mountain, McClure Pass, the Aspen and Snowmass ski areas, and a bunch of other excellent landmarks. To get to the trailhead, drive 2.5 miles south from the intersection of Highways 82 and 133 (just outside Carbondale), then turn left on Prince Creek Road, drive about five miles, stay right, and look for the parking area at Dinkle Lake.

Carbondale is also close to a bunch of easier trails (and more challenging ones, for that matter). The 3.7-mile **Middle Thompson Trail** begins about 7.4 miles west of Carbondale: take County Road 108 to County Road 305, turn left, drive about four miles, then take the right fork onto County Road 306, before parking at

a lot uphill. The trail passes a variety of pretty meadows, aspens, streams, and wildflowers. The **Lake Ridge Lakes Trail,** at 1.5 miles, is especially great for cyclists, running past lakes and oak brush before opening up to Mount Sopris views. To get here, take County Road 108 to County Road 305, turn left, drive about four miles, then stop at the intersection with County Road 306 and park at the old railroad grade; head uphill, past Middle Thompson Creek, about 1.5 miles to the trailhead sign.

Some anglers believe the best part of the Roaring Fork River, which plummets from 12,095-foot Independence Pass, is where it meets the Crystal River just outside Carbondale. Packed with trout, this middle part of the Roaring Fork is especially popular in the early season (that is, before late July, when it's a bit too low). The 13 miles of this river between Carbondale and Basalt are considered Gold Medal Waters. Also excellent for fishing: the lower Roaring Fork, which extends from Carbondale to Glenwood Springs and is known for its 5–8-pound fish; and the Colorado and Fryingpan Rivers, both roughly 15 minutes away by car. An excellent fishing resource for this area is Mike Shook's *The Complete Fly Fishing Guide to the Roaring Fork Valley,* available along with numerous other Colorado fishing guides and maps at www.flyfishguide.com/flyfishguide/Fryingpan.html. Finally, **Alpine Angling Adventure Travel** (995 Cowen Dr., Suite 102, Carbondale, 970/963-9245 or 800/781-8120, www.roaringforkanglers.com) rents equipment, organizes guided tours, and provides maps and other information.

Several campgrounds in the Maroon Bells–Snowmass Wilderness, not far from Carbondale, are among the prettiest in the state. To get to **Avalanche Creek Campground** (White River National Forest, 900 Grand Ave., Glenwood Springs, 970/945-2521), take Highway 133 south from Carbondale, drive 12.5 miles, turn left at the "Avalanche Creek" sign, and drive 2.5 more miles to the parking area at the end of the campground. It's near the great Avalanche Creek hiking trail, which

THE "SUBURBS" OF SKI TOWNS

Technically, Edwards isn't a suburb of Vail, and Carbondale isn't a suburb of Aspen, but both nearby towns give visitors a chance to experience chichi ski resorts without busting their budgets. Here are a few examples of where to stay if there's no place remotely affordable in Aspen, Vail, Keystone, Breckenridge, or Winter Park.

EDWARDS (VAIL)

Just 15 miles west of Vail along I-70, Edwards is the fastest-growing town in Eagle County and stuffed with surprisingly great restaurants, including **Juniper** (97 Main St., Suite E101, 970/926-7001, www.juniper-restaurant.com, 5:30-10 P.M. daily) and **Zino Ristorante** (27 Main St., 970/926-0777, www.zinoristorante.com, 5-9 P.M. daily). True bargain-hunters should stop by the **Vail Valley Cares Thrifty Shops** (34510 U.S. 6, Suite C2, 970/926-7134, www.vailvalleycares.com, 10 A.M.-6 P.M. Mon.-Fri., 10 A.M.-4 P.M. Sat.), which sells $3 CDs and $6.50 designer jeans.

CARBONDALE (ASPEN)

Less slick and streamlined than Edwards, Carbondale is a 130-plus-year-old mountain town (elevation 6,181 feet) located underneath the beautiful, near-13,000-foot Mount Sopris. Outdoors enthusiasts frequently drop by en route to Aspen, rent a pair of cross-country skis, and wind up so happy with the **Spring Gulch Nordic Council** (springgulch@sopris. net, www.springgulch.org) and its 50 miles of groomed trails that they never get any farther. Although prices for everything have been slowly rising since the town started its growth cycle in the early 1990s, Carbondale is still far more affordable than Aspen, 30 miles away. Try the woodsy **Ambiance Inn** (66 N. 2nd St., 970/963-3597 or 800/350-

1515, www.ambianceinn.com, $90-100); the restaurant **six89** (689 Main St., 970/963-6890, www.six89.com, 5:30-9 P.M. Tues.-Sun.); and, for a huge thrift-store selection, including $20 cashmere sweaters, **Misers Mercantile** (303 Main St., 970/963-3940, 10 A.M.-5:30 P.M. Mon.-Fri., 10 A.M.-5 P.M. Sat., 10 A.M.-3 P.M. Sun.).

DILLON AND SILVERTHORNE (KEYSTONE/BRECKENRIDGE)

Budget-conscious locals know that staying overnight regularly in Keystone to access the resort's amazing slopes and terrain parks is pretty much impossible, so they stop at the twin I-70 shopping towns of Dillon and Silverthorne. The hotels and restaurants are pretty much the affordable-chain variety, but the **Outlets at Silverthorne** (46-V Rainbow Dr., 866/746-7686, www.outletsatsilverthorne. com, 10 A.M.-8 P.M. Mon.-Sat., 11 A.M.-6 P.M. Sun.) often derail shopping enthusiasts from hitting the slopes (Breckenridge is 16 miles away, Keystone is 16 miles, and even Vail is just 32 miles) in a timely fashion.

FRASER (WINTER PARK)

Winter Park isn't nearly as pricey as neighboring Vail, Breckenridge, or Keystone, but Fraser is nonetheless popular among ski bums as a quiet, rural, sneeze-and-you-miss-it alternative. Stay at the plainspoken **Pinnacle Lodge** (108 Zerex St., 970/722-7631, www.pinnaclelodge.com, $130-220) and grab a drink at the **Crooked Creek Saloon** (401 Zerex St., 970/726-9250, www.crookedcreeksaloon. com, 11 A.M.-1:30 A.M. Mon.-Fri., 8 A.M.-1:30 A.M. Sat.-Sun.), both on Zerex Street, otherwise known as U.S. 40, the narrow road connecting Fraser to Winter Park, five miles south.

leads to broader areas such as the Hell Roaring Trail and East Creek Trail. These routes are especially popular with horseback-riders and backpackers.

In the winter, cross-country skiers swear by the **Spring Gulch Nordic Council** (springgulch@sopris.net, www.springgulch. org), which has 50 miles of groomed trails of varying degrees of difficulty north of Mount Sopris. Note that the trails are not patrolled, so bring a bit of backcountry experience.

For more information about outdoor

activities in Carbondale, including official U.S. Forest Service maps and rules about pets and wildlife, contact the **Sopris Ranger District** (620 Main St., 970/963-2266).

Carbondale's superb golf courses complement those in Aspen: **Aspen Glen** (0545 Bald Eagle Way, 970/704-1905, www.aspen-glen. com, $131 guests) was designed by Jack Nicklaus and is located along the Roaring Fork River, while the public **River Valley Ranch** (303 River Valley Ranch Dr., 970/963-3625, www.rvgolf.com, $95) is 520 acres at the base of Mount Sopris.

Entertainment and Events

At the intimate **Steve's Guitars** (19 4th St., 970/963-3304, http://stevesguitars.net), numerous guitars hanging from the ceiling supplement mostly local musicians playing live music.

During a long weekend in late July, the 40-plus-year-old **Carbondale Mountain Fair** (www.carbondalearts.com/mountain-fair) draws local rock bands, student recitals, drum circles, and a puppet-and-mask theater to Sopris Park, along Main Street. For this event, camping is allowed behind Carbondale Middle School.

Shopping

Carbondale's Main Street shopping district isn't quite as world-class as its neighbor to the southeast, but a few shops are worth the day trip. One is the **Roadside Gallery** (320 Main St., 970/963-9333 or 866/963-9332, www. roadsidegallery.com, 9 A.M.–6 P.M. Mon.– Fri.), which sells paintings and photos of classic American road signs—like a neon "Mom's Café" and a "Lum's Chop Suey" festooned

with a green-and-yellow palm tree. **Lulubelle** (320 Main St., Suite 100, 970/510-5141, www. lulbellecarbondale.com, 10 A.M.–6 P.M. Mon.– Sat.) is a women's clothing boutique selling all the hipster brands—Tano Handbags, Paige Denim, Alternative Apparel, and the like.

Accommodations

The Roaring Fork Valley's most distinctive hotels are in Aspen, of course, and the Redstone Castle is 18 miles away in Redstone. But Carbondale has a couple of distinctive and affordable properties, including the **Ambiance Inn** (66 N. 2nd St., 970/963-3597 or 800/350-1515, www.ambianceinn.com, $90–145). Its best room is the Aspen Suite, which has a wide redwood deck in addition to an indoor bar and sun room.

Food

Carbondale's best restaurant is **six89** (689 Main St., 970/963-6890, www.six89.com, 5:30–9 P.M. Tues.–Sun., $9–30), in a dimly lit mountain house that looks so comforting you expect meat loaf and chicken noodle soup to be the only items on the menu. Instead, six89 offers grilled octopus, buffalo-style veal sweetbreads, and slow-roasted Berkshire pork with a palisade peach barbecue sauce—in addition to the comforting burgers, steaks, and salmon dishes, of course.

Information

The **Carbondale Chamber of Commerce** (981 Cowen Dr., Suite C, 970/963-1890) runs the visitor-focused www.carbondale. com, while the **Town of Carbondale** (511 Colorado Ave., 970/963-2733, www.carbondalegov.org) provides information more tailored to residents.

Vail and Vicinity

It's possible to spend a few days in Aspen and have the time of your life without even thinking about skiing. Not so with Vail. Yes, there are luxurious things here—some of the hotels, restaurants, and shops are the best in the Rockies—but the entire culture revolves

around preparing for the slopes, skiing, and relaxing afterward. Skiers will find no problem with that arrangement; the resort's back bowls and tree-filled basins were world-renowned even before President Gerald Ford visited here in the 1970s. But nonskiers, especially in winter, may find Vail Resorts' "company town" overcrowded and obsessed with moguls and goggles.

Vail has been the white-gold standard for skiing since the resort opened in 1962, in what was once practically a ghost town. Although business dipped somewhat after 9/11, leading to a desperate plunge into deals and bonus amenities, Vail's charm and luxury remain intact. The central Vail Village area is a heavy concentration of fireplace-equipped lodges and restaurants with hopping outdoor patios, and it's fun to wander around even when the skiers come clomping back from the slopes over the central wooden covered bridge. The new Adventure Ridge (on the side of a mountain and accessible only via the Eagle Bahn Gondola) is a late-night family fun center with a bar, restaurant, laser tag, and "thrill sleds."

The resort isn't as hoity-toity as Aspen, but the shopping has become almost as important (and expensive) as the skiing. "Ski-in, ski-out" restaurants and lodges are right up against the mountains, so customers barely have to take their skis off to take a break.

The Vail resort is the anchor of Vail Valley, the broad area around I-70 that includes Eagle, Beaver Creek (a super-high-class resort that rivals Vail's skiing), Minturn, Arrowhead, and Edwards. The White River National Forest surrounds the area, and local entrepreneurs provide mountain biking, horseback riding, rock climbing, hot-air ballooning, and, yes, llama trekking. The area can be visitor-heavy in summer, especially during festivals such as the Teva Mountain Games, the Brews and Chili Festival, and the Annual Vail Jazz Party, so watch for off-season deals.

Over the years, Vail's surrounding towns have developed a charm and personality of their own. Beaver Creek, a few miles west down I-70, is a gated resort that caters to luxury tourists; park in a garage, get off an elevator, and run into a row of art galleries with small $7,500 paintings and $8,500 sculptures. Although Minturn, off I-70 between Vail and Beaver Creek, has doggedly tried to protect

© STEVE CRECELIUS / VISIT DENVER

Vail Village aglow with Christmas lights, with the Gore Range in the background

ASPEN AND THE SKI TOWNS

its rural-town feel, developers are on the warpath; for now, its down-home restaurants and inns are the best places in Vail Valley to escape. And the quality of Edwards's restaurants has recently grown to match the quantity of its condos.

HISTORY

If not for imperialistic explorers and gold miners, the Utes might still be frolicking around the mountains of Vail, peacefully enjoying the region's dramatic peaks and valleys. Scratch that—they'd probably be making tons of money from skiing, just as Vail Resorts does today. But as the story goes, Irishman "Lord" George Gore and American Jim Bridger bushwhacked into Vail in the 1850s, paving the way for miners and railroad men to suck out the gold and silver and transport it to civilization beyond the Rockies. More and more miners showed up and pushed the Utes off the land; the vengeful Utes set fire to thousands of acres of trees, causing severe deforestation that happened to be just right for skiing.

Eventually the miners took off and left the bruised valley to become sheep farmers. It stayed quiet until 1939, when construction engineer Charlie Vail built U.S. 6 from Denver. But even then, Vail was a sleepy mountain town until World War II, when the U.S. Army's 10th Mountain Division used the area's backcountry trails for survival training. Some of those troops returned after the war as veterans, including Pete Seibert, who with several partners carried out a lavish plan to build a ski resort. They started building in 1962.

The officially incorporated Town of Vail arrived four years later—along with the first gondola in the United States, two double chairlifts, and before long, restaurants, hotels, and a medical clinic. Its reputation as a ski area exploded worldwide in the mid-1970s—thanks to the Utes' choppy, bumpy, tree-lined paths—and sometime resident Gerald Ford became president in 1974. Like the rest of Colorado's ski-resort towns, Vail has become much more sophisticated (some would say corporate) since then, adding more and more trails, year-round

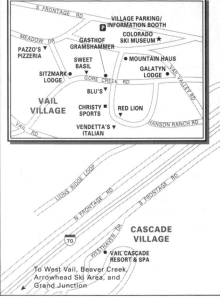

gondolas and chairlifts, tennis tournaments, and hot-air balloon rides.

SIGHTS
Colorado Ski Museum

The small Colorado Ski Museum (231 S. Frontage Rd. E., 970/476-1876, www.ski-museum.net, 10 A.M.–7:30 P.M. daily winter, 10 A.M.–5:30 P.M. daily spring–fall, free), on the third floor outside the Vail Village parking garage, is one of the few local attractions that rarely draws long lines—which is a shame, because the snowboarding and skiing histories presented here, along with the equipment and clothes of U.S. Olympic heroes such as Billy Kidd and Nelson Carmichael, put the lifts and moguls outside into perspective. I wasn't aware, for example, that inventor Tom Sims built the first snowboard in 1963 and later used one as a stuntman in the 1985 James Bond movie *A View to a Kill.* Also, the first-ever snowboard competition was in nearby Leadville.

Betty Ford Alpine Gardens

Given the underwhelming nature of his

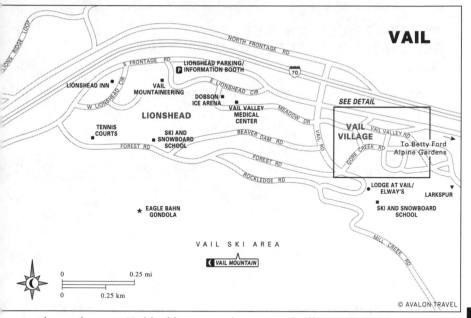

presidency, the many Vail buildings named after Gerald R. Ford can seem comical at first (the man skied there in the 1970s, for heaven's sake; he didn't win any Olympic luge medals!), but the late president and his wife, Betty Ford, who died in 2011, made numerous contributions to Vail Valley over the years. The Betty Ford Alpine Gardens (183 Gore Creek Dr., 970/476-0103, www. bettyfordalpinegardens.org, dawn–dusk daily, free), located in Gerald R. Ford Park, not far from Gerald R. Ford Amphitheater, is a sprawling park filled with mountain-grown flowers of every type, from roses and hyacinths to *Hymenoxys grandiflora*. Even if you're not big into flower classification, the waterfalls and rock gardens are worth wandering around during spring and summer.

SPORTS AND RECREATION
◖ Vail Mountain
Colorado skiers constantly debate the particulars of resorts—Keystone's night trails or Breckenridge's expert runs? Copper Mountain's convenience or Aspen's luxury? But Vail transcends all arguments. The mountain is 11,500 feet high, with 193 trails over 5,289 acres, and it ranges from the seven naturally formed and beautifully bumpy Back Bowls to the long, steep Front Side, which caters to beginners but has a few expert trails. The tree-filled Blue Sky Basin has only 645 acres, but no matter how many skiers show up on a given day at Vail, the trails are always secluded and almost eerily quiet. High-speed lifts, too, mean few bottlenecks.

Vail can be a bit tricky to traverse, and it doesn't look like much when you first encounter the mountain from the base area. But the higher up you go, the more complex the chutes and moguls become. "It can take an hour to get to where you want to be on the mountain, but once you're there, it's incredible," says Ryan Anderson, a Denver native and 21-year Colorado skiing and snowboarding veteran.

Beginners should plan to stick with the Front Side, notably the Lost Boy trail, which seems to last forever and has great views of the mountain range. (Conversely, beginners should avoid the Back Bowls and Blue Sky Basin, which have exactly zero green trails.)

TEN SKI TRAILS WHOSE REPUTATIONS PRECEDE THEM

Deborah Marks, senior editor at Boulder-based *Ski* magazine, generously took time out of her glamorous schedule of snowcat-skiing excursions to provide this list of Colorado's 10 top (or at least *very notable*) runs:

1. **Arapahoe Basin/Pallavicini:** An expert, double-black-diamond trail off the Pallavicini lift is named after the Pallavicini Couiloir on the highest peak in Austria. While it's not the most difficult run at A-Basin (the East Wall holds that claim), it's certainly the signature trail. A very long and steep bump run, it tests even the best skiers.

2. **Loveland/Porcupine Ridge:** Loveland's southern boundary runs right along the Continental Divide. From the top of Lift 9, you can look east into the Loveland Basin or west toward A-Basin and Summit County.

3. **Breckenridge/Devil's Crotch:** Devil's Crotch, off the north side of Peak 9, accessed from the E Chair, is a gnarly bump run that's super-steep.

4. **Vail/Riva's Ridge:** Not only is this one of the longest runs in Colorado (four miles), it's also one of the most historic. In 1942 the U.S. Army's 10th Mountain Division (its first alpine unit) climbed and skied over Riva's Ridge in Italy to attack a German corps during World War II. The 10th was made up of volunteers, recruited for their climbing and skiing abilities. After the war, it was the men of the 10th Mountain Division who more or less built the American alpine skiing industry. Bob Parker, who was a member of the 10th and one of the first VPs at Vail and later an editor at *Skiing Magazine,* named his favorite run at Vail after the Italian ridge. The run at Vail is a long, meandering intermediate trail with a few steep pitches. It is groomed pretty regularly, so it's a great family trail.

5. **Beaver Creek/Golden Eagle:** Golden Eagle, which you can access from the Cinch Express lift or the Birds of Prey lift, is another double-black-diamond trail that

Experts should proceed immediately to the mountain's east side, notably the Prima and Highline trails, which are filled with sharp bumps and log chutes. Check the resort website at www.vail.com, or call 970/496-4800 or 800/805-2457, for lift information, directions, and weather reports. Lift tickets generally run $108 per day.

For skiing and boarding tricksters, Vail has three terrain parks, including **Golden Peak,** located under the Riva Bahn, halfway up the mountain along Chair 6. It has 33 features, 12 jumps from 10 to 65 feet, a 500-foot-long, 18-foot-deep half-pipe, and a couple of smaller pipes.

The **SnowSports School** (970/754-8245 or 800/475-4543, http://vail.snow.com/winter/ss.asp) gives private and group lessons for all skill levels, and 850 instructors speak 30 different languages. The two sales offices are at the bases of Lionshead and Golden Peak. And Vail Village is, naturally, packed with ski-and-snowboard rental shops—try **Christy Sports** (293 Bridge St., 970/476-2244, www.christysports.com) or **Vail Sports** (492 E. Lionshead Circle, 970/476-3600, www.vailsports.com), which has several central locations throughout the resort.

Other Winter Sports

Vail Resorts offers lessons and rentals for many different skiing activities—cross-country, telemarking, snowshoeing, and snowmobiling. For lessons, which run about $65 for three hours, call 970/479-3210. If you plan to venture out on your own, be careful; not everything that looks like a ski trail is really a ski trail. The **Eagle-Holy Cross Ranger District** (24747 U.S. 24, Minturn, 970/827-5715), **Eagle Ranger District** (125 W. 5th St., Eagle, is also the site of the only men's World Cup downhill race in the United States. When it's not groomed, it's a long, steep, gnarly bump run. When it is groomed, it's still steep and gnarly – only minus the bumps.

6. **Snowmass/The Big Burn:** Snowmass is known as the most family-friendly of all the mountains. That reputation can be attributed to The Big Burn, which is an expansive intermediate trail. It was the first trail in the United States to be shamelessly marketed as "intermediate."

7. **Telluride/Palmyra Peak and Black Iron Bowl:** This is probably the best, most scenic, most spectacular hike-to, inbounds terrain in the state, if not the country. It opened in the 2007-2008 season. I skied it recently and *oh, my God.*

8. **Mary Jane/Outhouse:** When it comes to single-word monikers, Outhouse ranks right up there with Madonna: Anyone who has skied in Colorado for any length of time knows of its reputation. It is a long,

grueling bump run. The moguls are like small Volkswagen Beetles. Mary Jane is known as Colorado's best place for bumps, and Outhouse is the biggest, toughest bump run there.

9. **Steamboat/Shadows:** Everyone knows about Steamboat's trademarked Champagne Powder, but it is also the best glade skiing in the state. None of the gladed trails at Steamboat are very steep, but that's what makes them so much fun. You can just float down through the powder at a nice, comfortable, and safe pace. Shadows is 4,600 feet long – almost a mile – and it covers nearly 2,000 feet of vertical.

10. **Echo Mountain:** Terrain parks and freestyle skiing are exploding right now. For its fans and participants, moving downhill is of no interest, so park-only areas are popping up around the country. Echo Mountain is on the Front Range, only 30 minutes from Denver, so it's great for quick trips. It's basically a skate park on snow.

970/328-6388), and **Colorado Avalanche Information Center** (303/499-9650, http://avalanche.state.co.us) give free advice on safety as well as directions.

The **10th Mountain Hut Association** (1280 Ute Ave., Suite 21, Aspen, 970/925-5775, www.huts.org) offers tours on trails all around Summit County, including Vail Pass (which has a trailhead at an elevation of 10,580 feet) and Commando Run (which is accessible by car near Mill Creek but more easily by gondola). Also, **Paragon Guides** (970/926-5299, www.paragonguides.com) offers backcountry skiing and hut-to-hut tours that last 3–5 days each. Snowmobile rentals are available via **Nova Guides** (719/486-2656, www.novaguides.com), which also runs the nearby Pando Cabins.

Vail's **Activities Desk** (970/476-9090) will direct you to the right arena.

Hiking and Biking

Hundreds of miles of biking and hiking trails run in and out of Vail Valley, including many on Vail Mountain itself—start with the pretty, one-mile Eagle's Loop. Later, step up a few notches in difficulty and take Kloser's Klimb, a steep hike up 1,000 vertical feet. Then go straight down six miles from Eagle's Nest through groves of aspen trees. Just outside of Vail, down I-70 about five miles to the northeast, is the entrance to Eagle's Nest Wilderness, hundreds of acres of snowcapped peaks, beautiful lakes and creeks, and aspen and spruce trees.

The Vail area is home to **Mount Holy Cross,** one of the most dramatic and popular fourteeners due to a mysterious cross pattern etched into its rocks. When snow falls, it highlights the cross even more. But the best way to see the cross is to climb nearby **Notch Mountain.** To

© MATT INDEN/WEAVER MULTIMEDIA GROUP/COLORADO TOURISM OFFICE

a wildflower hike near Vail

get there, go west from Minturn on I-70; exit onto U.S. 24, then go four miles to Forest Road 707; turn right and drive eight miles to the Fall Creek Trailhead; pick up the Notch Mountain Trail after 2.5 miles on the Fall Creek Trail.

For bicycle rentals, as well as tours and repairs, try **Vail Bike Tech** (555 E. Lionshead Circle, 970/476-5995 or 800/525-5995, www.vailbiketech.com), near the Eagle Bahn Gondola. Vail Mountain trail information is at www.vail.com: click on "summer" at the bottom and look for recreational activities, and call the **Dillon Ranger District** (680 Blue River Pkwy., Silverthorne, 970/468-5400, www.dillonrangerdistrict.com) or the **Eagle-Holy Cross Ranger District** (24747 U.S. 24, 970/827-5715) about outside-the-town hikes and bike rides.

Camping

Hidden Treasure Yurt (off I–70, 16 miles south of Eagle, near New York Mountain, 800/444-2813, www.backcountry-colo-rado-yurt.com) rents two yurts to campers in Eagle County. The yurts sleep eight people with bunk beds and are available in summer and winter, with a wood stove, a propane stove for cooking, and bright propane lamps. Guests bring their own sleeping bags.

Golf

The Vail area has more than 18 golf courses, including some at hotels and lodges such as the private **Sonnenalp Golf Club** (1265 Berry Creek Rd., Edwards, 970/477-5372, www.sonnenalp.com/activities/golf, $80–130 guests). The **Vail Golf Club** (1778 Vail Valley Dr., 970/479-2260 or 888/709-3939, http://vailgolfclub.net/golf.cfm, $45–80), an 18-hole, par-72 course, is at 8,200 feet in elevation, which means the ball will fly 10 percent farther (in theory) than at sea-level courses.

NIGHTLIFE

The Tap Room (333 Bridge St., 970/479-0500, www.taproomvail.com, 11 A.M.–1:30 A.M. daily) is a cozy après-ski drinker's haven with a central fireplace. **Samana Lounge** (228 Bridge St., 970/476-3433, www.samanalounge.com, 9:30 P.M.–2 A.M. daily, reduced hours off-season) is a nice change of pace from the reggae and hippie bands that dominate the local music scene. The martini lounge's DJs play electronic dance music, with a jazzy, chill-out feel toward the end of the night.

For live music, **Sandbar Sports Grill** (2161 N. Frontage Rd., 970/476-4314, www.sandbarvail.com, 11 A.M.–2 A.M. daily) caters to a young, hippieish crowd, booking plenty of reggae bands, Grateful Dead tribute acts, and DJs who play the same. **The Club** (304 Bridge St., 970/479-0556, www.theclubvail.com) also specializes in live music, by local and national country acts and singer-songwriters such as Scott Munns and Steve Meyer.

Just down the highway from Vail, in Eagle, the cleverly named **The Back Bowl** (I-70 Exit 147, Eagle, 970/328-2695, www.thebackbowl.com, 4 P.M.–midnight Mon.–Fri., noon–1 A.M. Sat., 11 A.M.–midnight Sun.) begins the day as a café and sports bar (seven TV screens!) and transforms at night into a 20-lane bowling alley with comfy couches and swanky lounge areas surrounding the lanes.

Vail has a healthy après-ski bar scene, centered on Vail Village. When I recently ventured to the **Red Lion** (304 Bridge St., 970/476-7676, www.theredlion.com, 11 A.M.–close daily), a guitarist was covering the Eagles' "Hotel California" on the jammed outdoor patio in the middle of winter. So it's that kind of place. **Vendetta's Italian Restaurant** (291 Bridge St., 970/476-5070, http://vendettasvail.com, 11 A.M.–2 A.M. daily) is a pizza place that has developed into a village nighttime hangout. Inside the flag-covered, over-the-top-European Gasthof Gramshammer hotel, **Pepi's Bar & Restaurant** (231 E. Gore Creek Dr., 970/476-5626, www.pepis.com, 11:30 A.M.–3 P.M. and 5–9 P.M. daily) supplements its wild game- and veal-dominated menu with plenty of beverages. **The George** (292 E. Meadow Dr., 970/476-2656, 6 P.M.–2 A.M. daily) is a friendly English-style pub.

EVENTS

The **Bravo! Vail Valley Music Festival** (970/827-5700 or 877/812-5700, www.vailmusicfestival.org), running late June–early August, started with a handful of people and musicians in 1987 but has grown to crowds of more than 60,000 people. Among the attractions: the Dallas Symphony Orchestra and the New York Philharmonic.

Held in late July–early August at the Gerald R. Ford Amphitheater, the **Vail International Dance Festival** (970/777-2015 or 888/920-2787, www.vaildance.org) began in 1989 with the Bolshoi Ballet Academy. It continues to focus on ballet, although recent attractions such as the Fly Dance Company, a Houston hip-hop and break dancing outfit, give it a fun, modern edge.

Late spring's **Vail Film Festival** (970/476-1092, www.vailfilmfestival.org) is hardly Cannes, or even Telluride, but it draws a nice selection of up-and-coming movie premieres, including 2004's acclaimed *Before Sunset*.

Some 5,000 hungry people attended the latest **Taste of Vail** (various locations in Vail Valley, 970/926-5665, www.tasteofvail.com), a charity event that showcases hundreds of local and national chefs, restaurants, winemakers, and foods from pork-belly sandwiches to maple bourbon foie gras *panna cotta*. The festivities include seminars with prominent chefs and riesling experts along with mountaintop picnics.

SHOPPING

Not surprisingly, most of Vail's top shops are geared to skiers, and in Vail Village, it's hard to swing a pole without whacking into a boot store. Among the most prominent are **Pepi Sports** (231 Bridge St., 970/476-5206, www.pepisports.com, 10 A.M.–6 P.M. Mon.–Thurs., 10 A.M.–7 P.M. Fri.–Sat.), which makes a big point of shaping footwear to fit your foot, and **Charter Sports** (716 W. Lionshead Place, 888/295-9797, www.chartersports.com, 7 A.M.–10 P.M. daily, reduced hours off-season), in the Lion Square Lodge.

Vail is a cornucopia of high-end galleries

and shops—and while it's not as shopping-conscious as pricey neighbor Aspen, travelers often come here just for the stores. Among them: the fine-jewelry **Currents** (285 Bridge St., 970/476-3322, www.currentsfinejewelers.com, 10 A.M.–9 P.M. daily winter and summer, 10 A.M.–5 P.M. daily fall and spring), the upscale cowboy-clothing **Axel's** (201 Gore Creek Dr., 970/476-7625, www.axelsltd.com, 10 A.M.–6 P.M. Sun.–Wed., 10 A.M.–8 P.M. Thurs.–Sat.), the Italian-clothing **Luca Bruno** (40 E. Meadow Dr., 970/476-1667, www.lucabruno.com, 10 A.M.–6 P.M. daily), and the **Masters Gallery at Vail** (100 E. Meadow Dr., 970/477-0600, www.mastersgalleryvail.com, 10 A.M.–8 P.M. Mon.–Sat., 10 A.M.–5 P.M. Sun.), which sells many colorful and vivid paintings by artists such as James Jensen and Carrie Fell. Beyond the path, **Pismo Fine Art Glass** (122 E. Meadow Dr., 970/476-2400, www.pismoglass.com, 10 A.M.–6 P.M. daily) sells handblown glass collections that twist into exotic shapes, like Brian Brenno's *Blue Hat with Turquoise Flower* ($800).

ACCOMMODATIONS

Vail's best hotels are crowded in the central part of town—mostly Vail Village and Golden Peak—and some of the best are within a few hundred yards of the slopes. Now that the economical Roost Lodge in West Vail has closed, the only way to find a truly affordable hotel is to try outlying areas such as Minturn, Eagle, or Edwards. (Comfort Inn has an outlet in Eagle and another in Vail itself.) Skiers know to factor in high-season lodging prices, and lift-ticket packages are often the best deals. Prices drop dramatically in the off-season. And don't ignore condos; they're everywhere.

$100-150

In Edwards, which has become sort of a Vail suburb in recent years, **The Inn and Suites at Riverwalk** (27 Main St., Edwards, 970/926-0606 or 888/926-0606, www.innandsuitesatriverwalk, $120–180) has an outdoor pool, mountain views in many guest rooms, free parking (not something you typically get in Vail), and free shuttles to the Vail and Arrowhead ski areas.

Some of the most affordable guest rooms in the Vail Valley are in Eagle—**Silverleaf Suites** (315 Chambers Ave., Eagle, 970/328-3000 or 877/324-5328, www.silverleafsuites.com, $101) has a ski resort–style stone fireplace in the lobby, but otherwise it's pretty standard stuff.

$150-200

The **Lionshead Inn** (705 W. Lionshead Circle, 970/476-2050 or 800/283-8245, www.lionsheadinn.com, $149–289) is a functional skiers' hotel that just happens to be in one of the best locations in town—in the middle of the Lionshead area, less than a block from the Eagle Bahn Gondola and Chair 8. The exercise and game rooms are a nice plus.

$200-300

In case Vail didn't look enough like an Austrian ski village, the **Gasthof Gramshammer** (231 E. Gore Creek Dr., 970/476-5626 or 800/610-7374, www.pepis.com, $245–295) has the old-script lettering and women in Bo Peep outfits (at least, as depicted on the website) to correct the oversight. Run since 1964 by former Olympic skier Pepi Gramshammer and his wife, Sheika, the brightly colored inn has a party atmosphere, with happy-hour skiers populating an outdoor patio even in the middle of winter.

The Lodge at Vail (174 E. Gore Creek Dr., 970/476-5011 or 877/528-7625, http://lodgeatvail.rockresorts.com, $259–329) had been open for exactly one month when the first gondola opened on Vail Mountain in 1962—and things have worked out pretty well for both the skiing industry and the lodge ever since. It's prime real estate, just a few steps from the slopes in Vail Village, and the best guest rooms have superb views of the mountain. There's also a heated outdoor pool, hot tubs, high-speed Internet access, and The Wildflower, one of the best restaurants in Vail.

The **Sitzmark Lodge** (183 E. Gore Creek Dr., 970/476-5001 or 888/476-5001, www.

sitzmarklodge.com, $255–295) is probably the town's best deal if ski-slope proximity is your primary concern. It's in Vail Village, ensconced between slopes, restaurants, and shops, and the prices aren't out of control. The guest rooms work just fine, like a more personable Marriott, and amenities like the year-round outdoor pools are a nice touch.

$300-400

The **Galatyn Lodge** (365 Vail Valley Dr., 970/479-2418 or 800/943-7322, www.thegalatynlodge.com, $375) emphasizes luxury, convenience, and privacy; it's at the center of Vail Village, but its stone-covered building doesn't broadcast itself to the crowds outside. (Unlike, say, the Gasthof Gramshammer, which screams, "Look at me!") The guest rooms are large and colorful, with air-conditioning, high-speed Internet access, DVD players, and fully equipped kitchens.

Directly next to Gore Creek, the luxurious **Vail Cascade Resort & Spa** (1300 Westhaven Dr., 970/476-7111 or 800/282-4183, www.vailcascade.com, $300–544) has amenities galore, from the 78,000-square-foot Aria Club & Spa, which even has its own basketball court, to heated outdoor swimming pools and hot tubs. The resort's recent $30 million renovation means one extremely important thing to summer visitors: air-conditioning!

Another comfortable lodge at the center of Vail Village is **Mountain Haus** (292 E. Meadow Dr., 970/476-2434 or 800/237-0922, www.mountainhaus.com, $350–650), whose fat, inviting lobby couches and armchairs hint at what to expect inside. Many of the guest rooms have stone fireplaces and balconies.

FOOD
Snacks, Cafés, and Breakfast
Although **Blu's** (193 E. Gore Creek Dr., 970/476-3113, www.blusrestaurant.com, 9 A.M.–11 P.M. daily, $23) is a pricey lunch-and-dinner establishment known for its something-for-everybody menu, including ribs, chicken-fried steak, tuna, and lasagna, I particularly recommend the brunch, which is both

light and filling, especially the oatmeal with brown sugar on the side.

Casual
Vail is especially indulgent of skiers who need pizza right away. **Vendetta's Italian Restaurant** (291 Bridge St., 970/476-5070, http://vendettasvail.com, 11 A.M.–2 A.M. daily, $15) is famous locally for the "snow pig"—a pie with sausage, hamburger, and ham, which pretty much covers the main food groups. **Pazzo's Pizzeria** (122 E. Meadow Dr., 970/476-9026, www.itsblank.com/pazzos, 11 A.M.–9 P.M. daily, $12) is perfectly located in Vail Village, just between the covered bridge and the parking lot, so it's almost always packed without even trying. The pizza is a little greasy and the service uneven on crowded nights, but the sandwiches are excellent, and it's a great place to relax, meet people, and not have to venture too far from the slopes.

The food at the **Red Lion** (304 Bridge St., 970/476-7676, www.theredlion.com, 11 A.M.–1 A.M. Mon.–Fri., 10 A.M.–1 A.M. Sat.–Sun., reduced hours off-season, $14) is perfect for skiers on a budget—wings, ribs, microbrews, burgers, fries, and onion rings. The location is perfect too, at the center of Vail Village, just steps from the slopes and hotels.

Upscale
Steak-and-potatoes specialist **Elway's** was supposed to open in The Lodge at Vail (174 E. Gore Creek Dr., 970/476-5011) as of Thanksgiving 2011. Former Broncos football great John Elway's namesake restaurant was supposed to replace one of Vail's best restaurants, Wildflower. Hours and other specifics were unknown at press time.

The only thing holding back the **Larkspur** (458 Vail Valley Dr., 970/754-8050, www.larkspurvail.com, 5–9 P.M. daily, reduced hours in summer, $32) is its location (inside the ski-in, ski-out Golden Peak Lodge), adjacent to a hotel lobby of boot-clomping skiers and screaming parents and kids. If you're looking for a peaceful meal, be sure to get a table as far into the restaurant as possible, with a full view of the nearby slopes; the food ranges from salmon to veal to beef. There's also a smaller Larkspur toward the entrance of the hotel that serves deli-style snacks and quick breakfasts.

Sweet Basil (193 E. Gore Creek Dr., 970/476-0125, www.sweetbasil-vail.com, 11:30 A.M.–2:30 P.M. and 6–10 P.M. daily, $29) is thicker and more luscious than even the best of Vail's gourmet restaurants—the fish isn't just fish, it's pan-roasted swordfish with tempura green beans and herb olive oil mashed potatoes. The apple pie isn't just apple pie, it's caramel apple tart with dark rum and ginger ice cream.

The **Game Creek Restaurant** (278 Hanson Ranch Rd., 970/754-4275, www.gamecreekclub.com, 5–8:30 P.M. Thurs.–Sat., 11 A.M.–2 P.M. Sun. summer, 5:30–9 P.M. Tues.–Sat. winter, $82 for 3 courses, $92 for 4 courses, $102 for 5 courses) isn't exactly a quick walk from your hotel; it involves gondola and snowcat rides straight up the mountain, into the Game Creek Bowl. More foie gras here, along with lamb chops, filet mignon, and a dessert whose name alone creates a sort of Pavlovian response: roasted chestnut ganache cake.

INFORMATION AND SERVICES

Check www.vail.com before making a trip here—its main thrust is the ski slopes, of course, so it has powder and weather updates, but the site is also filled with lodging and food information. Call 970/479-2100 or 866/650-9020 or visit www.vailgov.com for Town of Vail information, 800/842-8062 for Vail Resorts customer service, or 970/754-4888 for area weather and snow reports.

The **Vail Valley Medical Center** (181 W. Meadow Dr., 970/476-2451, www.vvmc. com) is based in Vail, but it serves all the valley towns—Beaver Creek, Minturn, Eagle, Edwards, and the rest.

GETTING THERE

Even before you see the first green Vail sign off I-70, heading east from Denver, you'll notice the condominiums. They're everywhere in Vail, and the ski village itself isn't until the second exit. That's where visitors will want to go; a huge parking garage is on the outskirts of the village, and while it fills up during prime ski times, it's almost always possible to find a spot. The third exit is West Vail, which is more of a regular town, with supermarkets, affordable restaurants, and somewhat cheaper-than-usual gas stations (although the gas prices here are a good $0.30 per gallon higher than in Denver or Boulder).

Vail has its own airport, the **Vail/Eagle County Airport** (219 Eldon Wilson Rd., Gypsum, 970/328-2680, www.eaglecounty.us/airport), with service to 13 U.S. cities on six major airlines. For the independently wealthy, there's also the **Vail Valley Jet Center** (871 Cooley Mesa Rd., Eagle, 970/524-7700, www.vvjc.com).

GETTING AROUND

A town-run **bus service** (970/479-2178, www.vailgov.com) serves numerous stops throughout Vail, including the Vail Run resort, the Sandstone Creek Club condo, Ford Park in the middle of town, and a variety of chain hotels. In the winter, it runs roughly 6 A.M.–2:10 A.M. daily, and summer hours are slightly reduced. Check the website for elaborate maps and schedules.

Vail Valley Taxi and Transportation (970/524-5555, www.vailtaxi.com) offers 24-hour shuttle service between the towns in Vail Valley and also goes to the Vail/Eagle County Airport.

The **Colorado Mountain Express** (970/754-7433 or 800/525-6363, www.coloradomountainexpress.com) shuttles skiers between the Vail ski resort and the Eagle airport to Denver International Airport, Glenwood Springs, Aspen, and other ski-oriented locations. Another shuttle, based in Beaver Creek, stops every 20 minutes at various points around the resort as well as Arrowhead, Avon, and Bachelor Gulch; call 970/949-1938 for a schedule. A bus service goes between Vail and Beaver Creek (970/328-3520). Taxis and shuttles are also available from Denver International Airport.

BEAVER CREEK

Since it opened in 1980, Beaver Creek has never tried to be the next Vail. It's too many miles west down I-70, for one thing, and buried within the town of Avon. But it has more than discovered its niche: luxury and class. The shops, hotels, and restaurants are several steps up in elegance from, say, Blu's in downtown Vail Village. Just know what you're getting into before you go; even the redbrick strip of art galleries immediately outside the central parking area can induce serious sticker shock.

Beaver Creek is a sort of gated community; driving in through Avon, the surrounding small mountain town off I-70, you have to identify yourself to a guard in a booth. The resort is more self-contained than even Vail or Keystone, and it has the feel of a super-outdoor-mall, complete with a network of escalators and a charming ice-skating rink in the middle of one of the plazas. The ski trails of Beaver Creek link to Bachelor Gulch and Arrowhead, both of which are in quaint surrounding towns on the same level of luxury (check out the home prices).

As for the slopes: The skiing is designed with all three skill levels in mind, with Beaver Creek Mountain summit available purely for beginners.

Sports and Recreation

Many skiers trek to Beaver Creek when Vail is mobbed, but that standard operating procedure hardly does the resort's slopes justice. Beaver Creek's 109 trails—not counting the 25 at Bachelor Gulch and 12 at Arrowhead—are equally distributed for beginners, intermediates, and black-diamond experts. Its deceptively steep Birds of Prey course, which starts at an elevation of 11,427 feet, was the site of four men's World Cup races, and its Grouse Mountain runs are legendarily (and strenuously) bumpy.

Skiing the village-to-village route from Beaver Creek to Bachelor Gulch to Arrowhead

Beaver Creek's mountain views are just as spectacular in the summer as they are in the winter.

© STEVE KNOPPER

ASPEN AND THE SKI TOWNS

and back again is one of the area's great charms. Bachelor Gulch generally has better powder but not as many expert runs, while Arrowhead is three resorts removed from Vail, so it's hardly ever filled with people. The resort has terrain parks, of course: **Park 101,** for beginners; **Zoom Room,** with 20–30-foot jumps for those with slightly more experience; **The Rodeo,** with 40–60-foot jumps for experts, plus highly technical rails, boxes, and logslides; and the **Half Barrel Half Pipe,** which is about 375 feet long and has 18-foot walls.

Beaver Creek's **Ski & Snowboard School** (800/842-8062) gives lessons (in the $150 range, but many packages are available) for all skill levels. Kids, women, snowboarders, Nordic skiers, and downhill racers can choose from a variety of classes, clinics, and private lessons. For rental equipment, try **Beaver Creek Sports** (111 Beaver Creek Plaza, Avon, 970/745-5400, www.beavercreeksports.com), which also rents bikes for the many area trails. It's probably easiest to reserve a rental-and-lift-ticket package online in advance. Lift tickets generally run about $108 per day.

The resort's best backcountry ski trails—more than 20 miles of them—are at **McCoy Park,** which is accessible from the Strawberry Park Express lift (number 12). Snowshoes are allowed on the lift. Warning: Although there are equal numbers of beginner, intermediate, and advanced tracked trails, there are many uphills, and it's easy to get exhausted at 9,840 feet. The **Beaver Creek Nordic Sports Center** (970/754-5313, 8:30 A.M.–4 P.M. daily Dec.–Apr.) rents cross-country skis and snowshoes and can answer questions about local trails.

One of the central charms of Beaver Creek Village Plaza is the year-round **ice-skating rink** (970/845-0438, noon–9 P.M. daily), just past the strip of art galleries beyond the parking garage. A Zamboni polishes the 150- by 65-foot rink every three hours, and $14 (including admission) rental skates are available at a nearby booth.

The **Red Sky Golf Club** (1099 Red Sky Rd., Wolcott, 970/754-4259 or 866/873-3759,

www.redskygolfclub.com, $195–250 guests) is a swanky private joint with segments designed by pros Tom Fazio and Greg Norman. Also on the premises is a golf academy, which at $320 per day isn't cheap but at a student-to-teacher ratio of four to one ensures plenty of personal swing attention. The **Beaver Creek Golf Club** (103 Offerson Rd., Avon, 970/754-5775, www.beavercreek.com/golf/beaver-creek-golf-club.aspx, $89–185) isn't quite as breathtaking as Red Sky, but it's a decent course with nice views. Robert Trent Jones Jr. designed the 18-hole course. Some hotels have golf facilities too, including the **Club at Cordillera** (0097 Main St., Edwards, 970/569-6480, www.cordillera-vail.com, $150–225), which has courses designed by the likes of Jack Nicklaus and Hale Irwin.

Deciding whether to **hike** in Vail or Beaver Creek is a toss-up—the only difference is that Vail tends to be more crowded during the spring and summer. As in ski season, Beaver Creek's big draw is the **Village-to-Village Trail,** a three-mile one-way hike through aspen trees with views of the Gore Range beyond the forest. To get there, take Village Road beyond Beaver Creek, and the trailhead is just past Elk Track Road on the right; after walking to Bachelor Gulch, you can turn around or call from the Ritz Carlton to arrange a shuttle pickup.

Beaver Creek Mountain itself has 50 miles of hiking-and-biking trails, including the popular **Beaver Lake Trail** and new **Royal Elk Trail,** both of which are easy jaunts to Beaver Lake. The **Beaver Creek Information Center** (970/845-9090) has more information on trails. **Beaver Creek Sports** (126 Riverfront Lane, 970/748-3080; Beaver Creek Mountain, 970/754-6221) rents bikes for roughly $50 for four hours. The **Beaver Creek Hiking Center** (970/754-5373, www.beavercreek.com/the-mountain/hiking-summer.aspx, spring–summer) provides guided hikes.

Entertainment and Nightlife

The **Vilar Center for the Arts** (68 Avondale Lane, 970/845-8497 or 888/920-2787, www.

An outdoor ice-skating rink is lit up at night in Beaver Creek.

vilarpac.org) is a 530-seat theater at the center of Beaver Creek Village (just down the escalator from the ice-skating rink). It gets big names, but mostly of the genteel variety: soul legend Al Green, jazz singer Madeleine Peyroux, Michael Flatley's *Lord of the Dance,* country singer Clint Black, and various Broadway-style theater and dance acts.

One of the area's most popular karaoke nights (Friday) is at **Loaded Joe's Coffeehouse and Lounge** (82 E. Beaver Creek Blvd., Avon, 970/748-1480, www.loadedjoes. com, 7 A.M.–1:30 A.M. daily), which also has DJ-run dance nights, an open-mike night, movie nights, and group guitar lessons.

The Beaver Creek–Avon bar scene has a few must-swill spots: the **Dusty Boot** (St. James Place, 210 Offerson Rd., Beaver Creek Village, Beaver Creek, 970/748-1146, www.dustyboot. com, noon–10 P.M. daily), which is primarily a family-friendly steakhouse but serves margaritas all the time; the **8100 Mountainside Bar & Grill** (inside the Hyatt Beaver Creek, 50 West Thomas Place, Avon, 970/827-6600,

7–11 A.M., noon–2:30 P.M., and 5:30–10 P.M. daily); the **Gore Range Brewery** (0105 Edwards Village Blvd., Bldg. H, Edwards, 970/926-2739, www.gorerangebrewery.com, 11:30 A.M.–10 P.M. Mon.–Sat., noon–10 P.M. Sun.), whose originals include Fly Fisher Red Ale and Biker Stout; **Coyote Café** (210 The Plaza, Village Hall, Beaver Creek, 970/949-5001, www.coyotecafe.net, 11 A.M.–1 A.M. daily), which has DJs, dancing, and occasional karaoke; and the slope-side **Beaver Creek Chophouse** (15 W. Thomas Place, Beaver Creek, 970/845-0555, www.beavercreekchophouse.com, 11 A.M.–9 P.M. daily), where the steaks are large, the wine list is long, and the martinis have names like the "ruby redlicious tini."

Shopping

The art galleries along the redbrick path from the parking garage to the Beaver Creek Village have window-shopping prices that may well blow your mind. **The Sportsman's Gallery Ltd. & Paderewski Fine Art** (Beaver Creek

Plaza, 970/949-6036, www.sportsmansgallery. com, 10 A.M.–9 P.M. daily, reduced hours off-season) recently displayed an $8,500 bronze elk and a small Ogden M. Pleissner watercolor of a yellow-and-orange mesa for $7,500. **J. Cotter** (5 Market Square, 970/949-8111, www.jcotter-gallery.com, 9:30 A.M.–6 P.M. daily) specializes in fine art and jewelry, and recently showed a two-foot-tall purple-crystal rock. Perhaps the most unique store in the Beaver Creek area is **Christopher & Co.** (0105 Edwards Village Blvd., Edwards, 970/926-8191, www.christo-pherco.com, 10 A.M.–5 P.M. Mon.–Sat.), which has a gigantic stash of vintage entertainment and art posters, from a pen-and-ink French Buster Keaton handbill to scenic mountain images from many different eras and locations.

Accommodations

Beaver Creek hotels are extremely expensive, but plenty of cheaper deals are available up the highway in Vail, Minturn, Edwards, and Eagle.

The most luxurious hotel in the Vail Valley, the **(Ritz-Carlton Bachelor Gulch** (0130 Daybreak Ridge, Avon, 970/748-6200, www. ritzcarlton.com/resorts/bachelor_gulch, $549–749) is in a beautiful, sprawling building that's as big as a town and nestled underneath a mountain. There's a private golf club, the Red Sky, on the premises, as well as a spa (sorry, a "coed rock grotto") and various one-of-a-kind accoutrements. For example: The hotel makes its own dogs, a St. Bernard called Bachelor and an Irish retriever named Miner, available for hikes. Obviously demand is highest during ski season, but my wife and I found an excellent deal (less than $200) for a room overlooking the valley in May a few years ago. We had the place just about to ourselves, with plenty of solitude and no waiting at the bars. The downside: With no crowds, many of the best restaurants are closed.

The incredible mountain views distinguish the **Park Hyatt Beaver Creek Resort & Spa** (136 E. Thomas Place, Avon, 970/949-1234, http://beavercreek.hyatt.com, $599–899) from every other Hyatt.

"Luxury lodging" reads the sign on the

front of the **Poste Montane** (76 Avondale Rd., 970/845-7500 or 800/497-9238, www.poste-montane.com, $200–575), and it's a believable claim. The white building, topped with brown wooden roofs, is directly at the bottom of the Beaver Creek shopping area and escalators, and visitors wander out wearing cowboy boots and Stetsons. The guest rooms are huge, and bath-robes are available.

The **Charter at Beaver Creek** (120 Offerson Rd., 970/949-6660 or 800/525-2139, www.thecharter.com, $365) is a beautiful property, both inside and out, with dark-blue roofs and elegant flowery bedspreads and thick mattresses in even the smallest of guest rooms (which is to say, two beds). It has a spa, a pool, three restaurants, and excellent views of the re-sort, ski slopes, and a multitude of trees.

In addition to a prime location among the trees on the resort slopes, **The Pines Lodge** (141 Scott Hill Rd., 970/754-7200 or 866/605-7625, http://pineslodge.rockresorts.com/info/rr.asp, $220–240) has a sort of quiet dignity—ski-boot heaters are in all the guest rooms, and some have incredible panoramic mountain views. The Grouse Mountain Grill is one of the resort's best restaurants.

The **Lodge & Spa at Cordillera** (2205 Cordillera Way, Edwards, 970/926-2200 or 800/877-3529, www.cordilleralodge. com, $295–395) has sadly gone the way of Watergate—nice place to stay, but nobody will think of it as merely a place to stay ever again. This is where police arrested basketball star Kobe Bryant in summer 2003 for alleg-edly raping a young employee (charges were later dropped). It's a great hotel—a long, white complex on the side of a mountain with four restaurants and four golf courses.

The **Beaver Creek Lodge** (26 Avondale Lane, 970/845-9800 or 800/525-7280, www. beavercreeklodge.net, $299–649) has always been a decent place to stay, in the European mode with large guest rooms and a central lo-cation. But owner Richard Kessler gave it a multimillion-dollar facelift in 2004, and sud-denly it's a condo-lodge filled with red suede lobby curtains and even grommets. The guest

the lobby of the Park Hyatt Beaver Creek Resort & Spa during winter

rooms have fireplaces and wireless Internet access.

Food

A ranching and farming community in the 1880s, the town of Edwards, a few miles west of Beaver Creek off I-70, has developed a reputation for diverse and affordable restaurants. Among the more interesting: **Sato** (56 Edwards Village Blvd., Suite 120, Edwards, 970/926-7684, www.satosushiedwards.com, 11:30 A.M.–2 P.M. and 5–10 P.M. Mon.–Fri., 5–10 P.M. Sat.–Sun., $20), one of the only sushi joints in the region; **The Gashouse** (34185 U.S. 6, Edwards, 970/926-3613, www.gashouse-restaurant.com, 11 A.M.–10 P.M. daily, $18), an old log-cabin steakhouse with serious happy hours; **Fiesta's New Mexican Café and Cantina** (57 Edwards Access Rd., Edwards, 970/926-2121, www.alacarvail.com/pdf/fiestas.pdf, 11 A.M.–9:30 P.M. Mon.–Fri., 7 A.M.–10 P.M. Sat.–Sun., $12), which combines Mexican and New Mexican food into one blue-corn enchilada; and **Juniper** (970

Main St., Edwards, 970/926-7001, www.juniperrestaurant.com, 5:30–10 P.M. daily, $34), at which chef Mike Irwin's concept of "comfort fusion" involves roasted butternut squash soup with ginger.

Located just past the redbrick gallery path from the parking lot to the resort village, authentic-Italian **Toscanini** (60 Avondale Lane, Avon, 970/754-5590, www.toscaninibeavercreek.com, 5:30–9:30 P.M. daily, $32) is relatively affordable, despite the preponderance of women in fur coats who file out after dinner.

The **Grouse Mountain Grill** (141 Scott Hill Rd., Beaver Creek, 970/949-0600, www.grousemountaingrill.com, 5:30–10 P.M. daily summer, 5–10 P.M. daily winter, $36) is inside The Pines Lodge, in the middle of a forest on the side of its namesake mountain. Although it serves fancy fish and duck dishes, its house specialties are of the slabs-of-meat variety—elk rib chop, beef tenderloin steak, and New York strip, all in the mid-$30 range. As with the guest rooms, the mountain views are awesome.

Vista (676 Sawatch Dr., Edwards,

970/926-2111, www.vista-arrowhead.com, 11:30 A.M.–2:30 P.M. and 5–9 P.M. daily, $32) has the entrées and the white-linen air of an upscale restaurant, but it's built on a homey bar with a big wine list and has down-home touches like a kids menu that kids actually like.

Beaver Creek founder George Townsend supposedly built the log-cabin structure that houses **Mirabelle** (55 Village Rd., 970/949-7728, www.mirabelle1.com, 3:30–9 P.M. Mon.–Sat., reduced hours off-season, $36) as the town's first residence in the early 1880s. It's still a beautiful building, with hardwood floors and elegant rugs, and it adds French touches like foie gras and Dover sole meunière ($45) to what is otherwise a typically diverse menu of elk, chicken, steak, and seafood.

To get to **Beano's Cabin** (Larkspur Bowl, 970/754-5762 or 866/395-3185, www.beavercreek.com/groups/group-venues/beanos-cabin.aspx, 5:30–8:45 P.M. daily early Dec.–early Apr., 5:30–8:45 P.M. Thurs.–Sun. Memorial Day–Labor Day, $99 for 5 courses), on the side of the Grouse Mountain, diners must hail a snowcat and sleigh in the winter or a shuttle van or wagon ride (or even a horse) in the summer. Try the pan-seared pheasant breast or the Colorado lamb loin. Note that diners have to be more than seven years old and weigh less than 235 pounds in order to travel there safely.

In addition to the woodsy scenery and the food—try the veal loin and mustard-crusted veal breast ($32) or the wood-oven-roasted lobster ($45)—the main thing you need to know about **Splendido** (17 Chateau Lane, 970/845-8808, www.splendidobeavercreek.com, 5:30–10 P.M. daily winter, 5:30–10 P.M. Tues.–Sun. summer, $46) is that it has a piano bar, and a good pianist.

Information

The Beaver Creek ski resort has a comprehensive website (www.beavercreek.com) that includes dining and lodging listings.

MINTURN

The streets of this century-old mining and railroad town are invitingly quiet even on a Saturday night during ski season. It's just a few exits west of Vail off I-70, in a pretty spot beneath the hills where Gore Creek and the Eagle River meet. And it's an oasis between always-mobbed Vail to the east and super-affluent Beaver Creek to the west. The shops and galleries are quaint, the Minturn Inn is a little out of the way but well worth searching for, and two or three of the downtown restaurants are among the best in the area.

Minturn became a town in 1904, long before Vail was incorporated, and workers settled here for years before the railroads closed, mining died out, and skiing took over as the region's major industry.

The tiny mountain town's growth prospects took a significant hit after the 2008 recession. It seems that a developer had promised city officials $180 million in financial benefits if they supported a long-planned, almost mythical nearby ski resort known as Battle Mountain. But the recession hit the town hard, developers' budgets cratered, and Minturn abruptly reverted to sleepy mountain tourist town. "Minturn remains in limbo, and its residents are alternately resigned and upset," wrote Patrick Doyle in a *5280* magazine investigation in 2011 titled "The Last Resort."

So while Minturn doesn't have quite the "rising resort town" feel it had four or five years ago—the venerable Chili Willy's restaurant closed not long ago, which some locals have interpreted as a sign—it still makes an excellent getaway from crowded Vail or tony Beaver Creek and retains its small-mountain-town charm. Don't be surprised if you sidle up to The Saloon for a beer and find two Hummers parked outside and several pairs of ski boots and ski poles leaning against the 1901 building out front.

Nightlife

Minturn's bar scene revolves around the deceptively divey-looking **The Saloon** (146 N. Main St., 970/827-5954, www.minturnsaloon.com, 3:30 P.M.–close daily winter, 4 P.M.–close Sun.–Fri., 1 P.M.–close Sat. summer), in a wooden structure that (according to various legends) has housed gambling rings and basketball games since it was built in 1901. It has sit-down food of the upscale Mexican variety on one side, drinks on the other, and various stuffed moose heads and Gerald R. Ford Invitational Golf Tournament posters all over the walls.

Other Main Street restaurants are more notable for their drinks than their food. These include **Kirby Cosmo's BBQ Bar** (474 Main St., 970/827-9027, www.kirbycosmos.com, 11:30 A.M.–8:30 P.M. daily), which serves pizza and barbecue to go with live local music and many different kinds of beer.

Minturn Cellars (107 Williams St., 970/827-4065) has the usual chardonnays, rieslings, merlots, and cabernet sauvignons—and tasting rooms, of course. Call first, as hours vary, especially during the winter.

Accommodations

Built in a 1915 log-cabin home and refurbished by an enterprising ski-bum couple in 1995, the (**Minturn Inn** (442 Main St., 970/827-9647 or 800/646-8876, www.minturninn. com, $149–179) has comfortable wooden guest rooms with lots of space and large beds and couches. It's a friendly local spot, with chefs taking orders for breakfast personally from a large kitchen off the main dining room.

Food

Don't let the name of the **Minturn Country Club** (131 Main St., 970/827-4114, www. minturn-country-club.com, 5–10 P.M. daily Dec.–mid-Apr., 5:30–10 P.M. daily late Apr.–Nov., $28) fool you: "The only thing missing is the golf course," goes the slogan. From the outside, it looks like a wooden-walled dive, with pool tables and old framed pictures. But the cook-your-own steak dinners are just $16, and chicken and fish are available.

The diner-style **Turntable Restaurant** (160 Railroad Ave., 970/827-4164, http://turntablerestaurantminturn.com, 7 A.M.–3 P.M. Mon.–Wed., 7 A.M.–9 P.M. Thurs.–Sun., $8) serves steaks, burgers, and other American-type food in the motel of the same name.

Shopping

The shops along Main Street in Minturn are a break from the eye-popping prices of, say, Beaver Creek. **Holy Toledo** (Main St. and Toledo Ave., 970/827-4299, http://sites. google.com/site/vailheathr/holytoledo2, 10 A.M.–6 P.M. Mon.–Fri., 10 A.M.–4 P.M. Sat.–Sun.) is a consignment shop for men and women that carries all the top brands—Versace, Betsey Johnson, Chanel, and the like. **Mountain Pedaler** (161 Main St., 970/827-5522, www.mountainpedalar.com, noon–6 P.M. Mon., 10 A.M.–6 P.M. Tues.–Fri., 10 A.M.–4 P.M. Sat.) is a well-situated bike shop that saves cyclists from having to venture into crowded Vail to grab a quick sprocket or tire-repair kit before a long mountain ride.

Information

The **Town of Minturn** (302 Pine St., 970/827-5645, www.minturn.org) has a website that conspicuously says nothing about the recent Battle Mountain problems, but it's nonetheless informative for visitor preparation.

Breckenridge

Exactly 393 people lived in Breckenridge in 1960, and residents feared the area just west of the Continental Divide would dwindle into a ghost town. But a year later, the Rounds and Porter Lumber Company of Wichita, Kansas, received a permit to build a ski area, and within a few months, 17,000 visitors had showed up to ride the two-chair ski lift. Breck has grown steadily ever since, and while nine companies, including Aspen and Vail resorts, have owned the resort, it continues to expand. The one constant during the years of booms and busts has been incredible Tenmile Range backdrops, easily accessible from downtown.

For skiers, Breckenridge has always been a contradiction. The mountain's four peaks, all of which are around 13,000 feet in elevation, are challenging and fun, especially for expert skiers. A gondola between Peak 7 and Peak 8 mostly solved these problems after it was built in 2006, but some still complain.

Also, Breckenridge was one of the first Colorado resorts to embrace the once-renegade sport of snowboarding, sponsoring a major national competition in 1986 and continuing to tailor runs for one-board visitors. (Some boarders, however, dislike navigating the many paths between the runs.)

The town of Breckenridge, with its 100 restaurants, 500 hotels, and 2,300 condos, is among the most diverse and affordable of all the Summit County resort areas. From the pizza-and-burger joint Downstairs at Eric's to the tony and beautiful Café Alpine, not to mention reasonable prices and wide-open areas for parking and walking, the experience for visitors is top-notch. Breckenridge is also a big area for history buffs—gold was first discovered here in 1887, and the Washington Gold Mine is one of several remnants from that era offering tours; also, the 12-block downtown Breckenridge district has more than 250 historic buildings.

Perhaps more than any other Summit County ski area, Breckenridge thrives in spring and summer as well. It's on the Colorado River, and fishing, kayaking, and white-water rafting opportunities are numerous. Plus, there's a golf club and about a zillion festivals, from Genuine Jazz to the Toast of Breckenridge.

HISTORY

Believe it or not, some people still show up in Breckenridge for reasons other than skiing, mountain biking, hiking, or feasting in local bars and restaurants. Of all the Summit County ski towns, Breckenridge has the most historical riches—350 such structures, including 250 in the National Register of Historic Places.

Breckenridge became an official town in 1859, when somebody discovered gold in the hills and miners from all over the United States rushed to become part of the boom. By 1860,

the town had more than 8,000 miners and merchants and a bar, the Gold Pan Saloon, that continues to operate downtown. At the turn of the 20th century, miners erected a Methodist church, a railroad, a boarding house, and a school, and they sent a four-boat Navy expedition down the Blue River to the Colorado, hoping to find a water passage to the Pacific. It didn't work. Miners discovered the town's biggest gold nugget, at 13.5 pounds, in 1887.

Gradually, through the early 20th century, mining of gold, silver, lead, zinc, and other metals slowed down, especially when U.S. officials demanded that metal be melted down and sent to help in World War II. The Country Boy Mine was among the last to close, after a flood in 1945, and residents deserted the town—just 393 people were left in the early 1960s.

But skiing took over in 1961, even before the completion of I-70, and the industry became successful enough to prop up Breckenridge for the next four decades. Early creaky lifts gave way to a high-speed quad lift in 1981, and for the 2006–2007 season, the resort peaked with 1,650,321 visitors.

SIGHTS
Historic District

When people refer to Breckenridge's Historic District, they usually mean the 12-square-block area of downtown bounded by Main, High, and Washington Streets and Wellington Road. While touring this area, you may note that one thing hasn't changed—miners hung out in the same buildings and streets that townies and tourists use today.

The **Breckenridge Heritage Alliance** (309 N. Main St., 970/453-9767, www.breckheritage.org) offers walking tours (1 and 2:30 P.M. Thurs.–Sun., $10) beginning at the Welcome Center (203 S. Main St.). The 75-minute tours, which require no reservations, hit downtown historical sites, including the Alice G. Milne House and the W. H. Briggle House, along with the school, the courthouse, and churches. Although the heritage alliance focuses on all the mining towns in Summit County, it takes particular interest in Breckenridge, with tours of

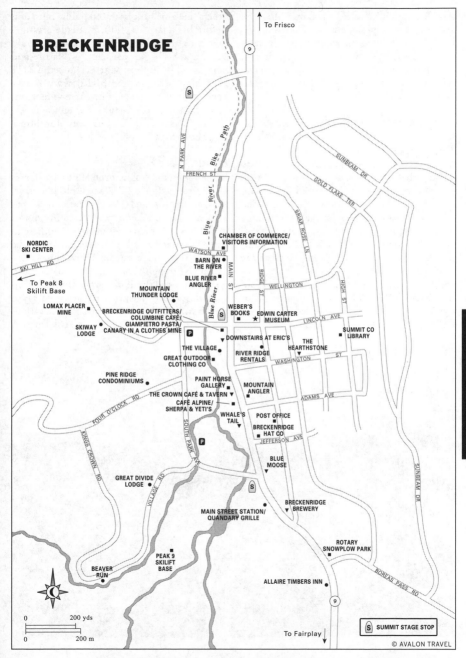

BRECKENRIDGE

To Frisco

9

To Peak 8
Skilift Base

NORDIC
SKI CENTER

SKI HILL RD

N PARK AVE

Bike Path

FRENCH ST

Blue River

WATSON AVE

SUNBEAM DR

GOLD FLAKE TER

CHAMBER OF COMMERCE/
VISITORS INFORMATION

BRIAR ROSE LN

BARN ON
THE RIVER

BLUE RIVER
ANGLER

MOUNTAIN
THUNDER LODGE

Blue River

MAIN ST

RIDGE ST

WELLINGTON

HIGH ST

LOMAX PLACER
MINE

BRECKENRIDGE OUTFITTERS/
COLUMBINE CAFÉ/
GIAMPIETRO PASTA/
CANARY IN A CLOTHES MINE

WEBER'S
BOOKS

EDWIN CARTER
MUSEUM

LINCOLN AVE

SUMMIT CO
LIBRARY

SKIWAY
LODGE

P

DOWNSTAIRS AT ERIC'S

THE VILLAGE

RIVER RIDGE
RENTALS

THE
HEARTHSTONE

WASHINGTON ST

GREAT OUTDOOR
CLOTHING CO

PINE RIDGE
CONDOMINIUMS

PAINT HORSE
GALLERY

MOUNTAIN
ANGLER

ADAMS AVE

FOUR O'CLOCK RD

THE CROWN CAFÉ & TAVERN

CAFÉ ALPINE/
SHERPA & YETI'S

WHALE'S
TAIL

POST OFFICE
BRECKENRIDGE
HAT CO

JEFFERSON AVE

KINGS CROWN RD

SOUTH PARK AVE

BLUE
MOOSE

GREAT DIVIDE
LODGE

VILLAGE RD

P

S

BRECKENRIDGE
BREWERY

MAIN STREET STATION/
QUANDARY GRILLE

SUNBEAM DR

ROTARY
SNOWPLOW PARK

PEAK 9
SKILIFT
BASE

BEAVER
RUN

BORAS PASS RD

ALLAIRE TIMBERS INN

9

0   200 yds

0   200 m

To Fairplay

S SUMMIT STAGE STOP

© AVALON TRAVEL

the Washington Mine, Edwin Carter Museum, and Rotary Snowplow Park. For those who prefer riding to walking, **Breckenridge Pedicabs** (970/423-7196, www.breckenridgepedicabs. com) provides tours ($25–85) focusing on history plus others dealing with beer, wine, and local hotspots in general.

Edwin Carter Museum

Had it existed in 1859, People for the Ethical Treatment of Animals would surely have enlisted Edwin Carter, a gold rush miner who noticed that Summit County deer and bison were growing strange deformities. He attributed the mismatched antlers and two-headed calves to chemicals used for placer mining, a technique for extracting gold from streambeds. Eventually, Carter switched from mining to naturalism and traveled all over the Rockies collecting samples and learning taxidermy. His work helped scientists learn about the adverse effects of mining on local wildlife, and his log-cabin home (filled with 3,300 full-sized specimens of bears, bison, elk, and

others) became his office and public museum. Before his death in 1900, he made arrangements to sell his collection to what would become the Denver Museum of Nature and Science. The Edwin Carter Museum (111 N. Ridge St., 970/453-9022, www.breckheritage.com/pages/edwin-carter-museum, 11 A.M.–3 P.M. Tues.–Sun., $3) contains few of those specimens, but it has lots of information about his life.

Mines

In the 1880s, the **Washington Mine** (465 Illinois Gulch Rd., 970/453-9767, www.breckheritage. com, tours 1 P.M. and 2:30 P.M. Sat. June–Sept., $15) was one of the largest mines in an area crawling with them—30 men worked here in five main shafts of gold and silver ore stretching more than 10,000 feet underground. It was heavily active through about 1905 and stayed open on and off until the 1960s, when the local mining industry effectively died out and gave way to the ski industry. Tickets are available at various Breckenridge sites, including the Information

© MATT INDEN/WEAVER MULTIMEDIA GROUP/COLORADO TOURISM OFFICE

Breckenridge

Cabin (309 N. Main St.); the mine itself is about a 20-minute drive from downtown.

Other historic mines in or near town include the **Lomax Placer Mine** (301 Ski Hill Rd., 970/453-9767, www.breckheritage.com/pages/lomax-placer-mine-tour, tours 1 P.M. and 2:30 P.M. Sat. June–Sept., $15) and the still-operating-for-visitors **Country Boy Mine** (0542 French Gulch Rd., 970/453-4405, www.countryboymine.com, 10 A.M.–4 P.M. daily Memorial Day–Labor Day, reduced hours fall–winter).

Rotary Snowplow Park

Rotary Snowplow Park (189 Boreas Pass Rd., 970/453-9767, www.breckheritage.com/pages/rotary-snowplow-park, $5) contains a 108-ton snowplow, built in 1901, with intimidating blowing and cutting fans that once cleared narrow railroad tracks. These monstrosities were so big that half a dozen steam-driven locomotives had to push them up Boreas and Fremont Passes. Although the cabin is restored, the plow no longer operates, so don't get any big ideas about driving it down Main Street.

Valley Brook Cemetery

The graves at the circa-1882 Valley Brook Cemetery (near Airport Rd. and Valley Brook Rd., 970/453-9767, free, private tours by appointment, $10) include that of Baby Eberlein, whose remains were moved here from Breckenridge's first cemetery in 1997. Most of the hand-carved headstones are unmarked, and they likely belong to miners too poor to pay for their own burials.

Peak 8 Fun Park

In the summer, the **Breckenridge Fun Park** (Ski Resort Peak 8, 970/496-4700 or 800/536-1890, www.breckenridge.com/peak-8-fun-park.aspx, 10 A.M.–6 P.M. daily late June–Labor Day, 10 A.M.–6 P.M. Fri.–Sun. Labor Day–late Sept.) turns a ski area into a kid-oriented outdoor-activity center. The centerpiece is an especially twisty alpine slide, but the park also includes a bungee-cord chair-ride contraption that allows people to bounce *really*

high, a panning-for-gold area, a maze, and, for the grown-ups, a pleasant ski-lift ride up the hill. The rides are fairly expensive if your kids demand that you take them multiple times, so consider shelling out $65 for an all-day unlimited SuperPass.

SPORTS AND RECREATION
Downhill Skiing and Snowboarding

Skiing and snowboarding are Breckenridge's primary cultural, recreational, and financial base—with a capacity for almost 37,000 skiers taking 27 lifts up the four peaks. Experts are fiercely loyal to the runs, choosing Breck over its more basic neighbor Arapahoe Basin and the more glamorous Vail—some feared the recently opened Peak 7 would be swamped with beginners, but it has its share of difficult 45-degree slopes.

The primary complaint about Breck is navigating the narrow cross-country "catwalks" that connect the runs on the front of the mountain. This is especially pronounced among snowboarders, who have come to love the resort for its long-standing support of the younger sport but can't stand the leg-cramping "cross-country snowboarding" required to traverse the catwalks. But the recently built six-passenger SuperChair, among other lifts, has helped skiers reach the back of the mountain, filled with wide-open bowls and tree-filled runs.

According to difficulty, Breckenridge's downhill skiing trails break down like this: easiest, 15 percent, including a portion of the Four O'Clock, which at 3.5 miles is the area's longest run; more difficult, 33 percent, including seven new runs on Peak 7; most difficult, 20 percent, including the bumpy Pika, Ptarmigan, and Forget-Me-Not trails; and expert, 32 percent, with the tree skiing of Peak 9 and the South Side of Peak 10, a desolate spot filled with bumps and glades.

Breck's five terrain parks are among the most famous in the world, catering to both experts and beginners: The **Freeway Super Park** has huge jumps and pipes; the **Gold King Pipe** is 14 feet; and **Park Lane** has a complicated route of rails, boxes, jumps, and jibs. For more information, including a variety of YouTube action videos, go to www.breck1080.com.

The one-day walk-up rate for lift tickets during the high season is roughly $92, but local newspapers and websites offer deals. Many of the town's lodges offer packages, and, of course, season passes are excellent deals for frequent skiers. Child-care facilities are available for all ages at the Peak 8 **Children's Center** (888/576-2754), among other places; the resort recommends making reservations at least two days in advance. And many businesses along Main Street rent equipment; believe me, you won't have trouble finding deals on the slopes or in town.

The resort's **Ski & Ride School** (888/576-2754) has programs for beginners of all ages and also offers private lessons. It's best to reserve a slot in advance.

For weather and snow updates on Breckenridge, check www.breckenridge.com and click on "weather report."

Cross-Country Skiing and Other Snow Sports

Nordic skiing, which most people know as cross-country, is big in Breckenridge, especially given the off-the-slope trails that link the downhill runs together. The **Breckenridge Nordic Center** (1200 Ski Hill Rd., 970/453-6855, http://breckenridgenordic.com) provides access to numerous groomed trails and gives lessons; the **Gold Run Nordic Center** (Clubhouse Dr., 970/547-7889, www.townofbreckenridge.com), with nine miles of trails, also rents skis and provides lessons.

Of course, backcountry skiers can choose from an almost unlimited terrain of mountain trails. Just be careful, especially in tricky weather conditions, and check out the trails in advance by contacting the **Dillon Ranger District** (www.dillonrangerdistrict.com).

For hut-to-hut skiers, the **Summit County Huts Association** (524 Wellington Rd., 970/453-8583, www.summithuts.org) makes

four tiny cabins available for skiers to spend the night while on a run.

A number of companies throughout the area give **snowmobiling** and **dogsledding** tours—try **Good Times Adventures** (6061 Tiger Rd., 970/453-7604 or 800/477-0144, www.goodtimesadventures.com) or, for general information, **Colorado Mountain Activities** (970/547-1594, www.coloradomountainactivities.com). Santa Claus obsessives should contact **Nordic Sleigh Rides** (373 Gold Flake Court, 970/453-2005, www.nordicsleighrides.com) or **Breckenridge Sleigh Rides** (970/453-0222, www.brecksleighrides.com, www.countryboymine.com).

Ice-Skating

Breckenridge has two ice-skating options: **Maggie Pond,** at the Village at Breckenridge, and the **Stephen C. West Indoor and Outdoor Ice Arenas** (0189 Boreas Pass Rd., 970/547-9974, www.townofbreckenridge.com), which has two National Hockey League–sized rinks and capacity for 475 spectators. Both rent skates.

Hiking and Biking

Yes, it is possible to enjoy yourself outside in Breckenridge while wearing plain old shoes or boots. Hundreds of miles of hiking and biking trails, of all levels of difficulty, snake through the Central Rockies. In Breckenridge, the 0.5-mile **Sapphire Point Overlook** begins on Swan Mountain Road between Breckenridge and Keystone and has superb views of Dillon Reservoir and the mountains. The 10-mile **Peaks Trail** is a plunge from Breckenridge to Frisco; to get to the trailhead, go south on Highway 9 from I-70, turn right on Ski Hill Road, and go past Peak 8 for about 0.6 miles to the parking area. **Spruce Creek Trail,** 3.1 miles, allows 4WD vehicles for half the trail; the trailhead is accessible by taking Highway 9 south from Breckenridge, then turning right at Spruce Creek Road and driving to the top of the hill. **Gold Hill Trail,** 3.1 miles, off Highway 9 between Frisco and Breckenridge, is a challenging up-and-down path that overlooks

TERRAIN PARKS: WHEN SKIING ISN'T TERRIFYING ENOUGH

Inspired by skateboard parks, terrain parks were born in the early 1990s, when the Vail ski resort opened what it then called a "snowboard park." They're basically obstacle courses for boarders and skiers, with structures known as jibs. These include: thin metal bars called rails, which curve in every direction, including up and down; jumps, as in ski jumps, only shallower, trickier, and usually closer together; boxes, a wider type of rail; and pipes, or narrow concave tubes that resemble bobsled runs. Just about every Colorado ski resort has some kind of terrain park, all of which have on-site classes for skiers and boarders of all ages. Here are five of the best:

* Keystone's **A51 Terrain Park** (970/496-4500 or 800/328-1323, www.keystoneresort.com/a51/home.aspx) has some of the most diverse features in the state, roughly 100 total, beginning with the three huge jumps of Main Street. Goldrush Alley is steep, with alternating jumps and rails, while Park Lane has smaller jumps for beginners.

* **Breckenridge** (800/536-1890, www.breck1080.com) has five terrain parks, most famously Freeway, renowned for its three huge jumps in a row, sending boarders and skiers spinning high into the air, but also Park Lane, sort of a miniature version of Freeway, with smaller jumps, boxes, and jibs, and Bonanza, a hilly practice area. The half-pipes are at Freeway (this one is especially huge), Trygves, and Eldorado.

* Formerly a failed ski resort called Squaw Pass, **Echo Mountain Park** (19285 Hwy. 103, Idaho Springs, 303/325-7347, www.echomtnpark.com) opened in 2006 as an extreme-sports paradise that doesn't involve an epic trip from Denver along I-70. It has 16 trails, a freestyle terrain known as "The Junkyard," and a collection of colorfully painted boxes, rails, and curvy ramps that lead to gasping elevations.

* **Vail** (970/754-8245, www.vail.com) has two terrain parks, most notably Golden Peak, or "GP," located about halfway up Chair 6. It has 12 jumps, from 10 feet to 65 feet, and the photos of flying skiers on the resort's Facebook page are enough to make you dizzy while sitting at your desk. There are also 33 boxes, rails, hitching posts, and lift towers. The park also recently added Bwana Park, more of a beginner's area, with two small jumps and more easygoing features such as log slides.

* **Woodward at Copper Mountain** (505 Copper Rd., Copper Mountain, 888/350-1544, www.woodwardatcopper.com) is best known for the Barn, a 19,400-square-foot indoor training facility with huge ramps and pipes ending in foam pits, as well as elaborate gymnastics and tumbling equipment. It's a safe way to practice for the real thing outside – like a 22-foot superpipe, the rail-filled Eagle Jib Park, and a series of steep jumps all in a row known as the Catalyst.

ASPEN AND THE SKI TOWNS

the Blue River Valley and Tenmile Range. **Quandary Peak,** 6.75 miles round-trip, goes straight up, well above 14,000 feet in elevation—it's a long, difficult hike with amazing panoramic views of nearby Crystal Peak, the Gore Range, Mount Democrat, and, at the top, Grays and Torreys Peaks. To get started, take Highway 9 south from Breckenridge; turn west on County Road 850; turn right on County Road 851; and look for trailhead signs on the

right side of the parking area. The weather changes quickly on this mountain, so an early start is key.

Another popular route is **Boreas Pass to Baker's Tank.** Here, hikers follow the route of mining trains that traveled from Breckenridge to South Park. The end point is Baker's Tank—an old historic water tank that the steam trains used to refill before they turned around. This hike is six miles round-trip, with a little climbing at the start. From the Breckenridge Conoco station at the south end of town on Highway 9, take Boreas Pass Road east. Watch for the trailhead on the east side of the road after you pass the winter trail closure gate.

The 33-mile **Colorado Trail/Kenosha Pass** route is only for experienced cyclists, although it's mostly easy up-and-down riding. The hard part is on the way down from 11,880-foot-high Georgia Pass, about 12 miles into the route, where you'll encounter roots, rocks, and other technical barriers. But the scenery is astounding, with views of a huge cross-section of Summit County and various fourteener and thirteener peaks. Fans of this trail say it's most scenic when the aspens turn gold in the fall. Be sure to check a recent Colorado Trail map for reroutes. To get to the route from Denver, drive south toward Buena Vista on U.S. 285; the trailhead is seven miles southwest of Grant, at the top of Kenosha Pass.

The **Dillon Ranger District** website (www. dillonrangerdistrict.com) is an amazingly thorough resource for hiking trails in Breckenridge, Dillon, Silverthorne, Frisco, and Keystone—many of which run into each other in this small interconnected region.

Many information-center employees and hotel concierges will give out trail maps and may even know something about the terrain. Or try **Daniel's Cabin Information Center** (309 N. Main St.) or the **Breckenridge Welcome Center** (Blue River Plaza, 970/453-6018).

If it goes really fast up and down hills, chances are it's a sport and Breckenridge offers some form of it. Silverthorne's **CBST Adventures** (970/668-8900, www.coloradobikeandski.com), short for Colorado Bike and Ski Tours, gives instruction for snowshoers, rock climbers, hikers, rafters, kayakers, offroad drivers, and cyclists. The guides are experienced, and some of the trips include lodging.

Fishing

Most visitors think of Colorado as a dry, landlocked state—and truthfully, nobody will mistake Breckenridge for San Francisco or Norfolk, Virginia, anytime soon. But the bodies of water can be even more exhilarating because you don't expect to encounter them. The town is directly on the Colorado River, and **Maggie Pond** is one of thousands of miles of lakes, streams, and reservoirs with fishing options. For lessons, equipment, and tours, there's **Blue River Anglers** (281 Main St., Frisco, 970/668-2583 or 888/453-9171, www. blueriveranglers.com), **Mountain Angler** (311 S. Main St., 970/453-4669, www.mountainangler.com), and **Breckenridge Outfitters** (101 N. Main St., Suite B, 970/453-4135, www. breckenridgeoutfitters.com).

Golf

Jack Nicklaus designed the town's sloping 27-hole course in 1985, then added another nine holes in 2001. As Colorado Rockies pitchers will sadly attest, balls fly faster and straighter in high altitudes than they do at sea level, so enjoy the long whacks—and the surrounding views. The **Breckenridge Golf Club** (0200 Clubhouse Dr., 970/453-9104, www.townofbreckenridge. com, $62–109) is at an elevation of 9,324 feet.

Horseback Riding

Breckenridge Stables (Breckenridge Ski Resort, Peak 9, 970/453-4438, www.breckstables.com) employs expert horse trainers to lead groups of experienced and inexperienced riders high into the mountains—reaching elevations of more than 10,000 feet. Breck Stables supplements its breakfast ($75), dinner ($89), and regular 1.5-hour rides (8 A.M.–4 P.M., $60) with private lessons and, in the winter, sleigh rides. The route goes up Peak 9 of the ski resort. Other than the sleigh rides, the stables are open mainly late spring–early fall.

White-Water Rafting

Breckenridge's location on the Colorado River, combined with extreme snowpack in the winter and heat in the summer, makes it prime territory for white-water rafting. Most of it takes place just outside the town, and most rafting outfits will shuttle large groups to various river launches.

The main Breckenridge-based rafting company is **Colorado Whitewater Rafting** (505 S. Main St., Suite A-10, 970/423-7031 or 800/370-0581, www.breckenridgewhitewater.com), which offers routes for beginning and advanced rafters. The Clear Creek route, which launches at Idaho Springs, is about 45 minutes from Breckenridge; Gore Canyon, which launches at Kremmling, is about 70 minutes away. The Gore Canyon route is part of the Colorado River and includes both a crazed rock-strewn Class V trip and the serene "Upper C," which floats gently among beautiful vistas and rock formations and includes a side trip to a hot springs.

Fitness

The **Breckenridge Recreation Center** (880 Airport Rd., 970/453-1734, www.townofbrecknridge.com) is a typical public-gym complex, with racquetball and basketball courts, aerobics classes, weight machines, and two indoor swimming pools. At 69,000 square feet, it's the first building you see on the way into town on Highway 9.

ENTERTAINMENT AND EVENTS

Summit County has a live-music scene built primarily around young skiers and jamming rock bands, and Breckenridge entered the club world a few years ago with **Three20South** (320 S. Main St., 970/547-5320, www.three-20south.com), formerly Sherpa & Yeti's, which regularly packs the place with hip-hop acts and dance DJs, plus local bands and occasional national touring acts like Fishbone, once-notorious rappers 2 Live Crew, and blues band North Mississippi Allstars. Also a well-known restaurant dating to the 1850s, the **Gold Pan Saloon** (103 N. Main St., www.thegoldpansaloon.com, 970/453-5499, noon–11:30 P.M. daily) regularly puts on DJs and Colorado bands. The **Blue River Bistro** (305 N. Main St., 970/453-6974, www.blueriverbistro.com, 11 A.M.–midnight Sun.–Thurs., 11 A.M.–2 A.M. Fri.–Sat.) has live music most nights, and **The Whale's Tail** (323 S. Main St., 970/453-2221)

sometimes puts on live comedy and music. **Cecelia's** (520 S. Main St., 970/453-2243, www.cecilias.tv, 2 P.M.–2 A.M. daily) is mostly a cigar-and-martini bar, but it also schedules weekly DJ-run dance nights and occasional local bands.

A sizable portion of tourists are college students and young international visitors, many of whom like to stay up all night drinking mountain brews. Cheap drink specials, from $2 domestic drafts to two-for-one margaritas, are not hard to find in Breckenridge. Bars for this scene include the **Breckenridge Brewery** (600 S. Main St., 970/453-1550, www.breckbrew.com, 11 A.M.–10 P.M. daily); slope-side, outdoor-patio-equipped **Coppertop Café and Bar** (Beaver Run Resort, 620 Village Rd., 970/453-6000, 11 A.M.–8:30 P.M. daily, closed off-season); **Napper Tandy's** (110 E. Lincoln Ave., 970/453-4949, www.nappertandysbreck.com, 3 P.M.–2 A.M. daily, reduced hours off-season), an Irish pub in the same spot as the Salt Creek restaurant; **The Dredge Boathouse** (180 W. Jefferson St., 970/453-4877, www.dredgerestaurant.com, 5 P.M.–midnight daily), a somewhat upscale restaurant floating on the Blue River with a very affordable bar on the second floor; **Jake's Dive Bar** (100 N. Main St., 970/547-0110, www.jakesdivebar.com, 11:30 A.M.–2 A.M. daily), which, exactly as its name implies, has tolerable food to go with a down-home townie atmosphere and extremely cheap drinks; and **Mi Casa Mexican Restaurant** (600 S. Park Ave., 970/453-2071, www.micasamexicanrestaurant.com, 11:30 A.M.–10:30 P.M. daily), which has 99-cent tacos and a 3–6 P.M. daily cantina happy hour. Located in the Riverside Mountain Lodge, the **Fireside Lounge** (100 S. Park Ave., 970/453-4711, 3–11 P.M. daily, reduced hours off-season) could be classified après-ski if that highfalutin term weren't so incongruous with $1.50 drafts, darts, and foosball.

The **Breckenridge Music Festival** (970/453-9142, www.breckenridgemusicfestival.com) is spread out among several venues—mostly the downtown Riverwalk Center—between June and September. It stars

ASPEN AND THE SKI TOWNS

the Breckenridge Music Festival Orchestra, which is diverse enough to handle symphony pieces, patriotic Fourth of July anthems, and sometimes even big-band swing. In January, if eerie ice princesses give you pleasure, try the **Budweiser International Snow Sculpture Championships** (970/453-3187, ext. 3, or 970/547-3100, www.gobreck.com), but if Norse gods of snow are more your thing, there's the **Ullr Festival** (888/251-2417, www.gobreck.com), which includes a wacky costumed parade down Main Street and other cold-weather events. There's also the June **Breckenridge Festival of Film** (www.breckfilmfest.com, 970/453-6200), which in recent years has showed indie gems like *La Vie en Rose* and *A Guide to Recognizing Your Saints,* and the **Breckenridge Beer Festival** (970/453-2234, http://alwaysmountaintime.com/ksmt), which runs in different months every year.

SHOPPING

Breckenridge, especially a five-block section of Main Street, is a picturesque shopping area marketing to all types of skiers: a T-shirt shop is just a few doors down from a sign advertising "teak and mink." Expensive knickknacks and bumper stickers with slogans about how it's better to fall off a ski slope than to fall off your living-room sofa are available everywhere, along with more practical (and familiar) businesses such as Sunglasses Hut and Starbucks. Prices at ski towns are generally a little higher than elsewhere, but Breckenridge shops are reasonable compared to some of the other Summit County resorts.

For a small mountain resort town with a population of just more than 2,400, Breckenridge sure has a lot of shops—more than 200 in all, from galleries of horse paintings to vegetable-based glycerin soaps. One of the best is the **Paint Horse Gallery** (226 S. Main St., 970/453-6813, www.painthorsegallery.com), including, yes, paintings of horses, and a lot of Navajo weavings and sculpture of them as well. **Canary in a Clothes Mine** (114 S. Main St., 970/547-9007, http://canaryinaclothesmine.com, 10:30 A.M.–8:30 P.M. daily,

reduced hours off-season) is a high-end alternative to the many goofy T-shirt shops along Main Street; a hillbilly-style "True Love" T-shirt costs $54, and a hand-painted Virgins Saints and Angels Jesus and Mary belt is a steal at $178. **Weber's Books** (100 S. Main St., 970/453-4723, www.webersbooks.com, 9 A.M.–9 P.M. daily, reduced hours off-season) is a cozy shop in a Victorian house.

Outlets for practical skiwear are everywhere—try the nine ski-area locations of **Breckenridge Sports** (535 S. Park Ave., 970/453-3000, www.breckenridgesports.com, 9 A.M.–4 P.M. daily) or the one location of **Great Outdoor Clothing Co.** (211 S. Main St., 970/547-2755, www.greatoutdoorclothing.com, 10 A.M.–6 P.M. Sun.–Thurs., 10 A.M.–7 P.M. Fri.–Sat.)—but for impractical skiwear the best option is **Breckenridge Hat Co.** (411 S. Main St., 970/453-2737, www.breckenridgehatcompany.com, 9 A.M.–9 P.M. daily), which sells mullet wigs, Christmas-tree hats, and Rastafarian ski-helmet covers.

ACCOMMODATIONS

With 2,300 condos and 500 hotels, Breckenridge is equipped for almost any tourism surge. Rates during the peak seasons—January–March and late June–early September, plus holidays—tend to be the highest, but scan the newspapers and websites for package deals. Summer (Memorial Day–late Sept.) can also be crowded and pricey due to local festivals and picnicking Rocky Mountain travelers. The best month for skiers is April, a surprisingly snowy month in recent years, with deals on lodging, lift tickets, and restaurants. Other good-deal months are June, September (which benefits from 70°F late summers), and October, which is often balmy in Colorado and has the best travel deals of all.

The town offers central reservation information at http://gobreck.com (click on "Lodging") and 888/251-2417.

$100-150

Strategically located for history buffs—it's on a mining claim from the 1850s and is next door to the Summit Historical Society's miner tribute Lomax Placer Gulch—**Skiway Lodge** (275 Ski Hill Rd., 970/453-7573 or 800/472-1430, www.skiwaylodge.com, $135–195) has three suites and five regular guest rooms. All have private balconies, and while the wooden floors and ornate shelves give the guest rooms a certain antique feel, the ambience is basic and functional.

The beloved bed-and-breakfast **(Barn on the River** (303B N. Main St., 970/453-2975 or 800/795-2975, www.breckenridge-inn.com, $129–219) has spectacular scenery on the bank of the Blue River with the mountains in the background. The four queen guest rooms include fireplaces, and all have private balconies.

$150-200

A classic log-cabin ski lodge with mountain views from the main-deck hot tub, the **Allaire Timbers Inn** (9511 Hwy. 9, 970/453-7530 or 800/624-4904, www.allairetimbers.com, $149) fills up its 10 guest rooms, from basic lodge rooms to suites, quickly during ski season. The stone fireplaces, door-to-door coffee delivery, four-poster beds in some guest rooms, and short walk to Main Street give it a friendly, practical feel.

$200-300

Beaver Run Resort and Conference Center (620 Village Rd., 970/453-6000 or 800/265-3560, www.beaverrun.com, $210–240) is owned by the Premier Resorts chain and feels a little corporate, but it offers ski-in, ski-out access to the Beaver Run Super Chair and the Quicksilver Six lifts at the base of Peak 9. There aren't a lot of frills, but 500 guest rooms and seven restaurants are on the premises, including the Copper Top.

The spa is the main draw at **The Lodge & Spa at Breckenridge** (112 Overlook Dr., 970/453-9300 or 800/736-1607, www.thelodgeandspaatbreck.com, $215–250), which is a little removed from town and the ski slopes but overcompensates with extra luxury. Most of the standard guest rooms have mountain views—which is to say, spectacular views overlooking

the Continental Divide—and the suites are panoramic.

The Village at Breckenridge (535 S. Park Ave., 970/453-5192 or 800/400-9590, http://breckresorts.com/villageatbreckenridge, $215–245) is the monster place to stay in Breckenridge, as it's sprawled out on 14 acres at the base of the ski resort and a 10-minute walk from the Main Street shops and restaurants. It has a variety of guest rooms, from small no-frills studios to large three-bedroom luxury condo suites, all with ski-in, ski-out access to the six-person Quicksilver Super6 chairlift. On the premises are hot tubs, the Blue Sage Spa, an indoor pool, two restaurants (the Park Avenue Pub and The Maggie), a ski school for adults and children, and even The Village at Breckenridge Fly Fishing School. It's not particularly creative to simply book a room at The Village, but it's simple, usually available, and convenient.

The **Great Divide Lodge** (550 Village Rd., 970/547-5550 or 800/400-9590, http://breckresorts.com/greatdividelodge, $225–285) is a smaller but just-as-modern alternative to The Village at Breckenridge, with 208 guest rooms in a rectangular tree-lined building 50 yards from the ski resort's Peak 9 base. The hot-tub area overlooks the mountains, but the key reason for staying here (at least in the winter) is location.

Mountain Thunder Lodge (50 Mountain Thunder Dr., 970/547-5650 or 800/400-9590, http://breckresorts.com/mtnthunderlodge, $240–385) is a little more removed from the slopes than its sibling properties, The Village and the Great Divide Lodge, but the wooden lodge has an old-school log-cabin quality, and its primary luxuries are in-room stone fireplaces, outdoor hot tubs, and a large heated pool with surrounding heated decks. A shuttle takes guests to the slopes. The Mountain Thunder and Great Divide Lodges and The Village are run by Vail Resorts, the big ski-resort company that owns a big part of Vail and Keystone.

$300-400

The **Hyatt Main Street Station** (505 S. Main

St., 970/547-2700, www.hyattmainstreetstation.hyatt.com, $329–499) may look like a standard Rocky Mountain condo from the outside (note the green and brown wood panels), but it goes out of its way to provide cozy luxury—gas fireplaces, large kitchens, and whirlpool spas are in every guest room. Watch for deals during the off-season.

The primary advantage of **Pine Ridge Condominiums** (400 Four O'Clock Rd., 970/453-6946 or 888/840-4170, www.pineridge.com, $304) is its proximity to ski trails—many of the slope-side units are located directly on the popular Four O'Clock ski run. Each unit has a hot tub, a washer-dryer, and a full kitchen, but if you're looking for rustic mountain charms, you'd probably be better off at, say, the Allaire Timbers Inn. Keep an eye out for specials: During some event and off-season weekends, guest rooms can be as cheap as $119.

River Ridge Rentals (233 South Ridge St., Unit A, 970/547-9975, www.riverridgerentals.com, prices vary by property) rents about 30 quaint homes in Breckenridge, including the beautiful old **The Victorian,** about a block away from Main Street and the gondola, and the five-bedroom **River Lodge,** which is in a log-cabin building near the river and a golf course.

FOOD

For a small ski town, Breckenridge is crammed with restaurants—more than 100 in all, from greasy breakfast to fancy breakfast, sports-bar lunch, and high-end multicourse dinner.

Snacks, Cafés, and Breakfast

The Crown Café and Tavern (215 S. Main St., 970/453-6022, 10 A.M.–10 P.M. daily, www.thecrowncafe.com, $7) serves coffee and breakfast all day and basics like lasagna and tuna salad for meals, but its specialties are the sweet stuff—try the baked brie with chipotle raspberry sauce, then tour the pastry case.

The **Blue Moose** (540 S. Main St., 970/453-4859, 7 A.M.–1 P.M. daily, reduced hours off-season, $8) and the **Columbine Café** (109 S. Main St., 970/547-4474, 7:30 A.M.–1:30 P.M. Mon.–Fri., 7:30 A.M.–2:30 P.M. Sat.–Sun., $8)

serve breakfast along with coffee, dessert, and sandwiches.

Casual

After a day on the bright-white slopes, walking into the dungeon-like sports bar **Downstairs at Eric's** (111 S. Main St., 970/453-1401, www.downstairsaterics.com, 11 A.M.–midnight daily, $8) might cause temporary blindness. But the disconcerting feeling quickly passes, and the cheerful servers, 120 brands of beer, TVs suspended everywhere (if you're interested in that sort of thing), and old-school video games give this Main Street fixture charm. The food is affordable and very solid, from buffalo burgers to pizza. For pizza, though, you might want to go with an expert: **Giampietro Pasta & Pizzeria** (100 N. Main St., 970/453-3838, www.giampietropizza.com, 11 A.M.–9:30 P.M. daily, $13). The **Quandary Grille** (505 S. Main St., 970/547-5969, 11 A.M.–10 P.M. daily, $20) has $5 lunch and $10 dinner specials in its barn-shaped building next to pretty Maggie Pond; the fare is burgers, fries, and burritos in addition to some higher-end dishes like ribs and steak.

Upscale

Voted "Top Dinner for the Whole Family" in *5280* magazine, **(The Hearthstone** (130 S. Ridge St., 970/453-1148, www.hearthstonerestaurant.biz, 4 P.M.–close daily, $29) is in a 100-year-old Victorian and has a wine list that seems miles long. Its menu is an elegant mix of comfort food (try the three-onion soup) and exotic experiments (granola-crusted elk chop)—plus an affordable prime rib dish for the kids. Formerly Pierre's Riverwalk Café, **Relish** (137 S. Main St., 970/453-0989, www.relishbreckenridge.com, 4–9 P.M. daily, reduced hours off-season, $25) is a meat-and-potatoes and tofu restaurant that puts the slightest twist on familiar dishes—like sheep's-milk cheese gnocchi with portobello mushrooms and lamb meatloaf. **Taddeo's Ristorante Italiano** (535 S. Park Ave., 970/547-5959, www.taddeosristorante.com, 4–9 P.M. Sun.–Thurs., 4–10 P.M. Fri.–Sat., $17) is one of Breckenridge's best and most filling restaurants—try the Fat Tony, or five meatballs with marinara, as an appetizer.

INFORMATION AND SERVICES

Several official Breckenridge websites contain useful information on the ski area and the town as well as lodging, restaurants, shopping, and other amenities: www.breckenridge. com, www.gobreck.com, and www.townof-breckenridge.com. For general inquiries, call 970/453-2913.

For major hospital care, the nearest facility is the **Vail Valley Medical Center** (181 W. Meadow Dr., Vail, 970/476-2451, www.vvmc. com). However, Breckenridge has smaller facilities, including the **Breckenridge Community Clinic Emergency Center** (base of Peak 9 in the ski area, 970/453-1010, www.stanthony-mountainclinics.org/breckenridge).

GETTING THERE

I-70 connects to Highway 9 in the Dillon-Silverthorne area, and the two-lane route is considerably more icily treacherous than the interstate. Take Highway 9 south into Breckenridge, and keep going until it turns into Main Street. You can't miss the ski area in the snowcapped mountains in front of you, to the right; Main Street is a row of shops, restaurants, and galleries several blocks long. Street parking is available, but pay attention to the signs.

GETTING AROUND

The free **Summit Stage** bus (970/668-0999, www.summitstage.com, 6 A.M.–1:30 A.M. daily year-round) stops at numerous locations in Breckenridge, including City Market and the Breckenridge Recreation Center. It also serves nearby Dillon, Silverthorne, and Frisco.

Breckenridge Pedicabs (970/423-7196, www.breckenridgepedicabs.com) is a bicycle-and-cart service that provides tours, local rides, and prearranged transportation for special events. Most rides cost $10.

Keystone

For years, hard-core skiers considered Keystone a fun but visitor-heavy resort that never quite got enough snow, worth perhaps just a brief stop on the way to Copper Mountain or Breckenridge. Millions of dollars in renovations have changed that mentality: "This isn't the same place you remember from that icy night-skiing experience a decade ago," opined *Ski* magazine. A $4.5 million snowmaking system took care of the ice problem; the resort expanded its acreage considerably and added several bowls above the tree line geared to expert skiers. Another $1 million brought restaurants, bars, and nightclubs to the River Run base area.

Unlike Breckenridge, Aspen, or Vail, Keystone is a village built for the ski industry. Upon arriving in town for the first time, you might wonder where all the shops and restaurants have gone—and the answer is "up the slopes." Some of the town's best amenities, such as the 11,444-foot-high Alpenglow Stube restaurant and the Outpost Lodge, are accessible only via ski lift.

Both River Run and Lakeside Village are affordable and heavy on the visitors, and the best restaurants have high-class food to match the views. The Keystone Ranch, built in the 1930s, is a self-contained mountain playground that includes a golf course, and decades of visitors have come to associate the entire resort with the ranch experience. Note that many cost-conscious skiers avoid shopping at the villages entirely, opting instead to park in Dillon or Silverthorne, about 20 miles away, and take reasonably priced shuttles to the base mountains.

Keystone summers are eventful as well, and the resort enthusiastically rents mountain bikes for its hundreds of miles of trails, some of which overlook the magnificent Grays and Torreys Peaks. It's also just removed from the

Colorado River, which, in tandem with the small Keystone Lake, means boating, whitewater rafting, fishing, and kayaking. Check out the River Run Blues and the Bluegrass & Beer festivals in July as well.

SPORTS AND RECREATION
Skiing and Snowboarding

Keystone has three peaks: Dercum Mountain (11,640 feet, with a variety of terrain as well as the A51 Terrain Park), North Peak (11,660 feet, with especially long and bumpy trails), and the Outback (11,980 feet, known for its tree skiing in the North and South Bowls). Although Dercum Mountain, geared for beginners, once dominated the resort, its upgrades have attracted numerous experts, including training members of various U.S. ski teams. (Dercum Mountain, by the way, is named for Max and Edna Dercum, who founded the resort in 1970.)

Keystone's major distinction from other resorts is night skiing; the resort keeps 15 halogen lamp–lighted trails open at night and sponsors events such as moonlight snowshoe tours and "36 Hours at Keystone," attracting snowboarders and skiers who don't mind the weird shadows that mysteriously appear on the moguls. Night skiing is offered on 15 trails throughout the resort at all skill levels as well as in the A51 Terrain Park. Huge floodlights allow riders to see where they're going, and because nighttime frequently brings out more party-oriented riders, Keystone offers a large tubing hill known as Adventure Point (800/354-4386, www.keystoneresort.com, $33 per hour). Hours vary, so check with the resort before making night plans.

Keystone's skiing in general sometimes gets a bad rap from locals and experts, who perceive it as prime territory for families and beginners—the resort's Incubator Beginner Park, on the Freda's Way run about halfway up North Peak, has basic rails and rollers for the less coordinated. Also, the **Ski & Snowboard School** (800/255-3715), at the base Mountain House, offers lessons for adults and classes and day-care programs for kids age two months to

14 years. But in truth, Keystone's easiest trails make up just 19 percent of the three peaks; more difficult runs account for 32 percent, and the most difficult runs are almost half. The resort has 3,148 acres of total skiable terrain.

The A51 Terrain Park has dozens of rails, wall rides (including one painted like the American flag), and a superpipe close to the ski lift. The park is organized according to experience level—Freda's Incubator, on the northeast side of the park, accessible from the Peru Express lift, is for beginners; Main Street, for experts, is near the A51 Park Lift; and Park Lane, between the other two areas, is for intermediates. Check www.keystoneresort.com/a51/home.aspx for videos documenting the jibs and tricks at all the areas.

Some Keystone skiers swear by the central North Peak, filled with long drops unencumbered by trees and crowds; others prefer more technical terrain such as the twisty Bergman Bowl and the steep and rocky Erickson Bowl. Thanks to rugged snowcat vehicles, it's easier than ever before to access these bowls, high atop North Peak with views of Grays and Torreys Peaks in the distance. Bypassing North Peak is a little tricky, involving a gondola transfer or two, but for experts searching for difficult runs, The Grizz and Bushwhacker on the dense Outback Mountain are the places to be.

The easiest way to buy lift tickets ($89 in the most recent ski season) is online at www.keystoneresort.com (click on "Winter Accommodations" and "Lift Tickets"), or call 970/496-4589 or 800/344-8878. As usual, watch the local papers and ask at your hotel for package deals. The **Children's Center** (River Run, 800/255-3715) has day-care accommodations for kids age two months to six years—and has a special learn-to-ski program for three-year-olds.

Keystone Sports (River Run Village, 970/496-4619, www.keystonesport.com) is one of many centrally located stores that rents skis and equipment and sells winter clothing. It's in both the Mountain House base area and River Run village. The average price is about $20, rising to more than $36 for higher-end packages, but deals are more common in Dillon or Silverthorne, or even in Denver or Boulder.

The Keystone website offers a reliable and frequently updated weather report (www.keystoneresort.com/ski-and-snowboard/snow-report.aspx). Snow conditions are available at 970/496-4111, and road conditions are at 970/668-1090 (Summit County) and 303/639-1234 (Colorado).

Cross-Country Skiing

Keystone's **Nordic Center** (155 River Course Dr., 970/496-4275, www.keystoneresort.com/activities/nordic-center.aspx) offers lessons and rental equipment. The center is at the edge of 45 miles of White River National Forest trails. In addition to skiing, the center focuses on skating, snowshoeing, tubing, and telemarking.

Golf

The hub of Keystone golf is **Keystone Ranch** (1239 Keystone Ranch Rd., 970/496-1520, $55–170), a sprawling, beautiful area filled with trees and a nine-acre lake. It also has some of the resort's best lodging (at the Keystone Ranch condos) and food (the Keystone Ranch restaurant). The club's par-72, 7,090-yard course, designed by Robert Trent Jones Jr. in 1980, is fairly traditional on the first nine holes, but it switches to more mountainous terrain on the second. Another course, the Keystone River Course, opened in 2000 and winds through dense forest on the back nine. Both courses have amazing mountain views, but the Keystone River Course overlooks the Continental Divide.

Ice-Skating

The frozen five-acre **Keystone Lake** (800/354-4386) is "the largest Zamboni-maintained outdoor skating rink in North America," according to the resort website, and any superlative involving a Zamboni is fine by me. Seriously, the lake is spectacular, the air is clear, and skates and hockey sticks are available for reasonable rental fees.

Fishing

Keystone Resort (800/354-4386) offers fly-fishing lessons, although they're on the pricey side. Also pricey is **Summit Guides** (22138 U.S. 6, 970/468-8945, www.summitflyfish.com), which sells equipment and gives wading and floating tours throughout Summit County, including Keystone.

ENTERTAINMENT AND NIGHTLIFE

The Keystone bar scene is small but lively: For foosball, local rock bands on most nights, and free Pabst Blue Ribbon beer, **The Goat Soup and Whiskey Tavern** (22954 U.S. 6, 970/513-9344, www.thegoattavern.com, 3 P.M.–2 A.M. daily, reduced hours off-season) is a longtime favorite for the younger ski crowd. Also serving live music on a regular basis is the **9280 Tap House** (River Run, 970/496-4333, 11 A.M.–10 P.M. daily), a Mexican restaurant that goes heavy on the margaritas. **Greenlight** (River Run, 970/496-3223) transforms from a mild-mannered snack bar and après-ski hangout to a throbbing disco-ball dance club 9:30 P.M.–1:30 A.M. nightly. **Kickapoo Tavern** (129 River Run Rd., Unit A1, 970/468-0922, www.kickapootavern.com, 11 A.M.–10 P.M. daily, closed off-season) is a cavernous restaurant and bar with a large stone fireplace, long wooden tables, and stools as far as the eye can see. The **Tenderfoot Lounge** (22010 U.S. 6, 970/496-3715, www.keystonelodge.rockresorts.com, 4–10 P.M. daily), inside the Keystone Lodge & Spa, is a relaxing spot with a fireplace and occasional live entertainment. The **Snake River Saloon** (U.S. 6, 970/468-2788, www.snakeriversaloon.com, 4–10 P.M. daily) has high-class food (escargot for $12!) to go with the usual beer specials and mostly local rock bands and other live entertainment on certain nights.

EVENTS

Keystone has no major entertainment draw like the Telluride Bluegrass Festival or the Breckenridge Music Festival, but October's **Wine in the Pines** (www.wineinthepines.org) brings some 1,000 people to sample more than

ASPEN AND THE SKI TOWNS

500 vintages. The benefit for Cerebral Palsy of Colorado includes a gourmet food tasting and a winemaker's dinner.

SHOPPING

Most of Keystone's stores are in the **River Run** condominium district, not far from the ski lifts, but others are scattered throughout Lakeside Village, the Mountain House base area, and elsewhere in town. (Many residents and day-trippers, however, opt for the outlet stores in nearby Dillon and Silverthorne.) Among the gems: **Amazonias** (0195 River Run Rd., 970/262-6655, 10 A.M.–6 P.M. daily, closed off-season), selling hand-knit sweaters, and local chain **Gorsuch** (Buffalo Lodge, 100 Dercum Square, 970/262-0459, www.gorsuch. com, 8:30 A.M.–7 P.M. daily, reduced hours off-season), which rents equipment and sells stylish ski jackets and corny snowflake sweaters alike.

ACCOMMODATIONS

With more than 1,500 lodging units, **Keystone Resort** (run by Vail Resorts, 970/496-4500 or 800/328-1323, www.vailresorts.com, www.keystoneresort.com) has a lock on the market. But it does a pretty good job, offering diverse properties such as the 1880s Ski Tip Lodge and the golf-centric Keystone Ranch, along with a wide range of restaurants and outdoor activities as well as a shuttle that stops at most properties and the ski area. Many of the hotels, apartments, and condos listed here belong to the resort. The resort is divided into seven basic areas—East, North, and West Keystone, all somewhat removed from the slopes; Mountain House, the "base camp" at the bottom of the ski area; Keystone Ranch, golf-course territory; and Lakeside and River Run Villages, both centrally located "towns" equally close to amenities and the slopes. These are given in lieu of addresses as locations below.

For many Keystone skiers, location is the most important criteria when picking a lodge. Some of the more central and affordable properties include **Gateway Mountain Lodge** (23110 U.S. 6, 877/753-9786, www.keystoneresort.com, $189–289), which has a liquor store on the premises; **Aspen Ridge** (North Keystone, 877/753-9786, www.keystoneresort.com, $147–213), condos with superb views from the Tenderfoot Mountain Ridge; and **Riverbank Condominiums** (River Run, 877/753-9786, www.keystoneresort.com, $144). Note that many condos require a five-night minimum, although shorter stays may be available during the off-season.

The resort's general lodging numbers are 970/496-4500 and 800/328-1323.

$100-150

Not to be confused with the Ski Tip Condominiums, **Ski Tip Lodge** (0764 Montezuma Rd., 877/753-9786, www.keystoneresort.com, $135–190) was a stagecoach stop in the 1880s. Keystone founders Max and Edna Dercum bought it in the 1940s as a private home and turned it into an early ski lodge. Although Keystone Resort bought the lodge in the 1970s, it's still intimate and quaint, with individually decorated guest rooms, a central fireplace, and an acclaimed restaurant.

$150-200

At the center of Keystone Village, the **Keystone Lodge & Spa** (22101 U.S. 6, 970/496-3712, www.keystoneresort.com, $191) aims for luxury (check out the spa, sauna, and indoor-outdoor pool) above the intimate charm of the Ski Tip Lodge. Every room has a nice view of Keystone Mountain and the Snake River. It's also incredibly convenient, with ice-skating and bike rental within a short walk and the slopes within a short shuttle ride.

$200-300

Cabin in the Pines (North Keystone, 877/753-9786, $201–288) is a woodsy condominium complex with three-bedroom units. The **Inn at Keystone** (23044 Hwy. 6, 970/496-4825, www.keystoneresort.com, $219–239) is a plain but inexpensive hotel on U.S. 6, with a jazz bar and restaurant on hand. It's closer to nightclubs such as The Goat and the Snake River Saloon than it is to the slopes, but it's within 300 yards of the Mountain House base area.

Over $400

Keystone Ranch (006 Goldenrod Circle, 888/222-9298, $650) is the prime spot for golfers, immediately next to the Robert Trent Jones, Jr.–designed course, but Melville House is an upscale multiple-bedroom property available for rent.

FOOD
Casual

The Mountain House ski-area base underwent renovations in the early 2000s, and family-oriented quickie restaurants such as **Black Diamond Pizzeria** (Mountain House, 970/496-4020 or 970/496-4386, 8 A.M.–5 P.M. daily, closed off-season, $6) sprang up for skiers whose three-year-olds are unable to sit still for a six-course Alpenglow Stube meal. The pizza isn't bad at all; neither is the beer. Also, the **Timber Ridge Food Court** (North Peak, 970/496-3156, 9 A.M.–3 P.M. daily), at the top of prime skiing territory, has a variety of quick-and-cheap hamburger and Asian noodle dishes. The food isn't anything special, but you can't beat the convenience—or the views.

It's unlikely that many Irish immigrants live in Keystone, but the **Cala Inn** (40 Cove Blvd., 970/468-1899, www.calainn.com, 11 A.M.–11 P.M. Mon.–Thurs., 10 A.M.–midnight Fri.–Sat., 11 A.M.–10 P.M. Sun., $13) is one of those classic Irish joints with shepherd's pie and fish and chips to go with unlimited Guinness.

Upscale

Dinner prices can easily get to the $100 range, not including wine from the extensive list, but the 🄲 **Alpenglow Stube** (North Peak, 800/354-4386, 11 A.M.–1:30 P.M. and 5:30–8:30 P.M. Thurs.–Sat., 5:30–8:30 P.M. Fri.–Sat., 10:30 A.M.–1:30 P.M. Sun., closed off-season, $99 for 7 courses) is worth it for the scenery alone. It's a North Peak gondola ride up to 11,444 feet, with a six-course meal of elegant dishes like duck foie gras and roast chestnut and butternut squash tartlet. They also let you replace your ski boots with slippers—and no, this isn't a typo—warmed in the oven.

Real-life cowboys probably don't come to the **Keystone Ranch** (1437 County Rd. 150, 800/354-4386, 6–8:45 P.M. Tues.–Sat., reduced hours off-season, $75 for 5 courses, $42 for 2 courses) golf-course restaurant anymore—I'm pretty sure Roy Rogers and Dale Evans didn't eat foie gras trio sautéed with pumpkin oil—but the Old West paraphernalia and decor is fun to look at. Located in a 1930s cattle-ranch homestead, the restaurant offers six-course meals with boar and buffalo specialties.

The restaurant at the comfortable and welcoming 🄲 **Ski Tip Lodge** (0764 Montezuma Rd., 970/496-4950 or 800/354-4386, www.keystoneresort.com, 5:45–8:45 P.M. daily, reduced hours off-season, $69 for 4 courses) turns mahimahi, roast prairie quail, and veal into high-class comfort food. From the fireplace to the rich coffee and dessert (best eaten in the lounge), the Ski Tip is as soothing as a post-ski hot chocolate.

The **Bighorn Steakhouse** (22101 U.S. 6, 970/496-4386 or 800/345-4386, www.keystoneresort.com, 5–9:15 P.M. daily, reduced hours off-season, $35), in the Keystone Lodge & Spa, is unsurprisingly focused on steaks, but it also serves chicken, venison, corn-and-bean soup, and seafood. The dining room's huge wide windows provide a beautiful view of Keystone and the mountains. The Tenderfoot Lounge has live music on Friday and Saturday nights.

INFORMATION AND SERVICES

Just about everything Keystone—ski area, town, lodging, shopping—falls under the Keystone Resort umbrella (970/496-2316 or 877/625-1556, www.keystoneresort.com).

There are no major hospitals in Keystone, although emergency facilities are located in nearby Breckenridge and Vail. The ski area has a **Mountain First Aid** squad (970/496-3810) and a **Ski Patrol** (970/496-3180). Also nearby is **Lake Dillon Fire-Rescue** (401 Blue River Pkwy., Silverthorne, 970/513-4100, http://ldfr.org).

GETTING THERE AND AROUND

Keystone is tucked at the bottom of Loveland Pass, just removed enough from I-70 to make the drive interesting during a blizzard. From Denver, take I-70 west through Georgetown and Idaho Springs, but turn east on U.S. 6 (at the Silverthorne/Dillon exit) a few miles before hitting the Eisenhower Tunnel. After passing the Loveland ski area, the beautiful Loveland Pass overlooking the Continental Divide, and Arapahoe Basin, continue on the narrow, twisty, two-lane highway until you plunge into Keystone. Compared to Vail or Breckenridge, the town itself is a little hard to spot—just green-and-brown wooden condo buildings everywhere. It's only about nine miles from Breck up Highway 9, making a two-resort vacation simple.

The small and self-contained Keystone has its own little bus stop, serving most of the condos, hotels, restaurants, and ski shops in the area. To check the pickup locations and schedule, call 970/496-4200. **Colorado Mountain Express** (970/468-7600, www.coloradomountainexpress.com) and **Fresh Tracks** (970/453-4052, www.freshtrackstransportation.com) provide transportation among Keystone, Vail, and other nearby areas.

LOVELAND SKI AREA

Few out-of-towners travel all the way to Colorado to ski at the **Loveland Ski Area** (I-70 Exit 216, near Georgetown, 303/569-3203 or 800/736-3754, www.skiloveland.com)—for one thing, there's no lodging—but day-tripping locals swear by this 13,010-foot-tall mountain that averages 400 inches of snow. Opened in 1936, the mountain rises above the Continental Divide, which means great scenery, and while the lifts can be poky and the wind intense, it gets some of the best powder in the region. Nine lifts serve more than 90 runs, an equal mixture for beginners (Loveland Valley) and experts (Loveland Basin). Rental shops and a ski school (303/571-5580, ext. 170) are easily accessible from the base area, and parking is plentiful. Like every other ski resort

in Colorado over the past decade, Loveland also added a terrain park, which doesn't draw the world's top snowboarders but does put on the Tall Tees & Tacos competition in late March and late April.

Loveland Pass, directly up U.S. 6, has a scenic area overlooking the Continental Divide about 10 miles from the ski area. Whether you're skiing or exploring, the area makes for a nice stop en route to Keystone or Breckenridge.

◖ ARAPAHOE BASIN

If Vail and Aspen are for skiers serious about their clothes, A-Basin (28194 Hwy. 6, Keystone, www.arapahoebasin.com, 970/468-0718 or 888/272-7246) is for skiers serious about their partying. It's the highest ski area in the United States, with a base elevation of 10,780 feet and a summit of 13,050 feet; it's Summit County's first ski area, built in the 1940s, and it maintains its rickety charm; and due to its elevation and a relatively new snow-making machine, it stays open later than any other Colorado resort. As a result, locals fill the parking lots for "Beachin' at the Basin" tailgate parties through June or July.

Aside from an on-site cafeteria and bar, A-Basin itself has almost nothing by way of restaurants or hotels. Its clientele tends to be day-trippers up from Boulder or Denver, or out-of-town visitors who've settled in nearby Dillon or Silverthorne and shuttled between their hotel and the base.

Most visitors to the old-school resort will find it unsurprising that Arapahoe Basin began with just one sturdy tow rope for a ski lift. And to get to the bottom of the rope, skiers had to ride in a U.S. Army weapons carrier that was pulled by a 4WD vehicle. That was in 1946, and the resort still seems like a throwback.

Sports and Recreation

A-Basin offers few frills aside from its internationally known extreme runs. (One longtime Colorado skier calls it "scary-ass terrain.") Best known is the Pallavincini, thought to be the longest and steepest in Colorado, but it is filled with double-black diamond (which is to say, expert) runs that attract locals who aren't so obsessed with drinking hot chocolate in the lodge afterward. It's also just west of the Continental Divide—almost on top of it—and the views are excellent. The two terrain parks, **Treeline** and **High Divide,** have more than a dozen features each, including the narrow, curved Rainbow, and the long, angular A-Box.

The **Ski School** (888/272-7246, www. arapahoebasin.com, $80 pp half day) promises groomed runs for beginners ("or your money back!"). Lift tickets tend to be affordable ($69), and the slopes aren't as crowded as those of Vail or Steamboat Springs. Rental equipment is available at the base area.

Nightlife
Post-ski A-Basin drinkers have pretty much one choice without venturing to nearby Keystone or Breckenridge: the **Sixth Alley Bar**

(A-Frame base lodge, 970/513-5705, 11 A.M.–5:30 P.M. Mon.–Fri., 10:30 A.M.–5:30 P.M. Sat.–Sun., closed off-season), which has cheap drinks and that's pretty much it. Live bands sometimes play outside in May.

Services
The ski area has a patrol for emergency services. Otherwise, medical resources are available in nearby Breckenridge, Silverthorne, and Vail.

Getting There
Driving to A-Basin can be tricky in bad weather, as it involves a trip up the twisty, two-lane U.S. 6 (after exiting I-70) to Loveland Pass. The base area is at the very bottom of the steep highway. Just six miles beyond the area is Keystone, so skiers from that resort may want to venture to a different experience.

Dillon, Silverthorne, and Frisco

DILLON AND SILVERTHORNE
Ski-resort regulars drive past suburban-looking twin towns Dillon and Silverthorne and think *cheap shopping.* Both towns have huge factory outlets with many name brands and are generally more affordable than the shops populating nearby resort base areas and tourist districts. Both are also worth a stop—and not just for the many convenient chain hotels, restaurants, and ski-slope park-and-ride shuttles. Silverthorne (pop. 3,500) is along the Blue River and has many parks and out-of-the-way spots for anglers and kayakers. The 125-year-old Dillon (pop. 2,800) is best known for the 9,000-foot-high marina-equipped Lake Dillon, a favorite for sailboaters, and its history as a stagecoach stop in the 1880s.

History
In the 1950s, the state government gave Dillon an ultimatum: Everybody move, or you'll drown. Drought had struck Denver, the capital city 70 miles to the east, so the Denver Water Board decided to dam the Blue River.

This turned out to be a massive undertaking. Dillon townspeople had to sell their property and move by 1961. Workers cut a 1,700-foot-long tunnel from solid rock, built a shaft 233 feet deep, and submerged the town under 150 feet of water. (The dam, located underneath Lake Dillon, is no longer visible, but you can see the location by driving east from Frisco to Dillon on Dam Road.) That was the *third* time Dillon moved.

Dillon became a town in 1883, when stagecoach riders established a trading post in the region (then, as now, the town was a prime midpoint for city dwellers traveling to pretty mountain towns). The town first moved closer to the Utah and Northern Railroad; later, it moved to be near the Blue, Tenmile, and Snake Rivers. Its third move was to the shore of the Denver Water Board's reservoir. And that's where the town—which swells to 5,200 people in the winter, thanks to condos and hotels—stands today.

Silverthorne's history is slightly less colorful. Its name comes from Judge Marshall

Silverthorn, who in 1880 made a gold-mining claim called the Silverthorn Placer on what would become the town of Silverthorne. The border between the two towns is blurred, so many passersby refer to them interchangeably.

Sports and Recreation

Unburdened with the crush of downhill skiing, Dillon and Silverthorne focus on other outdoor sports, both in winter and summer. The activity centers on picturesque **Lake Dillon,** on the edge of Dillon and Frisco. The **Dillon Marina** (970/468-5100, www.dillonmarina.com) rents pontoons, sailboats, and runabouts ($105–210 for 2 hours) as well as offering **sailing** lessons (call in advance). Even oceanfront aficionados from San Francisco and Boston will find the 26 miles of shoreline a relaxing way to spend a nonsnowy afternoon. For **anglers,** the lake is packed with brown and rainbow trout.

The Old Dillon Reservoir, which was the reason the town of Dillon moved for the third and final time in the early 1960s, recently closed due to fallout from pine-beetle deforestation. However, the **Old Dillon Reservoir Trail** remains one of the more popular hiking, biking, and cross-country skiing routes in Dillon. From the town, head east on Dillon Dam Road, turn left past Heaton Bay Campground, then park in the area near a trail-marker sign. The easy trail is only 0.75 miles each way, just a bit uphill through the forest and part of the way around the placid reservoir. Also in Dillon are two **Dillon Nature Preserve** trails, both beginning at the parking lot on U.S. 6 one mile east of Tenderfoot Street. Both trails are two-mile loops around meadows and forests, with pretty views of the Rockies.

Lesser-known but just as beautiful, **Boulder Lake** is accessible via trailheads in Silverton. To get to one of them, take Highway 9 north from I-70, turn left on Rock Creek Road, go about 1.2 miles on the gravel road, and turn left at the "Rock Creek" sign. The trail is about 2.7 miles each way, passing through meadows en route to Boulder Lake; watch for moose. The more difficult trail to Boulder Lake starts

sailboats on Lake Dillon

© MATT INDEN/WEAVER MULTIMEDIA GROUP/COLORADO TOURISM OFFICE

at the same trailhead but is six miles each way and climbs roughly 1,500 feet.

Cross-country skiers can spread out on miles of trails at Silverthorne's **Nordic Center** (Raven Golf Course, 2929 Golden Eagle Rd., Dec.–Mar.), which is run by the Town of Silverthorne (970/262-7300, www.silverthorne.org). Silverthorne also has an **ice-skating park** (Hwy. 9 and Hamilton Creek Rd., Dec.–Jan.).

About 27 miles north of Silverthorne on Highway 9 is the tiny town of Heeney, which is known for the **Green Mountain Reservoir** (www.greenmountainreservoir.com), a pretty little out-of-the-way body of water that's open in the summer for boating, fishing, and Jet-Skiing, if you bring your own. The small **Heeney Marina** (151 County Rd. 1798, 970/724-9441, www.heeneymarina.com, Memorial Day–Labor Day) rents pontoons and small and large fishing boats ($40–120 for 2 hours). Several good wilderness trails surround Heeney as well, including the two-mile **Cataract Lake Loop,** a wildflower-heavy trail (seasonal, mid–late June) that passes by pretty Cataract Falls. To get to the trailhead, go north on Highway 9 from Silverthorne, turn left onto Heeney Road (also known as County Rd. 30), turn left onto Cataract Creek Road, and go 2.5 miles to the trailhead and parking area. Sadly, the annual **Heeney Tick Festival** has been shut down since 2000, so you'll have to swallow your suspense regarding the next Tick Festival King and Queen.

The Dillon Ranger District also runs the **Green Mountain Reservoir Campground** (970/468-5400, www.dillonrangerdistrict.com, $10 per vehicle plus $5 per vehicle per day), which has seven large campsite areas, both around the reservoir and halfway up the Cataract Lake Loop.

For more information on trails and outdoor activities, contact the **Summit County Chamber of Commerce** (Frisco, 970/668-2051, www.summitchamber.org). Another superb trail resource, especially on the Web, is the **Dillon Ranger District** (680 Blue River Pkwy., Silverthorne, 970/468-5400, www.dillonrangerdistrict.com).

Although the best golf courses in the area are in Keystone, a just-as-scenic and not-so-pricey option is the **Raven Golf Club at Three Peaks** (2929 N. Golden Eagle Rd., Silverthorne, 970/262-3636, www.ravengolf.com, $45–165), a tree- and lake-filled 18-hole course designed by Alister MacKenzie.

Nightlife

Like the rest of Silverthorne and Dillon, the bars here are no-nonsense. For a quick, cheap drink, try the **Dillon Dam Brewery** (100 Little Dam St., Dillon, 970/262-7777, www.dambrewery.com, 11:30 A.M.–11:30 P.M. daily), a brewpub whose homemade flavors include Dam Lyte and Wildernest Wheat. Check the website for drink specials. Live bands play Thursday nights during winter and summer. For a more upscale experience, there's **D'Vine Wine** (358 Blue River Pkwy., Unit G, Silverthorne, 970/468-9377, www.winerysilverthorne.com, noon–7 P.M. Fri.–Sun. and Tues.–Wed., noon–8 P.M. Thurs.), which carries the requisite merlots and cabernet sauvignons and allows visitors to make their own wine.

Shopping

Many visit the Silverthorne-Dillon area purely for the mall-type shopping—common in big cities and suburbs, but an unexpected luxury in the middle of a Rocky Mountain blizzard. The **Outlets at Silverthorne** (246-V Rainbow Dr., Silverthorne, 970/468-5780 or 866/746-7686, www.outletsatsilverthorne.com, 10 A.M.–8 P.M. Mon.–Sat., 11 A.M.–6 P.M. Sun.) has 50 stores split up into three "villages" on opposite sides of I-70; Tommy Hilfiger and the Gap are to the north, while Nike and Levi's outlets are to the south.

Accommodations

Many of the hotels in Dillon and Silverthorne are of the Holiday Inn variety—with rates far lower than accommodations in nearby Keystone and Breckenridge—but there are a few bed-and-breakfasts nestled between the hills and lakes. The **Mountain Vista Bed and Breakfast** (358 Lagoon Lane, Silverthorne, 970/468-7700 or 800/333-5165, www.colorado-mtnvista.com, $79–135) is a centrally located, no-frills hotel with three guest rooms.

Food

The **Dillon Dam Brewery** (100 Little Dam St., 970/262-7777 or 866/326-6196, www.dambrewery.com, 11:30 A.M.–10 P.M. daily, $15) is a brewpub with pretty much everything you could want on the menu (try the San Luis pepper duck, $19) and several kinds of homemade beers. For steaks of all shapes and sizes (and, yes, chicken and fish), the **Historic Mint** (347 Blue River Pkwy., Silverthorne, 970/468-5247, www.mintsteakhouse.com, 4:30–10 P.M. daily, $25) lets you cook slabs on 1,100°F flaming rocks. Located in a can't-miss-it square white building, the restaurant has been here since 1862 and has the antiques and decor to prove it.

Information and Services

The **Town of Dillon** (275 Lake Dillon Dr., 970/468-2403, www.townofdillon.com) has straightforward information for travelers. The Town of Silverthorne information line is at 970/262-7300, or go to www.silverthorne.org. While there's no hospital in the Dillon-Silverthorne-Frisco area, **Lake Dillon Fire-Rescue** (401 Blue River Pkwy., Silverthorne, 970/262-5100, http://ldfr.org) provides emergency services.

FRISCO

Although it doesn't draw as many I-70 travelers as neighboring Dillon and Silverthorne, let alone booming resort areas like Vail or Breckenridge, Frisco is a woodsy mountain town with decent hotels and restaurants. First discovered by the Utes, Frisco was overrun with beaver-trapping mountain men in the early 1800s; the gold rush later that century brought mines, railroads, hotels, saloons, and more people. The boom ended in 1918, and the Great Depression lowered the population to exactly 18 people. "Frisco persevered," its website reads, "and by 1946 the population had

increased to 50." Thanks to ski traffic, it's up to 2,800 today.

History

The **Frisco Historic Park** (Frisco Historical Society, Main St. and 2nd St., 970/668-3428, www.townoffrisco.com/activities/historic-park-museum, 10 A.M.–4 P.M. Tues.–Sat., 10 A.M.–2 P.M. Sun. winter, 9 A.M.–5 P.M. Tues.–Sat., 9 A.M.–3 P.M. Sun. summer, free) is a 10-building district anchored on the old Frisco Schoolhouse, which today houses a museum. Some of the buildings, including the gazebo Ches's Place, are open for public tours. Just don't commit any crimes against history or you'll land in The Historic Jail.

Sports and Recreation

Despite the misleading name, **Frisco Bay** isn't a standalone body of water—it's part of the Dillon Reservoir—but it does have its own marina on the east end of Main Street. The town of Frisco runs the **Frisco Bay Marina** (970/668-4334, www.townoffrisco.com/

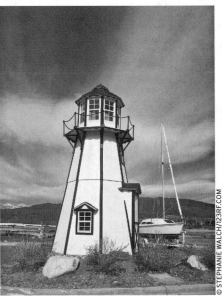

lighthouse in Frisco

© STEPHANIE WALCH/123RF.COM

frisco-bay-marina), which rents sailboats and offers storage for canoes and kayaks.

Frisco has several excellent hiking-and-biking trails. One of the most difficult is **Meadow Creek,** a 4.7-mile climb from town to 11,900-foot Eccles Pass. To get there, take I-70 to exit 203, then go around the traffic circle until you see the U.S. Forest Service sign. Turn right onto that gravel road and follow it to the parking area. It's a pretty trail, through aspens and pines, overlooking Dillon Reservoir and the Upper Blue Valley. A little easier, or at least shorter, is **Mount Royal/Masontown,** which is one mile to Mount Royal or two miles to Masontown, an old mining town destroyed by an avalanche in 1926. Look for the trailhead near the parking lot at the east end of Main Street in Frisco. This trail is especially beautiful, with amazing views of the Tenmile Range, Dillon Reservoir, the Continental Divide, and, in the southeast, the 13,370-foot peak Mount Guyot.

Nightlife

Frisco's townie bar extraordinaire is the **Backcountry Brewery** (720 Main St., 970/668-2337, www.backcountrybrewery.com, 11:30 A.M.–11 P.M. Sun.–Thurs., 11:30 A.M.–midnight Fri.–Sat.), a nightlife party-time kind of place that serves burgers, wraps, pizza, and, of course, beer. There's also **Upstairs at Jonny G's** (409 Main St., 970/668-5442, www.jonnygs.com, 4 P.M.–2 A.M. Mon.–Sat., 10:30 A.M.–2 A.M. Sun.), which has hip-hop DJ nights, karaoke, and occasional live bands.

Accommodations

Don't be put off by the huge moose head hanging above the stone fireplace in the **Hotel Frisco** (308 Main St., 970/668-5009 or 800/262-1002, http://hotelfrisco.com, $99–189); it just contributes to the woodsy quality of this bed-and-breakfast. Huge foothills are visible right outside the front door, and the hotel's Main Street location is at the center of Frisco's historic district.

Food

Open since the 1940s, the **Blue Spruce Inn** (20 Main St., 970/668-5900, www.thebluespruce.com, 4 P.M.–2 A.M. daily, $30) specializes in large steaks (and the occasional fish or chicken dish). Its homey bar has chicken wings aplenty, and somebody named Doowop Denny plays during happy hour every Sunday afternoon.

Silverheels at the Ore House (601 Main St., 970/668-0345, www.silverheelsrestaurant.com, 4–10 P.M. Mon.–Wed., 11:30 A.M.–10 P.M. Thurs.–Sun., $25) is a great place to get $9 salmon crab cakes. Despite its nautical theme, including a Wednesday sushi night, Silverheels is best known for inexpensive dishes, from pork chops to stuffed chiles rellenos.

For breakfast, don't miss the **Log Cabin Café** (121 Main St., 970/668-3947, www.logcabincafe.co, 7 A.M.–2:30 P.M. daily, $8), in a 1908 log cabin, serving renowned three-egg omelets and other classic breakfasts. It's also open for lunch and dinner.

Finally, the **Alpine Market and Deli** (301 Main St., 970/668-5535, www.alpinemarketfrisco.com, 9 A.M.–6 P.M. daily, $8) is a friendly little Whole Foods–style supermarket with a bonus: an amazing deli in the back with super-fresh meats, breads, vegetables, and cheeses. It's a great quick place to stop off I-70 between the ski resorts and Denver (look for the blue highway sign).

Information

The **Town of Frisco**'s Town Hall is at 1 Main Street. Contact town officials at 970/668-5276 or www.townoffrisco.com.

COPPER MOUNTAIN

Chuck Lewis built Copper Mountain on 280 acres in 1971, and thanks to three huge mountain peaks, thousands of miles of ski trails, and a word-of-mouth reputation that attracts non-snobby skiers, it has since expanded to 2,433 acres. The resort continues to grow as owner Intrawest Corp. continues to expand its village area after spending hundreds of millions of dollars through the late 1990s and early 2000s. Copper's village area isn't a city in the Vail sense, but the pedestrian village Burning Stones Plaza has high-priced condominiums and restaurants as well as nice touches like ice-skating rinks and sledding hills. Copper Mountain is simple to find, along I-70 about seven miles west of Frisco.

Sports and Recreation

Copper (209 Ten Mile Circle, 888/219-2441, www.coppercolorado.com) remains one of the best-laid-out ski areas in the state, with three peaks, all more than 12,000 feet high, and more than 2,400 ski acres. The runs are conveniently removed from each other so experts on the bumpy eastern side and beginners in the Union Creek area don't collide at the bottom. Lift tickets cost roughly $79 per day. The resort's **Woodward at Copper** terrain-park program offers a variety of parks and features, including a 22-foot superpipe, a kids area, and an expert-only playground called **Catalyst** known for extra-tall rails, boxes, and jumps. A few of the parks, including Catalyst, are open during the parts of summer when snow is still on the ground.

A full-day adult lesson at the **Ski & Snowboard School** (866/549-9934, www.coppercolorado.com) costs $119, and separate classes are available for snowboarders and kids. The resort also provides rental equipment (970/968-2318) that's fairly reasonable, especially compared to Aspen or Vail.

Aside from skiing, Copper's other two big outdoor sports are cycling and golf. **Mountain bikers** can rent steeds at **Gravitee** (Tucker Lodge, 0164 Copper Rd., 970/968-0171, http://gravitee.com, $25–45 per day) or **Peak Sports** (214 Ten Mile Circle, www.coppersports.com, 970/968-2372, $47 per day) and use the resort's American Eagle lift to access trails such as the moderate Shrine Pass (including a nine-mile drop) and the more advanced Searle Pass. **Golfers** can try the 18-hole, par-70 Pete and Perry Dye–designed **Copper Creek Golf Club** (Wheeler Place, 866/286-1663, $29–67), which starts underneath towering pine trees and meanders into an abandoned mining-town area.

Nightlife

Most Copper denizens of the night rotate between a few hot spots: **Endo's Adrenaline Café** (209 Ten Mile Circle, 970/968-3070, www.endoscafe.com, 11 A.M.–7 P.M. daily), which has DJs and a dance floor and promises "body shots and dancing on the bar nightly"; **JJ's Rocky Mountain Tavern** (102 Wheeler Circle, East Village, 970/968-3062, www.jjstavern.com, 10 A.M.–9 P.M. daily, reduced hours off-season), with live music Wednesday–Saturday and drink specials; the **Storm King Lounge** (The Village at Copper, 970/968-2318, 4–10 P.M. daily, reduced hours off-season), specializing in martinis; and **Jack's Slopeside Grill** (The Village at Copper, 970/968-2318, 8 A.M.–6 P.M., reduced hours off-season), also with live music on a regular basis.

Shopping

Hang around the shops at Copper Mountain for a while and you'll notice a theme: skiing. **The Mountain Adventure Center** (The Village at Copper, 970/968-2318, ext. 45621, 8 A.M.–8 P.M. daily) rents and sells high-quality ski equipment and winter clothing. The **Surefoot Boot Fitting Co.** (0184 Copper Circle, Suite A5, 970/968-1728, www.surefoot.com, 8:30 A.M.–6 P.M. daily, reduced hours off-season) expands its repertoire from ski boots to cowboy boots. **Kokomo** (Taylor's Crossing, 970/968-2327, 9 A.M.–9 P.M. daily in ski season) sells clothes, gifts, pottery, and visitor-focused artwork.

Accommodations

Copper Mountain Resort (209 Ten Mile Circle, 866/841-2481, $215–261) is pretty much the only game in town, lodging-wise, but it makes up for the lack of choice with high quality guest rooms and amenities—try the Cirque, a relatively new building with three pools, French architecture, and washer-dryers in every room. The new Village at Copper is the centerpiece area,

snowboarding at Copper Mountain

near most of the restaurants and shops, but the East Village is closer to the mountain. Resort guests can buy $10-per-day passes to the Copper Mountain Athletic Club, which has a huge indoor pool, spas, steam rooms, and saunas. Be sure to ask about lift-ticket packages. Of course, budget-conscious visitors can book rooms at hotels in nearby Frisco, Silverthorne, and Dillon.

Food

While booming music and a huge, grizzled ski-in, ski-out crowd won't make anyone mistake **Endo's Adrenaline Café** (209 Ten Mile Circle, 970/968-3070, www.endoscafe. com, 10:30 A.M.–10 P.M. Mon.–Thurs., 10:30 A.M.–11 P.M. Fri.–Sat. winter, 11 A.M.–7 P.M. daily summer, $9) for a New York City chophouse, the sandwiches are gigantic and the food is better than you'd expect.

JJ's Rocky Mountain Tavern (102 Wheeler Circle, East Village, 970/968-3062, www.jjstavern.com, 11 A.M.–9 P.M. daily, reduced hours off-season, $20) has the feel of a brewpub, but the food is high-class—try the gourmet Thai pizza with shrimp, snow peas, and pineapple.

Information

The ski resort (209 Ten Mile Circle, 866/841-2481 or 888/219-2441, www.coppercolorado.com) has all the information you'll need.

Winter Park and Vicinity

Revered for its treacherous moguls and expert ski runs, the five-mountain Winter Park is a step up from spare townie-oriented resorts such as Copper Mountain and Arapahoe Basin. Owner Intrawest Corp. has expanded Winter Park significantly in recent years, broadening the base village and building a new gondola that runs from downtown to the ski area. But loyal Winter Park fans worry that (1) Intrawest will do away with Colorado's only Nordic ski jumps besides Steamboat Springs and (2) somebody will smooth out the moguls. Bumper stickers throughout the Front Range read: "Save Our Bumps." (The bumps are probably safe, though.)

Of Winter Park's five mountains—Winter Park, Mary Jane, Vasquez Cirque, Vasquez Ridge, and Parsenn Bowl—Mary Jane is the most respected, especially for its long mogul runs and steep chutes. The resort is also the exact midpoint between snooty Aspen and Vail and the lower-key Arapahoe Basin and Copper Mountain. Its mountainside resort village, which has been significantly expanded and renovated, includes low-key but elegant condos, hotels, and restaurants, including the Zephyr Mountain Lodge and local favorite Deno's Mountain Bistro, as well as affordable shops.

Created in 1940, the ski resort overwhelms the nearby town of Winter Park, which encompasses 7.5 square miles and has 999 full-time residents, according to the latest U.S. Census. The town is well worth visiting, especially during spring and summer, when crowds keep away and hundreds of miles of trails are wide open for cyclists and hikers. The resort, which has 50 miles of its own trails, is on the eastern edge of town, and a shuttle runs between the town and the resort throughout ski season. Many opt to stay at nearby (and smaller) Fraser as well.

SPORTS AND RECREATION
Downhill Skiing and Snowboarding

Winter Park itself is the most diverse of the resort's three ski areas, with runs for all skill levels and terrain parks and a half pipe for expert skiers and boarders. Its Groswold's Discovery Park, at 20 acres, is popular for beginners and riders trying to avoid extreme twists, trees, and bumps. Mary Jane ("No Pain, No Jane") is world-renowned for its seemingly endless mogul runs and steep chutes—almost all geared toward experts. Vasquez Ridge is the opposite extreme; it's a little out of the way, accessible via the Pioneer Express lift, but many leisurely skiers prefer long, easygoing runs like Stagecoach and Sundance. Lift tickets run about $85.

Of the 3,060 total acres of skiing at Winter Park, Mary Jane, which opened in 1976, has the longest runs, including some at 4.5 miles. It's also the tallest mountain, at 12,060 feet. And at the very top of the mountain it has the Parsenn Bowl, which has incredible views and is especially popular after a blizzard.

The resort's terrain park includes six areas, one superpipe, and 85 total features—begin with **Starter Park,** which has wide, low rides, then move on to the small **Ash Cat** to test out new tricks, and work up to **Re-railer** or **Dark Territory,** which is so treacherous that the resort requires riders to fill out an extra waiver and watch additional safety videos.

Winter Park's ski school is open to adults and children, and it gives private and group lessons. A full-day adult session is $109–119, including lunch; call 800/729-7907 to make a reservation. Several shops at the ski area rent equipment for skiers and boarders: **West Portal Rental** (970/726-1662), at the base of the mountain, also offers free overnight storage, and **The Jane Shop** (970/726-1670) is based exclusively at the Mary Jane base area.

Finally, the base area is home to the **National Sports Center for the Disabled** (970/726-1540 or 303/316-1540, www.nscd.org), which began in 1970 as a ski lesson for young Denver amputees. It has since grown to thousands of members of all ages and offers a variety of ski and snowboard programs in the winter.

Information about Winter Park's ski area, along with lodging, food, recreation, and other activities, is at www.winterparkresort.com, or call 303/316-1564 or 970/726-1564.

Cross-Country Skiing

It's not uncommon while driving toward Winter Park on I-70 or U.S. 40 during a heavy snowfall to see backcountry skiers and snowboarders schlepping their equipment along the bushwhacked trails on the side of the road. Use these trails at your own risk, as many of them are unexplored and unmarked. For skiers preferring more organized cross-country trips, there's the **Devil's Thumb Ranch** (3530 County Rd. 83, Tabernash, www.devilsthumbranch.com, 800/933-4339, day pass $18, ski and snowshoe rentals $20), seven miles from Winter Park, with about 75 miles of groomed trails through the woods. The YMCA-run **Snow Mountain Ranch** (1101 County Rd. 53, Granby, 800/777-9622, www.ymcarockies.org) offers about 62 miles of backcountry skiing trails, including two that are open at night. Both areas provide equipment and are open to snowshoers. The ranch also has an accessible campground ($30–40) and seven yurts, which sleep 6–8 people ($89). It's great for little kids, although it isn't exactly a haven of wilderness privacy. Activities here include scavenger hunts, horseback riding, volleyball, crafts, an indoor pool, a climbing wall, a gym with basketball courts, and fishing on a heart-shaped reservoir. In winter, there are miles of snowshoe and cross-country ski trails for all levels.

Use extreme caution when tackling **Berthoud Pass** (U.S. 40, http://boc123.com/berthoudpass/berthoudpass.cfm), once a classic Colorado ski area built in 1937. Its lifts have long been removed, the base lodge will soon be gone, and what's left are 65 trails spread over 1,200 acres. "Please do not ski this area without the proper gear and knowledge," reads the website, listing no beginner trails, 26 percent expert, and 74 percent advanced. South of Winter Park off U.S. 40, Berthoud Pass is affiliated with the **Boulder Outdoor Center** (2525 Arapahoe Ave., Suite E4-228, Boulder, 303/444-8420, www.boc123.com), which rents equipment and provides trail information.

Hiking and Biking

Winter Park Resort shifts from skiers to cyclists in the summer, offering the Zephyr Express chairlift to the mountain summit—and 50 trails of varying difficulty. They're marked similarly to the ski trails, with green Fantasy Meadow and Tunnel Hill trails for beginners and black Mountain Goat and Icarus trails for more experienced riders. The resort offers lessons, guided tours, and equipment rental (800/979-0328). **Trestle Bike Park** is for expert cyclists and extreme riders who like plenty of big rocks, branches, and other "features" in their path as they whoosh downhill along 37 miles of trails. Also, **TreadFest** (303/293-5311, http://events.nscd.org) is a two-day charity competition, benefiting the American Red Cross and the National Center for the Disabled, that is laid-back and open to all ages. Registration costs $75.

Beyond the resort are more than 600 miles of trails for cyclists and hikers, but they're spread out and hard to find if you don't prepare beforehand. An easily accessible trailhead for casual hikers and cyclists is at the intersection of U.S. 40 and Winter Park Drive; it leads to paths including Moffat Road, an old railroad route with some of the ties still embedded in the dirt road. **Winter Park Guide** (970/887-0776, www.winterparkguide.com) will send you a trail map for a fee.

Windsurfing

Northwest of Winter Park, near a small town called Parshall, **Williams Fork Reservoir** is an artificial 1,860-acre body of water that allows fishing (including northern pike and kokanee), boating (two ramps), and camping. It's also one of the few spots in the Rockies for windsurfing enthusiasts. The reservoir is run by **Denver Water** (www.denverwater.org/Recreation/WilliamsFork), but for more information, contact the **Colorado Division of Wildlife** (6060 Broadway, Denver, 303/291-7227).

Golf

The **Pole Creek Golf Club** (6827 County Rd. 51, Tabernash, 970/887-9195 or 800/511-5076, www.polecreekgolf.com, $29–44) has several high-elevation courses, including the tree-lined Meadow, Ranch, and Ridge, which at nine holes each are available for 18-hole combinations. The private **Grand Elk** (1300 Ten Mile Dr., Granby, 970/887-9122, www.grandelk.com, $24–49) was designed by PGA hero Craig Stadler and is a more standard 18-hole course near the woods.

NIGHTLIFE

In the past, Winter Park has had clubs devoted to live music and dance floors. Today, bands still perform here and there, but it's mostly as an appetizer in bars and hotels, such as Deno's or the Ranch House Restaurant at Devil's Thumb. The best-known such venue is **The Pub** (78260 U.S. 40, www.winterparkpub.com, 970/726-4929, 3 P.M.–2 A.M. daily), which has excellent happy hour specials and draws the younger post-ski crowd. **Randi's Irish Saloon** (78521 U.S. 40, 970/726-1172, 4–9 P.M. Mon.–Fri., 11 A.M.–9 P.M. Sat., 11 A.M.–9 P.M. Sun.) is famous locally for its mashed potatoes and shepherd's pie—and is also known to play host to a live musician or two. Inside the Winter Park Mountain Lodge, **Moffat Station Restaurant and Brewpub** (81699 U.S. 40, 800/726-3340, www.winterparkhotel.com/Moffat.html, 7–10 A.M. and 4–10 P.M. daily) supplements its microbrews with tasty snacks such as buffalo meatloaf.

The bars in Winter Park are similar to those in Breckenridge or Keystone: affordable and unpretentious, with a mix of young skiers and townies. The central slope-side burgers-and-beer hangout is the **Derailer Bar** (76 Parsenn Rd., 970/726-5514), at the base of Winter Park Mountain. Others include the **Five Mountain Tavern** (100 Winter Park Dr., 800/472-7017, www.vintagehotel.com/restaurant, 2–9 P.M.

daily Nov.–Apr.), inside the Vintage Hotel, which serves a wide range of martinis, beer, and something called the Five Mustard Giant Hot Pretzel in a cozy bar named for Winston Churchill; and the **Sushi Bar** (78707 U.S. 40, 970/726-0447, www.ineedsushi.com, 4–10 P.M. Mon.–Thurs., 4–11 P.M. Fri.–Sat., reduced hours off-season), which bills itself, accurately, as Winter Park's only sushi bar, and has a 4–6 P.M. happy hour.

ACCOMMODATIONS
Under $100

Although the **Sundowner Motel** (970/726-9451 or 800/521-8279, www.thesundownermotel.com, $80–130) has more in common with a Best Western than a Hyatt Regency, it's at the center of town and is sort of a tradition among price-conscious local skiers.

Also centrally located, the **Gasthaus Eichler** (78786 U.S. 40, 970/726-5133 or 800/543-3899, www.gasthauseichler.com, $89–179) has the look of a corny European hotel, complete with dark-brown trim and flags, but it's actually quite nice, with whirlpool tubs in every room and excellent package deals that include rooms and one of the three on-site restaurants (Dezeley's may be the most elegant, but the Fondue Stube is the most fun).

About 30 miles from Winter Park, just off I-70 on the way up U.S. 40, the **Peck House** (83 Sunny Ave., Empire, 303/569-9870, www.thepeckhouse.com, $75–135) claims to be the state's oldest hotel. Built in 1860, the building was once a destination spot for mining-boom tourists, including P. T. Barnum and Ulysses S. Grant, and its Old West charm remains. The guest rooms have a timeless quality, some all in red and others with quaint patterned wallpaper.

$100-150

From the moment you walk into the lobby and spot the stone fireplace, huge picture windows overlooking the mountains, and log-built everything, the **Wild Horse Inn** (1536 County Rd. 83, 970/726-0456, www.

wildhorseinncolorado.com, $135–265) screams "Rocky Mountains!" It has three cabins, seven guest rooms, and tiny luxuries like in-house massages and chess sets near the fireplace.

The **Inn at SilverCreek** (62927 U.S. 40, Granby, 970/887-4080 or 888/878-3077, www.silvercreekgranby.com, $101–141) sacrifices location—it's about 20 miles from the ski resort—for amenities. Its 342 guest rooms are tall, with a modern feel, and it has a heated outdoor pool, racquetball and outdoor volleyball courts, a beauty shop, exercise facilities, and a complimentary shuttle to the resort.

The **Winter Park Mountain Lodge** (81699 U.S. 40, 866/726-5151, www.winterparkhotel.com, $115–125) is the first hotel you see upon driving into Winter Park on I-70. It's large and boxy, with mountains all around, and the guest rooms are nice but not spectacular.

The **Rocky Mountain Chalet** (15 County Rd. 72, Fraser, 970/726-8256 or 866/467-8351, www.therockymountainchalet.com, $129–149) is a hotel and hostel with private guest rooms on one floor and dorm rooms on the other. It's not the most luxurious lodge in Colorado ski country, but it allows people to experience the Rockies on a tight budget.

$150-200

Vintage Hotel (100 Winter Park Dr., 800/472-7017, www.vintagehotel.com, $185–235) has the look and feel of a Radisson or a Marriott, but skiers swear by it for the heated outdoor pool, tavern, and ski shop on the premises. The rates are very reasonable, even during high season.

$200-300

With the **Zephyr Mountain Lodge** (201 Zephyr Way, 970/726-8400 or 877/754-8400, www.zephyrmountainlodge.com, $255–265), you're paying for location—it's the only Winter Park lodging at the base of the ski area. As a result, most of the guest rooms have mountain views, and the small outdoor hot-tub area draws a hard-partying ski-bum crowd.

FOOD

Winter Park's restaurants are hardly in the foie gras and caviar class of its culinary neighbors, such as Vail, Aspen, and even Breckenridge, but they have a casual townie feel, and many serve first-rate pub food.

Snacks, Cafés, and Breakfast

Although it doesn't look like much in its Park Plaza strip-mall location, the **Rise and Shine** (78437 U.S. 40, 970/726-5530, www.basecampbakery.com, 7 A.M.–2 P.M. daily, $9) is a quickie place that serves excellent sandwiches and baked goods. **Carver's Bakery and Café** (93 Cooper Creek Way, 970/726-8202, http://carvers-wp.com, 7 A.M.–2 P.M. daily, $9) is another great breakfast joint, especially notable for its blueberry pancakes.

Casual

Deno's Mountain Bistro (78911 U.S. 40, 970/726-5332, www.denoswp.com, 11:30 A.M.–10 P.M. daily, $27) is a Winter Park institution with a colorful past—previous owners recall keeping a gun under the bar in case the tough, sleeping-in-the-trunks-of-their-cars ski-bum crowd became too rowdy. Today, Deno Kutrumbos's 1900-era restaurant serves large steaks and is best known for its huge wine list, although let's just say that while it fits the ambience of Winter Park itself, it's not the most luxurious spot in town.

Upscale

The stone floors, walls, and fireplace at **The Lodge at Sunspot** (Zephyr Express Lift, 970/726-1446, hours vary, full menus in winter, reduced à la carte menu at one restaurant in summer) hint at the relaxed mountaintop feel of this restaurant area at the top of the Zephyr Express Lift. The **Provisioner** is a buffet with sliced turkey and ham, and the **Coffee Shop & Bakery** serves drinks and scones, but the main draw is **The Dining Room,** with its multicourse menu ($59) of elk, beef, deer, or fish.

The **Devil's Thumb Ranch House Restaurant and Saloon** (City Rd. 83, 970/726-5633 or 800/933-4339, www.

devilsthumbranch.com, 4–9 P.M. Wed.–Sun., $20) has a distinct Rocky Mountain flavor, like the 3,700-acre guest ranch it sits on. Antelope and steak are big here, but the menu goes for variety, with fish and turkey as well as an extensive children's menu. It's about a 15-minute drive west of Winter Park.

INFORMATION AND SERVICES

Information about Winter Park's ski area, along with lodging, food, recreation, and other activities, is on www.winterparkresort.com, or call 303/316-1564 or 970/726-1564.

Winter Park has no hospital per se, but the nearby **St. Anthony Granby Medical Center** (450 E. Agate Ave., 970/887-7400, www.granbymedicalcenter.org) provides care and emergency services—and a helicopter for severe illness or injuries. And, of course, both Winter Park and Mary Jane have ski patrols.

GETTING THERE AND AROUND

To get to Winter Park, take I-70 west from Denver; Idaho Springs is the first major mountain town before U.S. 40, which leads north to Winter Park. Just a few miles west of the U.S. 40 exit, also off I-70, is Georgetown. Both Idaho Springs and Georgetown are dinky towns, excellent for a quick stop.

The first town you reach after exiting the interstate is Empire, a tiny mountain town with a gas station. A word about Empire: Don't speed as you pass through town (trust me). Upon arriving in Winter Park, the resort is on the immediate left, while the town is farther up U.S. 40 and lasts for about a mile.

Winter Park is also accessible via the **Ski Train** (303/296-4754), which advertises scenery "seen only by train passengers and goat herders." It starts at Denver's Union Station and goes 67 miles, past historic mining sights and through 29 tunnels.

Once in Winter Park, there's a free town shuttle called "The Lift" (970/726-4163) that stops at most hotels and condos and, of course, the ski area.

GEORGETOWN

After climbing all over the Colorado Rockies in a vain search for gold, prospector George Griffith finally had his "eureka!" moment in 1859. For years after that, "George's Town" was miner territory, and travelers from all over the world dislodged more than $200 million in gold, silver, copper, and lead. Today, Georgetown is a tiny, quiet mountain town where sightings of bighorn sheep and reasonably priced condominiums provide the most excitement—but many of the abandoned mineshafts and brick buildings remain, so it's possible even now to roughly imagine what those gold-mining days must have looked like.

The town is far less exciting today, although it serves as a pretty introduction for first-time Rocky Mountain visitors headed up I-70 to Steamboat Springs, Vail, Aspen, and the rest. Georgetown is about 56 miles southeast of Winter Park; to get here, take U.S. 40 to I-70, then head west for 3–4 miles. Check out the restaurants while you're here, and some of the reasonably priced hotels aren't bad either.

Sights

In the late 1960s, it was a massive undertaking to carve the **Eisenhower Memorial Tunnel** (www.dot.state.co.us/eisenhower/welcome.asp) just west of Georgetown along I-70; it's a hole 55 feet wide and 45 feet high through solid mountain rock underneath the Continental Divide. The project began in spring 1968, but it quickly bogged down due to weather conditions and worker inefficiency at 11,000-foot altitudes. The first tunnel was supposed to open three years later, but it was delayed until 1973; its twin didn't open until 1979. At some point during the $108 million project, one of its 1,140 workers declared: "We were going by the book, but the damned mountain couldn't read." Until the Eisenhower was completed, travelers had to navigate the far more treacherous Loveland Mountain Pass, which even today is a twisty two-lane road that's frightening during the snow season. The square two-lane tunnel, planned as early as 1937 despite geologists' concerns about cutting into

downtown Georgetown

the rock, has essentially given Denverites and other visitors easy access to the heart of the Colorado Rockies. Without it, the ski-resort towns are lost.

The town's biggest tourist attraction is the **Georgetown Loop Historic Railroad** (I-70 Exit 226, near Silver Plume, 888/456-6777, www.georgetownlooprr.com, $25), a 1929 steam locomotive that pulls a narrow-gauge train on six miles of track from Georgetown and Silver Plume. It's not as scenic as, say, the Durango & Silverton Narrow Gauge Railroad in southwestern Colorado, but the tree-filled hills are pretty, and the massive bridge makes for a dramatic trip.

British-born William A. Hamill, the town's best-known silver baron, lived in **Hamill House** (305 Argentine St., 303/569-2840, www.historicgeorgetown.org, 10 A.M.–4 P.M. daily Memorial Day–Sept., noon–4 P.M. Sat.–Sun. Oct.–Dec., $4) after it was built in 1867 (it was expanded in 1979). Hamill's high-class tastes extended to the walnut woodwork, hand-painted wallpaper, and marble fireplaces, and

Historic Georgetown Inc. has restored and preserved these original artifacts.

The **Hotel de Paris** (409 6th St., 303/569-2311, www.hoteldeparismuseum.org, 10 A.M.–5 P.M. Sat., noon–5 P.M. Sun. May and Oct.–late Dec., 9 A.M.–5:30 P.M. Mon.–Sat., noon–5 P.M. Sun. June–Sept., $5) was one of the fanciest hotels and restaurants in Colorado during the mining era. French miner Louis Dupuy bought the building, originally a bakery, and expanded it into a hotel in 1970 after an accident cut his mining career short. Today, it's a museum.

Sports and Recreation

At **Grays and Torreys Combo**, near Silver Plume, hikers can bag two fourteeners in one moderate climb. At 14,270 feet, Grays is the highest peak on the Continental Divide and one of the easier fourteeners. To find the trailhead, take I-70 west to Exit 221 at Bakerville, go south to Forest Road 189, and follow the signs to Grays trailhead. The hike to both summits is 8.25 miles round-trip with an elevation gain of 3,600 feet. When afternoon storms roll in, many hikers bail out after hitting only Grays. There's a separate trail down for this scenario. For more details, visit www.14ers.com.

Mount Bierstadt is another beginners' fourteener near Georgetown. Peak-baggers love it because it has a straightforward route, it's easy to find, and it has nice views from the top. Take I-70 west to Exit 228 at Georgetown, and follow the signs about 12 miles to Guanella Pass; the trailhead is near the east-side parking area at the top of the pass. It's a seven-mile round-trip hike to the summit and back, with steep switchbacks and a 2,850-foot elevation gain.

Accommodations

The guest rooms at **Georgetown Mountain Inn** (1100 Rose St., 303/569-3201 or 800/884-3201, www.georgetownmountaininn.com, $81–92) have distinctive styles and decorations—the Colorado Room has pine walls and a steel drawing of the Georgetown Loop Railroad on the bed's headboard, and the Antique Room is filled with elegant but slightly spooky paintings and curvy lamps from the mining days.

Silver Heels Guest Suites (506 6th St., 303/569-0941 or 888/510-7628, www.silverheelsguestsuites.com, $135–165) are two apartment rooms (the Merry Widow and Baby Doe suites) above the Buckskin Trading Co. in downtown Georgetown. Both rooms are hard to snag in the high season, so make reservations early.

The **Geneva Park Campground** (www.reserveamerica.com, 303/275-5610, $14) is 17 miles south of Georgetown, on Clear Creek County Road 381, then west on Forest Service Road 119. It's a tent-only experience that favors kids and families. Visit in the spring and you'll see a crop of blue columbines. It's also a hotspot for fall color, with golden aspen trees shimmering against bright blue skies. Be sure to stash food in your car—bears like to camp here too.

Food

Mother's Saloon (601 14th St., 303/569-2080,

11 A.M.–11 P.M. Sun.–Thurs., 11 A.M.–2 A.M. Fri.–Sat., $8) is known for its cheeseburgers, Philly cheesesteaks, and pork tenderloin. It's a true townie bar, with football pools and trivia nights.

The **St. James Tea Room** (614 Rose St., 303/569-3100, http://saintjamestearoom.com, 9 A.M.–6 P.M. daily, $8) is in an 1870s-era restaurant and hotel, and the yellow building still has an Old West feel. Almost everything on the menu is homemade, including the deviled eggs and black walnut cookie that come with the historic combo ($7) and the finger snacks that go with the afternoon tea ($18).

Information

The **Town of Georgetown** (404 6th St., 303/569-2555 or 888/569-1130, www.town.georgetown.co.us) is a good resource for local services.

IDAHO SPRINGS

The first mountain town you hit while driving I-70 west from Denver, Idaho Springs seems like a touristy miner district at first—but certain things about it are breathtaking and addictive. To some skiers and mountain-town explorers, for example, a trip to the high country isn't complete without a thick-crust pizza at the downtown BeauJo's. And up Highway 103, just beyond Echo Lake, is the Mount Evans Scenic and Historic Byway, a 28-mile drive straight up a 14,265-foot peak with views of the Front Range.

First discovered by the Ute and Arapaho people—who considered the local hot springs to be sacred healing waters—sleepy Idaho Springs became a new kind of town when George Jackson found gold in the creeks. It's hard to believe, just by looking at the black-and-white Old West photos in the town's Heritage Museum and Visitors Center, that local miners once provided $2 million worth of gold ore to the U.S. Mint.

Sights

In addition to the **Heritage Museum and Visitors Center** (2060 Miner St.,

303/567-4382, www.historicidahosprings.com, 9 A.M.–5 P.M. daily Sept.–May, 8 A.M.–6 P.M. daily June–Aug., free), several Idaho Springs sights celebrate the town's legacy as a late-1800s mining metropolis. The most popular is the **Phoenix Gold Mine** (Trail Creek Rd., 303/567-0422, www.phoenixmine.com, 10 A.M.–6 P.M. daily, $15), which bills itself as the oldest running family-owned gold mine and allows visitors to keep any of the gold fragments they unearth in the old sand-and-bucket style.

The **Argo Gold Mill and Museum** (2350 Riverside Dr., 303/567-2421, www.historicargotours.com, 9 A.M.–6 P.M. daily, $15) also relives the good old days—specifically 1913, when miners completed the 22,000-foot Argo Tunnel to transport gold from the mine to buyers in outlying areas. The mill sold more than $100 million of ore at a time when prices were $18–35 per ounce; the tunnel closed in the 1940s after an accident left four miners dead.

The **Charlie Tayler Water Wheel** (City Hall Park, south side of I-70), at the base of Bridal Veil Falls, was built in 1890 by a miner who attributed his longevity to never bathing or kissing women. The **Underhill Museum** (1416 Miner St., 303/567-4709, www.historicidahosprings.com, 11 A.M.–5 P.M. Thurs.–Mon.) is an information center and gift shop in a building once owned by Colorado surveyor and mining engineer James Underhill and his wife, Lucy. Finally, the entire **Miner Street** has the wooden-structure feel of an Old West boomtown, with the Victorian buildings to prove it.

Built into the side of a mountain between 1903 and 1911, **Indian Springs Resort** (302 Soda Creek Rd., 303/989-6666, www.indianspringsresort.com, 9 A.M.–10 P.M. daily, $14–16) remains a great place to take a bath—or a hot tub in a "geothermal cave," or a steam, or a mud bath. Chief Idaho of the Utes was said to have called the baths "the healing waters of the great spirit."

St. Mary's Glacier looks like a glacier only after a particularly wet summer and cold winter. It's accessible to hikers who want to wander less than one mile to the base for a view of the lake; those who want to see the Continental Divide from a much higher, more bumpy summit; and those who want to climb the 13,294-foot James Peak in the distance. A sign on the 10-mile drive to the base reads "injuries and fatalities occur each year": In the early 1990s, a fisherman was trapped under a boulder in bad weather and had to cut off his own leg.

Is St. Mary's really a glacier? "It is pretty small, and if we lived in Alaska, we probably would not call it a glacier," David Bahr, a scientist with the University of Colorado's Institute of Arctic and Alpine Research, told the *Denver Post* in 1998. "But since we live in Colorado, we take what we can get." Note that the lakes are private, parking is available only in a small lot north of the glacier trail, and fishing is illegal. Property owners in the nearby towns of Alice, St. Mary's, and Winterland are extremely particular about these rules and regularly push the Forest Service to discourage visitors.

"Oh My Gawd Road" is so-named not because of the New Yorkers who drive through here on the way to Vail or Aspen but because its 2,000-foot climb straight uphill is filled with treacherous curves. Just as it did in the 1870s, when it was built, the road takes fortune-seekers from Idaho Springs (I-70 Exit 241) to Central City and Black Hawk, which today are popular low-stakes gambling towns.

◖ Mount Evans Scenic and Historic Byway

This 28-mile byway climbs to a 14,265-foot summit with some of the greatest mountain views in all the Rockies—the entire Front Range and the Continental Divide are visible here. On the way up, you'll pass Echo Lake (10,600 feet), Lincoln Lake (11,700 feet), and Summit Lake (12,830 feet), along with trailheads leading to 100 miles of hiking and mountain-biking paths. It's also a great area for nature-lovers, as the Mount Goliath Natural Area, between Echo and Lincoln Lakes, has bristlecone pines, flag trees, and other plants characteristic of the region. Oh, and if you see a bighorn sheep (with curly horns) or a white mountain goat, don't chase it—they bite and ram, and rangers charge a fine for feeding them.

Although the byway closes mid-September–Memorial Day, it's worth getting out during winter for a glimpse of snowdrifts as high as 75 feet on the road. To get to the byway, drive I-70 west from Denver, take Exit 240 in Idaho Springs, and follow Highway 103 to Echo Lake. The **Clear Creek Ranger District** (101 Chicago Creek Rd., Idaho Springs, 303/567-3000, www.fs.usda.gov) off Highway 103 in Idaho Springs has more information about the mountain.

Food

There are Chicago pizza, New York pizza, Italian pizza, and, thanks to 🄲 **BeauJo's** (1517 Miner St., 303/567-4376, www.beaujos.com, 11 A.M.–9:30 P.M. Sun.–Thurs., 11 A.M.–10 P.M. Fri.–Sat., $13), "mountain pizza." The crusts are thick (and best served with honey),

the cheeses blend perfectly, and the napkin drawings on the walls are fun for kids. Even the football players from my high school were unable to pass "The Challenge"—a 14-pound hamburger-and-sausage pie free to any two eaters who complete it in under an hour (and $64 otherwise). Because it is, in fact, possible to eat too much pizza, **Buffalo Restaurant & Bar** (1617 Miner St., 303/567-2729, www.buffalorestaurant.com, 11 A.M.–10 P.M. daily, $16) is a nice alternative, serving burgers, black-bean chili, fajitas, and other made-from-buffalo items.

Information and Services

The **City of Idaho Springs** is at 303/567-4421 or www.idahospringsco.com.

Serious medical issues should be handled in Denver, but the **Meadows Family Medical Center** (115 15th St., 303/567-2668) has an outlet in Idaho Springs.

Steamboat Springs

When Norwegian Carl Howelsen set up a wooden ski jump in Steamboat Springs in 1912, he had no idea he was inventing a multi-million-dollar Colorado tourism industry and indulging people's wintertime obsessions all over the world. It's not hard to see what drew him to the place. Located in the Yampa River Valley, the former ranching and farming (but not mining!) community is about an hour removed from I-70 and has some of the most awesome Rocky Mountain views in Summit County.

Steamboat Springs, at an elevation of almost 7,000 feet, is known as "Ski Town USA." Its sprawling Steamboat Mountain Village has a variety of restaurants (the crab-and-elk Café Diva and the coffee-and-bagel Winona's nicely capture both sides of the food spectrum), hotels, and diversions such as Strawberry Park Natural Hot Springs, about seven miles outside Steamboat.

Note that unlike most of the ski areas along I-70 and the Continental Divide, Steamboat

is a self-contained trip unto itself. Once you're here, you pretty much stay here (unless, of course, you have several weeks to kill on a vacation).

HISTORY

The Utes were believed to have lived in this region as early as the 1300s, but it didn't officially become "Steamboat Springs" until 1865, when three French fur-trappers traveled down the Yampa River and heard what sounded like a paddlewheel steamer. It turned out to be a gurgling mineral spring.

Nine years later, hunter James Harvey Crawford discovered the Yampa Valley region, staked a claim, and brought his family to Steamboat. The town grew slowly after that—a newspaper here, a general store and hotel there—and mail carriers figured out how to traverse the difficult snowy cliffs on skis and snowshoes. The growth accelerated irreversibly in 1913, when Norwegian visitor Howelsen arrived in 1912 and started "ski-jumping" off a wooden platform—and teaching local kids how to do the same.

Borrowing from Howelsen, local ranch-family heir Jim Temple spearheaded the Steamboat Ski Area, which opened in 1961 with a creaky lift known as the Cub Claw. By the late 1960s, Steamboat was equipped with five new chairlifts, a restaurant on top of Thunderhead Peak, ski-patrol buildings, and other facilities—which locals called the "million-dollar building boom." But Steamboat's biggest draw for skiers is Champagne Powder, a naturally occurring light and dry snow that's so distinctive that the resort actually copyrighted the name.

SIGHTS
Tread of Pioneers Museum

Although it's not as comprehensive as Vail's Colorado Ski Museum, the Tread of Pioneers Museum (800 8th St., 970/879-2214, http://yampavalley.info/treadofpioneers.asp, 11 A.M.–5 P.M. Tues.–Sat., $5) has a history-of-skiing exhibit to go with its displays on Routt County pioneer life, Native American artifacts, and vintage firearms. It's in a 1908 Queen Anne–style Victorian home with authentic early-1900s furniture and decor.

Hot Springs

The **Old Town Hot Springs** (136 Lincoln Ave., 970/879-1828, www.steamboathotsprings.org, 5:30 A.M.–9:45 P.M. Mon.–Fri., 7 A.M.–8:45 P.M. Sat., 8 A.M.–8:45 P.M. Sun., $15) is the granddaddy of Rocky Mountain hot springs, with an 82°F Olympic-sized lap pool, a 350-foot waterslide, and three hot pools registering 98–103°F. The downtown complex offers fitness equipment, including weight-lifting machines and treadmills, yoga and kickboxing classes, and five hot springs.

Strawberry Park Hot Springs (44200 County Rd. 36, 7 miles west of Steamboat, 970/879-0342, www.strawberryhotsprings.com, 10 A.M.–10:30 P.M. Sun.–Thurs., 10 A.M.–midnight Fri.–Sat., $10) isn't as popular as the Health & Recreation Center, and it isn't quite as well maintained. Kids under 18 aren't allowed after 6 P.M. The thermal pools reach as high as 105°F, and guests are guaranteed soaks of at least an hour. In the winter, a separate company, **Sweet Pea Tours** (970/879-5820, www.sweetpeatours.com, $25), carts hot-springs visitors along snowy roads, many of which require chains for cars during the winter.

SPORTS AND RECREATION
Downhill Skiing and Snowboarding

The **Steamboat Ski Resort** (2305 Mount Werner Circle, 970/879-6111, www.steamboat.com) comprises six mountains with summits of more than 10,000 feet along with 165 trails spread over 65 miles. The resort is known for its snowfall, called Champagne Powder, and the tree-filled bumpy terrains are diverse and fun. Lift tickets are roughly $97 per day. Other than those at Winter Park, the 15 trails of Steamboat's **Howelsen Ski Area** (845 Howelsen Pkwy., 970/879-8499, www.steamboatsprings.net) make up the only run for aspiring jumpers in Colorado.

Steamboat's venerable **Mavericks Superpipe** is 450 feet long and 56 feet wide with 18-foot walls; next to it is one of the resort's four terrain parks. This one is best known for its Mini-Mav pipe for beginning riders. It also has the usual rides and jibs—sliders, rainbows, and something called "S" mailboxes.

In addition to the Champagne Powder—which can get a little *too* deep after a blizzard for some skiers' tastes—Steamboat's biggest draws are tree-lined terrain, wide runs for cruisers, fast lifts, and near-oppressive sunshine. One of the best spots for tree skiing is Twistercane, a short but rough stretch of aspens between the black-diamond Twister and Hurricane runs. Although the runs are fast and smooth, they're not long, so take full advantage of quads like the Storm Peak and Sundown.

Warning to the least experienced: Of the 142 ski trails on 2,939 acres, just 13 percent are for beginners.

Olympic skier Billy Kidd directs the **Steamboat Springs Ski & Snowboard School** (800/299-5017), which at $103–139

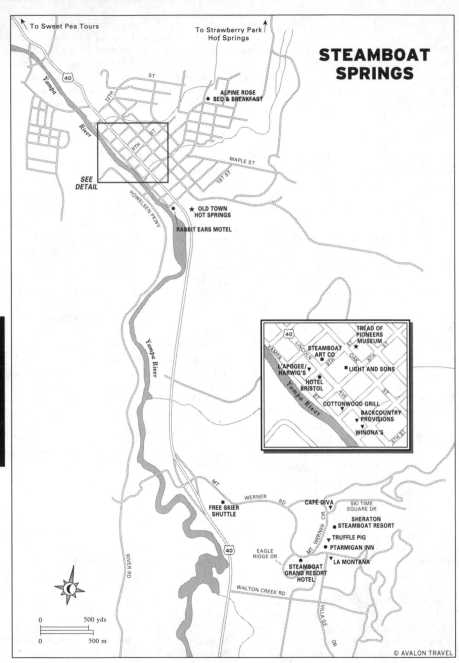

STEAMBOAT SPRINGS

To Sweet Pea Tours

To Strawberry Park Hot Springs

Yampa River

40

ST

12TH

8TH

SEE DETAIL

ALPINE ROSE BED & BREAKFAST

MAPLE ST

1ST ST

HOWELSEN PKWY

★ OLD TOWN HOT SPRINGS

RABBIT EARS MOTEL

Yampa River

Detail:

40

LINCOLN

YAMPA

5TH

STEAMBOAT ART CO

L'APOGEE/ HARWIG'S

HOTEL BRISTOL

COTTONWOOD GRILL

Yampa River

TREAD OF PIONEERS MUSEUM

OAK

7TH

8TH ST

★

■ LIGHT AND SONS

AVE

BACKCOUNTRY PROVISIONS

WINONA'S

MT

WERNER

RD

FREE SKIER SHUTTLE

CAFÉ DIVA

SKI TIME SQUARE DR

MT WERNER CIR

SHERATON STEAMBOAT RESORT

TRUFFLE PIG

PTARMIGAN INN

LA MONTANA

EAGLE RIDGE DR

STEAMBOAT GRAND RESORT HOTEL

40

RIVER RD

WALTON CREEK RD

VILLAGE DR

0   500 yds

0   500 m

© AVALON TRAVEL

© MARCO REGALIA/123RF.COM

sunset on ski slopes, Steamboat Ski Resort

per day offers a range of group and private lessons for adults, kids, and skiers with special needs. Kidd's **Performance Center** takes a high-tech, high-attention approach to expert lessons—instructors use handheld cameras to study skiers' strengths and weaknesses, and the ratio of students to teachers is just six to one. Although many sports-equipment stores rent skis and snowboards in town, **Steamboat Ski & Sport Pro Shops** (970/879-0740 or 877/237-2628) are one-stop shopping for all ages and skill levels.

Cross-Country Skiing

The **Steamboat Ski Touring Center** (Clubhouse Dr., 970/879-8180, www.steamboatnordiccenter.com) is a family-owned backcountry skiing school and shop with access to several excellent trails around Steamboat.

Elkhorn Outfitters (37399 N. Hwy. 13, Craig, 970/824-7392, www.elkhornoutfitters. com) makes 15 miles of groomed trails (for snowshoeing and inner-tubing as well) available to a total of eight skiers per day, and serves lunch and rents equipment. One disadvantage: It's 15 miles north of Craig, about 40 minutes west of Steamboat, so a long shuttle ride is part of the deal. Also renting equipment is **Ski Haus** (1457 Pine Grove Rd., 970/879-0385 or 800/932-3019, www.skihaussteamboat. com). For more information on backcountry and Nordic skiing, contact Steamboat Central Reservations (877/237-2628).

Hiking and Biking

The **Medicine Bow-Routt National Forest** area is 2.2 million acres of parks and forest land extending from Steamboat Springs through southern Wyoming. Among the many official and unofficial routes for hikers and mountain bikers is the **Mountain View Trail,** a moderate six-mile trek connecting Mount Werner to Long Lake and giving access to another 25 miles of summer hikes. The easiest way to get there is by riding the resort's Silver Bullet Gondola to Thunderhead and following trailhead signs to the top.

Spring Creek Trail is an easy four-mile ride

that goes uphill immediately. Start in town at the intersection of Amethyst and Maple Streets; go up a dirt road to the Mountain Park; follow Spring Creek; at the second bridge, turn around, then return to the starting point.

Also close by are the massive **Fish Creek Falls,** the **Mount Zirkel Wilderness Area,** and **Steamboat and Pearl Lakes.**

During summer, most of the resort's ski trails transform into mountain-biking trails. Lift tickets are available for the gondola for $8, and the resort's main ticket office (970/879-6111 or 877/783-2628) rents bikes and gives cycling lessons and clinics. If the ski area seems too crowded with visitors trying to ride mountain trails, try the historic ski jump **Howelsen Hill** (across the river from downtown on Howelsen Pkwy.). It's just as good for mountain biking as it is for skiing; you fly through the air either way.

Golf

The nine-hole **Steamboat Golf Club** (26815 W. U.S. 40, 970/879-4295 or 866/479-4295, www.steamboatgolfclub.com, $38) has water hazards, including a stream that cuts through one of the fairways. Designed by Robert Trent Jones Jr., the 18-hole course at the **Sheraton Steamboat Golf Club** (1230 Steamboat Blvd., 970/879-1391, www.rollingstoneranch-golf.com, $65–95) has views of the Flat Top Mountains in the distance and occasionally attracts uninvited bears and other wildlife.

Horseback Riding

There are tons of ranches in the Steamboat Springs area, which means tons of horseback riding—the 1,000-acre **Del's Triangle 3 Ranch** (55675 Routt County Rd. 62, Clark, 970/879-3495, www.steamboathorses.com) gives rides to ages six and older during summer and winter. **Saddleback Ranch** (37350 Routt County Rd. 179, 970/879-3711, www.saddlebackranch.net) offers two rides per day along with calf-roping demonstrations.

NIGHTLIFE

Steamboat Springs is a great place for late-night bar crawls, with several not-too-fancy,

not-too-grubby slope-side bars and a restaurant-packed downtown that's easy and fun to wander.

The town's primary place to catch live bands is **The Tugboat Grill and Pub** (1860 Mt. Werner Rd., 970/879-7070, 11:30 A.M.–midnight Sun.–Thurs., 11:30 A.M.–2 A.M. Fri.–Sat.), a local fixture with great happy-hour specials and a relaxed après-ski vibe that attracts a younger crowd. The grill is famous for its beautiful Butch Cassidy–era wooden bar but is more popular these days for its outdoor patio and bar food, ranging from burritos to wings.

Other slope-side bars geared to the après-ski crowd include the **Bear River Bar & Grill** (2300 Mt. Werner Circle, 970/871-5165, 11 A.M.–6 P.M. daily winter–spring) and the aptly named **Slopeside Grill** (1855 Ski Time Square, 970/879-2916, www.slopesidegrill.com, 11 A.M.–2 A.M. daily, reduced hours off-season), which also serves pizza and ribs.

Removed from the slopes, the **Rio Grande** (628 S. Lincoln Ave., 970/871-6277, www.riograndemexican.com, 11 A.M.–10 P.M. Sun.–Thurs., 11 A.M.–11 P.M. Fri.–Sat.) may be a Front Range chain, but this outlet at the center of town is always packed with margarita-loving skiers and townies; also serving Mexican food and margaritas is **Cantina** (818 S. Lincoln Ave., 970/879-0826, 11 A.M.–2 A.M. daily). **Mahogany Ridge Brewery & Grill** (435 Lincoln Ave., 970/879-3773, 4 P.M.–close daily) serves homebrews with big main courses like ribs and chipotle chicken pot pie. The **Old Town Pub** (600 Lincoln Ave., 970/879-2101, www.theoldtownpub.com, 11:30 A.M.–10 P.M. daily) specializes in standbys like steak and beer, with occasional live music, and for sports enthusiasts, the **Tap House** (729 Lincoln Ave., 970/879-2431, www.thetaphouse.com, 11:30 A.M.–2 A.M. daily) has the usual multiple TV screens.

SHOPPING

Shopping at Steamboat is confined to the ski-resort base village (which has Ski Time Square, Gondola Square, and Torian Plum Plaza), Old Town Square (7th St. and Lincoln Ave.), and the five-block downtown. Of these, downtown has the most unique and affordable shops, including the **Steamboat Art Company** (903 Lincoln Ave., 970/879-3383, www.steamboat-art.com, 10 A.M.–7 P.M. daily), with $475 photos of old-time skiers and pewter martini glasses; **F.M. Light & Sons** (830 Lincoln Ave., 970/879-1822, http://fmlight.com, 8:30 A.M.–10 P.M. Mon.–Sat., 9 A.M.–9 P.M. Sun.), a clothing store that opened in this very spot in 1905; and **Romicks Into the West** (402 Lincoln Ave., 970/879-8377, 10 A.M.–6 P.M. Mon.–Sat., 11 A.M.–5 P.M. Sun., reduced hours off-season), where the proprietor is U.S. Ski Team member turned furniture maker Jace Romick.

ACCOMMODATIONS
$100-150
The motel with the strange pink bunny on the sign, the **Rabbit Ears Motel** (201 Lincoln Ave., 970/879-1150 or 800/828-7702, www.rabbitearsmotel.com, $109–179) has basic and luxury guest rooms, some overlooking the Yampa Valley. Opened in 1952, the Rabbit Ears isn't exactly in its renaissance phase, but it's centrally located (although it's three miles from the base area, the free city bus stops nearby), fun, and affordable.

Hotel Bristol (917 Lincoln Ave., 970/879-3083 or 800/851-0872, www.steamboathotel-bristol.com, $129–189) is a pretty little lodge with 24 guest rooms that include colorful wool blankets and sharp Old West paintings and photos. Then–police chief Everett Bristol built the place in 1948; it was a bed-and-breakfast for years.

The **Alpine Rose Bed & Breakfast** (724 Grand St., 970/879-1528 or 888/879-1525, www.alpinerosesteamboat.com, $125–155) is in a hot-pink three-story building with blue trim. If that's not your color, don't be scared off—the guest rooms are simple and elegant, with nice touches like the odd fireplace or old-fashioned wooden bed frame. Also, there's a wooden deck and hot tub.

$150-200
No longer a Best Western, as it was for many

years, the privately owned **Ptarmigan Inn** (2304 Apres Ski Way, 970/879-1730 or 800/538-7519, www.steamboat-lodging.com/prop-bestwestern.shtml, $150–250) has the best spot in town, at the base of the Mount Werner/Steamboat ski area. It's all about the skiing, with complimentary valet ski storage, an on-site ski shop, a daily après-ski happy hour, and slope-side dining at the Snowbird Restaurant and Lodge.

$300-400
The **Sheraton Steamboat Resort & Conference Center** (2200 Village Inn Court, 970/879-2220, www.starwoodhotels.com, $339–399) is just a few hundred yards from Steamboat's base ski area. The resort complex includes four restaurants, including a Starbucks, the fancy Sol Day Spa, the Morningside Tower (with 23 luxury condos), and a seven-hole golf course.

Over $400
The **Steamboat Grand Resort Hotel and Conference Center** (2300 Mt. Werner Circle, 970/871-5500 or 877/306-2628, www.steamboatgrand.com, $399–429) is a massive mountainside hotel with 327 guest rooms at the base of the ski mountain. With a pool, an exercise center, and 17,000 square feet of meeting space, it's a favorite of business visitors.

Relais & Châteaux's **Home Ranch** (54880 Routt County Rd. 129, Clark, 970/879-1780, www.homeranch.com, $475–585) isn't for spontaneous locals or day skiers—the Old West–style complex requires a two-night minimum stay, and it's a few miles north of Steamboat. But it's amazingly charming and comfortable, with beds and tables made out of logs, a fully stocked refrigerator (and cookie jar) in the lobby, and horseback riding almost any time of day. The restaurant is one of the area's best.

FOOD
Snacks, Cafés, and Breakfast
Backcountry Provisions (635 Lincoln Ave., 970/879-3617, http://backcountryprovisions.

com, 7 A.M.–5 P.M. daily, $8) is a crowded deli with a huge sandwich selection.

Winona's (617 Lincoln Ave., 970/879-2483, 7 A.M.–3 P.M. daily, $8) is a great drop-in breakfast and sandwich joint with a long menu, from tofu scrambles ($7) to banana almond pancakes ($5). It reeks of healthfulness.

Casual

La Montana (2500 Village Dr., 970/879-5800, www.lamontanasteamboat.com, 5–9:30 P.M. daily, reduced hours off-season, $22) has 25 kinds of tequila and almost as many flavors of margaritas, but its major selling point is basic Tex-Mex food. Some of the entrées can be a little pricey (like the scallops Veracruz, for $27), but the basic enchiladas are $13, the fish tacos are $16, and the kids menu is the deal you'd expect. Tip: Fill up on the guacamole sauce.

Upscale

Café Diva (1855 Ski Time Square, 970/871-0508, www.cafediva.com, 5:30–9 P.M. daily, $28) opened in 1998 as a white-tablecloth kind of place that serves foie gras and chocolate fondue along with regional standards like elk tenderloin and duck confit. Its location, not far from the ski lifts, gives it an automatic crowd.

Housed in the 1880s-era Harwig Building—which includes a built-in wine cellar with 10,000 bottles—◖ **L'Apogee/Harwig's** (911 Lincoln Ave., 970/879-1919, www.lapogee.com, 5–11 P.M. daily, $31) offers a dish for every conceivable eating preference. If you don't eat the veal Oscar ($29), there's always the New Orleans jambalaya ($19) or the pistachio chicken ($24). The two restaurants used to be separate operations, but they've gradually merged, so it's just one building and one menu.

At the base of the ski gondola, **Truffle Pig** (2250 Apres Ski Way, 970/879-7470, http://trufflepigrestaurant.com, 4–9 P.M. Tues.–Sat., $30) has an all-star chef: Ezra Duker, who worked at the Napa Valley's renowned French Laundry. The menu emphasizes tapas, from oysters to sliders, but Duker's specialty is gnocchi.

Chefs Michael Fragola and Peter Lautner bring their elegant Asian-food expertise to **Cottonwood Grill** (701 Yampa St., 970/879-2229, www.cottonwoodgrill.com, 5:30–9:30 P.M. or 10 P.M. daily, $29), which serves a variety of Thai (pork tenderloin), Chinese (Peking duck), Cambodian (hot pot), and other dishes (Yampa Valley lamb pot stickers). Don't forget the sake.

INFORMATION AND SERVICES

The main Steamboat Ski Resort number is 970/879-6111, but www.steamboat.com will tell you just about all you need to know. For updated snow reports, call 970/879-7300, and for lodging reservations, 877/783-2628.

Steamboat Springs has a major hospital: the **Yampa Valley Medical Center** (1024 Central Park Dr., 970/879-1322, www.yvmc.org). And, of course, the resort has a ski patrol for slope-side emergencies.

GETTING THERE AND AROUND

Steamboat is accessible via I-70, driving west from Denver, like most of the other ski resorts, but it's surprisingly far away—3–4 hours depending on weather. In snowy conditions, the trip up U.S. 40 from Winter Park can be treacherous, so handle the hairpin curves and steep declines with care. From I-70, take Exit 232 to U.S. 40, and follow it almost 100 miles beyond Empire and Winter Park.

Some of the hotels provide their own town shuttles, but the best local-transportation deal is the **SST** (970/879-3717), a free shuttle that runs 6:30 A.M.–10:30 P.M. daily among the resort, condos, grocery stores, restaurants, and hotels.

GRAND JUNCTION AND NORTHWEST COLORADO

If northwest Colorado has an unofficial capital city, it's Grand Junction, which appears in the middle of nowhere on the map—Telluride is several hundred miles south, Denver is a four-hour drive east, and the closest ski resorts are the dinky ones in touristy Glenwood Springs and Grand Mesa. Although it's flat and quiet, with far more churches than nightclubs, Grand Junction is part of the Grand Valley, a rich outdoor area of massive mesas, gnarled sandstone formations, natural arches, dry canyons, and scenic lakes.

The Grand Valley is at the Colorado and Gunnison Rivers, near the Little Book Cliffs (flat, steep mountains that look a little like the Grand Canyon and extend for miles), the 10,000-foot-tall Grand Mesa and its surrounding national forest, and the 23,000-acre Colorado National Monument. Few visitors come to this region for the nightlife—or even the hotels, which skew plain and modest—but the cycling, cross-country skiing, and accompanying mountaineering outfits are world-class (try the REI outlet in Grand Junction or Summit County Mountaineering in downtown Glenwood Springs).

Because of its mild weather and rich soil, the Grand Valley is a major agricultural outpost, with farms, ranches, and orchards everywhere. Grapes became a huge part of the harvest in the late 1800s; the state's first winery, Ivancie, opened in 1968; and quiet Palisade has grown into the state's primary vineyard region.

There's one other unexpected attraction in northwest Colorado: dinosaurs. They roamed this part of the world millions of years ago, leaving behind fossils and bones. Dinosaur National Monument is a scenic hiking area

HIGHLIGHTS

◖ **McInnis Canyons National Conservation Area:** Home to the Black Ridge Canyons Wilderness, this outdoor paradise west of Grand Junction encompasses red-rock cliffs, waterfalls, and natural arches and spires. It's great for hiking and biking (page 225).

◖ **Kokopelli's Trail:** Bring a bike and 3-4 days' worth of free time – and get in shape. Beginning west of Grand Junction, the 135-mile trail, very rocky in parts, climbs from 4,400 feet to 8,500 feet in elevation, rubbing against the Colorado River en route to Moab, Utah (page 230).

◖ **Colorado National Monument:** A sort of mini-Grand Canyon, with twisted, reddish rocks that arch over roads and recall Morrison's Red Rocks Park and Colorado Springs' Garden of the Gods, Colorado National Monument is filled with trails, bike paths, and huge, flat mesas (page 233).

◖ **Dinosaur Journey:** The best part of this Fruita museum – not to be confused with Dinosaur National Monument to the north – is the robotic arms that let you experience shambling dinosaur movements directly (page 234).

◖ **Little Book Cliffs Wild Horse Range:** More than 30,000 acres of breathtaking canyons and plateaus aren't enough – about 115 wild horses – pintos, roans, browns, and palominos – run free in this sprawling range thanks to a long-ago act of Congress (page 235).

◖ **Grand Mesa National Forest:** With the 11,000-foot Leon Peak, the beautifully blue Butts Lake, and several excellent hiking and biking trails, the Grand Mesa is one of the state's most dramatic outdoor enclaves (page 238).

◖ **Dinosaur Quarry:** The scenery and hiking are amazing on the Colorado side of Dinosaur National Monument, but the Utah side has this quarry, where 1,500 *Stegosaurus*, *Tyrannosaurus rex*, and other fossils are embedded in a wall and visitors can hunt for thousands more (page 254).

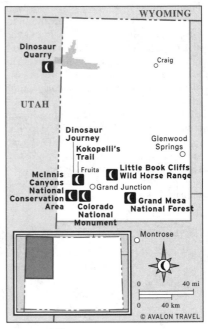

LOOK FOR ◖ TO FIND RECOMMENDED SIGHTS, ACTIVITIES, DINING, AND LODGING.

at the northwest tip of the state; on the Utah side, it turns into a museum and outdoor playground for amateur paleontologists and kids obsessed with stegosaurs and pterodactyls.

PLANNING YOUR TIME

The stretch of I-70 from Denver to Grand Junction is about four hours of driving, and Glenwood Springs, Rifle, and Palisade are pleasant stopovers along the way. Glenwood Springs is also a sort of gateway to Aspen, and many skiers who don't want to pay Aspen's high hotel and restaurant rates book lodging at the Hotel Colorado or the Hotel Denver. Cedaredge, Grand Mesa, and Delta bunch up along Highway 65 south of Palisade.

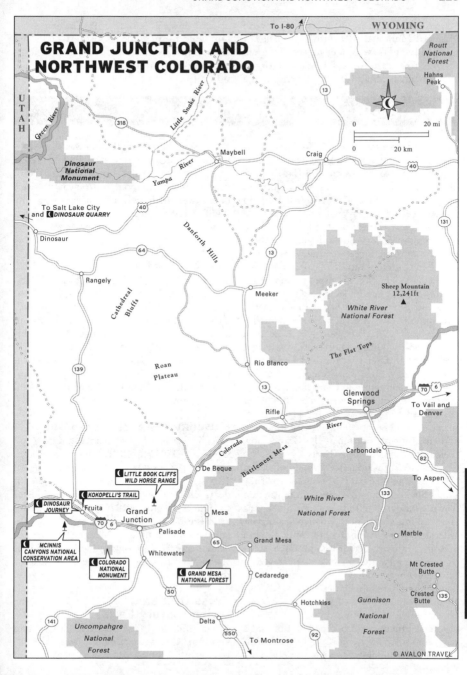

GRAND JUNCTION AND NORTHWEST COLORADO

WYOMING

To I-80

Routt National Forest

Hahns Peak

UTAH

Green River

318

Little Snake River

Maybell

Craig

13

Dinosaur National Monument

Yampa River

40

0   20 mi

0   20 km

131

To Salt Lake City and ◖DINOSAUR QUARRY

40

Danforth Hills

Dinosaur

64

13

Rangely

Meeker

Sheep Mountain 12,241ft ▲

White River National Forest

Cathedreal Bluffs

Roan Plateau

Rio Blanco

The Flat Tops

139

13

Glenwood Springs

70 6

To Vail and Denver

Rifle

Colorado River

82

Carbondale

To Aspen

◖LITTLE BOOK CLIFFS WILD HORSE RANGE

De Beque

Battlement Mesa

133

◖KOKOPELLI'S TRAIL

Fruita

Grand Junction

Mesa

White River National Forest

Marble

◖DINOSAUR JOURNEY

70 6

Palisade

65

Grand Mesa

◖MCINNIS CANYONS NATIONAL CONSERVATION AREA

Whitewater

◖COLORADO NATIONAL MONUMENT

◖GRAND MESA NATIONAL FOREST

Cedaredge

Mt Crested Butte

Crested Butte

135

50

141

Uncompahgre National Forest

Delta

550

To Montrose

Hotchkiss

92

Gunnison National Forest

© AVALON TRAVEL

GRAND JUNCTION

Some of the many entrances to Colorado National Monument are within 10 miles of Grand Junction's western edge, and the town of Dinosaur, adjacent to Dinosaur National Monument, is about 80 miles north on the up-and-down Highway 139. The trip from Dinosaur to Steamboat Springs, including Craig at just about the midpoint, is three hours straight uphill, and you'll notice the altitude shift.

Grand Junction and Vicinity

In almost every direction of this mid-size agricultural town is an adventure. The Grand Mesa, to the south, is a flat-topped, 10,000-foot-tall mountain; the Book Cliffs, to the north, have the feel of an inverted Grand Canyon—2,000 feet tall, red, yellow, and completely flat, stretching 100 miles into Utah; and even the Palisade orchards and vineyards, to the east, have a certain cherry- and apricot-filled natural beauty. These outdoor sights make Grand Junction a hot spot for mountain biking, hiking, snowshoeing, and fishing.

Grand Junction's history is rooted in the Meeker massacre, a clash between 1870s reformer Nathan Meeker, whose namesake town is still about 100 miles northeast of the city, and resentful Utes that resulted in 11 dead white men. Whites demanded retribution, and Ute leaders agreed to a compromise—a retreat beyond Colorado's western borders. After that, freed from the pesky Indians, settlers formed new cities, including Grand Junction, so named for its location at the Grand (now Colorado) and Gunnison Rivers.

The city's founders, Kansas politician George Crawford and Michigan attorney James Bucklin, assembled the Grand Junction Town Company in 1881, and within a year they had installed a local newspaper, a mayor, aldermen, and a major railroad. With no Utes around, nearby miners felt comfortable stopping in the city, and some of them stayed to farm sugar beets and build farms and ranches. Thanks to more sophisticated Grand Valley irrigation systems, locals exported crops of apricots, cherries, and grapes.

Grand Junction has boomed and busted a few times since then—in the 1900s, oil drillers and uranium miners set up operations along the Western Slope, and the city was a key stopover for these new businesspeople. The market continued through the bust of the early 1960s; hiking, museums, and tourism have since taken over. Although its population is only 40,000, Grand Junction is the largest town between Denver and Salt Lake City.

SIGHTS
The Art Center
The Art Center (1803 N. 7th St., 970/243-7337, www.gjartcenter.org, 9 A.M.–4 P.M. Tues.–Sat., $3) shows 300 works focusing on Colorado and the West, with an emphasis on historic Native American artifacts. The exhibitions are usually Southwestern-style—colorful paintings of Colorado National Monument and other mountain-desert concoctions—but now and then brilliantly weird works like Paul Pletka's bird skeletons creep in.

Museum of Western Colorado
The Museum of Western Colorado (462 Ute Ave., 970/242-0971, www.wcmuseum.org, 10 A.M.–3 P.M. Tues.–Sat. Oct.–Apr., 10 A.M.–5 P.M. Tues.–Sat. May–Sept., $6.50) deals with many angles and time periods of the Old West, from a 1921 fire truck to a firearms exhibit of Winchesters, carbines, pistols, and a 15th-century Spanish cannon. An education tower has geology and weather exhibits at the top, but many make the climb just for the views.

Cross Orchards Living History Farm
From 1896 to 1923, the Red Cross Land and Fruit Company ran a 243-acre, 22,000-tree farm of apples, pears, and peaches that

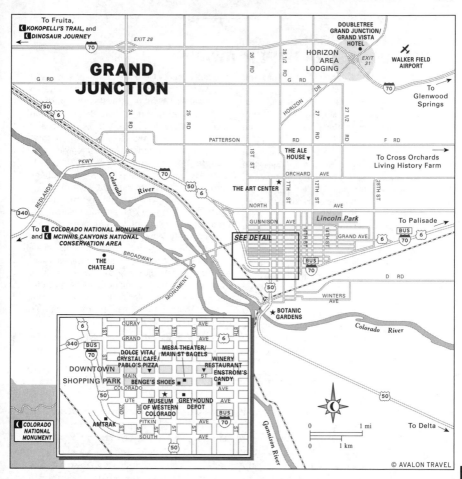

GRAND JUNCTION

dominated Grand Junction's economy and geography. It has long since closed, but preservationists bought four acres of it in 1980 and turned the site into the Cross Orchards Living History Farm (3073 F Rd., 970/434-9814, www.wcmuseum.org/crossorchards.htm, open for special events, tours, and rentals), which shows much of the original farm equipment and 19th-century kitchen and pantry facilities.

McInnis Canyons National Conservation Area

Created in 2000, this 122,240-acre forest-

and-valley area (2815 H Rd., 970/244-3000, www.blm.gov/co/st/en/nca/mcnca.html), formerly known as Colorado Canyons, extends from western Colorado into Utah. Its centerpiece is the Black Ridge Canyons Wilderness, a picturesque area of red-rock cliffs, waterfalls, rocks, and natural arches and spires (and deer, mountain lions, and bighorn sheep, if you're really, really quiet). Operated by the U.S. Bureau of Land Management, the massive area is about 10 miles west of Grand Junction and is popular with hikers and cyclists.

Inside the McInnis area, with nine massive

WILD, WILD HORSES
(YOU CAN'T DRAG THEM AWAY)

Thanks to a 1971 law protecting horses and burros lucky enough not to be born in captivity, some 29,000 of these wild animals roam 10 Western states – including about 800 in five Colorado "herd management areas." And actually, you *can* drag them away, for adoption, as long as you meet rigorous Bureau of Land Management (BLM) guidelines, like owning a corral with a six-foot high fence as well as a covered trailer. These rules, for the most part, protect the horses from harm – but stuff happens; in 2005, six wild horses were purchased in Cañon City and then resold to a slaughterhouse.

Over the past 30 years, Colorado public land for wild horses has shrunk by more than 40 percent, to about 400,000 total acres. In part, this is because nearby ranchers consider them a nuisance, saying they fight with cattle herds to forage for food. More recently, the BLM under the Bush administration opened the broader areas where some wild horses live to oil and gas drilling. The BLM is attempting to evict all 120 horses at one such spot, the West

Douglas County Herd Area south of Rangely in northwest Colorado, to the East Douglas area near Meeker. Wildlife activists aren't thrilled: "The BLM is zeroing out herds or reducing them to ridiculous levels in Colorado and across the West," Andrea Lococo, a consultant with the Washington-based Animal Welfare Institute, told *The Denver Post*. In 2005, BLM officials thinned out the Colorado populations by rounding up more than 350 horses.

Nonetheless, you can still visit wild horses in the following four areas, all of which contain campsites. I highly recommend this experience. My family recently visited the Little Book Cliffs wild-horse area and, although we were hoping to see horses, we weren't prepared for the majestic site of five or six free, beautiful animals loping casually along a dirt path across the valley from us. It was one of the most breathtaking nature experiences I've ever had in Colorado.

• **Little Book Cliffs:** The best-known wild-horse area is northeast of Grand Junction, about 2,300 feet up the glades, in a rugged,

natural arches that extend from natural sandstone and cliffs that rise 500–700 feet from the ground, **Rattlesnake Canyon** (King's View Rd., west of Colorado National Monument, 970/244-3000, free) is a great uncrowded spot for a nature walk. It's just a little hard to get in. The easiest entrance—one that doesn't involve floating down the Colorado River and climbing up a canyon—is a 13-mile drive along the rugged Black Ridge Access Road, which takes you to the trailhead. Don't even consider it during rain or snow. And 4WD vehicles can get here from the high end of Rim Rock Road. Maps are available from the nearby Bureau of Land Management office.

SPORTS AND RECREATION
Biking

Moab, Utah, is less than two hours away, and

it's a haven for sandpaper-like slickrock trails. But cyclists who aren't in the mood for all that slipping and sand gravitate to Grand Junction and nearby Fruita—and miles and miles of single-track trails. Unlike Moab, also a Motocross haven, the trails here were designed specifically for mountain biking. Annual biking events include the **Rose Hill Rally** (970/242-5940, www.stmarygj.org, early May), the **Mountains to the Desert Ride** (Telluride to Gateway Canyons, 970/931-2458, http://m2dbikeride. com, late Sept.), the **Fruita Fat Tire Festival** (www.fruitamountainbike.com, Apr.), and **18 Hrs. of Fruita** (970/858-7220, www.emgcolorado.com, May), in which cyclists attempt to do the most loops around Highline State Park in 18 hours.

Here are the trails:

Pet-e-kes, located in the Lunch Loops

cliff-heavy, 36,000-acre canyon land. To get to the Tellerico Loop Trail, take 1st Street in Grand Junction to I Road, turn left, and then turn right at 25 Road. Stay on 25 past a canal as the road turns to dirt; veer right to a fenced area, and park in the parking lot. The horses are about 600 yards past the fence, roughly to the northwest. The horses in this area, as well as Spring Creek and Sandwash Basin, are the most colorful – pintos, duns, grays, and roans, in addition to the more common bay, sorrel, and brown horses. For information, contact the **Grand Junction Field Office** (2815 H Rd., Grand Junction, 970/244-3000).

- **Spring Creek Basin:** At 20,455 acres, Spring Creek is the state's smallest wildhorse area, but the terrain is extreme, from rolling hills to steep mountain climbs. Elevations range 6,000-7,500 feet. From Montrose, go 18 miles south on Highway 141 to Gypsum Gap; turn south on County Road 19Q; after 5.2 miles, turn east on BLM Road 4010; the entrance is about 3.5 miles from there. Contact the **Mancos/Dolores Field Office** (29211 Hwy. 184, between Mancos and Dolores, 970/882-7296).

- **Sandwash Basin:** From Craig, head 31 miles west to Maybell, then hit Highway 318, heading northwest for about 17 miles, until you come to an entrance. Dress properly for the weather on this hilly, 160,000-acre plot in northwest Colorado – temperatures jump to more than 100°F in the summer and drop to -30°F in the winter. Contact the **Little Snake Field Office** (455 Emerson St., Craig, 970/826-5000).

- **Piceance/East Douglas Creek:** The 225 bays, blacks, sorrels, and browns as well as a few grays, buckskins, palominos, and pintos are 19 miles north of Rifle on Highway 13, near the intersection of Piceance Creek Road and Ryan Gulch Road. In addition to horses, these 195,000 acres filled with aspens and sagebrush contain antelope, elk, eagles, hawks, coyotes, and rattlesnakes – so watch your step! Contact the **White River Field Office** (73544 Hwy. 64, Meeker, 970/878-3800).

area, was named after Pete Larson and his dog Kes. Larson, an avid trail runner and mountain biker, worked for the Bureau of Land Management (BLM) and National Park Service. This was one of his favorite trails. It offers an intermediate ride in an otherwise challenging trail area. From Grand Junction, go west on Highway 340, then left on Monument Road. The trailhead is 1.5 miles on the left.

To get to **Prime Cut** and **Zippidy-do-da,** travel eight miles northwest of Grand Junction on I-70 to Exit 19, take Maple Street to North 3/10 Road, and then to 18 Road. In the BLM's 18 Road parking area, look for the post that marks where the single-track begins. Follow Prime Cut to Zippidy-do-da. You can also take a shuttle and just do the downhill part of Prime Cut for an easier ride. Prime Cut was built for beginners, and Zippidy is part of the nearby Book Cliffs trail system; both rides are among the most popular in the Fruita area.

The Ribbon has the biggest slick rock in the area; it's 7.2 miles round-trip with a 1,671-foot elevation change (mostly downhill). To get to it, go west of Grand Junction on Grand Avenue, turn left on Monument Road, turn left on D Road, turn right on Rosevale Road, then take a right on Little Park Road. The Ribbon trailhead is 3.1 miles along on the left.

Troy Built Loop is a strenuous, eight-mile ride with vertical uphills, technical descents, and rocky sections. Go 15 miles west of Grand Junction on I-70 to Exit 11, cross under the highway to a gravel frontage road, and look for the trailhead. Advanced riders should try other trails in this area, such as **Free Lunch, Holy Cross,** and **Lemon Squeezer.**

Because temperatures frequently rise to

WHERE TO BIKE WITH A WHOLE LOT OF PEOPLE

© GRAND JUNCTION VISITOR & CONVENTION BUREAU

mountain biking in Grand Junction

Although cycling fanatics tend to congregate in northwest Colorado (particularly Grand Junction, Rifle, and Fruita), the Durango area (flat, surrounded by the irresistibly high San Juans), and Boulder (perhaps the most bike-friendly city in the United States), the varied terrain of Colorado makes it prime territory for races and two-wheeled events of all kinds. Here's a Top 10:

Durango: For serious riders, the Memorial Day weekend **Iron Horse Bicycle Classic** (www.ironhorsebicycleclassic.com) is a bear of a straight-up, 50-mile course that begins in 4,500-foot-high Durango and climbs to Silverton's 10,000-foot-plus mountain passes. The race's origins are with brothers John and Tom Mayer, the former a railroad brakeman and the latter a cyclist, who decided to race man versus machine in the 1880s. In 1972 a group of 36 riders took up Tom's cause and inaugurated the grueling mountain ride. Today, there's a race for experienced cyclists and a citizens' ride for everybody else.

The long-running **Ride the Rockies** (303/954-6700, www.ridetherockies.com), in late June, is a weeklong climb through some of the most beautiful mountain scenery in the state. It's a tough trip, with slogs of 49–92 miles per day, with one day of rest, hitting Telluride, Crested Butte, and Buena Vista before landing in Breckenridge. The highest mountain pass, Cottonwood, at more than 12,000 feet, comes on the second-to-last day – so get in shape before registering!

Buena Vista: The **Buena Vista Bike Fest** (www.bvbf.org), just before Memorial Day, is a ride west through the mountains along Highway 82 from Buena Vista to Twin Lakes to Aspen. Participants can take 35-, 50-, or 62-mile routes depending on their endurance and skill levels. It begins in McPhelemy Park, north of the town's only traffic light, and while the route is a little insane, it's worth it for the amazing mountain scenery.

Grand Junction: Beginning and ending at Canyon View Park, the early-May **Rose Hill Rally** (24 Rd. exit off I-70, 970/255-7731) offers 62-mile and 31-mile courses through mostly flat farmland during a very mild time of year. It's sponsored by the nearby St. Mary's Hospital (www.stmarygj.org) and a local mortuary-crematory – which, I promise, isn't an omen for cyclists who aren't in the greatest of shape.

Denver: The **Denver Century Ride** (www.denvercenturyride.com), in mid-June, begins at Sports Authority Field at Mile High, climbs to Lookout Mountain west of town, winds through Red Rocks Park, and winds up on a pretty urban route. Riders can take 100-, 62-, and 22-mile routes.

Castle Rock: Somewhat counterintuitively sponsored by a major car company, the early-June **Elephant Rock Cycling Festival** (303/282-9020, www.elephantrockride.com) begins and ends at the Douglas County Fairgrounds outside Castle Rock between Denver and Colorado Springs. The half-dozen courses range 8–100 miles, including a 25-mile off-road route that runs mostly on unpaved roads. Many routes have steep hills.

Fort Collins: Although the USA Cycling Collegiate Road National Championships recently relocated to Madison, Wisconsin, the Fort Collins area is home to two other cycling events – **Fort Collins Cycling Festival** (970/481-8455, www.fccyclingfest.com) in late June, a nine-mile climb up Rist Canyon and a fast plunge back into Poudre Canyon; and **Horsetooth Double Dip,** a two-day 180-mile ride in late August from Fort Collins to Estes Park. Both begin at Colorado State University.

Copper Mountain: In early August, **Colorado Cyclist Copper Triangle** (303/282-9020, www.coppertriangle.com) starts high, at the Copper Mountain ski resort in the northern Rockies, and goes higher, over three mountain passes, beginning with the 11,300-foot Fremont Pass, with a few killer downhills in between. The one-day course is 78 miles.

Fruita: The **Fruita Fat Tire Festival** (970/858-7220, www.fruitamountainbike.com) begins in late April with four days of downtown Fruita partying, beer gardens, and informal samplings of surrounding bike trails, like the smooth dirt paths through meadow-dominated scenery in the Book Cliffs area near 18 Road. It continues the following weekend with an 18-hour coed race – beginning at midnight, with campsites available in numerous locations along the way – through the town's many rugged hills.

Gunnison: The **Colorado Rocky Mountain Bike Tour** (720/379-5593, www.crmbt.com) is a 472-mile route over a week in early August. The up-and-down course goes through some of the state's most spectacular country, from the valleys surrounding the Blue Mesa Reservoir to the Rockies in Aspen and Vail to the final plunge into Salida and Gunnison. Organizers help set up lodging, and camping is plentiful.

about 100°F in the summer, don't forget to bring lots of water.

Grand Junction and Fruita are jammed with bike shops. In Grand Junction, try **Ruby Canyon Cycles** (301 Main St., 970/241-0141, www.rubycanyoncycles.com), which offers a place to ship bikes for cross-country rides. They have staff mechanics and can arrange tours for you. In Fruita, the staff at **Over the Edge Sports** (202 E. Aspen Ave., 970/858-7220, www.otefruita.com) helps cyclists find campsites. Join one of the group rides the shop organizes Wednesday evenings.

◖ Kokopelli's Trail

A gnarly 135-mile bike trip that begins about 15 miles west of Grand Junction and cuts straight into Moab, Utah, Kokopelli's Trail is a 3–4-day trip that's part steep bushwhacking and part smoothed-out Jeep roads. It climbs from 4,400 feet to 8,500 feet and rubs against the Colorado River before shooting back up and dropping down into Utah's canyons. To get to the trailhead, go west on I-70 out of Grand Junction and exit at Luoma; turn left at the top, take the next right, turn left at the truck station, and go about 0.5 miles until you can park along the road.

Just off Kokopelli's Trail, the 3.5-mile **Horsethief Bench** is a single-track loop; take I-70 to Loma, turn right on the Exit 15 access road, and follow it to Kokopelli's Trailhead. Horsethief branches off to the left after you follow Mary's Loop for 1.6 miles.

The **Colorado Plateau Mountain Bike Trail Association** (970/244-8877, www.copmoba.org) is a long-running group of cyclists that sets up and maintains trails in the areas and sponsors biking events. For rentals and guided local tours, try **Over the Edge Sports** (202 E. Aspen Ave., Fruita, 970/858-7220, www.otefruita.com).

Hiking

Highline Lake Trail is an easy 3.5-mile loop around the lake in Fruita's Highline Lake State Park. The trail is open to bikes and horses in addition to pedestrians. Mule deer and shorebirds may show up to greet hikers. The trail begins at the east boat ramp and follows the boundary of the park. The strenuous five-mile **Cactus Park** is in Big Dominguez Canyon, which has waterfalls and boulders covered with ancient rock art. The trailhead is about 22 miles south of Grand Junction. Take U.S. 50 south, turn right on Highway 141, go eight miles, turn left at the "Cactus Park" sign, then drive seven more miles to the trailhead.

Camping

The **Rabbit Valley/Trail Through Time** (Fruita, 26 miles west of Grand Junction on I-70, 970/244-3000, free) is a desert hike-in campground near the Utah border. It has interpretive trails with dinosaur bones and prehistoric rock art. Parents, be warned: There's a steep cliff right next to the campground. Also, bring your own water. **Colorado River State Park** (Clifton, 970/434-3388, http://parks.state.co.us/parks/jamesmrobbcoloradoriver, $16, plus $7 entrance fee) has showers and water and takes reservations. North of Grand Junction, the 31-campsite **Highline Lake State Park** (near Hwy. 139 and Q Rd., Loma, 303/858-7208, www.parks.state.co.us/parks/highlinelake/Pages/HighlineLakeHome.aspx, $16, plus $7 entrance fee) has hot showers (coin-operated), laundry, and water, and it is near the Kokopelli mountain-bike trail. Another selling point: You can set a tent on grass instead of dusty dirt and sagebrush. Also along Kokopelli: **McInnis Canyons** (970/244-3000, free), which is no-frills but has quick access to all the best trails; and the **Book Cliffs** (970/244-3000), near bike trails and the wildhorse refuge area.

ENTERTAINMENT AND EVENTS
Nightlife

The Ale House (2531 N. 12th St., 970/242-7253, www.breckbrew.com/food/alehouse.html, 11 A.M.–2 A.M. daily) is part of the statewide Breckenridge Brewery chain and draws a late-night clientele. The menu is high-end bar food—nachos, chicken wings, sandwiches, all very good—and, of course, beer, including a signature brew.

Events

The city's biggest music festival is the late-June **Country Jam** (800/780-0526, http://co.countryjam.com), which draws gigantic mainstream-country acts such as Lady Antebellum, Alan Jackson, and Little Big Town. The three-day festival draws Stetson-wearers from all over the West, so plan for traffic during that weekend, and reserve hotels early.

Entertainment

Main Street is filled with interesting restaurants, cafés, and shops, but everything seems to close around 8 or 9 P.M., even on the weekends. One exception is the **Mesa Theater and Lounge** (538 Main St., 970/241-1717, www.mesatheater.com), which snags midlevel national music acts like the Young Dubliners and Warrant (!) and attracts a healthy regimen of kids out front on otherwise-boring nights. Also downtown: weird street art.

The **Grand Junction Symphony Orchestra** (970/243-6787, www.gjsymphony.org) gives concerts all year, including special events like kids shows.

SHOPPING

Downtown Grand Junction has a comfortable, historic feel, with shops such as the outdoor-outfitting **Summit Canyon Mountaineering** (461 Main St., 970/243-2847, www.summitcanyon.com); **Toys for the Fun of It** (519 Main St., 970/248-3511, http://toysforthefunofit.com, 10 A.M.–6 P.M. Mon.–Sat., 11 A.M.–3 P.M. Sun.), where owner Mike Allen occasionally shows off his juggling skills; and **New York Moon Boutique** (200 W. Grand Ave., Suite 3B, 970/242-2013, http://newyorkmoongj.com, 10 A.M.–6 P.M. Mon.–Sat.), a clothing shop mostly for young women (shoes and purses, with hipster brands like Ed Hardy) that doubles as a salon.

Particularly unique: **Enstrom's Candy** (701 Colorado Ave., 970/683-1000, www.enstrom.com, 7 A.M.–8 P.M. Mon.–Fri., 8 A.M.–8 P.M. Sat., 10 A.M.–4 P.M. Sun.), a Colorado chain specializing in nutty toffee; the funky **Girlfriends** (316 Main St., 970/242-3234, 10 A.M.–5:30 P.M. Mon.–Sat.), which has couches to go with clothes and gifts; **Razzmatazz!** (552 Main St., 970/245-8318, 9:30 A.M.–5:30 P.M. Mon.–Fri., 9:30 A.M.–5 P.M. Sat.), which sells hipster jewelry, dresses, and handbags; and **Benge's Shoes** (514 Main St., 970/242-3843, 10 A.M.–5 P.M. Mon.–Sat.), which sells plenty of cool brands (Diesel and Mephisto) despite being the second-oldest shoe store (or so they say) in Colorado.

ACCOMMODATIONS

Glenwood Springs, Aspen, and even Redstone, just a few miles east along I-70, are known for their distinctive luxury hotels, but Grand Junction is mostly chains—you're more likely to find a La Quinta or Comfort Inn than a bed-and-breakfast. As a result, the best places to stay are the high-end chains.

The eight-story **Doubletree Grand Junction** (743 Horizon Dr., 970/241-8888, www.doubletree.com, $154–174) has 273 guest rooms and amenities like wireless Internet, a horseshoe pit, and a 5,000-square-foot ballroom downstairs. It's sort of *the* place to stay in Grand Junction, although it's a little plain and (in places) needs work.

Comfortable and reliable, **Main Street Suites** (225 Main St., 970/242-2525, www.hawthorn.com, $119–159) is a centrally located, relatively new brownstone with a free breakfast buffet and all the basic amenities.

The Grand Vista Hotel (2790 Crossroads Blvd., 970/241-8411 or 800/800-7796, www.grandvistahotel.com, $79) is a six-story building with an indoor and outdoor pool and a lobby lounge with karaoke every Thursday and Saturday night.

The Chateau (2087 Broadway, 970/255-1471 or 866/312-9463, www.tworiverswinery.com, $92–145) is better known as Two Rivers Winery, but it's also a French-style bed-and-breakfast directly underneath the Book Cliff

Mountain Range. The winery produces chardonnay, merlot, cabernet sauvignon, and riesling, and hopes to hit 10,000 cases soon.

Willow Pond Bed and Breakfast (662 26 Rd., 970/243-4958 or 877/243-4958, www.grandjunctioncoloradobedandbreakfast.com, $125) is in a 1916 farmhouse, with three wide, uncluttered guest rooms on the second floor. It is so named because of, yes, a willow tree and a small pond. Adding to the ambience, local singer-songwriters occasionally perform in the large yard.

FOOD

Befitting a meat-and-potatoes kind of city, **The Winery** (642 Main St., 970/242-4100, www.winery-restaurant.com, 4:30–9 P.M. daily, $25) specializes in steak and chicken dishes—nothing fancy—and a fine-dining experience that includes stained-glass windows, brick walls, and plants.

◖ **Dolce Vita** (336 Main St., 970/242-8482, www.dolcevitagrandjunction.com, 11 A.M.–9 P.M. Tues.–Sat., $16) is perhaps the best restaurant in town, a family-run northern Italian restaurant that serves wine-marinated portobello mushrooms and scaloppini chicken with angel-hair pasta, grilled red onions, a brandy cream sauce, and (the surprise ingredient) strawberries.

The restaurant part of the Tomorrow Hill Bed & Breakfast, the **Crystal Café & Bake Shop** (314 Main St., 970/242-8843, www.tomorrowhillfarm.com/CrstlCafe.html, 7–10:15 A.M. and 11 A.M.–1:45 P.M. Mon.–Fri., 8 A.M.–noon Sat., $16) is known for a super-sweet breakfast menu of apple pancakes and banana-nut French toast, but its dinners of steak and seafood are worth trying as well.

Across the street from Dolce Vita, **Pablo's Pizza** (319 Main St., 970/255-8879, www.pablospizza.com, 11 A.M.–8:30 P.M. Sun.–Thurs., 11 A.M.–9 P.M. Fri.–Sat., $15) has a knack for unusual flavor combinations—try the roasted garlic, walnut, and goat cheese pesto, the pepper-and-sausage Big Daddy's Rajun Cajun, or the peanut-sauce-and-shrimp Bangkok Express.

Main Street Bagels Artisan Bakery & Café (559 Main St., 970/241-2740, www.mainstreetbagels.net, 6:30 A.M.–6:30 P.M. Mon.–Sat., 7 A.M.–3 P.M. Sun., $7) is a rare bohemian enclave in a conservative city. The *chai,* bagels, and cinnamon rolls are homemade, and it's a Wi-Fi hot spot.

INFORMATION

The **Grand Junction Chamber of Commerce** (360 Grand Ave., 970/242-3214, www.gj-chamber.org) has tons of information about the city, and the **Grand Junction Visitor & Convention Bureau** (740 Horizon Dr., 970/244-1480 or 800/962-2547, www.visitgrandjunction.com) is helpful as well. The *Grand Junction Daily Sentinel* (www.gjsentinel.com) is the local metropolitan paper.

The **Town of Fruita** (325 E. Aspen Ave., 970/858-3663, www.fruita.org) carries sparse information about the small town not far from Grand Junction.

Opened in 1992, Grand Junction's community radio station **KAFM** (88.1 FM, 1310 Ute Ave., 970/241-8801, www.kafmradio.org) has programs devoted to blues, bluegrass, Americana, jazz, and public affairs. The city's TV news channels include **KREX** (CBS/Fox, Channel 5, www.krextv.com), **KJCT** (ABC, Channel 8, www.kjct8.com), and **KKCO** (NBC, Channel 11, www.nbc11news.com).

Area hospitals include **St. Mary's Healthcare** (2635 N. 7th St., 970/298-2273 or 800/458-3888, www.stmarygj.org), the only high-level trauma center in the area, and **Community Hospital** (2021 N. 12th St., 970/242-0920, www.yourcommunityhospital.com).

The main **U.S. Post Office** is at 241 North 4th Street.

Allowing you to wash your clothes are **Washboard Laundromat** (2692 U.S. 50, 970/255-9520) and **Econ-O-Wash Laundromat** (2401 North Ave., 970/245-9965).

GETTING THERE AND AROUND

The easiest way to get to Grand Junction is by flying into the **Grand Junction Regional Airport** (2828 Walker Field Dr.,

970/244-9100, www.walkerfield.com), with 19 departures a day, mostly on major airlines like Frontier, Delta, United, and American and serving primarily western Colorado and eastern Utah. **American Spirit Shuttle** (970/523-7662, www.americanspiritshuttle. net) is a charter service that takes travelers from anywhere in Grand Junction to the airport. Advance reservations are required, and prices vary. The shuttle also serves Aspen, Vail, Steamboat Springs, Telluride, and Crested Butte. Most major rental-car services are also on-site.

The city-run bus service is **Grand Valley Transit** (970/256-7433, http://gvt.mesacounty. us), which charges $1.50 for rides throughout Grand Junction, including stops at the airport and nearby Fruita and Palisade. Buses run 5:15 A.M.–7:15 P.M. Monday–Saturday.

◖ COLORADO NATIONAL MONUMENT

A sort of mini–Grand Canyon, with gnarled, reddish rock formations that recall Colorado Springs's Garden of the Gods or Morrison's Red Rocks Park, Colorado National Monument is a 20,500-acre haven for hikers, bikers, wildlife watchers, and campers. Its main artery is the narrow 23-mile Rim Rock Drive, which seems to have the perfect mesa-top, valley, or canyon view at the edge of every hairpin curve. (At one point, the road seems to burrow straight into the rock. Known as "Half Tunnel," this artificial structure was such a difficult accomplishment in the 1930s that 11 workers died when the roof collapsed.)

Credit for exploring the monument's many trails, most famously the Canyon Rim Trail above Wedding Canyon, goes to John Otto, saluted on a plaque as "trail builder, promoter, and first custodian"—in 1911, he became the first modern explorer to preserve the area. Today, it's run by the **National Park Service** (Fruita, 970/858-3617, www.nps.gov/colm, $10 per vehicle, $5 per hiker, cyclist, or motorcyclist), and the 6,000-foot-high mesas and cliffs and complex horizontal sandstone formations are worth a long visit.

The numerous hiking trails here range from 0.5-mile scenic strolls to 17-mile scrambles up canyon walls. The easier ones include the flat one-mile (one-way) **Canyon Rim,** which runs along the top of Wedding Canyon, opening to a deep view of curved red-and-orange rocks and monoliths and the Book Cliffs in the distance; the 0.5-mile **Coke Ovens,** which follows a downward path to a view of the namesake rocks, which look like a row of jolly round cartoon characters; and the 1.75-mile **Serpents Trail,** which has 50 switchbacks and was known as "the crookedest road in the world" when it was a main path into the park. More difficult trails are the steep six-mile

MIKE THE HEADLESS CHICKEN DAYS

Every September the serious people of Fruita, a small town just north of Colorado National Monument, gather downtown to drink beer, eat chicken, drive in car shows, and dance in contests. The occasion? A Wyandotte rooster from 1945 who legendarily lived for 18 months after farmer Lloyd Olsen – whose wife, Clara, demanded chicken for dinner – swung an ax and chopped off his head.

This miracle of science (the explanation goes that the ax missed Mike's brain stem, and a clot formed to stop him from losing too much blood) draws thousands of people to experience Mike the Headless Chicken Days. Colorado's nuttiest and most macabre festival this side of Nederland's annual Frozen Dead Guy Days, Mike the Headless Chicken Days operates under this inspirational motto: "It is great comfort to know you can live a normal life, even after you have lost your mind." PETA is apparently not invited.

For more information on the festival, contact Mike the Headless Chicken Days headquarters (325 E. Aspen Ave., Fruita, 970/858-3663, www.miketheheadless-chicken.org).

© GRAND JUNCTION VISITOR & CONVENTION BUREAU

Colorado National Monument

Monument Canyon, which overlooks some of the Monument's best-known rock structures, such as Kissing Cousins and Coke Ovens; seven-mile **Ute Canyon,** which goes straight into perhaps the most breathtaking of the Monument's several canyons, with its long orange horizontal stripes, and ends up following pleasant streams and pools; and, perhaps most difficult of all, the steep, undeveloped No **Thoroughfare Canyon.**

Featured in the 1985 Kevin Costner flick *American Flyers,* the Monument's primary bike trail is its centerpiece: 23-mile **Rim Rock Drive,** which is actually 33 miles if you count the local connecting roads outside the park. As drivers know, there are few paved paths in the United States as scenic as this one, but cyclists are often frustrated with the car traffic and the tunnels. The ascents can be tough at first, but after a few miles the path flattens out. (Trivia: *American Flyers* incorrectly called the park "Monumental National Park." The route was also one of the stages of the Coors Classic, an international cycling race, but that

ended in 1986, when local officials decided they didn't want to close the park every year for crazed fans.)

While spending time inside the monument, you'll almost certainly notice mule deer, foxes, and squirrels, but keep an eye out for desert bighorn sheep, coyotes, mountain lions, and bobcats. Bird-watchers may be lucky enough to happen upon golden eagles, red-tailed hawks, canyon wrens, and turkey vultures.

The park has one official campground, **Saddlehorn** (970/858-3617, www.nps.gov/colm/planyourvisit/campgrounds.htm, year-round, $20), which has 80 sites, flush toilets, water during the summer, and grills—but no electric hookups or showers, and wood fires aren't allowed. Backcountry camping is also possible within the park.

The **visitors center** (970/858-3617) is about four miles into the monument area and gives out trail maps.

◖ Dinosaur Journey

Across from the western monument site, this "paleontologist's playground" (550 Jurassic Court, Fruita, 888/488-3466, www.museumofwesternco.com/visit/dinosaur-journey, 9 A.M.–5 P.M. daily, $8.50) is just off I-70 a few miles west of Grand Junction. Run by a company that specializes in robot dinosaur replicas, the elaborate museum is more impressive than even the dinosaur exhibits in Dinosaur National Monument to the north. Its life-size fossil reconstructions of *Dilophosaurus, Utahraptor,* and *Tyrannosaurus rex* are animated so visitors can control them with buttons and levers. On-site paleontologists work in a lab that's open to public viewing, and the interactive exhibits for kids include an earthquake simulator.

Accommodations

Aside from small, plain chain motels, the **Saddlehorn Campground** (Colorado National Monument, 970/858-3617, www.nps.gov/colm/planyourvisit/campgrounds.htm, year-round, $20) is the primary lodging in the area—it has 80 sites, including flush toilets

GRAND JUNCTION

and sinks, and allows charcoal grills but not wood fires. Located in a piñon forest near the visitors center, the campground has pretty valley views.

Food
Nearby Fruita is no metropolis, and the restaurants are mostly of the Subway, Wendy's, and McDonald's variety, but the **Fiesta Guadalajara Restaurant** (103 U.S. 6/50, 970/858-1228, 11 A.M.–10 P.M. Mon.–Sat., 11 A.M.–9:30 P.M. Sun., $10) is a family Mexican joint worthy of its Southwestern location—the chiles rellenos and fajitas come in huge portions.

PALISADE
Unless you're a wine enthusiast, you might have no idea, upon driving from Glenwood Springs west to Grand Junction on I-70 past dinky Palisade, that this is the winery capital of Colorado. Seventy-five percent of the state's vineyards are here, most give tours, and as a bonus, the blink-and-you'll-miss-it kind of town has tan-and-red mesas in every direction and the Colorado River charging past the railroad tracks.

A longtime agricultural town, 2,600-resident Palisade was renowned even among the Utes for its rich soil. It began to produce peaches, cherries, and, of course, grapes after the U.S. Bureau of Reclamation built irrigation canals, including a Colorado River dam that created the Highline Canal and several large ditches. Today, the mild weather makes for a 182-day growing season—perfect for peaches.

Wineries
Palisade's Vinelands area has more than a dozen wineries specializing in a wide range of wines—riesling, chardonnay, merlot, cabernet sauvignon, and Budweiser. (Just kidding on that last one.) The four wineries listed here have no fees for tastings, although Plum Creek charges $2 pp for groups with more than 15 people, and adds that visitors get the money back via discounts on wine sales.

One of the best Palisade marketers is

Carlson Vineyards (461 35 Rd., 970/464-5554 or 888/464-5554, www.carlsonvineyards.com, 10 A.M.–5:45 P.M. daily), a down-home place where "wine is not treated as the nectar of snobs"—names like Prairie Dog Blush and Cougar Run Fat Cat Muskrat reinforce the point.

Founded in 1978, **Colorado Cellars Winery** (3553 E Rd., 970/464-7921, www.coloradocellars.com, 9 A.M.–5 P.M. Mon.–Fri., 10 A.M.–5 P.M. Sat.) is the state's oldest and largest vineyard, specializing in peach, raspberry, plum, and cherry wines, along with something called Roadkill Red.

The website for **Garfield Estates Vineyard and Winery** (3572 G Rd., 970/464-0941, www.garfieldestates.com, 11 A.M.–5 P.M. daily Mar.–Dec., noon–5 P.M. Mon.–Fri. Jan.–Feb.) delivers an impassioned defense of rosé—it's not just "white zin," don't you know. It has "more complexity than many whites but not the heavy tannins of a full-blown red."

Most renowned in the area is probably **Plum Creek Winery** (3708 G Rd., 970/464-7586, www.plumcreekwinery.com, 10 A.M.–5 P.M. daily), which boasts of all the gold, double-gold, and silver medals its 1998 Cabernet Franc, 1992 Grand Mesa, and numerous others have won over the years.

The **American Spirit Shuttle** (970/523-7662, www.americanspiritshuttle.net, 1–5 P.M. Sat., $200 for groups of 1–6) offers driving tours of many of the Palisade and Grand Junction wineries.

◖ Little Book Cliffs Wild Horse Range
The Little Book Cliffs Wild Horse Range (2815 H Rd., 970/244-3000, www.blm.gov/co/st/en/fo/gjfo.html, free), eight miles northeast of Grand Junction, is 30,261 acres of low, rocky canyons and high, flat plateaus that rise from 5,000 to 7,421 feet. And one other thing: wild horses. About 115 of them—bays, blacks, grays, pintos, roans, browns, and palominos—are running free, like a sequel to *The Black Stallion*. They're mostly descendants of horses who fled nearby ranches over the last two centuries; some have blood that can be traced to 1800s Native

NORTHWEST COLORADO WINERIES

- **Canyon Wind Cellars,** 3907 N. River Rd., Palisade, 970/464-0888, www.canyonwindcellars.com

- **Carlson Vineyards,** 461 35 Rd., Palisade, 970/464-5554, www.carlsonvineyards.com

- **Colorado Cellars Winery,** 3553 E Rd., Palisade, 800/848-2812, www.coloradocellars.com

- **Confre Cellars,** 785 Elberta Ave., Palisade, 970/464-1300

- **DeBeque Canyon Winery,** 3943 U.S. 6, 1.5 miles east of Palisade, 970/464-0550, www.debequecanyonwinery.com

- **Garfield Estates Vineyard and Winery,** 3572 G Rd., Palisade, 970/464-0941, www.garfieldestates.com

- **Grande River Vineyards,** 787 Elberta Ave., Palisade, 970/464-5867, www.granderiverwines.com

- **Graystone Winery,** 3352 F Rd., Clifton, 970/523-6611, www.graystonewine.com

- **Plum Creek Winery,** 3708 G Rd., Palisade, 970/464-7586, www.plumcreekwinery.com

- **Reeder Mesa Vineyards,** 7799 Reeder Mesa Rd., Whitewater, 970/242-7468, www.reedermesawines.com

- **Meadery of the Rockies,** 3701 G Rd., Palisade, 970/464-7899 or 800/720-2558, www.rocky-mountain-meadery.com

- **St. Kathryn Cellars,** 785 Elberta Ave., Palisade, 970/464-9288 or 877/464-4888, www.st-kathryn-cellars.com

- **Two Rivers Winery,** 2087 Broadway, Grand Junction, 970/255-1471, www.tworiverswinery.com

- **Whitewater Hill Vineyards,** 220 32 Rd., Grand Junction, 970/434-6868, http://whitewaterhill.com

a vineyard beneath a butte, Palisade

© DENISE CHAMBERS/WEAVER MULTIMEDIA GROUP/COLORADO TOURISM OFFICE

GRAND JUNCTION

American owners or, even earlier, to Spanish traders. Thanks to schoolchildren writing to their representatives, Congress passed the Wild and Free-roaming Horses and Burros Act in 1971, which is why hiking, biking, and mountain climbing in this massive area can be so dramatic. I visited recently with my family, and even though we were hoping to see horses, we were shocked when several of them appeared, calmly trotting on a dirt path in the hills above us.

Sports and Recreation

Because it's near Grand Junction, a huge **mountain-biking** area, Palisade is home to a few excellent rides as well. **Mount Garfield,** four miles round-trip, shows beautiful views of the Little Book Cliffs area—and maybe some wild horses will appear in the distance. Officials warn that this trail can be steep, slick, and challenging, especially when wet. To get to the trailhead, take I-70 to Exit 42, turn south on 37 3/10 Road, then take the first right (G 7/10 Rd.), wind through some homes, come through a tunnel under the highway, and look for the Mount Garfield parking area.

Entertainment and Events

Palisade's many orchards come together every August for the **Palisade Peach Festival** (3rd St. and Main St., among other locations, 970/464-7458, www.palisadepeachfest.com), which claims attendance of something like 18,000. You've never seen so much fuzz in your life, and vendors set up booths for barbecue, corn, and pancakes—plus, there's an afternoon car show.

Throughout the summer **Grande River Vineyards** (I-70 Exit 42, 970/464-5867, www.granderiverwines.com) sponsors relatively big-name blues, country, folk, and flamenco music stars, such as recent headliner Blues Traveler. Its festival is called **Heard It Through the Grapevine.**

Accommodations

Most of the lodging in Palisade is generally small, plain, and motel-style. For good deals, try the **Mesa View Motel** (424 W. 8th St., 970/464-0539, $59–72) and the **Wine Country Inn** (777 Grande River Dr., 970/464-5777 or 888/855-8330, www.coloradowinecountryinn.com, $139–249), which looks like an oversized barn but is in a perfect location underneath the mesas along I-70 and within walking distance of downtown Palisade and several vineyards. The **Peach Valley Lodge Bed and Breakfast** (3939 U.S. 6, 970/464-1323, www.peachvalleylodgebandb.com, $79–129) isn't the lap of luxury, but the owners make up for it with attention to detail, like old-fashioned frame beds, sofa chairs, and friendly artwork on the walls.

Food

The **Palisade Café** (113 W. 3rd St., 970/464-0657, www.palisadecafe.com, 11 A.M.–8 P.M. Mon.–Wed., 9 A.M.–9 P.M. Thurs., 8 A.M.–9 P.M. Fri.–Sat., 8 A.M.–3 P.M. Sun., $6) is your standard breakfast-and-lunch restaurant—omelets and sandwiches of all kinds—with paintings on the walls and a homey atmosphere. And pie. Plenty of pie.

In an old brick building, the **◖ Slice O' Life Bakery** (105 W. 3rd St., 970/464-0577, 8 A.M.–4:30 P.M. Tues.–Fri., 8 A.M.–3 P.M. Sat., $4) is Palisade's biggest claim to fame (other than the wineries, of course). Locals rave about the homemade baked goods, from sweet rolls to fruitcakes, and the bakery serves sandwiches for lunch.

Information

Try the **Palisade Chamber of Commerce** (319 Main St., 970/464-7458, www.palisadecoc.com) for general city services.

GRAND JUNCTION

Grand Mesa and Vicinity

GRAND MESA

Although this part of Colorado is dry and hot, a trip up the 11,000-foot Grand Mesa, the world's largest flat-topped mountain, leads to a dramatically different world. The sagebrush gives way to spruce and fir trees, the heat disappears, lakes pop up in every direction, and what was a bumpy desert turns into a nature lover's paradise of fishing holes, hiking trails (try the 10-mile Crag Crest), and 13 campgrounds.

In the Utes' days, the 50-square-mile area encompassing Grand Mesa was known as "Thunder Mountain"—until the U.S. government pushed the Utes to Utah and southwestern Colorado reservations in the 1880s. The Grand Mesa became an official national forest in 1892 by decree of President Benjamin Harrison.

◖ Grand Mesa National Forest

The best-known **hiking-and-biking** trail in the 346,219-acre Grand Mesa National Forest (2250 U.S. 50, Delta, 970/874-6600, www.fs.usda.gov) is the **Crag Crest National Recreation Trail,** a 10-mile loop that curves around three lakes, with other lakes on the outside—bring a camera for the spectacular view of Butts Lake, a glittering blue one-mile-long body of water surrounded by fir, spruce, and aspen trees. As for the mesa itself, its lava indentations can inspire geologists for hours. Consider hiking the 11,234-foot Leon Peak, on the forest's eastern edge, which is the Grand Mesa's tallest point and overlooks Gunnison Peak, the West Elk Mountains, and the San Juan Range.

To get to the trailhead from I-70, take the Highway 65 exit and go south about 35 miles to Forest Road 121, turn left, drive another 2.5 miles, bear left, and watch for signs about one mile ahead. Note that lightning is common on this popular trail, and it can get cold even when the weather below indicates otherwise. For

Crag Crest, Grand Mesa

© GRAND JUNCTION VISITOR & CONVENTION BUREAU

GRAND JUNCTION

maps and other information, contact the U.S. Forest Service's district office (2777 Crossroads Blvd., Grand Junction, 970/242-8211).

The forest has some of the best **fishing** in Colorado—mostly rainbow trout, but also brook and cutthroat. There are 300 lakes, so it's hard to pick just one, but the 10,000-foot-high **Carson Lake** (from Hwy. 65 south, take Rim Drive Rd. southwest 3 miles to Carson Lake Rd. and follow it for about 2 miles) has 12-inch cutthroat and some rainbow.

Contact the **Colorado Division of Wildlife** (711 Independent Ave., Grand Junction, 970/255-6100, http://wildlife.state.co.us/fishing) for maps, licenses, and information on conditions and laws.

Sports and Recreation

World-class skiers probably wouldn't plan a trip around **Powderhorn Ski Resort** (Hwy. 65, 20 miles south of I-70, 970/268-5700, www.powderhorn.com), but it's a great unexpected place to drop in if you happen to be traveling in the area during winter. The resort has 600 groomed acres, plus another 1,000 acres for backcountry skiers, with a summit elevation of almost 10,000 feet, four lifts, and trails for all skill levels. The ski trails run along the contours of the mesa. The resort also has three terrain parks, **Top Cut, Maverick, and Rustler's,** with the usual mix of boxes, rails, jumps, and other features. Lift tickets cost about $56.

Accommodations

Unlike the rest of northwest Colorado, the Grand Mesa area has several quaint, elegant inns and resorts; if you're planning to visit Colorado National Monument or Grand Junction, consider using this area as a base. Perhaps the best is ◖ **Mesa Lakes Resort** (3619 Hwy. 65, 12 miles south of Mesa, 970/268-5467 or 888/420-6372, $50–285), a log cabin next to a lake (fishing gear is available at the resort) in the middle of a forest. Several miles of groomed cross-country skiing trails are on the site, and the lodge serves prime rib nightly with live country singers in the background.

Also overlooking a lake—actually two lakes,

both filled with trout—is the ◖ **Thunder Mountain Lodge** (20658 Baron Lake Dr., 16 miles north of Cedaredge, 970/856-6240 or 877/470-6548, $55 pp), built in 1956. It's in the forest itself among a clump of spruce trees and has 11 cabins, most with kitchens. Also on the premises are the Over the Top Restaurant and snowmobile rentals.

At the Powderhorn Ski Resort, lodging is available at **Goldenwoods Condominiums** (4828 Powderhorn Rd., Mesa, 970/268-5040, www.goldenwoodscondos.com, $139–189).

The Grand Mesa National Forest has 13 full-service campgrounds, but perhaps the most striking is **Vega State Park** (15247 N. 6/10 Rd., 12 miles east of Collbran, 970/487-3407, $7), which is in an alpine meadow next to a high-elevation lake. The park is big with hikers, cyclists, cross-country skiers, and snowmobilers, and the complex has four campgrounds ($16), one of which is just for tents. Call first to find out which areas have electricity and heat—don't worry, none of them have phones or TV sets.

CEDAREDGE

This town of 1,200 people is the midpoint between the flat Grand Canyon–like mesas to the north and the rounder, greener, taller San Juans a little farther south. It is tiny and easy to miss on the map, but it also has 300 lakes, an elevation of 6,100 feet and the mild orchard-friendly climate to go with it, and, like many small towns in northwestern Colorado, a huge variety of mountain-biking trails.

Fifteen minutes south of Cedaredge—along Highway 65, also known as the Grand Mesa National Scenic and Historic Byway—is the Grand Mesa, a flat-topped mountain that extends 10,000–11,000 feet above sea level. The scenery is incredible: Rainbows and dramatic sunsets are common, and the San Juans are visible in the distance. The elevation makes everything cool, even as late as June or July, so bring a coat.

Sights

Pioneer Town (Hwy. 65, 970/856-7554, www.pioneertown.org, 10 A.M.–4 P.M. Mon.–Sat.,

1–4 P.M. Sun. Memorial Day–Sept., $3) is a 23-building wooden-sidewalk area two blocks south of downtown that recreates frontier life in the late 1800s. There's a working blacksmith shop (just in case your horse's feet get tired), a railroad depot, a schoolhouse, a fruit-packing shed, several ranch silos, a saloon, and the popular Doris Doll and Toy House.

Sports and Recreation
The **DeerCreek Village Golf Club** (500 SE Jay Ave., 970/856-7781, www.deercreekvillage-golf.com, $20–37) is an 18-hole course (that is, two nines) with the Grand Mesa in the distance and lots of trees and water.

Shopping
The Apple Shed (250 S. Grand Mesa Dr., 970/856-7007, www.theappleshed.net, 9 A.M.–5:30 P.M. Mon.–Fri., 9 A.M.–4 P.M. Sat.–Sun.) is a complex of shops and galleries with an emphasis on local artists—most notably the owner, Connie Williams, who does watercolor landscapes and abstract acrylics. The shops are of the seasonal knickknack variety, including tiny snowmen, teapots, and Christmas stockings.

Accommodations
I personally would not have thought to combine a llama-breeding farm with a bed-and-breakfast, but the 【 **Cedars' Edge Llamas B&B** (21575 Hwy. 65, 970/856-6836, www.llamabandb.com, $95–110) has both llamas and guest rooms, so what else are the owners supposed to do? Aladdin, Emma, Mini T, and others cost roughly $250 each to take home, although as of this writing all but one were sold. And if that isn't enough scenery, the bed-and-breakfast is within viewing distance of the Black Canyon of the Gunnison National Park and the Grand Mesa National Forest. The rooms are colorful, with many blues and peaches, and breakfast in bed is available.

The **Aspen Trails Campground** (199975 Hwy. 65, 970/856-6321, $12), three miles north of town, specializes in motorcycle

rallies, so if you're lost in this area and happen to stumble upon a bunch of llamas and Harley riders, that's a sign you're in Cedaredge. There's a central fireplace, camper cabins, RV sites, a tent area, and a gift shop.

Food
Wildfire Pizzeria and Wine Bar (500 SE Jay Ave., 970/856-6200, 11 A.M.–9 P.M. daily, $20) is in view of the golf course, with a nice wine list to go with pizza and Italian food in general.

Information
The **Cedaredge Chamber of Commerce** (245 W. Main St., 970/856-6961, www.cedaredgecolorado.com) shares a website with the town government.

DELTA
Almost 50 miles south of Grand Junction, on the Gunnison River near the picturesque Escalante Canyon, Delta is a small (pop. 3,900) agricultural town known for its orchards and several large Main Street murals painted in the 1980s (thus the nickname "City of Murals"). Although it has a couple of OK restaurants and chain hotels, it's not exactly a destination, and many visitors prefer nearby Cedaredge.

Sights
The Fort Uncompahgre History Museum (205 Gunnison River Dr., 970/874-1718, 9 A.M.–3 P.M. Mon.–Fri., $3.50) is on the site of a heavily trafficked 1828 fur-trading post. As a small-town museum, it's pretty elaborate: There's a "trade room" that includes furs, guns, knives, and beads; a "hide room" that once stored deer and beaver skins; and guides dressed as settlers, traders, Native Americans, and cowboys.

Accommodations
The **Riverwood Inn** (677 U.S. 50 N., 970/874-5787 or 888/213-2124, http://riverwoodinn.net, $62–75), which includes an RV park, is a one-story, 14-room hotel that's a step above the chains in the area. Half of the rooms overlook the Gunnison River.

Food

Formerly the Delta Fireside Inn, **Miller's Deitch Haus** (820 Hwy. 92, 970/874-4413, 6–10 A.M., 11:15 A.M.–2 P.M., and 4:30–8 P.M. Mon.–Tues. and Thurs.–Sat., 11:15 A.M.–2 P.M. Wed., $10) is a buffet-style Mennonite restaurant that serves just about everything travelers need—a coffee bar in the morning, six different meats and casserole dishes in the evening, a soup-and-salad bar, and a rotating list of homemade pies.

Information and Services

The **Delta City Hall** (360 Main St., 970/874-7566, www.delta-co.gov) is a great resource for locals, but travelers will probably prefer the **Delta Area Chamber of Commerce** (301 Main St., 970/874-8616, www.deltacolorado.org).

The **Delta County Memorial Hospital** (1501 E. 3rd St., 970/874-7681, www.deltahospital.org) serves Delta as well as Cedaredge, Grand Mesa, and other towns and attractions in the area.

Glenwood Springs

The last ski town for travelers heading west on I-70 from Denver, Glenwood Springs is perfectly situated between Aspen to the south, Vail to the east, and Grand Junction to the west. It has a tiny ski resort, but the town is far more famous for its namesake springs—two natural hot pools, one of which is 405 by 100 feet, both in a giant tourist-trap area near the regal but worn Colorado Hotel.

Due to its proximity to high-end Aspen, you'd think Glenwood Springs would be a ritzy kind of mountain town—and it was, from the late 1800s to the mid-20th century, when Teddy Roosevelt and Al Capone used to stay downtown. Today, it's actually modest and tourist-oriented, with the large hot-springs pool on one side of town and a strip of low-key shops and cafés on the other. Both

© MATT INDEN/WEAVER MULTIMEDIA GROUP/COLORADO TOURISM OFFICE

a bird's-eye view of Glenwood Springs

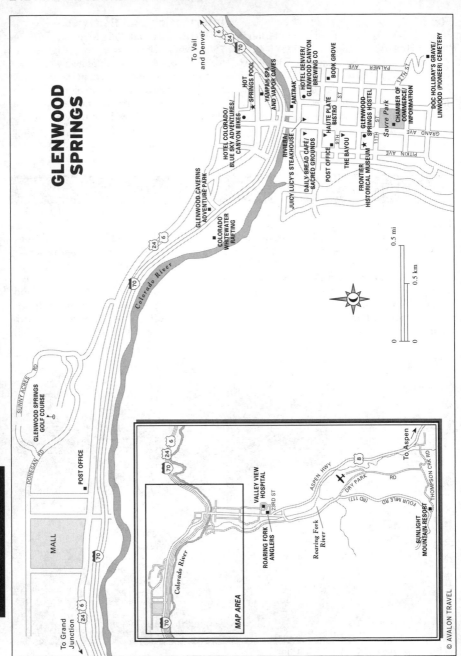

GRAND JUNCTION

GLENWOOD SPRINGS

To Vail and Denver

HOT SPRINGS POOL

YAMPAH SPA AND VAPOR CAVES

AMTRAK

HOTEL DENVER/ GLENWOOD CANYON BREWING CO

BOOK GROVE

PALMER AVE

HOTEL COLORADO/ BLUE SKY ADVENTURES/ CANYON BIKES

RIVIERA

HAUTE PLATE BISTRO

GLENWOOD SPRINGS HOSTEL

DOC HOLLIDAY'S GRAVE/ LINWOOD (PIONEER) CEMETERY

GLENWOOD CAVERNS ADVENTURE PARK

JUICY LUCY'S STEAKHOUSE

DAILY BREAD CAFÉ/ SACRED GROUNDS

POST OFFICE

THE BAYOU

CHAMBER OF COMMERCE/ INFORMATION

Sayre Park

GRAND AVE

PITKIN AVE

8TH ST

9TH ST

11TH ST

PLAZA ST

COLORADO WHITEWATER RAFTING

FRONTIER HISTORICAL MUSEUM

Colorado River

0   0.5 mi

0   0.5 km

SUNNY ACRES RD

GLENWOOD SPRINGS GOLF COURSE

POST OFFICE

DONEGAN RD

MALL

To Grand Junction

MAP AREA

VALLEY VIEW HOSPITAL

23RD ST

ROARING FORK ANGLERS

Colorado River

ASPEN HWY

DRY PARK RD

To Aspen

Roaring Fork River

FOUR MILE RD (RD 117)

THOMPSON CRK RD

SUNLIGHT MOUNTAIN RESORT

© AVALON TRAVEL

historic hotels, the Colorado and the Denver, show their age, and travelers wishing for more luxury should proceed to Aspen.

The western route from Denver and the ski resorts into Glenwood Springs is amazingly scenic. The Colorado River, which today runs along I-70, created a 17-mile stretch known as Glenwood Canyon, and it's very difficult to concentrate on the road while staring up at the towering red-and-brown canyon walls. This is also a rich area for wildlife-viewing— elk, Rocky Mountain bighorn sheep, coyotes, rabbits, and mule deer are known to pop their heads out from time to time.

HISTORY

The Utes considered the springs sacred for centuries, and, after fiercely protecting their land from other tribes, they happened upon ailing explorer Richard Sopsis, a U.S. military captain, and took him to the springs for healing in the 1860s. A decade later, silver miners from nearby Leadville flooded the town, displaced the Utes, and colonized it for themselves.

The springs' reputation grew quickly in American culture as well: Annie Oakley and Doc Holliday visited here in the 1880s, but Holliday, suffering from tuberculosis, died about six months after he showed up.

By 1893, thanks to the Denver and Rio Grande Railroad and the luxurious swimming pool–equipped Hotel Colorado, Glenwood Springs became a resort town for travelers en route to California. Some of these big-money visitors stayed permanently, and for years Glenwood Springs's polo teams won national titles.

Just to show how things have changed over 150 years, the hot springs are now a popular spa; formerly the Yampah ("big medicine" in Ute) Valley Springs, they're known today as the Hot Springs Pool.

SIGHTS
Hot Springs Pool

Hot Springs Pool (401 N. River St., 970/945-6571 or 800/537-7946, www.hotspringspool.com, 7:30 A.M.–10 P.M. daily Memorial Day–Labor Day, 9 A.M.–10 P.M. daily Labor

Hot Springs Pool, Glenwood Springs's biggest tourist attraction

GRAND JUNCTION

Day–Memorial Day, $13.75–18.75) is built around two natural pools, heated constantly to almost 100°F, and while the minerals aren't harmful to your skin or eyes, swimming for too long a period will make you blink a *lot* (consider bringing eye drops). The large pool is longer than a football field, and the small one is just 100 feet long. The pools aren't quite as sacred as they were in the days of the Utes or when luminaries like Doc Holliday and Annie Oakley showed up in Glenwood Springs to experience their healing qualities. Given the 107-room lodge on the premises, plus a spa, shops, and miniature golf, the pool is among the biggest tourist attractions in western Colorado. Go during the off-season to avoid crowds. To check out the pool before indulging, climb the large footbridge overhead and spy on all the swimmers.

Yampah Spa & Salon

The Yampah Spa & Salon (709 E. 6th St., 970/945-0667, www.yampahspa.com, 9 A.M.–9 P.M. daily, $12), subtitled "The Hot Springs Vapor Caves," turns yet another Ute tradition into modern tourism. The three underground caves get hotter and hotter—at a top temperature of 125°F—until you feel like the stresses have seeped out of your pores. Of course, the salon offers all the beauty products and spa treatments one could possibly want.

Glenwood Caverns Adventure Park

Glenwood Caverns Adventure Park (5100 Two Rivers Plaza Rd., 800/530-1635, www.glenwoodcaverns.com, 10 A.M.–6 P.M. Sun.–Fri., 10 A.M.–10 P.M. Sat. fall–winter, 9 A.M.–9 P.M. daily summer, $22) is a gigantic theme park built on the natural caves and mazes of the Glenwood Caverns and Fairy Caves, which opened as a tourist attraction in 1887. It takes 127 steps to get down, so make sure you're in shape before descending. To get to the cave entrance, take the 4,300-foot-long Iron Mountain Tramway gondola, which floats over the Rockies and brushes the tops of trees. There are cave tours of varying lengths and intensity, and the Panorama Trail is a nice outdoor walk in summer or snowshoeing trip in winter. New attractions include the 3,400-foot Alpine Coaster, a 1,300-foot Giant Swing, and a 32-foot climbing wall.

Frontier Historical Museum

The Frontier Historical Museum (1001 Colorado Ave., 970/945-4448, www.glenwoodhistory.com, 11 A.M.–4 P.M. Mon.–Sat. May–Sept., 1–4 P.M. Mon. and Thurs.–Sat. Oct.–Apr., $3) documents the fascinating history of Glenwood Springs, from the time Captain Sopsis "discovered" the springs with his Ute encounter to Doc Holliday's ultimate demise here in 1887. (Holliday, for the record, is buried in Linwood Cemetery, just east of the town. Nobody knows the exact location of his grave.) The museum contains 5,000 photos from the Old West days and offers guided tours and a gift shop.

SPORTS AND RECREATION
Fishing and Other Water Sports

Field & Stream's February 2008 issue named Glenwood Springs the number 1 town for anglers to live in—beating the likes of Mountain Home, Arkansas, and Traverse City, Michigan. The main reason is geography. Glenwood is at the junction of the Roaring Fork and Colorado Rivers, and trout-filled wonderlands like the Eagle River and the Gunnison River are within close driving distance. Another reason is the weather—300 days of sun per year. And the final reason is the economy—unlike Aspen, Telluride, and the other ritzy ski towns, Glenwood Springs and the rest of northwestern Colorado are affordable and easygoing.

As the 1,450-mile-long **Colorado River** flows from 12,000 feet of elevation in the northern Rockies down to the flatter Glenwood Springs area, it merges with the Roaring Fork River and gets slower and wider in many parts, making it a particularly rich stretch for anglers. The entire river is packed with trout—cutthroat, rainbow, brook, and brown. An excellent access point is the South Canyon exit off I-70, west of Glenwood Springs. Note that this stretch of the Colorado is incredibly beautiful, running down the center of Glenwood Canyon.

Helpful in the fishing department is **Roaring Fork Anglers** (2205 Grand Ave., 970/945-0180, www.roaringforkanglers.com), which rents equipment, provides guided tours and fly-tying classes, and gives tips and directions on its website.

Sixteen-mile Glenwood Canyon, on I-70 just east of town, has rapids that rage quite nicely during spring and summer. Several local outfits offer guided tours, including **Rock Gardens** (1308 County Rd. 129, 800/958-6737, www.rockgardens.com), which has both easygoing scenic family tours and hard-core trips for adventure travelers; **Colorado Whitewater Rafting** (2000 Devereux Rd., 970/945-8477 or 800/993-7238, www.coloradowhitewaterrafting.com), which has full-day, half-day, and short kids trips; and **Blue Sky Adventures** (319 6th St., 970/945-6605 or 877/945-6605, www.blueskyadventure.com), in the Hotel Colorado. The cost for rafting trips ranges $30–75 for a half-day trip, more for private guided tours.

This stretch of the Colorado River is also open to swimmers, kayakers, and other lakegoing types. For regulations, weather conditions, and other information, contact the local **Division of Wildlife Office** (50633 U.S. 6/Hwy. 24, 970/947-2920). Another excellent resource on this subject is the **Bureau of Land Management** (2815 H Rd., Grand Junction, 970/244-3000, www.blm.gov/com).

Mountain Biking

For about 17 miles east of Glenwood Springs along I-70 and the Colorado River, **Glenwood Canyon** has a well-maintained 16-mile bike path with plenty of picnic areas and rest stops along the way. It's easy to find; begin at Two Rivers Park (Centennial St. and Devereux Rd.), which has a band shell, near the center of town.

Also, the White River National Forest isn't far from these parts, and many choose to bring their own bikes or rent equipment in Glenwood Springs before heading down to the trails of Aspen. Otherwise, try **Canyon Bikes** (526 Pine St., 970/945-8904 or 800/439-3043, www.canyonbikes.com), in the Hotel Colorado, for rentals, maps, and trail advice.

Skiing and Snowboarding

Skiing started as an off-and-on sport in Glenwood Springs in 1940, and it truly took hold in the mid-1960s when the **Sunlight Mountain Resort** (10901 County Rd. 117, 970/945-7491 or 800/445-7931, www.sunlightmtn.com, 9 A.M.–4 P.M. daily winter) opened about 10 miles up Four Mile Road. Today, it's hardly the biggest resort in northern Colorado, but it has 67 trails, 470 acres of ski terrain, vertical drops of 2,010 feet, and a collection of steep runs known as Extreme Sunlight. The summit is almost 9,900 feet, more than 4,000 feet higher than the town of Glenwood Springs, and the incredible views at the top are of Mount Sopsis and the Elk Mountain Range. It also has the **Pump Haus Terrain Park,** with jump lines of several sizes and various rails, boxes, and log jibs. Bonus for cross-country skiers: 20 miles of trails through a valley between Sunlight Mountain and Williams Peak.

Lift tickets cost $55 per day for adults, with cheaper prices for kids and seniors. The **Ski and Snowboard School** gives lessons to adults and kids for $100 per day, which includes ski rental and lift ticket.

Although it's at the center of downtown, a few miles from the skiing, the **Sunlight Mountain Ski and Bike Shop** (309 9th St., 970/945-9425, www.sunlightmtn.com) is affiliated with the resort.

EVENTS

Strawberry Days (Sayre Park, Highland Park, and Grand Ave., 970/945-6589, www.strawberrydaysfestival.com) is a three-day festival in late June with all the trimmings—a parade, local bands, a pancake breakfast, the 5K "Strawberry Shortcut" run, a food court, art, crafts, and something called the Valley View Hospital Auxiliary Pie Day.

SHOPPING

The touristy area of Glenwood Springs centers on the hot springs, near the Hotel Colorado and the Hotel Denver, where a huge bridge overlooks the city. But the best shopping is a few blocks away, along 9th Street, an area of comfortable, modern cafés and tourist and townie stores alike.

Book Grove (801 Blake Ave., 970/384-0992, www.bookgrove.com, 10 A.M.–5:30 P.M. Wed.–Sat.) is a charming store specializing in used and out-of-print titles. **Treadz** (812 Grand Ave., 970/928-0620, www.treadzshoes. com, 10 A.M.–6 P.M. Mon.–Sat., 10 A.M.–5 P.M. Sun.) is a shoe store for women with emu and bear-paw boots and funky scarves.

ACCOMMODATIONS

Built in 1806 as an art deco palace, the **Hotel Denver** (402 7th St., 970/945-6565 or 800/826-8820, www.thehoteldenver.com, $99–179) has a three-story atrium and (in most guest rooms) views of the springs outside. Like the Hotel Colorado, it has a historic charm that screams "famous people once stayed here"— but it hasn't been appropriately restored in years. Several interesting historical artifacts are in the lobby, including an 1885 Weber piano, a tile floor laid in 1921, and an old grandfather clock that has stood here since the 1930s. The lower guest rooms are the cheapest, but they're a little noisy due to the train station next door. The Glenwood Canyon Brewing Company, for food and beer, is on the first floor.

Not far from the Sunlight Mountain Resort, the **Sunlight Mountain Inn** (10252 County Rd. 117, 970/945-5225, www.sunlightinn.com, $76–149) is a woodsy New West lodge with fireplaces in many of the guest rooms (and the lobby) and plenty of room to store your skis and poles. Some of the packages include coupons for nearby horseback-riding trails, skiing, snowmobiling, and hot springs.

Once the most luxurious place to stay between New York City and Los Angeles—Al Capone, Teddy Roosevelt, William Taft, Molly Brown, Doc Holliday, and assorted other luminaries and gangsters stayed here in the late 1800s—the **◖ Hotel Colorado** (526 Pine St., 970/945-6511 or 800/544-3998, www.hotel-colorado.com, $142–192) is on the National Register of Historic Places and retains much of its elegance from the old days, although its fanciness has worn down over the years. Known as "the grande dame" after it was built in 1893, the hotel was famous for its Italian-style design and various elaborate waterfalls and shooting fountains. Imported Italian wallpaper, antiques, and interesting black-and-white portraits of former guests Capone, Roosevelt, and others almost reproduce the Old West ambience, but more modern adventurers will appreciate the convenient lobby locations of Light Circle Massage, Canyon Bikes, and Blue Sky Adventures. The indoor-outdoor restaurant on the main floor is charming, and it has a three-course dinner theater ($45–55).

FOOD

The **Riviera Restaurant** (702 Grand Ave., 970/945-7692, www.rivierarestaurantgws.com, 4:30–11 P.M. daily, $22) is the most modern of Glenwood Springs's downtown restaurants, despite its old-school neon sign out front. It's full of colorful paintings as well as plenty of seafood, a long dessert menu, and a longtime recipe known as Mabel's Prime Rib.

Across the lobby from the Hotel Denver, the **Glenwood Canyon Brewing Company** (402 7th St., 970/945-1276, http://glenwood-canyon.com, 11 A.M.–11 P.M. Sun.–Thurs., 11 A.M.–midnight Fri.–Sat., $12) is a brewpub with big wooden booths, sports on television, a bunch of tasty beers (my preference is the Grizzly Creek Raspberry Wheat, in which you can taste the raspberries even more than the beer) and a steady hand for basic dishes such as steak, chicken-fried steak, ribs, and enchiladas.

With a gigantic breakfast-and-lunch menu that includes burritos, omelets, granola, and a zillion kinds of toast, **Daily Bread Café** (729 Grand Ave., 970/945-6253, 7 A.M.–2 P.M. daily, $8) specializes in mushroom bisque ($7) and deli sandwiches ($7–9).

The Bayou (919 Grand Ave., 970/945-1047, 4–10 P.M. Mon.–Sat., 10:30 A.M.–10 P.M. Sun., $15), relocated recently to a historic downtown building, is perhaps the only New Orleans–style restaurant in the mountains of Colorado, and it's a good one—specializing, of course, in gumbo, étouffée, blackened fish and chicken, red beans and rice, and menus describing certain spices as "hurt me." Mardi Gras masks hang on the wall, the staff provides goofy entertainment, and you can raise a glass to the Crescent City.

Formerly the 8th Street Deli, **Haute Plate Bistro** (205 8th St., 970/945-5011, www.8thstreetdeli.com, 11 A.M.–3 P.M. Mon.–Sat., $8) is an easygoing and somewhat hippieish deli that seats just eight people and has breakfast burritos, sandwiches, and desserts. The salad dressings are homemade. A little bigger is **Sacred Grounds** (725 Grand Ave., 970/928-8804, www.sacredgrounds.biz, 7:30 A.M.–4:30 P.M. daily, $7), one of those roomy delis that chalk-prints its huge menu across several blackboards. "Build Your Own Sandwich" is usually a straightforward instruction, but here it involves numerous kinds of cheeses, vegetables, wraps, spreads, and breads. The homemade brownies are delicious.

Juicy Lucy's Steakhouse (308 7th St., 970/945-4619, www.juicylucyssteakhouse.com, 11 A.M.–9:30 P.M. Sun.–Thurs., 11 A.M.–10 P.M. Fri.–Sat., $20), just underneath the bridge on the touristy side of town, has the feel of a Boulder brewpub, if a little older. But its 14-ounce New York sirloin ($28) and center-cut pork chop ($17) are about as far from vegetarian-friendly Boulder as you can get.

INFORMATION AND SERVICES

Glenwood Springs's **Chamber of Commerce** is at 1102 Grand Avenue; call 970/945-6589 or 888/445-3696 or check out www.glenwoodchamber.com. The local paper is the *Glenwood Springs Post Independent* (www.postindependent.com).

The primary medical-care facility here is **Valley View Hospital** (1906 Blake Ave., 970/945-6535, www.vvh.org), but the federally funded **Mountain Family Health Centers** (1905 Blake Ave., Suite 101, 970/945-2840, www.mountainfamily.org) also makes doctors, nurses, and nurse practitioners available for emergencies and regular care.

GETTING THERE AND AROUND

Ride Glenwood Springs (101 W. 8th St., 970/384-6400, www.ci.glenwood-springs.co.us/transpo/1a-1.htm, 6 A.M.–10 P.M. daily, hours vary) is a free bus service that hits most of the central spots in town. Also, the **Roaring Fork Transportation Authority** (970/925-8484, www.rfta.com) provides a shuttle among Aspen, Snowmass, Glenwood Springs, and several of the smaller towns in between.

If you have a small plane and know how to fly it, try **Glenwood Springs Airport** (970/618-0778, www.glenwoodspringsairport.com).

The Northwest Corner

GRAND JUNCTION

RIFLE

Like many of the small towns near Grand Junction, Rifle is a hub for mountain bikers, hikers, cross-country skiers, and hunters—Teddy Roosevelt came here in 1901 to hunt bears—without a whole lot to do in town. Well, there is one thing: Drop by a bar and start an argument with locals about how the town got its name. One of many legends has it that an explorer in the 1800s left his rifle leaning on a tree. Upon his return to camp, he realized his error and wrote "Rifle" on the only map anybody had. The name stuck.

The scenery surrounding Rifle is incredible—mesas, cliffs, sagebrush parks, woodlands of piñon and juniper trees, the Elk Mountains, Gore Range, Grand Mesa, and Flat Tops. Trails are everywhere, and it's common to pass cars toting bikes, skis, and, yes, rifles.

Sights

Rifle Falls State Park (5775 Hwy. 325, 14 miles north of Rifle, 970/625-1607, http://parks.state.co.us/parks/riflefalls, $7) is named for a triple waterfall that goes over limestone

Rifle Falls State Park

cliffs. Within the cliffs are dark and scary caves—bring a flashlight, especially if you plan to explore a famous 90-foot room beneath the falls. The 100-acre state park first opened in 1883 to local ranchers, and by 1910 the Rifle Hydroelectric Plant had split the waterfall into three streams. Consider visiting in winter, when the falls create ice crystals on the vegetation.

Ice and rock climbers swear by the 1,305-acre **Rifle Gap State Park** (Hwy. 325, 9 miles north of Rifle, 970/625-1607, http://parks.state.co.us/parks/riflegap, $7), beneath the thick Grand Hogback sandstone, which is filled with waterfalls and caves. It also has a 350-acre reservoir, popular among boaters, fishers, swimmers, divers, and windsurfers as well as ice fishers and skaters in the winter. Art-history trivia: Renowned outdoor artists Christo and Jeanne-Claude built an orange curtain that stretched across the entire valley in 1971; winds knocked it down, they rebuilt it a year later, and the second curtain lasted just

24 hours. So, there's no curtain anymore, but a commemorative site on Rifle Creek recalls the huge environmental display.

The **Rifle Falls Fish Hatchery** (11466 Hwy. 325, 970/625-1865, 8 A.M.–4 P.M. daily, free), run by the Colorado Division of Wildlife, produces the most trout in the state. It's open for viewing but not fishing. It's upstream of Rifle Falls.

Sports and Recreation

Mountain-biking trails spread like tentacles from Rifle into the surrounding mountains and cliffs. The town recommends a trail three miles north of town, off JQS Road, which is on Highway 13 north of I-70—look for a small break in the guardrail. The rocky dirt road goes seven miles up the Roan Cliffs, overlooking Rifle at the top. Numerous Jeep trails and narrow biking roads are also off JQS Road. The **Rifle Information Center** (200 Lions Park Circle, 970/625-2085 or 800/842-2085, www.riflechamber.com), on the Colorado River, provides detailed mountain-biking trail maps.

Also, watch the main Rifle website (www.rifleco.org) for information about races and group biking events. **Roan Cliff Chaos,** in mid-July on the JQS Road trails, is a popular one.

The only cycling shop in Rifle, Colorado Custom Cycles, recently closed, so renters have to trek to Glenwood Springs—**Canyon Bikes** (319 6th St., 970/945-8904 or 800/439-3043, www.canyonbikes.com) is downtown in the Hotel Colorado.

The easiest place to find fish is outside the Rifle Information Center (200 Lions Park Circle), next to the Colorado River, and many local shops will set you up a littler farther inside the rapids. **Boating** and **fishing** are big at the trout- and bass-packed Rifle Gap State Park, which has a paved boat ramp.

The Rifle area is disproportionately packed with outdoors-supply stores, including **Timberline Sporting Goods** (101 E. 3rd St., 970/625-4868, www.timberlinesports.com) and **Up Close on the River** (1060 Grand Ave., Silt, 970/876-2665, www.upcloseontheriver.com).

Three miles north of Rifle, the 18-hole **Rifle Creek Golf Course** (3004 Hwy. 325, 970/625-1093, www.riflecreekgc.com, $33–43) is in the shadow of the Hogback Range and has plenty of trees and water hazards.

Accommodations

Rifle's lodging is mostly low-end chains and low-overhead motels, so most visitors will probably want to stay in nearby Grand Junction or Glenwood Springs. But there is one campground: Although you probably won't want to set up a tent underneath the 60-foot triple waterfall—and probably not in the limestone caves underneath the falls, either—**Rifle Falls State Park** (5775 Hwy. 325, 970/625-1607, $16) is a photogenic place to camp. A daily park pass is an additional $7. Swimming is available in the creek, but call first to find out whether electricity and heat are available where you plan to stop.

Food

As with hotels, Rifle is mostly chains (and fast-food ones at that). But there are a few distinctive local joints, including **Columbine Restaurant** (3004 Hwy. 325, 970/625-9201, www.riflecreekgc.com, 9 A.M.–8 P.M. daily, $14), at the Rifle Creek Golf Course, which tops off an easy day of golf with plenty of wiener schnitzel ($13), steak, chicken, and trout.

Information and Services

The **Rifle City Hall** (202 Railroad Ave., 970/665-6400, www.rifleco.org) is geared more toward residents than visitors, but it's somewhat helpful. The **Rifle Chamber of Commerce** (200 Lions Park Circle, 970/625-2085 or 800/842-2085, www.riflechamber.com) lists local businesses, shops, and restaurants. The town newspaper is the *Rifle Citizen Telegram* (www.citizentelegram.com).

The **Grand River Medical Center** (501 Airport Rd., 970/625-1510, www.grhd.org) is the main hospital in Rifle, but it has spin-off locations throughout the area, including elsewhere in Rifle and Parachute.

MEEKER

The 2,200 people who live in Meeker must be pretty thrilled that their town is forever linked with the word *massacre*. But such is history. The Meeker Massacre began with journalist and teacher Nathan C. Meeker, a well-known reformer of the 1800s who had founded the town of Greeley and wanted to convert the Utes into the white vision of church-attending farmers. The Utes didn't respond well to his advances, and in September 1879, Meeker requested reinforcements from the U.S. Army.

The Utes ambushed Major Thomas Thornburg, who was on his way to Meeker's White River area with a relief contingent, killing him and 13 of his troops. The Utes continued into Meeker's agency and slaughtered not only the would-be reformer but 11 other men—and took several women and children captive and burned down Meeker's agency. The women and children were released after 23 days, but the damage was done; the "Utes must go!" movement became more shrill and powerful overnight, and the Utes lost their bargaining leverage. By 1880, Chief Ouray agreed in Washington to move his people to Utah.

The town of Meeker as we know it began three years later, when the U.S. government established a fort and sold it to local settlers. Today, three of these log cabins house the White River Museum in downtown Meeker. A marker commemorating the massacre site is on Highway 64, four miles west.

Located about halfway between I-70 and U.S. 40, on the west end of the White River National Forest, Meeker is like many small northwestern Colorado towns—a haven for outdoor activities, but not much else. The hiking, fishing, horseback riding, rafting, snowmobiling, and especially hunting are popular given the proximity to the White River Forest, the Flat Tops Wilderness, and the White River Valley.

Sights

The photo near the front door of the **White River Museum** (565 Park St., 970/878-9982, www.meekercolorado.com/museum.

htm, 9 A.M.–5 P.M. daily mid-Apr.–Nov., 10 A.M.–4 P.M. daily Dec.–early Apr., free) was taken three years after the U.S. military left Meeker in the late 1880s. The museum's three log cabins were a barracks until the government sold them to settlers; today, they're filled with photos (including many of doomed reformer Nathan Meeker and his family), period dresses, hats, jewelry, and, um, a Victorian wreath made of human hair. Perhaps most historically important is the actual plow with which Meeker dug up the Utes' pony racetrack, which led to the Meeker Massacre.

The **Flat Tops Trail Scenic Byway** (U.S. Forest Service, Blanco District, 317 E. Market St., 970/878-4039, www.meekercolorado.com/byway.htm) is an 82-mile passage through the ranches, mines, lakes, and woodlands of the original White River Plateau Timberland Reserve, set aside in the 19th century. It's a pretty drive from Meeker to Yampa and hits just a few small towns in between, so be sure the gas tank is full before you take off. Also, the road gets slippery and treacherous when it rains.

Entertainment and Events

Meeker Classic Sheepdog Trials (970/878-5510, www.meekersheepdog.com) is a five-day celebration in early September of really smart dogs who tell sheep what to do. The winner gets $25,000, so you'll see some of the best fetching, outrunning, and herding in the world, and some expert human whistling as well. A pancake breakfast, art contest, crafts, and various dog-therapy workshops are on hand.

Accommodations

Built in 1896, **The Meeker Hotel and Café** (560 Main St., 970/878-5255, www.themeekerhotel.com, $87–136) is a brick structure filled with elk and mule deer trophies and a vivid lobby painting of the Meeker Massacre. Its 24 guest rooms include a few large suites, and they're all colorful and orderly, with beds matching the meticulously patterned wallpaper. The café is as historic as the hotel, having served Billy the Kid, both President Roosevelts,

and Gary Cooper, and it continues to emphasize heavy comfort food like chicken-fried steak and mashed potatoes with gravy.

Food

Meeker is so small that just eight restaurants are listed with the Chamber of Commerce—and a couple of those aren't even in the city limits. In the Meeker Hotel, the **Meeker Café** (560 Main St., 970/878-5062, www.themeekerhotel.com/dining-in-meeker.php, 8 A.M.–9 P.M. Mon.–Sat., 8 A.M.–2 P.M. Sun., $14) is most famous for serving such guests as Teddy Roosevelt, Franklin D. Roosevelt, and Gary Cooper since it opened in the late 1800s. Today, it's a vision of hardwood—floors, tables, chairs, and the odd stuffed deer head on a brick wall.

Information and Services

Between the **Town of Meeker** (www.meeker-colorado.com) and the **Meeker Chamber of Commerce** (710 Market St., 970/878-5510, www.meekerchamber.com), travelers should get just about anything they need to know about this small historic town.

Pioneers Medical Center (345 Cleveland St., 970/878-5047, www.pioneershospital.com) is a small, homey hospital serving this area since 1950.

CRAIG

A city of 8,100 people, Craig is tantalizingly close to Colorado's most popular ski areas, particularly Steamboat Springs, about a 45-minute drive to the east. Craig itself, however, is flat and filled with nothing. Well, that's not totally true—the **Grand Old West Days** brings bull-riding, bands, and a parade to town every Memorial Day, and the Museum of Northwest Colorado has an interesting collection of guns and other cowboy memorabilia.

But as with Rifle, Rangely, Palisade, and other small towns in northwest Colorado, Craig is also a popular spot for outdoor recreation—particularly hunting and fishing in the Yampa and Green Rivers and Trappers Lake. Otherwise, it's a long, empty drive down U.S. 40 between Dinosaur and Steamboat Springs, so think of Craig as a last-ditch gas-and-snacks option.

And if you're really desperate for scenery, the three-smokestack **Craig Station** is the largest coal-fired energy plant in Colorado. It's about six miles south of town.

Sights

In the city park downtown, early-1900s mining and railroad magnate David Moffat's greenish-black **Marcia Car** (U.S. 40, 970/824-5689, free), named for his daughter, is available for tours and private viewings. Recently restored, the car once transported Moffat up and down his Denver Northwestern & Pacific Railroad line to inspect the construction. Although Moffat planned to extend the line to Salt Lake City, he and his investors fell short of funds and had to stop in Craig—nonetheless, from 1913 to 1947 it was known as the Denver & Salt Lake Railroad. It's across the street from the Craig Chamber of Commerce.

The **Museum of Northwest Colorado** (590 Yampa Ave., 970/824-6360, www.museumnwco. org, 9 A.M.–5 P.M. Mon.–Fri., 10 A.M.–4 P.M. Sat., free) is yet another Colorado museum that delves into the romantic Old West days of cowboys and outlaws, miners, and ranchers. This one's specialty is cowboy gear—chaps, saddles, spurs, guns, and other memorabilia from Bill Mackin's 50-year-old collection. Another striking artifact is the bronze statue (by Sheridan, Wyoming, artist Jerry Smiley) of local gunfighter James Robinson, whose tall hat and casual manner capture the lazy-eyed renegade spirit of those times.

The **Browns Park National Wildlife Refuge** (1318 Hwy. 318, Maybell, 970/365-3613, www.fws.gov/brownspark) is about 30 miles west of Craig, 53 miles northwest of the Maybell intersection of U.S. 40 and Highway 318, and the pretty waterfall-and-canyon area is somewhat infamous for having hid Butch Cassidy and other Wild West outlaws. The 13,455-acre area is along the Green River, and its main function today is to provide a habitat for Great Basin Canada geese and ducks. It's a great place for **bird-watching**—golden eagles and peregrine falcons occasionally fly overhead—as well as spotting antelope, bighorn sheep, and elk.

Sports and Recreation

The Yampa River is just one of the **fishing** spots (mostly pike and trout) around Craig—one good vantage point is east on U.S. 40 for seven miles. For more information on this or the Green River, Freeman Reservoir, Trappers Lake, Lake Avery, Elkhead Reservoir, or any of the other bodies of water in the area, contact the **Sportsman Information Center** (360 E. Victory Way, 970/824-3046). For fishing and hunting license and map information, try **Craig Sports** (504 W. Victory Way, 970/824-4044, www.craigsports.net).

The well-maintained, tree-filled, 18-hole **Yampa Valley Golf Course** (2179 Hwy. 394, 970/824-3673, www.yampavalleygolf.com, $25–38) doubles as a cross-country skiing zone in the winter.

Accommodations

The Holiday Inn is the primary place to stay in Craig, but some prefer to go all the way to Steamboat Springs rather than deal with a nondescript chain hotel. Campers have a better option: **Freeman Reservoir Campground** (Hwy. 13, 12 miles north of Craig, 970/824-5689, $12), which has 17 campsites, running water during some parts of the year, and easy access to many hiking and biking trails.

Food

The **Golden Cavvy** (538 Yampa Ave., 970/824-6038, 5:15–9 P.M. Mon.–Thurs., 5:15–10 P.M. Fri.–Sat., 5:15–8 P.M. Sun., $11) is a cheap, everything-on-the-menu kind of restaurant on the site of a hotel that burned down years ago (its huge fireplace remains). House specialty: fried stuff.

Information and Services

The **Moffat County Visitors Center** (360 E. Victory Way, 970/824-5689) and **Craig Chamber of Commerce** share a website at www.craig-chamber.com.

Craig has a small hospital: **The Memorial**

GRAND JUNCTION

Hospital (750 Hospital Loop, 970/824-9411, www.thememorialhospital.com).

RANGELY

Although Rangely didn't officially become a town until 1947, it has been a thoroughfare for Fremont Indians, Utes, Spanish explorers en route from Mexico to California, early American pioneers and cattle-herders, and, after World War II, so many new oilmen that they had to live in makeshift trolley cars.

The oil boom has long since died out, and Rangely's popularity has slowed to a trickle—mostly history buffs searching for Native American artifacts, off-road mountain bikers heading to the Raven Rims and other trails, coyote and elk watchers, and outdoors enthusiasts looking for a mesa or sandstone cliff. About 2,100 people live in the city, and most travelers come for the accessibility to parks and mountains.

Sights

The **Canyon Pintado National Historic District** (beginning 3 miles south of Rangely on Hwy. 139, 970/675-8477) took its name ("painted canyon" in Spanish) in 1776 when traveling missionaries discovered Native American glyphs and art on the rocks. They're pretty extraordinary—Utes and Fremonts "pecked" them onto the sides of mountains using large rocks, and some resemble hands and bowls popping out of tiny urns. Native Americans carved them between the years 600 and 1300, and the elaborate artwork distinguishes this district, which stretches roughly 15 miles along Highway 139, from the surrounding Douglas Creek Valley. Contact the **Rangely Chamber of Commerce** (209 E. Main St., 970/675-8477, www.rangely.com/rock-art.htm) to find out where all the glyphs are.

Sports and Recreation

Kenney Reservoir (Hwy. 64, five miles east of Rangely) is on the White River, directly below the 20-year-old Taylor Draw Dam. It's stocked with black crappie, channel catfish, and rainbow trout—and if you happen to catch an endangered pikeminnow, Colorado Division of

Wildlife park officials request that you throw it back immediately. **Fishing** at the reservoir requires a license, available at the **Rangely Chamber of Commerce** (209 E. Main St., 970/675-8477, www.rangely.com/fishing.htm); for fishing reports and other information, the Division of Wildlife is at 303/297-1192.

Accommodations

Super-cheap hotel chains and bargain motels are the standard in Rangely, so for lodging I'd recommend Grand Junction, about an hour's drive south. Campers can stay at the relatively new **Buck 'N' Bull RV Park & Campground** (2811 E. Main St., 970/675-8335, $30), which has hookups for electricity and water and is near Kenney Reservoir and the Canyon Pintado National Historic District.

Food

Los Tres Potrillos (302 W. Main St., 970/675-8870, 11 A.M.–9 P.M. Mon.–Sat., $10), which complements its tacos and fajitas with wall-hanging sombreros and pottery.

Information and Services

The **Town of Rangely** (209 E. Main St., 970/675-8477, www.rangely.com) has information about the town itself in addition to the dinosaur monument and other nearby activities. The **Rangely District Hospital** (970/675-5011, www.rangelyhospital.com) is at 511 South White Avenue.

DINOSAUR

Dinosaur is a tiny town with a couple of small restaurants, a large and run-down green dinosaur statue, a visitors center, and a couple of shops. It's famous mostly for its proximity to Dinosaur National Monument, a sprawling area of incredible mountain hikes and 1,500 genuine dinosaur fossil bones on the Colorado-Utah border.

The monument is not the kind of place you can pass through on a side trip from Grand Junction or Moab. The Dinosaur Quarry is on the Utah side, about a 20-minute drive from the town of Dinosaur, and completely

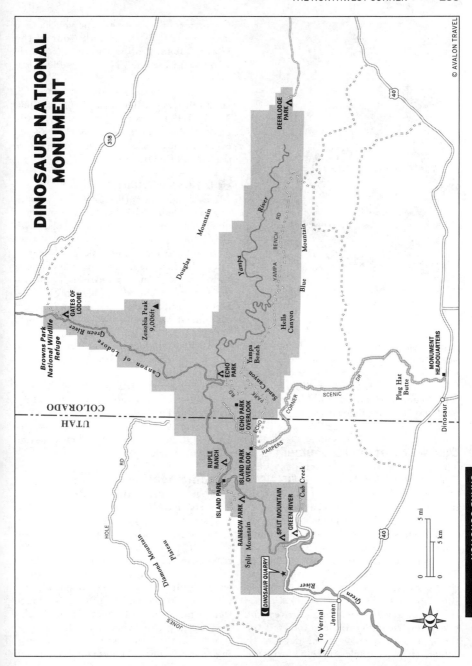

DINOSAUR NATIONAL MONUMENT

© AVALON TRAVEL

GRAND JUNCTION

318

40

COLORADO
UTAH

Browns Park
National Wildlife
Refuge

GATES OF
LODORE

Green River

Douglas

Mountain

Zenobia Peak
9,006ft

Canyon of Lodore

Yampa

River

BENCH
RD

YAMPA

Blue

Mountain

Hells
Canyon

DEERLODGE
PARK

ECHO
PARK

Yampa
Bench

Sand Canyon

PARK
RD

ECHO
PARK
OVERLOOK

ECHO

RUPLE
RANCH

ISLAND PARK
OVERLOOK

HARPERS

CORNER

SCENIC

DR

MONUMENT
HEADQUARTERS

Plug Hat
Butte

Dinosaur

ISLAND PARK

RAINBOW PARK

ISLAND PARK

SPLIT MOUNTAIN

GREEN RIVER

Cub Creek

Split Mountain

HOLE

RD

Diamond Mountain
Plateau

JONES

DINOSAUR QUARRY

Green

River

To Vernal

Jensen

40

Green

River

5 mi

5 km

0

0

© MATT INDEN/WEAVER MULTIMEDIA GROUP/COLORADO TOURISM OFFICE

Dinosaur National Monument

inaccessible during the winter. The Colorado side is mostly superb hiking and scenery, particularly trails like Echo Park Drive and the Canyon of Lodore, but the trailheads aren't immediately evident, and many visitors will need to spend some time talking to the monument's rangers.

Dinosaur National Monument

The Colorado side of Dinosaur National Monument (4545 E. U.S. 40, 970/374-3000, www.nps.gov/dino) has little to do with dinosaurs, but it's terrific for hiking, biking, and camping. The trails aren't suitable for in-and-out side trips, but the monument offers many guided tours and information for bushwhacking—try **Journey Through Time,** a 62-mile Harpers Corner Road drive that hits numerous scenic overlooks on the Blue Mountain Plateau, Echo Park, and the Yampa Bench. Some hikes, drives, and bike rides, including Ruple Point Trail and the path to Echo Park, take all day and are completely inaccessible during bad weather.

Another good tour—this one you have to take yourself—is the 11-mile **Tour of the Tilted Rocks,** leading through extremely scenic areas and a few Native American history sites.

The Colorado side's **visitors center** (U.S. 40, 2 miles east of Dinosaur, 970/374-3000, 9 A.M.–4:30 P.M. daily Memorial Day–early Oct., free) has dinosaur souvenirs plus knowledgeable employees who can help you navigate the hard-to-find trails.

Dinosaur Quarry

The Utah-side quarry (Hwy. 149, 7 miles north of Jensen, Utah, 435/781-7700, www.nps.gov/dino) is perhaps best known as "the place with all the dinosaur bones." It began in 1909, when paleontologist Earl Douglass explored northeastern Utah, came across thousands of bones, and shipped them to a Pittsburgh museum for display. Fascinated, President Woodrow Wilson named the site Dinosaur National Monument; within a few years, the National Park Service started work on the quarry. Today, more than 1,500 fossil bones are embedded in a rock layer on a wall of the quarry's visitors center; imprints of bones are visible throughout the quarry grounds. The bones belonged to 11 kinds of dinosaurs, roughly half of the species found in North America—*Stegosaurus, Dryosaurus, Allosaurus, Camptosaurus,* and others who lived roughly 150 million years ago during the Jurassic period.

Accommodations

Neither Dinosaur nor its nearest town, Rangely, have much by way of cozy hotels, so consider staying in Grand Junction to the south or Craig to the east. Sleep-on-the-ground types have six campgrounds ($8) to choose from inside Dinosaur National Monument. On the Utah side are **Green River, Split Mountain,** and **Rainbow Park;** the Colorado side has **Echo Park, Deerlodge Park,** and **Gates of Lodore.** All are in perfect locations for campers of all ages who want to sit through classes or seminars during their vacations. For more information call

GRAND JUNCTION

DINOSAURS IN COLORADO

Dinosaur Quarry, in Dinosaur National Monument, marks the area where early-20th-century paleontologist Earl Douglass discovered thousands of bones and reassembled them to determine what the 165-million-year-old monstrosities looked like. Many of the species he uncovered were traced to what is now Colorado and other Western states, including:

- **Apatosaurus:** The 34-ton, 75-foot-long, skinny-necked brontosaurus first showed up in Morrison; excavators in the National Monument found a skull from it in the early 1900s.

- **Camarasaurus:** Also known as "chamber lizard," this 35-60-ton species has a "small version" and a "large version." Both are huge and were discovered in Garden Park.

- **Diplodocus:** Discovered in Garden Park, this tall, skinny dinosaur was 75-85 feet long and weighed "only" 13 tons.

- **Stegosaurus:** Another of the best-known dinosaurs – at least to kids who read books about them and watch *The Flintstones* reruns – *Stegosaurus* was relatively small but protected itself from sharp-toothed munching with hard spines along its back. It was first found in Morrison, where Red Rocks Park houses a dinosaur exhibit today.

- **Ceratosaurus:** Also found in Garden Park, this meat-eating dinosaur had a rare horn.

For more information on these and other dinosaurs, check out Dinosaur National Monument's official website (www.nps.gov/dino).

970/374-3000 (Colorado) or 434/781-7759 (Utah), or visit www.nps.gov/dino.

Food

The **Massadona Tavern Steak House & RV Campground** (22927 E. U.S. 40, 20 miles east of Dinosaur, 970/374-2324, 4–8:30 P.M. Mon.–Fri., 11 A.M.–8:30 P.M. Sat.–Sun. $12) is one-stop shopping for many campers—the tavern has burgers and steaks, of course, and is a little hard to find. If you want a baked potato, call before 5 P.M.

B&B Family Restaurant (120 Brontosaurus Blvd., 970/374-2744, 8 A.M.–9 P.M. daily, $9) is indicative of the entire town of Dinosaur—fun but run-down, with *Flintstones*-inspired Brontoburgers and Plateosaurus steaks. (As far as I know, the meat doesn't come from actual dinosaurs, and I'm especially confident it doesn't come from Dino.)

Information

The Town of Dinosaur itself has no official online resources, but surrounding **Moffat County** information is at www.co.moffat.co.us.

GRAND JUNCTION

TELLURIDE AND THE SOUTHERN MOUNTAINS

The northern Rocky Mountains get all the press in Colorado, but the San Juans, which provide the majestic backdrops for Telluride, Ouray, Silverton, Lake City, and Pagosa Springs, are worth the long and often harrowing drives southwest from Denver. The San Juan Mountains encompass about 12,000 square miles, or roughly one-eighth of the state, and have numerous fourteener peaks, such as Uncompahgre and Wetterhorn, just northeast of Ouray. They're part of a 2-million-acre national forest filled with hiking trails and ski slopes, but they're more spread out and less compact than their northern mountain neighbors. Every time I drive through the San Juans en route to the Telluride Bluegrass Festival or an overnight in pretty Ridgway, I'm overwhelmed by the valleys, plains, small lakes, and red-and-yellow flat peaks. Certain parts have the look and feel of the Badlands in South Dakota, even though they're in a whole different world.

The San Juans, though, aren't all there is to southwest Colorado. Crested Butte is the northern tip of this region, and it has its own namesake mountain—a hulking, pyramid-shaped peak that provides some of the state's best (if most isolated) skiing. The Four Corners area, in the far southwest corner of the state, is so named because you can touch Colorado, New Mexico, Arizona, and Utah at the same time. The area's mesa-and-canyon scenery rivals the chunks of Rocky Mountains in Aspen or Vail. The Black Canyon of the Gunnison National Park, with a 12-foot-thin stretch of river visible far down a mesa cliff,

HIGHLIGHTS

◖ Redstone Castle: John Cleveland Osgood is the early-1900s coal-and-railroad magnate behind this 42-room mansion, which dominates a gem of a one-road town south of Aspen and north of Crested Butte (page 268).

◖ Bridal Veil Falls: With a funky 19th-century power station at the top, this tall waterfall is the first thing you notice upon driving into Telluride (page 279).

◖ Telluride Ski Resort: Two thousand-foot drops down the majestic San Juan Mountains, trails perfectly groomed for experts and beginners, and a free gondola make Telluride some of the best (and perhaps most underrated) skiing in the state (page 279).

◖ Ouray Ice Park: Make sure your carabiners are tight when scrambling up these massive manmade ice cliffs on the edge of a historic mining town (page 292).

◖ Black Canyon of the Gunnison National Park: Hold tight to the railing as you stare from the North or South Rim straight down mesa cliffs into a 40-foot-wide river at the bottom; only the best kayakers paddle below (page 298).

◖ Durango & Silverton Narrow Gauge Railroad: The prettiest commute in Colorado involves a two-hour, 45-mile trip from Durango to Silverton and back via 1920s-era locomotives that once hauled ore out of the San Juans (page 305).

◖ Mesa Verde National Park: Perhaps the finest ghost town in the world, the large and scenic park is home to abandoned cliff dwellings from the A.D. 1200-era Anasazi civilization (page 314).

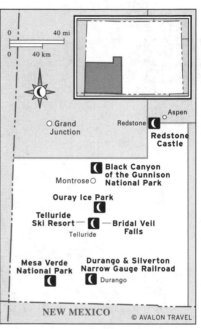

LOOK FOR ◖ TO FIND RECOMMENDED SIGHTS, ACTIVITIES, DINING, AND LODGING.

is at the edge of a spectacular park area with several reservoirs, all open for fishing and boating.

Also fascinating is the area's history. Creede, in the eastern shadow of the San Juans, is where Jesse James's killer, Bob Ford, was shot and killed, and historic gold- and silver-mining towns such as Ouray and Lake City are such serene tourist areas these days that it's easy to forget the violent mayhem that went on in the Old West. Four Corners, including Durango, Cortez, and Mesa Verde National Park, is filled with elaborate Native American ruins—in some cases, entire abandoned communities that have been carefully archaeologically preserved.

Finally, of course, there's skiing—the resorts in Telluride and Crested Butte are world-renowned, and the lesser-known hills near Durango and Pagosa Springs have the added advantage of being uncrowded. One tip: If you're driving south from Aspen, stop in tiny, touristy Redstone and have a picnic by the river.

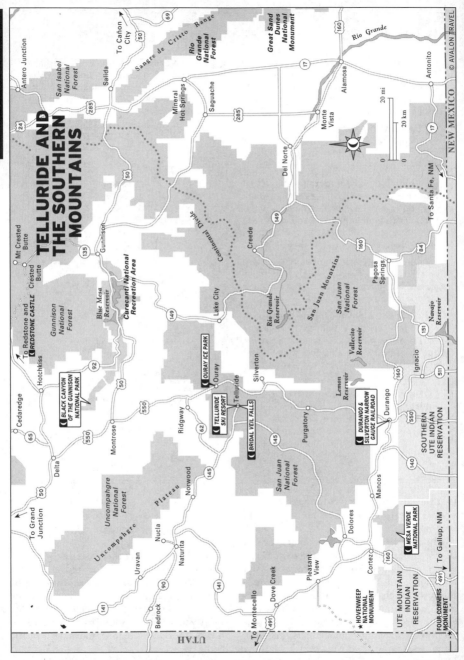

TELLURIDE AND THE SOUTHERN MOUNTAINS

© AVALON TRAVEL

PLANNING YOUR TIME

The small airports of Durango, Montrose, and Gunnison are mostly reliable, but they serve small carriers, and in nasty weather conditions it's probably best to fly into Denver International Airport. From Denver, Telluride is roughly a six-hour drive by car—the most direct route is U.S. 285 southwest to tiny Poncha Springs, then west on the super-scenic U.S. 50, which passes Monarch Pass, the Continental Divide, pretty Blue Mesa Reservoir, and the hills and valleys of Curecanti National Recreation Area (Black Canyon of the Gunnison National Park is just a short drive up Hwy. 347). From Montrose, go south on U.S. 550 through Ridgway and Ouray and follow the signs to Telluride.

To get to Crested Butte in the summer, the fastest and easiest route is I-70 west to Glenwood Springs, then south on Highways 82 and 135, the last leg of which becomes bumpy and difficult. You'll cross Kebler Pass, although it's closed in the winter, which makes Crested Butte the most isolated major ski resort in the state—to get there from Denver, the indirect route of U.S. 285 south to U.S. 50 west to Highway 135 north is one of the few good options. These are the main highlights of southwest Colorado, although pit-stop towns such as Pagosa Springs (east of Durango), Gunnison (south of Crested Butte), Cortez (near the Four Corners, west of Durango), and Redstone (along Hwy. 82 en route to Crested Butte) have their charms as well.

Crested Butte and Vicinity

"The last great ski town," as locals call it, is a relaxed little historic area that lionizes its gold-mining years just as hard-partiers are streaming down the slopes in kilts, pink-bunny costumes, or no clothes at all. It's one of Colorado's most beloved ski resorts, but it's hard to get to, especially when ski conditions are best—heavy snowfall can close Kebler Pass, 110 miles south of Aspen along Highway 135, forcing travelers to use the longer unpaved Highways 82 or 133 or other tricky roads.

Like Aspen and Telluride, Crested Butte has turned into a bit of a rich person's playground over the past few years, and the gap between homeowners and ski bums stands to get wider with the Muellers' high-class upgrades. Crested Butte actually refers to two separate areas, connected by shuttle bus—the pastel-colored, Victorian-lined 1880s mountain town that has the feel of a funkier Breckenridge or Steamboat Springs, and the 40-plus-year-old ski resort two miles uphill that's officially known as Mount Crested Butte.

The town's personality remains far different from hoity-toity Aspen and hippie-swamped Telluride—in addition to naked skiers, Crested Butte is a magnet for extreme sports

and mountain bikers. The resort plays host to the **Winter X Games,** the **U.S. Extreme Freeskiing Championships,** and the **U.S. Extreme Boarderfest,** among others, and even in a state renowned for its mountain biking, Crested Butte is consistently where all the cyclists go. You can ride 40 miles up Pearl Pass to 12,700 feet in elevation on a Saturday and visit the Mountain Bike Hall of Fame & Museum on a Sunday. Just bring lots of water.

HISTORY

When miners discovered $350,000 worth of gold in Washington Gulch, Crested Butte shifted from a roaming ground for Utes, explorers, and fur traders to a key stopover for frantic wealth-seekers. This was in the 1860s, and areas such as Washington and Armstrong Gulches, Crystal River, and Gold Creek produced millions of dollars for gold-panners. Prosperity led to colonization: In 1874, Sylvester Richardson founded the Gunnison agricultural colony, which evolved into Gunnison County, a big ranching area.

The gold boom led to a silver boom in the 1870s and 1880s, and 25,000–40,000 people streamed into town, followed by two

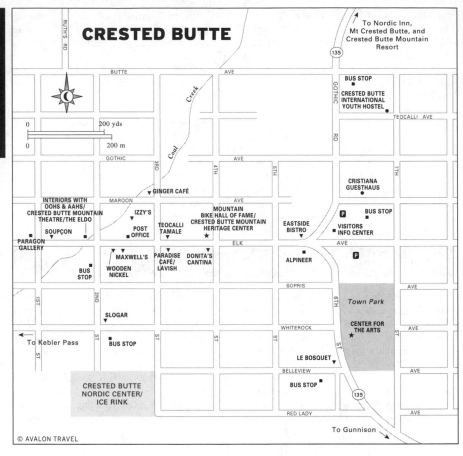

CRESTED BUTTE

To Nordic Inn, Mt Crested Butte, and Crested Butte Mountain Resort

BUS STOP
CRESTED BUTTE INTERNATIONAL YOUTH HOSTEL

GINGER CAFÉ

CRISTIANA GUESTHAUS

INTERIORS WITH OOHS & AAHS/
CRESTED BUTTE MOUNTAIN THEATRE/THE ELDO

IZZY'S

MOUNTAIN BIKE HALL OF FAME/ CRESTED BUTTE MOUNTAIN HERITAGE CENTER ★

BUS STOP

EASTSIDE BISTRO

VISITORS INFO CENTER

SOUPÇON

POST OFFICE

TEOCALLI TAMALE

PARAGON GALLERY

MAXWELL'S

PARADISE CAFÉ/ LAVISH

DONITA'S CANTINA

ALPINEER

WOODEN NICKEL

BUS STOP

SLOGAR

SOPRIS AVE

Town Park

CENTER FOR THE ARTS ★

WHITEROCK AVE

To Kebler Pass

BUS STOP

LE BOSQUET

BELLEVIEW AVE

BUS STOP

CRESTED BUTTE NORDIC CENTER/ ICE RINK

RED LADY AVE

To Gunnison

© AVALON TRAVEL

200 yds
200 m

narrow-gauge railroads and mining camps of some 3,500 people each. The silver industry went bust in 1893, but Crested Butte and its mountain-valley neighbor, Gunnison, survived into the 1950s thanks to their resources of cows and coal. The Mount Crested Butte ski area opened in the early 1960s, ensuring the town would continue to thrive, even without gold and silver.

SIGHTS

The town of Crested Butte is about three miles from the mountain and resort village, and it's worth visiting, particularly in the summer when the crowds aren't quite so intense. The village is a lovingly preserved National Historic District of colorful Victorian buildings, some of which have retained their identities as saloons and banks. Wandering downtown is a great way to kill a lazy summer Saturday, and the large park along 6th Street often has live music and kids events.

Mountain Bike Hall of Fame & Museum

The best part of the **Mountain Bike Hall of Fame & Museum** (331 Elk Ave., 970/349-6817, www.mtnbikehalloffame.com, noon–6 P.M.

© GUNNISON-CRESTED BUTTE TOURISM ASSOCIATION

Crested Butte

daily winter, 10 A.M.–8 P.M. daily summer, closed off-season, $3 donation) is the old photos showing how the bikes themselves have evolved—from the rubber hose that veterinary surgeon John B. Dunlop attached to his son's bike in 1887 to the V-shaped handlebars of the 1974 Cupertino riders to the sleeker, more engineered rides of today. Located inside the free **Crested Butte Mountain Heritage Museum,** the Mountain Bike section is as important to cyclists as Vail's Colorado Ski Museum is to downhillers.

SPORTS AND RECREATION
Downhill Skiing

Although 12,162-foot-high **Crested Butte Mountain Resort** (12 Snowmass Rd., 800/810-7669, www.skicb.com) has allowed itself to get a little run-down in recent years, pushing ski traffic to other resorts, its new owners are aggressively renovating the place— and emphasizing beginner and intermediate runs, although the area is famous for its intimidating peaks, advanced and expert terrain,

and friendliness toward snowboarders and extreme-sports aficionados. A new base village, Mountaineer Square, is in the works, with 93 planned residences, a spa, and a convention center, and co-owner Tim Mueller tells *Ski:* "There's been an overemphasis on the extreme. We also have good beginner and intermediate terrain. Crested Butte should be marketed more as a family place."

But first, something for the experienced thrill-riders: Extreme Limits, 583 acres of deliberately ungroomed, incredibly steep trails with trees that seem to block every turn. And that's just the bowls that are open to the public. For events such as the U.S. Extreme Freeskiing Championships (early Mar.), mountain officials open routes like The Hourglass and Catch and Release, filled with sharp rocks and unexpected twists. Most of the double-diamond runs are at the top—take the Twister Lift to the High Lift. Also at the resort are a 400-foot-long, 17-foot-deep superpipe and three terrain parks, including the beginner-focused **Painter Boy** and the more expert-oriented **Cascade.**

For skiers who prefer more humane terrain, the Keystone lift gives access to gentle runs such as Poverty Gulch and Mineral Point; toward the bottom, Houston is easy to find and ride for kids. Both the Paradise and Teocalli lifts lead to intermediate runs—the former with long chutes like Forest Queen and Canaan leading to the East River area, the latter into the half-pipe. Overall, the resort's 1,058 acres of ski trails break down to 15 percent for beginners, 44 percent intermediate, and 41 percent advanced and expert. Lift tickets are roughly $90, depending on the time of year.

Crested Butte's **Ski & Ride School** (Gothic Center, 800/544-8448, www.skicb.com/cbmr/mountain/lessons.aspx) gives lessons for all ages but is especially good for kids ages 3–16. Group workshops are roughly $90 for a half day, and, as with all ski areas, private lessons are considerably more expensive. The resort has on-site ski rental at the Gothic Center (888/280-5728), but **Crested Butte Sports Ski & Bike Shop** (35 Emmons Rd., 970/349-7516 or 800/970-9704, www.crestedbuttesports.com) is also a good option.

Cross-Country Skiing

With gigantic wilderness areas sprawled in every direction—Maroon Bells–Snowmass, the Raggeds, and Collegiate Peaks—Crested Butte's backcountry skiing opportunities are just about unlimited if you're careful. Among them: **Slate River Gulch,** about 4.5 miles from the Gothic Road exit off Highway 135, leading two miles from Nicholson Lake (at 8,920 feet) to Oh-Be-Joyful (9,100 feet); **Washington Gulch,** about 2.6 miles from the same Gothic Road exit, which passes empty valleys and tree-filled mountaintops, including Anthracite Mesa, White Rock Mountain, and the breathtaking Snodgrass Mountain; and **Ditch Road,** south of town on Highway 135, off Forest Road 738 near Brush Creek Road, a less-strenuous route near some pretty ranch country. Note that avalanches aren't common, but they've been known to happen in these parts. The **Alpineer** (419 6th St., 970/349-5210, www.alpineer.com) rents equipment and

can answer most questions about weather conditions and routes.

The **Crested Butte Nordic Center** (620 2nd St., 970/349-1707, www.cbnordic.org) maintains a 15–20-mile network of groomed tracks that go through the town's historic area, along the East River, and through forests and recreation paths. It also sponsors guided tours, nighttime ski parties, and a four-mile hike to the Forest Queen Hut in Gothic. You can rent equipment here too.

Hut-to-hut skiing isn't as formal here as it is, say, in Telluride or Aspen, but **Adventures to the Edge** (970/209-3980, www.swissmountainguide.com) leads trips to the Elkton Huts, above Gothic Mountain and Elkton Ridge, a path that includes a steep drop into a ravine and a difficult climb. The owner-guide, Jean Pavillard, is based in Crested Butte, but does most of his business online and has no storefront in town. **Crested Butte Mountain Guides** (Elk Ave., 970/349-5430, www.crestedbutteguides.com), in a small log cabin behind the post office, does guided three-mile trips to the Forest Queen Hut in nearby Gothic, and the route is far easier, with incredible views of the Maroon Bells–Snowmass Wilderness and Gothic Mountain.

Hiking

It's easy to find hiking in Crested Butte; visit Crested Butte's backcountry-skiing trails—Maroon Bells–Snowmass, the Raggeds, and Collegiate Peaks—in the summer and start walking. And there are tons of trails beyond that, from the **Upper Loop Trail,** an easy 3.4-mile walk southeast of Mount Crested Butte on Hunter Hill Road through aspens and meadows to the difficult-but-beautiful **Crested Butte Summit Trail,** which begins at the resort visitors parking area and leads through tall trees and choppy tundra. **Judd Falls** goes two miles from the Gothic Campground, on the north side of town, and the Silver Queen chairlift provides access to numerous trails filled with skiers and boarders during the winter. **Green Lake** is a scenic and steep nine-mile (round-trip) walk with a reward at the end: a high alpine lake with great fishing. To find it, go to the Crested Butte Nordic Center (620 2nd St.) and follow the well-marked signs for Green Lake. Trail runners follow this route every July during the annual "Grin and Bear It" event.

Lower Loop and Upper Loop trails are the perfect way to work off dinner, as they're next to many of Crested Butte's visitors condos. To get there, go north on 1st Street, then west on Butte Avenue, which turns into Peanut Lake Road; park along the fence before Peanut Mine, and the trailhead is across the road from the mine. The lower loop is an easy two-mile hike appropriate for kids and families. If you want to make it a longer jaunt, add the Upper Loop.

And watch for wildflowers, particularly in mid-July, when the **Crested Butte Wildflower Festival** (818 Red Lady Ave., 970/349-2571, www.crestedbuttewildflowerfestival.com) guides more than 100 different hikes ($40–70 each) throughout the area, usually during the festival—botanists are generally the leaders, and the slots tend to fill up quickly.

Mountain Biking

Some say Crested Butte tinkerers came up with the original mountain bike, and while that's impossible to verify, it's easy to observe the unusually high bike-to-car ratio and conclude that this is the mountain-biking capital of the world, or at least of Colorado. Rides are everywhere. On a recent summer driving trip down County Road 12, over **Kebler Pass**—which my three-year-old daughter nicknamed the "Bumpy Cow Road" due to its washboard bumps and cows grazing in the middle of the dirt road—we passed at least half a dozen huffing-and-puffing cyclists. It's a challenging, spectacular ride if you're in shape.

Perhaps the most famous local ride is **Pearl Pass**, site of the annual "Klunker Tour" that began in 1976 when a group of crazed riders took makeshift bikes with fat tires, pedals, a chain, and handlebars up this 40-mile pass from Crested Butte to Aspen. The trail continues to attract cyclists by the dozen—albeit with more sophisticated rides—and most even make it, although the top altitude of 12,700 feet is nothing to take lightly. It's open to cars too.

Check out the **Mountain Bike Hall of Fame** website (www.mtnbikehalloffame.com) for descriptions of more than a dozen bike trails, including **Deer Creek,** a steep, almost-18-mile ride beginning in nearby Gothic and weaving through meadows and cow paths straight into Mount Crested Butte, and the wildflower-filled **Teocalli Ridge,** which begins two miles south of Crested Butte on Brush Creek Road and climbs up Teocalli Mountain into Middle Brush Creek. There are a couple of ways to reach the Deer Creek trail (fans prefer it because it's open to bikes only—no motorcycles or ATVs). If you start riding in Gothic, veer left at the intersection of Deer Creek Road and West Brush Creek Road and take it all the way to the Teocalli Ridge Trail. Teocalli is known for its glorious wildflowers. You'll have to work for those views, though, because the 25-mile trail rises 2,200 vertical feet.

Other popular Crested Butte bike trails include **401 Trail Loop,** which many local mountain-bikers call the best trail in Colorado. How can you beat views of the Maroon Bells to the east, and colorful wildflowers that tickle your ankles as you zoom through scenic aspen meadows? This 14-mile intermediate-to-advanced trail finishes with a downhill section into the parking lot. To get here, take Gothic Road 4.5 miles to Schofield Pass, then veer right onto Trail 401's well-maintained single track. Check with the **U.S. Forest Service** (970/641-0471) to make sure a pile of snow won't clog up your brand-new nubby tires. Sometimes the snow pack sticks around until July 4. The **Crested Butte Mountain Bike Association** (970/355-9582, www.cbmba.org) offers up-to-date weather-condition reports.

Lower Loop, 2.5 miles, has an easier grade for beginners. It's close to town and overlooks Crested Butte. Half of the Lower Loop is accessible for wheelchair users. To find it, go north on 1st Street, then west on Butte Avenue, which turns into Peanut Lake Road; park along the fence. The trailhead is across the road from Peanut Mine.

Strand Hill Trail, a 17-mile (round-trip) adventure with a 1,500-foot elevation gain, has a tough creek crossing: Water can be waist high during wet years. To find the trailhead, go south on Highway 135 to Brush Creek Road. Travel east about four miles, and then take the dirt road on the right. When the road comes to a T, veer left to find the trail.

Many local hotels rent bikes, as does **Crested Butte Sports** (35 Emmons Rd., 970/349-7516 or 800/970-9704, www.crestedbuttesports.com) and the **Alpineer** (419 6th St., 970/349-5210, www.alpineer.com). **Crested Butte Mountain Guides** (970/349-5430, www.crestedbutteguides.com) offers guided tours (some from vans) to trails long and short, easy and hard. And for mountain-biking events, you can't beat late June's **Crested Butte Bike Week** (970/349-5430, www.ftbw.com), which is all about the riding, the tricks, and the partying; reggae legends Toots and the Maytals performed here in 2011.

Fishing

With trout wiggling through the nearby Taylor, Gunnison, and East Rivers, Crested Butte is a surprisingly excellent place for fly-fishing. For reports on conditions and other basic information, visit the Gunnison–Crested Butte Vacations website (www.gunnisoncrestedbutte.com); for equipment, maps, and tour guides, **Three Rivers Resort & Outfitting** (130 County Rd. 742, Almont, 9707/641-1303 or 888/761-3474, www.3riversresort.com) is one of several reliable and knowledgeable local shops.

Camping

The backcountry **Gothic Valley** bursts into bloom—with columbine, lupine, and daisies—during July. To get here, drive from town to the ski area, and then keep going north to the town of Gothic. Look for a campground a couple of miles beyond Schofield Pass. At an elevation of 9,600 feet, it's tiny and straightforward, with just four sites, including toilets and trash cans

but not much else. The Copper Lakes Trail and Judd Falls are other good areas in the Gothic Valley to view the wildflowers.

Golf

The centerpiece of **The Club at Crested Butte** (385 Country Club Dr., 970/349-6127 or 800/628-5496, www.theclubatcrestedbutte.com, $75–135) is a Robert Trent Jones Jr.–designed course—but it also has tennis courts, a swimming pool, a spa, and a high-class restaurant. If you can afford to be a member, you can't beat the views.

ENTERTAINMENT AND EVENTS

Most of the town's numerous outdoor festivals—including the late-July **Crested Butte Music Festival,** the **Tour de Forks** in July–August, and a weekly film series—are arranged through the **Crested Butte Center for the Arts** (606 6th St., 970/349-7487, www.crestedbuttearts.org). The center puts on art exhibits, plays, concerts, and speakers.

The nonprofit **Crested Butte Mountain Theatre** (403 2nd St., 970/349-0366, www.cbmountaintheatre.org) puts on dramas, musicals, and comedies all year, from *Footloose* to *Charlie Cox Runs with Scissors.*

A number of bars have lively happy hours, including **Lobar Restaurant and Lounge** (303 Elk Ave., 970/349-0480, www.thelobar.com, 5:30 P.M.–close daily), which has sushi, Thursday karaoke night, and live jazz on Sunday; and the **Wooden Nickel** (222 Elk Ave., 970/349-6350, 4 P.M.–close daily) steakhouse. For live music on top of cheap booze, **The Eldo** (215 Elk Ave., 970/349-6125, http://eldobrewpub.com, 3 P.M.–2 A.M. daily) is a microbrewery that snags many of the reggae, bluegrass, folk, and jam bands when they come through town; the sign out front says, "A sunny place for shady people." Over in the mountain village, the **Trackers Bar and Lounge** (620 Gothic Rd., Mt. Crested Butte, 970/349-4228, hours vary) has an area for live music and is where many skiers begin partying before shambling closer to town as the night goes on.

SHOPPING

Crested Butte's shopping is on par with Breckenridge or Steamboat Springs—lots of little shops, most geared toward visitors. The gold and diamond rings, necklaces, and bracelets are of surprisingly elegant quality given the ramshackle Old West look of the **Ice Mountain Jewelry** (311 6th St., 970/349-6331 or 800/863-2375, www.icemountainjewelry.net, 10 A.M.–5 P.M. Mon.–Sat.) building downtown. The **Paragon Gallery** (132 Elk Ave., 970/349-6484, http://paragongallery. org, 10 A.M.–7 P.M. daily) is a local artists' co-op that has in recent years displayed Jim P. Garrison's photography, Bren Corn's jittery, colorful paintings of people, and others.

On the clothing front, **Lavish** (234 Elk Ave., 970/349-1077, www.lavishcb.com, 10 A.M.–8 P.M. daily, reduced hours off-season) stocks funky, high-end stuff for women—Skagen watches, Maxx handbags, Hilary Druxman jewelry, and the like. **Interiors with Oohs & Aahs** (326 Elk Ave., 970/349-0303, www.interiors-oohsandaahs.com, 10 A.M.–6 P.M. Mon.–Fri., 10 A.M.–4 P.M. Sat.) specializes in large antique furniture—all very comfortable (we sat on some of it)—and various Western knickknacks.

ACCOMMODATIONS

As with most Colorado ski towns, condominiums are often more affordable than hotels—especially if you want to do your own cooking or stay with a large group. The listings at the community website **Visit Crested Butte** (www.visitcrestedbutte.com/condominiums) are up-to-date and reliable.

$100-150

The family-owned **Nordic Inn** (14 Treasury Rd., 970/349-5542 or 800/542-7669, www.nordicinncb.com, $113–155) is a homey, European-style ski-village lodge with large guest rooms and an outdoor hot tub. The room rates reflect a deliberate lack of frills.

The **Cristiana Guesthaus** (621 Maroon Ave., 800/824-7899, www.cristianaguesthaus.com, $105–120) is the same idea as the Nordic Inn—family-owned, small, wooden, European-style, strategic location down the street from the ski-resort shuttle—but a step down in elegance. It does have a sundeck, sauna, large lobby fireplace, and continental breakfast included.

Eight miles south of town, the **Pioneer Guest Cabins** (2094 Cement Creek Rd., 970/349-5517, www.pioneerguestcabins.com, $119–171) is a collection of eight streamside 1930s-era log cabins in Gunnison National Forest. The smartly decorated cabins use the soothing wood floors and staircases to their advantage, and while staying in one of the four historic cottages is a little like camping in the woods, the four mountain cabins are more luxurious than rustic.

$150-200

The ski resort's **Grand Lodge Resort & Suites** (6 Emmons Loop, 800/810-7669, www.skicb.com/cbmr/grand-lodge.aspx, $165–175) is perhaps the easiest place in town to find a room during heavy season, with 246 guest rooms, including 105 suites. When my family visited, we found the guest rooms to be large and comfortable, the staff friendly, the amenities thorough (including an indoor-outdoor pool), and the views gorgeous, but the hotel lacks a bit in personality.

The **Lodge at Mountaineer Square** (620 Gothic Rd., Mt. Crested Butte, 800/810-7669, www.skicb.com/cbmr/lodging/mountaineer-square-lodge/mountaineer-amenities. aspx, $185–325), part of the huge, recently built conference facility Mountaineer Square, has 95 guest rooms of all sizes, plus an indoor-outdoor pool and a hot tub, and a convenient mountain-village location near shops and restaurants. It's also run by the ski resort.

$200-300

In 2006, **Elevation Hotel & Spa** (500 Gothic Rd., Mt. Crested Butte, 800/810-7669, www.skicb.com/cbmr/elevation-hotel-and-spa.aspx, $229–269) surprised locals by replacing the Club Med, which had upgraded with a $6 million renovation. Run by the ski resort,

Elevation is more streamlined and business traveler–oriented and less kid-friendly, with a mixture of elegant and modern suites and large guest rooms. Most of the guest rooms have outdoor balconies, small kitchens, and fireplaces.

FOOD
Snacks, Cafés, and Breakfast
In business since the late 1980s, **Paradise Café** (303 Elk Ave., 970/349-6233, http://paradisecafecrestedbutte.com, 7–11 A.M. and 11:30 A.M.–3 P.M. Mon.–Sat., 7:30 A.M.–noon Sun., $6) specializes in standard breakfast dishes—burritos, skillets, pancakes, French toast, and so forth. Its lunchtime deli sandwiches, burgers, and soups are almost as captivating. Serving excellent deli sandwiches on homemade bread, **Izzy's** (Elk Ave., behind the post office, 970/349-5630, 7 A.M.–2 P.M. Wed.–Sun., $8) is well known for its dessert crepes, homemade bagels, muffins, and cookies.

Casual
In an 1882 building that ran as a saloon during the coal-mining boom, the refurbished **Slogar** (2nd St. and Whiterock St., 970/349-5765, 5–9 P.M. daily, $16) is a local comfort-food fixture serving skillet-fried chicken, biscuits, coleslaw, mashed potatoes, and steaks.

Formerly the Buffalo Grille & Saloon, **Eastside Bistro** (435 6th St., 970/349-9699, www.eastsidebistro.com, 5–10 P.M. Mon.–Fri., 10 A.M.–2 P.M. and 5–10 P.M. Sat.–Sun., $30) doesn't have quite as much buffalo left on its menu, aside from the occasional buffalo rib eye—but plenty of high-class dinners like the halibut with summer succotash.

Teocalli Tamale (311½ Elk Ave., 970/349-2005, www.teocallitamale.net, 11 A.M.–9 P.M. daily, $9) is a burrito bar in a small pink-and-purple building with benches out front. Take one to go and stroll on Elk Avenue.

Don't let the hideously bright-colored facade scare you off: **Donita's Cantina** (330 Elk Ave., 970/349-6674, www.donitascantina.com, 5:30–9 P.M. daily, $14) is a loud and usually packed Mexican restaurant that has great salsa, fajitas, and $2 margaritas.

The light-green **Ginger Café** (311 3rd Ave., 970/349-7291, 11 A.M.–10 P.M. daily, $11) has the look of a tiny one-room Asian restaurant, but many of its dishes have a surprising Indian feel—I had a great spicy mixture of grilled chicken, peppers, and onions.

On the mountain are the **Paradise Warming House** (base of Paradise lift, 970/349-2274, www.skicb.com) and the **Butte 66 BBQ Roadhouse** (Treasury Center, base of the ski area, 970/349-2999, www.skicb.com, 11 A.M.–6 P.M. daily)—both open only in winter.

Upscale
At the base of the Twister chairlift—an elevation of about 10,500 feet—the **Ice Bar at Uley's Cabin** (lunch 970/349-2275, dinner 970/349-4554, 9 A.M.–5 P.M. daily winter, $25) is an intimate après-ski eatery that serves decent high-end dishes like blue-corn chiles rellenos stuffed with mesquite-smoked rainbow trout. The outdoor deck is the best drinking spot on the mountain.

Brooklyn-born chef Scott Greene may have picked a corny name for the log-cabin 【 **Soupçon** (127 Elk Ave., 970/349-5448, www.soupconrestaurant.com, dinner seatings 6 P.M. and 8:15 P.M. daily, $39), but he did cook with Charlie Trotter in Chicago, so diners should give him a pass. Other reasons to do so: pistachio-crusted pheasant breast ($28), a marinated Sonoma quail entrée ($11), and dishes like foie gras and frog legs.

Maxwell's (226 Elk Ave., 970/349-1221, www.maxwellscb.com, 11 A.M.–10 P.M. daily, $30) is a downtown steakhouse with some nice additional touches—a huge wine list, buffalo burgers, goat-cheese croquettes, and chicken and fish alternatives.

Le Bosquet (6th St. and Belleview Ave., 970/349-5808, 5:30–9 P.M. daily, $30) is a French-tinged family restaurant that has operated in Crested Butte since 1976—with nothing extreme on the menu, just rack of lamb, hazelnut chicken, salads, soups, and the like.

INFORMATION AND SERVICES

The **Crested Butte Mountain Resort** (12 Snowmass Rd., 970/349-2222 or 800/810-7669, www.skicb.com) maintains weather reports, ski conditions, and a trove of dining, lodging, and nightlife information on its website; the phone operators are fairly helpful too. Also informative are the **Gunnison-Crested Butte Tourism Association** (202 E. Georgia Ave., Suite B, Gunnison, 800/814-7988, www.gunnisoncrestedbutte.com), **Visit Crested Butte** (www.visitcrestedbutte.com) and the **Crested Butte-Mount Crested Butte Chamber of Commerce** (601 Elk Ave., 970/349-6438, www.cbchamber.com). The **Town of Crested Butte** (507 Maroon Ave., 970/349-5338, www.townofcrestedbutte.com) has general information about local services and emergencies. The local daily is the *Crested Butte News* (www.crestedbuttenews.com).

The **Gunnison Valley Health System** (711 N. Taylor St., Gunnison, 970/641-1456, www.gvh-colorado.org) is a hospital complex based in Gunnison, but it covers Crested Butte and surrounding areas as well.

GETTING THERE AND AROUND

Crested Butte is one of the more difficult ski resorts to reach in Colorado, as the easiest driving route—over Kebler Pass Road, south from Aspen along Highway 135—is closed after the first fall snowstorm. That leaves the southern entrance into town—coming in from the opposite direction, north on Highway 135. This approach adds at least an hour, especially in snowy weather, as drivers from Denver have to take U.S. 285 rather than the much faster I-70, then head west on U.S. 50. No matter how Crested Butte residents try to spin it, the town is a huge pain to reach during ski season.

These winter realities aside, the easiest way to get to Crested Butte from out of state remains flying into Denver International Airport, renting a car (or taking a shuttle), and driving in. But connecting flights from Denver to **Gunnison-Crested Butte Regional Airport** (711 W. Rio Grande Ave., Gunnison, 970/641-2304), including United Express and other major carriers, are convenient much of the year. The regional airport also has most major car rental agencies, including Hertz and Dollar.

The free **Mountain Express** (970/349-5616, www.mtnexp.org, 7:35 A.M.–11:50 P.M. daily, reduced hours off-season) is a brightly painted bus that runs among the town, the ski resort, and various condominium locations all day and most of the night.

REDSTONE

Built as a coal-mining area in the late 1800s, serving the regional railroads, Redstone has since transformed into a charming little artist-and-tourist hot spot with a beatific park next to the Crystal River. The town is basically one long block, Redstone Boulevard, with the tourist-trap castle and historic inn on one end and a campground on the other. The boulevard runs along the river, and quaint structures like the one-room museum, the general store, and the Highline Foot Bridge are at the center of town.

Sights

You're definitely in Redstone once you see the cave-like **Coke Ovens** on the west side of Highway 133. The Colorado Fuel and Iron Co.'s John Cleveland Osgood constructed these large beehive pod structures in the 1890s, which gave him the ingredients for the Crystal River Railroad, transporting the coke from Carbondale to Pueblo. This area boomed in the mining years, but neither the ovens nor the railroad have been in business here for decades.

Once Colorado's third-largest industrial town, **Marble** (Marble Tourism Association, 201 E. Marble St., Suite B, 970/987-2870, www.marbletourismassociation.org) is today a ghost town about 17 miles south of Aspen where workers once extracted precious building materials from the Colorado Yule Marble Quarry and sent them to the Lincoln Memorial in Washington, D.C., and elsewhere. After the **Crystal Mill** closed in the mid-1900s, the workers took off, even though the mill still stands (and is frequently photographed) about eight miles east of the old town, accessible only via 4WD vehicle. Today, Marble is a quiet and picturesque area amid numerous hiking trails, rivers, and some of the best Rocky Mountain scenery in the state.

At the center of Redstone is the **Redstone Museum,** a one-room log cabin that has no phone number or even staff members but includes some artifacts in glass cases—like a Redstone Band bass drum, 20th-century letters, and silverware and plates from the old Big Horn Inn.

C Redstone Castle

John C. Osgood built this 42-room mansion (58 Redstone Blvd., 970/963-9656, www.redstonecastle.us, tours 1:30 P.M. daily Memorial Day–Labor Day, 1:30 P.M. Fri.–Mon. Labor Day–Memorial Day, $15) for $2.5 million in 1902. Known as Cleveholm Manor at the time, it was one of the most lavish and beautiful estates in the state, and his list of celebrity guests included Teddy Roosevelt, John D. Rockefeller, and Buffalo Bill. It sits on 150 acres, with red roofs on all the towers, as well as a carriage house, a barn, and other buildings. Inside the castle itself are high-class touches (even for today) such as Persian rugs and Tiffany lamps.

Sports and Recreation

Nestled between world-renowned ski areas such as Crested Butte, Aspen, and Snowmass, Redstone doesn't even bother competing with its own facilities. Instead, the town is perfect for **horseback riding. Avalanche Outfitters** (17843 Hwy. 133, 970/963-1144, www.redstonestables.com) provides guided trail rides ($50 per hour). Sleigh-ride tours are available in the winter. The **Mount Sopris Nordic Council** (www.springgulch.org), in nearby Carbondale, is a great resource for area cross-country skiing trails.

Shopping

One thing Redstone has is lots of galleries and knickknack shops. My then-three-year-old daughter loved the teddy bear–filled **Wild Horse Enterprises** (0306 Redstone Blvd., 970/963-8100, 10 A.M.–6 P.M. daily, mostly closed in winter), a friendly tourist-type store filled with jewelry, antiques, and scratched musical records. (I picked up a 1950s gem called *Music for Private Eyes* by somebody named Ralph Marterie and his Marlboro Men.)

Accommodations

Another John C. Osgood construction, the C **Redstone Inn** (82 Redstone Blvd., 970/963-2526, www.redstoneinn.com, $75–160) was originally a 20-room building that housed workers in the local coal mines and railroads. After Osgood lost his company in a stock war and the mines and ovens closed, he returned, a chastened man, and spent the rest of his life renovating this property. Today, the red-roofed inn has the elaborate Old West charm of the Hotel Colorado in nearby Glenwood Springs; there's a first-floor dining room overlooking a pool, a stately wooden staircase, chandeliers and period wallpaper, and friendly employees.

Food

The **Redstone General Store** (292 Redstone Blvd., 970/963-3126, www.redstonegeneralstoreonline.com, 9 A.M.–6 P.M. daily), at the center of town, sells snacks and ice cream to go with expensive gas—which has been a problem for Redstone tourism in the era of $4-plus per gallon. But aside from the store and the **Crystal Club Café** (467 Redstone Blvd., 970/963-9515, usually 4:30–9:30 P.M. Wed., 11:30 A.M.–9:30 P.M. Thurs.–Mon., $16)—which offers soup, pizza, and sandwiches—it's hard to find a decent meal on Redstone Boulevard. It's best to stock up in nearby Carbondale, about 20 miles north, or go all the way to Aspen or Crested Butte.

Information

Redstone's official community website is at www.redstonecolorado.com; its community association (303 Redstone Blvd.) has no phone number.

GUNNISON

If a helicopter dropped you into the center of Gunnison, you might wonder why anybody visits this 5,300-resident town at all. Aside from a few nice shops, a decent arts-and-theater center, a small college, and a few homey places to eat breakfast and lunch, there's really nothing here. But drive (or bike) a few miles in any direction and you'll see why so many people visit this town—it's less than 30 miles south of Crested Butte, just east of the breathtaking Curecanti National Recreation Area and at the meeting point of the Gunnison River and Tomichi Creek. As a result, visitors flood the local Comfort Inn and other chains.

In nice weather, plan to fight for hotel space and wait in line for Sunday-morning breakfast as hunters, fishers, cyclists, and other outdoors lovers have long since realized that this is a far cheaper alternative to staying in Crested Butte or Telluride. Other than that, Gunnison is basically a small, pleasant ranching town where the Utes hunted and fished more than 150 years ago. Its most obvious landmark is a giant white "W" (for the local Western State College) on the side of Tenderfoot Mountain, a chunk of hill overlooking the city to the east.

Sights

Although it looks a little ramshackle from the outside, the **Pioneer Museum** (803 E. Tomichi Ave., 970/641-4530, www.gunnisoncrestedbutte.com/activity/pioneer-museum, 9 A.M.–5 P.M. Mon.–Sat., 11 A.M.–5 P.M. Sun. Memorial Day–Sept., $7) is a well-maintained and surprisingly elaborate complex of 1800s buildings and artifacts, including a bright yellow narrow-gauge train engine, an original post office, and various arrowheads, dolls, and toys. Ask for directions to **Aberdeen Quarry,** on Beaver Creek a few miles south of town, which supplied granite for the Colorado State Capitol building.

Sports and Recreation

The **Dos Rios Golf Club** (501 Camino del Rio, 970/641-1482, $70), about 1.5 miles west of Gunnison on U.S. 50, has 18 holes and a restaurant.

downtown Gunnison in summer

Curecanti National Recreation Area

The first time I took U.S. 285 to U.S. 50 from Denver to Telluride—I had driven I-70 on previous trips—I was unprepared for the majesty of Curecanti National Recreation Area (102 Elk Creek, U.S. 50 between Gunnison and Montrose, 970/641-2337, www.nps.gov/cure), a collection of three dark-blue reservoirs underneath yellow-and-pink mesas and canyons that rival South Dakota's Badlands.

In addition to being a massive fishery of kokanee salmon, the 26-mile-long **Blue Mesa Reservoir** is the largest body of water in the state. Created by the 390-foot Blue Mesa Dam in 1965, the reservoir is Utopia for fishing enthusiasts, with perch, white sucker, and trout of all kinds to go with the salmon. The reservoir has two marinas catering to anglers and sailors: **Elk Creek** (on Blue Mesa Reservoir, 15 miles west of Gunnison, 970/641-0707, www.bluemesares.com, May–Sept.) and the smaller **Lake Fork** (on Blue Mesa Reservoir, 15 miles west of Gunnison, 970/641-0707, www.bluemesares.com, May–Sept.). Both rent pontoons ($55–60 per hour) and fishing boats ($20 per hour) and provide guiding fishing tours ($325 for up to 4 people for 4 hours). Both have gift shops, but Elk Creek is the only one with a restaurant (**Pappy's**, 970/641-0707, breakfast daily, lunch and dinner Mon.–Fri., $9) and boat-repair facilities. Blue Mesa is also

the best of the three Curecanti reservoirs for ice-fishing—particularly at Iola Basin, accessible along U.S. 50 driving west from Gunnison into the area.

Morrow Point Reservoir is for slightly more adventurous hikers and paddlers. To get here, locate the Pine Creek Trail, one mile west of the U.S. 50/Highway 92 junction and up a steep road. Then climb down 232 steps—the hard part is getting back up!—and plop your canoe or kayak into the river. The 12-mile-long reservoir begins with fast rapids but calms down quickly, allowing paddlers to enjoy amazing scenery like the 100-foot Chipeta Falls. Watch for the "fluffy muffin," a big wave in the first mile that's perfect for diving and surfing (!). A National Park ranger guides the **Morrow Point Boat Tour** (Elk Creek Visitors Center, U.S. 50, 15 miles west of Gunnison, 970/641-2337, ext. 205, 10 a.m. and 12:30 p.m. Wed.–Mon. Memorial Day–Labor Day, $15) for 1.5 miles along this reservoir. The fishing in this reservoir is almost as good, and more secluded, than that of the Blue Mesa Reservoir; look for trout, yellow perch, white suckers, kokanee salmon, and crayfish.

Anyone planning to paddle scenic six-mile **Crystal Reservoir,** with its tricky back-currents and protruding rocks, should be experienced and prepared for rapidly changing weather and dam conditions. Wear a lifejacket—which should go without saying for

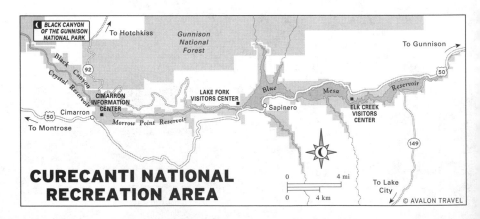

CURECANTI NATIONAL RECREATION AREA

© AVALON TRAVEL

all Colorado paddling trips. The access point is off the Mesa Creek Trail north of Cimarron, and you have to hike a few hundred yards to get to the reservoir access point. Nearby in this area: the **Gunnison Diversion Tunnel,** built in 1909, a National Historic Landmark. The tunnel is not accessible via the reservoir; to get here, take the unpaved, winding, closed-in-winter East Portal Road, beginning on U.S. 50 in Cimarron.

Curecanti's seven hiking trails range from the flat, easy, 1.5-mile **Neversink** to the steep, strenuous, six-mile **Hermit's Rest.** Neversink is recommended for bird-watchers—it begins five miles west of Gunnison on U.S. 50 and follows a stream near a great blue heron rookery. Hermit's Rest begins on Highway 92, about 17 miles west of the intersection with U.S. 50. It descends about 1,800 vertical feet along the Morrow Point Reservoir shore into a camping and picnicking area, and it has little shade, so bring water. The most breathtaking of the seven trails is the **Curecanti Creek Trail,** beginning at the junction of Highway 92 and U.S. 50. It begins easily enough, with an easy walk from Pioneer Lookout Point's north rim overlooking the Black Canyon of the Gunnison River, but it soon descends 900 feet straight into the river. The Curecanti Needle, a 1,000-foot-high granite cliff, towers above the river at the end of this hike. Be warned: Even the easiest hikes in this area are subject to extreme heat (you might want to plan your trip for October or April), and weather changes. Bring water!

The Curecanti area contains 10 campsites of wildly varying terrain. On one extreme is **Gateview,** in the middle of a thin, deep canyon at the south end of the Blue Mesa Reservoir's Lake Fork Arm. To get to these six campsites with few amenities, take Highway 149 seven miles west of Powderhorn, then turn north on the gravel Blue Mesa Cutoff Road. On the other extreme is the easily accessible **Elk Creek** ($12), which has 160 campsites, flush toilets, showers, a fish-cleaning station, and electrical outlets for a small fee; it's 16 miles west of Gunnison on U.S. 50 on the Blue Mesa shore. Check www.nps.gov/cure/planyourvisit/camping.htm for information on the other campsites.

For more general Curecanti information, contact the **National Park Service** (102 Elk Creek, Gunnison, 970/641-2337, www.nps.gov/cure). In addition to the Elk Creek Visitors Center, the **Cimarron Visitors Center** (U.S. 50, about 20 miles east of Montrose, 970/249-4074) is within Curecanti National Recreation Area, and it has the usual information—as well as some fancy old trains and railroad exhibits.

Entertainment
The **Gunnison Arts Center** (102 S. Main St., 970/641-4029, www.gunnisonartscenter.org, 11 A.M.–7 P.M. Tues.–Fri., noon–5 P.M. Sat.) is a vibrant community center with three gallery spaces, a theater for community and children's productions and the occasional movie, plus space for dance, art, quilting, and book-appreciation classes. The center also presents a free summer "Sundays at Seven" concert in the park a few blocks away.

Shopping
The shopping in Gunnison is on the quirky side, with the occasional toy shop and bookstore around the corner from **Traders Rendezvous** (516 W. Tomichi Ave., 970/641-5077, www.coloradoantlers.com, 9 A.M.–5 P.M. Mon.–Fri., 10 A.M.–2 P.M. Sat.), an everything-goes type of place that spreads its elk heads and moose rugs all over the sidewalk on sunny summer mornings; its website offers mounts, skulls, antlers, rugs, and furs. Artier and more seasonal is **Hope and Glory** (234 N. Main St., 970/641-1638, 9 A.M.–6 P.M. Mon.–Sat., 11 A.M.–4 P.M. Sun.), which sells pottery, candles, and various holiday accoutrements—and, in half of the store, flowers.

Accommodations
Given its proximity to Crested Butte and Telluride, Gunnison has a surprising lack of distinctive privately owned hotels; when my family stayed here, we picked the Comfort Inn, which is generic and across the street from a

Wal-Mart, but it has a pool and large guest rooms and met our needs.

A Ramada Inn until recently, the **Gunnison Alpine Inn and Suites** (1011 Rio Grande Rd., 970/641-2804, www.gunnisonalpineinn.com, $59–129) is a half step more interesting than a chain hotel. It has a small heated indoor pool, a hot tub, and suites equipped with microwaves and refrigerators.

Food

Gunnison is a small town with a large tourist population during certain times of the year, which means one thing: overcrowded restaurants. (You can always pull over on one of U.S. 50's side roads overlooking the Blue Mesa Reservoir and leisurely eat a picnic lunch.) Expect to wait in line for any of the three side-by-side restaurants at the corner of North Main and Tomichi Streets: the **W Café** (114 N. Main St., 970/641-1744, http://thewcafe.com, 7 A.M.–2 P.M. Thurs.–Tues., $8), an old-fashioned diner with wood paneling, chicken-fried steak sandwiches ($8), steak and eggs ($10), and breakfast burritos ($8); the **Firebrand Delicatessen** (108 N. Main St., 970/641-6266, 7 A.M.–3 P.M. Tues.–Sun., $8), with homemade soups and deli sandwiches along with friendly snapshots all over the walls; and **The Bean** (120 N. Main St., 970/641-2408, http://thebeancoffeehouseandeatery.com, 6:30 A.M.–8 P.M. Mon.–Fri., 7 A.M.–8 P.M. Sat.–Sun., $6), which supplements its coffee, pastries, and sandwiches with cozy couches, sculptures, and paintings on the walls along with kids toys.

For dinner, **Pie-Zan's NY Pizzeria** (730 N. Main St., 970/641-5255, 11 A.M.–9 P.M. Mon.–Sat., $11) serves hand-tossed New York–style pizza with barely a hint of grease—and delivery is fast.

The fancy sit-down place in town is **Garlic Mike's** (2674 Hwy. 135, 970/641-2493, www.garlicmikes.com, 5–9:30 P.M. Mon.–Sat., 10 A.M.–12:30 P.M. and 5–9:30 P.M. Sun., $20), whose signature dish is a pepper-crusted filet mignon in a cognac mustard-cream sauce—and there's also a Sunday champagne brunch buffet.

Information and Services

The **Gunnison Country Chamber of Commerce** (970/641-1501, www.visitgunnison.com) is at 500 East Tomichi Avenue.

The **Gunnison Valley Health System** (711 N. Taylor St., 970/641-1456, www.gvh-colorado.org) is a 24-bed hospital with facilities for emergencies, trauma, and altitude-related injuries and ailments.

South of Gunnison

Lake City and Creede are tiny towns across the Continental Divide from each other along Highway 149. Both have rich Old West history—Lake City was the site of Alferd Packer's cannibalization of five companions during an 1874 blizzard, while Creede boomed to more than 10,000 people in the 1890s after a local prospector found a silver vein along the Rio Grande River. Both are south of Gunnison and just southeast of Montrose; Lake City is about 50 miles northwest of Creede, but leave extra time for the drive through the curvy San Juans.

LAKE CITY

Lake City is where Colorado's most infamous resident, Alferd Packer, ate his five companions while they were trapped for days in a mountain blizzard in 1874. The six men had left Chief Ouray's camp near what would later become Montrose in February, and Packer's next sighting was two months later, at the Los Pinos Indian Agency, with somebody else's rifle and hunting knife. Authorities arrested him, and it came out that Packer killed one of his men—in self-defense, he said—and ate him and at least one of the others. Although he was sentenced for murder, a judge reduced it to manslaughter, and Packer served 17 years of a 40-year sentence, living in Littleton until his death in 1907.

Packer has since become sort of a wacky Colorado historical icon, the inspiration for

Lake City's Alferd Packer Jeep Tour and Barbecue and the University of Colorado-Boulder's Alferd Packer Grill. There's even a local monument, the **Alferd Packer Memorial,** on Highway 149 near Lake San Cristobal.

Lake City itself is largely oblivious, these days, to Packer's deadly shenanigans. It's a pretty tourist town of just 250 people surrounded by the Uncompahgre and Rio Grande forests, and its large National Historic District includes numerous classic Victorian buildings.

Sights

The **Silver Thread Scenic Byway,** or Highway 149, was a mining road in the 1870s and has long since expanded to a modern paved highway. En route to South Fork, about 75 miles to the south, it passes some of southwest Colorado's most beautiful scenery, in the Gunnison and Rio Grande National Forests, as well as several historic mining areas and the Rio Grande valley.

Sports and Recreation
FISHING
Lake San Cristobal (Hwy. 149), about five miles south of town, came into being about 700 years ago when something called the Slumgullion Earthflow flowed into the Gunnison River and created a large body of water. The Slumgullion is no longer a threat to the lake, which is plopped inside the Gunnison National Forest and is one of the best fishing spots in the area. Also, while the lakeshore is private property, numerous public trails are nearby, leading to 14,000-foot mountains such as Redcloud, Sunshine, and Handies.

For more information on the forests, hiking trails, and fishing, contact the **U.S. Forest Service** (2250 U.S. 50, Delta, 970/874-6600, www.fs.fed.us/r2/gmug). For local fishing equipment, guided tours, and general advice, try **Dan's Fly Shop** (723 Gunnison Ave., 970/944-2281 summer, 970/252-9106 winter, www.dansflyshop.com).

HIKING
Lake City is close to five 14,000-foot-tall

peaks: Uncompahgre, Handies, Redcloud, Wetterhorn, and Sunshine, all of which have hiking opportunities of varying levels of difficulty. **Uncompahgre** is the state's sixth-highest fourteener, but one of the easiest to climb—a 16-mile (round-trip) hike with a 3,309-foot elevation gain. There are two trailheads. To get to Nellie Creek, follow the sign to Engineer Pass in Lake City, then take the dirt Henson Creek Road for about nine miles before turning right on Nellie Creek Road; after that, you need a 4WD vehicle to go the next 15.5 miles; you'll see a parking lot, from which you hike 7.5 miles to the trailhead. To get to Matterhorn Creek, follow the sign to Engineer Pass in Lake City, then take the dirt Henson Creek Road for about nine miles to Nellie Creek Road; go beyond Nellie Creek Road another four miles; take North Henson Creek Road for about two miles before parking at the trailhead. Visit www.14ers.com for more information on which routes are safest during different times of the year.

One of the more challenging trails, more than 11 miles long, leads from the Gunnison River to Redcloud Peak to Sunshine Peak; the beginning of the hike is 2.5 miles south of town on Highway 149. Go about 16.5 miles on Cinnamon Pass Road and look for the trailhead on the right. The elevation climbs quite a bit, so bring water.

Accommodations
Lake City isn't a huge bed-and-breakfast area—neither is nearby Gunnison, for that matter—but there are a couple of decent B&Bs if you can't make it all the way to Crested Butte or Ouray. A triangular log cabin in a forest with seven guest rooms and a wood fireplace, the **Old Carson Inn** (8401 County Rd. 30, 505/301-5111, www.oldcarsoninn.com, $220 per night, 3-night minimum) is large and homey, with plenty of room for kids but no pets.

Food
The **Sportsman's Texaco BBQ Station** (173 S. Gunnison Ave., 970/944-2525, www.sportsmanstexaco.com, 7:30 A.M.–2 P.M. and

5–9 P.M. daily, reduced hours in winter, $8) is a hidden Lake City gem—a burger-and-barbecue joint that doubles as a bona fide Texaco service station ($65 per hour for repairs). It's run by a couple—a former insurance agent and real-estate appraiser—who followed a dream almost-retirement to this pretty mountain town. The station sponsors a "backyard concert series," drawing reasonably big country-music names such as Suzy Bogguss and local singer-songwriter Chuck Pyle.

Information

The **Lake City/Hinsdale County Chamber of Commerce** (800 N. Gunnison Ave., 970/944-2527 or 800/569-1874, www.lakecity.com) will tell you everything you need to know about local restaurants, hotels, outdoor sports, and Alferd Packer.

CREEDE

Today, just 850 people live in picturesque Mineral County, of which Creede is the only town, tucked into the east side of the San Juan Mountains. But in 1890, after Nicholas Creede came across a silver vein near the Rio Grande River, its population surged to 10,000. This led to an intense fortune-seeking explosion, even by Colorado standards—travelers poured into the county, building "tent towns" such as Amethyst and Jimtown and pulling tons of silver out of the Holy Moses, Last Chance, and Kentucky Belle mines.

Creede wound up exporting more than $1 million in silver by 1892, transporting much of it via Colorado Springs businessman William Palmer's extended railroad line. Then the questionable characters showed up: Bob Ford, who allegedly killed Jesse James, opened a saloon and was killed in a gunfight here; Poker Lulu Swain, known as the Mormon Queen, became one of the town's more infamous call girls; and Bat Masterson and Calamity Jane lived here. Opined the *Creede Candle:* "Creede is unfortunate in getting more of the flotsam of the state than usually falls to the lot of a mining camp."

Today's Creede isn't nearly as exciting, but like nearby Salida, Buena Vista, and Gunnison, it's a pit-stop town among numerous outdoor attractions—several fourteeners are within striking distance, notably San Luis Peak, and the Silver Thread National Scenic Byway (Hwy. 149) leads to pretty North Clear Creek Falls and the sparkling Wheeler Geologic Area.

Sights

Upon its discovery in the early 1900s, locals favorably compared the **Wheeler Geologic Area** (about 24 miles east of Creede) to Colorado Springs's Garden of the Gods and even the Grand Canyon. Formed 30 million years ago out of volcanic ash, some of which has cemented and some of which remains loose and fragile, the area is filled with mountain-sized pointy peaks and wild-looking stripes and sandstone-colored patterns. It's pretty hard to get here, though: You drive about seven miles southeast on Highway 149, then turn north onto Pool Table Road/Forest Road 600 for another 10 miles. Look for the dusty remains of the former Hanson's Sawmill, then drive another 14 miles to the area's fence—but you'll need a 4WD vehicle for the last stretch. Cars aren't allowed into the area, so bring sturdy hiking boots.

A one-hour drive along Highway 149 north from Creede, **North Clear Creek Falls** is a striking 100-foot waterfall that's frequently photographed due to its proximity to the main road.

The **Creede Historic Museum** (17 Main St., 719/658-2303, www.museumtrail.org/creedehistoricmuseum.asp, 10 A.M.–4 P.M. daily Memorial Day–Labor Day, free), in an 1890s-era wooden depot, has an old roulette wheel, a come-hither saloon painting of a woman, a horse-drawn hearse, and other interesting artifacts from Creede's wild days.

The **Underground Mining Museum** (503 Forest Rd. 9, 719/658-0811, www.museumtrail.org/creedeundergroundminingmuseum.asp, 10 A.M.–4 P.M. daily summer, 9:30 A.M.–3 P.M. Mon.–Fri. spring and fall, $7) is a long, flat structure built into the side of a hill, although it never was a working mine.

Instead, the exhibits recreate old blacksmith shops and elevator-like "hoists" along with several ore and rock specimens.

Entertainment

USA Today once named the **Creede Repertory Theatre** (124 N. Main St., 719/658-2540, www.creederep.org) one of the "10 best places to see the lights way off Broadway." The performers are surprisingly talented for such a small town, and the theater rotates a wide variety of well-chosen productions, from musicals like *How to Succeed in Business Without Really Trying* to mining-history dramas like *Slabtown*.

Accommodations

Open only May–September, the **Antlers Rio Grande Lodge** (26222 Hwy. 149, 719/658-2423, www.antlerslodge.com, $129) is next to the Rio Grande River about five miles southwest of town. It rents weekly cabins and has spaces for RV camping, but the motel rooms are the best deal—including a porch and a swing, from which you can fish for trout in the river.

Sheepherders drive dozens of fuzzy white animals across the grounds of **Cottonwood Cove** (13046 Hwy. 149, 719/658-2242, www.cottonwoodcove.com, $90–130) a few times a year, adding a surreal touch to the friendly cabins and lodge rooms. The complex, which also allows RV camping ($26), is south of Creede, halfway to South Fork along Highway 149.

Known as Zang's Hotel in the late 1800s, when Creede had some 100 hotels to accommodate the miners and miscreants, the light-blue **Creede Hotel** (120 N. Main St., 719/658-2608, www.creedehotel.com, $105–115) has four guest rooms named after notorious local characters—Calamity Jane, Poker Alice Tubbs, Soapy Smith, and Bat Masterson.

The **Wason Ranch** (Hwy. 149, 719/658-2413 or 877/927-6626, www.wasonranch.com, 3-bedroom cottage or 6-bedroom ranch house $325–350) is an old horse ranch that belonged to explorer and Civil War soldier M. V. B. Wason in the 1800s, and today it rents modern, furnished log cabins along the Rio Grande River.

Food

Most of the restaurants in tourist-heavy Creede are at the hotels—try the Riverside Restaurant in the Antlers Lodge—and the rest are of the down-home variety, mostly burgers and burritos. **Kip's Grill** (5th Ave. and Main St., 719/658-0220, http://kipsgrill.com, 11 A.M.–8 P.M. daily, $13) serves tacos, burgers, and homemade salsa and has occasional live music. **Café Olé** (112 N. Main St., 719/658-2880, 7:30 A.M.–2:30 P.M. Tues.–Wed. and Fri.–Sat., 7:30 A.M.–8 P.M. Thurs., $8) has homemade baked goods, deli sandwiches, and on Thursday evenings, pizza.

Information

The **Creede/Mineral County Chamber of Commerce** (719/658-2374 or 800/327-2102, www.creede.com) has a detailed visitor-oriented website full of restaurant and hotel listings and a bunch of interesting history.

Telluride and Vicinity

So many hippies have settled in Telluride—with its exhilarating clean air, 8,237-foot elevation, and waterfall-covered mountains casting shadows over Colorado Avenue—that this utopian middle-of-nowhere town has become a sort of laid-back southwestern Colorado metropolis. My first trip to Telluride was in 1988 to visit a friend who was taking a break between college and career; the town was still roomy and relaxed. Colorado Avenue had a few shops and bars, a sizable number of residents wore dreadlocks and the look of having stayed up all night, and the Victorians within a few blocks of downtown were surrounded by open space and muddy culverts. It was totally different on my most recent trip: Sturdy, modern houses had filled in every bit of the downtown open space, high-end restaurants are on every

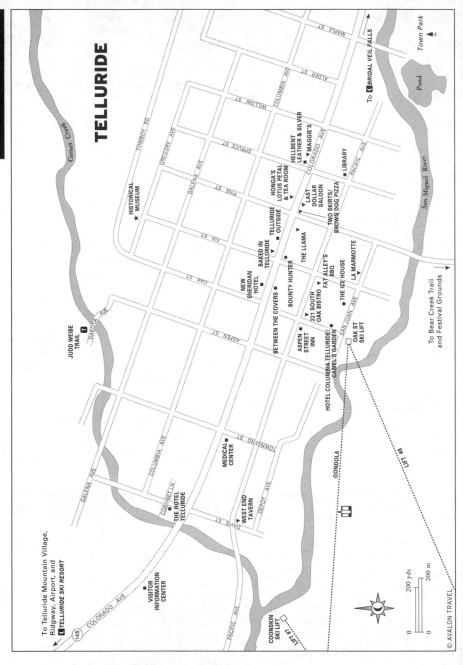

TELLURIDE

To Telluride Mountain Village,
Ridgway, Airport, and
◾TELLURIDE SKI RESORT

145

VISITOR
INFORMATION
CENTER

To ◀BRIDAL VEIL FALLS

Town Park

Pond

San Miguel River

Cornet Creek

HISTORICAL
MUSEUM

JUDD WEIBE
TRAIL

THE HOTEL
TELLURIDE

WEST END
TAVERN

COLORADO AVE

GALENA AVE

MEDICAL
CENTER

COLORETT LN

TOWNSEND ST

DEPOT AVE

PACIFIC AVE

DAVIS ST

ASPEN ST

FIR ST

OAK ST

PINE ST

SPRUCE ST

WILLOW ST

ALDER ST

MAPLE ST

GREGORY AVE

TOMBOY RD

DAKOTA AVE

COLUMBIA AVE

PACIFIC AVE

COLORADO AVE

NEW
SHERIDAN
HOTEL

BETWEEN THE COVERS

BAKED IN
TELLURIDE

TELLURIDE
OUTSIDE

BOUNTY HUNTER

221 SOUTH
OAK BISTRO

ASPEN
STREET
INN

HOTEL COLUMBIA TELLURIDE/
CAMEL'S GARDEN

THE LLAMA

FAT ALLEY'S
BBQ

THE ICE HOUSE

LA MARMOTTE

HONGA'S
LOTUS PETAL
& TEA ROOM

LAST
DOLLAR
SALOON

TWO SKIRTS/
BROWN DOG PIZZA

HELLBENT
LEATHER & SILVER

MAGGIE'S

LIBRARY

SAN JUAN AVE

OAK ST
SKI LIFT

GONDOLA

LIFT 8

To Bear Creek Trail
and Festival Grounds

COONSKIN
SKI LIFT

LIFT 7

0   200 yds
0   200 m

© AVALON TRAVEL

© MATT INDEN/WEAVER MULTIMEDIA GROUP/COLORADO TOURISM OFFICE

biking down Telluride's main drag

block of Colorado, and the people wandering the streets wore far more jewelry than I remembered.

"The Next Aspen," as some have pejoratively called Telluride over the years, is a bit of an exaggeration: The town's average home price (including land and condos) was $1,015,806 in 2009, according to the Telluride Association of Realtors; that's about $400,000 lower than it was before the recession but still reflects incredible growth, considering the number was $485,600 in 2000. But in recent years celebrities such as Gen. Norman Schwarzkopf, Oprah Winfrey, and Donald Trump have moved to the area, at least part-time; home prices have skyrocketed; and while hippies continue to peruse the "free box" at the center of town, they're pretty much priced out of the housing market. So while the town's lazy, comforting vibe has given way to a certain sprawl, it's still one of the most magnificent cities in the state, with 14,000-foot Mount Wilson and Bridal Veil Falls literally at the end of town. My latest trip was in late September, when the leaves

had turned bright yellow and snow had fallen in the peaks for the first time; most visitors arrive during ski season, but I highly recommend a trip during this spectacular time of year.

Although Butch Cassidy robbed banks here in the late 1800s, Telluride was a sleepy little nothing town until roughly 1971, when the ski resort opened—and ever since, it has been a haven for skiers of all kinds along with hikers, mountain climbers, cyclists, and off-roaders. It's one of those places in Colorado where the weather always seems to be superb—even during a blizzard—and the air is cleaner than any place you've ever been. Leading the annual roster of events is the Telluride Bluegrass Festival, which started in 1974 as a gathering of local bluegrass mavericks and has grown into a four-day institution of bluegrass, country, blues, and rock, from Emmylou Harris to Wilco.

HISTORY

After the Utes hunted here and Spanish explorers stumbled on and named the San Juan Mountains, prospectors drifted here with the

1858 Colorado gold boom—and discovered gold in the San Juans. Telluride's first claim was in 1875, by John Fallon, in Marshal Basin; the town attempted to establish itself as "Columbia" five years later, but the U.S. Post Office denied the name due to the mining camp in Columbia, California. Telluride was so-named because: (1) Tellurium is an element associated with gold deposits, although it doesn't exist in this area; or (2) "To hell you ride!" is what friends, family, and squeamish prospectors told gold-diggers heading for the southwest mountains. Believe your own theory.

For awhile in the 1890s, after the railroad came to town, miners from all over the world traveled to the area, boosting Telluride's population to 5,000—along with saloons, gambling dens, and what the official Telluride website calls "a much-heralded red-light district." Butch Cassidy and his Wild Bunch showed up to begin a notorious career of bank robbing (among other things) at the San Miguel National Bank. But the mining boom ended, many locals joined the military during World War I, and by the 1960s the population had dropped to less than 600. As with Vail and Aspen, however, skiing came to the rescue.

Locals built a ski area out of a ridge in the early 1970s, and by decade's end, entrepreneurs Ron Allred and Jim Wells had figured out how to profit from it—they added a mountain village, snowmaking equipment, new lifts, beginner-focused terrain, and, in 1996, a free gondola. But owing to Telluride's remote location—Denver is at least a five-hour drive in good weather conditions, and who really comes to Colorado through Durango?—the town remained mostly isolated and dominated by locals. Throughout the 1970s, starry-eyed hippies dominated local boards and enacted severe restrictions on growth.

Growth happened anyway, especially after the town built a regional airport in the late 1980s, and Telluride quickly started growing from an out-of-the-way mountain gem to a booming rich person's playground. The housing prices have spun out of control, and as with Aspen, celebrities are some of the few who can

afford to live among the population of 2,000. Still, thanks to smaller nearby towns such as Ridgway, Ouray, and Silverton, the area is still popular with hippies and ski bums, and its 14 summer festivals and the construction of the Peaks Resort and Telluride Mountain Village ensure tourists will be streaming through here for decades to come.

SIGHTS
National Historic Landmark District

Like most of the mountain towns in Colorado, Telluride aggressively memorializes its gold-mining heritage—particularly in the 14-building downtown-centered National Historic Landmark District, including the San Miguel County Courthouse (301 Colorado Ave.), built in 1887 as the county's first courthouse; the Rio Grande Southern Railway Depot (Townsend St. and San Juan Ave.), built in 1891 and converted to Harmon's Restaurant 100 years later; and most famously, the totally refurbished **New Sheridan Hotel & Opera House** (231 W. Colorado Ave.), built in 1895 with telephones and velvet curtains, and still a well-known hotel and restaurant.

One of these buildings, the former

CELEBRITIES OF TELLURIDE (PART-TIME, AT LEAST)

- Tom Cruise and Katie Holmes
- Oprah Winfrey
- Gen. Norman Schwarzkopf
- Ralph Lauren (actually in nearby Ridgway)
- Susan Saint James and Dick Ebersol
- Jerry Seinfeld

Sources: *The Denver Post, Rocky Mountain News*

Miner's Hospital, today houses the **Telluride Historical Museum** (201 W. Gregory Ave., 970/728-3344, www.telluridemuseum.com, 11 A.M.–5 P.M. Mon.–Wed. and Fri.–Sat., 11 A.M.–7 P.M. Thurs., 1–5 P.M. Sun. summer, 11 A.M.–5 P.M. Fri.–Wed., 11 A.M.–7 P.M. Thurs. fall–spring, $5), which has 20,000 historical artifacts and 2,000 photos focusing on the mining era. Guided audio tours are available.

A local historian, Ashley Boling, runs **Historic Tours of Telluride** (970/728-6639, by appointment), covering the buildings in the National Historic Landmark District and many other sights.

Bridal Veil Falls

This impossible-to-miss waterfall overlooking Telluride is the easiest and most obviously spectacular **hiking, biking,** and **off-roading** trail in the area, and it begins at Pandora Mill on the east side of town; the trail is about 1.8 miles long and is steep and difficult, but most hikers in decent shape can make it without

much trouble—particularly in fall, spring, and summer. It's almost impossible to get to the base of the falls during winter, although portions of the trail are accessible all year—and it's even possible to hike beyond the falls in good weather to pretty sights such as Blue Lake and Silver Lake. If you have a 4WD vehicle, you can maneuver the dirt road most of the way, but you will eventually have to get out and walk. To get to the trail, drive through Telluride along Highway 145 until the road turns to dirt. Look for a parking area just beyond that point. The falls are part of the Uncompahgre National Forest; for more information, contact the **U.S. Forest Service** (2250 U.S. 50, Delta, 970/874-6600, www. fs.fed.us/r2/gmug).

SPORTS AND RECREATION
Telluride Ski Resort

The greatest quality of this skiing utopia—after the majesty of the San Juan Mountains and the natural drops of the 2,080-foot Bushwacker and intimidating early-spring bump runs like Mammoth—has always been seclusion. The Telluride Ski Resort (970/728-7335 or 800/778-8581, www.tellurideskiresort.com) is in the middle of nowhere, a long and twisty five-hour drive from Denver and 65 miles from Durango, the nearest "regular" city; locals and regulars alike have long prized their wide-open terrain, lack of lift lines, and hidden world of natural mountain beauty. The lift ticket to said world costs roughly $92.

But commerce and transportation have been chipping away at Telluride's seclusion for the past 10–15 years. In the late 1980s, the Telluride Regional Airport gave skiers a whole new way to reach the resort, and city officials hope to renovate the "notoriously dodgy" airport, as *Ski* magazine calls it, so 100-seat commercial jets can land as well. In recent years the resort has opened many once-remote areas to lift traffic, including the 12,250-foot-high Gold Hill, previously accessible only to ambitious hikers.

Lines or no lines, the skiing remains

© MATT INDEN/WEAVER MULTIMEDIA GROUP/COLORADO TOURISM OFFICE

Bridal Veil Falls

impeccable. Telluride's primary downhill areas are the long, steep, bumpy trails on the north side of the mountain—to get there from town, use Lift 8 to get to Lift 9, which leads to the self-explanatory Spiral Staircase and the bumpy Mammoth. Catering to beginning and intermediate skiers, Gorrono Basin, on the other side of the mountain, includes long cruises like See Forever and The Lookout as well as the snowboarding Sprite Air Garden Terrain Park. Also making skiers talk in rapturous tones is Prospect Bowl, a huge expansion of the ski area with runs that swerve around trees; it's accessible by several lifts, but many prefer the more rugged "hike-to" approach.

Telluride has four terrain parks for different skill levels: **Ute,** for beginners, with small jumps, a mini snow cross, and ride-on boxes; **2,** for intermediate riders, with small–medium-sized jumps, rollers, rails, and boxes, open Thursday–Sunday evenings in addition to day skiing; **Misty Maiden,** for high-intermediate riders, with slightly higher and more difficult jumps and tricks; and **Hoot Brown,** for experts, with the largest jumps in the resort. The 2 Park is accessible from Lift 2, Ute from Lift 11, and Misty Maiden and Hoot from Lift 4.

Keep in mind that the town of Telluride and the Mountain Village park are two distinct areas, separated by a mountain. But one of the resort's great advantages is the free gondola, an incredible 2.5-mile, 13-minute ride over ridges and valleys that begins in Telluride and ends in the village (and continues to a remote parking lot). The gondola is open year-round; on a recent trip to Telluride, I rode it at night, in the rain, and the return trip was like descending back into town via the space shuttle. The resort also has several impressive "hike-to" runs beyond the lifts.

Of the resort's more than 2,000 skiable acres, 23 percent are for beginners, 36 percent for intermediates, and 41 percent for advanced skiers or experts. The advanced terrain has expanded a bit in recent years. Eighteen lifts are available, including two gondolas, and the highest peak is Palmyra, which watches over Mountain Village and Telluride at 13,320 feet.

The **Telluride Ski & Snowboard School** (565 Mountain Village Blvd., 970/728-7507 or 800/801-4832, www.tellurideskiresort.com) gives lessons of all types—including classes for kids ages three and older. Full-day group lessons are roughly $300, while full-day individual lessons are $650.

Among the most prominent of the many local ski-rental shops are **Telluride Sports** (several locations, including 150 W. Colorado Ave., 970/728-4477 or 800/828-7547, www.telluridesports.com) and **Paragon Ski & Sport** (213 W. Colorado Ave., 970/728-4525, www.paragontelluride.com).

Cross-Country and Heli-Skiing

The best skiing away from the mountain begins at the **Telluride Nordic Center** (500 E. Colorado Ave., Town Park, 970/728-1144, www.telluridetrails.org/html/nordic_ctr.html, 10 A.M.–4 P.M. Sat.–Thurs., 10 A.M.–7 P.M. Fri. winter), which guides you to 10 miles of groomed trail in the Town Park area. The center rents skis and ice skates and gives cross-country lessons as well as ski and snowshoe tours. Note that the center's phone number works only during the winter.

The **San Juan Hut Systems** (970/626-3033, www.sanjuanhuts.com) ski route follows the Dallas and Alder Creek Trails, underneath huge peaks in the Mount Sneffels Range, from Telluride to nearby Ridgway and Ouray—with stops at five greenish huts, each with eight padded bunk beds, propane cook stoves and lamps, and no water (what do you think all that snow outside is for?). Intermediate skiing experience is recommended.

Finally, for well-to-do adventurers who *really* want to get away from the crowds, **Telluride Helitrax** (970/728-8377 or 877/500-8377, www.helitrax.net) uses a Bell 407 helicopter to drop skiers into remote locations such as the Hope Lake Basin, 13,000 feet above sea level. It's safe but pricey—numerous packages are available, including a six-run, single-day experience in the $800–900 range, and an exclusive private trip for $6,250 per hour. Telluride Helitrax is the only

Colorado company that does heli-skiing, and it claims just one injury since it was founded in 1982—a well-publicized 1994 incident involving supermodel Christie Brinkley, her friend, and a sputtering copter.

Ice-Skating

Telluride's Town Park, just before the mountains begin on the far side of town, has a nice ice-skating rink. Contact the **Telluride Nordic Center** (970/728-1144, winter only), for rentals. Mountain Village also has a free ice-skating pond in winter.

Hiking

Just north of Telluride, the **Sneffels High Line Trail** is a 14-mile loop that climbs strenuously from about 9,000 to 12,250 feet; the trail takes about seven hours, but it's worth it, given the views of the San Miguel Mountains, three fourteeners, Lizard Head Peak, and Dallas Peak. Connecting with the Sneffels Trail is **Jud Wiebe Trail** (north on Aspen St., near Cornet Creek), a curvy three-mile passage that isn't nearly as difficult.

South of Telluride along Highway 145, the 12-mile hard-and-steep **Lizard Head Trail** straddles the Uncompahgre and San Juan National Forests and is worth trying for the classic view of 13,113-foot Lizard Head Peak alone.

Finally, two of the most popular local trails are **Mount Wilson** (Hwy. 145, 11 miles southwest of Telluride), which climbs 4,000 feet in eight miles, including the hard-sloping final 400 feet; and **Bear Creek Falls,** a pretty and easy two-mile trail beginning at the end of Pine Street.

For information and maps, contact **Uncompahgre National Forest** (2250 U.S. 50, Delta, 970/874-6600, www.fs.fed.us/r2/gmug), the **Ouray Ranger District** (2505 S. Townsend Ave., Montrose, 970/240-5300), or the **Norwood Ranger District** (1150 Forest St., Norwood, 970/327-4261).

Biking

In summer, the **San Juan Hut Systems** (970/626-3033, www.sanjuanhuts.com) hut-skiing service turns into a mountain-bike adventure guide, leading cyclists 206 miles from Telluride to Moab, Utah, with huts every 35 miles. The route is mostly U.S. Forest Service dirt roads, beginning with the San Juan Mountains and ending in Utah's deserts and canyons. Bring a well-exercised body, as vehicles aren't allowed access to the huts.

Imogene Pass, between Telluride and Ouray, is a high, twisty, 17-mile road that some say is a route for courageous mountain bikers. But I'd add "crazy" and "death-defying" to that description.

For an easy warm-up ride to get used to the altitude, bike five miles out to Alta, a scenic mining ghost town that's on the National Register of Historic Places. It's surrounded by picturesque lakes. To find it, take Highway 145 six miles south of Telluride, toward Cortez, to Alta Lakes Road. Go about four miles to find the ghost town. Turn right to see the lakes.

Water Sports

Three major mountain rivers—the San Miguel, Dolores, and Gunnison—are within striking distance of Telluride, as are plenty of lakes. The San Miguel River, west of the city in the Ilium Valley, is packed with rainbow and brown trout and is especially great for fly-fishing in summer and fall; the hard-to-get-to Gunnison River has fees and complicated regulations; and the cutthroat-heavy Dolores River, on Highway 145 outside Cortez, is especially challenging.

Five lakes are within 15 miles of the city as well: Alta Lake (Hwy. 145, 9 miles southwest of Telluride), Priest Lake (Hwy. 145, 12 miles south of Telluride), Silver Lake (in Bridal Veil Basin), Trout Lake (near Priest Lake), and Woods Lake (Hwy. 145, 12 miles west of Telluride). For more information as well as equipment rental and guided tours, **Telluride Outside** (121 W. Colorado Ave., 970/728-3895 or 800/831-6230, www.tellurideoutside.com) is a terrific resource.

Like many riverside cities in Colorado,

Telluride is superb for white-water rafting; try **Telluride Outside** (121 W. Colorado Ave., 970/728-3895 or 800/831-6230, www.tellurideoutside.com) for tours of varying intensity along the San Miguel and Dolores Rivers.

Rock Climbing and Ice Climbing

Because rock climbing wasn't death-defying enough, locals have taken to the sport of ice climbing, which is big in Telluride and nearby Ouray. Both sports are dangerous, but for thrill-seekers they're irresistible in these towns of peaks, crags, cliffs, and boulders. Giving guided trips is the **San Juan Outdoor School** (300 S. Mahoney Dr., 970/728-4101 or 866/386-8743, www.tellurideadventures.com), which recommends at least four people to a group and gives a one-day course for the basics.

Horseback Riding

Longtime wrangler and mustachioed local character Roudy Roundebush of **Ride with Roudy** (970/728-9611, www.ridewithroudy.com) conducts scenic horseback-riding tours from his ranch barn about six miles from Telluride. He gives tours from another ranch, in Norwood, during the winter.

Golf

If you must come to Telluride for golf—as opposed to, say, listening to bluegrass or climbing to a waterfall—the **Telluride Golf Club** (565 Mountain Village Blvd., 970/728-7302, www.tellurideskiandgolfclub.com, $70–190) has 18 holes and remarkable views of Mounts Wilson and Sunshine.

Hang Gliding

The principals behind **Telluride Soaring** (Telluride Regional Airport, 1500 Last Dollar Rd., www.glidetelluride.com, 970/209-3497 or 970/708-0862, $180 per hour) are certified pilots Jeff Campbell and "Glider Bob," who guide one passenger at a time all over the skies of Telluride.

© MATT INDEN/WEAVER MULTIMEDIA GROUP/COLORADO TOURISM OFFICE

Teeing off at Telluride, watching your ball fly farther than it does at sea level, is a welcome experience.

ENTERTAINMENT AND EVENTS

Nightlife

Telluride's bar scene isn't as interesting as it was 100 years ago, when cowboys and gamblers regularly pulled guns on each other, but the mixture of old-school hippies, new-school trust-funders, and visitors looking for a good time makes for lively nights.

As of this writing, the **Fly Me to the Moon Saloon** (136 E. Colorado Ave.) was posting for-sale signs outside, which is too bad because it snagged the best live bands in town. Making up for its loss, somewhat, is **The Llama** (100 W. Colorado Ave., 970/728-5114, www.llamatelluride.com, 11:30 A.M.–9:30 P.M. daily, reduced hours off-season), which puts on local acts and hosts battles of the bands. It serves burgers and other bar food, but its in-house raw bar, Pescado, has sushi and sake.

Also playing host to occasional live acts is **Brown Dog Pizza** (110 W. Colorado Ave., 970/728-8046, www.browndogpizza.net, 11 A.M.–midnight daily).

Smuggler's Brewpub and Grille (225 S. Pine St., 970/728-0919, www.smugglersbrew.com, 11 A.M.–10 P.M. daily) brews in the basement and emerges with unique flavors such as Powder Night Espresso Porter and Knuckledragger Extra Pale Ale—in addition to homemade root beer and cream soda. Skiers hit this place regularly for the drinks, beer nuggets, and a snack called the Mountain Bloom Onion ($8).

An old standby is the **Last Dollar Saloon** (100 E. Colorado Ave., 970/728-4800, www.lastdollarsaloon.com, 3 P.M.–close daily), with a great jukebox and bartenders who know their way around a shot.

Across the mountain, at the Mountain Village, drinking can be had at **Allred's** (565 Mountain Village Blvd., 970/728-7474, www.allredsrestaurant.com, 5 P.M.–close daily), 1,800 feet above the city, with one of the best wine lists in town, plus a piano player Wednesday–Sunday nights.

Theater

In addition to being a historic building, the **Sheridan Opera House** (110 N. Oak St., 970/728-6363, www.sheridanoperahouse.com) is the only nice indoor stage in town—so it draws big music names, including hit singers James Taylor and Jimmy Buffett, bluesman John P. Hammond, and country star Dierks Bentley. It's also a renowned theatrical stage, having sponsored productions with actors like Mel Gibson, Patrick Stewart, and Carol Burnett over the years. The opera house is a nonprofit venue, benefiting the **Sheridan Arts Foundation** (110 N. Oak St., 970/728-6363), which brings the stars to town to work with promising young talent.

The **Telluride Repertory Theatre Co.** (970/728-4539, www.telluridetheatre.com) books local actors and productions into the Sheridan Opera House and onto the Town Park stage (and conducts workshops with thousands of schoolkids). The community-run **Telluride Council for the Arts & Humanities** (283 S. Fir St., 970/728-3930, www.telluridearts.com) and the **Ah Haa School for the Arts** (300 S. Townsend Ave., 970/728-3886, www.ahhaa.org) also run smaller-scale classes and workshops.

Festivals

Telluride has more than a dozen festivals in the summer alone, including the well-known Bluegrass Festival and the Wine Festival, both in late June. Although the film festival's reputation has grown considerably in recent years, the **Telluride Bluegrass Festival** (800/624-2422, www.bluegrass.com) remains the festival flagship. It's a spectacular event, with old-school bluegrass heroes such as Ralph Stanley on the same bill as new-school bluegrass experimenters like Béla Fleck and Sam Bush, and rock, country, and pop acts like John Hiatt and Wilco just to bring in the big crowds. Be sure to make hotel reservations long in advance, however; one year I camped just outside of town and could barely find a spot in a muddy, noisy area.

The town is so festival-heavy that residents have declared a weekend in late July "The Nothing Festival" (www.

telluridenothingfestival.com). Check out www.visittelluride.com (click on "Signature Events" under "Events & Festivals") to coordinate dates.

Early September's **Telluride Film Festival** (510/665-9494, www.telluridefilmfestival.org) is a sub-Sundance fest that draws serious film stars to town and broke *Sling Blade* and Ken Burns's *The Civil War.*

The **Wild West Fest** (970/728-6363, www.sheridanoperahouse.com/wild-west-fest) in early June brings disadvantaged kids to town for art, theater, and rodeo events; late June's **Telluride Wine Festival** (970/766-4335, www.telluridewinefestival.com) brings numerous master sommeliers to town.

The mid-August **Telluride Chamber Music Festival** (970/728-8686, www.telluridechambermusic.com) and early August's **Telluride Jazz Celebration** (970/728-7009, www.telluridejazz.com) round out the musical offerings.

SHOPPING

Open since 1974, the **Between the Covers Bookstore & Coffee House** (224 W. Colorado Ave., 970/728-4504, www.between-the-covers.com, 8 A.M.–9 P.M. Mon.–Fri., 9 A.M.–8 P.M. Sat., 9 A.M.–6 P.M. Sun., reduced hours off-season) is a great place for browsing, with an emphasis on local authors, tour guides, Colorado history, and relevant titles like Annie Gilbert Coleman's *Ski Style: Sport and Culture in the Rockies.*

Every mountain town that hopes to have any kind of tourist following contains at least one cowboy-hat store, and **Bounty Hunter** (226 W. Colorado Ave., 970/728-0256, www.shopbountyhunter.com) is Telluride's. Of course, "cowboy hat" is a little too limiting a description for a store that sells Outback explorers, derbies, and classic brown fedoras—plus boots.

Noteworthy galleries include **Hellbent Leather and Silver** (215 E. Colorado Ave., 970/728-6246, www.hellbentleather.com, 10 A.M.–7 P.M. daily), with solid handbags, wallets, belts, and hats, plus silver and gold jewelry; the **Telluride Gallery of Fine Art** (130 E. Colorado Ave., 970/728-3300, www.

telluridegallery.com, 10 A.M.–9 P.M. daily, reduced hours off-season), one of the town's oldest galleries, selling oil paintings and displaying an elaborate jewelry collection; and **Naturescapes Gallery** (100 W. Colorado Ave., 970/728-6359, www.naturescapesgallery.com, 10 A.M.–5 P.M. Mon.–Sat., closed off-season), showing a series of richly colorful mountain scenes by native Coloradoan Dale Malmedal.

Telluride Outside (121 W. Colorado Ave., 970/728-3895 or 800/831-6230, www.tellurideoutside.com, 8 A.M.–6 P.M. daily) sells fishing equipment and outdoor sports–type clothing and has knowledgeable guides who can walk you through all your adventure excursions, from rock climbing to heli-skiing. **Jagged Edge** (223 E. Colorado Ave., 970/728-9307, www.jagged-edge-telluride.com, 10 A.M.–8 P.M. daily) is more stylish than rugged, with Tibetan jackets, sports moccasins, thermoses, and water bottles.

In the Nugget Building, the first to carry modern electricity in the United States, **Two Skirts** (127 W. Colorado Ave., 970/728-6828, www.twoskirts.net, 10 A.M.–6 P.M. Mon.–Thurs., 10 A.M.–7 P.M. Fri.–Sat., 11 A.M.–6 P.M. Sun.) is a pink-bag women's-clothing store that targets women in T-shirts and jeans who occasionally like to wear expensive cashmere.

Dogs are big in Telluride, and so are their accessories: **Mountain Tails** (307 E. Colorado Ave., 970/369-4240, www.mountaintails.com, 11 A.M.–5 P.M. daily) sells Dog Bone Carabiners ($6), perfect for dog-obsessed rock climbers.

ACCOMMODATIONS
Under $100

Aside from campsites, it's pretty much impossible to find lodging under $100 in Telluride, unless you hit nearby mountain towns such as Ouray or Silverton. Unlike Aspen or Vail, where budget-conscious travelers can find deals in Basalt or Eagle, Telluride is isolated from its neighbors, and tiny nearby towns such as Pandora and Ophir have a few residents but aren't known for their visitor facilities.

$150-200

Built in 1891, rebuilt in 1894 after a fire, and elaborately refurbished in 1995, the **(New Sheridan Hotel** (231 W. Colorado Ave., 970/728-4351 or 800/200-1891, www.news-heridan.com, $179–199) is the best-known and most impressive historic site in a town that continually celebrates its gold-mining past. (Trivia: William Jennings Bryan announced his failed bid for the presidency here in 1896.) It's also a luxury hotel in a sturdy redbrick building, with 32 guest rooms and corresponding period furniture and antiques; hot tubs are on the roof, the breakfast and pantry pastries are amazing, and the on-site Chop House is one of the best high-end restaurants in a town full of them. Ask for a third-floor room overlooking Colorado Avenue; I woke up one morning, looked beyond the buildings across the street, and noticed the clouds in the mountains were almost at eye level. During the off-season, particularly September–October and March–April, the guest rooms are shockingly affordable.

The **Aspen Street Inn** (330 W. Pacific Ave., 888/728-1950, www.telluridehotels. com, $149–229) took over from the beloved San Sophia B&B not long ago. It still offers a breakfast buffet and luxurious guest rooms, but the hands-on staff attention is no longer there.

$200-300

The ski-in, ski-out **The Peaks Resort & Golden Door Spa** (136 Country Club Dr., 970/728-6800 or 800/789-2220, www.the-peaksresort.com, $229–259) is literally on a cliff in the middle of Telluride's Mountain Village. The views of Mount Wilson and various other peaks are incredible—you feel like you're standing in a beer commercial—and the 174 guest rooms and suites, 14 penthouse condominiums, and 10 private cabins are filled with CD players, huge down comforters, and terrycloth bathrobes. As for the spa, let's just say the Skier's Salvation Massage is aptly named.

(Camel's Garden (250 W. San Juan Ave.,

970/728-9300 or 888/772-2635, www.camels-garden.com, $234–421) has 35 guest rooms, suites, and condos that are pink and super-luxurious, with Italian marble bathrooms, balconies, and fireplaces. Whereas most quaint hotels in secluded mountain towns play up the antiques and Old West history, Camel's Garden is thoroughly modern, with immaculate shining hardwood floors and a facade that looks like a suburban-hipster townhouse complex. It's also home of Oak, an upscale restaurant.

A huge river-rock fireplace is the most impressive part of the **Mountain Lodge at Telluride** (457 Mountain Village Blvd., 970/369-5000, www.mountainlodgetelluride. com, $219–319), which is in a perfect location for skiers and has both standard hotel rooms and larger condominiums with kitchens.

Next to a pond, river, and wetlands, **The Ice House** (310 S. Fir St., 970/728-6300 or 800/544-3436, www.icehouselodge.com, $203–395) has a woodsy feel, mostly due to the balconies and mountain views in every room. It was remodeled in 2008, and all 10 suites have a wet bar, marble bathrooms, and antique Navajo rugs.

In a brown brick-and-wood building that's a cross between a ski condo and a college dorm, **The Hotel Telluride** (199 N. Cornet St., 866/468-3501, www.thehoteltelluride.com, $209–256) is a nice half step toward the luxury of The Peaks Resort or the New Sheridan. The Spa has deep-cleansing facials and Swedish massages; The Bistro serves a breakfast buffet; the lobby has comfortable leather sofas and wool rugs; and each of the 59 guest rooms has something called "The Incredible Bed."

$300-400

Also in a convenient spot for skiers, the **Inn at Lost Creek** (119 Lost Creek Lane, 970/728-5678 or 888/601-5678, www.innat-lostcreek.com, $290–475) is a high-end hotel that opened in 1988; it includes the 9545 Restaurant & Bar, which serves steak, duck breast, and other expensive dishes and has a hefty wine list.

A huge corner hotel downtown, the red-brick **Hotel Columbia Telluride** (300 San Juan Ave., 970/728-0660 or 800/201-9505, www.columbiatelluride.com, $350–495) opened in 1995 with 21 fireplace-equipped guest rooms, including two penthouse suites, plus a rooftop hot tub and the fancy Cosmopolitan Restaurant. The nearby gondola is a little noisy, especially in the summer.

For condominium information, contact the **Telluride & Mountain Village Convention & Visitors Bureau** (630 W. Colorado Ave., 970/728-3041 or 888/605-2578, www.visit-telluride.com).

FOOD

Before making a reservation, check the on-line **Telluride Dining Guide** (www.telluride-diningguide.com), a great resource that covers the best restaurants in town and inexpensive breakfast-and-sandwich gems.

Snacks, Cafés, and Breakfast

The two best things about the downtown bakery, deli, and café fixture **Baked in Telluride** (127 S. Fir St., 970/728-4775, www.discovercolorado.com/bakedintelluride, 5:30 A.M.–10 P.M. daily, $9) are (1) the pizza, and (2) it delivers after 5 P.M. and for free to the Mountain Village. Plus, the bread and bagels are homemade, the soup and sandwiches are cheap and plentiful, and the pasta dinners are $7. The Telluride institution survived a February 2009 fire and reopened in summer 2011.

Maggie's Bakery & Café (217 E. Colorado Ave., 970/728-3334, 7:30 A.M.–3 P.M. daily, $9) is your basic but rarely disappointing breakfast-and-burger joint, with bacon and eggs for the morning and sandwiches for lunch.

Casual

Fat Alley's BBQ (122 S. Oak St., 970/728-3985, www.discovercolorado.com/fatalley, 11 A.M.–10 P.M. daily, $10) is a haven for Telluride's "trustafarians"—which is to say, well-off locals who don't want to dump all their trust-fund money on meals at Allred's—and

others who need a break from white tablecloths and $800 bottles of wine. The tables are built for families, the beer is cheap, and the pork sandwiches and big plates of ribs are straight out of the South.

The **Floradora Saloon** (103 W. Colorado Ave., 970/728-8884, http://floradorasaloon.com, 11:30 A.M.–2:45 P.M. and 5 P.M.–close Mon.–Fri., 10 A.M.–2:45 P.M. and 5 P.M.–close Sat.–Sun., $15) has the feel of a townie brew-pub, but its bar food is unexpected—barbecue duck quesadilla and tacos, seafood gumbo, duck French onion soup, and blue cheese, bacon, and avocado burgers.

Siam Telluride (200 S. Davis St., 970/728-6886, www.siamtelluride.com, 5–10 P.M. daily, $15) is a Thai restaurant best known for its large multifaceted entrées ($25), including ahi tuna with vegetables, wrapped in dried seaweed, and chicken cordon bleu with shrimp, mango, and asparagus, wrapped in ham.

Upscale

To get to ⟨⟨ **Allred's** (565 Mountain Village Blvd., 970/728-7474, www.allredsrestaurant.com, 5:30–9 P.M. daily, $38), at 10,551 feet above sea level, you need to take a gondola to the top. The views of various 13,000-foot mountains are a bit distracting, but dishes like macadamia- and hazelnut-crusted soft-shell crab with Himalayan red rice, tropical fruit, and Thai coconut broth should drag your focus back to the table. The head chef is Bob Scherner, a former sous-chef for Charlie Trotter in Chicago. A concert pianist plays in the bar 7–10 P.M. Wednesday–Sunday.

⟨⟨ **Honga's Lotus Petal & Tea Room** (135 E. Colorado Ave., 970/728-5134, www.hongaslotuspetal.com, 6–10 P.M. daily, $23) has the best sushi bar in town, plus superb vegetarian and organic chicken and beef dishes. It's Asian fusion with an emphasis on Thai and Japanese, along with especially potent curry and fruit flavors—and a wide variety of cocktails from all over the world. The food arrives in large, colorful bowls that match the inviting, wide-open feel of the restaurant.

Inside the Hotel Columbia Telluride

downtown, the **Cosmopolitan** (300 W. San Juan Ave., 970/728-1292, www.cosmotelluride.com, 5–9 P.M. daily, $32) is most famous for its coffee-and-donuts dessert—a reference not to Krispy Kreme but to Southern beignets. The menu is long on fish—lobster corn dogs are more New England seaside bistro than New York City hot-dog stand—but the chicken and pork dishes are excellent as well.

La Marmotte (150 San Juan Ave., 970/728-6232, www.lamarmotte.com, 5:30–9:30 P.M. daily, $28) is one of those simple and confident French bistros that puts only six entrées on its dinner menu—the spinach-stuffed chicken breast is a highlight.

Southern chef Eliza H. S. Gavin used to cook at Galatoire's, the Cajun fixture on Bourbon Street in New Orleans, but at **221 South Oak Bistro** (221 S. Oak St., 970/728-9507, www.221southoak.com, 5:30–10 P.M. Tues.–Sat., 10 A.M.–1 P.M. and 5:30–10 P.M. Sun., $33), there's nary a red-beans-and-rice or jambalaya dish on the menu. Rather, the bistro is heavy on upscale fish and steak dishes, such as ruby red trout with spaghetti squash and wild mushroom ravioli ($21). Maybe it's because Gavin studied in Paris and the Napa Valley as well. There's a brunch one Sunday a month.

In the Mountain Village (in case you couldn't tell by the name), **La Piazza Del Villaggio** (117 Lost Creek Lane, 970/728-8283, www.lapiazzadelvillaggioristorante.com, 5:30–9 P.M. Mon.–Sat., $38) is an elegant little Italian *ristorante* that serves its share of risotto, *zuppa,* and gnocchi as well as succulent entrées such as sautéed veal loin cutlets and yellowtail with ginger and jalapeños.

INFORMATION AND SERVICES

Several websites deliver the basics about Telluride. The **Town of Telluride** (113 W. Columbia Ave., 970/728-2155, www.telluride-co.gov) has a directory of official phone numbers and sections on parks and recreation, history, and so forth. The **Telluride Ski Resort** (800/778-8581, www.tellurideskiresort.com) includes snow reports, weather maps, and hotel and restaurant listings as well as a "summer" page on hiking, cycling, and other non-skiing activities. Telluride's tiny newspaper is the **Daily Planet** (www.telluridenews.com), and www.telluride.com is a marketing site that emphasizes real estate but is reasonably informative.

The nearest major hospital is in Montrose, which may be impossible to reach in the dead of winter, but Telluride has a few medical facilities. The **Telluride Medical Center** (500 W. Pacific Ave., 970/728-3848, www.tellmed.org) provides 24-hour emergency care and has a trauma center. Within the center is the **Institute for Altitude Medicine** (970/728-6767, www.altitudemedicine.org), which offers clinical care and conducts studies for people operating at 8,000–12,000 feet of elevation. Another outlet is at 113 Lost Creek Lane, Suite A, in the Blue Mesa Building of the Mountain Village.

GETTING THERE AND AROUND

The **Telluride Regional Airport** (1500 Last Dollar Rd., 970/728-8600, www.tellurideairport.com) opened in 1984 and has since expanded to accommodate several major airlines—Frontier, America West, and United among them. Many connecting flights to Denver International Airport are available.

A free bus service, the **Galloping Goose** (970/728-5700, www.telluride-co.gov, 7 A.M.–9 P.M. daily, extended hours during festivals and ski season), loops through downtown Telluride, hitting stops at the gondola plaza, the library, the courthouse, and other central places. **Dial-A-Ride** (970/728-8888, 7 A.M.–1 A.M. daily mid-Nov.–mid-Oct.) is a free shuttle around Mountain Village.

"The most beautiful commute in America," boasts Telluride's website of the gondola (www.telluride.com/telluride/the-gondola.html, 7 A.M.–midnight daily late May–mid-Oct. and late Nov.–early Apr.), and it's no exaggeration, given the peaceful float over the mountains from downtown to Mountain Village.

The eight-passenger G cars are open 275 days a year; it's about 10 minutes from Station Telluride (near the corner of Oak St. and San Juan Ave.) to Station Mountain Village, and another 1.5 minutes to Station Village Parking. Passengers can transport bikes in some of the gondola cars.

Both Ridgway and Ouray are small towns en route to Telluride, just a few miles north along U.S. 550. Follow the signs to Telluride from either town. Silverton is harder to reach—to get there from Telluride, take Highway 145 south, turn left on County Road D65, left again on County Road 8, then take U.S. 550 south. **Mountain Limo** (970/728-9606 or 888/546-6894, www.mountain-limo.com) arranges van and limousine trips around the Telluride area, including to tiny mountain towns such as Silverton and Ouray.

OURAY

Ouray may look like the prettiest, most placid mountain town in the world, but the man who inspired its name was ambiguous and troubled. Known as "the white man's friend"—for better or worse—Taos, New Mexico–born Chief Ouray was the leader of the Utes beginning in the mid-1800s. He was by all accounts a great and brilliant man with a beautiful and equally stately wife, Chipeta, and the two were so well respected that they met personally with U.S. presidents Ulysses S. Grant and Rutherford B. Hayes.

When whites started settling on Western land that had belonged to the Utes for decades, Ouray preached compromise and conciliation. He signed treaties for the Utes to give up their land east of the Continental Divide in exchange for better conditions vis-à-vis white Americans. Many of his people considered him a traitor, and some even tried to kill him, but treaties and negotiations continued.

Until 1878: Tensions were high due to conflicts between the Utes and Colorado gold miners, and they peaked when reformer Nathan Meeker tried to push the Indians into a utopian farming arrangement like the one he famously set up in Greeley. Many Utes wouldn't take it, and they killed Meeker and seven other whites and took women and children captive; Ouray intervened on behalf of the hostages. Americans lost sympathy for the Utes, and in 1880 Ouray signed a treaty agreeing to leave Colorado and move to Utah.

Ouray died not long after that of natural causes, but his small southwestern namesake town, founded in 1875 as gold-mining territory, lives on as a quaint Old West tourist attraction. The Tabeguache Utes lived in this beautiful San Juan Mountains spot for centuries during warm weather until the miners took it over, building saloons, hotels, bordellos, and churches in pretty Victorian-style buildings—some of which stand on Main Street today. Mountains edge up against the town, and it's a hot spot for ice climbing.

Sights
The **Million Dollar Highway** is the skinny, treacherous two-lane section of U.S. 550 that veers up and down a mountain from out-of-the-way Ouray to secluded Silverton. Although crews keep it open year-round, it scared the hell out of me when I tried to make it one mid-spring day, when it didn't look especially threatening from the dry vantage point at the bottom. Ouray's section is known as **Red Mountain Pass,** an 1880s toll road for miners dragging gold ore out of town.

Laid-back Telluride hippies and other visitors have been filling Ouray's hot springs for decades—and before that, the Utes saw the natural waters as healing spirits. **The Historic Wiesbaden Hot Springs Spa & Lodge** (625 5th St., 970/325-4347 or 888/846-5191, www.wiesbadenhotsprings.com, $132–347) is an extraordinary hotel built above an underground vapor cave, open to visitors as a sort of natural jetted tub, that gets its heat during the winter from the adjacent natural hot springs. Those waters range 78–128°F, and it's the most soothing place to stay in southwestern Colorado. It's not to be mistaken for the **Ouray Hot Springs Pool and Fitness Center** (1200 Main St., 970/325-7073, www.cityofouray.com, 10 A.M.–10 P.M. daily Memorial Day–Labor Day,

© MATT INDEN/WEAVER MULTIMEDIA GROUP/COLORADO TOURISM OFFICE

families enjoying the Ouray Hot Springs

the 27 rooms over three floors. Today, the museum concentrates on mining, ranching, and railroading along with Native American culture and artifacts.

The **Bachelor-Syracuse Mine Tour** (1222 County Rd. 14, 970/325-0220 or 888/227-4585, www.bachelorsyracusemine.com, tours on the hour 9 A.M.–4 P.M. daily mid-May–mid-June and mid-Aug.–mid-Sept., 9 A.M.–5 P.M. daily mid-June–mid-Aug., $16) is a ride on a "trammer" (mine train) about 3,350 feet into Gold Hill, where visitors can pan for gold and learn about the Old West mining days. There's a gift shop, a blacksmith shop, and an outdoor café.

Sports and Recreation

The big-time **mountaineering** spot in Ouray is **Mount Sneffels,** which doesn't lend itself to official trails and well-marked paths; it's more for backcountry enthusiasts. One decently run trail up this 14,150-foot mountain peak involves a lot of uphill scrambling. To get to the trailhead from Ouray, take U.S. 550 south and turn onto Highway 361, otherwise known as Yankee Boy Basin Road. Follow the signs to the basin; it's a rough road, so a 4WD vehicle helps. Head toward Mount Sneffels and Blue Lakes Pass, and park where you have to stop. Then go on foot the rest of the way to the trailhead. Also, heed this warning from the **Ouray Trail Group** (www.ouraytrails. org): "Mount Sneffels is a climb—not a hike!… The upper part of the mountain, in the best circumstances, requires scrambling on steep slopes with loose rock, and much of the year requires ascending a steep couloir where an ice ax is essential."

Mount Sneffels is part of the **Sneffels Range,** encompassing its namesake fourteeners and numerous thirteener peaks. Many are located north and west of town, with accessible paths from Ouray itself. Somewhat easier than Mount Sneffels, but still no cakewalk, is **Teakettle,** which has a tricky preponderance of unhinged volcanic rock, common in this area. To get here, head south of Ouray along U.S. 550, turn right onto Highway 361, and

noon–9 P.M. Mon.–Fri., 11 A.M.–9 P.M. Sat.–Sun. Labor Day–Memorial Day, $10), a more conventional type of hot springs that also has exercise equipment in the fitness center.

Box Canyon Falls & Park (off U.S. 550, southwest Ouray, 970/325-7080 or 970/325-7065, www.cityofouray.com, 9 A.M.–5 P.M. daily May, 8 A.M.–8 P.M. daily Memorial Day–Labor Day, 8 A.M.–dusk Labor Day–Apr., $3) spills thousands of gallons of water every minute from Canyon Creek to a boxy rock formation 285 feet below. It's a pretty spot in a town where everything is a pretty spot, and the visitors center gives interactive geology lessons. A walkway and suspension bridge take you directly under the falls.

The **Ouray County Museum** (420 6th Ave., 970/325-4576, www.ouraycountyhistoricalsociety.org, 1–4:30 P.M. Thurs.–Sat. mid-Apr.–mid-May, 10 A.M.–4:30 P.M. Mon.–Sat., noon–4:30 P.M. Sun. mid-May–Sept., 10 A.M.–4:30 P.M. Thurs.–Sat. Oct.–Nov., $5) was a miners hospital from 1887 to 1964, and it's easy to imagine patients and doctors roaming

FOUR-WHEEL-DRIVING IN SOUTHWEST COLORADO

Rugged mountain roads make for 4WD paradise throughout much of Colorado, especially in the southwest, where the San Juans are drier, dirtier, and less explored than their Rocky neighbors to the north. Here are six excellent trails:

- **Dolores:** The drive up Highway 145 to Scotch Creek is filled with muddy holes and leads to serious lake and abandoned-mine territory.

- **Ouray:** The last stretch of County Road 361 (off U.S. 550) into Yankee Boy Basin is 4WD only, and the mountain views and wildflower-rich landscape are terrific.

- **Purgatory:** The route from here to Silverton atop Coal Bank and Molas Passes is an out-of-the-way tour of the area's steepest mountains and deepest valleys.

- **Ridgway:** The gravel County Road 10, just north of Ridgway off U.S. 550, leads to Owl

Creek Pass; the views of 11,781-foot Chimney Rock are great, and the drive isn't as strenuous as some other 4WD passes in the area. Try it in late summer or fall, when the trees are changing color.

- **Silverton:** Several tricky roads around Silverton lead to historic mining areas around town, including Engineer and Cinnamon Passes.

- **Telluride:** Tomboy Road, beyond North Fir Street, where the National Guard once put an end to a miners strike, goes over Imogene Pass, a thirteener, and has a nice vantage point overlooking Bridal Veil Falls.

For more information on 4WD driving in this area – or to a rent a Jeep or other vehicle – try **Silver Summit** (640 Mineral St., Silverton, 970/387-0240 or 800/352-1637, www.silversummitrvpark.com), one of many companies in the area that parks a bunch of Jeeps for rent on the side of the road.

---

drive about 6.5 miles to the Camp Bird mine entrance. From here—it helps to have a 4WD vehicle—keep heading uphill, past the road to Governor Basin to a visible restroom area in lower Yankee Boy Basin.

More manageable hiking trails in Ouray take visitors past such dramatic and colorful areas as Box Canyon Falls, Bear Creek Falls, and the Grizzly Bear Mine. One of the most popular is **Bear Creek Trail,** a difficult 4.2-mile (one-way) trip up and down narrow ledges to the Grizzly Bear and Yellow Jacket mines. En route, you'll see huge mountain peaks and, in the distance, the outline of the Grand Mesa. The trailhead is two miles south of town along U.S. 550; park beyond the south end of the tunnel. Much easier is the **Lower Cascade Falls Trail,** a pretty 0.25-mile hike to the base of the falls. To get here, walk in the uphill direction along 8th Avenue from the intersection with Main Street.

For more Ouray trails, the **Ouray Chamber**

Resort Association (800/228-1876, www.ouraycolorado.com/Hiking) posts an elaborate trail map with descriptions, and the volunteer-run **Ouray Trail Group** (www.ouraytrails.org) has even more detailed information.

Ironton Park has 3–4 miles of groomed **cross-country skiing** tracks, about nine miles south of town on U.S. 550. From U.S. 550, turn left on County Road 20, take the left fork, and follow the squiggly road until another fork. Turn left, and look for Ironton Park a bit up the road. There are five nice walks accessible from the trailhead, including **Colorado Boy,** a 0.6-mile loop along a stream that leads to an old mine. Another popular track is **Top of the Pines,** a four-mile path through a mesa-top meadow with vista views in every direction; to get here, start in nearby Ridgway, drive west, turn south on County Road 5, drive five miles, and turn right on Highland Drive. Another excellent trail is **Miller Mesa Road,** a roughly six-mile path maintained by a local resident; it leads through meadows and aspen forests, and the views of the Sneffels range are superb. To get here, take Highway 62 out of Ridgway, turn south onto County Road 5, drive about 5.5 miles, park at the end of the plowed road, and ski as the road continues. All of the aforementioned trails are also excellent for **snowshoeing** or hiking in the summer.

An excellent cross-country skiing and snowshoeing resource is the **Ouray County Nordic Council** (970/626-3347, www.ouraytrails.org), a branch of the Ouray Trail Group, whose members' phone numbers are on the website. The Council grooms the tracks in Ironton Park.

Numerous big rivers flow in Ouray County, and the **fishing** is generally excellent throughout the summer and much of the spring and fall. Start with the **Cimarron River,** just below Silver Jack Reservoir, accessible at Forest Road 858 near the **Big Cimarron Campground** (U.S. 550, near the south end of Ouray, $18), which has 19 tent sites. This area is known for its dry fly-fishing, and the lower part of the river has plentiful wild rainbow and brown trout. The **San Miguel River** (Hwy. 162, east of Ouray) can be hit-or-miss, depending on snowpack, but generally has enough rainbow and cutthroat trout to go around April–November. For hardier anglers, **Blue Lakes** is a recreation area with three lakes at elevations of 11,000 feet. The trout are huge. But to get here, you have to hike four miles into the Mount Sneffels Wilderness; take U.S. 550 south from Ouray, turn right at County Road 361, turn right at County Road 26A, turn left at County Road 26, and stay right for another 2.5 miles. Pay attention to weather conditions!

White-water rafting is a big deal in this area, thanks to the huge winter snowpack leading to intense summer rapids. Two of the best options are the **San Miguel River,** which drops roughly 7,000 feet from mountains to desert, leading to white-water rapids in the Class II–III range. In other words, it's fun but not hugely technical. **Scenic River Tours** (703 W. Tomichi Ave., Gunnison, 970/641-3131, www.scenicrivertours.com) will set you up with guides, rafts, and routes.

Another big-time sport in Ouray: **rock climbing.** The North Buttress section of Mount Sneffels is a tough but scenic climb. From Ouray, take U.S. 550 south and turn onto Highway 361. Follow the signs to the basin; it's a rough road, so a 4WD vehicle helps. Head toward Mount Sneffels and Blue Lakes Pass, and park where you have to stop. Then go on foot the rest of the way to the trailhead. For rock-climbing resources and guides, try **San Juan Mountain Guides** (970/325-4925, www.ourayclimbing.com).

Camping is a popular outdoor activity in the Ouray area. To get to the **Uncompahgre National Forest Amphitheater Campground** (877/444-6777, www.recreation.gov, $18), take U.S. 550 to the south end of Ouray, look for the campground sign, then drive one mile to the entrance. Locals call this part of the state "Little Switzerland." When you reach the campground, you'll see why: It has a glacial mountain backdrop and green meadows dotted with little alpine lakes.

© MATT INDEN/WEAVER MULTIMEDIA GROUP/COLORADO TOURISM OFFICE

ice climbers challenging themselves on a frozen waterfall in the Ouray Ice Park

◖ Ouray Ice Park

Featured in *Esquire* magazine in 2004, this ice park (Uncompahgre Gorge, 970/325-4288, www.ourayicepark.com) draws gearheads who can't be bothered with wimpy little excursions like extreme snowboarding. The owner of Ouray Hydroelectric bought the property in 1992, then (after procuring insurance, of course) allowed people to spray water all over it and climb to the top. Thanks to imaginative climbers and half-inch PVC pipe, the ice turned into art—blue, shiny, and crystallized—and then a popular sport with 40 different climbing paths in three areas of the city-leased park.

Shopping

Ouray's Main Street strip has a mixture of practical and arty shopping for various kinds of travelers. The best gallery is **Ouray Glassworks** (619 Main St., 800/748-9421, www.ourayglassworks.com, 10 A.M.–4 P.M. daily), where artist Sam Rushing blows his own bowls, hummingbird feeders, and various ornaments.

Accommodations

For a town this small, Ouray has a ton of hotels, inns, motels, and bed-and-breakfasts, many of which are elegant and distinctive (although you can, of course, stay at the Best Western Twin Peaks). Most are in historic buildings, and some, like the Beaumont and the St. Elmo, retain their stately ambience.

The ◖ **Beaumont Hotel** (505 Main St., 970/325-7000 or 888/447-3255, www.beaumonthotel.com, $119–159), which in its days as the "flagship of the San Juans" served Teddy Roosevelt, Herbert Hoover, and Belgium's King Leopold, opened in 1887 but spent 35 years as a large boarded-up shack. A renovation began in 1998, and today's version of the Beaumont includes a huge wooden lobby staircase, a salon and spa, and the Tundra Restaurant.

The **Ouray Hotel** (303 6th Ave., 970/325-0500 or 800/216-8729, www.ourayhotel.com, $50–150) isn't quite as refurbished and beautiful as the Beaumont, but it's in a solid

Victorian-style corner brick building erected in 1893 and restored a century later.

Along with mountainside hot tubs, the **Box Canyon Lodge & Hot Springs** (45 3rd Ave., 970/325-4981 or 800/327-5080, www.boxcanyonouray.com, $115–160) includes a small triangular lodge and guest rooms with free satellite TV service and DVD players.

The **China Clipper Inn** (525 2nd St., 970/325-0565 or 800/315-0565, http://ouray-lodging–inns.com, $135–159) is in a three-story Victorian just below the mountains, but its primary distinction is a nautical theme—all 12 guest rooms are named after famous clipper ships, from *Witch of the Seas* to *Flying Cloud*. Fortunately, pirates rarely walk the halls at night shouting, "Ar!"

Quaint and fancy, with flower-patterned wallpaper and frilly bedcovers, the **St. Elmo Hotel** (426 Main St., 970/325-4951 or 866/243-1502, www.stelmohotel.com, $125–190) is in a restored boxy-brick turn-of-the-20th-century building. It includes the Bon Ton and Buen Tiempo Restaurants.

True to its name, the **Riverside Inn** (1805 N. Main St., 970/325-4061 or 800/432-4170, www.ourayriversideinn.com, $44–110) includes several small wooden cabins adjacent to the Uncompahgre River as well as a fairly standard 18-room lodge. Hiking trails are all over the grounds.

Food

Most of Ouray's best restaurants are in Ouray's best hotels. The Beaumont's **Bistro** (505 Main St., 970/325-7000, www.beaumonthotel.com, 11 A.M.–9 P.M. Thurs.–Sat., 10:30 A.M.–2 P.M. Sun., $18) serves high-end steak, chicken, and fish from its second-floor perch overlooking Main Street. In the basement of the St. Elmo, the **Bon Ton Restaurant** (426 Main St., 970/325-4951, www.stelmohotel.com, 5:30–9 P.M. daily, $25) is Italian with frills—from pasta primavera to escargot and crawfish tails. And while the restaurant at the **Historic Western Hotel** (210 7th Ave., 970/325-4645 or 888/624-8403, www.historicwesternhotel.com, 4:30–10 P.M. daily, reduced hours off-season, $14) isn't as distinguished as the other two, it's a great family place for burgers and beer.

Information

The **Ouray Chamber Resort Association** (1230 Main St., 800/228-1876, www.ouray-colorado.com) maintains a most informative website, with plenty of dining, lodging, and shopping listings.

RIDGWAY

Whenever I go to the Telluride area, I like to avoid the "big city" and stay among the dirt roads and one streetlight of Ridgway, about half an hour south of Montrose. It looks like a sleepy mountain area, and although designer Ralph Lauren's Double RL Ranch is just south of town, time passes slowly here—it was once a major Western railroad hub and a serious ranching area, but not so much these days.

The 1969 John Wayne movie *True Grit* was filmed in Ridgway, and several monuments (including the True Grit restaurant) display Wayne memorabilia. For a cheap, quick trip to the San Juans, stay at the homey Chipeta Sun Lodge and make sightseeing runs to Telluride, Ouray, and Silverton.

Sights

Although the last train left Ridgway in 1951, the tiny green **Ridgway Railroad Museum** (U.S. 550 and Hwy. 62, no phone, ridgwayrailroadmuseum@ouraynet.com, www.ridgwayrailroadmuseum.org, 9 A.M.–4 P.M. daily June–Sept., 10 A.M.–3 P.M. Mon.–Fri. Oct.–May, free) maintains a number of photos and displays about the old days.

Sports and Recreation

It's hard to find sandy beaches in the mountains, but the **Ridgway State Park & Recreation Area** (28555 U.S. 550, 970/626-5822, http://parks.state.co.us/parks/ridgway) has a curvy lake filled with rainbow trout, large-mouthed bass, and yellow perch. The park has 5–6 pretty **hiking** trails, some of which go along the lake, and all of which are in the shadows of pristine mountain scenery. Try the **Enchanted Mesa Trail,** a 2.5-mile run with trailheads at the Pa-Co-Chu-Puk (north side of the park) and Dutch Charlie (south side) areas. It's a long and challenging trail, but it runs through several wildlife areas, where mule deer and elk mill around in a flat-top pasture. The park also has three camping areas, with 258 **campsites** (970/626-5822, www.parks.state.co.us/Parks/Ridgway/Camping/Pages/Camping.aspx) for RVs and trailers ($22) and another 25 for walk-in campers ($16), plus yurt facilities.

The park also offers a ramp for **boating** (8 A.M.–4 P.M. daily Mar.–Apr., 7 A.M.–9 P.M. Sun.–Thurs., 7 A.M.–10 P.M. Fri.–Sat. May–mid-Sept.) Check the park website (http://parks.state.co.us/parks/ridgway) for information about inspections.

White-water rafting enthusiasts should try the narrow canyons of the **Uncompahgre River,** which runs from the town of Ridgway to the Ridgway Reservoir. The rafting difficulty is in the easygoing Class II–III range, and the scenery is superb, especially for wildlife viewers and bird-watchers. **RIGS Fly Shop & Guide Service** (65 Sherman St., Suite 2, 970/626-4460 or 888/626-4460, www.fishrigs.com) leads white-water rafting tours and provides kayak and fishing equipment and resources.

For **hikers, bird-watchers, snowmobilers,** and **cross-country skiers, Owl Creek Pass** has shady aspen meadows, expansive views of Courthouse Mountain, Chimney Rock, and an impressive set of pinnacles to view or climb on Cimarron Ridge. The road to the trailhead is quite rustic, so a 4WD vehicle is strongly recommended, if not essential. Travel five miles north of Ridgway on U.S. 550, then east on Owl Creek Pass Road (County Rd. 8); after 16 miles, take West Fork Road west for two miles until you see the Courthouse Mountain trailhead.

Accommodations

I drove to the adobe (● **Chipeta Sun Lodge & Spa** (304 S. Lena St., 970/626-3737 or

800/633-5868, http://chipeta.com, $125–235) one March weekend for an impromptu two-day trip to Telluride and Silverton, and there were so few other guests that the front desk upgraded me to the second-floor hot-tub suite. Overlooking the San Juans, the room was incredible, and the hippie types who work at the lodge are sweet and helpful. It's a little more crowded, obviously, during high season, but not nearly as crowded as downtown Telluride.

Food

The **True Grit Café** (123 N. Lena St., 970/626-5739, www.truegritcafe.com, 11 A.M.–9:30 P.M. daily fall, 11 A.M.–8:30 P.M. daily winter, 11 A.M.–9 P.M. daily spring, 11 A.M.–10 P.M. daily summer, $12) is all burgers, fries, and beer but with friendly biker-and-hippie wooden-wall ambience—complete with John Wayne movie posters and paraphernalia on the walls. Don't waste your time looking for more elegant restaurants in the area, unless you're in the mood to drive to Ouray or Telluride. Note that the recent Coen Brothers remake of *True Grit*, sadly, was not filmed anywhere near here.

Information

The **Ridgway Area Chamber of Commerce** (150 Racecourse Rd., 970/626-5181 or 800/220-4959, www.ridgwaycolorado.com) website is mostly ads, but it posts some details about outdoor activities, food, lodging, and local businesses.

SILVERTON

Wander the streets of Silverton in March–April, when most of the skiers have gone home and the summer travelers have yet to arrive, and it's a 7- by 12-block clean-air Pleasantville in a valley of 14,000-foot peaks. The 500 townspeople mostly keep to themselves, although they're perfectly polite to visitors, who keep the Greene Street shops and hotels filled during high seasons. While Silverton boomed in the mining days, with 5,000 residents as late as 1912, isolation is a major part of its charm—the only way to get here (other than the Durango & Silverton Narrow Gauge

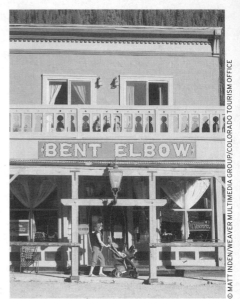

Silverton hearkens back to frontier days.

Railroad) is via the high hairpin curves of the Million Dollar Highway, the stretch of U.S. 550 that runs north from Durango and south from Ouray.

Note that most of the bars, shops, restaurants, and other services boom in the summer and dwindle to ghost-town status in the winter. The ski area is popular, but the sport is hardly big enough to populate the entire town à la Vail or Breckenridge. If you're planning to visit during the winter, be sure to double-check the seasonal business hours in advance.

Sights

The entire downtown area is a National Historic Landmark District, and it's pretty fun to imagine the crowded streets and overflowing saloons of the old days, from the 1880s to the 1910s, when miners left their ramshackle boarding houses to visit brothels on Saturday night and churches on Sunday morning. Among the historic buildings are the 1907 **San Juan County Courthouse** (1557 Greene St.), which still has a gold dome and a

TELLURIDE

© MATT INDEN/WEAVER MULTIMEDIA GROUP/COLORADO TOURISM OFFICE

clock tower; the 1902 **San Juan County Jail** (1559 Greene St.), now the San Juan County Historical Society; and the 1907 **Old County Hospital** (1315 Snowden St.), a boxy building that houses the *Silverton Standard and Miner* newspaper.

Silverton magazine will send a copy of a walking-tour map if you send $10 to Circle B Publishing (P.O. Box 705, Ridgway, CO 81432). Or click on "Maps" at the **Silverton Chamber of Commerce & Visitors Center** website (www.silvertoncolorado.com).

The most notable thing about the **San Juan County Historical Society** (1559 Greene St., 970/387-5838, www.silvertonhistoricsociety. org, 10 A.M.–5 P.M. Memorial Day–early Oct., $5) is its location—inside the old county jail, the first building on Court House Square, which was by several accounts consistently full during the mining years. Converted to a museum in 1965, the building's exhibits include old railroad passes, mining equipment, handguns, a recreated schoolroom and kitchen, and, of course, jail cells on the second floor.

The **Old Hundred Gold Mine** (721 County Rd. 4A, 970/387-5444 or 800/872-3009, www.minetour.com, 10 A.M.–4 P.M. daily mid-May–mid-Oct., tours on the hour, $18) opened in 1872 when three German brothers staked their claim to a gold vein called "Number Seven." Although it closed in 1973, the underground mine—45–50°F at all times—simulates the old days with mine-train rides and gold panning. Another gold-panning spot is the **Mayflower Mill** (Hwy. 110, two miles northeast of Silverton, 970/387-5838, www. silvertonhilstoricsociety.org, 10 A.M.–5 P.M. daily Memorial Day–Labor Day, $8.50), which closed in 1991. Mayflower opened in 1929 with a state-of-the-art (at the time) aerial tram, in which miners rode small ore buckets like modern skiers on a lift. Some of the guides in recent years have been actual former mine and mill workers, and they tell great stories. Gold-panning is free. As of early 2012, the mill was undergoing a large renovation.

The **Christ of the Mines Shrine** (on top of Anvil Mountain, three miles north of Silverton) is a 12-ton white-marble statue carved in Carrara, Italy, and erected as a miners' tribute in 1959. At the time, it was considered a good-luck charm for struggling Silverton. You can reach it by hiking a mile up 10th Street or driving along Shrine Road.

Silverton Mountain

Silverton Mountain (Hwy. 110A, 6 miles north of Silverton, 970/387-5706, www.silvertonmountain.com) is an exclusive ski resort that climbs from 10,400 feet at the base to almost 12,300 feet at the peak. By "exclusive," I mean it's open only to expert and advanced skiers—and the resort strongly recommends eight-person groups for the steepest and rockiest trails (guides are available). One chairlift serves just 40 people per day, and be sure to read the safety precautions under "General Info" on the website; the high altitudes can be dangerous—the resort recommends ginseng or Viagra (!) to overcome this—weather changes are quick and frequent, and the skiing is "the steepest, most adventure-filled lift-served skiing this side of Valdez, Alaska." All-day guided skiing costs $139, while unguided runs are $49 for a lift ticket.

Also check the **Colorado Avalanche Information Center** (325 Broadway, Boulder, 303/499-9650, http://avalanche.state.co.us) for weather conditions.

Sports and Recreation

Beginning skiers are better off at the weekend-only, town-operated **Kendall Mountain Recreation Area** (1 Kendall Mountain Place, 970/387-5228, http://skikendall.com, lift tickets $15), which also has hills for sledders and tubers, and free ice-skating at the **Silverton Town Rink** (with skate rentals at the visitors center nearby).

Cross-country skiers can veer off the established ski-resort paths at the **St. Paul Ski Lodge** (Red Mountain Pass, U.S. 550 between Silverton and Ouray, 970/799-0785, www. skistpaul.com), an old miner's cabin with six rooms for 22 people and several groomed trails nearby. For more information about trails in the area, contact **Silverton Snowmobilers** (970/387-5512, www.silvertonsnowmobilers. org).

Silverton Mountain (Hwy. 110A, 6 miles north of Silverton, 970/387-5706, www.silvertonmountain.com) transforms from a ski resort to an extreme-cycling playground during summer—one of the runs is evocatively known as the Chicken [Expletive Deleted] Drop. It's probably best to bring your own bikes—mostly because rental shops are hard to find in this isolated area. It's for advanced riders only. Parking is $22 per day, and scenic lift rides are $15 each.

Hikers swear by the **Bear Creek Trail,** a not-too-strenuous five-mile loop that passes through incredible mountain-and-valley scenery. North of Silverton on U.S. 550, about 10 miles after Red Mountain Pass, you'll see the trailhead signs on the right side of the road.

For campers, **Molas Lake Park** (U.S. 550, 6 miles south of Silverton, 970/387-5522, www. molaslake.com, $18) is a public park that has the highest elevation of any campground in the Lower 48 states, at 10,515 feet. No reservations are available, so arrive early.

Entertainment

The **Miners Union Theatre** (1069 Greene St., 970/387-5337, www.atheatregroup.org) plays host to movies, theater events, and a fine-arts youth camp; A Theatre Group is the local company that books all the shows. It used to be on the second floor of Miners Union Hall, but today puts on shows at various Ouray-area locations, most commonly in the Grand Imperial Hotel (1219 Greene St., 970/387-2557 or 800/341-3340, www.grandimperialhotel.com).

Shopping

The shops of Silverton are generally of the kitschy, touristy variety, so if you want to find practical sweaters or even books, Ouray and Telluride are better bets. The **Blair Street Emporium** (1147 Blair St., 970/387-5323, 10 A.M.–4 P.M. daily, reduced hours off-season), packed with Christmas decorations year-round, exemplifies this trend.

Accommodations

In a wide, blue 1882 building at the center of Greene Street, the **Grand Imperial Hotel** (1219 Greene St., 970/387-2557 or 800/341-3340, www.grandimperialhotel.com, $80–150) has become a little worn over the years, but it's still the most recognizable and one of the nicest hotels in town.

The well-maintained **Wyman Hotel & Inn** (1371 Greene St., 800/609-7845, www. thewyman.com, $115–175) has huge beds, whirlpool tubs in many of the guest rooms, and a gourmet breakfast; a candlelight dinner is included in more expensive packages.

Also downtown is the **Teller House Hotel B&B** (1250 Greene St., 970/387-5423 or 800/342-4338, www.tellerhouse.com, $89–139), built by a prominent brewer in 1896. It's still one of the best-known hotels in town, but be sure to ask about the facilities before showing up—the "European-style" rooms have shared baths.

The **Bent Elbow** (1114 Blair St., 970/387-5775 or 877/387-5775, www.thebent.com, $100–140) dates to 1907, having been run by such Old West characters as Big Tillie and later Effie and Snarky, the latter of whom lost the building in a fire and rebuilt it completely in 1968. The bright-red brick building is in the Victorian style, although it's obviously a bit more modern than the Victorian period, and the guest rooms have that historic feel, with feather beds and wooden ceiling fans.

Food

The top of the 1883 building that houses **Natalia's 1912 Restaurant** (1159 Blair St., 970/387-5300 May–Oct., 928/282-3073 Nov.–Apr., www.natalias1912.com, 11 A.M.–8 P.M. daily summer, 11 A.M.–3 P.M. daily fall, closed winter, $10) once said "Mattie B's"—a reference to the madam who ran a notorious bordello. Today, it's a restaurant with a splashy red-and-white facade that serves American, Italian, and Mexican dishes and a lunch buffet.

Handlebars (117 13th St., 970/387-5395,

www.handlebarssilverton.com, 10:30 A.M.–9 P.M. daily, $10) is a boisterous bar and restaurant with Old West knickknacks, from photos to bandannas, hanging all over the walls and ceiling. The food is homemade bar fare, like seven types of burgers (including Buffalo Bill's buffalo burger), baby back ribs, chicken-fried steak, and peach cobbler.

The **Avalanche Coffee House** (1067 Blair St., 970/387-5282, www.silvertoncoloradocoffee.com, 7 A.M.–3 P.M. daily, $7) is a homey blue shack of a coffee-and-sandwiches joint that serves espresso and homemade soups to cold and desperate skiers. The coffeehouse serves pizza on weekends along with beer and wine.

Information
The **Silverton Chamber of Commerce** (U.S. 550 and Hwy. 110, 970/387-5654 or 800/752-4494, www.silvertoncolorado.com) has tons of dining, lodging, and outdoor-activity listings.

Montrose

Every time you drive from Denver to Telluride, you pretty much have to go through Montrose, an ordinary town that's perfectly placed for a pit stop since gas stations, supermarkets, fast-food restaurants, and affordable accommodations line this stretch of U.S. 50. It's hard to believe so much natural beauty is within a short drive: Black Canyon of the Gunnison National Park, the San Juan Mountains, Curecanti National Recreation Area, and Gunnison River. Utopian mountain towns Telluride, Ouray, Ridgway, and Crested Butte are just down the road.

Montrose's history is about as eventful as the town itself—with one colorful exception. In 1873, gold-mining wannabes Oliver D. "Pappy" Loutsenhizer, Alferd Packer, and several others showed up in Ute territory en route to what is now Breckenridge, but they ran into Chief Ouray's valley camp. Ouray encouraged them to turn back, which Loutsenhizer and some of his friends did, but Packer and four other men went on. They landed in a Lake City blizzard, where the trapped Packer cannibalized his companions.

Loutsenhizer eventually returned with a friend, and in 1881 the two founded and named Montrose after a duchess in a Walter Scott novel. Within the next 20 years, the railroad and the Gunnison Diversion Tunnel turned Montrose into a fairly important farming town, specializing in cotton and sugar beets.

SIGHTS
Ute Indian Museum and Ouray National Park
The Ute Indian Museum and Ouray National Park (17253 Chipeta Dr., 970/249-3098, www.historycolorado.org/museums/ute-indian-museum-0, 9 A.M.–4:30 P.M. Mon.–Sat., 11 A.M.–4:30 P.M. Sun. July–Sept., 9 A.M.–4 P.M. Mon.–Sat. Oct.–Dec., $4.50) is on the 8.65-acre plot owned by Chief Ouray and his wife, Chipeta, in the 1800s. Ouray, whose namesake

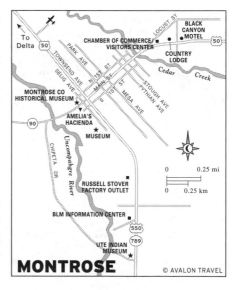

MONTROSE

© AVALON TRAVEL

town is about 30 miles south of Montrose, was the diplomatic Ute leader who befriended U.S. officials; he is considered a hero even though his willingness to compromise led to the Utes withdrawing from huge tracts of Colorado land. Built in 1956, the museum displays thousands of Ute photos and artifacts, and the grounds include a memorial park, Chipeta's crypt, and a plant garden.

Montrose County Historical Museum

The **Montrose County Historical Museum** (Main St. and Rio Grande Ave., 970/249-2085, www.montrosehistory.org, 9 A.M.–4 P.M. Mon.–Fri., 10 A.M.–2 P.M. Sat. mid-May–mid-Oct., by appointment mid-Oct.–mid-May, $6) is in the onetime Denver & Rio Grande Train Depot and, like many small Old West history museums in Colorado towns, displays wagons, farm tools, railroad memorabilia, Native American artifacts, and musical instruments.

© ALEXEY KAMENSKIY/123RF.COM
Black Canyon of the Gunnison National Park

◖ BLACK CANYON OF THE GUNNISON NATIONAL PARK

The unusually steep and scenic Black Canyon of the Gunnison National Park (Hwy. 347, office: National Park Service, 102 Elk Creek, Gunnison, 970/641-2337, www.nps.gov/blca, $15) gets much of the attention in this area as scenic landmarks go, and it's pretty amazing—a 53-mile cut of the earth that's 1,000 feet wide at the top with the 40-foot-wide Gunnison River at the bottom. But it's also a bit of a tourist trap, especially during summer, with a souvenir-selling visitors center, lines for outdoor restrooms, and a few crowded paths leading to points where you can look down the vertigo-inducing mesa cliffs into the sliver of river. Wildlife and birds are all over the place—in addition to commoners like hawks, wrens, ground squirrels, and chipmunks, sporadically making appearances are golden eagles, mountain lions, black bears, and even Rocky Mountain bighorn sheep.

You can check out the canyon in two fairly simple ways. The South Rim is about seven miles long, with 12 overlooks, and begins at the visitors center. To get there, take Highway 347 north from U.S. 50, then drive about six miles to the visitors center and hit one of scenic overlooks into the canyon. The North Rim's six overlooks are accessible via the gravel North Rim Road, beginning at the east end of Crawford State Park. Both the road and the North Rim Ranger Station, which is located near the entrance and contains information about the park, are closed during the winter.

A more difficult way into the canyon is the East Portal Road, a steep (16 percent grade!) and curvy path that begins in the northwest portion of Curecanti National Recreation Area, near the Gunnison Diversion Tunnel. One way to access the road is to start at Cimarron (U.S. 50, 18 miles east of the park).

The park offers several "official" hiking trails, four beginning at the South Rim and three at the North Rim. The easiest ones include the one-mile Rim Rock Nature Trail (South Rim), which overlooks the canyon, beginning at Campground Loop C and ending

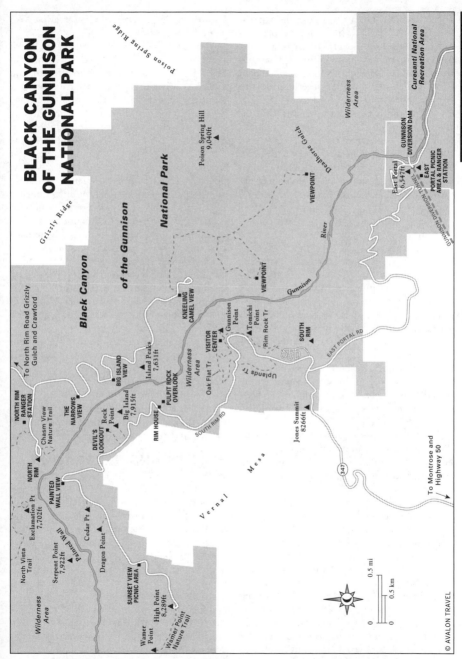

BLACK CANYON OF THE GUNNISON NATIONAL PARK

Poison Spring Ridge

Grizzly Ridge

Black Canyon

of the Gunnison

National Park

Poison Spring Hill 9,040ft

Deadhorse Gulch

Curecanti National Recreation Area

Wilderness Area

GUNNISON DIVERSION DAM

East Portal 6,547ft

EAST PORTAL PICNIC AREA & RANGER STATION

GUNNISON DIVERSION TUNNEL

VIEWPOINT

River

Gunnison

VIEWPOINT

To North Rim Road Grizzly Gulch and Crawford

KNEELING CAMEL VIEW

Island Peaks 7,631ft

BIG ISLAND VIEW

Wilderness Area

VISITOR CENTER

Gunnison Point

Tomichi Point

Rim Rock Tr

SOUTH RIM

EAST PORTAL RD

PULPIT ROCK OVERLOOK

Oak Flat Tr

Uplands Tr

NORTH RIM RANGER STATION

Chasm View Nature Trail

THE NARROWS VIEW

Big Island 7,915ft

Rock Point

RIM HOUSE

DEVIL'S LOOKOUT

SOUTH RIM RD

Jones Summit 8266ft

NORTH RIM

PAINTED WALL VIEW

Exclamation Pt 7,702ft

North Vista Trail

Serpent Point 7,922ft

Cedar Pt

Dragon Point

Vernal Mesa

347

To Montrose and Highway 50

Wilderness Area

Painted Wall

SUNSET VIEW PICNIC AREA

Warner Point

High Point 8,289ft

Warner Point Nature Trail

0.5 mi

0.5 km

0

© AVALON TRAVEL

at the Tomichi Point Overlook; the Chasm View Nature Trail (North Rim), just over 0.3 miles, which leads out of a forest to a scenic overlook that takes in the entire canyon; and the 0.7-mile Cedar Point Nature Trail (North Rim), which offers perhaps the best view of Painted Wall, which at 2,250 feet is the tallest cliff in the state. More strenuous trails include the two-mile Oak Flat Loop Trail (South Rim), which begins near the visitors center and traverses uphill switches and rocky paths, and the seven-mile Green Mountain Trail (North Rim), which has perhaps the best views of the canyon as well as the San Juans, Grand Mesa, and the West Elks.

It's also acceptable to bushwhack the incredibly steep paths down the valley into the river, but this approach is fraught with danger. The National Park Service recommends "only individuals in excellent physical condition should attempt these hikes" and warns of prevalent poison ivy, dead ends formed by steep cliffs, giardia in the water supplies, and unstable terrain. Even when you get to the river, the dangers persist—particularly slippery rocks. Bring tough hiking boots and plenty of water and be prepared to retrace your downward steps in order to get back up the cliffs. This area is accessible during winter, but be sure to bring an ice ax, crampons, snowshoes, and a rope.

Once you get into the river itself, via East Portal Road or scrambling down from the North or South Rim via one of the inner-canyon routes, the fishing is incredible. The trout streams are designated "Gold Medal" waters, which means, well, a whole lot of trout. Note that rainbow trout are catch-and-release, and live bait is forbidden.

Kayaking is big in the Gunnison River, but it's dangerous and recommended for experienced paddlers only. As with fishing, the access points are via East Portal Road or scrambling down the inner-canyon pathways from the North or South Rim. Of course, it's much harder to hike these hills carrying a kayak. Rafting is forbidden in this stretch of river; the National Park Service recommends the nearby

Gunnison Gorge National Conservation Area as an alternative.

You can tell just by the names of the Black Canyon cliffs—Painted Rock, Cimarron Slabs, Russian Arete, Checkerboard Wall, and so forth—that this area is a haven for rock climbers. The most popular areas for climbing—the North and South Chasm Walls—stretch roughly 1,820 feet from the tops of the rocks to the bottom of the canyon. Some climbs, such as the flat "Snake Dyke" flat route up a quartzite slab, are relatively easy, but all of them require experience, expertise, and preparation. **Skyward Mountaineering** (2412 Hidden Valley Dr., Grand Junction, 970/209-2985, www.skywardmountaineering.com) offers guided climbs, and its website contains detailed information about a number of routes. Also, numerous books about climbing, and adventure trips in general, have been written about the Black Canyon of the Gunnison—the National Park Service recommends Robbie Williams's *Black Canyon Rock Climbs* (Sharp End, 2001).

There are two campgrounds in the park. The one on the North Rim has 13 campsites (mid-May–mid-Oct., $12) in the forest and offers toilets, tables, grills, and water. The South Rim campground (year-round, $12) has 88 sites with the same amenities—and you can pay extra for electricity. Wood fires are prohibited in the canyon.

SPORTS AND RECREATION
Water Sports
The 14 miles of Gunnison River white-water at the bottom of Black Canyon National Park is not for the squeamish—the thin water passage is for expert **kayakers** only, and even some advanced paddlers have died trying. The water is cold all the time, the rocks are so close together that you can barely see the sun, poison ivy grows more than five feet high at some points, and the river is exclusively Class IV and Class V. If you must try, though, contact the **National Park Service** (102 Elk Creek, Gunnison, 970/641-2337, www.nps.gov/blca/contacts.htm) in advance.

Calmer waters are just west of the park, in the **Gunnison Gorge National Conservation Area** (Bureau of Land Management, 2465 S. Townsend Ave., Montrose, 970/240-5400, www.blm.gov/co/st/en/nca/ggnca.html). **Canoes** are kosher in this area, and several of Colorado's many white-water rafting outfits sponsor tours—try **Wilderness Aware Rafting** (Buena Vista, 719/395-2112 or 800/462-7238, www.inaraft.com) or the **Boulder Outdoor Center** (2707 Spruce St., Boulder, 303/444-8420 or 800/364-9376, www.boc123.com).

Fishing

Both the **Black Canyon of the Gunnison National Park** and the **Gunnison Gorge National Conservation Area** contain points where you can fish for brown and rainbow trout on the river. But getting there is hard, involving various 4WD-only routes and bushwhacking hikes. You'll need a free state fishing license, although the National Park Service gives out just a few, to whomever arrives first. It may be worth it: The Colorado Wildlife Commission considers this stretch of the Gunnison River "Gold Medal" waters, meaning 60 pounds of trout per surface acre. Just be sure not to swim or wade into the river.

Free permits are available through the **National Park Service** (970/641-2337, ext. 205, www.nps.gov/blca). Several local fishing shops provide information, guided tours, and equipment, including **Cimarron Creek** (317 E. Main St., Montrose, 970/249-0408, www.cimarroncreek.com).

Hiking

Bushwhackers can hike through Black Canyon of the Gunnison Park at any number of self-made trailheads—just be careful—but established (and safer) trails exist with views of both the top and the bottom. The two-mile **Oak Flat Loop** is just west of the park's **visitors center** (970/249-1914), about eight miles west of Montrose on U.S. 50, and descends briefly below the south rim. The easier three-mile

Exclamation Point begins on the North Vista Trail, leading due west from the ranger station on the north side of the park; you'll be able to walk right to the edge of the North Rim and stare 1,800 feet down to the river.

Gunnison Gorge National Conservation Area also has a few excellent hiking trails, including **Gunnison Gorge** itself, which begins about 9.5 miles north of Montrose on U.S. 550. Once you get to Falcon Road, turn right, drive 11.1 miles, turn right on Ute Road, and go 2.6 miles to the trailhead. It's not as breathtaking as the Black Canyon of the Gunnison, but the canyon views are nice.

To hike on local trails, you'll need a free permit from the **National Park Service** (970/641-2337, ext. 205, www.nps.gov/blca).

ENTERTAINMENT AND EVENTS

Although it mostly plays host to weddings and corporate events, the 600-seat **Montrose Pavilion** (1800 Pavilion Dr., 970/249-7015 or 800/982-2518) occasionally has dance, music, and theater events. North of Montrose, in tiny Olathe, the early-August **Olathe Sweet Corn Festival** (970/323-6006 or 866/363-2676, www.olathesweetcornfest.com) is a much bigger deal than you'd think, with big-name performers such as country singer Randy Travis supplementing the pancake breakfast, car show, and other corny events. (That's pronounced "Oh-LAYTH-uh," by the way.)

SHOPPING

Most of the shopping in Montrose is pretty generic, but the plain-looking **Russell Stover Factory Outlet** (2185 Stover Ave., 970/249-5372, www.russellstover.com, 9 A.M.–6 P.M. Mon.–Sat., 11 A.M.–6 P.M. Sun.) is a gigantic (7,500 square feet) building filled with chocolate and other gift candies. Disappointingly, there are no Oompa-Loompas or other psychedelic *Charlie and the Chocolate Factory*–style visions, but Stover does manufacture more than 100 million pounds of chocolate all over the United States every year.

ACCOMMODATIONS

Lodging in Montrose consists mostly of chains, but a few low-priced motels are good for a quick stop en route to Telluride, Ouray, Ridgway, or the Four Corners. The **Black Canyon Motel** (1605 E. Main St., 970/249-3495 or 800/348-3495, http://blackcanyonmotel.com, $50–60) has an outdoor pool, as does the wooden **Country Lodge** (1624 E. Main St., 970/249-4567, www.countrylodgecolorado.com, $69), where John Wayne reportedly stayed while filming *True Grit* in the 1960s.

About six miles from Montrose, the seven-room **Uncompahgre Bed & Breakfast** (21049 Uncompahgre Rd., 970/240-4000 or 800/318-8127, www.uncbb.com, $110–150) is slightly quainter than the other area hotels.

FOOD

Montrose is hardly an area around which to plan a gourmet trip, but it has a few distinctive restaurants, including **Amelia's Hacienda** (44 S. Grand Ave., 970/249-1881, www.ameliashacienda.com, 11 A.M.–9 P.M. Mon.–Fri., noon–9 P.M. Sat., noon–8 P.M. Sun., $10), one of the better Mexican restaurants in town.

INFORMATION AND SERVICES

The **Montrose Visitors and Convention Bureau** (1519 E. Main St., 970/249-5000 or 800/873-0244, www.visitmontrose.net) has up-to-date dining and lodging listings as well as city services.

Most of the tiny mountain towns in this area—Ouray, Ridgway, Silverton, and so forth—have little in the way of medical facilities. Telluride has a small hospital, but the biggest one in the region is the **Montrose Memorial Hospital** (800 S. 3rd St., 970/249-2211, www.montrosehospital.com).

GETTING THERE AND AROUND

The **Montrose Regional Airport** (2100 Airport Rd., 970/249-3203, www.montroseairport.com) services several major carriers, and it's a reliable alternative to Telluride's smaller airport in bad-weather conditions.

Durango

A college town with a lively Main Avenue, especially during summer, Durango is more of a real city than a scenic mountain hamlet like nearby Telluride. It's neither big (pop. 14,000) nor high (elevation 6,500 feet) nor amazingly popular with skiers. But its location on the Animas River (thus the name, which means "water town"), moderate climate, picturesque location underneath several huge mesas, and proximity to four Western states make it a pleasant place to pass through and an affordable place to live. The downtown area recalls Boulder's Pearl Street Mall, with its touristy shops and guitar-playing buskers, but it's also a practical place to make copies or buy CDs.

Durango began as a railroad town. After gold-mining drew thousands of people to the nearby San Juan Mountains, they incorporated Animas City, two miles north of what is Durango today; when the Denver and Rio Grande Railroad showed up within a few years, almost all 2,000 townspeople relocated to the new area. Durango officially became a town in 1881—a booming one, thanks to the railroad, although the 1893 silver crash forced many residents away and the rest into farming and ranching.

Durango lived on as a sleepy city for decades, but tourism gradually began to create growth. The city is within 30 miles of Mesa Verde National Park and Four Corners, as well as ski resorts such as Telluride and Silverton. Higher-end hotels, restaurants, and rows of tourist shops have sprung up in recent years to supplement attractions like the Durango & Silverton Narrow Gauge Railroad. Note that Durango is also a popular motorcycling hot spot—when my family stayed at the Strater Inn downtown, huge

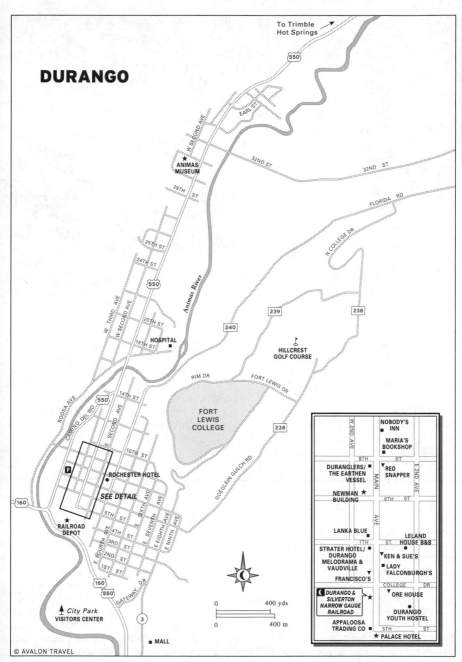

DURANGO

To Trimble
Hot Springs

550

EARL ST

W. SECOND AVE

★ ANIMAS
MUSEUM

29TH   ST

32ND ST

32ND   ST

FLORIDA   RD

N COLLEGE DR

25TH ST

24TH ST

550

Animas River

20TH ST

W. THIRD AVE

W. SECOND AVE

■ HOSPITAL ■

18TH ST

239

238

240

HILLCREST
GOLF COURSE

ROOSA AVE

CAMINO DEL RIO

550

14TH ST

RIM DR

FORT LEWIS DR

FORT
LEWIS
COLLEGE

238

E. SECOND AVE

10TH ST

GOEGLEIN GULCH RD

160

P

ROCHESTER HOTEL ●

SEE DETAIL

5TH   ST

E. SEVENTH AVE

SIXTH AVE

E. EIGHTH AVE

E. NINTH AVE

★ RAILROAD
DEPOT

E. FOURTH AVE

4TH   ST

3RD   ST

2ND   ST

1ST   ST

160

550

GATEWAY DR

▲ City Park
VISITORS CENTER

3

0   400 yds

0   400 m

■ MALL

© AVALON TRAVEL

Detail

W. 2ND AVE

NOBODY'S
INN ●

MARIA'S
BOOKSHOP ■

9TH   ST

DURANGLERS/ ■
THE EARTHEN
VESSEL

▼ RED
SNAPPER

E 2ND AVE

MAIN

NEWMAN ★
BUILDING

8TH   ST

AVE

LANKA BLUE ■

7TH   ST

LELAND
HOUSE B&B ●

STRATER HOTEL/ ●
DURANGO
MELODRAMA &
VAUDVILLE

▼ KEN & SUE'S

■ LADY
FALCONBURGH'S

FRANCISCO'S ▼

COLLEGE   DR

DURANGO &
SILVERTON
NARROW GAUGE
RAILROAD ★

▼ ORE HOUSE

DURANGO ●
YOUTH HOSTEL

APPALOOSA
TRADING CO ■

5TH   ST

★ PALACE HOTEL

downtown Durango

© SVEN BRUNSO/DURANGO AREA TOURISM

groups of bikers congregated regularly in hotel parking areas. One group was from France, riding vintage Harleys. If you're not a biker, make lodging plans that consider the noise.

SIGHTS
National Historic District

Some of Durango's downtown area has filled up with chain hotels and restaurants in recent years, but it remains a giant National Historic District with 86 buildings that have been preserved from the late 19th and early 20th centuries. The primary area is around 12th Street and Main Avenue, with buildings such as the 1895 **Palace Hotel** (429 Main Ave.), the 1882 **Railroad Depot** (5th St. and Main Ave.), the 1887 **Strater Hotel** (7th St. and Main Ave.), and the 1897 **Newman Building** (8th St. and Main Ave.). The second historic area, with rows of Victorian homes, is on 3rd Avenue, two blocks east of Main Avenue.

Trimble Hot Springs

The Utes used what is now Trimble Hot Springs (6475 County Rd. 203, 970/247-0111, www.trimblehotsprings.com, 9 A.M.–10 P.M. daily summer, 10 A.M.–9 P.M. Sun.–Thurs., 10 A.M.–10 P.M. Fri.–Sat. winter, $15) as "healing waters," and when rheumatism-plagued Frank Trimble settled here in 1884, he claimed to be healed. He also turned the springs into a tourist attraction (Marilyn Monroe is said to have experienced the healing powers). Today, there's an Olympic-sized pool and three "natural therapy" pools with temperatures are as high as 120°F.

Fort Lewis College

Known as Colorado's "campus in the sky," the 4,500-student Fort Lewis College (1000 Rim Dr., 970/247-7010 or 877/352-2656, http://explore.fortlewis.edu) is on top of a mesa, with red-roofed buildings surrounded by various cliffs and mountains. In an expanded and refurbished building with Masayuki Nagase's stone-obelisk *Passage of the Wind* sculpture out front, the **Fort Lewis College Art Gallery** (Art Bldg., 1000 Rim Dr., Room

© SVEN BRUNSO/DURANGO AREA TOURISM

the historic Strater Hotel

Crow Canyon Archaeological Center

Another superb Anasazi resource is Crow Canyon Archaeological Center (23390 Rd. K, 970/565-8975 or 800/422-8975, www.crow-canyon.org), which allows archaeology enthusiasts to work with professionals on dig sites and in labs. The center makes its exhaustive research available in publications and other resources. The Sand Canyon Pueblo Database, for example, analyzes a key Mesa Verde cliff-dwelling site and comprises over 2,000 color photographs, hundreds of maps, and other data. The center also sponsors adventure trips, with scientists and other experts as guides, to archaeological areas in this region as well as in Arizona, New Mexico, and elsewhere.

◖ Durango & Silverton Narrow Gauge Railroad

The railroad has defined Durango for most of the last 130 years, so it's fitting that the city's tourism business centers on the Durango & Silverton Narrow Gauge Railroad (479 Main Ave., 970/247-2733 or 877/872-4607, www.durangotrain.com, 8:30 A.M.–5:45 P.M. daily May–Oct., $86). This 45-mile line began in 1882 to haul gold and silver ore out of the San Juan Mountains, and it continued running despite the silver crash of 1893 and a devastating Spanish-flu outbreak in Silverton. It closed just before World War II, however, and reopened for tourism in 1947—and movie producers came to the area, filming the train in *A Ticket to Tomahawk, Around the World in 80 Days, Butch Cassidy and the Sundance Kid,* and several others. Today, the steam-powered, coal-fired, 1920s-era locomotives pull six passenger cars along a scenic, placid Animas River route at 18 miles per hour; it's perhaps the nicest commute in Colorado, with a two-hour layover in mountain-secluded Silverton.

101, 970/247-7167, www2.fortlewis.edu/art/ArtGallery.aspx, 10 A.M.–4 P.M. Mon.–Fri., noon–4 P.M. Sat.) displays student paintings and sculpture. The college's **Native American Center** (970/247-7221) supports a student population that is 16 percent Native American.

Chimney Rock Archaeological Area

Chimney Rock Archaeological Area (Hwy. 151, 3 miles south of U.S. 160, about 40 miles east of Durango, 970/883-5359 or 970/264-2287 off-season, www.chimneyrockco.org, 9 A.M.–4:30 P.M. mid-May–Sept.) may have been an Anasazi astronomical observatory 1,000 years ago—more likely, it was an agricultural area, as well as the site of 200 homes and ceremonial buildings, 27 work camps, and 91 other structures. Archaeologists are still investigating, but what's certain is Chimney Rock is a beautiful and fascinating 4,100-acre site on a high mountaintop within the Southern Ute Indian Reservation, with pinkish mesas and weird rock formations in every direction.

SPORTS AND RECREATION
Hiking and Biking

Durango, which played host to the inaugural World Mountain Biking Championships in 1990, is a huge mountain-biking town surrounded by hundreds of trails. They cut through forests and canyons, with views of La Plata Mountains and the Animas Valley, and armadas of crazed cyclists fill up the hotels and restaurants downtown throughout the summer. They compete for attention with the motorcyclists, who flock here from all over the world.

Every Memorial Day, a crazy group of cyclists gathers in Durango to see if they can ride faster than a speeding train. The resulting 50-mile race, known as the **Iron Horse Bicycle Classic** (www.ironhorsebicycleclassic.com), follows the railroad line from Durango to Silverton. It's the oldest continuous bike race in American history, dating to 1972. If you can't make the race, consider following the same path along U.S. 550 from Durango to Silverton and back; or take the Durango & Silverton Narrow Gauge Railroad uphill to Silverton, then ride mostly downhill on the way back to Durango. Watch out for cars, though: On a recent trip along this route, my family encountered numerous cyclists, but we were distracted by the incredible views of snowy peaks, sharp cliffs, bubbling rivers and waterfalls, and vivid mountainside colors. This route has some of the best scenery in the state.

Another scenic route is along U.S. 160, east out of Durango to Pagosa Springs. The 60-mile ride can be steep and is best for advanced cyclists. But if the ride causes sore muscles, don't worry: There's a soothing, steamy hot pool waiting for you at the end, in Pagosa Springs.

Trail-wise, an easy ride is **Animas Overlook** (north on Main Ave., left on 25th St., left at the fork in the road, to a parking area at milepost 7), a 0.5-mile stretch that overlooks the valley. More difficult is **Mountain View Crest** (north on Main Ave., right on 32nd St., left on County Rd. 250, right on Missionary Ridge Rd., right on Henderson Lake Rd.), about 28 miles outside of town, requiring a 4WD vehicle the last four miles. The uphill nine-mile hike is worth it, with amazing views of Pigeon and Turret Peaks and Chicago Basin in the Weminuche Wilderness.

Another easy, flat trail is **Baker's Bridge,** which locals call "the Long Valley," a 30-mile loop through the Animas Valley. Find the beginning on North Main Avenue near the City Market in Durango. Turn right on 32nd Street, then left on County Road 250. After the bridge, turn left on County Road 550 and take it to Hermosa. Turn right on County Road 203 to head back to Durango.

The 20-mile loop **Colorado Trail/Hoffheins Connection,** for advanced riders, is mostly single track with a lot of variety: steep climbs, numerous downhills, cool forests, streams, and views of the San Juans. From Durango, go west on 25th Street, which turns into Junction Creek Road. Stay left at that intersection; the Colorado Trail begins to the left, where the pavement ends. Once you pass the area called "Gudy's Rest," watch for the Hoffheins Connection trail in about 200 yards, then veer left.

Another popular 20-mile advanced ride, **Hermosa Creek** follows the creek from Purgatory to the village of Hermosa, about nine miles from Durango. This is a fast, downhill, single-track route with rocks, roots, and steep cliffs, plus two creek crossings. Bring fishing gear and you might just catch lunch along the way. A dirt road behind the Purgatory ski resort leads to the trailhead.

Durango-area bike shops include: **Mountain Bike Specialists** (949 Main Ave., 970/247-4066, www.mountainbikespecialists.com), whose owners Ed and Patti Zink helped organize the Iron Horse, and **2nd Ave. Sports** (600 E. 2nd Ave., 970/247-4511, www.2ndavesports.com), convenient for downtown visitors who need rentals or repairs.

To get to **Needle Creek Trail,** hikers can ride the Durango & Silverton Narrow Gauge Railroad to Needleton, then return on foot. It's a 16.6-mile walk. Not all of the trains stop at the right spot, so call ahead to make sure—or just tell the conductor you'll be hiking in from Needleton.

North of Bayfield, a tiny town about 20 miles east of Durango, another beautiful hiking spot is **Vallecito Lake,** a cool and shady spot under towering mountains and thick forests. The Missionary Ridge Fire of 2002, which burned 70,000 acres in just more than a month, took out a wide swath of trees in this area; former resident Paul McGinnis carved some of the dead trees into sculptures of firefighters and animals to mark the tragedy, and visitors can tour them via the "Tour of Carvings" road signs in the area. Meanwhile, hikers and cyclists will see signs for the trails surrounding the lake just about anywhere as they drive around it. The reservoir is also a popular place for picnics, fishing, motorboating, sailing, and camping. To get here, take U.S. 160 east from Durango, then take County Road 501 north from Bayfield; you'll pass a ton of tiny marinas and campsites.

For more information about hiking local trails—as well as rock climbing and other outdoor activities—contact the **San Juan Public Lands Center** (15 Burnett Court, 970/247-4874, www.fs.fed.us/r2/sanjuan), part of the U.S. Forest Service.

Fishing

Fly-fishing spots are all over the Durango area—in the San Juan River and Weminuche Wilderness, among others—but perhaps the best known is just below Navajo Dam, about an hour's drive from the city. **Duranglers** (923 Main Ave., 970/385-4081 or 888/347-4346, www.duranglers.com) is one of several local angling shops that sell maps and equipment and offer fishing advice. It gives guided tours as well.

Golf

The Durango area has two major golf courses. The 18-hole, 7,000-yard **Dalton Ranch Golf Club** (589 County Rd. 252, 970/247-8774, www.daltonranch.com, $69–89) is six miles north of Durango, above the Animas River and below the San Juan Mountains. The public 18-hole **Hillcrest Golf Course** (2300 Rim Dr., 970/247-1499, www.golfhillcrest.com, $36) is near Fort Lewis College.

Camping

The **San Juan National Forest Junction Creek Campground** (near 25th St. and Forest Rd. 171, 5 miles west of Durango, 970/247-4874, $17) is close to Durango but feels remote. The 500-mile Colorado Trail, which ends in Durango, passes right by the campground. You can also fish, enjoy panoramic views of the San Juans, ride a mountain bike, or take the train to Silverton.

A bit farther from town, the **Miller Creek and Florida Campgrounds** (Lemon Reservoir, near County Rd. 240 and County 243, off County Rd. 501, 16 miles from Durango, 970/247-4874, $14) is a peaceful alternative to its more popular neighbor, Vallecito Reservoir, which is abuzz with Jet Skis and motorboats. At this site, the small Miller Creek campground is two miles north of the concrete dam

YURTOPIA

Because hauling a tent up a mountain is too much of a pain, many Colorado campsites provide yurts – cylindrical huts based on the lattice-and-felt structures used in Central Asia and Mongolia for centuries. **Mancos State Park,** 27 miles west of Durango off U.S. 160, makes two yurts available year-round. They have lattice walls and ceilings as well as wooden doors and floors and such luxuries as a propane heater, gas-log fireplace, futons and bunk beds, and a ceiling fan. Reservations are possible at 303/470-1144 or 800/678-2267, and yurts cost $60 per night plus an $8 reservation fee. Other campsites with similar yurt arrangements include **Pearl Lake State Park,** two miles west of Steamboat Springs, and **Golden Gate Canyon,** one mile north of Golden. For general yurt-camping information, check the Colorado State Parks website (parks.state.co.us).

Oh, and the **Colorado Yurt Company** (28 W. South 4th St., Montrose, 800/288-3190, www.coloradoyurt.com) will sell you a yurt for $5,800-10,000.

on the south end, with only 11 sites and a boat launch. The Florida Campground, with 20 sites, sits on the north end of the lake.

Horseback Riding

D bar G Outfitters (north of Lemon Reservoir, about 20 miles northeast of Durango, 970/385-6888, www.dbarg.com) recently took my family up a rocky mountain path overlooking Lemon Reservoir. The guides are personable and kid-friendly, and the horses are easy to handle. In tiny Mancos, north of Mesa Verde National Park, **Rustler's Roost Ranch** (5964 County Rd. 41, Mancos, 970/533-1570 or 800/758-1667, http://rustlersroostranch. com) gives rides from two hours to full days overlooking Weber Canyon, Mancos Valley, and Mesa Verde.

White-Water Rafting and Other Summer Sports

Mild to Wild (50 Animas View Dr., 970/247-4789 or 800/567-6745, www.mild2wildrafting.com) is based in Durango but gives rafting tours all over southwestern Colorado as well

kayaking on rapids near Durango

© MATT INDEN/WEAVER MULTIMEDIA GROUP/COLORADO TOURISM OFFICE

as Arizona and Utah. The Durango-area trips mostly focus on the Animas River—the lower portion is more easygoing, for beginners, while the upper Animas is mostly for experts. In addition, Mild to Wild offers Jeep tours and packages involving Narrow Gauge Railroad rides. Also focusing on the Animas River, at least locally, is **Mountain Waters Rafting** (643 Camino del Rio, 970/259-4191 or 800/585-8243, www.durangorafting.com).

Rock climbers can do their own trips on area San Juan peaks such as Engineer Mountain, Snowdon Peak, and Vestal Basin—or they can hire an outfitter such as **Southwest Adventure Guides** (1111 Camino del Rio, Suite 105, 970/259-0370 or 800/642-5389, www.mtnguide.net), founded in 1989, which leads trips for climbers, mountaineers, hikers, and cyclists.

ENTERTAINMENT AND EVENTS
Theater

The **Durango Melodrama & Vaudeville** (699 Main Ave., 970/375-7160, www.durangomelodrama.com) puts on weird and funny shows that involve mustache-twirling villains, damsels in distress, and lots of slapstick comedy. The 600-seat **Fort Lewis College Community Concert Hall** (1000 Rim Dr., 970/247-7657, www.durangoconcerts.com) hosts theater and concerts that include the San Juan Symphony, country singer Steve Earle, bluesman Taj Mahal, and soul legend Booker T. Jones and the M.G.'s.

Events

Just 11 musicians played the first **Music in the Mountains** (1063 Main Ave., 970/385-6820, www.musicinthemountains.com, mid-July–mid-Aug.) in 1987; today, the chamber, pops, classical, and orchestra festival has expanded to a three-week extravaganza starring renowned musicians from all over the world.

Nightlife

Of the many places to drink until very late at night in Durango, the **Diamond Belle**

Saloon (699 Main Ave., 970/247-4431, www. diamondbelle.com, 11 A.M.–midnight daily) is the most surreal—it's an Old West ragtime piano bar, with period music and costumes. According to legend, author Louis L'Amour always stayed in the Strater Hotel room above the Diamond Belle to help set the mood for his novels. Not long ago, my family stayed in this very room (number 222) and was pleasantly surprised not to hear any of the honky-tonk piano or saloon noise below. (However, we certainly did hear the muffler-challenged bikers drive down Main Avenue on a regular basis, and even the white-noise machines helpfully provided next to our beds did little to muffle the sound.)

A more conventional tavern—with large murals on the walls—is the European-style **Lady Falconburgh's Barley Exchange** (640 Main Ave., 970/382-9664, www.ladyfalconburgh.biz, 11:30 A.M.–1:45 A.M. Mon.–Thurs., 11:30 A.M.–midnight or later Sat.–Sun.). To give you some idea of the ambience, the website depicts the stately Ms. Falconburgh declaring, "Yowza! 38 Beers on Tap!"

The **Irish Embassy** (900 Main Ave., www.theirishembassypub.com, 970/403-1200, 10:30 A.M.–midnight daily) has Irish food, Irish music, Irish beer, and, presumably, a few quiet words to mark St. Patrick's Day every year. And the **Bar D Chuckwagon** (8080 County Rd. 250, East Animas Valley, 970/247-5753, www.bardchuckwagon.com, 5:30–9:30 P.M. daily Memorial Day–Labor Day) is an old-fashioned (since 1969) barbecue joint with the veteran comedy-and-music troupe Bar D Wranglers as a backdrop.

About 25 miles from Durango, the **Sky Ute Casino & Lodge** (14324 Hwy. 172 N., Ignacio, 970/563-7777 or 888/842-4180, www.skyutecasino.com) has the best gambling (blackjack, slots, and so on) in the state if you don't count Black Hawk, Central City, or Cripple Creek.

SHOPPING

Durango's downtown has become increasingly touristy in recent years, and many of the shops and galleries have stepped up their business with the growth. **Maria's Bookshop** (960 Main Ave., 970/247-1438, www.mariasbookshop.com, 9 A.M.–9 P.M. daily) is a comfortable little store with hardwood floors and not a single employee named Maria. The **Appaloosa Trading Co.** (750 Main Ave., 970/259-1994, www.appaloosadurango.com, 9 A.M.–10 P.M. daily) sells handcrafted silver and leather items, from belt buckles to books. **Southwest Sound** (922 Main Ave., 970/259-5896, 10 A.M.–8 P.M. daily) is a great old-fashioned CD store, in case you thought they no longer existed.

Gallery-wise, the **Toh-Atin Gallery** (145 W. 9th St., 970/247-8277 or 800/525-0384, www.toh-atin.com, 9 A.M.–6 P.M. Mon.–Sat., 10 A.M.–5 P.M. Sun.) has been selling Navajo rugs and Native American jewelry since 1957. Artist and goldsmith Gary McVean runs **Lanka Blue Jewelry** (701 Main Ave., 970/247-9448, www.lankablue.com, 10 A.M.–6 P.M. daily), specializing in gold and silver set *naja* amulets, once believed in Spanish culture to ward off the evil eye. **The Earthen Vessel** (115 W. 9th St., 970/247-1281, www.earthenvessel.com, 10 A.M.–5:30 P.M. Mon.–Sat., 10 A.M.–4 P.M. Sun.) sells pottery made by Colorado artists. Specializing in home furnishings, with a mix of modern comfort and Old West looks, is **Tippy Canoe** (925 Main Ave., 970/247-1010, www.tippycanoehome.com, 10 A.M.–6 P.M. Mon.–Sat., noon–5 P.M. Sun.).

ACCOMMODATIONS
$100-150

Nobody's Inn (920 Main Ave., no phone, www.nobodysinn.com, $119–169) operates on an intriguing *Seinfeld*-like concept—it's run by nobody. Guests let themselves in using an electronic code-and-key system, make their own beds, put their own mints on their own pillows, then let themselves out. "We thought, when we go traveling, what do we want?" owner Linda Ward told the *Orange County Register*. "We want to be left alone." Appropriately, the four guest rooms are named Somebody, Anybody, Everybody, and Homebody, and they're brightly colored and comfortable, with weird modern-art touches like a giant image of a scissors on the wall of Homebody's Room.

$150-200

Built in 1887 by a Cleveland pharmacist, the **(Strater Hotel** (699 Main Ave., 800/247-4431, www.strater.com, $180–290) is a classic redbrick fortress with hand-carved turrets and flourishes; it has survived fires and market crashes, and it underwent a massive renovation in the early 1980s. The hotel claims the world's largest collection of Victorian walnut furniture, and while that's difficult to verify, the guest rooms certainly make a case, with four-poster beds, elaborately patterned love seats, and other antiques. It's the most centrally located hotel in town, in the middle of Main Avenue, with free parking in several lots and within walking distance of restaurants, shops, and the railroads.

The **Rochester Hotel** (721 E. 2nd Ave., 970/385-1920 or 800/664-1920, www.rochesterhotel.com, $169–219) is a rectangular brick box of a building that has operated as a hotel in this spot since 1892. Naturally, it plays up

© ROCHESTER HOTEL/DURANGO AREA TOURISM

the Rochester Hotel

the Old West history, with guest rooms based on Durango-filmed movies such as *Around the World in 80 Days* and *Viva Zapata!*—framed Hollywood posters are in each of the 12 guest rooms, adding to what the owners call the "funky cowboy" look.

The Rochester Hotel's owners, Diane and Kirk Komick, also run the **Leland House B&B** (721 E. 2nd Ave., 970/385-1920 or 800/664-1920, www.rochesterhotel.com, $169–219), across the street in a two-story 1927 brick apartment building. Breakfast is in the Rochester Hotel.

The **Apple Orchard Inn** (7758 County Rd. 203, 970/247-0751 or 800/426-0751, www.appleorchardinn.com, $160–185) is a sprawling complex of a stone-chimney house and six cottages in the middle of the Animas Valley. In addition to a pond (complete with geese) and homemade bread and chocolate-chip cookies, the five-acre property has an outdoor hot tub as well as rocking chairs and swings on each cottage patio.

FOOD
Snacks, Cafés, and Breakfast

Best early in the morning or late at night, **Carver Brewing Company** (1022 Main Ave., 970/259-2545, http://carverbrewing.com, 6:30 A.M.–10 P.M. daily, $12) opens with kid-friendly breakfast menus and closes with eight on-tap beers and a comfortable outdoor *biergarten* out back.

Casual

A raucous Mexican joint, **Gazpacho** (431 E. 2nd Ave., 970/259-9494, www.gazpachorestaurant.com, 11:30 A.M.–10 P.M. daily, $12) is popular with the student crowd.

Upscale

Reopened and renovated after a 2008 fire, **Seasons** (764 Main Ave., 970/382-9790, www.seasonsofdurango.com, 11:30 A.M.–2:30 P.M. and 5:30–10 P.M. daily, $26) is part of a two-restaurant chain (the other is in Albuquerque) centered on an open kitchen with a wood-burning grill and rotisserie. Locals rave about the mashed potatoes and green chili–covered sweet potatoes, although most of the dinner menu is steak, chicken, and seafood.

Only a baby, relatively speaking, in Old West Durango, the **Ore House** (147 E. College Dr., 970/247-5707, www.orehouserestaurant. com, 5–11 P.M. daily, $30) was established in 1972 and serves gigantic cuts of beef ($19–69) as well as lobster and poultry.

The Red Snapper (144 E. 9th St., 970/259-3417, www.redsnapperdurango.com, 4–10 P.M. daily, $30) broadcasts "Fresh Seafood Steak & Prime" on its awning, but aficionados know its primary strengths are not steak and prime but oysters, salmon, orange roughy, lobster tail, and shrimp cocktail. The numerous fish tanks make you feel hungry and guilty at the same time.

Francisco's Restaurante y Cantina (619 Main Ave., 970/247-4098, www.franciscos-durango.com, 11 A.M.–9 P.M. Mon.–Sat., 10 A.M.–9 P.M. Sun., $18), as you may have surmised, serves Mexican food—which owners Francisco and Claudine Garcia and their kids have been cooking since 1968. The menu is fairly typical—enchiladas, fajitas, and the like—with a few unique touches such as asparagus, potato, and poblano cream soup.

Ken & Sue's Place (636 Main Ave., 970/385-1810, www.kenandsues.com, 11 A.M.–2:30 P.M. and 5–9 P.M. Mon.–Thurs., 11 A.M.–2:30 P.M. and 5–10 P.M. Fri., 5–10 P.M. Sat., 5–9 P.M. Sun., $17) is an Asian-influenced American restaurant with heavy sauces to go with high-end combinations like potato-encrusted trout and lobster ravioli.

East by Southwest (160 E. College Dr., 970/247-5533, www.eastbysouthwest. com, 11:30 A.M.–2:30 P.M. and 5 P.M.–close Mon.–Sat., 5 P.M.–close Sun., $29) is one of Durango's few sushi places, at the center of town in a clean, modular bar well populated with students, travelers, and visiting parents.

INFORMATION AND SERVICES

The **City of Durango** (949 E. 2nd Ave., 970/375-5000, www.durangogov.org) has information on transportation, parks and recreation, and most city services. For travel listings, including dining and restaurants, try the **Durango Area Tourism Office** (111 S. Camino del Rio, 970/247-3500, www. durango.org). The local newspaper is the *Durango Herald* (www.durangoherald.com).

The local medical facilities include **Mercy Regional Medical Center** (1010 Three Springs Rd., 970/247-4311, www.mercydurango.org); the small physician-owned **Animas Surgical Hospital** (575 Rivergate Lane, 970/247-3537, www.animassurgical.com); and a walk-in clinic, **Durango Urgent Care** (2577 Main Ave., 970/247-8382, www.durangourgentcare.com).

GETTING THERE AND AROUND

The **Durango-La Plata County Airport** (1000 Airport Rd., 970/247-8143, www.du-rangogov.org/airport) serves the Four Corners region via carriers America West Express, United Express, and others. **Durango Transit** (970/259-5438, www.durangogov.org/transit) runs buses and trolleys well into the night.

PURGATORY VILLAGE

Although it's still known colloquially as "Purgatory," Purgatory Village is actually the ski-town area inside Durango Mountain Resort, about 20 miles north of Durango on U.S. 550. It's a great friendly little ski area, with an elevation of almost 11,000 feet and trails that start off bumpy but smooth out as you go—as a result, it's perfect for beginners, even if nearby Crested Butte and Telluride skiers scoff. The village is filled with restaurants and bars as well as the massive Lodge at Tamarron, on 750 acres in the middle of the woods—and the resort has an alpine slide and biking trails in the summer.

Sports and Recreation

Of the 88 ski trails at **Durango Mountain Resort** (1 Skier Place, 970/247-9000)—40 miles overall—about 20 percent are for beginners, 35 percent advanced and expert, and the rest intermediate. Ten chairlifts serve the established trails, although the **San Juan Ski Co.** (Purgatory Lodge, inside Backcountry

Experience, Durango Mountain Resort, 800/208-1780, www.sanjuanski.com) gives snowcat access and guided tours to another 35,000 ungroomed acres—a great experience for bushwhackers. Full-day lift tickets for the ski resort cost roughly $67.

The resort has two places for lessons, the **Adult School** (970/385-2149) and **Kids Mountain Adventure** (970/385-2149), both of which offer group and individual lessons in the $55–100 range.

During summer, the resort converts to **mountain biking** terrain, some of which is pretty hard-core, given that the World Mountain Bike Championships were here in 1990. But the 50 miles of trails include plenty of lighter, more scenic territory, and rentals (970/247-9000) are available on the premises.

The Glacier Club (600 Glacier Club Dr., 866/521-8575, www.theglacierclub.com, guests $100–150) has three private nine-hole **golf** courses amid dramatic views of mesa cliffs.

Accommodations

The Lodge at Tamarron (U.S. 550, 15 miles north of Durango, 970/247-9000 or 800/525-0892, www.durangomountainresort.com, $99–151) is a gigantic cliff-side property with guest rooms of many different sizes, from sleeper-sofa studios to kitchen-equipped condo suites. It has a spa, a pool, hot tubs, and tennis courts.

The resort offers lodging at several properties, most notably the slope-side **Purgatory Village Condominium Hotel** (1 Skier Place, 800/982-6103, $100–219), which has some of the best views in the resort, plus fireplaces in most guest rooms and a four-bedroom penthouse whose atrium overlooks the Demon ski run. It has several properties, from condos to hotel studios and suites.

Food

The resort itself has several decent-enough restaurants, but to get to the good stuff you have to get out of the village. The **Last Run Grill** (49617 U.S. 550, 970/247-1215, 7:30 A.M.–11 P.M. Wed.–Sun., $15), about one mile north of the resort, has pasta, steak, and chicken—the basics. The **Sow's Ear** (48475 U.S. 550, 970/247-3527, www.sowseardurango.com, 4–9 P.M. daily, $25) is in a condominium complex one mile south of the resort, serving homemade bread and desserts as well as steak, seafood, pasta, and poultry. It's pretty hard to find oysters on the half shell ($15 per dozen) anywhere else around here. There's live music on some nights.

Cortez and the Four Corners

Tiny Cortez is the last town in Colorado en route to the Four Corners—the area where Colorado, Utah, New Mexico, and Arizona meet—and remains sacred to several Native American groups that live on nearby reservations.

Cortez itself is one of those Colorado towns that doesn't look like much when you drive through—lots of fast-food restaurants, hotel chains, and old trailer park–style buildings scattered everywhere—but it's within striking distance of scenic plains, mesas, cliffs, and mountains and has galleries and shops on the main drag. Also, this is Native American country, with dances every week and art and rug dealers everywhere.

Cortez's main draw, though, is its proximity to Mesa Verde National Park, which at first glance is just another Colorado nature preserve filled with canyons and mesa cliffs; what sets it apart are the ghostly Anasazi cliff dwellings, tall and remarkably well preserved, with 200 elaborately detailed rooms that resemble apartments and hotels. Archaeologists have traced their origins to A.D. 550.

SIGHTS
Four Corners Monument

The Four Corners Monument (U.S. 160, about 38 miles south of Cortez, 928/871-6647, http://navajonationparks.org/htm/four-corners.htm, 8 A.M.–5 P.M. daily Oct.–Apr.,

7 A.M.–8 P.M. daily May–Sept., $3), run by the Navajo Nation, is the only place in the United States where you can touch four states at the same time. The brass-and-granite manhole-like monument reads: "Four states here meet in freedom under God."

Cortez Cultural Center

The Cortez Cultural Center (25 N. Market St., 970/565-1151, www.cortezculturalcenter.org, 10 A.M.–9:30 P.M. Mon.–Sat. Memorial Day–Labor Day, 10 A.M.–5 P.M. Mon.–Sat. Nov.–May, free) is a boxy building designed and painted in tribute to the Mesa Verde's cliff dwellings. The complex contains a museum, dedicated mostly to Ute, Navajo, and Anasazi culture and heritage, but it also sponsors traditional Native American dances; sells pottery, books, and CDs; and has a cultural park with a tepee.

Hovenweep National Monument

Hovenweep National Monument (McElmo Route, 970/562-4282, www.nps.gov/hove, 8 A.M.–5 P.M. daily, $3) is a dramatic 20-mile stretch of canyons and mesas containing six prehistoric villages on the border of Colorado and Utah. Built by the Anasazi between about A.D. 500 and 1300, the dwellings are architecturally similar to those at Mesa Verde National Park, and some are built directly on top of boulders and canyon rims. They look precarious, but they've survived since roughly the late 1200s, when an estimated 2,500 people lived here. (Cultural note: The commonly used word *anasazi,* in Navajo, means "enemy to our peoples," so many descendants prefer the more neutral term "Ancestral Puebloans.") A Mormon explorer discovered the ruins in 1854, and by 1923, President Warren G. Harding declared the area part of the National Park System.

It's possible to enter the monument from either the Colorado or Utah side—the access roads are only intermittently paved and a little precarious—but many start at the visitors center and Square Tower Group. To get here, take County Road G (McElmo Canyon Rd.) from Cortez, or Highway 262 from White Mesa, south of Blanding, Utah. The most difficult path is a dirt road from Highway 666, near Pleasant View.

SPORTS AND RECREATION

The views at the 18-hole **Conquistador Golf Course** (2018 N. Dolores Rd., 970/565-9208, www.cityofcortez.com, $22–28) are of La Plata Peak, Mesa Verde National Park, and Sleeping Ute Mountain; beware the trees on hole 5.

ENTERTAINMENT

It's pretty far from Black Hawk and Central City around here, so if you're lonely for slot machines and blackjack, the **Ute Mountain Casino** (3 Weeminuche Dr., Towaoc, 970/565-8800 or 800/258-8007, www.utemountaincasino.com) is run by the Ute reservation in nearby Towaoc.

SHOPPING

Cortez and its surrounding little towns are a great area to pick up Native American knickknacks and artistic works—among the best shops are **Cliffrose High Desert Gardens** (27885 U.S. 160, 970/565-8994, http://cliffrosegardens.com, 9 A.M.–6 P.M. Mon.–Sat., 10 A.M.–5 P.M. Sun.), specializing in hard-to-find plants, and the **Notah Dineh Trading Company and Museum** (345 W. Main St., 800/444-2024, www.notahdineh.com, 9 A.M.–6 P.M. Mon.–Sat.), known for its large handcrafted rugs, including an elaborate one called *Two Grey Hills,* for which weaving began in 1960.

ACCOMMODATIONS

The Best Western and the Comfort Inn are the only hotels in Cortez that get three stars from AAA. Nonetheless, the **Cortez Mesa Verde Inn** (640 S. Broadway, 970/565-3773 or 800/972-6232, www.cortezmesaverdeinn.com, $59–88) is a pretty entertaining place to hang around. It has live music (mostly local acts) in the lounge, a decent home-cooking restaurant, and a pool.

FOOD

The economic downturn hasn't been kind to Cortez restaurants, but **J. Fargo's**

(1209 E. Main St., 970/564-0242, 11 A.M.–9 P.M. Mon.–Fri., 7 A.M.–9 P.M. Sat.–Sun., $10) survives. It's an all-purpose family restaurant and brewpub that serves pizza, burgers, spaghetti and meatballs, ribs, steak, sandwiches, and an intriguing appetizer of onion petals with cactus sauce and ranch dressing ($7).

INFORMATION AND SERVICES

Several local websites provide information on Cortez: the **City of Cortez** (210 E. Main St., 970/565-3402, www.cityofcortez.com), the **Cortez Area Chamber of Commerce** (928 E. Main St., 970/565-3414, www.cortez-chamber.org), and the local newspaper, the *Cortez Journal* (www.cortezjournal.com). Also, the **Colorado Welcome Center** (928 E. Main St., 970/565-8227, www.mesaverdecountry.com) is in Cortez City Park at the center of town.

    Southwest Memorial Hospital (1311 N. Mildred Rd., 970/565-6666, www.swhealth.org) serves Cortez and the Four Corners area.

◖ MESA VERDE NATIONAL PARK

Walking into this 80-square-mile area of right-angle cliffs and deep canyons is like stumbling onto an entire ghost civilization. Here are massive stone villages, complete with buildings, towers, pools, and an odd-shaped checkerboard of rectangular windows and protruding, brick-shaped stones—everything a town would need, that is, except the people. The residents of these cliff dwellings were the Anasazi, also known as Ancestral Puebloans, who lived here from roughly A.D. 550 to 1300 and built their homes during the last 75–100 years of that period. The Anasazi took off, inexplicably, at the end of that period, leaving their empty homes behind, and they went undiscovered until around 1888, when local ranchers came upon the Cliff Palace, Spruce Tree House, and Square Tower House. Eighteen years later, the abandoned dwellings became a national park, and almost 500,000 visitors continue to arrive every year—so it's best to drop by anytime other than summer to avoid the crowds.

Mesa Verde National Park

Sights

The **Chapin Mesa Archaeological Museum** (20 miles from the park entrance, 970/529-4465, www.nps.gov/meve/planyourvisit/museum.htm, 8 A.M.–5 P.M. daily mid-Oct.–early Nov., 8 A.M.–6:30 P.M. daily early Apr.–mid-Oct., 9 A.M.–5 P.M. daily Jan.–early Apr. and early Nov.–late Dec.) is an educational first stop within the park, with dioramas, historical information, and a 25-minute orientation film about the Ancestral Puebloans. Here, you can talk to rangers about setting up guided winter tours (three times a day) or self-guided spring, summer, and fall tours. Even more practically, it's a great place to check in before beginning to explore the park, and a comfortable place to rest afterward, with a book store, a gift shop, a snack bar, bathrooms, and plentiful free water.

Within the park, visitors are allowed to explore just two of the dwellings on their own. To get to the magnificent **Spruce Tree House,** begin at Chapin Mesa and walk about 0.25 miles downhill to the dwelling. Erected between A.D. 1211 and 1278, this 130-room, 80-kiva house is the third-biggest complex at Mesa Verde, with room for 80 residents. Check it out in the late afternoon, when the sun brightens even the darkest corners.

Also accessible by foot, via a 0.75-mile (round-trip) path, is **Step House,** so-named for its rocky canyon-wall steps, and **Long House,** the park's second-largest dwelling. The route to Step House and Long House begins at the Wetherill Mesa kiosk within the park. (There isn't much by way of museums or displays at Wetherill Mesa, just a pit stop for the tram and ranger-guided tours.) Self-guided tours are available early March–early November (Spruce Tree House) and Memorial Day–Labor Day (Step House).

The other three dwellings are accessible only via guided tour. Even today, one of these, **Cliff Palace** (early Apr.–early Nov.), looks like a sprawling civilization, built underneath a long, thick, orange-and-black rock formation. It's the largest known cliff dwelling in North America, with 150 rooms and 23 kivas, and visible mortar, stones, plaster, and other original building material. Less celebrated but just as interesting are **Long House** (Memorial Day–Labor Day) and **Balcony House** (late Apr.–early Oct.).

Hiking

Although it doesn't pass by any cliff dwellings, **Petroglyph Point** is a moderate 2.8-mile hike with close-up views of ancient rock art, including handprints, mystical spirals, and hunting scenes. Drive 10 miles from Cortez on U.S. 160 to the park entrance, then go 20 miles south to the park headquarters. The trailhead is near the museum at park headquarters.

Accommodations

Within the park, Aramark runs most of the lodging and food areas, including the **Far View Lodge** (602/331-5210 or 800/449-2288, www.visitmesaverde.com, $102–164), which has well-furnished if pretty basic guest rooms and balconies that overlook amazing Mesa Verde views and, in the distance, glimpses of the three neighboring states. The lodge also has a Southwestern restaurant, the Metate Room, and sponsors guided tours and Navajo rug–weaving demonstrations. Roughing-it types will prefer the **Morefield Campground** (4 miles from the park entrance, 800/449-2288, www.visitmesaverde.com, May–mid-Oct., $23–33), which has 435 campsites (and a pancake breakfast) in a grassy area. You might see deer or wild turkeys.

Food

In addition to the Far View Lodge's Metate Room, as well as a marketplace and cafeteria within the park, there's **Millwood Junction** (U.S. 160 and Main St., Mancos, 970/533-7338, www.millwoodjunction.com, 11 A.M.–2 P.M. and 4–10:30 P.M. Mon.–Fri., 5:30–10:30 P.M. Sat.–Sun., $20). It's known for its Friday-night seafood buffet, although it also serves steak, chicken, and beer and wine.

Information and Services

Mesa Verde (U.S. 160, 970/529-4465, www. nps.gov/meve, entry $10 per vehicle, $3 for guided cliff-dwelling tours) is accessible at a few different points.

Getting There and Around

The park has one entrance, roughly halfway between Cortez (to the west) and Mancos (to the east) along U.S. 160. The entrance is about 47 miles west of Durango.

The **Chapin Mesa Archeological Museum** and the park headquarters, including a U.S. Post Office, is about 20 miles from the U.S. 160 entrance, and the **Far View Visitors Center** is 15 miles from the highway and has paths and a tram up the scenic route to **Wetherill Mesa** (summer only) and **Ruins Road,** leading to Spruce Tree House.

DOLORES

The main reason for visiting tiny Dolores, near the southwest corner of the state, is the **fishing**—particularly at **McPhee Reservoir,** which, after Blue Sky Reservoir, is the largest body of water in Colorado. Other fishing spots are Groundhog Lake, Narraguinnep Reservoir, and the Dolores River, which was formed from a 1968 irrigation dam, runs through the town, and is stocked with many kinds of trout.

The Colorado Division of Wildlife has stocked more than 4.5 million fish in McPhee Reservoir since 1987, including bluegills, crappies, trout, bass, kokanee salmon, and catfish. It's also a popular boating area, thanks to the **McPhee Marina** (25021 Hwy. 184), run by the U.S. Forest Service (15 Burnett Court, Durango, 970/247-4874).

Halfway between Durango and Telluride, Dolores is also an affordable alternative to either of those places for Mesa Verde National Park visitors; it's 20 miles from the park. For a truly out-of-the-way experience, drive a little farther up the highway to even-tinier towns like Mancos and Rico.

Sights

About three miles west of town, the **Anasazi Heritage Center** (27501 Hwy. 184, 970/882-5600, www.blm.gov/co/st/en/fo/ahc.html, 9 A.M.–5 P.M. daily Mar.–Oct., 10 A.M.–4 P.M.

daily Nov.–Feb., $3) collects the results of the Anasazi archaeological efforts of the past several decades. On display are 3 million artifacts—small items like blankets and sandals as well as larger remnants like corn-grinding instruments and a reconstructed pit house; visitors can also explore three archeological sites near the center.

Sleeping Ute Mountain, to the southwest, looks exactly as its name suggests—a gigantic reclining man wearing a headdress. The Utes believed he was a warrior god who helped ward off evil, and that he descended into some kind of coma after being wounded in battle.

The **Galloping Goose Museum** (5th St. and Hwy. 145, 970/882-7082, 9 A.M.–5 P.M. daily, free) recalls Dolores's days as an important railroad connection between Durango and Ridgway. This museum is the town's original train depot, including the 72-year-old *Galloping Goose No. 5,* a restored narrow-gauge car that carried mail and occasionally tourists through the San Juan Mountains roughly 1932–1952.

About nine miles west of Mesa Verde National Park, the **Canyons of the Ancients National Monument** (County Rd. CC, north and west of the intersection of Hwy. 184 and U.S. 491, 970/882-4811) is a 164,000-acre, mesa-heavy area of 5,000 archaeological sites—the highest concentration of such sites in the United States. Scientists believe the Anasazi hunted and gathered here through about 7500 B.C., and Ute and Navajo people lived off the land until European and American settlers showed up in the 1700s and later. Some of the more substantial evidence includes cliff dwellings and 420-room houses, sacred hot springs, and sweat lodges. Perhaps the most impressive site is the **Lowry Pueblo National Historic Landmark,** in the north part of the monument, a 40-room dwelling built in roughly A.D. 800 and restored in the 1960s to its (perhaps) original form, including large sacred kiva chambers.

The Bureau of Land Management, which runs Canyons of the Ancients, suggests visitors stop by the **Anasazi Heritage Center** (27501

Hwy. 184, 970/882-5600), which can answer any questions about the monument.

Accommodations

Did we say Dolores was affordable? It's true, but an exception would be to stay in the beautiful hand-built cabins at **Dunton Hot Springs** (52068 West Fork Rd., off County Rd. 38, 970/882-4800, www.duntonhotsprings.com, $1,000–1,800). They may look from the outside like miners' shacks from the 1800s, but they're lovingly put together, with small luxuries like brick fireplaces, thick beds, wide couches, and a wooden, foresty ambience. Also included on the site of a restored ghost town are a saloon, a dance hall, outdoor hot-springs pools, a library, and a chapel. Guests can "rent the town" for up to 42 people.

There's not much the **Circle K Guest & Dude Ranch** (27758 Hwy. 145, 970/562-3826 or 800/477-6381, www.ckranch.com, $50–177) can't do. In its wilderness location near the Dolores River, it has affordable motel rooms, wooden cabins for up to 11 guests, and large lodge rooms, and it provides tours and equipment for horseback-riding, fly-fishing, hunting, and river-tubing. Although its street address is in Dolores, it's technically a bit northeast, near Rico.

For those who prefer streamlined motels without ghost towns or fly-fishing guides, the **Dolores Mountain Inn** (701 Railroad Ave., 800/842-8113, www.dminn.com, $65–104) provides guest rooms with air-conditioning, cable TV, Wi-Fi, and maybe a Navajo rug or two on the wall for Southwestern spirit.

Camping is plentiful in Dolores. Among the numerous facilities are **Priest Gulch** (27646 Hwy. 145, 970/562-3810, www.priestgulch.com, $20–38), popular for its proximity to prime fishing on the Dolores River, McPhee Reservoir, and elsewhere. It has an RV park, lodge, cabins, and 88 two-person campsites.

Information

Get information about Dolores at the **Dolores Chamber of Commerce and Visitors Center** (201 Railroad Ave., 970/882-4018, www.doloreschamber.com).

Pagosa Springs and Vicinity

Tiny, touristy Pagosa Springs is the highlight of a broad three-town area in south-central Colorado around the San Juan National Forest. It's at the intersection of U.S. 160 and U.S. 84. To get from there to Creede, due north, take U.S. 160 across the Continental Divide and veer left onto Highway 149. From there, follow the Colorado River southeast, along Highway 149, to get to Del Norte.

PAGOSA SPRINGS

For centuries, Native Americans prayed and conducted fire ceremonies around **The Spring,** in this mild area in the shadow of the San Juan Mountains. It's a collection of 13 tubs known as "healing waters"—medicine men and American settlers swore by them, and today's New Age types insist they're better than ibuprofen. This hilly little town of 1,500 people is built around the springs as well as a stretch of the San Juan River that cuts through the center.

A sprawling campus of pools by the side of the river, the Springs Resort dominates the town—it's even located on Hot Springs Boulevard. Just above the pools, crossing the river bridge, is the main drag, Pagosa Street/U.S. 160, a tourist hot spot full of restaurants, malt shops, knickknack stores, and bakeries. As you walk along the bridge overlooking the San Juan River, feel free to gawk at people baking in the pools. Also, when my family visited on a recent summer vacation, we spent half an hour watching several (apparently) slumming white-water rafting guides attempt to propel their raft up some steep rocks against the rapids. Every time, they failed, laughed uproariously, then took a few swigs of beer and tried again as the entire resort watched.

FIVE GREAT HOT SPRINGS

Pretty much every section of Colorado has hot springs, and pretty much every one of them will boast of temperatures ranging 90–120°F, connections to the Utes' old "healing waters," and sources trickling down from mountain rivers and rising up from underground cracks. Most of these pools have lodging as well as massage and spa facilities. Prices refer to all-day passes.

The mother ship for Colorado hot springs is Pagosa Springs, a tiny tourist town in which the plentiful pools make up for a lack of gourmet restaurants and fine hotels. **The Springs Resort & Spa** (165 Hot Springs Rd., 970/264-4168, www.pagosahotsprings.com, 7 A.M.–1 A.M. daily June–early Sept., 7 A.M.–11 P.M. Sun.–Thurs., 7 A.M.–1 A.M. Fri.–Sat., mid-Sept.–May, $20) is the dominant hot spot, with more than 20 pools of various temperatures, all overlooking the San Juan River. The big pool in the center is earmarked for families, but the adults-only Serendipity Pool, with its six-foot waterfall, provides a respite from children. Wooden bridges with rope ladders separate the pools.

While lazing in the **Dunton Hot Springs** (52068 W. Fork Rd., off County Rd. 38, Dolores, 970/882-4800, hours vary, $115 for "lunch and soak" package), a luxurious ghost town-style resort near Durango, meditate by considering how the water became so cozy:

Dunton's hot springs are controlled by tectonic forces associated with the Triassic Dolores Formation. The springs are located on the trace of a north trending fault and encompass an area of approximately 0.3 square miles.

Got that? The springs come in three outdoor pools, a bathhouse, a cabin, and a river, and the mountain scenery and rustic buildings are part of the appeal.

It's pretty much impossible to visit Glenwood Springs, west of the ski towns along I-70, and say, "I wonder where the hot springs is." The **Glenwood Hot Springs** (401 N. River St., 970/945-6571 or 800/537-7946, www.hotspringspool.com, 7:30 A.M.–10 P.M. daily Memorial Day–Labor Day, 9 A.M.–10 P.M. daily Labor Day–Memorial Day, $13–19) is right there, huge, under the bridge along the 6th Street tourist strip. The Olympic-sized pool is usually jammed with visitors during the summer, so to avoid having to dodge babies and beach balls, stake out an off-season month for optimal free-floating. The water comes from a Yampah spring, in the mountains south of the Colorado River, but the management adds plenty of chlorine, so keep your eyes shut underwater.

It's unlikely that the bathers at **Orvis Hot Springs** (1585 County Rd. 3, Ridgway, 970/626-5324, www.orvishotsprings.com, 9 A.M.–10 P.M. daily, $14) look like the hot topless blond in the website photos, but we felt inclined to include one "clothing optional" hot springs for the purposes of diversity. Orvis has seven soaking areas, including a large pond, into which the hot water flows from a variety of underwater crevices.

Cottonwood Hot Springs Inn & Health Spa (18999 County Rd. 306, Buena Vista, 719/395-6434, www.cottonwood-hot-springs.com, 8 A.M.–midnight daily, $10) is in the woods in the middle of nowhere, five miles from downtown Buena Vista, a short hike from 14,000-foot Mount Princeton. The inn isn't known for its luxury – just a long, flat, wooden building painted bright blue, with wagon wheels and Old West paraphernalia for ambience. But floating on a cluster of kids' noodles in one of the 94–110°F pools, staring up at the peaks and blue sky, is the kind of meditative experience people want from their hot springs.

© MATT INDEN/WEAVER MULTIMEDIA GROUP/COLORADO TOURISM OFFICE

hot-springs soakers relaxing at the Springs Resort in Pagosa Springs

Sports and Recreation

DOWNHILL SKIING

Many avid Colorado skiers haven't heard of the **Wolf Creek Ski Area** (U.S. 160, top of Wolf Creek Pass, between Pagosa Springs and South Fork, 970/264-5639, www.wolfcreekski.com), but they're missing out, because this small middle-of-nowhere area has six lifts, 1,600 acres of trails, a top elevation of almost 12,000 feet, and snowfall averages of more than 465 inches a year. Lift tickets are in the range of $54 per day.

GOLF

The **Pagosa Springs Golf Club** (1 Pines Club Place, 970/731-4755, www.golfpagosa.com, $79) has three 18-hole courses in view of the San Juan Mountains.

Shopping

Hodge Podge (124 Pagosa St., 970/264-9019, 10 A.M.–5 P.M. daily) is one of those tourist-friendly shops that sells all manner of porcelain miniatures, from angels to horses, as well as a smattering of books, games, and clothes.

Accommodations

Two hotels in tiny Pagosa Springs provide access to the springs; you don't have to book a room to have a soak, but both hotels charge a fee for day visitors to the springs.

The **(Springs Resort** (165 Hot Springs Blvd., 970/264-4168 or 800/225-0934, www.pagosahotsprings.com, $189–220) is a sparse, pinkish, adobe-style hotel with 18 hot-springs pools of varying sizes in lieu of a backyard. It's a great place to relax, with trees and rocks strewn around the pools, which range 83–114°F—try the aptly named Lobster Pot, one of the hottest—and an amazing view of the San Juan River. The largest pool is lukewarm and popular among kids and families. The resort ably tends to guests' comfort, providing towels and towel drops as well as a relaxing on-site spa. The least expensive guest rooms are extremely small.

The big spring, about 50 by 74 feet, is at the **Spa at Pagosa Springs** (317 Hot Springs Blvd., 970/264-5910 or 800/832-5523, www.pshotsprings.com, $75–125), and the hotel is a little more basic and less expensive than the Springs Resort.

Although the two hot-springs hotels are

pretty much the best places to stay in Pagosa Springs, a worthy alternative is the **Pagosa Lodge** (3505 W. U.S. 160, 970/731-4141, www.pagosalodge.com, $110–125), which has a heated indoor pool, a nice old fireplace in the lobby, and access to a bunch of Pinon Lake trails on the lodge grounds.

Food

The **Pagosa Baking Company** (238 Pagosa St., 970/264-9348, http://pagosabakingcompany.com, 7 A.M.–5 P.M. daily, $5) sells muffins, breakfast burritos, cinnamon rolls, and quiche along with plenty of coffee and espresso drinks for travelers waking up from a night of hot springs.

In a 1912 cottage with a leafy backyard, **Alley House Grille** (214 Pagosa St., 970/264-0999, www.alleyhousegrille.com, 5–9 P.M. Mon.–Sat., $25) is not revolutionary, but customers rarely complain about what they get—steak, scallops, bruschetta, eggplant pizza, and grilled polenta. The owners also run **Farrago Market Café** (175 Pagosa St., 970/264-4600, 11 A.M.–8 P.M. daily, $8), a restaurant and beer garden down the street.

The **Elkhorn Café** (438C Pagosa St., 970/264-2146, 6:30 A.M.–8 P.M. Mon.–Sat., 7:30 A.M.–8 P.M. Sun., $10) serves sandwiches and burgers.

The Mexican family joint **Tequila's** (439 San Juan St., 970/264-9989, http://chatosytequilas.com/teq_home.html, 11 A.M.–10 P.M. Sun.–Thurs., 11 A.M.–11 P.M. Fri.–Sat., $16) is the most noticeable restaurant in town, overlooking the river and visible from the resort pools. It's also surprisingly good, if a hair overpriced, with well-cooked beef and chicken dishes and tasty margaritas.

Information

Between the **Pagosa Springs Chamber of Commerce** (970/264-2360 or 800/252-2204, www.pagosaspringschamber.com), the **Town of Pagosa Springs** (551 Hot Springs Blvd., 970/264-4151, www.townofpagosasprings.com), and **Pagosa.com** (www.pagosa.com), you'll find just about everything you need to know before traveling to Pagosa Springs.

DEL NORTE

Once the "Gateway to the San Juans," Del Norte became a town in 1872, after various Native American groups set up camp here for centuries and the first Spanish explorers arrived with their families in the mid-1800s. It's a tiny town with few hotels or restaurants, but plenty of rock climbing, biking, cross-country skiing, and fishing opportunities in the area.

Sights

The **Rio Grande County Museum and Cultural Center** (580 Oak St., 719/657-2847 or 877/365-9487, www.museumtrail.org/riograndecountymuseum.asp, 10 A.M.–4 P.M. Tues.–Fri., 10 A.M.–2 P.M. Sat., donation) focuses on artifacts from the Native American and Spanish-explorer eras—with an emphasis on John C. Frémont's 1848–1849 expedition into the San Juan Mountains, during which 10 explorers died of exposure before the rest were rescued.

Sports and Recreation

Near the New Mexico border in south-central Colorado, **Penitente Canyon** (13308 W. U.S. 160, 719/657-3321, www.blm.gov/co/st/en/fo/dnfo.html) has transformed over the past century from a worshipping area for the devout Roman Catholic sect known as Los Hermanos Penitentes to a U.S. Bureau of Land Management–run haven for rock climbers. *Climbing* magazine has written about the area, which includes nearby Rock Garden, Sidewinder, and Witches Canyons. To get to the recently renovated area, with new camping facilities, drive about three miles north of town on Highway 112, then follow the signs.

Information and Services

The **Del Norte Chamber of Commerce** (580 Oak St.) is at 719/657-2845 or www.delnortechamber.org.

The main hospital in this area, serving small towns such as Creede, Monte Vista, and South Fork, is the **Rio Grande Hospital** (0310 County Rd. 14, 719/657-2510, www.rio-grande-hospital.org).

COLORADO SPRINGS AND THE GREAT SAND DUNES

With Pikes Peak as the eternal attraction, Colorado Springs is the big-city anchor of south-central Colorado—including flat Pueblo to the south, the gambling town Cripple Creek to the west, the Great Sand Dunes National Park to the southwest, and various pretty small-highway drives leading to Salida, Buena Vista, and La Junta. Coloradoans addicted to the axis of Boulder, Denver, and Aspen often scoff at the Colorado Springs area, with its conservative military-and-family values and corny mining-era tourist attractions, but the scenery is incredible and it has a diversity of restaurants and hotels (notably The Broadmoor) perfect for budget-conscious visitors.

Beyond Colorado Springs, the south-central region is where the Rockies end—and flat cities such as Pueblo (the third-largest city in the state) and Alamosa (significantly smaller, with a population of 8,000) have far more in common with the landscape of neighboring New Mexico than the Rocky Mountain ski-resort towns to the north. But many other underrated mountain ranges are just beginning here, from the Sangre de Cristos to the numerous 14,000-foot peaks outside Salida. This region also has a rich Native American and Latin American heritage, as Mexico City immigrants came here in the 1800s by wagon train after they'd explored the Southwestern states. Highlights of this area include Great Sand Dunes National Park, which resembles a lunar landscape and has several 900-foot hills for climbing and "sand-skiing."

COLORADO SPRINGS

HIGHLIGHTS

◖ **Pikes Peak:** It isn't the tallest mountain in Colorado, but Colorado Springs visitors will immediately recognize why 1880s gold miners all over the United States considered it a snow-capped beacon (page 329).

◖ **North Cheyenne Cañon Park:** This 1,600-acre preserve is filled with birds and animals of all types along with waterfalls, trees, and all the nature you could possibly want outside of Pikes Peak (page 331).

◖ **Garden of the Gods:** Yes, it's a tourist trap, but the large and twisted red-rock formations are perfect backdrops for an impromptu picnic or hiking excursion (page 339).

◖ **Bishop Castle:** Colorado's answer to the Mitchell Corn Palace, of Mitchell, South Dakota, is Rye resident and amateur turret-builder Jim Bishop's obsession since 1969. Check out the 160-foot tower (page 347).

◖ **Arkansas River White-Water Rafting:** While Salida has its watery charms, I recommend the outfitters along the river in nearby Buena Vista, who claim, with some justification, the "best white-water rafting in the state" (page 354).

◖ **Great Sand Dunes National Park and Preserve:** Just north of Alamosa, the constantly shifting dunes are a cross between the Grand Canyon and the surface of the moon. Try the sand-skiing (page 357).

◖ **Colorado Gators:** Truly, no trip to Colorado is complete without a $100 alligator-wrestling lesson (page 358).

◖ **San Isabel National Forest:** A 1-million-acre area spread through south-central Colorado, this forest includes the beautiful Sangre de Cristo Mountains, Cuchara Pass, and many lakes and peaks full of hiking trails, campgrounds, and nature-watching opportunities (page 360).

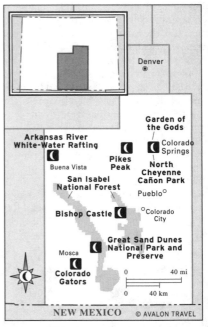

LOOK FOR ◖ TO FIND RECOMMENDED SIGHTS, ACTIVITIES, DINING, AND LODGING.

PLANNING YOUR TIME

It's tempting to look at the flat route between Colorado Springs and Trinidad and say, "No problem, I'll just cruise at the 75-mph speed limit down I-25 and hit everything in a few days." That may be possible, but you'll miss an entire state's worth of scenic and historic routes. The out-of-the-way highway drives, such as Highway 69 from Walsenburg through Westcliffe to Cañon City, are surprisingly beautiful, with the Wet Mountains on one side and the Sangre de Cristo Mountains on the other. And even tiny towns that look unappealing from the highway—from big Pueblo to tiny Walsenburg—contain interesting historic museums, public art displays, and generally mild-weather biking, hiking, and white-water rafting areas.

To explore the south-central region by car, plan at least 4–5 days. Spend a weekend in

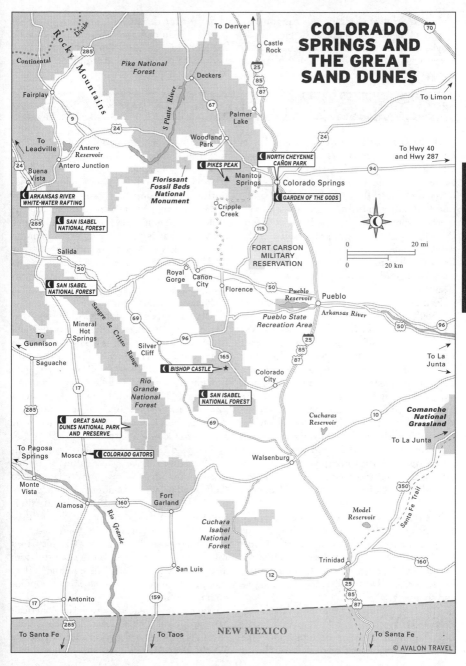

COLORADO SPRINGS AND THE GREAT SAND DUNES

To Denver

70

Castle Rock

Continental Divide

Rocky Mountains

285

Pike National Forest

Deckers

25
85
87

To Limon

Fairplay

9

67

Palmer Lake

24

Woodland Park

94

To Hwy 40 and Hwy 287

24

To Leadville

Antero Reservoir

Antero Junction

◖ PIKES PEAK

◖ NORTH CHEYENNE CAÑON PARK

Manitou Springs

Colorado Springs

Buena Vista

24

◖ ARKANSAS RIVER WHITE-WATER RAFTING

Florissant Fossil Beds National Monument

Cripple Creek

◖ GARDEN OF THE GODS

285

◖ SAN ISABEL NATIONAL FOREST

115

0   20 mi
0   20 km

Salida

50

FORT CARSON MILITARY RESERVATION

◖ SAN ISABEL NATIONAL FOREST

Royal Gorge

Cañon City

Florence

50

Pueblo Reservoir

Pueblo

Arkansas River

50

96

To Gunnison

Mineral Hot Springs

69

96

Pueblo State Recreation Area

85
25
87

To La Junta

Saguache

Silver Cliff

◖ BISHOP CASTLE ★

165

Colorado City

285

17

Sangre de Cristo Range

Rio Grande National Forest

◖ SAN ISABEL NATIONAL FOREST

Cucharas Reservoir

10

Comanche National Grassland

To La Junta

◖ GREAT SAND DUNES NATIONAL PARK AND PRESERVE

69

To Pagosa Springs

Mosca

◖ COLORADO GATORS

Walsenburg

Monte Vista

Alamosa

160

Fort Garland

Rio Grande

350

Santa Fe Trail

Model Reservoir

Cuchara Isabel National Forest

San Luis

12

Trinidad

160

17

Antonito

159

25
85
87

To Santa Fe

To Taos

NEW MEXICO

To Santa Fe

285

© AVALON TRAVEL

Colorado Springs checking out the touristy Garden of the Gods and nearby Cripple Creek; maybe a day or two in Pueblo, pausing for a leisurely tour of downtown; and the remaining days on some of the beautiful drives, including U.S. 50 near the Royal Gorge, Highway 12 between Trinidad and Walsenburg, and the entirety of Great Sand Dunes National Park outside Alamosa. Come to think of it, take a week.

Colorado Springs and Vicinity

With the U.S. Air Force Academy and Focus on the Family headquarters in the same town, Colorado Springs is the state's conservative counterweight to Boulder, about two hours to the northwest. But regardless of their politics, both cities share one thing in common: spectacular mountain scenery. The 14,110-foot Pikes Peak has drawn visitors from all over the world, notably in 1893, when Katharine Lee Bates climbed to the top in a prairie wagon, then on a mule, and wrote "America the Beautiful."

Founded in 1871, Colorado Springs boomed as a gold-rush town in the 1890s, then boosted its population at the beginning of World War II when it sold land to the U.S. military. Fort Carson sprang up in the south, and the Air Force Academy opened in the 1950s, the first of several important Air Force facilities, and later, the North American Aerospace Defense Command (NORAD). This heavy artillery—along with the heavy views of Focus on the Family, an influential conservative Christian group that has achieved worldwide notoriety for its opposition to marriage equality and other issues—balances out the light mountain air and laid-back hot spots such as Garden of the Gods and The Broadmoor hotel.

Today, 6 million people visit Colorado Springs every year, and while the obvious draws include Pikes Peak, Garden of the Gods, the Cheyenne Zoo, and the U.S. Olympic Training Center, the Springs (pop. 370,000) has a big-city feel with a diversity of restaurants and shopping.

HISTORY

Like so many regions of Colorado, the Pikes Peak area's first settlers were Native Americans—beginning with the Utes, before 1300, then the Apaches, Comanches, Cheyenne, and Arapaho. Then the rest of the country started talking about gold. In 1858, during an economic depression, two groups of prospectors responded to sketchy reports of nuggets in gold mines by flooding the area between what is now Denver and Colorado Springs. Pikes Peak was their beacon, but they landed at Cherry Creek, outside Denver, and successfully panned for "color" a few months later. Thus began the gold rush that established Colorado as a state.

Miners founded Colorado Springs—actually, the area between Colorado Springs and Manitou Springs known as Colorado City—in 1858. But the first to truly develop the town was William J. Palmer, a railroad baron who brought track to the area he called "Fountain City" in 1871. He also bought 10,000 acres and, in his own moral image, designed churches, parks, and playgrounds, leaving the saloons to Colorado City.

The gold rush didn't produce many multimillionaires that year, but Palmer's railroad lured thousands of people, mostly farmers, to Colorado Springs—the population grew from 987 in 1870 to 7,949 in 1880. The city's fortunes went way up, then way down, until the early 1890s, when prospectors discovered massive gold deposits in the nearby Cripple Creek mines, and Colorado Springs began to boom again. Suddenly it was "Little London," a ritzy mountain town that was especially popular among the British.

After silver replaced gold as the American standard in the 1920s, Colorado Springs went through another bad period, but just before World War II, the city shrewdly offered

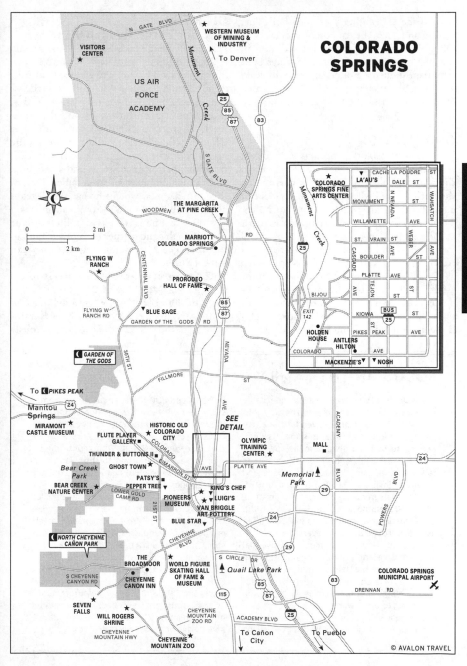

COLORADO SPRINGS

N GATE BLVD
VISITORS CENTER ★
WESTERN MUSEUM OF MINING & INDUSTRY ★
↑ To Denver
US AIR FORCE ACADEMY
Monument Creek
S GATE BLVD
25 85 87 83

COLORADO SPRINGS

WOODMEN
THE MARGARITA AT PINE CREEK ▼
RD
MARRIOTT COLORADO SPRINGS ●
0   2 mi
0   2 km
FLYING W RANCH ★
CENTENNIAL BLVD
PRORODEO HALL OF FAME ★
FLYING W RANCH RD
BLUE SAGE ▼
GARDEN OF THE GODS RD
85 87
30TH ST
☾ GARDEN OF THE GODS
NEVADA
FILLMORE
ST
AVE

COLORADO SPRINGS FINE ARTS CENTER ★
LA'AU'S ▼
CACHE LA POUDRE ST
DALE ST
WAHSATCH
Monument Creek
MONUMENT
N NEVADA
ST
25
WILLAMETTE
AVE
ST. VRAIN
ST
WEBER
AVE
CASCADE
ST
BOULDER
AVE
ST
BIJOU
PLATTE
TEJON
AVE
ST
ST
EXIT 142
KIOWA
BUS 25
ST
ST
HOLDEN HOUSE ●
PIKES PEAK
AVE
ANTLERS HILTON
COLORADO
AVE
MACKENZIE'S ▼
NOSH ▼

To ☾ PIKES PEAK
Manitou Springs
24
MIRAMONT CASTLE MUSEUM ★
HISTORIC OLD COLORADO CITY ★
SEE DETAIL
FLUTE PLAYER GALLERY ■
COLORADO
OLYMPIC TRAINING CENTER ★
MALL ●
ACADEMY
24
THUNDER & BUTTONS II ■
GHOST TOWN ●
BIMARRON ST
AVE
PLATTE AVE
Memorial Park
BLVD
POWERS BLVD
Bear Creek Park
PATSY'S ▼
PEPPER TREE ▼
29
BEAR CREEK NATURE CENTER ■
LOWER GOLD CAMP RD
PIONEERS MUSEUM ★
KING'S CHEF ▼
LUIGI'S ▼
VAN BRIGGLE ART POTTERY
24
21ST ST
BLUE STAR ▼
☾ NORTH CHEYENNE CAÑON PARK
CHEYENNE BLVD
29
THE BROADMOOR ●
WORLD FIGURE SKATING HALL OF FAME & MUSEUM ●
S CIRCLE DR
Quail Lake Park
COLORADO SPRINGS MUNICIPAL AIRPORT ✈
S CHEYENNE CANYON RD
CHEYENNE CANON INN ●
85 87
83
DRENNAN RD
SEVEN FALLS ★
WILL ROGERS SHRINE ★
CHEYENNE MOUNTAIN ZOO RD
115
ACADEMY BLVD
CHEYENNE MOUNTAIN HWY
CHEYENNE MOUNTAIN ZOO ★
To Cañon City
To Pueblo
25
© AVALON TRAVEL

land to the U.S. military—which built Fort Carson and, later, the Air Force Academy. The Olympic Training Center followed, and in the 1970s and 1980s, Colorado Springs built a tourism industry around its generally mild weather and sights such as Pikes Peak, Garden of the Gods, and the Cheyenne Mountain Zoo.

ORIENTATION

From Denver, Colorado Springs is a straight shot down I-25 south—beware of rush hour, though, because the interstate narrows in the Springs, and when there's an accident or bad weather, traffic can back up for hours. The prime business-and-restaurant district is at the center of town, roughly the corners of Colorado and Platte Avenues, with the quiet Acacia Park as the anchor. Touristy spots such as Pikes Peak, Manitou Springs, Garden of the Gods, and Ghost Town line up along U.S. 24 due east of town. To the south, I-25 extends to Pueblo, Walsenburg, and Trinidad, and it is the main route to Santa Fe, New Mexico.

SIGHTS
U.S. Air Force Academy

For a while there, the U.S. Air Force Academy (I-25, 14 miles north of downtown Colorado Springs, 719/333-2025, www.usafa.af.mil, visitors center 9 A.M.–5 P.M. daily) limited visitors due to post-9/11 security issues. Today, several spots are open to the public: the three-level, 17-spire, triangularly modern Cadet Chapel, which occasionally puts on public organ concerts; Arnold Hall, a student center with a performance stage and a cafeteria; and the Field House sports complex, including Clune Arena, where the basketball team plays. Established in 1954, the academy is on 18,000 acres and is filled with military-plane paraphernalia and statues such as a tribute to the Tuskegee Airmen, an African American military unit.

You'll get better-than-usual access to everything via **Gray Line of Denver** (303/394-6920 or 800/472-9546, www.grayline.com, 8:30 A.M. May–Dec., $95), which tours training cadets and a B-52 display, and generously

FOCUS ON THE FAMILY

Focus on the Family, located in an impeccable green-and-brown complex on the way into Colorado Springs from Denver, has an altruistic name and a spiritual mission. Its goal, according to child-development specialist and founder James Dobson, is to "turn hearts toward home" using "reasonable, biblical and empirical insights." Since it formed in 1977, the Christian group has grown to 74 ministries with 1,300 employees, and Dobson's radio broadcasts have an audience of 200 million listeners around the world every day.

The group is one of the most controversial conservative and antigay organizations in Colorado, if not the United States. In a characteristic article on the Focus website, one author declares that homosexuality is "wrong, according to God's word."

Evangelical Christians received much of the credit for President George W. Bush's elections in 2000 and 2004, and Focus on the Family still regularly flexes its political muscle, although its power has waned somewhat after Dobson retired and Barack Obama, a Democrat, became president. That reputation, as well as savvy marketing to the evangelical crowd, makes the Focus headquarters in Colorado Springs an extremely attractive destination for conservative visitors. Some 2 million guests have dropped by the welcome center since it opened in 1994, and the headquarters provides kid-friendly attractions like a three-story slide, soda shop, birthday-party room, and various theaters and rides.

If you're interested in setting up a visit or a tour, contact Focus on the Family (8685 Explorer Dr., 719/531-3328, www.focusonthefamily.com). Tours are free; check the website for hours, which vary by season. They're unavailable during chapel services.

samples the $3.8 million donation-driven visitors center. The tours are based out of Denver and start and end at the Cherry Creek Mall.

Olympic Training Center

Open since 1978, the Olympic Training Center (1 Olympic Plaza, 719/866-4792 or 888/659-8687, www.teamusa.org, store and visitors center 9 A.M.–5 P.M. Mon.–Sat., 11 A.M.–5 P.M. Sun., tours 9 A.M.–4:30 P.M. Mon.–Sat. summer, 9 A.M.–4 P.M. Mon.–Sat. fall–winter, free) has massive facilities for young athletes hoping to be the next Mary Lou Retton or Pocket Hercules. The Aquatic Center houses the biggest pool you've ever seen, and no, you can't dive in or start lifting weights.

Seven Falls

Seven Falls (2850 S. Cheyenne Canyon Rd., 719/632-0765, www.sevenfalls.com, 9 A.M.–5:15 P.M. Mon.–Thurs., 9 A.M.–9:30 P.M. Fri.–Sat., $9.25) refers to both the waterfall, which cascades down 181 feet over seven steps on a granite cliff, and the one-mile drive up a scenic canyon. The falls are open at night most of the year—they're elaborately lit during holidays—and there are trails for bikers and hikers.

Cheyenne Mountain Zoo

Cheyenne Mountain Zoo (4250 Cheyenne Mountain Zoo Rd., 719/633-9925, www.cmzoo.org, 9 A.M.–6 P.M. daily May–Labor Day, 9 A.M.–5 P.M. daily Labor Day–Apr., $17.25) is your basic city zoo, only much higher above sea level than usual. It has 500 animals, including an impressive giraffe herd, and the zoo claims the most prolific breeding program in the world, with 185 giraffe births since 1954.

Inside the zoo, the **Will Rogers Shrine of the Sun** (4250 Cheyenne Mountain Zoo Rd., 719/578-5367, 9 A.M.–3 P.M. daily Labor Day–Memorial Day, 9 A.M.–4 P.M. daily Memorial Day–Labor Day) is so-named because Broadmoor and Cheyenne Mountain

Cheyenne Mountain Zoo

Zoo founder Spencer Penrose was a friend of the great humorist. After Rogers died in a 1935 plane crash in Alaska, Penrose erected this five-story oblong granite shrine in the zoo.

Ghost Town

One large building houses an entire Ghost Town (400 S. 21st St., 719/634-0696, www. ghosttownmuseum.com, 9 A.M.–6 P.M. Mon.–Sat., 10 A.M.–6 P.M. Sun. June–Aug., 10 A.M.–5 P.M. Mon.–Sat., 10 A.M.–5 P.M. Sun. Sept.–May, $6.50), including a sheriff's office, a jail, a saloon, a general store, and a central museum, which also has gold panning.

Old Colorado City Historical Society

When miners and railroaders turned the Pikes Peak region into a boomtown in the late 1800s, the city's tough-talking saloon district was known as "Colorado City," and Old Colorado City Historical Society (1 S. 24th St., 719/636-1225, http://history.oldcolo.com,

11 A.M.–4 P.M. Tues.–Sat., free) preserves the old buildings, now housing much gentler galleries and shops.

Colorado Springs Pioneers Museum

The Colorado Springs Pioneers Museum (215 S. Tejon St., 719/385-5990, www.cspm.org, 10 A.M.–4 P.M. Tues.–Sat., free) has 40,000 books, quilts, pottery, a huge collection of Native American artifacts, and mining and agricultural items. It includes the **Starsmore Center for Local History,** a research library focusing on the Pikes Peak region, and recently added the *Pedal Power* exhibit, documenting cycling history in the Pikes Peak region.

ProRodeo Hall of Fame and Museum of the American Cowboy

At the front of the ProRodeo Hall of Fame and Museum of the American Cowboy (101 ProRodeo Dr., 719/528-4764, www.prorodeohalloffame.com, 9 A.M.–5 P.M. Wed.–Sun.

© MATT INDEN/WEAVER MULTIMEDIA GROUP/COLORADO TOURISM OFFICE

Colorado Springs Pioneers Museum

winter, 9 A.M.–5 P.M. daily summer, $6) stands a statue of Casey "The Champ" Tibbs, who, as the story goes, had a bronze heart welded into his chest containing the words "Ride Cowboy Ride." He's one of more than 160 riders enshrined at this Old West museum, featuring calf-ropers' actual saddles and boots, horses' silver halters, and various art and artifacts. It's easy to spot the museum by the bronco statue off I-25, but call first, as it can close at unexpected times.

Western Museum of Mining and Industry

A dynamite-blasting machine and actual steam engines are among the explosive highlights of the Western Museum of Mining and Industry (225 N. Gate Blvd., 719/488-0880 or 800/752-6558, www.wmmi.org, 9 A.M.–4 P.M. Mon.–Sat., $8), which also has scale models of actual Colorado mines and free guided tours every day. Plus: real burros!

Van Briggle Art Pottery Factory and Showroom

The Van Briggle Art Pottery Factory and Showroom (1024 S. Tejon St., 719/633-7729, www.vanbriggle.com, tours 9:30 A.M.–4:30 P.M. Sat., free) is a huge deal in the pottery world, as it opened in 1899 and collectors have prized its distinctive ceramic vases and bowls ever since. The tour includes a short video.

Bear Creek Nature Center

Ravaged by arson in 2000, the Bear Creek Nature Center (245 Bear Creek Rd., 719/520-6387, http://adm.elpasoco.com/Parks/Pages/BearCreekNatureCenter.aspx, 9 A.M.–2 P.M. Wed.–Fri., 9 A.M.–4 P.M. Sat., free) reopened two years later with bear- and coyote-fur exhibits and a huge collection of butterflies and insects. Two miles of woodsy hiking trails surround the small brown complex.

Colorado Springs Fine Arts Center

The Colorado Springs Fine Arts Center (30 W. Dale St., 719/634-5581, www.csfineartscenter.

org, 10 A.M.–5 P.M. Tues.–Sun., $10) is a big-time art museum, in a tall 1936 building designed by architect John Gaw Meem. Inside are paintings and sculpture by Georgia O'Keeffe, Ansel Adams, and John Singer Sargent, as well as a huge grand-lobby chandelier by Dale Chihuly. The museum is open for drinks and hobnobbing on some weekend evenings.

◖ Pikes Peak

Named for the 1806 explorer Zebulon Pike, Pikes Peak is not the tallest mountain in Colorado—that would be Mount Elbert—but it has a "purple mountain majesty" unparalleled in the state or the country. When Americans rushed west to search for gold in 1859, they shouted, "Pikes Peak or bust!"

All 14,110 feet of the mountain are open to visitors willing to travel a variety of ways—via the 19-mile, one-hour **Pikes Peak Highway** to the summit; the **Barr Trail,** which climbs 7,000 feet over the course of 13 miles; or the **Pikes Peak Cog Railway** (515 Ruxton Ave., Manitou Springs, 719/685-5401 or

Pikes Peak

800/745-3773, www.cograilway.com, times and dates vary, mostly closed in winter, $34), a nine-mile journey in an 1891-era passenger train along a stream. All modes of ascent are along scenic routes with views of Colorado Springs, Garden of the Gods, and all kinds of trees and wildlife.

Hiking trails are all over Pikes Peak and the surrounding foothills area. But it's a little hard to find resources and information about them in advance, considering the numerous groups that oversee the mountain, including the City of Colorado Springs, Teller County, and the National Forest Service. Don't let this gap deter you from taking on the mountain. As many enthusiasts of fourteeners say, Pikes Peak is the easiest and most accessible of these giant Colorado peaks for cyclists and hikers. Because the mountain traverses many vegetation and ecological areas, the wildlife-watching is some of the best in the state: Look for bighorn sheep, yellow-bellied marmots, black bears (at a distance), elk, deer, cougars, and a huge variety of birds.

The most famous and best-known Pikes Peak hiking path is **Barr Trail,** which is also the only trail to extend from bottom to top. Named after founder Fred Barr, who built it from 1914 to 1921, the trail begins above the Pikes Peak Cog Railroad Depot off Ruxton Avenue in Manitou Springs. The trail climbs from 6,720 to 14,110 feet, so bring water, watch for abrupt summer thunderstorms, and make sure you're physically equipped to handle the elevation change. Some 60,000 climbers traverse this path every year.

For many Pikes Peak climbers, the Barr Trail is a little too "middle of the road"—literally! On the "back side" of the mountain—the west side, opposite Barr Trail—there's the 12.5-mile (round-trip) **Crags Trail.** To get to the trailhead, take U.S. 24 west to Divide, turn south on Highway 67, then turn left at the sign for Crags Campground and drive to the end of the road. The trail begins slowly, but once you get to the base of the peak, it's pretty much straight uphill, for an elevation gain of 4,700 feet. Be sure to watch the trail markers, as straying

from the main drag can put you into rocky and far more difficult hiking territory.

Other Pikes Peak trails include **Devils Playground** (take U.S. 24 west to Cascade, then follow the Pikes Peak Toll Rd. to the parking lot), a 5.5-mile (round-trip) mostly moderate trail in which the spectacular views reward the brief rocky uphill scramble; and **Elk Park Trail** (from I-25, take Exit 41, travel west on U.S. 24 for 10 miles to Cascade, and then follow the Pikes Peak Toll Rd. for 13 miles to Glen Cove; the trailhead is at mile 14), a relatively easy and pretty 1,680-foot climb at high elevation. **Ring the Peak Trail** is an unofficial trail that attempts to link all the mountain trails into a 110-mile continuous loop. But only about 65 miles of trail, so far, are developed and maintained, so be prepared for disruptions. This route begins in Manitou Springs, near the intersection of Manitou and Ruxton Avenues; the trail is marked "Paul Intemann Memorial Nature Trail." It continues through Chipita Park, Catamount Reservoir, Horsethief Park, and other scenic areas. For more information and a map to various Ring points, click on the "Ring the Peak Trail System" link at **Friends of the Peak** (www.fotp.com) or visit the **Trails and Open Space Coalition** (1040 S. 8th St., 719/633-6884, www.trailsandopenspace.org).

Many of these trails, particularly Barr and Crags, are popular among backcountry skiers and snowshoers. Rentals are available at **Mountain Chalet** (226 N. Tejon St., 719/633-0732 or 800/346-7044, www.mtnchalet.com) and **Christy Sports** (1808 N. Academy Blvd., 719/597-5222, www.christysports.com).

The **North Slope Recreation Area** (www.springsgov.com, $4) is accessible from the Pikes Peak Highway, and it's open roughly May–September. It's a 2,267-acre park containing three reservoirs: Crystal Creek, North Catamount, and South Catamount. All three have hiking and mountain-biking trails and picnic areas and are open to paddling and fishing. You'll need your own equipment for all these activities.

Almost all the Pikes Peak trails allow cycling. Beware, though, the Barr Trail may be the primary artery up the mountain, but the uphill climb is murder for all but experienced cyclists. Some enterprising cyclists hitch rides to the top and coast down to experience Pikes Peak in a quick, scenic way.

Thousands of crazed runners partake in the **Pikes Peak Marathon** (www.pikespeakmarathon.org) up Barr Trail every August, and events from the Pikes Peak Auto Hill Climb to a New Year's fireworks display celebrate the mountain. At the top is the **Summit House** (8 A.M.–8 P.M. daily mid-June–Aug., 9 A.M.–3 P.M. mid-Apr.–mid-June), which has a gift shop and snack bar. For driving and weather updates, call 719/473-0208 or 800/318-9505.

Although camping is permitted throughout the mountain, Pikes Peak has one official campground: **Crags** (4.3 miles south of Divide, 719/553-1400, $11), which has 15 campsites for tents, RVs, and trailers. Somewhat less officially, **Barr Camp** (6.8 miles up Barr Trail, no phone, barrcamp@hughes.net, www.barrcamp.com) provides a 15-person cabin ($28), lean-to shelters ($17), and tent sites ($12).

The **Pikes Peak RV Park** (320 Manitou Ave., Manitou Springs, 719/685-9459, pikespeakrvpark7@aol.com, $30) is centrally located near a stream and the touristy parts of town.

Why can't I ski down Pikes Peak? you may be asking yourself. Actually, Pikes Peak had a small ski area until the 1990s, when it closed due to lack of snowfall. Every once in a while, a developer (the latest being John Ball, in 2008) floats the idea of opening up a new one. But remember—a ski area isn't just a ski area, it's a resort town of hotels, sporting-goods shops, bars, and other facilities. Environmentalists tend to be skeptical that such an undertaking could come into Colorado Springs without wrecking the city.

◖ North Cheyenne Cañon Park

North Cheyenne Cañon Park is a 1,600-acre tree-and-valley area that is almost as idyllic as Pikes Peak. It encompasses Helen Hunt Falls, Mount Almagre, and North Cheyenne

Creek and is home to black bears, mountain lions, deer, kingfisher birds, and broad-tailed hummingbirds.

Hikers should begin with the **Starsmore Discovery Center** (2120 S. Cheyenne Cañon Rd., 719/385-6086, www.springsgov.com, 9 A.M.–5 P.M. daily June–Aug., 9 A.M.–3 P.M. daily Apr.–May and Sept.–Oct.), which has maps, exhibits, and a climbing wall.

Bird-watchers should try the **Great Pikes Peak Birding Trail,** which begins one mile below nearby Seven Falls; they should also consider coming in May, during the **Hummingbird Festival.**

The **Helen Hunt Falls Visitor Center** (4075 N. Cheyenne Cañon Rd., 719/578-6146 winter or 719/633-5701 summer, www.springsgov.com, 9 A.M.–5 P.M. daily Memorial Day–Labor Day) is directly beneath the falls and sells trail maps and nature-history books as well as sponsoring hikes and nature workshops.

SPORTS AND RECREATION
Hiking and Biking

Tourist attractions such as Pikes Peak and Garden of the Gods are renowned for hiking, mountain biking, and rock climbing, but they can also be crowded at the best times of day and year. Less congested are Colorado Springs's multitudes of city trails, including a pathway from Palmer Park to Fountain Creek that links the **Pikes Peak Greenway** (damaged by a flood in 1999 and recently repaired) and the New Santa Fe and Fountain Creek regional trails.

Other city parks include the 165-acre **Blodgett Open Space,** in the northwest part of town, and the 1,680-acre **Cheyenne Mountain State Park,** underneath Cheyenne Mountain, which opened in 2004 near Fort Carson. For more information on city parks, contact the **Parks and Recreation Department** (719/385-2489), or click on "Play" at www.springsgov.com.

Golf

Golfing options include the city-run **Patty Jewett** (900 E. Espanola St., 719/385-6950, www.pattyjewettgolfshop.com, $28–30), an 18-hole, par-72 course whose restaurant has a nice view of Pikes Peak, and the 18-hole, par-71 **Valley Hi** (610 S. Chelton Rd., 719/385-6917, www.valleyhigolfcourse.com, $28–30), known for its beginners program and proximity to Pikes Peak and Cheyenne Mountain. Private facilities are at **The Broadmoor** (1 Lake Ave., 719/577-5790, www.broadmoor.com, $100–235), which has trees and sand bunkers underneath the mountains; Nicklaus Design renovated the 30-year-old Mountain Course in 2006. Finally, the **Colorado Springs Country Club** (3333 Templeton Gap Rd., 719/634-8851, www.cscountryclub.com, $45–65) is an 18-hole course built in 1925.

Camping

Kelsey (Jefferson County Rd. 126, near Castle Rock, north of Colorado Springs, 303/275-5610, www.recreation.gov, $15) is one of the best campgrounds in the National Forest Service's Buffalo Creek area, with nice forest cover and easy trails for hiking with kids. Kelsey has 17 campsites with tables, nonflush toilets, and fire rings, but no water.

In Bailey, **Wellington Lake Castle Mountain Recreation Area** (21843 Stoney Pass Rd., 303/838-5496, www.cameron-walker.com/cmr, $25–100) lets visitors camp or pay a small day-use fee to enjoy a private lake.

NIGHTLIFE

Colorado Springs is at heart a country-music town, and **Cowboys** (25 N. Tejon St., 719/596-1212, http://cowboyscs.com, 5 P.M.–close Wed.–Thurs., 4 P.M.–close Fri.–Sun.) is the capital—superstar Brad Paisley is one of many acts who have stopped here on the way up. Drinks, food, and two-stepping are taken for granted. On a slightly smaller scale, **The Thirsty Parrot** (32 S. Tejon St., 719/884-1094, www.thirstyparrot.net, 4 P.M.–2 A.M. Tues.–Sat.) grabs local acts like a Led Zeppelin tribute band and the Colorado Springs Big Jazz Band almost every night to go with its Caribbean theme.

Other live-music joints include the **Golden Bee** (1 Lake Ave., 719/577-5733, 11:30 A.M.–1:30 A.M. daily), a piano bar on The Broadmoor grounds that opened in 1961; **Thunder and Buttons II** (2415 W. Colorado Ave., 719/447-9888, www.thunderandbuttons.com, 11 A.M.–2 A.M. Mon.–Sat., 10 A.M.–2 A.M. Sun.), which hosts blues jams; and **Union Station** (2419 N. Union Blvd., 719/227-7168, http://unionstationrox.com, 11 A.M.–2 A.M. daily), an eclectic rock club with battle-of-the-bands events.

The **Loonees Comedy Corner** (1305 N. Academy Blvd., 719/591-0707, www.loonees.com) grabs almost-stars such as Chris "Crazy Legs" Fonseca.

SHOPPING

Colorado Springs may have the reputation of a conservative town, but funkier, more radical stuff is out there if you know where to find it. The Leechpit caters to punk rockers as well as former punk rockers trying to turn their babies into punk rockers, while Girl of the Golden West offers a distinctly feminist-pink take on Western-wear tradition. Of course, malls are plentiful, from the somewhat plain Briargate to the upper-crust shops that line the strip outside The Broadmoor.

Malls

Colorado Springs is packed with malls. The **Shops at Briargate** (1885 Briargate Pkwy., 719/265-6264, www.thepromenadeshopsatbriargate.com, 10 A.M.–9 P.M. Mon.–Sat., noon–5 P.M. Sun.) offers Pottery Barn, Ann Taylor, and Williams-Sonoma. **The Citadel** (750 Citadel Dr. E., 719/591-5516, www.shopthecitadel.com, 10 A.M.–9 P.M. Mon.–Sat., 11 A.M.–6 P.M. Sun.) has 160 stores, including Dillard's and Famous Footwear. A pricey 15-boutique strip, with salons, galleries, and a healthy-food market, is part of **The Broadmoor** hotel complex (1 Lake Ave.).

Galleries

The Flute Player Gallery (2511 W. Colorado Ave., 719/632-7702, www.fluteplayergallery.

com, 10 A.M.–5 P.M. Mon.–Thurs., 10 A.M.–6 P.M. Fri.–Sat., noon–5 P.M. Sun.) specializes in Southwestern jewelry, rugs, and furniture. Northeast of town, **Fountain Creek Productions** (11480 Black Forest Rd., Black Forest, 800/433-5858, www.fountaincreek. com, 8 A.M.–5:30 P.M. Mon.–Fri.) has wildlife sculptures, including marble lamp bases and pewter wolf statues. The **Bead Gallery** (1424 Kelly Johnson Blvd., 719/260-8560, http:// beadgallerycolorado.com, 10 A.M.–6 P.M. Mon.–Sat.) carries 2,000 types of beads, from National Football League charms to hex-cut delicas and gold and silver gewgaws.

Antiques and Flea Markets

With 400 vendors spread across 65,000 square feet, the **American Classics Marketplace** (1815 N. Academy Blvd., 719/596-8585, www.classicsmarket.com, 10 A.M.–6 P.M. daily) is one-stop shopping for this sort of thing. Just as sprawling is the outdoor **Colorado Springs Flea Market** (Platte Ave., 1 mile east of Academy Blvd., 719/380-8599, www.csfleamarket.com, 7 A.M.–4 P.M. Sat.–Sun.), where you can find everything from *Sesame Street* dolls to American flags of all shapes and sizes.

Clothing and Specialty Shops

Stop at **Patsy's** (1540 S. 21st St., www.patsys-candies.com, 719/633-7215 or 866/372-8797, 9 A.M.–6 P.M. Mon.–Fri., 10 A.M.–5 P.M. Sat., 11 A.M.–4 P.M. Sun.) for important traveling necessities such as chocolate, toffee, peanut-butter nuggets, and saltwater taffy.

A wall of old-fashioned black-and-red women's hats is one of many things that distinguishes the hipster-clothing store **Terra Verde** (208 N. Tejon St., 719/444-8621, www.terraverdestyle.com, 10 A.M.–6 P.M. Mon.–Sat., noon–5 P.M. Sun.), which also sells purses, jewelry, scarves, and one very old kaleidoscope.

The **Savory Spice Shop** (110 N. Tejon St., 719/633-8803, www.savoryspiceshop.com, 10 A.M.–6 P.M. Mon.–Fri., 10 A.M.–5 P.M. Sat., 11 A.M.–4 P.M. Sun.) is "like stepping into a magical storybook apothecary," writes the *Colorado Springs Independent,* citing the endless shelves of chilies, peppercorns, salts, seeds, and Jamaican allspice berries.

The Leechpit (802 N. Nevada Ave., 719/634-3675, http://leechpit.com, noon–7 P.M. Mon.–Sat.) is the perfect name for a store that sells vintage and punk-rock-style clothing and proudly boasts that its phone number spells 634-DORK. Its website proclaims, "Corporate Retail Sucks!" Also: "We like weird stuff."

Eve's Revolution (1312 Colorado Ave., 719/633-1357, http://evesrevolution.com, 10 A.M.–7 P.M. Mon.–Sat., noon–5 P.M. Sun.) is a consignment shop that carries brightly colored dresses from stylish brands such as Hazel and Ohm.

ACCOMMODATIONS

The Broadmoor is so dominant in Colorado Springs that it sucks all other luxury hotels out of the market—the only other options are nice but generic chains like the Antlers Hilton and the Marriott or tiny bed-and-breakfasts such as the Holden House and the Cheyenne Cañon Inn. Bargain hunters may want to avoid The Broadmoor, but its packages are generally affordable.

$100-150

In an 1895 peach-colored Victorian, **Our Hearts Inn** (2215 W. Colorado Ave., 719/473-8684 or 800/533-7095, www.inn-colorado-springs.com, $100–165) takes pains to be quaint and old-fashioned, with an actual white picket fence and in-room touches such as a classic radio and claw-foot bathtub.

The **Marriott Colorado Springs** (5580 Tech Center Dr., 719/260-1800, www.marriott.com, $131–169) is a massive, 309-room business-oriented hotel with 24,000 square feet of conference-room space and functional lodging befitting the national chain. It's a chain, of course, but it's *really big,* and the mountains are a spectacular backdrop.

A classic bed-and-breakfast with flowery pillows, cats roaming the halls, a porch swing, and knickknacks strewn about the lobby mantel and fireplace, the **Holden House** (102 W. Pikes Peak Ave., 719/471-3980 or 888/565-3980, www.holdenhouse.com, $145–155) is a family-owned inn in a restored 1902 Victorian.

Hyatt Place Colorado Springs (503 W. Garden of the Gods Rd., 719/265-9385, http://coloradosprings.place.hyatt.com/hyatt/hotels/place, $133–145) is centrally located for visitors, particularly those obsessed with Garden of the Gods. And it has typical Hyatt luxury—curved couches and modern furnishings in the lobby, guest rooms designed for business-traveler comfort, an outdoor pool, free Wi-Fi everywhere, and the like.

Recently renovated for $12 million, the **Crowne Plaza Hotel** (2886 S. Circle Dr., 719/576-5900 or 800/981-4012, www.cpcoloradosprings.com, $117–171) is funky and colorful in a flat white building that looks like a Holiday Inn with a hip makeover.

$150-200

The 121-year-old **Antlers Hilton Colorado Springs** (4 S. Cascade Ave., 719/955-5600, www.antlers.com, $159–189) underwent a $7.5 million renovation when it switched chains from the Adam's Mark to the Hilton. The downtown hotel doesn't look like much from the outside—just a boxy white building—but the mountain views are excellent, and free high-speed Internet access and the Judge Baldwin's microbrewery appeal to business customers.

Especially convenient for golfers, **The Lodge at Garden of the Gods Club** (3320 Mesa Rd., 719/632-5541 or 800/923-8838, www.gardenofthegodsclub.com, $169–305) has 75 guest rooms, some overlooking the Kissing Camels course, and others with nice views of Pikes Peak and Garden of the Gods. It's part of the same national chain as The Broadmoor, so the luxury (in the form of large wet bars, comfortable vinyl chairs and couches, and the like) is top-notch.

$200-300

◖ **The Broadmoor** (1 Lake Ave., 719/577-5775 or 866/837-9520, www.broadmoor.com,

an aerial shot of The Broadmoor hotel in Colorado Springs

© RICH GRANT / VISIT DENVER

$220–360) isn't so much a luxury hotel as a massive luxury complex, with its own lake, three golf courses, a spa, 11 restaurants, and 700 guest rooms. Its nickname, "the grande dame of the Rockies," seems like hyperbole until you actually stay here—the wide, puffy beds and frilly pillows whisper "slee-e-ep hee-e-ere for 15 straight ho-o-ours" and the impeccable Cheyenne Lake grounds just about magnetize you to the spot. Built in 1891 as a hotel and gambling casino, it transformed into a resort when Philadelphia entrepreneur Spencer Penrose took it over in 1916; it has been one of the state's best hotels ever since. Try the Charles Court restaurant, which has lake views and 600 wines.

All 316 guest rooms at the **Cheyenne Mountain Resort** (3225 Broadmoor Valley Rd., 719/538-4000 or 800/588-0250, www.cheyennemountain.com, $249–274) have private balconies and views of Cheyenne Mountain. Check regularly for packages—some come with free buffets at the Mountain View Dining Room.

FOOD

Colorado Springs is similar to Boulder in terms of dining variety, although it doesn't have the same number of experimental, exotic, or upscale restaurants. It does have at least a couple of strong choices for every kind of cuisine—Indian, Japanese, Mexican, French, Italian—and the prices are better than those at ski resorts. For more local restaurant information, search for reviews at *The Gazette*'s website (www.gazette.com).

Snacks, Cafés, and Breakfast

Long a local architectural joke, the **King's Chef** (110 E. Costilla St., 719/634-9135, www.kingschefdiner.com, 8 A.M.–2 P.M. Mon.–Thurs., 8 A.M.–2 P.M. and 9 P.M.–4:30 A.M. Fri., 9 P.M.–4:30 A.M. Sat.–Sun., $8) diner is in a purple, red, and yellow metal castle on the side of the road. But the food is serious: killer green chili, plus breakfast and deli sandwiches (at $7, the Reuben is a great deal). And it's open most of the night on weekends.

Casual

The best barbecue joint in town is **Bird Dog BBQ** (5984 Stetson Hills Blvd., Suite 200, 719/596-4900, www.birddogbbq.com, 11 A.M.–9 P.M. Mon.–Sat., 11 A.M.–8 P.M. Sun., $12), in a strip mall near a chain supermarket. The combination plate ($11) is the best deal, and brisket aficionados are advised to shop here before anywhere else in town. **A Second Cup** (13860 Gleneagle Dr., 719/481-6446, 6:30 A.M.–9 P.M. daily, $7) is a family restaurant (burgers, nachos, soup) that doubles as a brewpub at night.

Colorado Springs has numerous affordable ethnic restaurants. **India Palace** (5644 N. Academy Blvd., 719/535-9196, 11 A.M.–2:30 P.M. and 5–9:30 P.M. Sun.–Thurs., 11 A.M.–2:30 P.M. and 5–10 P.M. Fri.–Sat., $12), with a lunch buffet and the super-spicy lamb *roganjosh* ($12), is the best of five or six local Indian restaurants. **Kura** (3478 Research Pkwy., 719/282-8238, 4:30–9 P.M. Sun.–Thurs., 4:30–10 P.M. Fri.–Sat., $12) does raw fish and chicken teriyaki pretty well.

The Gazette's Nathaniel Glen estimates that (roughly) 95 percent of the Mexican immigrant–owned restaurants in Colorado Springs catering to Mexican-immigrant diners exist in a run-down area bounded by Galley Road, Academy Boulevard, and Union Boulevard. He dubs this the "Taco Triangle" and salutes the tongue tacos, beef-cheek tacos, posole soup, and shrimp-seviche tostados. There are tons of walk-up restaurants in this area, but Glen recommends **El Poblano** (980 N. Circle Dr., Suite A, 719/632-1971, 8 A.M.–8 P.M. daily), which is actually run by an El Salvadoran and specializes in *pupusa* (cornmeal, cheese, and refried beans wrapped in pigskin) with a side of cabbage-and-carrot relish.

On the subject of unusual tacos, **La'au's Taco Shop** (830 N. Tejon St., Suite 110, 719/578-5228, www.laaustacoshop.com, 11 A.M.–9 P.M. daily, $7.25) blesses students on the Colorado College campus with build-your-own combinations like chicken, mango, green papaya salad, hot peppers, onion, and, of course, cheese. It's pronounced "la-OWZ."

For more than two decades, **Mountain Shadows Restaurant** (2223 W. Colorado Ave., 719/633-2122, http://sites.google.com/site/mountainshadowsrestaurant/home, 7 A.M.–2 P.M. Sun.–Wed., 7 A.M.–8 P.M. Thurs.–Sat., $10) has been one step above a greasy spoon and best known for its $12 rib eye, an appetizer called the BFC (big fried cheese stick), large lunch sandwiches, and plentiful gravy.

Shinji's Sushi Bar (308 S. 8th St., 719/475-0669, 5–9 P.M. Mon.–Sat., $12) is named for its owner-chef-server, Tokyo transplant Shinji Shibuya. His modus operandi is to focus exclusively on sushi, with the freshest fish he can possibly find—without frills like chicken dishes for squeamish Americans. Shinji keeps the rolls tiny, like the rainbow roll, containing yellowtail, tuna, and salmon ($15) and the staple California roll ($5), for which he substitutes smelt roe and shrimp for the more common crab.

The Blue Star (1645 S. Tejon St., 719/632-1086, www.thebluestar.net, 11:30 A.M.–11 P.M.

Mon.–Fri., 3–11 P.M. Sat.–Sun., $23) has a casual bar (with excellent burgers) that's open all day and an elegant dinner menu with tapas (chicken basil meatballs, $7) and comfort food (chicken à la king, $17) of American and Asian persuasions.

Co-owner Gina Costley's parents moved from Chicago to open **Luigi's** (947 S. Tejon St., 719/632-7339, http://luigiscoloradosprings.com, 5 P.M.–close Tues.–Sun., $17) in 1958. The restaurant remains a master of Italian fixtures like spaghetti, linguine, pizza, and meatballs.

Danny's Corner Bistro (609 W. Midland Ave., 719/687-2233, www.dannyscornerbistro.com, 11 A.M.–3 P.M. and 4 P.M.–close daily, $20) is more or less comfort food, with standouts like fried green tomatoes, fried spinach, and Jack Daniels mashed potatoes. It's in a great location, with a cozy patio in fine view of Pikes Peak.

Upscale

The idea of **Cucuru Gallery Café** (2332 W. Colorado Ave., 719/520-9900, www.cucurugallerycafe.com, 10:30 A.M.–8 P.M. Tues.–Thurs., 10:30 A.M.–11 P.M. Fri.–Sat., 10:30 A.M.–4:30 P.M. Sun., $10) is to surround guests with a different type of artwork in every room. It's an entertaining concept, but it works mostly because the wine bar and tapas restaurant (steak, sausage, potatoes, chicken, and a grilled sweet peach full of goat cheese) has good food. Tango lessons are Tuesday nights.

If the combination of Ethiopian and Mediterranean food wasn't enough of an unusual merger, **Uchenna** (2501 W. Colorado Ave., 719/634-5070, www.uchennalive.com, 10 A.M.–9 P.M. daily, $11) is also a British tea house, a market, and an art exhibit. The sumptuous Ethiopian menu includes chicken *tibs, miser alech* (lentils), *shro wat* (chickpeas), and *atakilt* (string beans or cabbage); the Mediterranean menu has hummus, gyros, and…pizza.

The Margarita at Pine Creek (7350 Pine Creek Rd., 719/598-8667, www.coloradoeats.com/margarita, 11:30 A.M.–2 P.M. and 5:30–8:30 P.M. Tues.–Fri., 5:30–8:30 P.M. Sat., 10:30 A.M.–2 P.M. Sun., $38 for 5 courses) has nothing-special decor—plants everywhere, tiled floors—and straightforward, elegant Sunday brunch and prix fixe dinners, including one Mexican and two continental choices nightly. Saturday nights, a harpsichordist (yes, a harpsichordist) plays chamber music. It's perhaps most famous for the brunch—crabmeat eggs Benedict for those who prefer seafood for breakfast, and huevos rancheros for those who don't. But its revolving dinner menu ($33 for 3 courses) of catfish tempura, lamb T-bone steak, and crabmeat falafel appetizers are almost as good. The restaurant closes a bit early for dinner, but that makes diners more likely to experience the perfect view of Pikes Peak in the daylight.

For an over-the-top formal experience—where the waiters wear tuxedos—the **Pepper Tree** (888 W. Moreno Ave., 719/471-4888, www.peppertreecs.com, 5–9 P.M. Mon.–Sat., $34) specializes in steak (14-ounce chateaubriand, $33) and fish (Chilean sea bass, $26). And I dare you to not book a reservation after reading the name of this dessert: milk chocolate tulip cup filled with berries and cream, on a bed of bittersweet espresso mousse.

MacKenzie's Chop House (128 S. Tejon St., 719/635-3536, www.mackenzieschophouse.com, 11 A.M.–3 P.M. and 5–10 P.M. Mon.–Thurs., 11 A.M.–3 P.M. and 5–11 P.M. Fri., 5–11 P.M. Sat., 5–9 P.M. Sun., $25) is best known for classic American meals like the chophouse sirloin ($17), but also dips into Italian territory with dishes like gnocchi Bolognese ($24).

A longtime catering service that recently settled down and added a restaurant, **Blue Sage** (5151 Centennial Blvd., 719/332-1397, http://creativecateringsolutions.com, 11 A.M.–2 P.M. Mon.–Fri., $20) doesn't have a gigantic menu, but each of its dishes are a mixture of comfortable and surprising—ratatouille layered with eggplant, zucchini, squash, tomatoes, and peppers ($17); pork loin filled with chorizo, corn, pine nuts, and pineapple ($20), a grilled peach (from Palisade!) and white-chocolate mousse dessert.

Nosh (121 S. Tejon St., 719/635-6674, www.nosh121.com, 11 A.M.–9 P.M. Mon.–Thurs., 11 A.M.–10 P.M. Fri., 5–10 P.M. Sat., $19) is upscale in the food sense but not the price sense. Its definition of *fusion* means buffalo burgers ($12) are on the same menu as Thai fish-and-chips ($12) and pork tostada ($10). Befitting the name, the appetizer menu is long and varied, careening from polenta shrimp to Egyptian falafel, so the best way to experience this comfortable restaurant is with a few plates at the wine bar.

INFORMATION AND SERVICES

The City of Colorado Springs has a wide-ranging website at www.springsgov.com and a staff helpline at 719/385-2489. The Colorado Springs *Gazette* posts dining reviews and other visitor-friendly information at www.gazette.com. And pick up a free copy of the alternative weekly *Independent* (www.csindy.com), which also has news and snarky reviews of all types.

The top news-talk radio station is **KVOR** (740 AM, www.kvor.com), and the top music station is, unsurprisingly, country KCCY (96.9 FM, http://y969.com). The local television-news outlets are **KKTV** (CBS, Channel 11, www.kktv.com), **KOAA** (NBC, Channel 5, www.koaa.com), **KRDO** (ABC, Channel 13, www.krdotv.com), and **KXRM** (Fox, Channel 21, www.kxrm.com).

Memorial Hospital has more than a dozen locations in the Colorado Springs area; the main one is at 1400 East Boulder Street (719/365-5000, www.memorialhealthsystem.com). **Penrose-St. Francis Health Services** also runs a few hospitals in the city, including at 2222 North Nevada Avenue (719/776-5000, www.penrosestfrancis.org). **HealthSouth Rehabilitation Hospital of Colorado Springs** is at 325 Parkside Drive (719/630-8000, www.healthsouthcoloradosprings.com).

The central Colorado Springs **post office** is at 201 East Pikes Peak Avenue.

Centrally located laundries include **Spin Clean Laundromats** (646 Peterson Rd., 719/387-5959), **Austin Bluffs Coin Laundry** (4168 Austin Bluffs Pkwy., 719/260-6004), and **Sunshine Laundry** (1931 W. Uintah St., 719/634-3994).

GETTING THERE AND AROUND

The **Colorado Springs Airport** (7770 Milton E. Proby Pkwy., 719/550-1972, www.springsgov.com/airportindex.asp) is not only an efficient way to visit the area, it's often a more affordable option for Denver-region flights than Denver International Airport. Most of the major carriers fly here.

Like most big cities, Colorado Springs has a large transit system—**Mountain Metropolitan** (1015 Transit Dr., 719/385-7433, www.springsgov.com)—of buses and shuttles. The public buses run roughly 4 A.M.–9 P.M. daily, but check the website for specific routes. They stop all over the area, including downtown, the Garden of the Gods, and The Broadmoor. Fares are $1.75 per ride.

MANITOU SPRINGS

Built around the nine naturally carbonated springs at the center of town, Manitou Springs is the small-town addendum to Colorado Springs. (Bring your own cup, as French settlers did in the late 1800s, to enjoy a tasty natural soda pop.) While Colorado Springs is the second-largest city in Colorado, Manitou is a quaint bed-and-breakfast kind of town full of galleries, parks for visitors, and historic sights.

The springs themselves have fallen into disrepair and have been restored several times over the years—most recently in the 1980s, which was good timing, because spas and hot springs exploded in popularity in the following decade. The local chamber of commerce's **Mineral Springs Foundation** (354 Manitou Ave., 719/685-5089, http://manitoumineralsprings.org) provides maps and walking tours of the springs.

Sights

Cave of the Winds (100 Cave of the Winds Rd., 719/685-5444, www.caveofthewinds.com,

© STEVE KNOPPER

Manitou Springs is a quiet, pretty tourist town, full of shops and restaurants.

9 A.M.–9 P.M. daily summer, 10 A.M.–5 P.M. daily winter, $18–22) is a fascinating—and always warm—labyrinth of stalactites, stalagmites, flowers, crystal, and coral. Discovered and rediscovered many times over the centuries, it became a bona fide attraction in 1880, when two boys came upon it during an "Exploring Association" trip and started charging $1 admission. It can be cheesy, though, especially the elaborate summer laser shows.

The **Cliff Dwellings Museum** (U.S. 24, 719/685-5242 or 800/354-9971, www.cliffdwellingsmuseum.com, 9 A.M.–6 P.M. daily May–Sept., 10 A.M.–4 P.M. daily Dec.–Feb., 9 A.M.–5 P.M. daily Mar.–Apr. and Oct.–Nov., $9.50) documents a period as far back as A.D. 1100 when the Anasazi carved elaborate rooms into red-rock cliff homes. These replicas were built in 1906. The museum sponsors traditional Native American dances in the summer.

A long time ago, this was railroad magnate William J. Palmer's town, and his old estate **Glen Eyrie** (3820 N. 30th St., 719/634-0808 or 800/944-4536, www.navigators.org/us/

ministries/gleneyrie) was a 22-room frame house on 2,225 acres filled with red sandstone formations—giving it the nickname "Little Garden of the Gods"—with beautiful areas like the blue-and-brown General Palmer's Room, including an antique shower and a hand-carved wooden bed. The many surrounding trails are open to bikers and hikers, as are the volleyball, basketball, and tennis courts. Befitting Colorado Springs—and, hey, Palmer was a devout Quaker—the house is part of a Christian missionary organization.

In 1895 the **Miramont Castle Museum** (9 Capital Hill Ave., 719/685-1011, www.miramontcastle.org, 9 A.M.–5 P.M. daily summer, 10 A.M.–4 P.M. Tues.–Sat., noon–4 P.M. Sun. winter, $8) was the 14,000-square-foot home of French-born Jean Baptiste Francolon, a Catholic priest who lived here with his mother and six servants—they used 28 of the 46 rooms. Today, many of those rooms are lovingly reproduced after a renovation in 2000, and the exhibits include railroad and vintage doll collections.

THE SAGA OF GRAFFITI FALLS

In the foothills west of quaint, tiny Manitou Springs, just beyond the downtown district, Rainbow Falls was once the ultimate sunbathing spot. In recent decades, though, the Falls has fallen into disrepair, succumbing to trash, vandalism and high school parties and earning the nickname "Graffiti Falls."

But in 2010, El Paso County bought the falls from a private developer for $10 and immediately spent some $80,000 and organized volunteer crews to clean it up. "When we walked up in there, even though it was graffiti-scarred, it was a pretty place to have a picnic," Dave Rose, an El Paso County spokesperson, said at the time. "You could hear the highway, but you could also hear the water."

Today, the waterfall site is sort of two-faced. The concrete bridge of U.S. 24 rams right into the dirt beach next to the falls, and it's covered with colorful graffiti, some of it profane and some actually artistic. But the waterfall itself is so beautiful, spewing from the light-brown mountain facade, that it almost overcomes the urban clutter. The hike along a dirt path from the small parking area to the waterfall site is roughly 200 yards, with a wide view of the mountains in every direction. The overall feel is funky and scenic, and while you might avoid dropping by during high school ditch days, it's well worth grabbing a lunch from a downtown Manitou café, hiking 200 yards along a dirt path adjacent to the trickle-down stream, pulling up a comfortable rock to sit on, and then picnicking with your toes in the water.

To get to Rainbow Falls, take U.S. 24 west from Colorado Springs and exit on Manitou Avenue. Take this road west, toward the mountains, past the shops and cafés. Turn right on narrow Serpentine Road (the sign is a little hidden), then climb until the small dirt parking lot becomes visible on the left. Follow the narrow dirt path on foot to the waterfall. For information, call the county at 719/520-7529.

If a CD titled *The Flying W Wranglers Live in Concert with the Colorado Springs Philharmonic* doesn't scare you, the **Flying W Ranch** (3330 Chuckwagon Rd., 719/598-4000 or 800/232-3599, www.flyingw.com, shows 5 and 8 P.M. Fri.–Sat. Oct.–early May, 7 P.M. daily Memorial Day–Sept., $22) may be your kind of place. It's a working cowboy ranch with a chuckwagon supper and nightly entertainment by, yes, the Flying W Wranglers, who are sort of a combination of Riders in the Sky and Wayne Newton with a little Christian music thrown in.

Not to be confused with Redstone Castle in Redstone, the **Red Stone Castle** (601 South Side Rd., gailstuart@yahoo.com, http://redstonecastleofmanitou.com, tours by appointment) is in, well, a castle—built in the 1890s and maintained by a local family on a 20-acre estate. Under new ownership, it no longer provides lodging.

◀ Garden of the Gods

As the story goes, when two surveyors stumbled on a valley of towering, twisted, blood-red sandstone formations in 1859, the first declared it a "capital place for a beer garden." Responded the second man: "Beer garden! Why, it is a fit place for the gods to assemble." Thus the name Garden of the Gods (1805 N. 30th St., 719/634-6666, www.gardenofgods.com, 8 A.M.–8 P.M. daily Memorial Day–Labor Day, 9 A.M.–5 P.M. daily Labor Day–Memorial Day, free), which personalizes the big rocks with apt names like the Kissing Camels, Siamese Twins, and Tower of Babel. Archaeologists have found bowls and artifacts that prove people lived here more than 3,300 years ago, although it didn't become a park until railroad magnate Charles Elliot Perkins bought 240 acres for a summer home in 1879, and then declared it free to the public; his heirs sold it to Colorado Springs with that condition.

History and geology aside, though, the 1,350-acre park is prime territory for **hiking, rock climbing,** and **horseback riding.** Parks officials have in recent years added a Visitors

COLORADO SPRINGS

© STEVE KNOPPER

Garden of the Gods

& Nature Center, rock-climbing areas, school programs, and a film titled *How Did Those Red Rocks Get There?*

Some 15 miles of hiking trails run through the park. None of them are especially strenuous. The longest is the Chambers-Bretag-Palmer Trail, which loops three miles around just about the entire park; the shortest is the 0.5-mile Ridge Trail, which goes straight through the primary rock area. As long as you hew to the trails and do everything possible to avoid running into pedestrians or wildlife, you can drag your own bicycle around the park. Cyclists might consider timing their visit for the late-June **Starlight Spectacular** (Trails and Open Space Coalition, 1040 S. 8th St., Suite 101, 719/633-6884, www.starlightspectacular.org), an annual biking event that begins at midnight.

The red rocks here are a natural for rock climbing, which is allowed in the park as long as participants follow the rules—register in advance; use eco-chalk, available at the visitors center; and no sport-rappelling or scrambling. The climbs are mostly moderate, beginning

with the popular but often-crowded north ridge of Montezuma's Tower, and working up to the more strenuous Kindergarten Rock–New Generation, which contains risks of crumbling rock.

Guided horseback rides are available through **Academy Riding Stables** (4 El Paso Blvd., Colorado Springs, 719/633-5667 or 888/700-0410, www.academyridingstables.com). Private horse trailers are allowed too, as long as you park at the South Spring Canyon Picnic area; a trail map is available at the visitors center.

There is no camping in the park itself, but several campgrounds are nearby, including **Garden of the Gods Campground** (3704 W. Colorado Ave., 719/475-9450, www.colorado-campground.com, $42), which has showers, pools, big-screen TVs, a playground, and accommodations for RVs.

Shopping

Manitou Springs is the most touristy part of the Colorado Springs area, so scan the streets for shops and galleries, including **Cripple Creek**

Dulcimers (740 Manitou Ave., 719/685-9655, www.dulcimer.net, 10 A.M.–6 P.M. daily), which sells Appalachian-stringed instruments of all kinds (just in case you needed one), and **Nature of Things Chainsaw Art** (347 Manitou Ave., 719/685-0171, www.nature-ofthingschainsawart.com, 24 hours), which is self-explanatory. The **Business of Art Center** (513 Manitou Ave., 719/685-1861, www.the-bac.org, 11 A.M.–6 P.M. Tues.–Sat.) is a community-run collection of studios, galleries, and even a small theater for local artists—it displays everything from high schoolers' photographs to humorous live productions of Hans Christian Andersen stories.

Accommodations

A 20-room boarding house that thrived during the gold-mining boom in the 1850s, **The Cliff House** (306 Cañon Ave., 719/758-1000 or 888/212-7000, www.thecliffhouse.com, $120–230) hung around through the bust and became a resort hotel in 1914—Thomas Edison and Clark Gable were among the guests in that era. After a $9 million renovation in the late 1990s, the inn at the base of Pikes Peak now has 200 nice-looking guest rooms, including several elaborately furnished, pastel-colored, marble-decorated suites named for the old-time celebrities who stayed here in the 1910s.

Bed-and-breakfasts work perfectly in deliberately old-fashioned Manitou Springs, but only a couple of them are operating these days. The **1892 Victoria's Keep B&B** (202 Ruxton Ave., 719/685-5354 or 800/905-5337, www.victoriaskeep.com, $90–215) is in a powder-blue Victorian with a gazebo in the front, on a nice tree-lined spot not far from Pikes Peak. The **Agate Hill Inn** (Spencer Ave. and Cave Ave., 719/685-0685 or 877/685-0685, www.agatehill.com, $165–325) is almost as charming, renting large cottages with kitchenettes and gas-log stoves.

Food

After the **Craftwood Inn** (404 El Paso Blvd., 719/685-9000, www.craftwood.com, 5–8 P.M. daily, $35) switched from hotel to restaurant in 1940, stars such as Bing Crosby and Cary Grant were known to sit at window tables. It later closed and then reopened in 1988, and now specializes in wild game, including ostrich (a $14 appetizer), venison ($27), wild boar ($28), plus signature veggie dishes such as pistachio pesto ravioli ($20 for 2 as part of a combination plate).

The **Briarhurst Manor** (404 Manitou Ave., 719/685-1864 or 877/685-1448, www.briarhurst.com, 5–8 P.M. daily, $39, $44, and $49 set menus) is in a historic pink-sandstone building packed with a huge old-fashioned staircase, stained-glass windows, and even a vintage church pew. The food is just as distinctive: An à la carte menu includes diamondback rattlesnake ($20), bison carpaccio ($19), and dandelion-green salad ($7).

Although **Adam's Mountain Café** (110 Cañon Ave., 719/685-1430 or 719/685-4370, www.adamsmountain.com, 8 A.M.–3 P.M. and 5–9 P.M. Tues.–Sat., 8 A.M.–3 P.M. Sun.–Mon. May–Sept., 8 A.M.–3 P.M. and 5–9 P.M. Tues.–Sat., 8 A.M.–3 P.M. Sun. Oct.–Apr., $19) serves three meals a day, it's best known for the three-egg breakfast omelets ($8)—avocado, salmon, Santa Fe, or spinach. Acoustic guitarists play in the evenings and some mornings.

Formerly Pikes Pub and Grub, **The Black Bear Restaurant** (10375 Ute Pass Rd., Green Mountain, 719/684-9648, www.blackbearrestaurant.com, 5–8:30 P.M. Tues.–Sun., $20), just northwest of Manitou Springs, reverted to its original 1950s name when chef Victor Matthews bought it in 1999. Today it serves a *little* pub and grub so that snowed-in mountain residents can afford the food, but its specialties are high-end comfort meals like lacquered duck ($30) and a buffalo-and-beef burger ($10). Every Sunday, Matthews turns over the kitchen to students at his Paragon Culinary School.

Information

Although Manitou Springs is usually in the shadow of Colorado Springs, and you can find much information about the area at www.springsgov.com, the primary town resource is the **Manitou Springs Chamber of Commerce & Visitors Bureau** (354 Manitou Ave., 719/685-5089 or 800/642-2567, www.manitousprings.org). For information about Pikes Peak, visit www.pikes-peak.com.

PALMER LAKE

Built as a railroad town in 1871, Palmer Lake has become a tiny hiking-and-biking haven just east of the gigantic Pike National Forest and about 28 miles north of Colorado Springs along I-25. Although the population is only 2,000, it fills up every summer with hikers and cyclists and every winter with snowshoers and cross-country skiers. A 500-foot-wide star, erected on the side of Sundance Mountain, is a Christmas attraction. The town has lit it up throughout December annually since 1934.

Sights

In Woodland Park, about 20 miles west of Colorado Springs, the **Rocky Mountain Dinosaur Resource Center** (201 S. Fairview St., 719/686-1820, www.rmdrc.com, 9 A.M.–6 P.M. Mon.–Sat., 10 A.M.–5 P.M. Sun., $10.50) is run by local paleontologists Mike and J. J. Triebold, who've put many of their fossil collections, including "the world's smallest *T. rex*," a *Pachycephalosaurus*, and a *Mosasaur*, on display. The center offers tours and kids workshops.

Sports and Recreation

Palmer Lake itself was for years too shallow for **fishing,** but local volunteers have recently changed that—at least, when Colorado droughts take the summer off. The lake is next to the Santa Fe Regional Trailhead and El Paso County Park; call 719/481-2953 for directions and information.

The **Santa Fe Regional Trail,** 14 miles of narrow gravel **biking** and **hiking** paths, begins in Palmer Lake and runs through Monument to the border of the Air Force Academy in Colorado Springs. Trailheads are at 3rd Street and Baptist Road in nearby Monument and County Line Road in Palmer Lake.

While the town's reservoirs are closed to swimming and fishing, the pretty hiking, biking, and snowshoeing **Palmer Lake Reservoirs Trail** is open all year. To get to the Emory Hightower Trailhead, exit I-25 onto Highway 105, go four miles, turn left on South Valley Road, left again on Old Carriage Road, and then look for parking at the bottom of the curve.

Events

The Palmer Lake area, which includes Monument, doesn't have much by way of distinctive hotels, restaurants, or nightlife—but nearby Larkspur has the June–July **Colorado Renaissance Festival** (303/688-6010 or 877/259-3328, www.coloradorenaissance. com), a loopy celebration of medieval times that often recalls *Monty Python and the Holy Grail*. The annual dress-up extravaganza, complete with jugglers, jousters, maidens, and glassblowing artisans, is spread out over several summer weekends.

Information

The Palmer Lake website doesn't have amazingly great visitor information, but try it at www.ci.palmer-lake.co.us or call 719/481-2953.

CRIPPLE CREEK

After gold-rushers cried "Pikes Peak or bust!" in the late 1880s, they found what they were looking for—not at Pikes Peak but in Cripple Creek. Prospector Robert Womack found a small amount of gold ore in 1890, leading to production of $200,000 by the following summer, and the town wound up producing almost $20 million a year by the turn of the 20th century. Cripple Creek was a boomtown for years, and its mining legacy lives on today in both historic mine shafts and modern gold-processing plants.

The spirit of Cripple Creek, though, has completely changed in the age of legal low-stakes gambling. Like fellow small mountain towns Black Hawk and Central City, Cripple Creek is a shell of its former self, with casinos and parking lots taking away from the surrounding mountain views. Then again, gambling is pretty fun, as long as you don't get addicted—or double down on a 4 when the dealer has a 10 showing.

Sights

The **Mollie Kathleen Gold Mine** (9388 Hwy. 67, 719/689-2466 or 888/291-5689, http:// goldminetours.com, 8:45 A.M.–6 P.M. daily mid-May–mid-Sept., 9:45 A.M.–5 P.M. late Sept., 10 A.M.–4 P.M. daily Oct., $18) offers tours into a 1,000-foot-deep mine, more or less maintained as it was in 1891, when Mollie Kathleen Gortner and her family staked their claim. (According to legend, a town official told Mollie that women couldn't stake gold-mining claims, but she got her way by invoking her attorney-husband's name.)

Although gambling and other factors have turned nearby Victor, once a booming gold-rush area, into a depressing ghost town, the **Cripple Creek and Victor Narrow Gauge Railroad** (520 E. Carr St., 719/689-2640, www.cripplecreekrailroad.com, 10 A.M.–5 P.M. mid-May–mid-Oct., $13) is a fun, old-fashioned way to see the historical riches and modern casinos of Cripple Creek. Rides are 45 minutes long.

The **Cripple Creek District Museum** (5th St. and Bennett Ave., 719/689-2634, www. cripple-creek.org, 10 A.M.–5 P.M. daily mid-May–late Oct., 10 A.M.–4 P.M. Sat.–Sun. late Oct.–late May, $5) is a three-building down-town complex filled with maps, paintings, photos, and other artifacts from the mining era.

Twenty-six miles north of Cripple Creek, in tiny Florissant, the **Florissant Fossil Beds National Monument** (15807 Teller County Rd. 1, 719/748-3253, www.nps.gov/ flfo, 8 A.M.–6 P.M. Memorial Day–Labor Day, 9 A.M.–5 P.M. Labor Day–Memorial Day, $3 per week) is a huge mountain valley full of pet-rified redwoods and fossilized insects.

Sports and Recreation

About 33 miles northwest of Cripple Creek, near Lake George along U.S. 24, **Eleven Mile State Park** (Colorado State Parks, 4229 County Rd. 92, Lake George, 719/748-3401,

http://parks.state.co.us/parks/elevenmile) has a reservoir renowned for its **fishing.** Anglers can zone out staring at the long, flat Rocky Mountain vistas while dropping lines for rainbow and brown trout, kokanee, and pike. Boat fishing is allowed, along with sailing and paddling; an on-site marina rents boats. Beware of the dreaded zebra mussels!

The park also has several hiking trails—start with the 1.35-mile **Coyote Ridge Interpretive Trail,** which winds along a ridge and is in view of hundreds of different kinds of birds and wildlife. The park also has nine **campgrounds** ($14, more for electrical hookups).

Also in this area is **Spinney Mountain State Park** (Colorado State Parks, 4229 County Rd. 92, Lake George, 719/748-3401, http://parks. state.co.us/parks/spinneymountain), whose 2,550-acre reservoir is known statewide for its trophy trout and gold-medal waters. Tons of bird species hang out here, as do mule deer, pronghorn antelope, elk, and red foxes. Boat ramps are located on the north and south sides of the river, and all kinds of **boating** are allowed—as well as **windsurfing.**

Even farther north, in South Park, roughly 26 miles from Eleven Mile State Park, is a 175-acre oasis called **Tarryall Reservoir** (Colorado Division of Wildlife, 6060 Broadway, Denver, 303/291-7227). It's packed with rainbow, cutthroat, brown trout, and northern pike and is especially popular with families. To get here, take U.S. 285 from Denver to the town of Jefferson; from there, go south 16.5 miles on Park County Road 77.

Nightlife

Cripple Creek has around 20 working casinos, many of which have some form of live entertainment, even if it's just the Irish dance band at Creeker's Casino on St. Patrick's Day. Most of the casinos also have restaurants—Las Vegas gamblers will feel right at home at the buffets—and some even have lodging packages. The **Double Eagle Hotel & Casino** (400 E. Bennett Ave., 719/689-5000 or 800/711-7234, www.decasino.com), for example, has such contemporary acts as Juice Newton and

B. J. Thomas, who, if you're lucky and ask real, real nice, might play "Raindrops Keep Falling on My Head."

Accommodations and Food

The **Victor Hotel** (4th St. and Victor Ave., 719/689-3553 or 800/713-4595, www.victorhotelcolorado.com, $70–80), originally built in 1894, was delayed when excavators found a vein of gold in the foundation. The hotel burned down in 1899 along with the rest of Victor's businesses; owners rebuilt it as a bank, then changed it back into a hotel, although it was vacant for decades. In the early 1990s the tall, square hotel reopened again with a retro look—exposed brick walls in the guest rooms, with antique-style radiators and vintage photos.

While I acknowledge that casino buffets are awesome, most visitors will probably want to grab a meal in nearby Colorado Springs.

Information

Cripple Creek's website is thorough and colorful: www.cripple-creek.co.us. Its heritage center is at 9283 S. Hwy. 67 (877/858-4653).

Pueblo and Vicinity

For a major Colorado city in the shadow of the Rockies, Pueblo is surprisingly flat—in both senses of the word. Yes, there are historic sights, including the impressive Rosemount Museum Victorian mansion, and a few outdoor things to do, such as mountain biking and desert golfing, but compared to the huge mountains, fantastical rock gardens, and tourist traps of Colorado Springs and the bohemian food-and-lodging riches of Boulder, Pueblo is, well, boring. To residents, though, that just makes the area more pleasurable—*Money* magazine has ranked Pueblo in its Top 10 "most livable cities" several times in the past decade, owing to the low cost of living, diversity (its Hispanic population far outweighs those of Boulder and Colorado Springs), and proximity to mountains, golf courses, lakes, and hiking and biking trails.

If you wind up in Pueblo, save time for a long walk around downtown. The ambience is a mixture of urban and rural, and many of the tan-and-brown buildings are part of the **Union Avenue Historic District** (http://seepueblo.com), a central area of restaurants and galleries that thrived as brothels and gambling houses during the mining-boom years. And while Pueblo is more plains than mountains, its proximity to **Lake Pueblo** and its central **City Park** with two lakes, playgrounds, and a pool make it a surprisingly rich outdoor recreation area.

Watch for the **Union Avenue Train,** a black-and-red steam-engine replica complete with a coal car and a caboose, which shows up at various events and random spots around town.

HISTORY

Although Native Americans and Spanish explorers tinkered around this area for centuries, Pueblo truly became an American city in 1842, when "The Pueblo" opened as a trading post for travelers from the southern Rockies to Taos, New Mexico, and beyond. At first, American settlers established the post as competition to a prominent post in Santa Fe, but over the years, various Mexican and U.S. traders took it over and traded whiskey, blankets, and other goods to travelers between the Rocky Mountains, New Mexico, and Mexico. Locals also established Fort Pueblo, a small adobe structure, to defend the area.

But Pueblo almost died before it began—in 1854, when colonizing Fort Pueblo, settlers asked local Utes to celebrate with them during Christmas. The Americans got drunk, the Utes slaughtered them, and this "Christmas massacre" turned Pueblo into a ghost town, thought to be cursed, for the next 15 years.

The railroad arrived in 1870, and Pueblo became what historians Carl Abbott, Stephen J. Leonard, and David McComb call the "great iron and steel city of the New West."

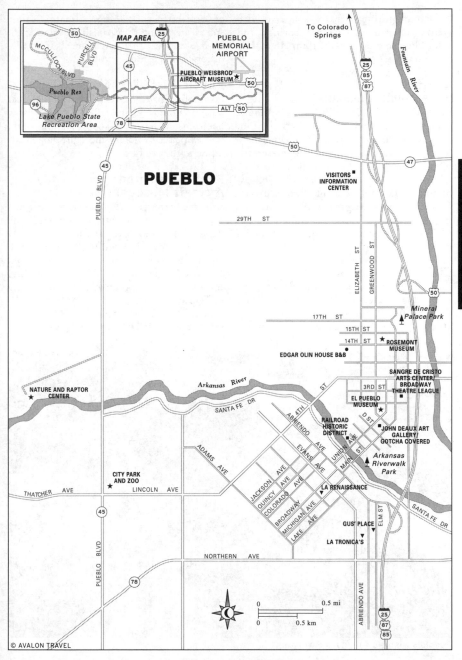

COLORADO SPRINGS

Its manufacturing business competed with Denver, outstripped Colorado Springs, and helped Pueblo grow into the third-largest city in the state.

SIGHTS
Rosemount Museum
Built for $60,750 in 1893, the Rosemount Museum (419 W. 14th St., 719/545-5290, www.rosemount.org, 10 A.M.–3:30 P.M. Tues.–Sat. Feb.–Dec., $6) is a carefully preserved, 37-room, 24,000-square-foot home-turned-museum with huge Tiffany chandeliers, beautiful oak staircases, a giant stained-glass window known as *Kingdoms of Nature,* and one strange anomaly: the McClelland Collection of World Curiosities, with lotus shoes and a mummy.

El Pueblo Museum
In a former trading post built in 1842, the El Pueblo Museum (301 N. Union Ave., 719/583-0453, www.historycolorado.org, 10 A.M.–4 P.M. Tues.–Sat., $5) is a stockpile

of local history, covering railroads, Native American groups, the Spanish arrival in 1540, businesses, and other developments from prehistoric times through 1900.

Pueblo Historical Society
For more history, try the Pueblo Historical Society (201 W. B St., 719/543-6772, www.pueblohistory.org, 10 A.M.–4 P.M. Tues.–Fri., free), which has a library and a gift shop in addition to the exhibits.

Pueblo Weisbrod Aircraft Museum
Airplane enthusiasts should extend their layovers at the Pueblo Airport, home of the Pueblo Weisbrod Aircraft Museum (31001 Magnuson Ave., 719/948-9219, www.pwam.org, 10 A.M.–4 P.M. Mon.–Sat., 1–4 P.M. Sun., $7), displaying military aircraft, including the Boeing B-29 bomber, used extensively in World War II, and a Huey UH-1 helicopter, like the ones seen on *M*A*S*H.* The **International B-24 Memorial Museum,** also

Pueblo's Historic Arkansas Riverwalk

© MATT INDEN/WEAVER MULTIMEDIA GROUP/COLORADO TOURISM OFFICE

on the premises, is in part a tribute to the airmen who trained in Pueblo.

Historic Arkansas Riverwalk

The Historic Arkansas Riverwalk (downtown, roughly bounded by Grand Ave., 1st St., Victoria Ave., and D St., 719/595-0242, www.puebloharp.com) is a 26-acre collection of pedestrian paths along the Arkansas River channel downtown. Bike routes lead to Lake Pueblo, and locally designed art and sculpture line the walkway. While wandering the area, check out the **Pueblo Levee Project** (719/546-0315), a 175,000-square-foot mural that made *Guinness World Records* as "World's Largest Mural." Some 1,000 artists have contributed to the sprawling patchwork painting since University of Southern Colorado students began the impromptu project one night in 1978. The styles range from graffiti to cartoons. To check it out, take the 1st Street exit from I-25, head south on Union Avenue, and turn right at the end of the Corona Avenue bridge.

Sangre de Cristo Arts Center

The Sangre de Cristo Arts Center (210 N. Santa Fe Ave., 719/295-7200, www.sdc-arts. org, 11 A.M.–4 P.M. Tues.–Sat., $4) has grown over the last three decades from a small two-building complex to 90,000 square feet of gallery space, with a $2 million budget and a theater. The large colorful paintings emphasize the Southwest, such as Bettina Steinke's *Early Morning Smile,* of a young Native American woman beaming on a cloudy day. The Buell Children's Museum, adjacent to the museum with bronze statues of kids playing, has make-your-own-art displays.

Bent's Old Fort National Museum

In La Junta, about 65 miles west of Pueblo, the reconstructed Bent's Old Fort National Museum (35110 Hwy. 194 E., La Junta, 719/383-5010, www.nps.gov/beol, 8 A.M.–5:30 P.M. June–Aug., 9 A.M.–4 P.M. Sept.–May, $3) is on the site of William and Charles Bent's original 1833 trading center for Plains Indians and trappers. For almost 16 years in the mid-1800s, the fort was among the only Santa Fe Trail settlements between Missouri and Mexico, and it was an oasis for travelers scratching through the desert.

◖ Bishop Castle

Bishop Castle (12705 Hwy. 165, Rye, 719/485-3040, www.bishopcastle.org), "always open [daylight hours] and always free," about 50 miles southeast of Pueblo in Rye, is either a genuine Wonder of the World (as its website claims with numerous exclamation points) or one man's loopy lifelong obsession. Jim Bishop started building the medieval architectural collage, whose tallest tower reaches 160 feet, in 1969 using stonemasonry know-how he picked up from books; a group called Friends of the Castle sent out Bishop's first-ever volunteer crew in 1999. The castle is impressive, full of stained-glass windows, turrets, stone-decorated walkways, tall stairways, and a gift shop. And, proclaims the website, "It won't be finished until the morning that Jim doesn't wake up again." Don't leave without picking up a Bishop Castle shot glass.

SPORTS AND RECREATION

The 9,600-acre **Lake Pueblo State Park** (Colorado State Parks, 640 Pueblo Reservoir Rd., 719/561-9320, http://parks.state.co.us/parks/lakepueblo) encompasses a large reservoir with two marinas and two boat ramps, 400 campsites, and numerous **hiking** and **biking** trails. As for the **fishing** at the reservoir, *Rocky Mountain News* outdoor writer Ed Dentry recently referred to it as "the big time." It's filled with trout, flathead catfish, walleye, wiper, bass, and catfish, and Dentry notes the state-record wiper (almost 27 pounds!) came from these very waters in 2004.

The **Nature and Raptor Center** (5200 Nature Center Rd., 719/549-2414, http://natureandraptor.org, 9 A.M.–5 P.M. Tues.–Sat., noon–5 P.M. Sun.), operated with the University of Southern Colorado, includes miles of trails, a hospital for injured hawks, volleyball and horseshoe courts, and a restaurant.

FOUR GREAT UNEXPECTED DRIVES

- **Scenic Highway of Legends:** Like the Spanish settlers and Native Americans before you, take Highway 12 from Trinidad through the San Isabel National Forest, including Cuchara Pass and Cordova Pass. Stop at tiny towns like Cokedale, Segundo, and Stonewall along the way for snacks.

- **U.S. 50 between Pueblo and Salida:** The stretch of highway west of Pueblo, through Cañon City and the Royal Gorge area, begins along the Arkansas River and remains in a pretty mountain valley for most of 100 miles. On the last stretch, as you ease into Salida, the bumpy snowcaps of the Sangre de Cristo Mountain Range become visible to the south.

- **Highway 69, from Walsenburg to Westcliffe:** If possible, take the long way from Walsenburg to Pueblo, rather than the flat and boring stretch down speedier I-25. This curvy two-lane road passes through the Sangre de Cristos on one side and the Wets (part of the San Isabel National Forest) on the other. The midway point is tiny Westcliffe, a beatific mountain town with a couple of bed-and-breakfasts and small roadside restaurants. Plan about 1.5 hours to get to U.S. 50, then another hour back east to I-25.

- **U.S. 160 from Walsenburg to Alamosa:** This 75-mile drive, over 9,413-foot North La Veta Pass, is notable for its mountain views and interesting rock formations. Before you hit Fort Garland, about 50 miles from Walsenburg, you'll see several 14,000-foot mountains to your right, including Little Bear Peak.

More information on Pueblo-area parks and recreation is at http://pueblo.us.

NIGHTLIFE

Gus' Place (1201 Elm St., 719/542-0755, 11 A.M.–close Mon.–Sat., noon–8 P.M. Sun.) is a classic local pub, a re-creation of which once landed at the Library of Congress's American Folklife Center to mark Italian American history. The pub is located in what was years ago a predominantly Italian neighborhood, although today's menu is Dutch. For more genteel live performances, the best venue is the **Broadway Theatre League** (210 N. Santa Fe Ave., 719/545-4721, http://broadwaytheatreleague.lbu.com), which has put on *Evita* and *Tommy* and hosted performances by Carol Channing and Marvin Hamlisch (both of whom undoubtedly wound up at Gus' Place after their shows).

SHOPPING

The mild weather and proximity to both New Mexico and the Rockies attracts a large community of artists to Pueblo, and many have galleries. Former local schoolteacher Lyle Clift's paintings of southwestern cliffs and vistas as well as his pottery and birdbaths are on display at his home **Deerfoot Studios** (405 Midnight Ave., 719/561-1575, http://deerfootstudios.net, call for appointment). For work by more local artists, the **John Deaux Art Gallery** (221 S. Union Ave., 719/545-8407, www.johndeauxartgallery.com, 11 A.M.–5 P.M. Tues.–Sat.) hangs paintings in an 1881 building that once housed a brothel, a casino, and a dance hall.

Female clothes hounds, especially those of the teenage pink-loving variety, will enjoy the family-run **Gotcha Covered** (230 S. Union Ave., 719/544-6833, 10 A.M.–5:30 P.M. Mon.–Fri.).

ACCOMMODATIONS

The hotels of Pueblo are mostly Best Westerns and Marriotts, and the classy Abriendo Inn recently went into foreclosure during the economic downturn. Surviving is the **Edgar Olin House Bed and Breakfast** (727 W. 13th St., 719/544-5727, www.olin-house.com,

$79–159), in a building that looks like three brick towers, with lovingly detailed guest rooms, some with small fireplaces and all with an Old West antique-ish ambience.

FOOD

La Tronica's (1143 E. Abriendo Ave., 719/542-1113, http://latronicas.com, 5–9 P.M. Tues.–Thurs., 5–10 P.M. Fri.–Sat., $15) remains a classic. It has been around since 1943, and Lyndon B. Johnson is among the dignitaries reputed to have dined here; it retains an old-fashioned quality, with comfort food like steak and fried chicken.

La Renaissance (217 E. Routt Ave., 719/543-6367, www.larenaissancerestaurant.com, 5–9 P.M. Tues.–Sat., $24) has a few vegetarian dishes, including the chiles rellenos ($12), but everything else has meat—many different kinds of steak plus chicken, duck, and lamb. It's all very juicy.

Angelo's Pizza Parlor (223 S. Union Ave., 719/544-8588, http://restaurantonline.biz/wwwroot/angelos, 11 A.M.–10 P.M. Mon.–Thurs., 11 A.M.–midnight Fri.–Sat., 11 A.M.–9 P.M. Sun., $12) is a family-run pizza place that serves Italian sandwiches in addition to inventive pies such as the "A.A.A. Plumbing," with chili peppers, sausage, and Tabasco sauce. The Union Avenue location is part of a Pueblo chain.

Every town needs a beloved sandwich shop like **DC's on B Street** (115 W. B St., 719/584-3410, 11 A.M.–2 P.M. Mon.–Tues., 11 A.M.–2 P.M. and 5:30–9 P.M. Wed.–Sat., $9), best known for the Pilgrim, a Thanksgiving dinner of a sandwich containing turkey, cranberries, and stuffing.

INFORMATION AND SERVICES

The **Greater Pueblo Chamber of Commerce** (302 N. Santa Fe Ave., 719/542-1704 or 800/233-3446, www.pueblochamber.org) and *The Pueblo Chieftain* (www.chieftain.com) have put up the extremely useful website www.pueblo.org, which has information about historic sites, restaurants, and art displays.

Pueblo's hospitals include **Parkview Medical Center** (400 W. 16th St., 719/584-4000, www.parkviewmc.com) and **St. Mary-Corwin Medical Center** (1008 Minnequa Ave., 719/557-4000, www.stmarycorwin.org).

CAÑON CITY

Bizarre but beautiful mountain town Cañon City is known for two things: prisons and a huge hole. The Royal Gorge is a 1,000-foot-deep canyon surrounded by rocky cliffs and treacherous peaks, and simply standing next to it is enough to give you vertigo. As for prisons, Cañon City built its first one in 1871, and today 7,500–8,500 convicts stay at 10 area facilities—including the supermax, which has housed super-villains such as Ted "The Unabomber" Kaczynski, original World Trade Center bomber Ramzi Yousef, and Oklahoma City bomber Timothy McVeigh. Area residents, believe it or not, love the prisons, as they give decent jobs to some 3,500 people.

Beyond those two things, Cañon City is a pretty little mountain town with creeks and fishing ponds throughout the valley west of Pueblo and northeast of the breathtaking Sangre de Cristo mountain range. Its downtown area of shops and galleries is a bona fide historic site, including mostly 1900s-era buildings, and is the place to visit if you're not in the mood for tourist attractions such as the Buckskin Joe Frontier Town and the Museum of Colorado Prisons. Also, the weather is frequently great, even in the winter, and Cañon City has plenty of hiking-and-biking trails, white-water rafting outlets, and a summer music festival.

Sights

A natural wonder some call the "Grand Canyon of the Arkansas River," the Royal Gorge formed 3 million years ago from a trickle of water, and its location was once home to dinosaurs. The Utes, among other Native American groups, set up camp here in the winter, and Spanish missionaries, fur traders, and trappers were among the early non-native settlers. In the late 1800s, after miners discovered silver on the Arkansas River, two railroads competed to build lines to cart ore from the high country—the Rio Grande won this "Royal Gorge War," which began with gunshots and ended in court.

There are several dramatic ways to experience the Royal Gorge, beginning with the **Royal Gorge Bridge & Park** (4218 County Rd. 3A, 719/275-7507 or 888/333-5597, www. royalgorgebridge.com, hours vary by season, $25), an 18-foot-wide bridge built in 1929 and suspended 1,053 feet up from the bottom. It's a little expensive to get in, and the 360-acre theme park is heavy on hot dogs and cowboy-hat shops, but the views are breathtaking, and the windy, wobbly walk across the bridge scares hundreds of thousands of visitors every year. To check out the gorge from the bottom, the **Royal Gorge Route Railroad** (401 Water St., 888/724-5748, www.royalgorgeroute.com, departure times vary by season, $33) is a 12-mile trip through the narrow valley, stopping to linger over the Royal Gorge suspension bridge and other sights. The railroad, heavily marketed by Cañon City, offers packages such as a "gourmet dinner car," a murder-mystery game, and a ride up front with the locomotive engineer.

Focusing on Cañon City's *other* claim to fame, the **Museum of Colorado Prisons** (201 N. 1st St., 719/269-3015, www.prisonmuseum. org, 8:30 A.M.–6 P.M. daily mid-May–Labor Day, 10 A.M.–5 P.M. Wed.–Sun. Labor Day–mid-May, $7) has such cheerful exhibitions as the hangman's noose used in the last Colorado execution, a lovingly preserved women's correctional facility from 1935, an actual gas chamber, and a gift shop. The creative visitor may want to bake a cake with a file in it before stopping by.

Connoisseurs of both wine and Benedictine monks will enjoy **The Winery at Holy Cross Abbey** (3011 E. U.S. 50, 719/276-5191 or 877/422-9463, www.abbeywinery.com, tasting room 10 A.M.–6 P.M. Mon.–Sat., noon–5 P.M. Sun. summer, hours vary in winter), with a monastery on the west side of the property and a Napa Valley–style wine-bottling facility on the east side. Visitors can tour both the abbey, which has impressive views of the Sangre de Cristo range, and the wine-making facility, with tasting in the pretty outdoor garden during the summer.

The **Dinosaur Depot** (330 Royal Gorge Blvd., 719/269-7150 or 800/987-6379, www. dinosaurdepot.com, hours vary by season, $4) documents the area's *really* old history, when dinosaurs roamed through the gorge. The region has produced many amazing fossils over the years, although some of the most famous have relocated to museums in Washington, D.C., and Denver; visitors to this museum will have to settle for a full-size replica of a *Stegosaurus* skeleton.

Accommodations

The Cañon Inn was once a fixture in this town, and even though it's now a **Quality Inn and Suites** (3075 E. U.S. 50, 719/275-8676, www.qualityinn.com/hotel-canon_city-colorado-CO027, $104–119), it still has the same plainspoken charm as it did when stars John Wayne, Jane Fonda, John Belushi, and James Caan stayed here over the years. It also has six indoor hot tubs and a heated pool.

In a restored 1890 Victorian downtown, the **Jewel of the Canyons Bed and Breakfast Suites** (429 Greenwood Ave., 719/275-0378, www.jewelofthecanyons.com, $99–119) has three guest rooms with a cozy turn-of-the-20th-century ambience—including one with a huge brass bed.

Food

Le Petit Chablis (512 Royal Gorge Blvd., 719/269-3333, www.lepetitchablis.com, 11:30 A.M.–1:30 P.M. and 5:30–8:30 P.M. Tues.–Thurs., 11:30 A.M.–1:30 P.M. and 5:30–9:30 P.M. Fri., 5:30–9:30 P.M. Sat., $25) is a high-class French joint with fresh seafood and pasta dishes, plus homemade bread and pastries. The menu changes daily.

Run by an Italian family that operated a cider mill and cherry orchard for years in Cañon City, ◖ **Merlinos' Belvedere** (1330 Elm Ave., 719/275-5558 or 800/625-2526, www.belvedererestaurant.com, 11:30 A.M.–1:30 P.M. and 4:30–10 P.M. Mon.–Fri., noon–10 P.M. Sat., noon–9 P.M. Sun., reduced hours fall–winter, $23) has served fettuccine with smoked salmon Alfredo sauce ($16) and manicotti ($14) since roughly 1946. Everything is homemade, and the bakery and pasta shop is a great find even if you don't stop for a meal.

El Caporal (1028 Main St., 719/276-2001, 11 A.M.–10 P.M. Mon.–Sat., 11 A.M.–9 P.M. Sun., $12) is an easygoing Mexican eatery with purple-and-pink tabletops. It has a massive menu of all combinations of tacos, enchiladas, burritos, and tostadas.

Information and Services

Cañon City (128 Main St., 719/269-9011) has an official website is www.canoncity.org.

The **St. Thomas More Hospital** (1338 Phay Ave., 719/285-2000, www.stmhospital.org) is one of the bigger facilities in the mountains beyond Colorado Springs and Pueblo.

Salida and Buena Vista

Salida and Buena Vista are small towns in sight of beautiful mountain scenery such as the Collegiate Peaks, the Sangre de Cristo range, and the White River National Forest. They're about 38 miles from each other—Salida is on U.S. 50, just east of U.S. 285, while Buena Vista is on U.S. 24, just north of U.S. 285 as it turns northeast to Denver. Both towns have a cozy, uncrowded feel, although they tend to fill up during summer as cyclists, hikers, and whitewater rafters fill up local hotels and inns. Salida, in particular, has a vibrant art-gallery scene, while Buena Vista is more of a traditional tourist town, with only a few upscale hotels and restaurants. Both are convenient stopping points for trips between Denver and southwest sights like Telluride, Mesa Verde National Park, Durango, and Four Corners.

SALIDA

Downtown Salida is a great place to kill a summer afternoon. For a town of just 5,500 people, it has some of the best art galleries in the state, and its colorful downtown district of restaurants, theaters, and little shops is built for tourists—with a little extra artistic oomph from pastel-colored restaurants and galleries with life-size wrought-iron animals spilling onto the sidewalks outside.

Salida's other great advantage is its proximity to extremely tall mountains, particularly the Sawatch Range, which seems to pop out of nowhere as you head north along U.S. 285. The Collegiate Peaks line the half-hour stretch of road from here to equally tiny Buena Vista, and on your left is a series of 14,000-foot peaks, including Mount Shavano, Tabeguache Peak, Mount Antero, and Mount Princeton. In addition to the 15 fourteeners surrounding Salida, the Arkansas River runs through town, the Sangre de Cristo Range is to the south, and the climate is so consistently mild that residents have dubbed it the "Banana Belt."

As a result, Salida, which in the late 1800s was a railroad town with legendarily tough saloons and flophouses, is a destination area for hikers, bikers, cross-country skiers, fishers, and white-water rafters. From Buena Vista, it's about 25 miles south on U.S. 285; from Cañon City, it's 50 miles west on U.S. 50.

Sports and Recreation

For truly excellent mountain **fishing,** make a pilgrimage almost any time of year to 14,433-foot-high Mount Elbert, the tallest mountain in Colorado, where the Arkansas River begins, popping and hissing its way down to the rest of the fourteeners in the area. The Colorado Division of Wildlife heavily stocks brown trout and rainbow trout here, and while several dozen fishing spots are accessible on the river, some are private.

Rafters will find it difficult to choose between Salida and Buena Vista, both near

BIGHORN SHEEP

Once, these huge rams and ewes, whose horns weigh 30 pounds apiece, roamed in the thousands from the top of the Canadian Rocky Mountains to the bottom of Texas. But thanks to pneumonia, disease, and parasites, the population of bighorn sheep, otherwise known as *Ovis canadensis*, has dwindled to hundreds, confined to pockets in the hills of Georgetown and Rocky Mountain National Park.

Check them out in the following places – and keep in mind, it's illegal to hunt, kill, or injure the state animal in any way.

The **Georgetown Wildlife Viewing Area** (Alvarado Rd., near I-70 Exit 228, Georgetown), in the small former mining town west of Denver, is a quiet, pristine place to watch a bunch of sheep on a hill. There's a town-wide viewing event in early November.

In mid-February, **Bighorn Sheep Day** (Garden of the Gods, 1805 N. 30th St., Colorado Springs, 719/634-6666, www.gardenofgods. com) provides a vantage point for the sheep who stay at lower elevations, around Garden of the Gods and Queens Canyon. (Some congregate higher up, on Pikes Peak, in the summer.) The free event includes wildlife-viewing stations, guided nature walks, and children's programs.

Hunting and disease cut down the bighorn sheep population considerably in the 19th and 20th centuries, but they started to make a comeback in the 1960s. Within a few decades, wildlife managers reintroduced them around the St. Vrain River and Cow Creek, near Boulder and Longmont. Today, about 650 of them live in **Rocky Mountain National Park** (1000 U.S. 36, Estes Park, 970/586-1206, www.nps. gov/room) – sometimes crossing U.S. 34 en masse on the north side of Horseshoe Park (there are signs; drive carefully).

The actual Bighorn Sheep Canyon, a stretch of the Arkansas River in Cañon City, is better known for its white-water rafting than its wildlife-viewing opportunities. However, the 60-mile stretch of U.S. 50 between Cañon City and Salida, in south-central Colorado, is a sheep-viewing sure thing, especially during winter. For more information, contact the **Colorado Division of Wildlife** (7405 U.S. 50, Salida, 719/530-5520).

superb Arkansas River rapids. Tour-guide outfits unique to Salida include **Canyon Marine Whitewater** (5620 E. U.S. 50, 719/539-4444 or 800/539-4447, www.canyonmarine.com) and **Whitewater Encounters** (14825 U.S. 285, 719/539-4680 or 800/255-5784, www. weraft.com).

Salida is also home to a small **ski** area—**Monarch** (23715 U.S. 50, 719/530-5000 or 888/996-7669, www.skimonarch.com), with 63 trails spread over 800 acres along the Continental Divide. The runs are mostly geared to experts, although 14 percent are for beginners and 28 percent for intermediate riders. The resort has five chairlifts, but nonetheless, this is a ski area of convenience—few would pick Monarch over Vail or Aspen. Lift tickets are in the $57 range.

One of the best **biking** trails in the state is the 32-mile **Monarch Crest,** which hits a section of the Continental Divide Trail. It rises about 1,000 feet to a peak height of more than 12,000 feet and rambles through dense forests, tight switchbacks, sharp rocks, and creeks. For a fee, the High Valley Bike Shuttle (6250 U.S. 285, Poncha Springs, 719/539-6089 or 800/871-5145, www.monarchcrest.com, 8 and 10 A.M. daily, $22) will take you and your bike from Poncha Springs to Monarch Pass Summit, an 18-mile trip along U.S. 50.

Bike rentals and equipment are available at **Absolute Bikes** (310 W. Sackett St., 719/539-9295, www.absolutebikes.com).

Shopping

Salida is stocked with antiques shops and art galleries, including **Antiques on First** (140 W. 1st St., 719/539-3353, 10:30 A.M.–5:30 P.M. Mon.–Sat., 11:30 A.M.–4:30 P.M. Sun., reduced hours fall–winter), with lamps, tables, books, a $45 bust of the poet Henry Wadsworth Longfellow, and an old box of acne medicine with the slogan "Rinse Away Your Blackheads." More modern is **Cultureclash** (101 N. F St., 719/539-3118, noon–6 P.M. Wed.–Sat.), an art and jewelry store with colorful paintings on display. The **Brodeur Art Gallery** (151 W. 1st St., 719/221-1272, www.brodeurart.com, 11 A.M.–5 P.M. Wed.–Sat., noon–4 P.M. Sun., reduced hours fall–winter, call for appointment) carries local artist Paulette Brodeur's colorful paintings of cats in spaceships and other wacky scenes.

Accommodations

Salida is filled with Best Westerns and Econo Lodges, plus the roadside fixture **Woodland Motel,** but two properties are more than generic and worthy of the dramatic mountain scenery surrounding the town. In a triangular brown house straight out of *The Sound of Music,* the tree-lined (**Tudor Rose** (6720 County Rd. 104, 719/539-2002 or 800/379-0889, www.thetudorrose.com, $90–185) has six guestrooms with large feather beds and views of several 14,000-foot mountains. More historic is the 1892-era building that houses the **River Run Inn** (8495 County Rd. 160, 719/539-3818 or 800/385-6925, www.riverruninn.com, $100–125), directly on the Arkansas River, with six private guest rooms and a shared third-floor "dormitory" that costs $30 pp and includes breakfast.

Food

Head to the downtown historic district for the distinctive bistros and wine bars. The **Laughing Ladies Restaurant** (128 W. 1st St., 719/539-6209, www.laughingladiesrestaurant. com, 11 A.M.–2 P.M. and 5 P.M.–close Mon. and Thurs.–Sat., 9 A.M.–2 P.M. Sun., $20) is run by experienced, Napa Valley-trained chefs who get the most out of standard dinner dishes—chili-grilled chicken breast ($21), barbecue duck ($22), and lamb steak ($23). They also run the **Downtown Bakery and Delicatessen** (124 F. St., 719/539-4248, 7:30 A.M.–6 P.M. Wed.–Sat., 7:30 A.M.–noon Sun.–Mon., $7.50).

Homier (and a little kitschier, in that country-kitchen kind of way) is the **Country Bounty Restaurant** (413 W. U.S. 50, 719/539-3546, www.thecountrybounty.com, 6:30 A.M.–9 P.M. daily summer, 7 A.M.–8 P.M. daily winter, $14), which starts with burgers ($8) and fries and moves into elk burgers ($10.50), pasta primavera ($10.25), and Atlantic salmon ($14.25). Check out the gift shop's large collection of porcelain dolls and various angels and lotions.

Amicas (136 E. 2nd St., 719/539-5219, http://amicassalida.wordpress.com/menus, 11:30 A.M.–9 P.M. daily, $10) is a fast-moving pizzeria and microbrewery with 15 kinds of pies, calzones, paninis, and eight desserts that include peanut-butter mousse ($6.65).

Information and Services

The **Salida Chamber of Commerce** is at 406 West U.S. 50 (877/772-5432, www.salidachamber.org).

Salida's primary hospital, the **Heart of the Rockies Regional Medical Center** (1000 Rush Dr., 719/530-2200, www.hrrmc.com) moved in 2008 to a much larger facility serving 20,000 patients in Salida and beyond.

BUENA VISTA

Although just 2,200 people live in Buena Vista today, it was once the home of 3,000 Utes, explorers believed, and during the gold-mining boom it had 36 bars. The scenery hasn't changed much—the Collegiate Range, with its eight 14,000-foot mountains, is to the west, and Brown's Canyon, which surrounds a surging stretch of the Arkansas River, is to the south. The town is big with hikers and bikers, and some call it the "capital for white-water rafting in the United States."

Sights

About 12 miles southwest of Buena Vista, the **Mount Princeton Hot Springs Resort** (15870 County Rd. 162, Nathrop, 719/395-2447 or 888/395-7799, www.mtprinceton.com) is a hotel and restaurant complex built around trickles of 135°F spring water. The natural

© MATT INDEN/WEAVER MULTIMEDIA GROUP/COLORADO TOURISM OFFICE

the Collegiate Range near Buena Vista

pools, used since prehistoric times, are in view of the 14,000-foot mountain ranges.

Formerly the Old Chaffee County Courthouse, site of a violent confrontation between rival Granite and Buena Vista officials in the 1880s, the **Buena Vista Heritage Museum** (506 E. Main St., 719/395-8458, www.buenavistaheritage.org/Heritage-Museum, 10 A.M.–5 P.M. Mon.–Sat., noon–5 P.M. Sun. Memorial Day–Sept., $5) displays mining-era clothing, furniture, and even a piano. Supposedly, the sheriff's wife used it to entertain prisoners in the county jail.

◀ Arkansas River White-Water Rafting

White-water rafting is the thing to do in Buena Vista, and the best place for it is on the Arkansas River, home of **Brown's Canyon.** The rapids are so intense here at this sharp drop-off that local adventure-sports companies have named them Zoomflume, Staircase, Devil's Punchbowl, and my personal favorite, Seidel's Suckhole.

Several outfitters sponsor tours, including **Performance Tours** (115 Gregg Dr., 800/328-7238, www.performancetours.com, $80–299), with trips of various lengths and durations; **Dvorak Expeditions** (17921 U.S. 285, Nathrop, 719/539-6851 or 800/824-3795, www.dvorakexpeditions.com, $50–1,625), whose offerings include elaborate 10-day trips; and **Buffalo Joe's** (113 N. Railroad St., 719/395-8757 or 866/283-3563, www.buffalojoe.com, $41–249), with a variety of trips.

Accommodations

The **Liar's Lodge** (30000 County Rd. 371, 719/395-3444 or 888/542-7756, www.liarslodge.com, $144–174) is an impressive log structure, with a 25-foot ceiling and a stone fireplace climbing all the way to the top. It's literally in the middle of the woods, on the bank of the Arkansas River.

On a woodsy two-acre plot just west of downtown, **Vista Court Cabins and Lodge** (1004 W. Main St., 719/395-6557 or 800/241-0670, $100–120) rents log cabins of various

WHITE-WATER RAFTING TOURS

Arkansas River white-water rafting

Don't go into a white-water rafting trip expecting a cakewalk – it's not like you can pull off to the side of the road, put on some special shoes, and run a river the way you'd hike a trail. First, unless you have a kayak and some experience, you'll need a commercial outfitter to set up the tour and provide the equipment. There are tons of them on the Internet, and I've listed several reliable ones throughout this chapter and book.

Secondly, prepare in advance: Wear a swimsuit, of course, and either tennis shoes or water sandals. Wool socks are OK. Bring waterproof sunscreen and, if you wear glasses, a string or Croakies. Waterproof cameras, with elastic bands, can easily be attached to life-jackets. Leave everything else – caps, jewelry, cotton clothing, wallets, keys – in the car. The outfitter will provide lifejackets and helmets if necessary.

Finally, call in advance to determine the trip's degree of difficulty. A Class I rapid is calm and easy, for kids and adults alike. Anything higher than a Class IV may require some heavy-duty paddling, so make sure you're in shape. Class VI is for professionals or experienced rafting teams only. Note that the water can be *freakin' cold* at almost all times of year save mid-July–early September, but the white-water rafting season officially begins around May. Most outfitters will rent wetsuits as well.

sizes, lodge rooms that have microwaves and small refrigerators, and a three-bedroom guest house. It's somewhat rustic, but that's part of the charm. Similarly wooden and rustic, **Thunder Lodge** (207 Brookdale Ave., 719/395-2245 or 800/330-9194, www.thunderlodge.com, $59–150) boasts roll-away beds, air mattresses, and free Wi-Fi, and its location, northwest of the town, is a plus.

Food

Unscientifically speaking, **K's Dairy Delite** (223 S. U.S. 24, 719/395-8695, 10 a.m.– 10 p.m. daily Apr.–Labor Day, 11 a.m.–8 p.m.

daily Labor Day–Oct., $5)—a walk-up hamburger and hot dog stand with frequent long lines during summer mealtimes—is the most popular restaurant in Buena Vista. For more advanced palates—or just people who feel like sitting inside at an actual table—**Mothers** (414 E. Main St., 719/395-4443, http://mothersbistrobv.com, 7:45 A.M.–5 P.M. Mon.–Sat., 9 A.M.–5 P.M. Sun., $10) serves sandwiches, pizza, quiche, coconut cookies, and apple strudel with walnuts and cinnamon.

Information
Contact the **Buena Vista Chamber of Commerce** (343 U.S. 24 S., 719/395-6612, www.buenavistacolorado.org) for more information.

WESTCLIFFE
Don't get so entranced by the mountainous scenery along Highway 69, northwest from Walsenburg, that you miss this in-and-out little town tucked away near the San Isabel National Forest. The seat of Custer County (pop. 3,500), Westcliffe has 700 residents and no stoplights. An old ranching town, Westcliffe is a local secret ensconced between the Sangre de Cristo and Wet Mountain Ranges. Although it's almost impossible to reach in the dead of winter—many of the hotels and restaurants are closed part of the year—Westcliffe is worth the out-of-the-way trip as an alternative to Walsenburg.

It's also a great base to explore the prettier areas of south-central Colorado.

Accommodations
About 10 miles south of town, the **Alpine Lodge** (6848 County Rd. 140, 719/783-2660, $65–80) offers small wooden two-bedroom cabins and has a restaurant and lounge. The ⟨ **Main Street Inn Bed & Breakfast** (501 Main St., 719/783-4000 or 877/783-4006, www.mainstreetbnb.com, $95–145, closed winter) is a beautiful little white-and-blue property at the center of town in an 1880-era building.

Food
Stop for a meal at **Garett Carlson's Westcliffe Feed Store** (116 N. 2nd St., 719/783-2771, http://westcliffefeedstore.com/FS, 5–9 P.M. Thurs.–Tues., $11), serving steak, fish, sandwiches, and four-cheese mushroom ravioli in an 1885-era building that once was an actual feed store. Go during happy hour, which serves two-for-one drinks, and stay for the occasional movie nights and live music.

Information
Contact the **Town of Westcliffe** (719/783-2943, www.townofwestcliffe.com) for more information; note that the unpaid town officials, while reachable via phone and email, are not available at a central town hall.

Alamosa and the Great Sand Dunes

With a population of 9,500, Alamosa is the metropolis of the San Luis Valley, the south-central Colorado plains area that extends about 125 miles north to south and 50 miles across. Given the incredible scenery in almost every direction, Alamosa is flat and plain, the only hint of outdoor adventure coming from the stretch of the Rio Grande River underneath a bridge through town.

While Alamosa has long been an agricultural center, notably for potatoes, and its Adams State College is one of the biggest

universities in the region, it's a sleepy town most notable for its proximity to other spots. Use the city as a base to visit the Great Sand Dunes National Park and Preserve, just to the northeast. For excitement, pretend you're visiting two centuries ago, when Pikes Peak discoverer Zebulon Pike was captured and taken prisoner to nearby Santa Fe, then a hostile area outside the United States.

Also near Alamosa are a several tiny but interesting towns—**Antonito,** about 30 miles south on U.S. 285, is home of both the

120-year-old steam-locomotive **Cumbres and Toltec Scenic Railroad** (U.S. 285, south end of Antonito, 719/376-5483 or 888/286-2737, www.cumbrestoltec.com, depot 7:30 A.M.–5:30 P.M. daily Memorial Day–mid-Oct., $91–165) and the Conejos River Guest Ranch, a comfortable spot to spend the night.

SIGHTS
Alamosa National Wildlife Refuge
The Alamosa region is a huge draw for **bird-watchers,** with the wet meadows and river oxbows of the Alamosa National Wildlife Refuge (9383 El Rancho Lane, 719/589-4021, www.fws.gov/alamosa/alamosanwr.html) giving homes to migrating songbirds and waterbirds along with mule deer, beavers, and coyotes.

Monte Vista National Wildlife Refuge
The Monte Vista National Wildlife Refuge (6120 Hwy. 15, Monte Vista, 719/589-4021, www.fws.gov/alamosa/Monte%20Vista.html) is also nearby, drawing 20,000 sandhill cranes in spring and fall—plus three endangered whooping cranes who like to pop up and freak out the birders.

Luther Bean Museum and Art Gallery
The Luther Bean Museum and Art Gallery (Adams State College, Richardson Hall, Room 256, 208 Edgemont Blvd., 719/587-7827, www2.adams.edu/lutherbean, 10 A.M.–2 P.M. Mon.–Fri., free) is known for its Native American pottery collection as well as Navajo and Rio Grande Valley weavings, antique furniture, memorabilia, and other items.

Jack Dempsey Museum
Completely unexpected is the Jack Dempsey Museum (412 Main St., Manassa, 719/843-5207, http://museumtrail.org/jackdempseymuseum.asp, 9 A.M.–5 P.M. Tues.–Sat. Memorial Day–Labor Day, free), some 23 miles south of Alamosa, where the 1919 heavyweight champion of the world grew up. The museum website refers to Dempsey as "Manassa's most famous figure," which makes sense, but I wonder what the competition would be. The museum is in the cabin where Dempsey grew up, and some of his championship gloves hang here.

◖ Great Sand Dunes National Park and Preserve
With pointy peaks, curvy bodies, various shades of brown, and shapes changing constantly in the wind, the Great Sand Dunes National Park and Preserve (11999 Hwy. 150, Mosca, 719/378-6300 or 719/378-6399, www.nps.gov/grsa, always open, $3 per week) looks like an alien landscape, or the kind of backdrop you'd see in a computer-animated movie. The dunes are like nothing else in Colorado, beginning with the flat, muddy Medano Creek and Sand Creek, then abruptly rising to sharp, rolling peaks and dipping just as sharply into mini valleys. No matter how old or out-of-shape you are, it is impossible to resist the urge to rush at full speed up one of the sandy hills, then crouch and drop into a roll down the other side. I can't remember when I've had so much dirt in my hair.

North America's tallest dunes are otherworldly and fascinating, extending 750 feet high, with the bottle-cap Sangre de Cristo Mountains in the background. Within the 30-square-mile area, a national monument since 1932, are alpine lakes, wetlands, aspens, and cottonwood trees, along with the alpine primrose and blue columbine flowers, peregrine falcons, white pelicans, tiger beetles, bobcats, and elk that go with them. The view from Highway 150 en route to the park entrance shows the massive dunes underneath the 11,000–13,000-foot peaks of the Sangre de Cristo Mountains in the backdrop. How did all this sand get here, anywhere from 12,000 to millions of years ago, as scientists estimate? Mostly, it blew up against the mountains with heavy winds, but streams, creeks, melting snow, and floods had something to do with it too.

The park is open all day every day, and some 300,000 visitors a year show up for camping,

© MATT INDEN/WEAVER MULTIMEDIA GROUP/COLORADO TOURISM OFFICE

The highest sand dunes in North America are found at the Great Sand Dunes National Park.

hiking, cycling, and, in the fall, sand-boarding. In late 2004, U.S. officials designated the dunes a national park, joining Rocky Mountain, Mesa Verde, and Black Canyon of the Gunnison in Colorado.

My family learned several survival tips for the Dunes on a recent midsummer visit: (1) Wear shoes with strong laces, as the dunes are littered with liberated sandals and flip-flops; (2) wear large sunglasses, as the wind whips up when you least expect it, even on mild 95°F days; (3) bring plenty of water, especially if you intend to hike the five or so miles to the top of the dunes, which can be an all-morning excursion at extreme elevation jumps from 7,500 to more than 13,000 feet; and (4) take advantage of the on-site shower facilities, or book a hotel or campsite nearby, or you'll be brushing sand out of different body parts for days.

Camping is available at a couple of places within the national park. The **Pinyon Flats Campground** (Hwy. 6, 10 miles east of Mosca, 719/378-6399, www.nps.gov/grsa/planyourvisit/campgrounds.htm, $20) is often crowded.

It has 88 campsites with toilets, tables, fire pits or grills, and showers. These fill up fast in the summer, so reserve a spot in advance. The private **Oasis Campground** (Hwy. 6, 10 miles east of Mosca, 719/378-2222, www.greatdunes.com, $20) has 70 campsites, all more shady and secluded than Pinyon Flats. Hot showers also come in handy, as do the nearby lodge (rooms $89), restaurant, gift shop, ice-cream socials, and horse rides. My family recently stopped by the restaurant to indulge in cloud-like bites of lemon and chocolate-cream pie. A local baker makes 10 different flavors to sell at the Oasis each day. You will probably want to sample all 10 of them.

🅲 Colorado Gators

Be forewarned. If you're in the Alamosa area and take one of the alligator-wrestling classes—yes, alligator-wrestling classes—you have to sign a liability waiver. According to *The Denver Post,* it reads in part: "I, ___, do hereby admit that if I'm crazy enough to willingly put my hands on an alligator, I deserve to get bit. Furthermore, I promise not to whine too much if I do get a few bumps and scrapes or even a flesh wound."

Waivers aside, the three-hour, $100 classes at Colorado Gators (9162 County Rd. 9 N., Mosca, 719/378-2612, www.gatorfarm.com, 9 A.M.–7 P.M. daily Memorial Day–Labor Day, 9 A.M.–5 P.M. daily Labor Day–Memorial Day, $15) are fairly safe if you follow the experts' instructions—i.e., stay far away from the sharp end of the 11-foot alligator. Also, the instructors are adept at pulling the gator's head back so his snout is facing straight up, then sticking their chins atop the gator's upright nose—don't do that yourself. It just seems like common sense. (Check out the surreal and very funny YouTube videos on the park's website.) Note that the wrestling classes are for grown-ups over age 18; kids have to make do as spectators of wrestling and exhibits like "Sir Kong," the 130-pound alligator snapping turtle.

Colorado Gators, also known as the San Luis Valley Alligator Farm, offers plenty of other entertainment for nonwrestlers. Two trained specialists regularly take on five or six of the more than 400 alligators. "There's a spot on my arm I haven't felt for four years," one of the wrestlers told *The Denver Post* in 2006. "But that's what helps keep us on our toes."

SPORTS AND RECREATION

Alamosa itself is merely a small town along the Rio Grande River, with little adventure to speak of. But it's near a bunch of out-of-the-way San Luis Valley spots revered by hikers, bikers, and rock climbers. Some of these excursions involve trips to other dinky nearby towns, like Monte Vista (to the northwest), Del Norte (a little farther northwest), and La Garita (due north along U.S. 285).

Rock climbers and hikers love **Penitente Canyon,** just outside of Del Norte, an easy three-mile round-trip for climbers of all skill levels. Some experts bemoan these climbs for being too short and too easy, but the valley views of the Sangre de Cristo range as well as the Great Sand Dunes keeps bringing them back. On the way into the canyon, you'll see the ancient rock art that graces towering sandstone walls; Penitente was named for some religious monks who used to live in this area. To get here, drive north from Del Norte on Highway 112, turn north on County Road 33, and follow this gravel road nearly 20 miles until you see the signs.

Anybody interested in the Colorado outdoors should load up the bike and the hiking boots and head to the **Rio Grande National Forest,** a 1,852-acre region encompassing the San Juan and Sangre de Cristo Mountains, the San Luis Valley, and the Rio Grande Del Norte—of the many mountain peaks, the elevations range from 7,500 feet to more than 14,000 feet. Trails are all over the area; for details, contact the forest supervisor's office (719/852-5941) or the **Conejos Peak Ranger District** (15571 County Rd. T-5, La Jara, 719/274-5193).

The **San Luis State Park** (Six Mile Lane, 13.5 miles north and 8 miles west of Blanca, 719/378-2020, http://parks.state.co.us/Parks/Sanluis) contains 2,054 acres of protected wetlands and is great for **wildlife viewing**—coyotes, rabbits, elk, songbirds, and snakes, among many others. The lake itself is open for boating and fishing.

A short, steep, winding trail past a creek leads to the **Zapata Falls Recreation Area** (20 miles from Alamosa, 5 miles south of Great Sand Dunes National Park, 719/274-8971). The views of the dunes and Sangre de Cristo Mountains are amazing, and the water and canyon breezes are perfect for a hot summer day. Look west for a huge herd of bison.

ACCOMMODATIONS

Most of the Alamosa-area hotels are chains, along with a few affordable inns and lodges, such as the **Great Sand Dunes Lodge** (7900 Hwy. 150 N., Mosca, 719/378-2900, www.gsdlodge.com, $95–105). The downtown Clarion-owned **Inn of the Rio Grande** (333 Santa Fe Dr., 719/589-5833 or 800/669-1658, www.innoftherio.com, $95) is a large white building with a small pool, an affordable on-site restaurant, and a large, popular-among-locals water park in the structure next door. About 30 miles away, in tiny Del Norte, the **AppleLodge Bed & Breakfast** (15081 W. U.S. 160, Del Norte, 719/657-2543 or 888/562-7753, www.applelodge.com, $99–119) has a huge stone fireplace and a small wooden hot tub, and it is generally cozy—but travelers should note the preponderance of Christian phrases like "enjoy the splendor and majesty of God's creation" on its website.

Thirty miles away in Antonito, the **Conejos River Guest Ranch** (25390 Hwy. 17, 719/376-2464, www.conejosranch.com, $98–125) is a pretty riverfront lodge whose innkeeper is named Shorty Fry.

FOOD

Next to a bowling alley a few miles north of U.S. 160, the **San Luis Valley Pizza Company** (2069 W. 1st Ave., 719/589-4749, www.sanluisvalleypizzacompany.com, 8 A.M.–9 P.M. Sun.–Tues., 8 A.M.–10 P.M. Wed.–Sat., $15) is an old-fashioned checkered-tablecloth pizza joint with beautifully fresh ingredients and enthusiastic service. Occasionally the cooks will put on a dough-twirling display for kids. The restaurant also delivers to hotels in the area.

I was sad to see the True Grits Steak House, in an old shack by the highway that John Wayne himself would have loved, recently closed. But you can get a similar type of food—burgers, steaks, sandwiches, and a lot of different types of beer—at the more modern **San Luis Valley Brewing Company** (631 Main St., 719/587-2337, www.slvbrewco.com).

INFORMATION AND SERVICES

Alamosa's **Visitor Information Center** (800/258-7597, www.alamosa.org) is in Cole Park.

Alamosa's hospital is the **SLV Regional Medical Center** (106 Blanca Ave., 719/589-2511, www.slvrmc.org).

CUCHARA VALLEY

One of the most breathtaking drives in Colorado—which is saying a lot, given the Rockies to the north and the San Juans to the southwest—the Scenic Highway of Legends passes through the mountainous **San Isabel National Forest,** the 10,000-foot **Cuchara Pass,** and the 11,248-foot **Cordova Pass.** It begins in Trinidad and forms a sort of smushy E shape before hooking up with U.S. 160, which extends to Walsenburg to the east and Fort Garland to the west.

The towns along this route are more significant for their history than for their modern amenities. **Cokedale,** founded in 1906, is a ghost town and National Historic Landmark District today, but once it was a massive coal-producing camp; **Segundo** was once popular among Spanish people coming up from Mexico, but today you're lucky if you can spot the gas station; and for more than a century **Stonewall** has been a popular spot for hunting and fishing.

Sights

The **Scenic Highway of Legends** (Hwy. 12) is just as rich with tales of fortune-seeking and war as it is with mountain scenery. In the 1800s, when Spanish explorers pushed north to the Spanish Peaks, they discovered gold, enslaved local Native Americans to help them dig, and then killed their poor helpers and destroyed the mine. But on their way south down Cuchara Pass, they encountered more Native Americans, who wiped them out—and, according to legend, or at least the Sangres.com website (http://sangres.com/shol), their gold remains in a river valley somewhere near Stonewall. Much later, Union soldiers pushed through the hills and valleys, leaving their names and initials on a rock at Scofield Ridge, just southeast of Trinidad.

C San Isabel National Forest

San Isabel is a sprawling, 1-million-acre collection of mountains, valleys, and lakes with corresponding hiking, biking, camping, and cross-country skiing opportunities. It includes the **Sangre de Cristo Mountains,** a stumpy set of snowcaps that begin in Poncha Pass, Colorado, and extend into Glorieta Pass, New

San Isabel National Forest's mountains and lakes offer numerous recreation opportunities.

Mexico, and include 10 peaks higher than 14,000 feet and more than 24 over 13,000 feet.

The **Spanish Peaks** have been a beacon for Native Americans, Spanish and French explorers, American settlers, and gold-rush fortune-seekers—they've been called many names, including *wahatoya,* an early Native American word meaning "breasts of the earth." Their best-known nickname is "Dos Hermanos," Spanish for "two brothers."

Sports and Recreation

Bear Lake is south of Cuchara off Highway 12; to get here, turn at the northern base of Cuchara Pass, head west on a dirt road, and drive about five miles. At 10,500 feet, the beatific tree-lined lake has 14 campsites, plus numerous trailheads for **hikers** and plenty of **fish.**

Another dirt road at the northern base of Cuchara Pass leads to **Blue Lake,** about four miles down the road; there are 15 campgrounds here, and the trailheads take hikers into the Sangre de Cristos.

For more information on bike-riding in the area, try **Spanish Peaks Cycling** (La Veta, info@spcycling.org, www.spcycling.org), which sponsors a 102-mile ride beginning in La Veta called the Stonewall Century and gives information about other rides and bike information in the Cuchara Valley area.

Accommodations

It's hard to find civilization along the Scenic Highway of Legends. La Veta, on Highway 12 near Walsenburg and the intersection of I-25 and U.S. 160, is a small resort town with several excellent places to stay. Those include **La Veta Inn** (103 W. Ryus Ave., La Veta, 719/742-3700, www.lavetainn.com, $119–139), in a square, tan building, which will rent out the entire 21-room hotel for $1,200 per night; and **Adagio Retreat** (818 S. Oak St., La Veta, 505/466-8385, www.alwaysonvacation.com/vacation-rentals/207253.html#contact, $155–400), in an early-1900s house in view of the Spanish Peaks, with croquet mallets and balls available on a spacious back lawn.

Food

The **Ryus Avenue Bakery** (129 W. Ryus Ave., La Veta, 719/742-3830, www.ryusavebakery. com, 7 A.M.–1:30 P.M. Tues., Thurs., and Sat., $6.50) serves healthy snacks, cinnamon rolls for breakfast, and deli sandwiches for lunch, but only three days a week. Grab a loaf of the home-cooked oatmeal cinnamon raisin bread for just $2.75.

The **Dog Bar and Grill** (34 Cuchara Ave. E., Cuchara, 719/742-6366, www.dogbarcuchara. com, noon–midnight Thurs.–Mon., $10) is exactly what the name implies—a fun, family-friendly restaurant with pizza, salads, burgers, mud pie, and, of course, hot dogs. A bonus is the outdoor patio, which often plays host to live bands. Note that as of early 2012, the restaurant and the entire surrounding shopping area was up for sale.

Information

Cuchara Valley shares a chamber of commerce with La Veta (http://lavetacucharachamber. com).

Trinidad and Walsenburg

TRINIDAD

The last Colorado town you encounter on I-25 south to New Mexico, Trinidad is a small collection of art galleries, historic Southwestern houses and museums, and a nearby recreation area with lakes and trails. But it wasn't always so peaceful: It was a key stop along the Santa Fe Trail in the late 1800s, and Old West villains such as Billy the Kid and Doc Holliday frequently stopped here to raise hell in the streets and casinos. The U.S. war against Mexico in 1847 led to tension and, occasionally, violence, such as the Christmas riot 20 years later, and the arrival of coal and the railroads led to a massive strike in 1914.

Trinidad has been more or less peaceful ever since, celebrating its history downtown with the six-mile **La Corazon de Trinidad** ("The Heart of Trinidad"). Even the unmemorable downtown buildings probably contain some kind of important history—the brick Carlisle Building (203 E. Main St.) is across the street from the city's first stagecoach stop and a hotel where Ulysses S. Grant stayed in 1880; according to legend, the entire county came out to escort him. With brick streets and century-old Victorian homes and churches, the downtown area is a nice pit stop before Santa Fe.

A small but weird footnote: Tiny, placid Trinidad is colloquially known as the "sex change capital of the world." It began in the 1960s, after a former Korean War MASH surgeon named Dr. Stanley Biber relocated here to become the town's general doctor. One day a woman showed up in his office and asked if he did "gender-reassignment operations." He had no idea what she was talking about, but agreed, and turned her into a man in 1969. Dr. Biber performed some 4,500 such surgeries before his death at age 82 in 2006.

Sights

Overlooking the Santa Fe Trail, the **Trinidad History Museum** (312 E. Main St., 719/846-7217, www.historycolorado.org/museums/trinidad-history-museum-0, 10 A.M.–4 P.M. daily May–Sept., by appointment Oct.–Apr., $8) is a complex of several historic buildings. Built in 1873, the **Baca House** is a two-story adobe house with Greek-style architectural flourishes and a small widow's walk out front—early Pueblo developer Felipe Baca and his wife, Dolores, bought it for 22,000 pounds of wool. The red- and blue-brick Victorian **Bloom Mansion** was the 1882 home of cattle baron Frank Bloom and his wife, Sarah, and the horn chair and porcelain figures inside recall the era. Also on the grounds is the **Pioneer Museum,** displaying covered wagons and other artifacts from Trinidad's early days as a town.

The **Arthur Roy Mitchell Memorial Museum and Gallery** (150 E. Main St., 719/846-4224, www.armitchell.org, 10 A.M.–4 P.M. Tues.–Sat., noon–4 P.M. Sun.

the historic Bloom Mansion in Trinidad

May–Sept., tours by appointment Oct.–Apr., $3) may look from the outside like a small supermarket, but it has some of the best Western memorabilia this side of Denver— Spanish folk art, classic cowboy paintings, and turn-of-the-20th-century photos. The mezzanine still has its original tin ceiling and horseshoe shape, and preservationists have maintained the hardwood floors and shiny white pillars.

Dinosaurs are the stars of the **Louden-Henritze Archaeological Museum** (Trinidad State Junior College campus, 600 Prospect St., Frudenthal Memorial Library entrance, 719/846-5508, www.trinidadstate.edu/index. php/archaeology-museum, 10 A.M.–3 P.M. Mon.–Thurs., free), which puts the fossil-digging work of Trinidad State Junior College archaeology students on display for the public. Highlights include the remains of a mosasaur, discovered while workers built a house in Trinidad.

The **Trinidad Trolley** (719/846-9843, ext. 133, www.historictrinidad.com) gives tours 8 A.M.–3 P.M. daily, stopping at all the local museums and historic sites.

Accommodations

Trinidad has a number of small motels and a few colorful bed-and-breakfasts befitting the town's arty, quiet downtown area. Wide, pink, and Victorian, the **Tarabino Inn** (310 E. 2nd St., 719/846-2115 or 866/846-8808, www.tarabinoinn.com, $84–89) is a bed-and-breakfast with local artists' paintings in the lobby and cherrywood bookshelves and stairs to offset the light hardwood floors. It's down the street from Trinidad Junior State College and within photo-shooting distance of Fisher's Peak and other pretty mountain scenes.

The **Stone Mansion Bed & Breakfast** (212 E. 2nd St., 719/845-1625 or 877/264-4279, www.stonemansionbb.com, $99–115) is in a shingle-covered 1904 Victorian with oak lobby furniture to match the staircase and ceiling beams. It has three guest rooms, but note that two of them share a bath.

Food

Sadly, the downtown Main Street Bakery and Café, which displayed local artists' work, has closed. In its place is the **Bella Luna Pizzeria** (121 W. Main St., 719/846-2750, 11 A.M.–3 P.M. and 5–9 P.M. Mon. and Wed.–Sat., noon–6 P.M. Sun., $18). For a sandwich alternative, try **The Café** (135 E. Main St., 719/846-7119, 7:30 A.M.–3 P.M. Mon.–Fri., 9 A.M.–2 P.M. Sat., $8), which serves cinnamon rolls and salads as well.

For Italian, **Nana and Nano Monteleone's Deli and Pasta House** (418 E. Main St., 719/846-2696, 10:30 A.M.–7:30 P.M. Wed.–Sat., $8) may have gnocchi Bolognese and gigantic deli sandwiches, but **Rino's Italian Restaurant** (400 E. Main St., 719/845-0949, www.rinostrinidad.com, 5–9 P.M. Wed.–Sun., $18) has singing waiters.

Information and Services

The City of Trinidad (719/846-9843, www.historictrinidad.com) is at 135 North Animas Street.

The **Mount San Rafael Hospital** (410 Benadicta Ave., 719/846-9213, www.msrhc.org) has been operating in one form or another since 1889.

WALSENBURG

It's tempting to look at a map and pick tiny Walsenburg, about one hour's drive north of Trinidad on I-25, as a transitional town for a trip from Denver to the Great Sand Dunes or Pagosa Springs. And the town clearly aspires to be a quaint tourist stop similar to Estes Park or Buena Vista—one hotel manager referred to it as "Little Mayberry." This tourism transformation hasn't quite been successful: When my family visited on a recent vacation, many of the downtown restaurants were boarded up, despite a string of interesting antiques shops along Walsen Avenue, including the Black Diamond and the Leanin' Tree. Also, a train runs through town at regular intervals all night, so keep that in mind when making lodging plans. Nonetheless, Walsenburg is strategically located, just south of Highway 69, and the indirect route to Pueblo on Highway 69 is a beautiful two-hour drive with the San Isabel National Forest on one side and the Sangre de Cristo mountain range on the other.

Accommodations

La Plaza Inn B&B (118 W. 6th St., 719/738-5700, www.laplazainnwalsenburg.com, $59–89) is a friendly bed-and-breakfast in a faded pink building between a flower store and a bookstore. Its owner clearly tries to make a lot out of a little, providing homey touches like a wall full of up-to-date magazines and guest rooms with stuffed animals and soft leopard-print bedcovers. However: Did I mention the train? The one with the very loud whistle? Ask about it before staying the night.

Food

This being the Southwest, try the popular Mexican joint **Corine's** (822 Main St., 719/738-1231, 9 A.M.–9 P.M. Sun.–Thurs., 9 A.M.–10 P.M. Fri.–Sat., $9).

THE EASTERN PLAINS

Having grown up in Detroit and lived for several years in Chicago, I've made the drive through endless Nebraska and Kansas to the eastern Colorado border via I-76 and I-80 almost a dozen times. The Eastern Plains are flat and uneventful prairie land compared to the vibrant Rocky Mountain regions of the state, but they have their exciting moments, unexpected gems, nature and wildlife viewing areas, and freakish roadside attractions if you know where to look. Driving into Colorado, you'll feel the car begin to climb around Sterling (home of the Overland Trail Museum, filled with Native American artifacts) and might consider a stop in Crook (home of the 7,000-acre Tamarack Ranch State Wildlife Area) or Fort Morgan (around the massive Pawnee National Grassland, which goes on and on and on but is a great spot for animal and bird-watching).

Unlike other parts of Colorado, the wide-open spaces, cornfields, and endless views of the horizon in eastern Colorado are just barely equipped for visitors. The motels in this large chunk of the state tend to be chains, and the restaurants lean more toward "truck-stop diner" than "elegant bistro"—a great thing if you're an enthusiast of burgers, ribs, and chicken sandwiches. The region's tourism industry is designed for drivers just passing through.

But wanderers will appreciate this part of Colorado—tiny history museums like the pink-and-red Genoa Tower in Limon are filled with Native American artifacts and Old West knickknacks, the reservoirs and tiny lakes are

© ANDREA GOLOD/WEAVER MULTIMEDIA GROUP/COLORADO TOURISM OFFICE

HIGHLIGHTS

◖ Pawnee National Grassland: A huge (193,060 acres) nature-watching area northeast of Greeley, Pawnee is full of mountain plover, burrowing owls, mule deer, coyotes, foxes, and snakes (page 370).

◖ Greeley Independence Stampede: Perhaps the biggest country-music festival in Colorado – certainly bigger than anything in Denver or Colorado Springs – the Stampede draws some 450,000 fans every June to see such big-name acts as Reba McEntire, Tim McGraw, and Faith Hill. Oh, and there's a professional rodeo (page 371).

◖ Living Trees: Bradford Rhea carves these massive sculptures out of actual trees in downtown Sterling – his best-known work includes the five 16-foot-tall giraffes of *Skygrazers* (page 378).

◖ Carson County Carousel: The rides on this unexpected and beautiful merry-go-round in the middle of nowhere (Burlington) cost only $0.25 – not much higher than they were before county fathers bought it for $1,200 and transported it from Elitch Gardens in Denver (page 380).

◖ Picket Wire Canyonlands: Near La Junta, this bumpy portion of the Comanche National Grassland contains 1,300 dinosaur footprints and rock art left over from early

human visitors some 1,500 years ago. It's also a great, flat, mild area for hiking and cycling, with plenty of wildlife (page 384).

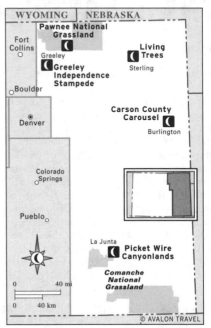

LOOK FOR ◖ TO FIND RECOMMENDED SIGHTS, ACTIVITIES, DINING, AND LODGING.

a big lure for pheasant hunters and fishers, and county fairs pop up even in the tiniest of towns. Northeastern Colorado centers on Greeley and Sterling, two conservative farming-and-ranching towns along I-76 east of Denver— Greeley is particularly famous for the Greeley Independence Stampede, a country music and rodeo festival that draws almost 400,000 every year. Southeastern Colorado—south of I-70 and east of Pueblo—includes Lamar (the "Goose Hunting Capital of the World"), Las Animas (whose Kit Carson Museum is a tourist monument of the kitschy persuasion, up there with the Mitchell Corn Palace and the World's Largest Badger), and, beyond that, a whole lot of open space.

PLANNING YOUR TIME

Greeley, Sterling, and Fort Morgan are the biggest cities in the High Plains region, and the drive there from Denver is an hour or two east along a major highway (I-76). It's easy to make a day trip to any of these towns; far more complicated is attempting to make a road trip out of the entire Eastern Plains region. Civilization is spread out, and covering Julesburg, Burlington, Lamar, Las Animas, and Limon will take a solid 10–12 hours.

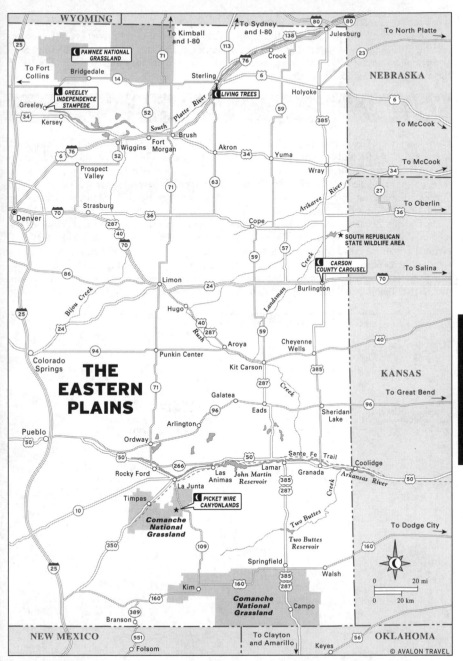

THE EASTERN PLAINS

It's best to spread out the trip—hit northeast towns like Sterling and Julesburg on one leg and Limon, Lamar, Las Animas, and the Comanche National Grassland at the bottom of the state. Of course, if you're driving west from Kansas or Nebraska to visit Denver or a ski resort, you'll encounter several of these towns on the way. Stop at a few tiny history museums for a break in the monotony.

Greeley

Here's where "Colorado turns into the Midwest," as my friend Jay Dedrick, who once lived in tiny Yuma and helped his father run the radio station there, describes the Eastern Plains. Greeley is a conservative farming, ranching, and beef-industry region that divides metropolitan Denver (about 55 miles to the west) from the flat eastern-Colorado plains leading to Kansas and Nebraska. Country-and-western music is the standard here, particularly during the Greeley Independence Stampede, a huge early-summer festival that annually draws 400,000 fans to hear the likes of Tim McGraw, Faith Hill, George Jones, Vince Gill, and Loretta Lynn.

The city was named after Horace Greeley of the *New York Tribune,* known for declaring, "Go West, young man, go West." Greeley's underling, *Tribune* agricultural editor Nathan C. Meeker, followed his advice in 1869 and colonized the area under a strict moral code—old-school concepts like temperance and religion to go with his more progressive farming and education ideas. By the time Greeley made his first and only visit the following year, Meeker's ideas had taken

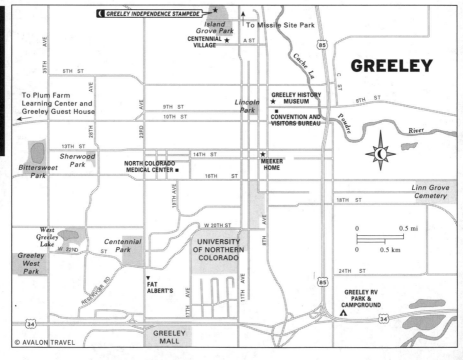

hold, and the wide streets were filled with trees, along with irrigation canals and nice houses; a newspaper, a schoolhouse, a courthouse, and what ultimately became the University of Northern Colorado followed within a few years.

Meeker had his comeuppance a few years later in northwest Colorado—the Utes didn't take to his patronizing reformist ideas and killed the journalist and his followers in what is now Meeker, Colorado—but his impact continues to be felt in the Greeley region. The city remains agricultural, religious, and conservative, and it's growing fast—the population jumped from 82,000 in 2002 to more than 90,000 in 2007. Today, it's packed with historical museums, proudly American restaurants, and ranches everywhere. And it has one thing it didn't have in the 1800s: one of the largest Hispanic populations in the state, at 30 percent.

SIGHTS
Centennial Village
Opened in 1976, Centennial Village (1475 A St., 970/350-9220, www.greeleygov.com/museums/centennialvillage.aspx, 10 A.M.–4 P.M. Tues.–Sat. late Apr.–Sept., weekdays $5, Sat. $6) is a sprawling, tree-lined, 32-building historic area—including the Union Pacific Depot, which regularly shows the *From Flame to Filament* exhibit about the history of lighting. The district of restored Victorian homes, vintage light posts, and brick plazas displays one-of-a-kind items such as a dress made of 42 rattlesnake skins (in the Shaw House) and a 1920 Federal truck. Guided tours are available—call in advance—but it's far less cumbersome to walk around the area yourself.

Meeker Home
The Meeker Home (1324 9th Ave., 970/350-9220, www.greeleygov.com/museums/meeker-home.aspx, tours by appointment, $3) is a modest, light-yellow, adobe-brick structure that reformer and Union Colony founder Nathan Meeker built when he arrived with his family in 1870. Many of the Meekers' original furnishings remain in the restored building. The guided tours are pretty interesting, delving

© STEVE KNOPPER

Greeley's Centennial Village is a 32-building historic area.

THE EASTERN PLAINS

into Meeker's history, his death, and his family's struggles afterward.

Greeley History Museum

The Greeley History Museum (714 8th St., 970/350-9220, www.greeleygov.com/museums/greeleyhistorymuseum.aspx, 8:30 A.M.–4:30 P.M. Wed.–Fri., 10 A.M.–4 P.M. Sat., free) opened in July 2005 with new collections of Front Range art and Weld County history.

Missile Site Park

An Atlas E, one of the first U.S. intercontinental ballistic missiles, is the main draw at Missile Site Park (10611 Spur 257, 970/304-6531, tours 7 A.M.–4 P.M. Mon.–Fri., call for reservations Sat.), a Cold War silo that was operational from 1961 to 1965. The missiles are no longer used, so don't worry about anything blowing up in your face when you visit the museum. Surreally, this one-time product of mutually assured destruction is now a park for kids, with a playground and restrooms.

Plumb Farm Learning Center

The Plumb Farm Learning Center (955 39th Ave., 970/350-9220, www.greeleygov.com/museums/plumbfarm.aspx, call to schedule tours) became a 160-acre farm in 1881 and is still owned by the same families on 2.5 acres—only now it's mostly known for agricultural programs, classes, and kids events like "Pets N' Popsicles" and "Baby Animals Days."

SPORTS AND RECREATION
Hiking and Biking

The primary place for outdoor Greeley activities is **Island Grove Regional Park** (501 N. 14th Ave., 970/350-9392, www.greeleygov.com/Parks/islandgrove.aspx), a 145-acre area filled with trees and grass, plus hiking-and-biking trails, various sports fields, and a pool. Beginning near Island Grove Park, along the Cache La Poudre River, the **Poudre River Trail** (11th Ave. and D St., east side of Island Grove Regional Park, 970/336-4044, www.poudretrail.org, dawn–dusk daily) is a 10-mile stretch that will ultimately extend another nine

miles to the Weld–Larimer county line. Until then, it runs between the cities of Greeley and Windsor and is a pleasant place to take a bike or a pair of in-line skates.

◖ Pawnee National Grassland

This 193,060-acre area (25 miles northeast of Greeley, 970/295-6600, www.fs.fed.us/r2/arnf) is Greeley's big nature-watching spot—birders go crazy over mountain plover and burrowing owls, and you can spot mule deer, coyotes, foxes, snakes, and the ever-present prairie dogs. It's a great place to hike, bike, camp, or ride a horse. Pick your spots in advance before traveling here: The Buttes, north from Highway 14 on County Road 103, are 300-foot-tall sandstone humps that make a nice backdrop for hiking and watching falcons and hawks. Otherwise, you'll wind up in an endless sea of green, green, and more green.

Golf

Greeley runs two municipal golf courses: the 18-hole **Boomerang Links** (7309 W. 4th St., 970/353-4653, www.greeleygov.com/golf/boomerang.aspx, $33), filled with ponds and other obstacles that pop out of nowhere; and the 18-hole **Highland Hills** (2200 Clubhouse Dr., 970/353-4653, www.greeleygov.com/golf/highlandhills.aspx, $33), which is much older (dating to 1959) than Boomerang Links and has more trees than ponds.

ENTERTAINMENT AND EVENTS

Part of the University of Northern Colorado's jazz studies program, the early-April **UNC/Greeley Jazz Festival** (Union Colony Civic Center, 701 10th Ave., 970/351-2577, www.unco.edu/arts/music/jazz_festival) puts together a wide variety of jazz and pseudo-jazz artists, from middle-school big bands to the great saxophonist Benny Golson. Many of them play together.

The UNC's **Little Theatre of the Rockies** (Norton Theatre, Gray Hall, 10th Ave. and 18th St., and Langworthy Theatre, Frasier Hall, 9th Ave. and 17th St., 970/351-2200,

Pronghorn, the fastest land animals in the Western Hemisphere, can be found in the Pawnee National Grassland.

http://arts.unco.edu/ltr) has been putting on big comedies and musicals since the 1930s—recent shows include *The Odd Couple* and *The Music Man.*

As for less theatrical nightlife, **Cactus Canyon** (1742 Greeley Mall, 970/351-8178, www.cactuscanyongreeley.com, 7 P.M.–2 A.M. Wed.–Thurs. and Sat., 5 P.M.–2 A.M. Fri.) is a butt-kicking country-and-western bar with mechanical-bull-riding contests straight out of *Urban Cowboy,* line-dancing straight out of Billy Ray Cyrus's days on the pop charts, and Daisy Duke's cutoff-shorts contests straight out of *The Dukes of Hazzard.*

Although **High Plains Chautauqua** (Aims Community College, 5401 W. 20th St., 970/352-3567, www.highplainschautauqua.org) sponsors historical tours of Greeley, old movies, musical events, and kids shows, it's best known for the actors who portray famous dead people—including Woody Guthrie, Franklin D. Roosevelt, and Joe Louis.

Greeley Independence Stampede

Although it began as a potato-farming festival in the late 1800s, this 10-day late-June extravaganza (600 N. 14th Ave., 970/356-7787, www.greeleystampede.org) has become so huge that many of its featured country-music performers don't even bother to play in nearby Denver the entire rest of the year. It's primarily a rodeo show—the finals have aired on ESPN and other TV channels—but the musical talent draws country fans from all over the United States. The list of headliners over the years reads like some combination of the Country Music Hall of Fame and the pop charts, including Loretta Lynn, George Jones, Ricky Skaggs, Vince Gill, Faith Hill, Brooks & Dunn, and Tim McGraw.

ACCOMMODATIONS

The **Greeley Guest House** (5401 W. 9th St., 970/353-9373 or 800/314-3684, www.greeleyguesthouse.com, $114–134) kind of looks like a retirement home on the outside, but the rooms are pretty and functional—including whirlpool tubs in the suites, high-speed Internet access, and fireplaces. Breakfast is complimentary.

Campers have a couple of viable options in

BIRD-WATCHING ON THE EASTERN PLAINS AND ELSEWHERE

When you wake up in the morning and realize you absolutely, positively must witness a ferruginous hawk or McCown's longspur that day, the Eastern Plains suddenly don't seem so flat and uneventful. Two of the best bird-watching spots in the state are **Pawnee National Grassland** (660 O St., Greeley, 970/346-5000), east of Fort Collins in the northeast, and **Comanche National Grassland** (27204 U.S. 287, 719/523-6591) in the southeast (and spilling into southern Pueblo), south of Springfield along the border with Oklahoma and New Mexico.

At first glance, Pawnee looks like endless grass, maybe with some hills and farms in the background. It's actually a treasure trove for birders, many of whom head off the main highway and trawl for gems on the back roads. Contact the Grassland's official office in nearby Greeley, or for a map of the bird routes, stop by Crow Valley Recreation Area (near County Rd. 77, north of Briggsdale), itself an excellent birding spot, with yellow-billed cuckoos and northern mockingbirds. At Pawnee, late spring–mid-summer, ferruginous hawks as well as mountain plover, long-billed curlews, Cassin's sparrows, and Chestnut-collared longspurs are in full flight. It's well worth delving into the Grassland for the buttes, where golden eagles and prairie falcons hang out in the spring, although it's against the rules to observe them too closely.

Comanche is famous for rare lesser prairie-chicken leks – its males, according to *National Geographic*, "gather in spring to 'dance' for females at dawn" mid-March–May. To find them, the magazine suggests, start at Campo, go eight miles east on County Road J, turn south on County Road 36, turn east at County Road G, then south at a gate before a culvert. Since the leks tend to congregate near high grassland areas, consider buying a map at the main office. Driving aimlessly around the area is recommended – if you're interested in bushtits, Chihuahuan ravens, grasshopper sparrows, Bewick's wrens, curve-billed thrashers, greater roadrunners, ladder-backed woodpeckers, and other birds that have inspired television-cartoon characters. Stop at the Carrizo Canyon Picnic Area, west of Campo, for a break with a bird backdrop.

In the southeastern town of Lamar, the late-February **High Plains Snow Goose and Birding Festival** (Colorado Division of Wildlife, 2500 S. Main St., Lamar, 719/336-6600, www.highplainssnowgoose.com) demonstrates that the difference between a lesser snow goose and a Ross goose is that the latter has "grinning patches" on its bill. In addition to the usual educational programs, there's a banquet.

Bonny Lake State Park (32300 YC Rd. 2, Burlington), a birder haven since it opened in 1951, abruptly closed in October 2011 and was folded into the **South Republican State Wildlife Area.** There's still a campground on this site, but the lake has been drained, hunting is encouraged, and it's unclear how all this will affect the bird-watching or what will eventually become of the park site. For more information, call 719/227-5200 or visit www.parks.state.co.us/Parks/bonnylake/Pages/BonnyLakeHome.aspx.

Beyond the Eastern Plains, Colorado is stuffed with amazing bird-watching areas. Fortunately for bird-watchers, it's far easier to spot a hawk than a dinosaur at the **Dinosaur Ridge HawkWatch** (16831 W. Alameda Pkwy.,

Morrison, 303/697-3466, www.dinoridge.com). The HawkWatch runs mid-March–early May, and people who look toward the 2,600-acre **Dakota Ridge Hogback** will notice hawks, of course, as well as eagles and vultures. Researchers from the **Rocky Mountain Bird Observatory** (14500 Lark Bunting Lane, Brighton, 303/659-4348, www.rmbo.org) are on hand to answer questions and give presentations.

Every spring, some 20,000 cranes stop at Monte Vista before flying north for the summer. They're so popular that the small southern town has inaugurated the **Monte Vista Crane Festival** (near U.S. 285 and U.S. 160, Monte Vista, www.cranefest.com), which has a wildlife photography workshop and craft fair. Also check out **Eckert Crane Days** (along U.S. 65, south of Cedaredge, www.eckert-cranedays.com) in mid-March, which includes speeches and panel discussions.

Bald eagles are no longer on the endangered-species list, but they're rare, and only a few of them nest in Colorado. The best time to spot them is October–early spring, and the early-February **Eagle Day Festival** (Lake Pueblo State Park, 640 Pueblo Reservoir Rd., 6 miles west of Thatcher Ave., Pueblo, 719/561-5300, www.eagleday.org) supplements the viewing with presentations and educational programs.

In the same part of the state, the four-day early-May **Ute Mountain-Mesa Verde Birding Festival** (registration at Cortez Cultural Center, 25 N. Market St., Cortez, 970/565-1151, www.utemountainmesaverdebirdingfestival.com) is one-stop shopping for more than 100 species of sparrows, finches, ducks, vultures, and titmice.

It's only half a day long, but the **Northern**

Colorado Birding Fair (Fossil Creek Reservoir Regional Open Space, Carpenter Rd., 1 mile west of I-25, Windsor, www.larimer.org/parks/birding_fair.htm, 970/679-4534) has events for rookie and advanced birders alike– including a scavenger hunt and owl presentations.

If your birding tastes run to the small and vibratory, the early-May **Hummingbird Festival** (Starsmore Discovery Center, 2120 S. Cheyenne Canon Rd., Colorado Springs, 719/385-6086) follows hummingbirds as they return home to North Cheyenne Canon Park after migrating for the winter.

More generally, some of the state's best birding areas include the **Colorado National Monument** (Fruita, outside Grand Junction, 970/858-3617), a utopia of red sandstone cliffs and swallows, jays, chickadees, and thrushes galore; **Fountain Creek Regional Park** (Nature Center, 320 Peppergrass Lane, Fountain, south of Colorado Springs, 719/520-6745), which offers classes like "Birds of Prey" and "Rowdy Raccoons" and where the marsh contains wood duck and Virginia rail and the trees attract Lazuli bunting and lesser goldfinch; **Arapaho National Wildlife Refuge** (953 JC Rd., Suite 32, Walden, 970/723-8202), a swampy area filled with ponds and sagebrush, attracting tons of ducks as well as yellow-headed blackbirds and Savannah sparrows; the Denver irrigation-lake area **Barr Lake State Park** (13401 Picadilly Rd., Brighton, 303/659-6005), where 350 species have shown up over the years, including horned larks and American goldfinches; and, perhaps most populous of all, **Rocky Mountain National Park** (1000 U.S. 36, Estes Park, 970/586-1206), whose mountains, lakes, and trees attract a huge diversity of birds, including broad-tailed hummingbirds, western wood pewees, plumbeous vireos, and Steller's jays.

THE EASTERN PLAINS

Greeley: the **Greeley RV Park & Campground** (501 E. 27th St., 970/353-6476 or 800/572-2130, www.greeleyrvpark.com, $28–30), which has 12 tent sites on a 10-acre plot between a farm and the highway; and the small campground at **Missile Site Park** (10611 Spur 257, 970/304-6531, $5), where you can fantasize about retaliating against the Soviet Union in the early 1960s.

FOOD

"Residents rejoice as Long John Silver's returns to town," read a Greeley *Tribune* headline in late 2007. As Greeley grows, its restaurants multiply—but the boom in recent years has mostly been in urban sprawl–type chain restaurants like Red Robin and the Olive Garden. In recent years, distinctive locals such as Potato Brumbaugh's, the State Armory, and the Canterbury Tea Room have closed. Yet a few stalwarts continue to thrive, even in Windsor, where a 2008 tornado decimated a huge chunk of the town, about 15 miles northwest of Greeley. The **Chimney Park Restaurant & Bar** (406 Main St., Windsor, 970/686-1477, www.chimneypark.com, 5–9 P.M. Mon.–Sat., 5–8 P.M. Sun., $25) suffered only minor wind damage. It continues to serve a high-end mix of porterhouse steaks, scallops, duck confit, and an alliterative appetizer known as *Bubalus bubalis* buffalo milk ricotta *gnudi*.

In Greeley itself, **Fat Albert's** (1717 23rd Ave., 970/356-1999, www.fat-alberts.com, 10:30 A.M.–9:30 P.M. Sun.–Thurs., 10:30 A.M.–10:30 P.M. Fri.–Sat., $14), is a family restaurant with chicken, steak, and sandwiches. The service is friendly and kids are everywhere.

Coyote's Southwestern Grill (5250 W. 9th St., 970/336-1725, 11 A.M.–9 P.M. Sun.–Thurs., 11 A.M.–10 P.M. Fri.–Sat., $9) is a Southwestern fixture in the west part of the city with a big outdoor patio and contemporary art on the walls. It's mostly the typical new-and-old Mexican you'd find in these parts, but with distinctive touches like tequila shrimp scampi.

JB's Drive-In (2501 8th Ave., 970/352-3202, 10 A.M.–10:30 P.M. Mon.–Thurs., 10 A.M.–11 P.M. Fri.–Sat., $6) is a family-run throwback with an actual malt machine, cheeseburgers for $1.79, chili dogs, and chicken tenders. It first opened as Jess' Sandwich House in the late 1930s, and Greeley residents have been regulars for decades.

INFORMATION AND SERVICES

The **Greeley Chamber of Commerce** (902 7th Ave., 970/352-3566, www.greeleychamber.com) has basic information about lodging, food, and businesses in the city. For more detailed municipal services, contact the **City of Greeley** (1000 10th St., 970/350-9750, www.greeleygov.com). The daily newspaper is *The Tribune* (www.greeleytribune.com), which doesn't have the most detailed restaurant or lodging reviews in the world but is somewhat helpful.

The **North Colorado Medical Center** (1801 16th St., 970/352-4121, www.bannerhealth.com) is the main hospital for the northeastern Colorado region.

GETTING THERE AND AROUND

The **Greeley Bus Service** (1200 A St., 970/350-9287) serves the entire city roughly 5:30 A.M.–8:30 P.M. daily; fares are $1.50 per ride. Pilots can fly into the **Greeley-Weld County Airport** (600 Airport Rd., Suite A, 970/336-3000, www.gxy.net)*, but commercial passengers should probably fly into Denver International Airport and drive the 55 miles northeast.

Fort Morgan

A plainspoken farming town about 20 miles east of Greeley, Fort Morgan is far less colorful than it was in the old days—just after the Civil War, the U.S. government built the fort and set Confederate rebels free from prison as long as they agreed to join the Union Army and fight Indians in the West. The fort's original purpose was to protect local immigrants and the mail service from Cheyennes and Arapahos, who had revenge on their minds after massive white settlements and the Sand Creek Massacre.

The uprisings eventually disappeared, and railroads, irrigation, ranches, and a canal popped up in the late 1800s. Teddy Roosevelt showed up in 1905, on a short train stop, and inspired 1,000 locals with a short speech about how great it was that hard work turned the Great Plains into a rich farming industry. In addition, the great big-band trombonist Glenn Miller was a high school football player here in the 1920s.

Fort Morgan has just a few hotels, all small chains such as Best Western and Super 8. For more distinctive options, nearby Sterling has a few nice bed-and-breakfasts, while Greeley is larger, with a broader range of accommodations.

SIGHTS

The **Fort Morgan Museum** (414 Main St., 970/542-4010, www.ftmorganmus.org, 9 A.M.–6 P.M. Mon., 9 A.M.–8 P.M. Tues.–Thurs., 9 A.M.–5 P.M. Fri.–Sat., donation) nicely samples all the important stuff about northeastern Colorado—sugar, agriculture, railroads, Glenn Miller, the original fort from the 1860s, and the town's well-kept historic buildings downtown.

SPORTS AND RECREATION
Biking
Although cycling is more popular in Boulder, the Rockies, and the mesas of northwestern Colorado, the Eastern Plains have one crucial advantage: They're flat. Rent bikes and ask for navigational assistance at **Bicycle Livery** (120 W. Railroad Ave., 970/867-2941, www.bicycle-livery.com), which knows its BMX bikes and tricycles equally well.

FOOD
The **Country Steak-Out** (19592 E. 8th Ave., 970/867-7887, www.countrysteakout. net, 6 A.M.–9 P.M. Tues.–Sat., 8 A.M.–2 P.M. Sun., $17) is a great old restaurant that seems like it has been here forever—actually since the 1920s—and serves steak and chicken dishes as if the cooks know exactly what they're doing. It's also one of those roadside places where truckers (of both the rig and pickup variety) pull right up to the building from the parking lot to follow the "Eat Beef" sign.

The city's classic Italian restaurant is **O Sole Mio** (322 Ensign St., 970/867-4836, www. myosolemio.com, 11 A.M.–2 P.M. and 5 P.M.–close Mon.–Fri., 5 P.M.–close Sat., $17), so go in with high risotto, gnocchi, parmigiana, and pasta expectations.

INFORMATION AND SERVICES
The **Fort Morgan Chamber of Commerce** (300 Main St., 970/867-6702 or 800/354-8660) has a somewhat helpful website (www. fortmorganchamber.org). Or try **City Hall** (110 Main St., 970/542-3960, www.cityof-fortmorgan.com) for more basic services. The *Fort Morgan Times* (www.fortmorgantimes. com) has regional news and entertainment listings.

Although Greeley's North Colorado Medical Center is the major hospital in northeastern Colorado, the **Sterling Regional MedCenter** (615 Fairhurst St., 970/522-0122, www.ban-nerhealth.com) has 36 beds as well as centers for trauma treatment and kidney dialysis.

THE EASTERN PLAINS

GLENN MILLER IN COLORADO

© NIKKIE COOPER / FORT MORGAN MUSEUM

a tribute to Fort Morgan's native son Glenn Miller at the Fort Morgan Museum

Before he became the best-known bandleader of the swing era, tromboning his way through 1930s hits like "Chattanooga Choo Choo" and "In the Mood," Iowa-born Glenn Miller lived in Fort Morgan and attended the University of Colorado. At Fort Morgan High School, he made the football team his senior year; the Maroons won the title in 1920, and Miller earned state honors as "the best left end in Colorado."

Although Miller scored a scholarship at the University of Northern Colorado, he had no desire to pursue a football career, thanks to his influential band director, Elmer Wells. Rather than attending his own high school graduation, he moved to Laramie, Wyoming, to join a big band. It broke up within a year, and Miller enrolled at the University of Colorado, where he stayed for two years. His college life centered on music, as he played in Holly Moyer's Jazz Band and did more arranging than studying.

The rest of Miller's story is close to legend: He quit CU to play with the Ben Pollack Orchestra in California (Benny Goodman was in the band as well), then moved with Pollack to New York City. Miller played for months in hit orchestras, arranging music for other big bands, and started the Glenn Miller Orchestra

in 1937. The most popular band in the United States, Miller's orchestra recorded 45 best-selling songs in 1940 and sold more than 1 million copies of "Chattanooga Choo Choo" two years later.

World War II made big bands more popular than ever, but the war also shot the genre in the heart. Miller left his hit-making orchestra to become a U.S. Army officer, but his military career lasted just two years. While flying over the English Channel, his plane disappeared and Miller was killed. James Stewart portrayed him in the 1953 movie hit *The Glenn Miller Story* – some of which was filmed on the University of Colorado at Boulder campus – and the university christened its Glenn Miller Ballroom the same year.

Today, Miller's famous bespectacled photo – with trombone – hangs as a framed black-and-white backdrop to his namesake CU ballroom. Surreally, over the years, bands such as Radiohead, Nine Inch Nails, and Jane's Addiction have performed with Miller smiling in the background.

Fort Morgan runs a Glenn Miller swing festival every June, with bands, food, and a historic tour. Go to www.glennmillerswingfest. com for more information.

Sterling

For a city of just 1,200 people, the farming-and-ranching town of Sterling has a disproportionate number of parks (12), huge trees, and stately Victorian homes whose long porches recall another era. The seat of Logan County, which includes tiny Atwood, Cook, Fleming, Iliff, and Merino, Sterling is the center of a booming agriculture-and-livestock area; cattle, alfalfa, corn, and sugar beets are the primary exports. The city is particularly obsessed with the latter: The **Sugar Beet Days** (www.sugarbeetdays.com) festival is in late September, with craft booths and food, around the downtown Logan County Courthouse.

Known as "The City of Living Trees"—a slogan derived from artist Bradford Rhea's towering downtown tree sculptures, carved straight out of the trees themselves—Sterling's modern roots are in farming. Its true roots are with the Cheyenne and Sioux, who lost the bloody Battle of Summit Springs to the U.S. Cavalry in 1869, paving the way for nonnative settlers. A railroad surveyor, David Leavitt, visited town in 1870 and liked it so much he started the first ranch here a year later; due to the town's geography along the South Platte River, other settlers streamed to the area, and Sterling boomed for years after its official foundation in 1881.

Each of the small towns in Logan County has a story: The county's first resident was Billy Hadfield, who settled on an island in the river just outside Atwood in 1871; a marker on U.S. 6 reveals the spot. Crook burned down twice before it was able to grow to a population of 300 in 1928. It's an interesting little area to visit if you're a history buff, although people experiencing Colorado for the first time might be disappointed with the lack of mountain scenery or dramatic views.

SIGHTS
Overland Trail Museum
The Overland Trail Museum (21053 County

© ANDREA GOLOD/WEAVER MULTIMEDIA GROUP/COLORADO TOURISM OFFICE

THE EASTERN PLAINS

A schoolhouse is one of many old buildings located at the Overland Trail Museum in Sterling.

Rd. 26.5, 970/522-3895, www.sterlingcolo. com, 9 A.M.–5 P.M. Tues.–Sat. Apr.–Oct., 10 A.M.–4 P.M. Tues.–Sat. Nov.–Mar., $2) is a tribute to the Old West pioneers and gold miners who went west in the 1860s, turning the Overland Trail, along the South Platte River through Nebraska and northeastern Colorado, into a veritable superhighway. Opened in 1936, the museum's centerpiece is a prairie village, including a barbershop, a general store, and a church.

🄲 Living Trees

Bearded sculptor Bradford Rhea earned a nuclear-science degree from the University of Colorado before his career took what you might call a sharp left turn. He moved to tiny Sterling, and since 1983 his scripture-influenced Living Trees (Columbine Park, U.S. 6 between S. 3rd Ave. and Division Ave., www.thesculptor.net) have defined the look and feel of "The City of Living Trees." The sculptures, including five 16-foot-high giraffes known as *Skygrazers* and two seven-foot rams carved out of an elm tree, weigh tens of thousands of pounds.

The Living Trees are beautiful and inspirational, but they're also a little surreal. On a recent trip to Sterling, I visited them for the first time and was surprised to learn that few people in town knew where they were. The sculptures, oddly, are far removed from the main highways, at random locations like Ramada Inns and out-of-the-way playgrounds in town parks. They spring up out of nowhere, with Rhea's inexplicable plaques at the bottom: *Skygrazers*, at Columbine Park, is described as "a congregation of spindling appendages fused in a mass of true beliefs." I took my spindling appendages and drove out of town after seeing that.

SPORTS AND RECREATION
Fishing

The outdoor sports in Sterling mostly involve water, thanks to **North Sterling State Park** (24005 County Rd. 330, 970/522-3657, http:// parks.state.co.us/parks/northsterling) and its massive **North Sterling Reservoir,** which, at 50 feet in some places, is one of the state's deepest reservoirs. There's a marina and three boat

ramps, and campers, fishers, boaters, and Jet Skiers tend to crowd the area during summers. It's also one of the prettiest places in northeastern Colorado to view the High Plains, especially with the setting sun as a backdrop.

Other fishing opportunities in the area include **Prewitt Reservoir** (U.S. 6, near Merino, 970/842-6300) and **Jumbo Reservoir** (U.S. 138, near Crook, 970/842-6300), both of which are big with sailors and bird-watchers: check out the gulls, jaegers, terns, swans, and scoters.

FOOD

Sterling's family-dining scene has been hurting ever since the spring of 2005, when a visiting entrepreneur bought the popular Shake, Rattle, & Roll diner for a reported $250,000, loaded it on a truck, and transported it to Carter Lake, Iowa. But the 60-year-old **J and L Café** (423 N. 3rd St., 970/522-3625, 5:15 A.M.–8 P.M. Mon.–Thurs., 5:15 A.M.–8:30 P.M. Fri.–Sat., 5:15 A.M.–2 P.M. Sun., $8) remains a classic downtown greasy spoon—try the steak-and-eggs breakfast—and a local favorite.

INFORMATION

The **Logan County Chamber of Commerce** (109 N. Front St., 970/522-5070 or 866/522-5070, www.logancountychamber.com) has a thorough website for such a small town. Or try Sterling's city government (421 N. 4th St., 970/522-9700, www.sterlingcolo.com). Also helpful is Sterling's daily newspaper, the *Journal-Advocate* (www.journal-advocate. com), which also covers a large part of northeastern Colorado.

CROOK

A ranching town that was once a key stagecoach stop on the Overland Trail, friendly, 148-resident Crook is about 30 miles northeast of Sterling and has two primary sightseeing opportunities. The small **Crook Museum** (4th St. and 4th Ave., 970/886-2713, call for appointment, donation), in a former Presbyterian church, contains Old West artifacts like a beautiful 1800s piano that somebody once bought for $0.50, and information about George Crook, an important U.S. general who scared the wits out of Native Americans for decades. He accepted Geronimo's surrender in 1866.

Crook is home to **Tamarack Ranch State Wildlife Area** (0.5 miles north of I-76 Exit 149, run by the Colorado Division of Wildlife, 303/291-7227, http://wildlife.state.co.us), a **bird-watcher's** paradise stuffed with rare species such as the red-bellied woodpecker, scarlet tanager, and black-billed cuckoo. The 7,000-acre plot along a river bottom is also a controlled hunting area.

JULESBURG

An agricultural town of about 1,500 people, Julesburg is just outside Colorado's northeastern border, and hitting Julesburg off I-76 after spanning Nebraska is almost as reassuring as hitting Burlington after spanning Kansas. The town is good for a pit stop—one of the state's eight welcome centers is here, off Exit 180, and the Fort Sedgwick and Depot Museums are brief diversions for Pony Express buffs. But if you've made it this far, why not drive the 188 miles west to Denver already?

Sights

A little removed from Sterling—almost 60 miles northeast of town, on Colorado's northern border with Nebraska—Julesburg is a former Pony Express town once known for its rough and nasty ways. Today, history-buff travelers mainly know it for the **Fort Sedgwick and Depot Museums** (114 E. 1st St., 970/474-2061, 10 a.m.–4 p.m. Tues.–Sat. and 1–4 p.m. Sun. Memorial Day–Labor Day, Fort Sedgwick only 9 a.m.–1 p.m. Mon.–Fri. Labor Day–Memorial Day, $1). The Fort Sedgwick Museum recalls the area's general history, while the Depot Museum focuses on the Pony Express. Both museums are in one flat brown building.

Accommodations

The **Budget Host Platte Valley Inn Motel** (15225 U.S. 385, 970/474-3336, www.budgethost.com/hotels/Budget_Host_Platte_Valley_Inn_Julesburg_CO.aspx, $66–72) is the best option in a hotel-challenged area. It's super-cheap and has a small restaurant.

Information and Services

The **Town of Julesburg** (970/474-3344, www.sedgwickcountyco.com) is at 100 West 2nd Street.

The 10-bed **Sedgwick County Memorial Hospital** (901 Cedar St., 970/474-3323) serves not only Julesburg but parts of southwestern Nebraska and northwestern Kansas.

Burlington

Although this town of 3,000 people was once a massive grain-shipping point, it is mostly known to drivers these days as "thank God, we're out of Kansas!" It's 13 miles from the Kansas border, and it's a huge relief to drivers who've just spanned that interminable state en route from Detroit or Chicago to Colorado.

Burlington today is an agricultural town—incorporated in 1888, and still the seat of Kit Carson County—and its primary attractions for visitors are historical, including Old Town, a collection of classic buildings and a beautiful old carousel. Check out the state visitors center nearby on I-70.

SIGHTS
Old Town

Old Town (420 S. 14th St., 719/346-7382 or 800/288-1334, www.burlingtoncolo.com, 9 a.m.–5 p.m. Mon.–Sat., noon–5 p.m. Sun., $6) is a collection of 20 restored century-old buildings—a bank, a blacksmith shop, a train depot, a law office (including an original wooden desk), a schoolhouse, a drugstore, and even doll houses (including one made of bread dough). To commemorate the proud era when "Burlington had six saloons and its share of female entertainment to go with it," in the words of the Old Town website, the restored

THE EASTERN PLAINS

© MATT INDEN/WEAVER MULTIMEDIA GROUP/COLORADO TOURISM OFFICE

a hand-carved armored horse on the Carson County Carousel

Longhorn Saloon showcases women doing the cancan throughout the summer.

◖ Carson County Carousel

Built in 1905, the Carson County Carousel (Kit Carson County Fairgrounds, north of I-70 Exit 437, 719/348-5562, www.kitcarsoncountycarousel.com, 11 A.M.–6 P.M. daily Memorial Day–Labor Day, $0.25 per ride, museum $1) and its 46 hand-carved horses, giraffes, and zebras were a fixture at Denver's Elitch Gardens amusement park until 1928. At that point, Elitch management sold the carousel and its elaborate pipe organ for $1,200 to Kit Carson County—the "extravagant expenditure" led to the political demise of certain county commissioners. It has given $0.25 rides in Burlington ever since.

ACCOMMODATIONS

The ◖ Claremont Inn (800 Claremont Dr., Stratton, 719/348-5125 or 888/291-8910, www.claremontinn.com, $169–309) is a little pricey for the middle of nowhere on the High Plains, but perhaps that's because it's the *only* quaint inn in the middle of nowhere on the High Plains. Built in 1995, it has six guest rooms with whirlpool tubs, one with a fireplace, and at least one is cleverly named: Out of Kansas.

FOOD

If you happen to be here at mealtime during a trip to the carousel or museum, the **Burlington Inn** (450 S. Lincoln St., 719/346-0336, www.burlingtoninncolorado.com, 11 A.M.–9:30 P.M. Tues.–Sun., $8) has a Chinese restaurant with the usual egg rolls and fried rice.

INFORMATION AND SERVICES

The **City of Burlington** (415 15th St., 719/346-8652, www.burlingtoncolo.com) has a bit of historical and visitor information on its website.

  Kit Carson County Health Service District (286 16th St., 719/346-5311, www.kccmh.org) is a small hospital near the Kansas border.

LIMON

Location has always been Limon's greatest asset—it's at the intersection of five major highways, including I-70, about 100 miles east of Denver, about 77 miles west of Burlington, and is the midpoint between northeastern and southeastern Colorado. The so-called "Hub City" had a similar advantage in 1888, when it was a workcamp site for miners and the Chicago and Rock Island Railroad used it as a key point between Kansas and Colorado Springs.

Today, with a population of 2,400, Hub City is more of a hub than a city; it's mainly known for downtown antiques shops, other small businesses, and a few museums. The town briefly became famous for the wrong reasons on June 6, 1990, when the biggest of several northeastern Colorado twisters touched down in Limon, destroying numerous buildings and killing phone service and power; amazingly, nobody died.

Sights

The **Limon Heritage Museum and Railroad Park** (899 1st St., 719/775-8605, 1–8 P.M. Mon.–Sat. Memorial Day–Labor Day, free) is packed with plains-related artifacts—the big displays include a one-room schoolhouse, a restored railroad depot (with a boxcar and five other train cars), and a windmill as well as a Native American tepee, art, and tools. There's also a playground with picnic tables in the outdoor park, which is open all year.

On an abandoned highway next to an unused stone restaurant building, the **World's Wonder View Tower** (30121 Frontage Rd., Genoa, 719/763-2309, 9 A.M.–5 P.M. daily Mar.–Sept., by appointment Oct.–Apr., $1) is a six-story, red-and-pink 1920s-era tower with "six states" scrawled on the side. (On a good day, from the top of the tower, visitors can apparently see six different states.) Inside is a kitschy collection of artifacts with no discernible theme: elk and jackalope heads, Elvis Presley stuff, fossil skulls, old books, a scattered rock collection, and Native American arrowheads. A fixture in *Roadside America* and, once upon a time, *Ripley's Believe It or Not,* this bizarre tourist attraction was known for years as the Genoa Tower Museum.

Accommodations

Limon has very few nice restaurants, other than fast-food chains and truck stops, but its small hotels aren't bad. "Traveling with a horse?" asks the **Craig Ranch Bed and Breakfast & Horse Motel** (50452 County Rd. 23, 719/775-2658, www.craigranchbandb.com, $81–91). If so, corrals are available for $5 per night. The B&B has people beds too—like the antique brass in the pretty pink Miss Molly's Room and the wooden family heirloom in Bill's Bunkhouse.

Information

The **Limon Chamber of Commerce** (205 E Ave., 719/775-9418, www.limonchamber.com) compiles online listings of restaurants, hotels, and other local businesses. For recreation and other city departments, contact the **Town of Limon** (100 Civic Center Dr., 719/775-2346, www.townoflimon.com).

Along the Santa Fe Trail

The Santa Fe Trail was a 1,200-mile stage-coach route that covered five states in the 1860s. Although the trail no longer exists as an official highway or road, it's still well-documented as a historic path, coming in from Kansas and going due west through Lamar, Las Animas, La Junta, and other small towns in southeastern Colorado. The trail runs along U.S. 50, curving slightly southwest from Las Animas, and turning into U.S. 350, roughly parallel with the Arkansas River. The Colorado portion of the trail was known to pioneers as the "Mountain Route," although then as now, it was flat Eastern Plains land. That designation is mostly due to the views of the Rocky Mountains in the western distance. The route isn't quite as celebrated or marked as well as, say, Route 66, but many of the small towns along the way have museums, celebrations, and markers devoted to its history. For more information on the trail, contact the **Santa Fe Trail Association** (1349 K-156 Highway, Larned, Kansas, 620/285-2054, www.santafetrail.org).

LAMAR

Lamar started with a fight: In 1866, cattleman A. R. Black owned most of the land on this uneventful Santa Fe Trail outpost along the Arkansas River, next to a key railroad depot, 30 miles from Kansas Territory and down the road from Las Animas and Denver. The U.S. government wanted to start a town on this strategic land and offered Black big money to give it up. Black refused. But the government outwitted him, buying nearby land from another rancher and hiring crews to move the railroad depot while Black was out of town.

The United States named the town after Lucius Quintius Lamar, President Grover Cleveland's secretary of the interior. It boomed for years, sometimes not so nicely, as cowboys and outlaws drove through regularly in the 1800s and early 1900s—four bank robbers even shot the president of First National Bank in 1928, wounding his son, kidnapping a worker, and getting away with almost $250,000.

Today, the heavily agricultural town is known as the "Goose Hunting Capital of the World."

Sights

The **Big Timbers Museum** (7515 U.S. 50, 719/336-2472, www.bigtimbersmuseum.org, 10 A.M.–5 P.M. Mon.–Sat. summer, 1–4 P.M. Mon.–Sat. winter, $3) is filled with relics from the late 1800s and early 1900s, when Lamar was an important trading post—a plow, a thresher, hay balers, a windmill, a wedding dress, a grand piano, a washing machine, and an impressive arrowhead collection. There's also a bunch of Civil War stuff, including a sword and uniforms.

Accommodations

Lamar's best hotels are chains—the Best Western is called a "Cow Palace"—but the **Chek Inn** (1210 S. Main St., 719/336-4331, www.chek-inn.com, $52–57) is somewhat more distinctive, and cheaper.

Information and Services

The **City of Lamar** (102 E. Parmenter St., 719/336-4376, www.ci.lamar.co.us) has all the information you need about the fire, police, and recreation departments, but not much on visiting.

Prowers Medical Center (401 Kendall Dr., 719/336-4343, www.prowersmedical.com) has just 20 beds and 200 staff members but serves 20,000 residents of southeastern Colorado.

LAS ANIMAS

About 20 miles west of Lamar, Las Animas is a flat, one-stoplight ranching town where the legendary Western explorer Kit Carson died in 1868. The town is new, relatively speaking, having formed as a riverside settlement called Las Animas City in 1867, after the Purgatoire River flooded and made nearby Fort Lyon

Las Animas, the last home of frontiersman Kit Carson

unlivable. Its name is derived from the Spanish name for that river—El Rio de Las Animas Perdidas en Purgatorio, meaning "the river of souls lost in purgatory." In other words, Las Animas is another way of saying "lost souls."

Due to its proximity to Bent's Fort, a thriving fur-trading post in what is now La Junta, about 22 miles away, Las Animas City thrived in its first few years. Wandering cowboys, soldiers, and explorers like Kit Carson populated the saloons and shops, and the population boomed to about 150 in the early 1870s. But the boom times ended quickly when the Union Pacific Railway routed track through the area and couldn't afford to go through Las Animas—which was "on the wrong side of the river," according to a 1999 report prepared for the Las Animas Urban Renewal Authority, quoted on the town's official website. After that came a very convoluted power struggle, with two railroad men who posed as 30 different squatters and grabbed more strategic land to the west. These men founded West Las Animas, built a stretch of railroad as well as

homes and businesses, and convinced locals in Las Animas City and nearby Boggsville to relocate. Eventually the city became simply "Las Animas" and thrived for years due to the railroad. Today its population is 3,300.

Twenty miles southwest of Las Animas, along U.S. 50, is **La Junta,** the seat of Otero County. Although it has some attractions, such as the community **Picketwire Theatre** (802 San Juan Ave., La Junta, 719/384-8320, www. picketwireplayers.org) and the **Bent's Old Fort** historical site, travelers mostly know this small town as the gateway to the Comanche National Grassland, a wide area extending south and southwest.

Sights

Las Animas's biggest attraction is the **Kit Carson Museum** (Bent Ave. and 9th St., 719/456-1914, www.phsbc.info/carson-museum.htm, noon–4:30 P.M. Mon.–Fri. Memorial Day–Labor Day, free), which opened in 1961 in a building that once housed German prisoners of war and, later, field-working

Jamaicans. But there are no monuments to Rastafarianism or Bob Marley here, just a top-notch collection of Old West memorabilia such as farming implements and Native American artifacts. Outside, there are numerous building replicas—a jail, a blacksmith shop, a house, and even a gallows.

A crucial fur-trading post along the Mexican border in the 1840s, **Bent's Old Fort** (35110 Hwy. 194 E., La Junta, 719/383-5010, www.nps.gov/beol, 8 A.M.–5:30 P.M. daily June–Aug., 9 A.M.–4 P.M. daily Sept.–May, $3) is a National Historic Site with a bookstore, guided tours, and special events like a re-creation of a freight-wagon ride along three miles of the old Santa Fe Trail. The fort was not only a place for local pioneers and Native Americans to come together peacefully during a tumultuous time, it also established nearby cities like Las Animas and Boggsville.

Named for Thomas O. Boggs, who founded a settlement along the Santa Fe Trail that became so huge it transformed into Boggsville, **Boggsville National Historical Site** (Hwy. 101, 2 miles south of Las Animas, 719/384-8054, 10 A.M.–4 P.M. daily May 1–Oct. 1, $15) is primarily remembered as Kit Carson's last home.

◖ Picket Wire Canyonlands

More than 1,300 once-muddy dinosaur footprints are evident within this large portion of the Comanche National Grassland, not far from La Junta. The area was once a dinosaur-filled tropical forest, with *Apatosaurus* and *Allosaurus* roaming near lakes during the Jurassic period 150 million years ago. Some of the first humans squatted here 1,500 years ago and left behind evidence of rock art; from the 1820s to the 1880s the grassland was scenery for pioneers traveling along the Santa Fe Trail; and after that, many families homesteaded in this area, and some remnants of their structures remain. For directions to these remnants, including the dinosaur tracks, contact the U.S. Forest Service (719/384-2181); another option is to participate in a guided audio tour of the grassland's historic sites in a 4WD vehicle.

The only way to access Picket Wire Canyonlands is via the Withers Canyon Trailhead. To get there from La Junta, go south on Highway 109 for 13 miles; turn right on County Road 802; turn left on County Road 25; turn left at Picket Wire Corrals onto Forest Road 500A, and follow that road for three miles to the parking area. There are five marked trails here of varying lengths, including a three-mile (one-way) path downhill into the canyon.

Sports and Recreation

Located in two wide areas—southwest of La Junta, and along the southeastern border with New Mexico—the 440,000-acre **Comanche National Grassland** (27204 U.S. 287, Springfield, 719/523-6591, www.fs.fed.us/r2/psicc/coma) is best known for its **wildlife viewing.** This includes rarely seen golden eagles, lesser prairie chickens, and swift foxes, along with coyotes, hawks, and wild turkeys.

Beyond Picket Wire Canyonlands, several recreation areas are located within both sections of the grassland, with picnic tables and hiking trails. The **Sierra Vista Overlook**, for example, begins 13 miles southwest of La Junta along U.S. 350, then 0.5 miles north on Highway 71. This three-mile route, marked by stone posts, goes along the Santa Fe Trail to the Timpas Picnic Area; if you walk up a bluff, you'll see an amazing view of the Spanish Peaks in the distance as well as the Rocky Mountains and a wide swath of prairie land. In the southern part of the grassland, **Picture Canyon** has a surrounding four-mile trail; to get there, take Highway 109 south from La Junta for 58 miles; turn left at U.S. 160 and go another 25 miles; turn right at County Road 18; after eight miles, turn right at the sign for Picture Canyon, and go another mile to the parking area. This is a pleasant path running through a vista and huge rock formations, but its primary draw is a collection of Native American petroglyphs on canyon walls, with clear images of deer and bighorn sheep.

Camping, biking, and hunting are permitted in Comanche National Grassland, but park officials do not provide routes, equipment, or facilities.

For more information on this area, contact the U.S. Forest Service (27204 U.S. 287, Springfield, 719/523-6591, www.fs.fed.us/r2/psicc/coma).

The **John Martin Reservoir State Park** (30703 County Rd. 24, Hasty, 719/829-1801, parks.state.co.us/parks/johnmartinreservoir), about 16 miles east of Las Animas near tiny Hasty, is the largest body of water in the southeastern part of the state. The area, formed by a dam, also includes the smaller Lake Hasty, with its own camping, picnicking, and fishing facilities, just to the east of John Martin Reservoir. It's a great place for a traveling break, with the 4.5-mile **Red Shin Hiking Trail,** named for a Cheyenne warrior who, according to local legend, had a dispute with another warrior over an Indian maiden, scrambled up a tall rock formation, and beat back all attackers; two boat ramps; the **Point Campground** and **Lake Hasty Campground,** providing a total of 213 campsites ($14), many with electrical hookups; and excellent fishing waters for bass, wiper, bluegill, drum, and catfish. The reservoir is especially fruitful for bird-watchers, as 400 species can be seen in Bent County, mostly within this area, including bald eagles and threatened and endangered species such as the piping plover and the least tern.

Although it's just nine holes, the **Las Animas Golf Course** (420 Country Club Dr., 719/456-2511, $15) is more than 2,900 yards long, designed by Ray Hardy, who was also responsible for the Hidden Hills course in north Texas.

Events

For four days in late April, **Santa Fe Trail Days** (719/456-0453) recalls the pioneers who drifted into Colorado along the Santa Fe Trail. The event is a town-wide party, including square dancing, a burger dinner at the high school, a run at the John Martin Reservoir, and a fishing derby at the city pond.

Accommodations

It's a chain, but the **Best Western Bent's Fort Inn** (E. U.S. 50, 719/456-0011, www.bestwestern.com, $70–80) is hard to ignore given its convenient location as well as amenities like a pool and a free town shuttle. Also, the website boasts that the inn is "minutes away from both the Bent County Correctional Facility and the Fort Lyon Correction Facility." Make of that what you will.

Food

Several of Las Animas's most distinctive restaurants have closed since the start of the economic downturn, but **Rivera's** (524 Bent Ave., 719/456-6078, 11 A.M.–2 P.M. and 5–8 P.M. Mon.–Thurs., 11 A.M.–2 P.M. and 5–8:30 P.M. Fri., 11 A.M.–8:30 P.M. Sat., 10 A.M.–4 P.M. Sun.) soldiers on, serving fajitas, enchiladas, and other Mexican fixtures. Its lunch buffet is only $6.50 most days.

Information

The **City of Las Animas** can be reached at 719/456-0422, and the surrounding **Bent County** provides local resources at www.bentcounty.org. The **Las Animas/Bent County Chamber of Commerce** (332 Ambassador Thompson Blvd., 719/456-0453) answers calls on the first try and pleasantly gives out directions and other local information.

BACKGROUND

The Land

With an area of more than 104,000 square miles, Colorado is the eighth-largest state, although with just 371 square miles of water, it's also one of the driest. The terrain varies wildly, from the prairies and dry mesa cliffs in the northwest to the San Juan Mountains in the southwest, through the massive Rocky Mountains in the west to the flat plains of the east. The southwest tip of Colorado is part of the Four Corners, where travelers can touch Colorado, Utah, Arizona, and New Mexico simultaneously.

Colorado's geography is an extension of its bordering states. The Continental Divide, the steep and bumpy upper edge of the Rocky Mountains, runs in a curvy, vertical, continuous path between New Mexico and Wyoming. Much of northern Colorado is as rugged and lush as Wyoming, while most of southern Colorado is as dry and desertlike as New Mexico. Similarly, Colorado's eastern plains match the flat, endless terrain of Nebraska and Kansas. Utah, in many spots, is the continuation of mesa cliffs, dry wilderness, and deep valleys.

Colorado's wild swings of altitude are legendary among residents and travelers, who have to put up with shortness of breath, nosebleeds, and other ailments as they climb sharply to the state's most beautiful places.

© OLIVIER LE QUEINEC/123RF.COM

The lowest point is the Arikaree River, at 3,350 feet, on the banks of the Arkansas River due west of Kansas near Wray; the highest is Mount Elbert, at 14,433 feet, southwest of Leadville. Elbert is just one of the 53 fourteeners in Colorado, including Pikes Peak, Mount Evans, and Longs Peak, all visible in large cities east of the Front Range, and there are numerous thirteeners as well.

Most of Colorado's population is clustered just east of the Rockies' Front Range in metropolitan Denver, the state capital, as well as college towns Boulder, Fort Collins, and Colorado Springs.

GEOGRAPHY

The Colorado region wasn't always full of mountains. Some 240–750 million years ago, in the Paleozoic era, the area was almost completely underwater. Toward the end of that era, mountains shot up as high as 10,000 feet, but many of the ranges eroded and gave way to flat land again. You can see evidence of these early ranges in Manitou Springs's Garden of the Gods and Morrison's Red Rocks Park, both strange-looking areas with gnarled, reddish rocks and hills that seem completely out of place among the massive Rockies. Huge sand dunes arose from this period as well.

The Mesozoic era, about 70–230 million years ago, brought dinosaurs and reptiles to the state—their fossils and footprints remain in places like Dinosaur National Monument, along the Utah border, and the Dinosaur Quarry in Red Rocks Park. But the Gulf of Mexico roared back into the area, the state was submerged in water once again, and the dinosaurs became extinct. Eventually the waters pulled back and the Rocky Mountains, as we know them, rose up.

Thanks to volcanic eruptions and rising mountains throughout the Cenozoic era (about 70 million years ago), tropical rainforests, large mountain lakes, and forests emerged all over the state. By the Pleistocene epoch, a little less than 2 million years ago, glaciers began their slow motions, creating huge and breathtaking mountain peaks and deep valleys as well as prairies, forests, and grasslands. Woolly mammoths took over from the preceding dinosaurs, and camels and horses appeared as well.

After the ice age ended, 20,000–25,000 years ago, humans showed up, early Native American hunters who wandered the mountains and valleys searching for mammoths and antelope to kill.

Rocky Mountains

Stretching from British Columbia to the Rio Grande River in New Mexico, the Rocky Mountains formed roughly 65–140 million years ago, during the Cretaceous period. Volcanoes and moving tectonic plates lifted massive chunks of rock high into the air, explaining the 10,000-foot elevations commonly seen today on the Rockies' dramatic east side, best viewed in Boulder and Rocky Mountain National Park. During the ice ages, from roughly 1.8 million to 11,000 years ago, gigantic glaciers moved south from Canada and moved around huge swaths of land, forming valleys and creating lakes with their runoff. A few such glaciers are still around in smaller form, including St. Mary's, outside Idaho Springs.

As a result of these prehistoric geological events, Colorado has some of the highest-elevation towns in the world, including Leadville (10,188 feet), along with more than 1,000 peaks above 10,000 feet. The elevation leads to great skiing, clean air, dramatic views, and, if you're not careful, shortness of breath.

The water and snowmelt coming down from Rocky Mountain peaks create one-fourth of the total U.S. water supply, and the rivers flow eventually into the Atlantic, Pacific, and Arctic Oceans.

Western Slope

Once you drive west from Denver or Boulder into the Rocky Mountains, you start to see fewer of the steep, dramatic drop-offs from mountain peaks to flatlands. Rather, the high country seems to go on and on. This part of the state, from the Continental Divide through the Utah border, is the Western Slope. Here the

COLORADO'S FOURTEENERS

Colorado has 53 mountain peaks more than 14,000 feet high (many are part of the San Juans, in the southwest part of the state), and some hardy outdoors enthusiasts make a sport out of climbing all of them. Here's a list:

Mountain	Elevation	Nearest Town
Mount Elbert	14,433	Leadville
Mount Massive	14,421	Leadville
Mount Harvard	14,420	Buena Vista
Blanca Peak	14,345	Alamosa
La Plata Peak	14,336	Buena Vista
Uncompahgre Peak	14,309	Lake City
Crestone Peak	14,294	Westcliffe
Mount Lincoln	14,286	Breckenridge
Grays Peak	14,270	Georgetown
Mount Antero	14,269	Salida
Torreys Peak	14,267	Georgetown
Castle Peak	14,265	Aspen
Quandary Peak	14,265	Breckenridge
Mount Evans	14,264	Georgetown
Longs Peak	14,255	Estes Park
Mount Wilson	14,246	Telluride
Mount Cameron	14,238	Breckenridge
Mount Shavano	14,229	Salida
Crestone Needle	14,197	Westcliffe
Mount Belford	14,197	Buena Vista
Mount Princeton	14,197	Buena Vista
Mount Yale	14,196	Buena Vista
Mount Bross	14,172	Breckenridge
Kit Carson Peak	14,165	Westcliffe
El Diente Peak	14,159	Telluride
Maroon Peak	14,156	Aspen
Tabeguache Peak	14,155	Salida
Mount Oxford	14,153	Buena Vista
Mount Sneffels	14,150	Ouray

Mountain	Elevation	Nearest Town
Mount Democrat	14,148	Breckenridge
Capitol Peak	14,130	Snowmass Village
Pikes Peak	14,110	Colorado Springs
Snowmass Mountain	14,092	Snowmass Village
Mount Eolus	14,083	Silverton
Windom Peak	14,082	Silverton
Challenger Point	14,081	Alamosa
Mount Columbia	14,073	Buena Vista
Missouri Mountain	14,067	Buena Vista
Humboldt Peak	14,064	Westcliffe
Mount Bierstadt	14,060	Georgetown
Conundrum Peak	14,060	Aspen
Sunlight Peak	14,059	Silverton
Handies Peak	14,048	Silverton
Culebra Peak	14,047	Alamosa
Ellingwood Point	14,042	Alamosa
Mount Lindsey	14,042	Alamosa
North Eolus	14,039	Silverton
Little Bear Peak	14,037	Alamosa
Mount Sherman	14,036	Leadville
Redcloud Peak	14,034	Silverton
Pyramid Peak	14,018	Aspen
Wilson Peak	14,017	Telluride
Wetterhorn Peak	14,015	Lake City
North Maroon Peak	14,014	Aspen
San Luis Peak	14,014	Creede
Mount of the Holy Cross	14,005	Minturn
Huron Peak	14,003	Buena Vista
Sunshine Peak	14,001	Silverton

Source: www.14ers.com

landscape varies wildly, from the mesas and cliffs near Grand Junction to the massive San Juan Mountain peaks to the miles and miles of flat ranching and farming land around Craig and Rifle.

The Continental Divide is the upper spine of the Rockies, which more or less follows the mountain range from British Columbia to the Rio Grande. (Adventurers can follow it by foot, on a long and challenging path known as the Continental Divide Trail.) Water flows in opposite directions on either side of the Divide—on the west side it goes to the Pacific Ocean, while on the east it goes to the Atlantic or the Gulf of Mexico.

Eastern Plains

Colorado's Eastern Plains are the western edge of the Great Plains states—Kansas, Nebraska, and Oklahoma. They took on their "lowlands" form during the Pleistocene epoch, a time of repeated ice ages, when Canadian glaciers moved south and, according to Donald E. Trimble's *The Geologic Story of the Great Plains,* "smoothed the contours and gave the land a more subdued aspect than it had before they came." The resulting valleys, grassland, and forest spread through the entire interior United States, through Kansas, Nebraska, Oklahoma, and northern Texas, and stopped at the edge of the Rockies.

The geologic area known as the Colorado Piedmont—roughly the base of the Front Range foothills, including Denver, the South Platte River valley, and the Arkansas River valley near Colorado Springs—formed some 28 million years ago when tectonic plates shifted in what is now the western United States. Some parts of this area, particularly Utah, boosted their elevations to more than 5,000 feet, and the resulting erosion had a massive impact on what is now Colorado. Sandstone fell away, the South Platte shifted, mounds of sedimentary rock gathered just beneath the Rockies, and the Pawnee Buttes formed in northeastern Colorado. This is where Pawnee National Grassland, from Greeley to Limon, stretches out today.

CLIMATE

Outside Colorado, people know the state from the extreme weather reports—massive blizzards, heavy droughts, fires due to extremely dry conditions, avalanches in the mountains, and so forth. But residents know that despite these dramatic weather events, the climate is generally mild, and the legend of 300 days of sunshine per year is not exaggerated. Humidity is pleasantly low in Colorado, a huge boon (especially for those without air-conditioning) during the few weeks of near-100°F temperatures in July–August.

One great thing about Colorado's blizzards: When they're over, the snow melts quickly, and within a few days it's spring again. In the mountains, the snow remains, but the sun warms everything, which explains why skiers at the big resorts are often able to glide around in light jackets and, occasionally, shorts.

Temperatures and conditions vary, often wildly, according to region and altitude. The higher you go in the mountains, the colder it gets, which makes for nice weather in July and potentially dangerous storm-and-avalanche conditions in December. The Eastern Plains and the flatlands in northwest Colorado tend to be warmer than, say, Denver, but generally these areas are milder than average as well.

Rocky Mountains

The average mountain temperature is 43°F, with very hot Julys (82°F average) and very cold Januarys (7°F average). Whenever traveling in the mountains, prepare for extreme temperature shifts, which are most dramatic in winter. Newspapers frequently report tragic stories of hikers leaving for a mountain excursion in mild weather who then get stranded without proper clothing or supplies when huge clumps of snow come out of nowhere. These shifts happen even in summer.

Whereas June is wet and humid throughout most of the United States, it's Colorado's driest month. That's a great advantage for outdoors enthusiasts, but it also creates droughts and forest-fire conditions. In 2002 and 2003, Colorado suffered particularly dry weather, and residents had to drastically cut down on water use (a few blizzards have helped bring the drought under control as well).

The most extreme wildfire in recent years was the 2002 Hayman Fire, in Pike National Forest, south of Denver, which damaged 138,000 acres, drove residents from their homes, and caused general panic for weeks. The cause was arson—park ranger Terry Lynn Barton pleaded guilty to setting the fire. The lessons: (1) Don't set forest fires; (2) Even accidental fires can spread to apocalyptic proportions in the dry season.

Boulder's Foothills have been plagued with forest fires in what seems like every summer. The biggest one lately was the Fourmile Canyon Fire, which spread to 6,388 acres and forced evacuations of more than 140 structures.

Western Slope

Because high mountains insulate the low valleys near Grand Junction, Palisade, and other northwestern Colorado cities, the weather is more consistent here than in the rest of the state. It can get hot in these parts during the summer, of course, but the nights are cool; winters tend to be a little colder than in the rest of the state. Note that winds can get fierce in Colorado, especially during winter: In 1997 they hit 120 miles per hour in the Routt National Forest outside Steamboat Springs, leveling millions of trees.

Eastern Plains

Eastern Colorado tends to share weather conditions with neighboring Nebraska and Kansas—low humidity, plenty of sunshine, frequent high winds, and temperatures reaching well over 100°F in the summer. Fortunately for the many farmers in the region, heavy rains tend to come during high growing season (Apr.–Sept.), although high winds dry the soil and lead to dust storms during winter. Chinooks, or dry and warm winds that fly off the Rockies during winter, are somewhat common here.

Elevations in the plains start out flat on Colorado's far eastern border, and then

aspen trees, a common sight in Colorado's mountains

© MARK HAYES/123RF.COM

gradually slant upward as travelers head west toward the Rockies. With these abrupt shifts in elevation come abrupt weather changes, so if you're traveling in this direction, be sure to pack appropriate clothing and supplies.

FLORA AND FAUNA
Flora

Because Colorado's climate and altitude vary wildly—rich soil and prime farming conditions on the Eastern Plains, drier soil in the High Rockies—some 3,000 plant species live in Colorado. These range from shrubs in the alpine zones to yucca plants, prickly pears, and colorful wildflowers in the foothills to short grass and sagebrush on the plains.

The highest growing areas in Colorado are considered the alpine zone, at roughly 11,400 feet and higher, where the extended winters are too frigid for most vegetation. Shrubs, grasses, and short trees contorted by high winds, heavy snows, and low temperatures are common at this altitude.

The subalpine zone—about 9,000–11,400 feet—is where mountain explorers find Colorado's best-known trees, the **aspens.** Although these white-bark trees often look skinny and twisted in the winter, like something you'd see in a Dr. Seuss book, they generate explosions of gold, red, and orange leaves in the summer and are among the best reasons for visiting Colorado in the fall. They give way to **lodgepole pine** trees, which have darker bark, as you go higher into the mountains.

At lower mountain altitudes, commonly seen trees include **ponderosa pine** (which can grow as tall as 150 feet), **Douglas fir,** and occasionally aspen and lodgepole pine. In the foothills, shrubs such as **skunk brush** and **wild plum** as well as **juniper** trees become more common as reservoirs, lakes, and streams reappear.

Gardening enthusiasts plan their entire years around spring and summer, when **wildflowers** of white, yellow, red, blue, purple, and orange appear on mountainside meadows all over the state—particularly rich areas include Rocky Mountain National Park, Loveland, and Aspen. The

columbine, the state flower

light-purple-and-white **columbine,** discovered by Edwin James during a Pikes Peak expedition in 1820, became the official state flower 79 years later, and it's still one of Colorado's prettiest attractions. There's nothing like hiking up a steep hill, reaching the summit, and seeing a green meadow filled with purple, blue, white, and yellow columbines.

The **Colorado State University Herbarium** (970/491-0496, http://herbarium. biology.colostate.edu) is an excellent local-flora resource.

Fauna

In many parts of Colorado, it's hard to find the line between human and wildlife dwellings—mountain residents, for example, must contend with black bears digging in their garbage, groups of hungry raccoons peering into their windows, skunks walking by their screen doors at the least convenient times, and coyotes, mountain lions, and foxes having altercations with their pet dogs and cats. But that's the charm of living in Colorado, home of 130

© MATT INDEN/WEAVER MULTIMEDIA GROUP/COLORADO TOURISM OFFICE

ENDANGERED SPECIES IN COLORADO

If you come across the following mammals, amphibians, birds, and fish, leave them alone. Contact the **Colorado Division of Wildlife** (6060 Broadway, Denver, 303/297-1192, http://wildlife.state.co.us) immediately. And above all, don't hunt them!

- Gray wolf
- Black-footed ferret
- Grizzly bear
- Lynx
- Wolverine
- Kit fox
- Boreal toad
- Whooping crane
- Southwest willow flycatcher
- Least tern (bird)
- Bonytail (fish)
- Razorback sucker (fish)

mammal species, 460 bird species, and 87 fish species, not to mention reptiles.

The aforementioned **black bears** live predominantly in western Colorado, but my parents, on the eastern edge of the foothills near Boulder, frequently report evidence of garbage violation. Some of the males can be as big as seven feet long and weigh 350 pounds, and they have sharp claws and teeth, so don't start any fights. *National Geographic* magazine's informative wildlife website, www.coloradoguide.com, has this advice for bear encounters: "Stay calm. As you move away, talk aloud to let the bear discover your presence. Back away slowly while facing the bear. Don't make eye contact. Don't run or make sudden movements. Speak softly to reassure the bear that no harm is meant to it."

Bighorn sheep, with their curly horns and changing colors, from sharp gray to dark brown, are commonly found in the Rockies, particularly at Mount Evans near Georgetown as well as Pikes Peak and Rocky Mountain National Park. When they fight, which is rare, they ram each other at a speed of 55 mph, and you can hear the resulting crash for miles. In short, don't make them angry. Slightly cuter but just as violent—they like to push each other off cliffs—are **mountain goats,** which despite name and appearance are actually part of the antelope family. They have black beards and horns and slumped shoulders and can be found sporadically around the Rocky Mountains—also tending to congregate at Mount Evans.

Long a source of food and clothing for Native Americans, **bison** are, at 10 feet long and weighing more than a ton, at least twice as big as a domesticated cow. They're also much more agile, able to run as fast as horses in some cases. Few run wild anymore in Colorado, but you can see herds of livestock along I-70, a few miles west of Denver, as well as north of Fort Collins and in a few other areas.

Many Colorado landowners, particularly in Boulder County, consider **prairie dogs** more irritating than rats, as the 16–20-inch-long critters eat grass and crops and burrow entire cities that can be as deep as 7 feet and as long as 16 feet. After much debate, Boulder County allowed landowners to kill the dogs as long as the owners make a good-faith effort to relocate them first.

Rocky Mountain elk are also seen regularly in the foothills, especially in Rocky Mountain National Park and Evergreen, outside Denver. The males have antlers that can weigh as much as 60 pounds. More common are **mule deer,** which peer out from the side of mountain roads and occasionally cross the roads. Don't blow off the yellow "deer crossing" signs; if you hit a deer at high speed, chances are your car will endure at least as much damage as the deer.

Finally, if anybody invites you to hunt for

jackalope, don't join the trip. Here's why: www.museumofhoaxes.com/tall-tales/jackalope.html.

Birds hang out everywhere in Colorado's forests, meadows, and cities—some of the more interesting ones include white-tailed ptarmigans, northern pygmy owls, greater prairie chickens, brown-capped rosy finches, three-toed woodpeckers, sharp-tailed grouse, pinyon jays, lark buntings, peregrine falcons, morning doves, ravens, wrens, robins, bluebirds, sparrows, blackbirds, orioles, mountain chickadees, turkeys, mockingbirds, titmice, and in some parts of the mountains, bald and golden eagles.

Although you generally have to get out of big cities like Denver, Colorado Springs, Pueblo, and Boulder to find them, Colorado's lakes provide surprisingly strong fishing opportunities. Some of the most common species are

brook trout, introduced in 1872 and common in high and cold streams and lakes; **cutthroat trout,** so populous in coldwater mountain streams, lakes, and rivers that they became Colorado's official state fish in 1994; the red-bodied **kokanee salmon,** which swims in warmer, shallower water near plants and trees; and the **largemouth bass,** a well-known warm-water fish that first joined Colorado's streams, rivers, ponds, and reservoirs in the 1870s.

Rarer fish in the state are the tiger muskie, pumpkinseed, orange spotted sunfish, and the endangered arctic grayling.

Contact the **Colorado Division of Wildlife** (6060 Broadway, Denver, 303/297-1192, http://wildlife.state.co.us, 8 A.M.–5 P.M. Mon.–Fri.) for information on endangered species, hunting, fishing, permits, and directions.

Environmental Issues

GAS DRILLING

The Energy Policy Act of 2005, one of President Bush's initiatives, opened the door for a Rocky Mountain drilling boom. Between 1999 and 2008, the federal Bureau of Land Management leased 5.2 million acres (an area the size of New Jersey) of Colorado land for new energy exploration. During that same period, the state experienced a sixfold rise in drilling permits, according to *The New York Times.*

One of the most controversial natural gas drilling spots is the Roan Plateau, which sits 180 miles west of Denver near Rifle. Conservation groups, industry leaders, local residents, and government regulators worked for seven years to put together a compromise that would leave the most pristine areas of the mesa for hunters and nature lovers. At the same time, the energy industry agreed to share a single drilling site as a way to minimize damage to the environment (an unprecedented move for the industry). But in 2008, the two sides had to shelve their carefully balanced plan when the Bureau of Land Management (BLM) took a radically different course. Officials decided

to lease all of the property on top of the plateau instead of protecting it. At press time, a coalition of 10 environmental groups had sued the BLM in U.S. District Court in Denver, and the case was still pending.

This issue has split environmentalists and political conservatives. "For Colorado, the risk is that the energy measure would let oil companies run roughshod over our landscape, particularly by exempting oil companies from clean water laws and by pushing oil shale and tar sand development," opined the generally liberal *Denver Post,* while the conservative *Rocky Mountain News* declared, "With oil prices over $60 a barrel…oil and gas drilling is going to happen. What's the point of making it slower and more expensive? That won't help the environment." During the 2008 presidential campaign, vice presidential candidate Sarah Palin famously rallied Republican supporters to chant, "Drill, baby, drill!"—in a slightly different context, but still relevant in this debate. President Obama has generally favored compromise and making certain lands open for drilling, but he hasn't dealt with the Colorado issues in particular. No doubt debate is still raging as you read this book.

OPEN SPACE

Coloradoans of all political persuasions love their open space—27 cities and nine counties in the state have rules protecting a certain amount of land from public or private use. Many of these local governments, as well as The Nature Conservancy, have earmarked hundreds of thousands of dollars to buy such land, mostly near the mountains, and preserve it from development.

It isn't always easy: In 2005 the Bush administration took away protections for 4.4 million acres of Colorado roadless areas. That doesn't mean developers have rushed in to tear trees out of the forests, but the state's governor at the time, Republican Bill Owens, created a task force to convene public hearings and make final recommendations. (Toward the end of his term, President Clinton had banned development on 58.5 million acres in the United States, but one of President Bush's first acts in office was to overturn these rules.)

Boulder, whose 43,000-acre strip of mountain and park land is one of the biggest in the United States, has debated for years just how much access to give hikers, bikers, and dog owners. Hard-core environmentalists say the land should be completely off-limits to bone-burying dogs and boot-wearing mountain climbers, while more moderate types say the land has no purpose if people can't use it. In early 2005, Boulder's city council compromised, declaring 13,000 acres "habitat conservation areas," with strict rules for staying on trails and leashing dogs, keeping 100 miles of trails open to everybody and about nine miles totally closed.

WATER CONSERVATION

During 20 drought-free years, Coloradoans became accustomed to using as much water as they wanted for showering, dishwashing, laundry, lawn care, and car washing. Then came the summer of 2002, when rainfall and snowpack dropped dramatically in the mountains,

and suddenly the dry state's drought tradition aggressively returned. Officials begged local residents to conserve water, restricting sprinkler systems to certain days of the week, and parks went almost overnight from lush and green to crinkly and yellow.

But Colorado residents were unperturbed, and they stopped taking long showers and leaving the sink running while they tossed their glasses into the dishwasher. By early 2003, thanks in part to a statewide blizzard that replenished some of the crucial mountain snowpack and filled certain key lakes and reservoirs, the drought warnings had subsided. In July 2005, despite an unprecedented heat wave, Denver Water's customers consumed 11.4 billion gallons of water, according to the *Denver Post,* compared to 12.9 billion gallons during the much cooler July 2000. Problem solved, right? Not necessarily. First, because Colorado residents followed the rules, water use went down, so entities such as Denver Water started to lose money—and had to raise the rates on water use. Second, although drought isn't as imminent a threat as it was in 2003, it still looms in many parts of rain-challenged Colorado.

MOUNTAIN PINE BEETLES

In the past few years, Colorado visitors who longed for the fragrant smell and cool beauty of mountain pines found only stark, depressing stands of dead trees. Some campers even encountered "closed" signs.

The campground closures will continue, National Forest Service officials say, as long as the mountain pine beetle keeps munching. That's because high winds might topple the dead trees and pose a safety threat to campers. The dead trees also increase the risk of forest fires.

With the help of prison work crews and private contractors, Forest Service officials are gradually making the rounds to the hardest hit areas, such as the Dillon Reservoir, to trim out the dead wood. Once the campgrounds are deemed safe, the Forest Service will re-open them. In 2008, for example, 17 of the

223 national forest campgrounds and picnic areas across Colorado and Wyoming were closed for the entire summer, and 14 sites had delayed openings.

Pine beetles have always existed in Colorado, but experts say a series of droughts and warm winters weakened the pine trees and made them more vulnerable to disease. In forests that do not have diverse types of trees (and have not been subject to beneficial controlled burns), the bugs have taken hold like never before. Scientists are calling them an epidemic. The Forest Service saved especially valuable areas with insecticides, but at this point, the beetles are winning.

Check the beetle status of any campground before visiting at www.fs.fed.us/r2/recreation/camping/campgroundlist.

History

THE FIRST SETTLERS

Ancient flint points found in the South Platte River indicate that people wandered Colorado as early as 15,000 years ago. They lived in what is now Weld County and hunted small game like deer and rabbits all over the state. Perhaps 1,000 years later, mammoths appeared on the Eastern Plains, and then were replaced by bison and smaller animals. For the next 4,500 years, inhabitants created villages, learned how to farm in river valleys, and created elaborate art on rocks and valley cliffs; some of these archaeological remnants can still be seen in western Colorado and elsewhere.

The Anasazi were the first in Colorado to truly build society and culture. They lived in what is today the Four Corners region, building elaborate cliff dwellings with sophisticated square-rock architecture and large, open kivas, or ceremonial rooms. The bulk of the structures survive today in Mesa Verde National Park, and other remnants of Anasazi culture are located along streams and rivers in western Colorado.

By A.D. 1300, in large part due to extreme weather events like floods, droughts, and heavy rainfall, Anasazi culture had almost completely died out. In its place came a new Native American group, the Utes, who started out in Utah and Nevada and, as they grew, explored and pushed into Colorado territory. Living during the winter in western river valleys, the Utes were thought to have raided the Anasazi's food storage areas—they were aggressive and resourceful and found ways to live through extreme drought conditions. Meanwhile, groups soon to be known as Navajos and Apaches moved into the state from the Kansas and New Mexico regions, massing near the San Juan River.

LATER SETTLERS
The Spanish

The first nonnative settlers, from roughly 1540 to 1580, were the Spanish, coming up from Mexico to continue their search for silver. They didn't find much silver, but they did like the scenery. When reports of pretty little villages along the Rio Grande reached Spanish leaders, explorer Juan de Oñate was dispatched to colonize the area. First, the Spanish took over New Mexico, intent on spreading Christianity to the native people—but the descendants of the Anasazi fought back, killing 400 Spaniards in 1680 and recapturing their land for a dozen or so years, until the Spanish returned and permanently quashed the Native Americans.

Their foothold thus established, the Spaniards began expeditions into Colorado in 1714 and 1719, mostly to fight the Utes, who despite a friendship pledge some 55 years earlier were making regular raids on Spanish farmers and others in New Mexico. Spanish troops also traveled through the Sangre de Cristo mountain range, from Taos, New Mexico, to the western Rockies, to fight the Comanches.

The Spaniards persevered, pressuring the Utes and Comanches into treaties, but more important to Colorado history was the Spanish colonization of Colorado. The Spanish would embark on the first key exploratory trips into Colorado's intimidating mountain ranges—explorer Juan de Rivera went into the San Juan Mountains and Gunnison River in 1765, and two friars, Dominguez and Escalante, traversed and named the Sangre de Cristo Range, the San Juan Mountains, and other locations in 1777.

The Louisiana Purchase and Zebulon Pike

By 1801, although the United States had been a bona fide country for 27 years, most of the West belonged to the Spanish—although rival France had battled for Colorado and other areas between the Mississippi and New Mexico for decades. That year, Spain gave up northern Colorado to the French. And two years later, the United States made the Louisiana Purchase, spending $15 million on southern property that virtually doubled the country's landmass. For Colorado, the purchase was especially significant because it led to negotiations that would define the territory's borders—the United States received part of the plains and the Front Range, while the Spanish maintained their hold on the rest of the Rockies and the western plateaus.

Into this rivalry between the Spanish and the Americans—with a little French and Native American tension on the side—hiked explorer Zebulon Pike. In 1806 he became the first American to truly investigate the Colorado territory, wandering into the south-central Rockies and naming Pikes Peak, which he said nobody could climb (of course, Dr. Edwin James, part of an official exploration party, scaled it in 1820). The next year, the Spanish captured and imprisoned Pike in Santa Fe, then released him shortly afterward.

After Mexico gained its independence, in 1821, the United States and Mexico put aside their differences and began a lucrative economic relationship. Beaver pelts and other kinds of fur were the most sought-after items for trade, and traders from Missouri to Santa Fe established the Santa Fe Trail, which cut around the Rockies in southeastern Colorado—avoiding treacherous terrain but often running into hostile Native Americans. Of the many trading posts along the route, the most famous was the adobe Bent's Fort, established in 1833 not far from Las Animas, where explorers, soldiers, and Cheyenne and Arapaho Indians could load up on food and supplies.

In 1846, when the Mexican-American War broke out, Bent's Fort was absorbed into the United States and transformed into a real fort, a training area for soldiers. The war lasted two years, and when the gunpowder had cleared, Mexico had agreed to a treaty ceding the entirety of what is now Colorado to the United States.

The Gold Rush

Rumors about gold in Colorado's Rocky Mountains circulated around the United States beginning in 1858, and that spring, 13 prospectors set out to the South Platte River to find it. After months of searching, they succeeded in early July, finding tiny gold deposits along Little Dry Creek, a few miles north of where Cherry Creek and the South Platte meet (this is where Denver sits today).

The ensuing rush built Colorado. Tens of thousands of miners, farmers, ranchers, outlaws, and gamblers moved to the mountains, creating human dramas and mythologies that reverberate today. According to legend, fortune-seeker William Larimer brought 30 men from Leavenworth, Kansas, in search of gold and wound up bribing a guard in St. Charles, near Cherry Creek and the South Platte River, to sign over the entire town while its founding fathers were out of town. Larimer named this new area Denver.

Denver started to grow, and its first newspaper, the *Rocky Mountain News,* was founded in 1859. But the early gold rush, which brought some 3,000 people to the area, turned out to be a bust, and many of those settlers headed dejectedly back to Kansas and Missouri. Those who stayed behind, however, were rewarded when the most determined miners started to bring back vials of gold from mines near Idaho

Springs and Clear Creek, both west of Denver in the eastern Rockies. This rush lasted several years, as an estimated 500 people a year moved to Colorado, numerous small towns sprouted up in the mountains, and Central City, Black Hawk, and Idaho Springs became havens for hard-drinking, hard-gambling, and hard-fighting miners.

Colorado officially became a U.S. territory in 1861, although the mines couldn't keep up production—gold discoveries dropped dramatically from 1860 to 1866, and with them went the population, with thousands of people moving out of the area yet again. In addition, Colorado was so isolated from other territories that many miners and their families had trouble dealing with the resulting depression. To build the state, boosters such as Larimer and first governor William Gilpin coaxed railroads to extend their lines to the area, helped modernize the mines, and encouraged farmers and ranchers to settle on the fertile Eastern Plains. Colorado would slowly boom again.

Conflicts with Native Americans

Needless to say, Native American groups weren't totally thrilled about settlers colonizing the land they'd been living on for centuries. The conflicts weren't pretty: In 1864, Cheyenne and Arapaho warriors murdered the Hungate family on its ranch some 30 miles from Denver, striking fear of war dances in the hearts of settlers for decades to come. American troops, led by Col. John Chivington, responded in kind, and set out with extermination in mind—he led a massacre of 500 Cheyennes, including many women and children, in southeastern Colorado. Even more infamously, religious-minded settler John Meeker, who had founded the city of Greeley, was killed along with several other whites after attempting to "reform" Native Americans according to Christian traditions. But this "Meeker massacre," in 1879, ultimately took away the leverage of Ute leaders such as Chief Ouray, who gave up wide swaths of Colorado land, allowing settlers to assume control of the state for good.

© ARINAHABICH/123RF.COM

During the mining boom years, fancy hotels, like the Beaumont in Ouray, sprouted all over Colorado.

The Bust

From 1870 to 1893, thanks to mines such as Gilpin and Clear Creek, which for a time produced more than $3.5 million a year worth of gold, Colorado's population boomed. The first railroad landed near Black Hawk in 1870, leading to many huge new industries, with stations built in Denver, Burlington, Grand Junction, Durango, Julesburg, and even tiny mountain towns such as Silverton. From roughly 1870 to 1880, the territory's population grew from about 40,000 to more than 124,000, and Colorado became a state in 1876. Fancy hotels sprouted all over the state—the Beaumont in Ouray, the Hotel Colorado in Glenwood Springs, the Sheridan in Telluride, and the Strater in Durango—and famous (and infamous) visitors such as Teddy Roosevelt, King Leopold of Belgium, and Doc Holliday stayed in the ornate rooms.

Silver mines also flourished during this period, particularly those in Leadville, as well as in Durango and other parts of the "Silver San Juans" in southwestern Colorado. However, beginning in 1873, the U.S. Congress started to deemphasize silver—the country discontinued silver dollars, and despite the protests of Colorado and other Western mining states, Congress stopped purchasing silver for good. Gold-mining held steady during this period, but the silver bust turned out to be foreshadowing for Colorado miners.

Gold production became wobbly in the 1900s, when mines started getting so deep they were too expensive to maintain, and World War I–era inflation knocked it out completely. While gold's value remained consistent, other commodities went up, and the economics of gold-mining made it obsolete.

Mines began to close, leading to a horrific domino effect throughout the state: Miners abandoned the towns they'd inhabited since the 1860s; Denver's population swelled, mostly with unemployed and homeless people; opulent hotels and stately banks closed; and entire boom towns such as Central City downgraded to ghost towns within a few months. Despite certain healthy industrial cities, like Redstone,

where coal workers thrived under magnate John Osgood, Colorado's fortunes changed from rich to poor.

Colorado was a roller coaster for the next three decades. Bloody strikes in mining towns like Cripple Creek and Telluride led to confrontations between management and labor. There were unexplained explosions, Colorado National Guard activations, labor-camp violence, and at the peak in 1914, an altercation near Trinidad resulting in dead strikers as well as women and children. The state economy recovered during a brief World War I–era silver boom, but it didn't last long, and by the Great Depression, farmers and ranchers lost everything, creating the gloom of poverty almost through World War II.

SCENERY, SKIING, AND TOURISM

As in the rest of the United States, Franklin D. Roosevelt's New Deal programs pulled Colorado out of its longtime funk—federal agriculture and public-works projects revived farmers and built new roads. Roosevelt's Civilian Conservation Corps planted 9 million trees, stocked lakes and streams with 2 million fish, and built Morrison's Red Rocks Amphitheatre, which remains one of the state's biggest tourism and entertainment draws to this day. World War II helped the economy too, as the military established huge training bases, such as Fort Carson, near Colorado Springs, and Buckley Field, near Denver.

Beginning in the 1950s, with major roads such as I-70 giving travelers access to the Rocky Mountains that ancient Native Americans and the Spanish explorers could never have imagined, Colorado truly began to market its scenic riches. Camping, fishing, and hunting drew thousands to mountain towns like Telluride, Durango, and Central City, and tourism became the state's third-largest industry in the 1950s and 1960s.

What really made the state take off, though, was skiing. The sport had been around as early as 1857, according to Abbott Fay's *A History of Skiing in Colorado,* when mountain guide Jim

Baker lost his way in the mountains east of Gunnison and built himself a pair of makeshift skis to climb a peak for a better view. Skiers were creative in the early days, with Army vehicles hauling adventurous types to a tow rope in the prechairlift era at Arapahoe Basin. Mountain mail carriers were some of the earliest adopters.

Thanks to pioneers such as Norwegian immigrant Carl Howelsen, who built Colorado's first ski jump in Steamboat Springs in 1914, skiing slowly developed a reputation among extreme-sports pioneers in the early 20th century. Visionary entrepreneurs plotted resorts in former mining towns like Breckenridge and uninhabited mountain regions like Vail, and by the 1960s, Vail, Breckenridge, Steamboat Springs, and Aspen were competing aggressively for tourist dollars. The moment skiing entered the international mainstream came in the early 1970s, when President Gerald Ford declared himself a Vail aficionado.

Today, skiing is a multibillion-dollar industry, with 28 total hills, 36,300 acres of skiable terrain, and 12 miles worth of mountain drops. Every major resort manufactures its own powder, expensive condominiums and affordable ski villages sit side by side in tourist-heavy but still quaint towns from Winter Park to Crested Butte, and extreme-sports festivals and outdoors magazines focus heavily on Colorado. The events of September 11, 2001, delivered a blow to the ski industry, along with the rest of world tourism, but it recovered for much of the early 2000s, although the ongoing economic downturn that began in 2008 has cut into attendance and resort profits yet again. Resorts market deals and packages as heavily as ever.

MODERN COLORADO

Many unexpected factors brought a variety of businesses to Colorado beginning in the 1950s. Mining boomed again—uranium this time—and prospectors with Geiger counters flooded Grand Junction and the Four Corners region searching for ore. Aspen took off as the world's posh playground, drawing celebrities and other hoity-toity types and boosting recreational tourism. The United States opened the National Center for Atmospheric Research in Boulder and the National Bureau of Standards in Denver, and businesses such as Martin Marietta Aerospace and IBM relocated to the area as well.

In the Rocky Mountains, the Eisenhower Tunnel opened in the early 1970s, offering easy driving passage from Denver to Vail, Aspen, Crested Butte, Glenwood Springs, and beyond. Denver overhauled its metropolitan area in the early 1960s, drawing numerous colleges and industries to town, and it began to emerge from its longtime reputation as a "cow town"—although plenty of farmers and ranchers lived nearby.

The city's latest rebirth happened in the 1990s, when Mayor Federico Peña spearheaded the state-of-the-art Denver International Airport, one of the largest in the country, and Major League Baseball moved to town in the form of the purple-and-black Colorado Rockies. Around the time of these developments came LoDo, a revitalization of the downtown warehouse-district areas, and in recent years, major transportation projects such as T-REX and FasTracks are establishing light-rail trains and other new transportation.

Government and Economy

GOVERNMENT

For years, Colorado was a "red state," in the vernacular of recent U.S. presidential elections, voting overwhelmingly for George W. Bush in 2000 and 2004 and generally electing Republican senators and representatives.

Things changed in 2008, when swing state Colorado voted for Democrat Barack Obama and key state representatives such as arch-conservative Marilyn Musgrave lost the seats they'd held for years. The majority of the state's residents, especially farmers and ranchers in the Eastern Plains and military families in the Colorado Springs area, are conservative, but in 2006 and 2010 the state elected two consecutive Democratic governors. "The People's Republic of Boulder," a college town filled with ex-hippies, is one of the most liberal cities in the country, and Denver isn't far behind.

As a result, Colorado elections wind up with such contradictory results as an overwhelming Bush victory in 2004 paired with Democrat Ken Salazar's ascension to the U.S. Senate the same year and state Democrats taking over the legislature for the first time in decades. More recently the state has taken on a distinctly purple hue, voting for Barack Obama in 2008 for president, Denver Mayor John Hickenlooper in 2010 for governor, and reelecting Sen. Michael Bennet the same year despite the Tea Party revolution.

Colorado has 64 counties, each with a board of commissioners, although Denver is run by a mayor and city council. As per Colorado's constitution, written in 1876, the state lawmaking body is the General Assembly, consisting of a Senate and a House of Representatives, with veto powers from the governor.

ECONOMY

Raising cattle and sheep and producing wheat, hay, corn, and sugar beets, among other things, have been the anchor of Colorado's economy since the mid-1800s. Farm market receipts are roughly $5 billion per year, according to Doug Freed's almanac *Colorado by the Numbers,* and farms are pretty much all you'll see if you

spend any time in Greeley, Sterling, Limon, or the rest of the Eastern Plains.

Other top business sectors include manufacturing (computer equipment is big), federal services (there are numerous military bases around the state, the Department of Defense spends about $5 billion here annually, and the U.S. Mint is in downtown Denver, not to mention prisons and airports), food processing, transportation and electrical equipment, and, particularly in the northwest, wineries and fruit orchards.

Also huge is tourism: Thanks mostly to the ski resorts, travelers spend some $8 billion a year in the state, from renting ski boots to buying T-shirts at the Greeley Independence Stampede rodeo and country-music festival.

Finally, Colorado cemented its reputation as a high-tech state during the Internet boom of the 1990s, when numerous startup companies formed in Denver, Boulder, Colorado Springs, and elsewhere, and large companies such as Sun Microsystems expanded their presence here. The resulting bust briefly damaged the economy—as with other states, Colorado officials had "irrational exuberance" and spent far too many millions on poorly thought-out projects like the Ocean Journey Aquarium in downtown Denver.

Although Colorado is lovingly remembered as a gold-mining state, most of those mines have shut down, leaving abandoned shafts all over the state. Colorado companies continue to mine gas, coal, gravel, and uranium.

The People

STATISTICS

More than 5 million people live in Colorado, as of the 2010 U.S. Census, and while the state has undergone some severe busts and depressions, most notably after gold and silver rushes in the late 1800s, it has never gone 10 years straight with a population decrease. Miners built the state, particularly Denver, Colorado Springs, and the small towns from the Front Range to the Western Slope, and while many of

those original regions have devolved into ghost towns or tourist areas, the layouts roughly remain the same.

Colorado is the third-fastest-growing state, with a population increase of 30 percent from 1990 to 2000. Although the state has traditionally had a dismally small African American population—just 4 percent, compared to 12.6 percent in the United States—it has a large and rapidly growing Hispanic populace. About

20.7 percent of the state is Hispanic, an increase from 17 percent in 2000—in Denver County, the number jumps to 32 percent—and many predict that Hispanics will account for one-quarter of the state's population by 2025.

Denver is easily the state's most diverse area, but some of the other large cities are almost disturbingly homogeneous. For all its other qualities, Boulder County's African American population is 0.9 percent, while its Hispanic population is 13.3 percent, far lower than its metropolitan neighbor, Denver County. (The African American population is basically steady, while Hispanics have increased.) For people visiting or moving from urban areas, this can make for culture shock.

ATTITUDES

Colorado is a divided state, politically and socially, in many ways. In most of Denver and Boulder, as well as Telluride and Aspen, you're likely to encounter "Rush Is Rong" bumper stickers, while signs for conservative candidates are far more common in Colorado Springs and the Eastern Plains. This makes for a bit of tension, as evidenced on radio talk shows and the letters pages of the *The Denver Post* and other newspapers.

Mostly, though, Colorado is a friendly, laid-back state, filled with individualists who've moved to the mountains to escape the stress of their more complicated lives in California or New York.

Arts and Culture

MUSIC

Some of the many thousands of people who came to Colorado in the 1960s and 1970s to ski, relax, and enjoy the mellow Rocky Mountain atmosphere were rock stars—and several of them stayed behind. Around the time they started making hit records in the mid-1970s, members of the Eagles held court regularly at Tulagi, the late, lamented nightclub near the University of Colorado campus in Boulder. Before long, rockers such as Stevie Wonder and Joe Walsh were living and recording at the $1,500-per-day-per-entourage Caribou Ranch in Nederland, and Elton John even titled an album *Caribou.*

For years afterward, Colorado had a reputation as a sort of summer home for rising rockers, especially gentle, country-leaning ones like Dan Fogelberg, Firefall, and Poco's Richie Furay, who retired from the music business to open his own ministry in Boulder County. From these seeds, as well as regular stops by the Grateful Dead through the mid-1990s, grew the local jam-band culture. Homegrown artists like Big Head Todd and the Monsters, the Samples, Leftover Salmon, and the String Cheese Incident used Red Rocks Amphitheatre as their home base and turned into solid

international touring acts. More recently, The Fray, a pop-rock band from Denver, became one of the most successful music acts in Colorado history, selling more than 2 million copies of its 2005 album *How to Save a Life.* Newer local acts such as the Flobots and singer-songwriter Danielle Ate the Sandwich may be on the brink of following The Fray into pop stardom.

Also serving this scene are numerous summer mountain festivals, such as the Telluride Bluegrass Festival, RockyGrass in Lyons, and Jazz Aspen Snowmass. For a thorough and lively study of pop music in Colorado, former *Denver Post* rock writer G. Brown's *Colorado Rocks!* is highly recommended.

The rodeo culture of the Eastern Plains spawned hundreds of thousands of country-music fans, and the Greeley Independence Stampede has become one of the biggest festivals this side of Cheyenne Frontier Days in Wyoming.

Opera, by contrast, isn't quite as big as it was in the late 1800s, when the most sophisticated miners gussied themselves up on a regular basis and headed to the Wheeler Opera House in Aspen or the Sheridan Opera House in Telluride. Nonetheless, many of these

SONGS ABOUT COLORADO

- A.J. Flynn, "Where the Columbines Grow" (state song)
- Bob Seger, "Get Out of Denver"
- Bowling for Soup, "Surf Colorado"
- Chuck Pyle, "Colorado"
- C.W. McCall, "The Silverton"
- C.W. McCall, "Wolf Creek Pass"
- Emmylou Harris, "From Boulder to Birmingham"
- Flying Burrito Brothers, "Colorado"
- Jackson Browne, "Bound for Colorado"
- Jimmie Dale Gilmore, "Another Colorado"
- John Denver, "I Guess He'd Rather Be in Colorado"
- John Denver, "Rocky Mountain High" (co-state song, as of 2007)
- John Denver, "Starwood in Aspen"
- Judy Collins, "The Blizzard (The Colorado Song)"
- Merle Haggard, "Colorado"
- Nitty Gritty Dirt Band, "Colorado Christmas"
- Stephen Stills, "Colorado"
- Warren Zevon, "Things to Do in Denver When You're Dead"
- Willie Nelson, "Denver"
- Xandra, "Colorado"

recently opened a fancy new opera hall, and the **Colorado Symphony Orchestra** do an excellent job of keeping classical, chamber, and opera music alive in the state.

THEATER

With Denver and Boulder acting as cultural centers—the University of Colorado's outdoor **Colorado Shakespeare Festival** is a must for bard devotees, and Denver has a strong collection of local theaters, including the **Denver Center Theatre Company**—Colorado is a surprisingly rich and diverse place to see a play. It's not New York City or Chicago, but the options, as you drive around the state, are as varied as the historical and goofy **Diamond Circle Melodrama & Vaudeville** in Durango and the colorful **Buell Children's Theatre** in Pueblo.

COWBOY POETRY

Long before there was such a thing as "country music," there was cowboy poetry—an around-the-campfire way of exchanging tall tales that was common in the Old West during the late 1800s and early 1900s. Here's a sample from the public domain, which modern cowboy poet Don Edwards revived on a recent album, reprinted on www.cowboypoetry.com:

> When I think of those good old days, my eyes with tears do fill
> When I think of the tin can by the fire and coyote on the hill.
> I'll tell you, boys, in those days old-timers stood a show,
> Our pockets full of money, not a sorrow did we know.
> But things have changed now; we are poorly clothed and fed.
> Our wagons are all broken and our ponies 'most all dead.
> Soon we will leave this country; you'll hear the angels shout,
> "Oh, here they come to Heaven, the campfire has gone out."

The best-known poets of this down-home literary style were men like Curley Fletcher,

historic old venues survive, sponsoring pop, rock, country, and jazz shows in addition to theatrical productions, and entities such as the **Denver Performing Arts Complex,** which who wrote *The Strawberry Roan,* and John Wallace "Captain Jack" Crawford, a Civil War soldier and later author of *Wher' the Hand o' God Is Seen and Other Poems.* This scene continues today, in cowboy-poetry gatherings around the country, of which Colorado is a large hub. Veterans such as celebrated Texas transplant Michael Martin Murphey, Boulder's Chuck Pyle, Westminster's Jon Chandler, and Denver's Liz Masterson continue to perform their material at bars, clubs, fairs, and statewide gatherings.

Some of the most popular events in this genre include the **Colorado Cowboy Poetry Gathering** (Arvada Center, 6901 Wadsworth Blvd., Denver, 720/898-7200, www.coloradocowboygathering.com) in January, around the time of the Stock Show; the **Rifle Rendezvous Festival** (970/625-0943, www.riflerendezvous.org), in July in tiny northwestern Rifle; the **Durango Cowboy Gathering** (970/749-2995, www.durangocowboygathering.org), in early October; and **A Gathering Under the Aspens** (970/487-3407, http://parks.state.co.us/Parks/vega), in early August at Vega State Park, near Collbran in northwestern Colorado.

SHOPPING

The best shopping districts in Colorado are part of the biggest cities—the **16th Street Mall** and **Larimer Square** in Denver, the **Pearl Street Mall** in Boulder, and **Old Town Square** in Fort Collins. But every tiny mountain town, from Ouray to Crested Butte, has its own strip of tourist-oriented, mom-and-pop–style shops that sell books, sunglasses, T-shirts, Western clothing, sports equipment, and organic foods. Most famous (and infamous) is Aspen, whose hoity-toity stores cater to the super-rich (or at least the super-rich–looking).

FOOD

Colorado restaurants are rarely listed in the glossy pages of *Esquire* and *Bon Appétit,* but the food here has touches of high class that rival anything in New York or Los Angeles. True gourmets should consider spending a few days in Denver for high-end restaurants such as **Mizuna** and **Rioja,** but they should also build an itinerary around Aspen, Beaver Creek, and Telluride. These mountain towns can't exactly choose from an unlimited pool of the best chefs and waitstaff, the way New York and Los Angeles eateries do, but they manage to attract some of the top talents in the world. Also worth visiting are hidden gems such as **Alice's Restaurant,** off the Peak-to-Peak Highway outside Boulder, and **Toscanini** in Beaver Creek.

Colorado also has a number of food-oriented festivals, including Aspen's **Food & Wine Classic,** Denver's **Great American Beer Festival,** the **Olathe Sweet Corn Festival,** and the **Annual Chili Pepper and Brewfest** in Snowmass Village.

Recreation

Colorado's marquee attraction is its outdoor scenery—towering mountains that pop up unexpectedly as you're driving to the grocery store, meadows and wildernesses that rival anything in the Swiss Alps, and some of the best skiing, biking, and hiking trails in the world. So the outdoors is the heart of Colorado's tourism industry, and casual outdoor wanderers and professional ski and bike racers alike spend serious time here for training and races. The range of outdoor activities is daunting: mountain biking in Crested Butte, fishing in Rifle, skiing in Aspen, and hiking in Rocky Mountain National Park.

PUBLIC LANDS

Colorado has 41 state parks—almost 219,000 acres of land and water overall—along with 4,000 campsites and 58 cabins and yurts that are open to the public. Daily vehicle fees are $3–7, and campsites range $7–20 depending on the amenities. The **Colorado State**

Parks main office (1313 Sherman St., Denver, 303/866-3437, http://parks.state.co.us) is in Denver.

In addition, the **U.S. Bureau of Land Management** (303/239-3600, www.blm.gov/wo/st/en.html) oversees 8.64 million acres of land, or 12.6 percent of the entire state, according to *Colorado by the Numbers*. Access to most lands is free, and campsites cost $3–10 per night.

The **U.S. Forest Service** manages 14 wilderness areas and national grasslands, including Routt National Forest outside Aspen. Day passes run about $5–8, and campsites are about $15 per night. The service has three park-ranger offices in the state (100 Main St., Walden, 970/723-8204; 2103 E. Park Ave., Kremmling, 970/724-3000; and 300 Roselawn Ave., Yampa, 970/638-4516). The main website (www.fs.fed.us/r2) has information on Wyoming, Kansas, Nebraska, and South Dakota as well.

Finally, the **National Park Service** (12795 Alameda Pkwy., Lakewood, 303/969-2500, www.nps.gov) maintains 15 parks, monuments, and historic trails in Colorado, including Rocky Mountain National Park, the Curecanti National Recreation Area, and Black Canyon of the Gunnison National Park. Day use is roughly $3–5.

OUTDOOR ACTIVITIES
Skiing

Consult individual chapters in this book for details about specific ski resorts—each one has a website with just about everything you need to know, from weather to lesson times—but suffice to say that "Ski Country USA" has some of the best skiing in the world, enough to satisfy a multibillion-dollar tourist industry. Numerous magazines—try *Ski* (www.skimag.com) and *Skiing* (www.skiingmag.com)—emphasize Colorado skiing, as do websites such as **Colorado Ski Country USA** (www.coloradoski.com) and the **Colorado Ski Resort Guide** (www.coloradoskicountry.com). Almost any sporting-goods store—and there are many scattered around the

resorts—will rent skis, boots, and poles in $24–30 one-day packages.

Backcountry and Nordic skiing—more commonly known as cross-country—are also popular at almost every Colorado ski resort as well as major parks and trails around Boulder, Rocky Mountain National Park, and elsewhere. The **Cross Country Ski Areas Association** (www.xcski.org) is an excellent resource, as are the resorts and the **Boulder Outdoor Center** (2707 Spruce St., Boulder, 303/444-8420 or 800/364-9376, www.boc123.com). Most sporting-goods stores rent equipment.

Snowboarding

Snowboarding used to be a renegade answer to skiing, but in the past decade it has become established as a legitimate alternative, the way punk rockers Green Day are an alternative to the Rolling Stones. (In Crested Butte, the downtown benches are snowboards with legs attached.) Every major ski resort in Colorado offers snowboard-oriented runs and bowls, and almost every ski shop rents equipment—the board is all you need, and you can rent one for $24–30 per day. There's such a thing as "cross-country boarding," but most snowboarders tend to hate it. It's truly a downhill-only sport. Just about every ski resort in Colorado today offers a terrain park for boarders (and skiers, too) who favor tricks and jumps as opposed to rote downhill runs.

Snowmobiling

You'd think snowmobiling would be almost as huge as skiing in Colorado, but mountain erosion limits the available trails, so there are restrictions on where and when you can indulge. Contact the **Colorado Snowmobile Association** (http://sledcity.com) about how to get started. Many mountain towns rent snowmobiles as well.

Hiking and Biking

Wherever you go in Colorado, you're bound to find some kind of scenic hiking trail—some of the best are in **Rocky Mountain National**

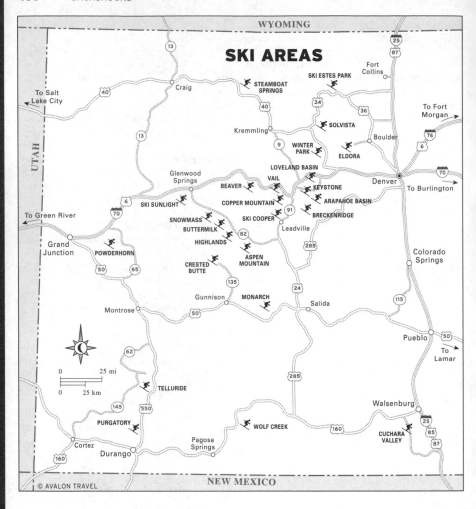

Park, **Chautauqua Park** in Boulder, the hike up to **Bridal Veil Falls** in Telluride, **Dinosaur National Park** in the northwest corner of the state, and **Curecanti National Recreation Area** east of Montrose.

Many of the aforementioned hiking and backpacking areas are open to cyclists as well. Some cities in Colorado, particularly Crested Butte, Grand Junction and neighboring Rifle, and Boulder, cater directly to cyclists, with police officers who actually enforce pedestrian-cyclist-motorist laws and designated lanes on the right side of the road. In addition, many of the well-known ski areas allow cyclists to pedal the slopes during late spring and summer, and if all else fails, just pick a mountain road and start riding upward. For more information on roads, conditions, renting equipment, or repairs, contact **American Cycling Association** (1135A S. Oneida St., Denver, 303/757-1892, www.americancycling.org).

© MATT INDEN/WEAVER MULTIMEDIA GROUP/COLORADO TOURISM OFFICE

placing the perfect cast near Rocky Mountain National Park

Fishing and Hunting

For a landlocked state far more famous for snow than water, Colorado has surprisingly rich fishing opportunities, from the narrow and dangerous **Black Canyon of the Gunnison National Park** east of Montrose to the **Cache La Poudre River** outside Fort Collins. You have to be 16 years old or older to buy a license—$26 per year for residents or $56 for nonresidents, and one-day and five-day licenses are available.

Hunting, especially of deer, pheasant, elk, and certain kinds of birds, is legal with a license (from $21 per day for small game to $41 for mountain lions). For both fishing and hunting, the **Colorado Department of Wildlife** (6060 Broadway, Denver, 303/297-1192, http://wildlife.state.co.us/hunt) doles out licenses, provides information, and enforces the various rules and restrictions.

Rock Climbing

Many adventure outfitters give rock climbing tours, but experienced climbers like to find the rocks on their own. Beware climbing without equipment, especially if you're new to

the sport. For more information, contact **Total Climbing** (www.totalclimbing.com), which sponsors courses and programs.

White-Water Rafting

White-water rafting is particularly popular along the Colorado River, and nearby towns such as Salida and Buena Vista are hot spots for the sport. Before finding an outfitter or guide and embarking on a trip, ask about the intensity level of the ride—some rafting trips are smooth and easy, others choppy and adventurous. For a fairly comprehensive list of guides, check out **Whitewater Rafting in Colorado** (www.raftinfo.com/colorado.htm).

SPECTATOR SPORTS

Denver is home base for professional teams in just about every sport—the National Football League's **Denver Broncos** (www.denverbroncos.com), Major League Baseball's **Colorado Rockies** (www.colorado.rockies.mlb.com), the National Basketball Association's **Denver Nuggets** (www.nba.com/nuggets), the National Hockey Association's **Colorado Avalanche** (www.coloradoavalanche.com), and even Major League Soccer's **Colorado Rapids** (www.coloradorapids.com). In addition, the state's major colleges, including the University of Colorado and Colorado State University, compete on a high level in most of the Division I sports.

Rodeos are also big in Colorado, especially during the **National Western Stock Show** (www.nationalwestern.com) every January in Denver and throughout the Eastern Plains.

INDOOR ACTIVITIES
Gambling
Three towns in Colorado—Black Hawk, Central City, and Cripple Creek—legalized limited-stakes gambling in 1991, and all three have more or less boomed (with the occasional bust) since then. Limited-stakes basically means you can do whatever you do in Las Vegas, from video poker to blackjack. The people-watching is almost as good as it is in Vegas, with an emphasis on cowboys, and some of the rickety country music played at the casinos makes the trip especially worthwhile.

A few Native American–reservation casinos are scattered throughout the state, including the **Ute Mountain Casino** in Cortez and the **Sky Ute Casino & Lodge** outside Durango.

Accommodations

HOTELS AND MOTELS
Trying to find a standard rate for a Colorado hotel is almost impossible, especially in the ski towns, where there's not just a high season (roughly late Nov.–early Apr.) and a low season (roughly early Sept.–early Nov. and late Apr.–mid-May). There's also a "holiday high season" (Christmas and Thanksgiving), a "summer high season," and a huge gap between weekend and weekday rates. The ski hotels, in particular, offer numerous packages and deals, some involving breakfast and luxuries like sleigh rides and guided tours. Also, scan the local papers (such as the Boulder *Daily Camera* or its website, www.dailycamera.com) for lift ticket–room packages, especially common at the big hotels.

The ritzier the ski area—like Aspen or Beaver Creek—the more expensive the room. Deals at Copper Mountain and Winter Park are usually quite affordable, and Coloradoans take advantage of them. Be sure to make reservations far in advance, especially during high season, because the best hotels fill up quickly.

In smaller towns that are less reliant on the ski season, rates tend to be more consistent. The Broadmoor, in Colorado Springs, is one of many high-end hotels that have surprisingly good deals in the middle of winter. Finally, consider staying just outside a ski resort—in Dillon, Silverthorne, or Frisco (or even Boulder or Denver)—and taking one of the shuttles or buses that traipse through the mountains.

BED-AND-BREAKFASTS
In Colorado, every town seems to have at least one small bed-and-breakfast, usually in a Victorian-style house or a woodsy log cabin, and they're generally a little more expensive than a standard hotel. Breakfast is included in the room rate, and in some cases, so are distinctive touches like dogs, cats, llama boarding (it's true!), and horse stables. Numerous websites list Colorado bed-and-breakfast facilities; **Bed and Breakfast Innkeepers of Colorado** (Colorado Springs, 800/265-7696, www.innsofcolorado.org) is one of the most reliable.

DUDE RANCHES
Dude ranches, or cabin-style hotels on actual ranches with horse stables, corrals, and instructors who give riding lessons, have been serving cowboy-hatted guests in Colorado since the 1870s. They can be good deals, especially for large groups with children, and are available in mountain areas like Winter Park and Grand County. Contact the **Colorado Dude and Guest Ranch Association** (Granby, 970/887-3128, www.coloradoranch.com).

CAMPGROUNDS AND HOSTELS

Camping is huge in Colorado—most campgrounds are open roughly Memorial Day–Labor Day—especially in prime scenery areas such as Rocky Mountain National Park and Colorado National Monument. The rates range from free to $25, and some spots offer running water, flush toilets, and electricity. Contact the **U.S. Forest Service** (303/275-5350, www.fs.fed.us/r2/recreation/camping) or the **State of Colorado** (303/866-3437 or 800/678-2267, http://parks.state.co.us/ reservations) about their respective facilities, or make reservations via a reliable camping-reservation website such as **Reserve America** (www.reserveamerica.com).

Hostels are rare in Colorado, but they exist, even at ritzy ski resorts. Others include the Rocky Mountain Inn near Winter Park and YMCA of the Rockies in Estes Park. For general hostel information, check the **Hostels.com** website (www.hostels.com) or contact **Hostelling International USA** (8401 Colesville Rd., Suite 600, Silver Spring, MD, 301/495-1240, www.hiusa.org).

ESSENTIALS

Getting There

BY CAR

Unless you happen to live in Wyoming, New Mexico, Utah, northeastern Arizona, or western Kansas or Nebraska, Colorado is a long drive from just about any destination. The main artery is I-70, which spans the state from east to west, cutting straight through the Rocky Mountains and providing easy access to most of the major ski resorts. I-25 also cuts through the state, south from Wyoming through Fort Collins, Denver (where it intersects with I-70), Colorado Springs, and Pueblo to northern New Mexico.

The smaller highways, including I-76 from Nebraska into Julesburg and U.S. 24 from Kansas into Burlington, are narrower but usually without much traffic as they climb slowly west into the Rockies.

BY BUS

Greyhound (800/231-2222, www.greyhound. com) provides the primary bus service into Colorado from all over the United States. The easiest way to plan a trip is to arrive in Denver, but the bus company provides service to Colorado Springs, Durango, Alamosa, Brush, Pueblo, Vail, and elsewhere. Check the website for routes and schedules.

© VISIT DENVER

BY AIR

The **Denver International Airport** (DIA, 8500 Pena Blvd., Denver, 303/342-2000, www.flydenver.com) and **Colorado Springs Airport** (7770 Drennan Rd., Colorado Springs, 719/550-1972, www.springsgov.com/airportindex.asp) are the two biggest airports in the state, with service by most of the major carriers. Some of the smaller regional airports make sense if you're flying into an area far from Denver. For those staying in Durango, Telluride, the Four Corners area, or other southwestern towns, try the **Durango La Plata County Airport** (1000 Airport Rd., Durango, 970/247-8143, www.durangogov.org/airport), which is served by several major airlines, including United Express, Frontier, and Southwest. For northwestern Colorado travelers, a better option is **Grand Junction Regional Airport** (2828 Walker Field Dr., Grand Junction, 970/244-9100, www.walkerfield.com), served by American, Frontier, United Express, Delta, and others. In general, though, air travelers should plan arrangements around DIA, which is centrally located and has easy access to rental cars, shuttles, buses, and taxis.

Getting Around

BY CAR

I-70 and I-25, which cut through the state, are wide and well maintained, with speed limits of 65–75 miles per hour in most places, and they accommodate plenty of traffic. During poor weather conditions and the occasional rock slide, however, I-70 can be frustratingly convoluted around the Eisenhower Memorial Tunnel and Idaho Springs. Denver and Colorado Springs also get extremely congested highways during rush hours.

Smaller roads, especially in the mountains, can be twisty and dangerous during poor weather, and some, such as the rocky road over Kebler Pass, from Highway 133 to Crested Butte, are impassable in the winter. Because of the uncertain terrain in mountainous areas, don't be surprised if the road abruptly shifts from paved to gravel. Many Colorado residents drive 4WD trucks and SUVs, and not for show—they need them merely to get out of their own driveways. Keep this in mind when renting a car. Snow chains help too.

Some of Colorado's highways have a history and personality of their own, including the **Scenic Highway of Legends** near Alamosa, the **Peak-to-Peak Highway** outside Boulder, and the **Million Dollar Highway** that connects Ouray with Silverton. As with Route 66 in the Midwest, many of these highways are fun to plan vacations around. Consider, for example, driving in from Kansas via U.S. 50, which follows the historic Santa Fe Trail, and continuing west into Colorado through Lamar, Las Animas, La Junta, and the Comanche National Grassland.

All the major rental-car chains do business in Colorado, including **Hertz** (877/826-8782, www.hertz.com), **Avis** (800/331-1212, www.avis.com), **Enterprise** (800/261-7331, www.enterprise.com), and **Dollar** (800/800-3665, www.dollar.com). All have outlets at Denver International Airport (http://flydenver.com/rentalcars) and many other airports throughout the state.

BY BUS

Most of the big cities have their own bus services, such as the reliable **RTD** (1600 Blake St., 303/299-6000, www.rtd-denver.com) of Denver and Boulder. And many of the ski resorts provide shuttle and bus transportation from condos to slopes and town to town. The **Roaring Fork Transportation Authority** (970/925-8484, www.rfta.com) provides bus service in Aspen and Glenwood Springs as well as among those two cities and smaller Rifle, New Castle, and Silt. The City of Colorado Springs runs the local **Mountain Metropolitan Transit** (1015 Transit Dr., Colorado Springs, 719/385-7433, www.springsgov.com) as well as **Front Range Express** (719/636-3739,

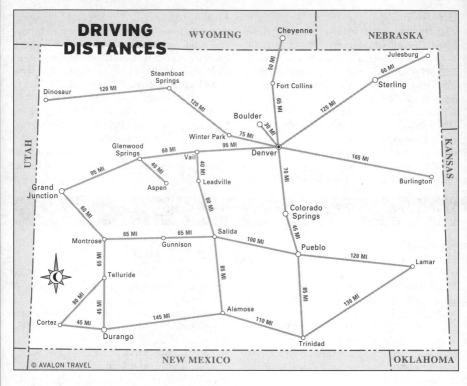

DRIVING DISTANCES

WYOMING
NEBRASKA
Cheyenne

UTAH
KANSAS

Julesburg
60 MI
Sterling
50 MI

Dinosaur
120 MI
Steamboat Springs
Fort Collins
125 MI
65 MI
120 MI

Boulder
30 MI
75 MI
Winter Park
95 MI
Glenwood Springs
60 MI
Vail
40 MI
Denver
165 MI
40 MI
Burlington
49 MI
Leadville
70 MI
Aspen
95 MI
Grand Junction
60 MI
60 MI

Colorado Springs
Montrose
65 MI
65 MI
Salida
100 MI
45 MI
Gunnison
Pueblo
120 MI
Lamar
65 MI
85 MI
Telluride
130 MI
80 MI
45 MI
85 MI

Alamosa
145 MI
110 MI
Cortez
45 MI
Durango
Trinidad

NEW MEXICO
OKLAHOMA

© AVALON TRAVEL

www.frontrangeexpress.com), which operates among Colorado Springs, Denver, Monument, and Castle Rock.

Numerous companies offer bus tours throughout Colorado. The best known is probably **Gray Line** (800/472-9546, www.grayline.com), which delivers travelers to Rocky Mountain National Park, Garden of the Gods, and many other locations, mostly in Colorado Springs and Denver. Smaller bus-tour companies include **Alpine Express** (Gunnison, 800/822-4844, www.alpineexpressshuttle.com), serving mostly northwestern Colorado, and **All Mountain Transportation** (Edwards, 970/949-9255 or 800/715-7634, www.vailrides.com), for the northern ski towns, including Aspen, Vail Valley, and Steamboat Springs.

If these services don't fit your travel plans between select cities in Colorado, try **Greyhound Bus Line** (800/231-2222, www.greyhound.com).

BY TRAIN

A state with a rich railroad pedigree, Colorado has numerous historic locomotives and fully operational narrow-gauge railroads in several towns, notably the **Durango & Silverton Narrow Gauge Railroad.** The **Royal Gorge Route Railroad** (719/276-4000 or 888/724-5748, www.royalgorgeroute.com) is a scenic two-hour ride in the Cañon City area. Also more for scenery than transportation is the **Leadville, Colorado & Southern Railroad** (326 E. 7th St., Leadville, 719/486-3936 or 866/386-3936, www.leadville-train.com), a 2.5-hour ride in northern Colorado overlooking spectacular 14,000-foot peaks.

Of course, the more practical **Amtrak** (800/872-7245, www.amtrak.com) has stations in Boulder, Denver, Fort Collins, Fort Morgan, Frisco, Grand Junction, Granby, Glenwood Springs, La Junta, Lamar, Trinidad, Vail, Pueblo, Colorado Springs, and Fraser, and the routes are convenient. The Glenwood Springs stop is especially nice, directly across the street from the Hotel Denver in the touristy part of town; I've never taken it, but several friends report that bystanders have a habit of mooning the train in this woodsy area as it roars by.

BY BIKE

Thanks to the mild weather, natural obstacles (like gigantic mountains), and varied terrain, Colorado is a haven for bicyclists. For decades, cycling stars from Davis Phinney and Connie Carpenter to Erin Mirabella have trained in cities like Boulder, Grand Junction, and Durango. Boulder, in particular, is a great place to ride around town and the surrounding mountains, as just about every major road has a bike lane and drivers actually respect the crosswalks.

Numerous biking events take place every year in Colorado, from the **Fort Collins Cycling Festival** to the **Aspen Cycling Criterium.** Biking tours pop up throughout the year too, including the **Bicycle Tour of Colorado** (303/985-1180, www.bicycletourcolorado.com), through Telluride, Durango,

Ouray, and elsewhere. **Colorado Bike and Ski** (970/668-8900, www.coloradobikeandski.com) organizes biking tours that begin in Frisco and focus on the northern Rockies ski towns.

For more information on biking in Colorado, contact **Bicycle Colorado** (1525 Market St., Denver, 303/417-1544, www.bicyclecolo.org). Many cities have amateur clubs, including the **Colorado Springs Cycling Club** (www.bikesprings.org) and the **Boulder Mountainbike Alliance** (http://bouldermountainbike.org). Finally, Boulder-based *Velo News* (www.velonews.com) thoroughly covers the local and national biking scenes.

TOURS

A number of companies arrange Colorado tours—by bus, 4WD vehicle, limo, hot-air balloon, van, horse, or just about any other way. Many of these are described in more detail in the individual regional chapters. **Colorado Tours** (www.coloradotours.net) will hook you up with everything from all-terrain-vehicle tours in Durango to dogsled tours in Leadville. **Colorado Sightseer** (303/423-8200 or 800/255-5105, www.coloradosightseer.com) gives guided bus tours, mostly of Denver, Colorado Springs, and Rocky Mountain National Park.

Tips for Travelers

TRAVELERS WITH DISABILITIES

Most of Colorado's big cities, particularly Denver, Colorado Springs, and Boulder, are well equipped with wheelchair ramps and easily accessible elevators and public buses. Some hiking and biking trails, fishing areas, and other outdoor-sports locations provide easier access than others for people with disabilities; resources for determining which is which include **Adaptive Adventures** (27888 Meadow Dr., Evergreen, 303/679-2770, www.adaptiveadventures.org), the **Colorado Division of Wildlife** (303/297-1192, http://wildlife.state.co.us), and

the **Breckenridge Outdoor Education Center** (970/453-6422 or 800/383-2632, www.boec.org). **Wilderness on Wheels** (303/403-1110, www.wildernessonwheels.org), based in the Denver suburb of Wheat Ridge, organizes hiking, biking, camping, and wildlife-watching activities for people with disabilities.

Many of the ski resorts have facilities for physically challenged skiers, such as the Eldora-based **Ignite Adaptive Sports** (303/442-0606, http://igniteadaptivesports.org). Winter Park's resort base area is the headquarters for the **National Sports Center for the Disabled** (970/726-1540, www.nscd.org).

GREEN TRAVEL TIPS

Avoid driving: Colorado is full of mass-transit services, including urban basics such as Denver's **Light Rail** (303/299-6000, www.rtd-denver.com/lightRail_subHome.shtml), which links the city to the suburbs; statewide **Amtrak trains** (www.amtrak.com, 800/872-7245) that begin at Denver's Union Station and branch out all over the state; and scenic railways like the **Durango & Silverton Narrow Gauge Railroad** (888/872-4607, www.durangotrain.com). In addition, shuttle services are becoming more efficient, canceling or combining routes when too few riders show up, driving at eco-conscious speeds on highways, and generally recycling or using recycled material around the office. **Green Ride** (888/472-6656, www.greenrideco.com) is an example of the latter, with routes from its Fort Collins base to Wyoming and Denver International Airport.

Bike regularly: Colorado cities such as Grand Junction, Boulder, Rifle, and Crested Butte are ridiculously bike-friendly, with rider lanes on just about every street, plentiful bike shops, generous pedestrian laws, and sympathetic police officers. Plus, Denver's **B-Cycle** (303/825-3325, www.denver.bcycle.com) provides racks of sturdy, $6-per-day red bicycles at key spots throughout the city, so bikeless types (and drunks stumbling out of downtown bars) have no excuse to overuse their cars.

Look for progressive hotels: Check the **"Green" Hotels Association** (713/789-8889, www.greenhotels.com) website for a list. These include the **Hotel Monaco** (1717 Champa St., Denver, 303/296-1717 or 800/990-1303, www.monaco-denver.com, $99-300), which employs environmentally friendly cleaning products, low-flow water systems, and designer recycling bins in the guest rooms; **Carr Manor** (350 E. Carr Ave., Cripple Creek, 719/689-3709, www.carrmanor.com, $100-400), which installed an $85,000 solar-power system in 2009, in addition to updating its old-fashioned radiators and heating units; and the **Hotel Columbia** (301 W. San Juan Ave., Telluride, 970/728-0660, www.columbiatelluride.com,

$350-495), which provides free parking for hybrid cars in addition to the usual lightbulb upgrades and encouragement of guests to reuse their towels and linens.

Shop green: Watch for boutiques that advertise sustainable materials, organic fibers, and fair labor practices. **Fancy Tiger** (1 S. Broadway, Denver, 303/733-3855, www.fancytiger.com, 10 A.M.-7 P.M. Mon. and Wed.-Sat., 10 A.M.-9 P.M. Tues., 11 A.M.-6 P.M. Sun.), a craft shop, stocks almost exclusively wool, cotton, and silk — no acrylics; **Giggling Green Bean** (3929 Tennyson St., Denver, 720/988-3725, 11 A.M.-5 P.M. Mon., Wed., and Fri., 11 A.M.-7 P.M. Tues. and Thurs., 10 A.M.-5 P.M. Sat., noon-4 P.M. Sun.) is a new-baby store that sells the Play All Day Hemp Fleece Flat Diaper ($6) and the Earth Mama Angel Baby Booby Tube ($25), with an organic-cotton shell; **Eco Ellie's** (3640 Walnut St., Boulder, 720/213-8876, www.ecoellies.com, 8 A.M.-5 P.M. Mon.-Fri.) sells organic mattresses, recycled porch furniture, and a huge variety of other stuff; and, in the Rockies, **Building for Health** (102 Main St., Carbondale, 970/963-0437 or 800/292-4838, www.buildingforhealth.com, 8 A.M.-5 P.M. Mon.-Fri.) sells hemp sheets, nontoxic paints, and natural-fiber carpets.

Try an eco-festival: Aspen holds the **Eco Fest** (downtown Aspen, www.aspenecofest.com) in early June, including stuff like a panel discussion on healthy eating and cooking, an art display made from recycled objects, and a green-tie fashion show in which everything is made out of duct tape or chopped-up rubber tires; the **Earth Day Fair** (Civic Center, downtown Denver, www.denvergov.org) runs on April 20, with exhibits and displays from dozens of companies and groups such as Greenpeace, Denver Recycles, and Environment Colorado; and **Earth Day at Red Rocks** (Red Rocks Amphitheatre, 18300 W. Alameda Pkwy., Morrison, http://windstarcoloradoconnection.org) is a free April 20 event with live music and displays by the Colorado Wolf and Wildlife Center, the Cloud Foundation, and others.

The U.S. National Park Service provides a lifetime **National Parks and Federal Recreational Lands Pass** for visitors with permanent disabilities; whoever carries one can enter any National Park with up to four passengers included. The catch is that you have to obtain it in person at the park in question. Also, you have to provide documentation, such as a physician's letter or paperwork from the Veteran's Administration or Social Security Disability Income.

SENIOR TRAVELERS

As in most states, Colorado's museums and other sights (and occasionally hotels and restaurants) often provide discounts for seniors. The U.S. National Park Service also sells a $10 lifetime **National Parks and Recreational Lands Pass** for access to parks and attractions throughout the state and the rest of the country. As with the people-with-disabilities pass, you have to show up in person at the park to buy it and provide documentation of your age.

A few outfits offer travel programs exclusively for seniors: **Senior Summer School** (800/847-2466, www.seniorsummerschool.com) teams with Colorado College to provide sightseeing trips at Pikes Peak, Garden of the Gods, and other Colorado Springs–area attractions; elder-focused **Road Scholar** (800/454-5768, www.roadscholar.org) has an international scope, but it oversees several trips and programs in Colorado, such as seven-day tours of the state's railroads and the Four Corners region, with meals and hotels included.

FOREIGN TRAVELERS

In order to gain access to most of the United States, including Colorado, most foreign travelers will need a **visa;** check the **U.S. Department of State's Bureau of Consular Affairs** website (http://travel.state.gov) to find out more specifics. Generally, European and Latin American nationals can avoid the visa process.

Like the other 49 states, Colorado's currency is the **U.S. dollar.** Currency exchanges are generally available at banks, hotels, and occasionally airports. The easiest way to get quick cash

is via **Automatic Teller Machines,** or ATMs, available at most banks, convenience stores, gas stations, stadiums and arenas, and occasionally restaurants. Many U.S. banks charge sky-high fees for nonnetwork ATM users, so pay attention to what you push "yes" for on the screen. Most Colorado establishments accept **traveler's checks,** particularly the best-known ones from Visa and MasterCard, as well as **credit cards.**

Expect to pay 15–20 percent of every restaurant bill in **tips;** if your party is large, the restaurant may levy this charge automatically. In hotels, the staff expects roughly $1–2 per bag for hauling your luggage to your room. Valet-parking attendants usually get $2–3. Bartenders generally expect $1 per drink.

If you're bringing a laptop or other **electronic** device, keep in mind Colorado, like the rest of the United States and most parts of Canada and Mexico, uses a 120-volt, two-prong plug. **Internet** users will be pleased to know that Colorado is a fairly advanced state when it comes to broadband connections and wireless Internet service; even the smallest hotels offer some version of this, sometimes for a fee in the $10-per-day range. Contact the hotel in advance to be sure.

TRAVELING WITH CHILDREN

The big cities have plenty of kid-oriented things to do, from the Buell Children's Museum in Pueblo to the Children's Museum in Denver. Most ski resorts give lessons to kids ages 3–16 and provide child care for all ages; check individual chapters for the resort contact information. Touring the mountains by car can be a little tough for infants; consider bringing Dramamine or another anti-motion-sickness drug (as per your doctor's advice, of course) before hitting the twisty highways. Also, some bed-and-breakfasts don't allow kids, so ask first before making hotel reservations.

GAY AND LESBIAN TRAVELERS

Homosexuality is, sadly, a political issue at the time of this writing, and Colorado's reception of openly gay men and women can depend on the area you visit. Boulder, Denver, and many of the mountain towns such as Telluride and Aspen are progressive, and several have passed laws banning discrimination against people based on sexual orientation. Colorado Springs, on the other hand, is the headquarters of the powerful Focus on the Family, which takes an unambiguous religious position that homosexuality is wrong. Another group, Colorado for Family Values, sponsored Amendment 2 in the early 1990s, which would have banned laws protecting gays and lesbians from discrimination had the U.S. Supreme Court upheld it.

Having said that, there are still those with unfavorable views toward gay men and women who live in Boulder and Denver and plenty of marriage-equality advocates who live in Colorado Springs. Somewhat incongruously, Boulder has few major gay clubs, while there are several in Pueblo and Colorado Springs; the scene is obviously larger in Denver. For more information, check out **The Center** (www.glbtcolorado.org).

Health and Safety

ALTITUDE SICKNESS
Upon climbing to thin-air elevations above 8,000 feet, you'll begin taking in less and less oxygen with every breath, so it's best to take it slow. Spread your hike into two or three manageable segments, or you could wind up with nausea, dizziness, headaches, or a bloody nose—and don't just dismiss these symptoms, as they could grow into more serious problems without rest and treatment (some doctors recommend the prescription drug Diamox). One of the best ways to prepare for strenuous high-altitude activity is to get in shape at a lower altitude, although even visiting professional sports teams have been known to keep emergency oxygen on the sidelines. Once you've stayed in Colorado for a few weeks, your body tends to get used to the elevation.

DEHYDRATION
Colorado is a dry state with extremely low humidity, and it's even drier at high elevations. Wherever you go, especially when exercise is involved, bring water. Don't ignore symptoms like thirst, dry lips (lip balm is big in Colorado), or dizziness, or they can develop into more serious problems.

SUNBURN
The higher you go in the mountains, the closer you get to the sun and the fewer barriers there are to prevent ultraviolet rays from reaching your body. Sunburn can lead to skin cancer, as any modern beachcomber knows, but the snow seduces many skiers into thinking the sun isn't a problem. Apply sunscreen regularly, preferably with a sun protection factor (SPF) of 15 or higher.

HYPOTHERMIA
Your body temperature needs to stay above 95°F or, in short, you're toast. Seriously, hypothermia is a bad situation; it's caused by exposure to long stretches of cold weather, and you might feel your heart rate and breathing slow down, lethargy, and general confusion. If at all possible, get to a hospital right away; if not, abandon wet clothing and get under a warm, dry blanket immediately. Under no circumstances should anybody rub your skin, apply heat directly, or give you alcohol. The best way to prevent hypothermia is to wear warm clothing (and bring emergency reserves with you in case your gloves get wet) and drink fluids.

FROSTBITE
If it's so cold outside that your skin turns blue and feels numb, you may have frostbite, caused by exposure to extreme freezing temperatures. It's usually easy to prevent this—cover yourself with wool or polypropylene clothing, and put on several layers. When it's incredibly cold outside—the kind of cold where you sniff and the sides of your nose stay frozen

together—consider not venturing out at all. If you do get frostbite, put the affected areas in warm water or cover them with warm clothing.

POISONOUS PLANTS

Yes, there are deadly plants in certain mountain regions of Colorado—be particularly wary of **water hemlock,** which have long, green, hollow stems that ooze a yellow liquid, often topped with tiny white flowers. Do not touch these plants! Even an ounce of the root is enough to kill a horse, less for a human. It causes paralysis and death. In general, unless you've taken a plant-identification course or studied books on the subject, it's best to avoid nibbling on strange plants, especially berries or mushrooms. For more specifics, A. P. Smith of Colorado State University maintains an excellent, searchable database called **Guide to Poisonous Plants** (http://southcampus.colostate.edu/poisonous_plants).

DANGEROUS ANIMALS

The most dangerous animals you're likely to find in large cities like Denver are pit bulls who violate a longstanding blanket ban. Elsewhere, about 3,000–7,000 mountain lions live in the state, and they're a little scary, with sharp teeth and mean looks, although attacks on people are rare—less than a dozen fatalities in the United States since 2003, according to the **Colorado Division of Wildlife** (many offices throughout the state, including 6060 Broadway, Denver, 303/297-1192, www.wildlife.state.co.us). If you encounter one, stay calm, back away slowly, try to appear larger by opening your jacket and raising your arms, and, if they don't retreat, fight back with sticks, rocks, or even bare hands. Black bears roam mountain areas and even nearby cities like Boulder or Fort Collins; the Division of Wildlife recommends staying far away and trying not to disturb these animals, which tend not to be aggressive toward humans unless they're wounded. Other potentially dangerous wildlife in Colorado includes certain types of snakes, large elk, and coyotes. Whatever you do, don't feed them.

GIARDIA

Backpackers and hikers need to protect themselves from *Giardia lamblia,* a single-celled parasitic infection of the intestine. You can contract this uncomfortable disease—leading to cramps, diarrhea, nausea, and other severe irritations—from contact with somebody else's stool or, more commonly, drinking infected water from an untreated lake or stream. Many recommend boiling the water or purifying it with iodine tablets, but my wife, who had giardia while hiking the Pacific Crest Trail in California, says iodine isn't reliable. She suggests buying *two* water-purification filters from a reputable mountaineering store and bringing both along in case one fails.

TICKS

Scary diseases such as Lyme disease and Rocky Mountain fever can come from ticks, but don't panic—they're hardly common. More likely, when you're hiking through the wilderness, you'll see a small black bug stuck to your skin and feel completely grossed out. The best way to get rid of it is simply to pull it off. If it has lodged inside the skin, pull and twist, being careful not to crush it, until it comes off. Afterward, clean the spot carefully (perhaps with hydrogen peroxide) and consider seeing a doctor. There's no fail-safe way to prevent ticks, but it helps to tuck in your clothing so there are no exposed areas. Also, in the shower after hiking, search your body to make sure you're clear of any ticks.

FIRST-AID KITS

On long hikes, bring a first-aid kit, which should include some form of identification, DEET or other insect repellent, bandages, a Mylar blanket, at least one kind of flare, aspirin, matches, a lightweight flashlight, sunscreen, motion-sickness medicine such as Dramamine, lip balm, and lots of water. It helps to take some kind of emergency rescue course before venturing out; contact **Crested Butte Outdoors** (Crested Butte, 970/596-2999, www.cboutdoors.com) to find programs in your area.

EMERGENCY AND MEDICAL SERVICES

The major cities in Colorado have plentiful hospitals and doctors' offices; check the individual region listings for information. Secluded towns like Crested Butte and Telluride are also well equipped for emergency services, mostly due to the large numbers of visitors they attract. Beware, though, when visiting smaller, more removed towns in the mountains or rural areas, as they are often several miles away from emergency care. If you plan to spend a long time in such an area, consider contacting the town hall first to check on services in advance. Ski towns big and small are generally excellent resources, as they're accustomed to injuries and altitude sickness and provide on-site staff.

CRIME

The latest Federal Bureau of Investigation statistics, for 2007, show major crime in Colorado has been dropping steadily—by about 1.8 percent for violent crime and 2.9 percent for property crime. The state roughly matches national crime trends. Bigger cities like Denver and Colorado Springs, of course, tend to be more dangerous than college towns like Boulder and Fort Collins and smaller rural areas. The beatific back-to-nature scenery in much of the state has a tendency to remove visitors' vigilance, but they should take the usual precautions, putting valuables in hotel safes, locking cars, and so forth.

Information and Services

MAPS

The first thing I did in researching this book was purchase the *Colorado Recreational Road Atlas* ($17) from **Mapsco;** sadly, it has closed its longtime Denver location and moved to Fort Worth, Texas, but the maps are still excellent and available at www.universalmap.com.

Also, the **American Automobile Association** (4100 E. Arkansas Ave., Denver, and several other locations in the state, 303/753-8800 or 866/625-3601) gives superb road maps, Triptiks, and TourBooks as well as roadside assistance to dues-paying AAA members. The *Colorado Atlas and Gazetteer* (DeLorme) is a strong topographical map.

TOURISM RESOURCES

If you can't find what you're looking for on its comprehensive website, the **Colorado Tourism**

Office (800/265-6723, www.colorado.com) will send material via snail mail. The **State of Colorado** (303/866-5000, www.colorado.gov) is somewhat more government-focused—note the smiling photo of the governor on the website—but answers questions and provides information as well.

TIME ZONES

Colorado is in the **mountain time zone**—two hours earlier than the East Coast, an hour earlier than the Midwest, and an hour later than the West Coast. The state adheres to most of the U.S. standards for **daylight saving time**—set clocks an hour forward on the second Sunday in March and an hour backward on the first Sunday in November.

RESOURCES

Suggested Reading

DESCRIPTION, TRAVEL, AND PHOTOGRAPHY

Caughey, Bruce. *The Colorado Guide*. Golden, CO: Fulcrum Publishing, 1991. A well-written and thorough (628 pages!) travel companion that first came out in the early 1990s.

Collier, Grant. *Colorado: Moments in Time*. Lakewood, CO: Collier Publishing, 2004. One of the best contemporary photo books on the state, with 160 images in all.

Fielder, John. *Best of Colorado*. Engelwood, CO: Westcliffe Publishers, 2002. Acclaimed nature photographer Fielder has written 30-some books and has specialized in Colorado for the past 20 years.

Fielder, John, and William H. Jackson. *Colorado: 1870–2000 II*. Englewood, CO: Westcliffe Publishers, 2005. Photographer Fielder's huge, leather-bound opus involved capturing Colorado images in exactly the same place where photographer Jackson captured them more than 135 years ago. A new edition adds another hundred photos.

Harris, Richard. *Hidden Colorado*. Berkeley: Ulysses Press, 1996, 1998, 2000. It doesn't quite live up to its billing as a guide to weird and offbeat places, but gives many good suggestions.

Muench, David. *Colorado II*. Portland, OR: Graphic Arts Center Publishing, 1987. Coffee-table book by a veteran wilderness photographer.

HISTORY

Abbott, Carl, Stephen J. Leonard, and David McComb. *Colorado: A History of the Centennial State*. Niwot, CO: University Press of Colorado, 1982, 1994. Exhaustively researched chronology, with emphasis on union struggles and industry. A little dense in places.

Arps, Louisa Ward. *Denver in Slices: A Historical Guide to the City*. Athens, OH: Swallow Press, 1959. Some of the information is outdated, but the stories are good.

Bancroft, Caroline. *Colorado's Lost Mines and Buried Treasure*. Boulder: Johnson Publishing, 1961, 1998. Originally written in 1961, veteran historian Bancroft's tiny book collects about 30 romantic vignettes of searching for treasure, ghosts, and similar romance in Colorado.

Bancroft, Caroline. *Silver Queen: The Fabulous Story of Baby Doe Tabor*. Boulder: Johnson Publishing, 1955, 1983. A colorful retelling of the sad mining-era tale of Leadville's Baby Doe Tabor.

Brown, G. *Colorado Rocks! A Half-century of Music in Colorado*. Boulder: Pruett Publishing, 2004. Exclusive interviews and colorful anecdotes about the likes of Jimi Hendrix, the Beatles, Billy Joel, the Eagles, the Fluid, and numerous others.

Byrd, Isabella. *A Lady's Life in the Rocky Mountains.* Norman, OK: University of Oklahoma Press, 1879. The Old West and gold rush days, from the perspective of an English explorer who wrote tons of letters.

Churchill, E. Richard. *Doc Holliday, Bat Masterson, and Wyatt Earp: Their Colorado Careers.* Leadville, CO: Timberline Books, 1974. A definitive history of Colorado's most infamous outlaws.

Dallas, Sandra. *Colorado Ghost Towns and Mining Camps.* Norman, OK: University of Oklahoma Press, 1984. The photos, by Dallas's daughter Povy Kendal Atchison, are the draw of this comprehensive book about 147 ghost towns, including Alice, near Idaho Springs, and Baltimore, near Rollinsville.

Danilov, Victor J. *Colorado Museums and Historic Sites: A Colorado Guide Book.* Boulder: University Press of Colorado, 2000. Comprehensive, but its prose is more like a dry list of facts than any kind of colorful narrative.

Fay, Abbott. *A History of Skiing in Colorado.* Montrose, CO: Western Reflections, 2000, 2003. A slice of Colorado history that's not covered in too many other books.

Fay, Abbott. *I Never Knew That About Colorado: A Quaint Volume of Forgotten Lore.* Montrose, CO: Western Reflections, 1997. Bizarre and surprising anecdotes about Colorado history, including the World War II bombing of the state.

Kreck, Dick. *Smaldone: The Untold Story of an American Crime Family.* Golden, CO: Fulcrum Publishing, 2009. The former veteran *Denver Post* columnist and local author tackles the 1930s North Denver mob scene run by Italian brothers Clyde and Eugene Smaldone with potboiler-ish panache.

Leonard, Stephen J., and Thomas J. Noel. *Denver: From Mining Camp to Metropolis.* Although Leonard and Noel write in a dry, fact-packed style, their books are Colorado's definitive historical resources; this Denver volume is a strong complement to *Colorado: A History of the Centennial State.*

Maclean, John N. *Fire on the Mountain: The True Story of the South Canyon Fire.* New York: William Morrow, 1999; New York: Pocket Books, 2000. A journalist's heavily detailed account of the 10-day forest fire in 1994 that killed 14 firefighters and cost the state more than $4.5 million.

Rockwell, Wilson. *The Utes: A Forgotten People.* Denver: Sage Books, 1956; Ouray, CO: Western Reflections, 1998. First published in 1956, former Colorado state senator Rockwell's *The Utes* was one of the first books to comprehensively survey the history and influence of this indigenous Colorado population.

Ruxton, George Frederick. *Mountain Men.* New York: Holiday House, 1966. An Old West explorer publishes his autobiography as it goes along, beginning in 1848, as a magazine series.

Schrager, Adam. *The Principled Politician: The Ralph Carr Story.* Golden, CO: Fulcrum Publishing, 2008. Schrager, a former 9News TV political reporter in Denver, became fascinated with this unexpected World War II–era opponent of interning Japanese Americans. He wrote former Colorado governor Carr's biography after spending long after-work hours poring over documents at the Colorado Historical Society.

Ubbelohde, Carl, Maxine Benson, and Duane A. Smith. *A Colorado History.* Boulder: Pruett Publishing, 2001. This classic history, on its eighth edition and counting, begins with the Ancestral Puebloans and other indigenous people in the southwestern Colorado Mesa Verde region and marches up to the present.

RECREATION

Cushman, Ruth Carol, and Glenn Cushman. *Boulder Hiking Trails*. Boulder: Pruett Publishing, 1995. One of the best and easiest-to-read guides to the many trails in this region.

Fielder, John, and Mark Pearson. *The Complete Guide to Colorado's Wilderness Areas*. Englewood, CO: Westcliffe Publishers, undated. Covers numerous hiking and biking trails and is a practical reference for visitors, but it's hard to search by location.

Outdoor Books & Maps. *Denver & Boulder Fishing Close to Home*. Castle Rock, CO: Adler Publishing, 2007. Anglers who'd rather stay in town than make an expedition to Rocky Mountain lakes, streams, and ponds will find this an indispensable resource.

Roach, Gerry. *Colorado's Fourteeners: From Hikes to Climbs*. Golden, CO: Fulcrum Publishing, 1999. Also, *Colorado's Thirteeners: 13,800 to 13,999 Feet, from Hikes to Climbs*. Golden, CO: Fulcrum Publishing, 2001. Comprehensive and easy-to-read guide to really, really tall mountains.

Warren, Scott S. *100 Classic Hikes in Colorado*. Seattle: The Mountaineers Books, 2001. Cherry-picks the best stuff, although it's not organized in any discernible regional order.

FICTION

Dallas, Sandra. *The Diary of Mattie Spenser*. Rockland, MA: Wheeler Publishing, 1997. An 1865-era historical novel by the author of *The Persian Pickle Club*.

Michener, James. *Centennial*. New York: Fawcett Crest, 1987. The classic Colorado novel set in a fake town, Centennial, and spanning 136 million years over more than 1,000 pages.

Stone, Irving. *Men to Match My Mountains: The Opening of the Far West, 1840–1900*. Garden City, NY: Doubleday, 1956. Written in the mid-1950s, this collection of fictional vignettes focuses on the U.S. move westward, and includes just as much on California as Colorado.

Waters, Frank. *Pikes Peak: A Family Saga*. Athens, OH: Swallow Press/Ohio University Press, 1971. A fictional re-creation of a mining-era family and how they dealt with unions, Native Americans, and the majesty of Pikes Peak itself.

ALMANACS AND ATLASES

Freed, Doug. *Colorado by the Numbers: A Reference, Almanac, and Guide to the Highest State*. Grand Junction, CO: Virga, 2003. More numbers, with a foreword by Colorado governor John Hickenlooper.

Noel, Thomas J. *The Colorado Almanac: Facts About Colorado*. Portland, OR: WestWinds Press, 2001. Numbers and demographics illustrating the state.

Internet Resources

For official, generally comprehensive, and often slightly saccharine travel information about Colorado, stick to the official sites run by chambers of commerce, ski resorts, tourism boards, and local governments. For more lively but perhaps not quite as reliable information, try blogs. A combination of both often gets you to where you want to go.

OFFICIAL TOURISM AND GOVERNMENT-RUN SITES
State of Colorado
www.colorado.gov
The official State of Colorado website, complete with links to state parks and information on hunting and fishing licenses.

Colorado.com
www.colorado.com

The most comprehensive travel website about Colorado, with directions to historic sites, ski resorts, visitors centers, and recreation areas.

Bureau of Land Management Colorado
www.blm.gov/co/st/en.html

The BLM website provides crucial information for state highlights, including wild-horse preserves, canyons, and Native American heritage centers.

Colorado Department of Transportation
www.cotrip.org

Before traveling anywhere in the mountains, check the Colorado Department of Transportation's website for traffic and weather conditions.

Dillon Ranger District
www.dillonrangerdistrict.com

This government site is a wonderful, comprehensive trove of trail resources, topo maps, and photos of hundreds of trails in Summit County—prime ski-resort territory in the northern Rockies.

Geology of National Parks
http://3dparks.wr.usgs.gov

For science enthusiasts, this government-run site covers the geological history of Colorado and other Rocky Mountain states and details the rock formations and other stony highlights you might find in national parks.

National Parks Service
www.nps.gov

As overseer of Mesa Verde National Park, Colorado National Monument, and dozens of others in the state, the NPS is a great resource for hikers, bikers, campers, bird-watchers, and other outdoors lovers.

NEWS AND MEDIA
Colorado Public Radio
www.cpr.org

The Colorado Public Radio page, with links to on-air broadcasts and information about politics, music, and culture.

SPORTS AND ENTERTAINMENT
Colorado Music Association
www.coloradomusic.org

The state's loosely organized network of musicians of all genres, from punk to bluegrass, comes together at Colorado Music Association meetings.

Colorado Ski Country USA
www.coloradoski.com

Colorado Ski Country USA is an excellent first stop before you make travel, hotel, and lift-ticket arrangements.

Colorado Sports Hall of Fame
www.coloradosports.org

Colorado doesn't have quite the athletic history of, say, California or New York, but out here in the podunks, us locals are mighty proud of the likes of John Elway, Byron "Whizzer" White, Goose Gossage, Doug Moe, and Babe Didrickson.

SkiNet
www.skinet.com

This Web partnership between *Ski* and *Skiing* magazines is a great resource for gear, trails, powder updates, and expert commentary. (Yes, the magazines are separate entities, although they're both owned by the same company and based in Boulder.)

ENVIRONMENT AND OUTDOORS
American Southwest
www.americansouthwest.net/colorado

This is another unofficial resource, but a great and very thorough one, about parks, such as Colorado National Monument, and outdoor activities in Colorado and other Southwestern states.

Colorado Environmental Coalition
www.ourcolorado.org
The Colorado Environmental Coalition is one of the state's largest protect-the-wilderness groups.

DesertUSA
www.desertusa.com
Similar to American Southwest, this site focuses on drier pastures, with an emphasis on wildlife and plants. It covers many of the major Colorado outdoors attractions.

Environment Colorado
www.environmentcolorado.org
Environmentalists can hit this advocacy site for updates on the latest issues and a chance to volunteer.

Friends of the Peak
www.fotp.com
Trying to find resources about outdoor activities on Pikes Peak can be frustrating, given the many entities that oversee the mountain. Friends of the Peak is one-stop shopping for maps, information, and answers.

14ers
www.14ers.com
Run by a Breckenridge resident, this site about Colorado's 14,000-foot-plus mountains is a wealth of great data, including a message board for avid hikers.

GORP
www.gorp.com
This outdoor-travel site contains many pages about Colorado, particularly a hiking guide that covers everything from prominent fourteeners to "dog-friendly Denver."

LocalHikes
www.localhikes.com
Hiking experts give directions and brief, useful descriptions for 80 trails in the Colorado

Springs area; 99 in Denver, Boulder, and Greeley; and 62 in Fort Collins and Loveland.

ProTrails Colorado
www.protrails.com/state.
php?stateID=CO
Here's another resource for outdoors enthusiasts, focusing on hiking and wildlife.

SummitNet
www.summitnet.com
Focusing on Keystone, Breckenridge, Vail, Copper Mountain, and Arapahoe Basin, this excellent resource provides outdoor-sports information for both winter and summer.

Trails and Open Spaces
www.trailsandopenspaces.org
This nonprofit group preserves bike paths, hiking trails, and other open spaces in the Colorado Springs area—and chronicles everything with maps and data on its website.

Trails.com
www.trails.com
Outdoors experts contribute detailed information about hiking and mountain-biking trails all over Colorado—the catch is, if you want maps and trailhead locations, you have to pay $50 for a subscription or give your credit-card information for a limited free trial.

Wildernet
www.wildernet.com
This interactive site invites skiers, hikers, snowshoers, and other outdoors enthusiasts to contribute maps, trail descriptions, and other trail information. It began in 1995 as part of Aspen.com and has expanded considerably.

OTHER RESOURCES
Colorado in the Yahoo! Directory
http://dir.yahoo.com/
regional/u_s__states/colorado
The Colorado directory at Yahoo! is an easy-to-flip-through guide to the state, including directions and statistical information.

ColoradoPols
www.coloradopols.com

Coloradoans and U.S. political observers won't want to miss this blog full of congressional-race information and snarky editorial commentary.

Colorado Vacation Directory
www.coloradodirectory.com

Although this site isn't comprehensive and the information is often advertising-driven, the hotels, restaurants, and other Colorado sites are searchable by name, town, and amenity. It's handy for beginning a vacation search.

Colorado Wines
www.coloradowine.com

Particularly in Palisade and other northwestern regions, Colorado is a surprisingly lively winery state. This site, run by the Colorado Wine Industry Development Board, contains resources and news about tastings and events.

Sangres
www.sangres.com

Run by a travel enthusiast who specializes in the Southwest, Sangres goes county by county in Colorado and unearths information on obscure areas you might not find elsewhere.

Santa Fe Trail Association
www.santafetrail.org

This site is a superb resource for the Santa Fe Trail, an important 1,200-mile stagecoach route that ran through five states, including Colorado, during the mid–late 1800s. Although the trail is now reduced to a historic route, the association provides maps and sightseeing information for following along.

University of Colorado
www.colorado.edu

Find information on enrollment, visitation, and tours at the University of Colorado's website.

Index

List of Maps

Acknowledgments

Special thanks to my wife, Melissa, a veteran of the Pacific Crest Trail in California, for tapping into her camping and hiking expertise in this expanded edition. She wrote far more eloquently than I ever could about trails and campgrounds, and shared her insight in a number of key areas. She and our daughter, Rose, age nine, accompanied me on an amazing vacation throughout southwest Colorado, from the Great Sand Dunes to Mesa Verde, and their insight and enthusiasm was invaluable. For the original edition, they accompanied me on several whirlwind driving trips to Vail, Montrose, Gunnison, Salida, and elsewhere, and took most of the photos in the Denver chapter. They provided insightful running commentary on the Pearl Street Mall, Denver Children's Museum, various kid-friendly restaurants and hotels, and the "bumpy cow road" outside Crested Butte.

Also extremely helpful were Stacy and Ryan Anderson, who provided a crucial overview of ski areas for this clueless nonskier; Bruce Schoenfeld, who generously shared his knowledge of Aspen and Vail restaurants, hotels, and general culture; Jay Dedrick of the *Rocky Mountain News,* who grew up on the Eastern Plains, went to school in Fort Collins, and shared his local-beer expertise; Tom Sullivan, who gave me a great late-night tour of the Minturn Inn; Tracy Ross of *Skiing* magazine; Peggy Gair of Royal Gorge Bridge & Park; Erik Wilmsen, a former Fort Collins resident who recommended bars and restaurants; John Lehndorff, my former editor at the *Daily Camera* in Boulder, food critic *extraordinaire,* and current *Aurora Sentinel* content director; my nephew Rob Knopper, a former Interlochen student, for the Aspen photo; Amy Storey, for the photo of Red Rocks during Easter services; and Jonathan Boonin, a gambling expert who ran down the casinos. For the new edition, I am so glad I made contact with Deborah Marks of *Ski,* a Boulder resident who wrote up the best state ski runs for free. I owe her many drinks.

Thanks to my magazine and newspaper editors for their understanding when I disappeared on a Friday for an impromptu drive to Trinidad or Grand Junction: Jonathan Ringen at *Rolling Stone,* Kevin Amorim at *Newsday,* Greg Kot and Kevin Williams at the *Chicago Tribune,* Adam Rogers at *Wired,* and MacKenzie Geidt at *Sunset.* Special thanks to Joe Rassenfoss, formerly of the late, lamented *Rocky Mountain News,* for giving the Avalon Travel people my name in the first place.

Finally, this book is dedicated to my parents, Morton P. and Dorothy Knopper, who were inspired to relocate our family from Michigan to Colorado in the 1980s. My dad died in August 2008 at his Boulder home overlooking the foothills.

Note: An important source for the *Background* and *Essentials* chapters as well as the history sections throughout the book was *Colorado: A History of the Centennial State* by Carl Abbott, Stephen J. Leonard, and David McComb (University Press of Colorado, 1994). Also helpful was Stephen Metzger's previous edition of *Moon Colorado* (Avalon Travel Publishing, 2002), particularly for history and information for the *Health and Safety* section; he cited the American Medical Association's *Encyclopedia of Medicine.*

www.moon.com

MOON.COM is ready to help plan your next trip! Filled with fresh trip ideas and strategies, author interviews, informative travel blogs, a detailed map library, and descriptions of all the Moon guidebooks, Moon.com is all you need to get out and explore the world—or even places in your own backyard. While at Moon.com, sign up for our monthly e-newsletter for updates on new releases, travel tips, and expert advice from our on-the-go Moon authors. As always, when you travel with Moon, expect an experience that is uncommon and truly unique.

**KEEP UP WITH MOON ON FACEBOOK AND TWITTER
JOIN THE MOON PHOTO GROUP ON FLICKR**

MAP SYMBOLS

▭▭▭	Expressway	**【**	Highlight	✗	Airfield	⚑	Golf Course
▭▭▭	Primary Road	○	City/Town	✈	Airport	🅿	Parking Area
▭▭▭	Secondary Road	◉	State Capital	▲	Mountain	▰	Archaeological Site
▭▭▭	Unpaved Road	⊛	National Capital	✦	Unique Natural Feature	⛪	Church
------	Trail	★	Point of Interest				
··········	Ferry	●	Accommodation	🌴	Waterfall	⛽	Gas Station
▭▭▭	Railroad	▼	Restaurant/Bar	▲	Park		Glacier
▭▭▭	Pedestrian Walkway	■	Other Location	⛳	Trailhead		Mangrove
▥▥▥	Stairs	▲	Campground	⛷	Skiing Area		Reef
							Swamp

CONVERSION TABLES

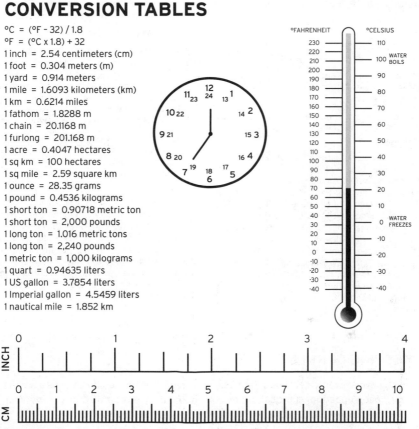

°C = (°F - 32) / 1.8
°F = (°C x 1.8) + 32
1 inch = 2.54 centimeters (cm)
1 foot = 0.304 meters (m)
1 yard = 0.914 meters
1 mile = 1.6093 kilometers (km)
1 km = 0.6214 miles
1 fathom = 1.8288 m
1 chain = 20.1168 m
1 furlong = 201.168 m
1 acre = 0.4047 hectares
1 sq km = 100 hectares
1 sq mile = 2.59 square km
1 ounce = 28.35 grams
1 pound = 0.4536 kilograms
1 short ton = 0.90718 metric ton
1 short ton = 2,000 pounds
1 long ton = 1.016 metric tons
1 long ton = 2,240 pounds
1 metric ton = 1,000 kilograms
1 quart = 0.94635 liters
1 US gallon = 3.7854 liters
1 Imperial gallon = 4.5459 liters
1 nautical mile = 1.852 km

MOON COLORADO

Avalon Travel
a member of the Perseus Books Group
1700 Fourth Street
Berkeley, CA 94710, USA
www.moon.com

Editor and Series Manager: Kathryn Ettinger
Copy Editor: Christopher Church
Graphics Coordinator: Darren Alessi
Production Coordinator: Darren Alessi
Cover Designer: Darren Alessi
Map Editor: Kat Bennett
Cartographers: Heather Sparks, June Thammasnong
Indexer: Greg Jewett

ISBN-13: 978-1-61238-121-3
ISSN: 1085-2697

Printing History
1st Edition – 1992
8th Edition – May 2012
5 4 3 2 1

KEEPING CURRENT

If you have a favorite gem you'd like to see included in the next edition, or see anything that needs updating, clarification, or correction, please drop us a line. Send your comments via email to feedback@moon.com, or use the address above.